D1604180

THE ARGUMENT OF THE ACTION

SETH BENARDETE

THE ARGUMENT OF THE ACTION

ESSAYS ON GREEK POETRY AND PHILOSOPHY

Edited and with an Introduction by Ronna Burger and Michael Davis

THE UNIVERSITY OF CHICAGO PRESS
CHICAGO AND LONDON

Seth Benardete is professor of classics at New York University. His recent books include *The Tragedy and Comedy of Life* and *The Bow and the Lyre.* Ronna Burger is professor of philosophy at Tulane University. Michael Davis is professor of philosophy at Sarah Lawrence College.

The University of Chicago Press, Chicago 60637
The University of Chicago Press, Ltd., London

Printed in the United States of America
09 08 07 06 05 04 03 02 01 00 5 4 3 2 1

ISBN (cloth): 0-226-04251-0

Library of Congress Cataloging-in-Publication Data

Benardete, Seth.
The argument of the action : essays on Greek poetry and philosophy / Seth Benardete ; edited with an introduction by Ronna Burger and Michael Davis.
p. cm.
Includes bibliographical references and index.
ISBN 0-226-04251-0 (alk. paper)
1. Greek literature—History and criticism. 2. Greek drama (Tragedy)—History and criticism. 3. Philosophy, Ancient. 4. Homer. Iliad. 5. Plato. I. Burger, Ronna, 1947– . II. Davis, Michael. III. Title.
PA3061.B46 2000
880.9′001—dc21
99-087699

♾ The paper used in this publication meets the minimum requirements of the American National Standard for Information Sciences—Permanence of Paper for Printed Library Materials, ANSI Z39.48-1992.

CONTENTS

PREFACE

There are many reasons to welcome a collection of essays by Seth Benardete. His writings on Greek poetry and philosophy cover a range few have equaled. As at home with Herodotus as he is with Homer, and with Sophocles as he is with Plato and Aristotle, Benardete is never guilty of narrowly specializing even though his command of the texts he interprets is unrivaled. Because he has not determined in advance what philosophers, historians, or poets are allowed to say, he is open to whatever they do say, scrupulously following their arguments with a care born of the expectation that these authors have everything to teach him.

The essays collected here span more than thirty years' work, from Benardete's studies of the *Iliad,* the subject of his dissertation, to his recent rethinking of Plato's *Theaetetus, Sophist,* and *Statesman.* Several of these pieces are transcriptions of lectures, published here for the first time; others appeared in books now out of print. We have long thought that collecting them into one volume would not only make more accessible what we have found in many cases to be the most illuminating commentary on the text in question, but would also provide a helpful way into Benardete's book-length works.

Benardete's unique imprint takes many forms: in the paradoxical formulations through which he sometimes expresses his insights, in the subtle linguistic analyses—of puns, etymologies, metaphoric extensions of literal usage—through which he uncovers the argument in the very language of the texts he interprets, in the Platonic playfulness that pervades his thinking. In these and other ways, Benardete's readings seek to capture "the argument of the action"—the title of this volume—and it is precisely in this capacity that they open up a radically new perspective on what might have seemed a familiar work. Of course, the very features of Benardete's writing that accomplish this with such brilliance are also a source of its difficulty and resistance to simplification. On a work of such grand scale as Plato's *Republic,* Benardete's interpretation especially challenges the reader to keep in mind the manifold threads he weaves into the intricate pattern of the whole. The essays in this volume, while in some ways no less demanding, offer the advantage to which Aristotle points in the *Poetics* when he compares the plot of a drama to a living animal, whose beauty depends not only on the arrangement of its parts, but also on a size that allows the design of the whole to be perceived as a whole.

Gathering these studies together is for us an expression of profound gratitude. Here, as so often elsewhere, Benardete has been our guide. In the last essay in this collection, he traces to Leo Strauss much of what seems to characterize his own work. This generosity, which might initially strike one as misplaced and excessively modest, points rather to the paradoxical experience of learning from another only after coming to understand for ourselves, although we then realize that we had been directed in some way by the other from the start. This experience lies at the heart of the practice of philosophy as interpretation. What is strikingly characteristic of this practice as Benardete carries it out is the depth of understanding he achieves through an uncanny ability really to see the surface of things, which in turn enables him to see what ordinarily obscures this surface. In recalling us to the hidden surface of things, these essays, and Benardete's work as a whole, exemplify what he once called "the being of the beautiful."

Acknowledgments

We have consulted with Seth Benardete on which writings to include in this collection and on the order in which they appear. In general we wish to extend our thanks for permission to include previously published writings. The particulars will be found in the bibliography listing Benardete's works. The Earhart Foundation provided a grant to assist us in the preparation of this volume. We would also like to thank Barbara Witucki, who typed the manuscript, and Robert Berman, whose advice was, as always, greatly valued.

INTRODUCTION

For Seth Benardete, all particular questions, when one follows them far enough, lead to the question of philosophy, and "what philosophy is seems to be inseparable from the question of how to read Plato."[1] Accordingly, Benardete's work in general may be said to be concerned with articulating the core of Platonic philosophy. It is no wonder, then, that over half of the essays in this volume deal with Plato. At the same time, since almost half do not, in what sense can these twenty essays on Greek poetry and philosophy be said to constitute a whole?

The poets present an "understanding of the city, particularly of its subpolitical foundations, and of the law, particularly the sacred law, [which] would remain in darkness were it not for the light Plato brings to them."[2] Because the Platonic dialogue raises to the level of argument the issues darkly embedded in the stories of the poets—above all those "experiences of the soul that are situated on the other side of the frontier of the law"[3]—it furnishes Benardete with a key to unlock the meaning of these stories. It does so, however, in a form that shows just how deeply the Platonic dialogue is indebted to poetic drama.[4] To discover the path from Plato to the poets requires recognition of the path from the poets to Plato; Benardete can make such powerful use of the one because he is so attuned to the other.

For Benardete, as for so many before him in the philosophic tradition, the way to poetry lies through tragedy, and "tragedy seems to raise a claim that by itself it is the truth of life."[5] The general formula for this truth is *pathei mathos*—learning through suffering, experiencing, or undergoing.[6] In its original location in the parados of Aeschylus's *Agamemnon* (177), *pathei mathos* is meant by the chorus to articulate the universal condition for human understanding. Poetry generally, and dramatic poetry in particular, present us with an artificial experience from which we are to learn something real. We do not have to commit incest to understand Sophocles' *Oedipus Tyrannus.* Still, one cannot simply skip to the conclusion of the play to appropriate its teaching, for what we get at the end depends on what we have experienced in the beginning and the middle. Story or plot is thus the "soul of tragedy."[7]

Pathei mathos cuts considerably deeper than this, however. For Benardete, the initial difficulty of tragedy lies in the tension between plot and character: Oedipus's fate looks inevitable, but he does not seem to deserve it.[8] The two may first be reconciled by seeing that his story—killing his father and marrying his mother—can be understood as an image of his character—his willful disposition to be his own man. The initial discrepancy between plot and character thus moves us to reevaluate Oedipus's character. That in a way he does deserve his fate is poetic justice and seems to make the play still more beautiful. Yet when we follow Benardete's lead, we discover troubling details; the perfect plot begins to unravel. Oedipus arrives in Thebes and is married to Jocasta before she can possibly know that Laius is dead. And he solves the riddle of the Sphinx to rid Thebes of a plague that can only barely have begun—Oedipus may even be the first person to whom the Sphinx speaks. Reflecting on difficulties like these, we discover that it is not just Oedipus whose anger and willfulness lead him to ignore plot difficulties (for example, that the one witness to the killing of Laius claimed that the company was attacked by robbers whereas Oedipus was alone), and not just Oedipus whose will to get at the truth causes him to embrace a conclusion that cannot possibly be true; it is rather Thebes itself that does so, and not only Thebes. Our own willfulness has also been engaged. We are so swept along by what seems the perfect plot that we suppress our knowledge of troublesome details that do not hang together. As Benardete puts it so vividly, there are "trapdoors" in the way things unfold.[9] If we somehow contrive to fall through the trapdoor in the plot of the *Oedipus* with our eyes open, we discover that the play means something quite different from what we first thought it to mean. We arrive at a conclusion—it is not simply the tragedy of an individual man but the tragedy of political life as such—to which we could come only by first having missed it, blinded by the "obvious."[10] To learn, we must first have erred, for learning amounts to disclosing the underlying reasons for such errors. *Pathei mathos.*

Philosophy generally reflects this same pattern; the Platonic dialogue, in its representation of Socratic philosophy, makes the pattern thematic. What Benardete discovers in the Platonic dialogue is akin to what Aristotle identifies as the "complex plot" of tragedy, whose incidents must unfold one as the consequence of another and yet contrary to expectation.[11] It is, more specifically, the function of reversal and recognition, on which such a tragic plot pivots, that has its philosophical equivalent in the Platonic dialogue.[12] It is not sufficient, therefore, to articulate the formal structure of the dialogue as a whole constituted of parts; this structure must be understood in relation to the sequential unfolding of the argument, which—not despite but because of the reversal it undergoes—proves finally to have been governed by a deeper necessity.[13]

There is, of course, an established modern tradition that recognizes the Platonic dialogue as a literary form characterized by the juxtaposition of speeches and deeds, which are to be interpreted in light of each other. This tradition insists on the inseparable connection of the content of a dialogue with its form, so that no proposition can be rightly understood except in its proper place; it is aware that speeches in a dialogue must be understood in light of the characters who utter them, recognizes Plato's deliberate use of contradiction as a literary device, and so refrains from any pretense of understanding Plato better than he understands himself.[14] Still, if such interpretation assumes that a Platonic dialogue produces among its readers a continuum of levels of understanding in which the teaching deepens but does not differ qualitatively, it falls short in the decisive respect; for "once argument and action are properly put together, an entirely new argument emerges that could never have been expected from the argument on the written page."[15] It is this new argument, which emerges through an action of its own, that makes the Platonic dialogue a whole. In reconstructing it, Benardete discloses how every dialogue reproduces in itself the conversion *(periagōgē)* of the philosopher in the cave, wrenched from his position facing shadows on the wall and turned in the opposite direction toward the light.

An intentional flaw in the flow of the apparent argument—Plato's "trapdoor"—induces us to drop beneath the surface to uncover the source of movement that reveals the real argument.[16] The *Phaedo* provides a striking example. In one of the most famous passages in Plato, Socrates presents an intellectual autobiography designed to account for what he calls his "second sailing in search of the cause" (99d). According to Socrates, he rejected Anaxagorean mind as a cause of all things because it did not account for the goodness of the order that it imposed. Now, Socrates has just used his own situation as an example of what Anaxagorean cosmology cannot account for. To explain why he is in prison and not running down the road to Megara, we must understand that it seems better both to him and to the Athenians that he remain in prison, take the poison, and die. But Socrates' reasons and the reasons of the Athenians look like contrary causes of the same effect: "If Socrates does what he does by mind, the Athenians cannot have done what they did by mind, for otherwise mind would be irrational in reaching the same conclusion through opposite routes."[17] Whatever Socrates' reasons may be for judging his death at this time to be good, he must mean, given the definition of death assumed from the outset of the dialogue, that it is good for his body and soul to be separated. But how, then, could a teleological account ever explain why it is best for things to be arranged as they are, with body and soul united in a living being? Discovering this incoherence forces us to leave behind the causal analysis of death as a physiological phenomenon and to reinterpret, in light of the deeper argument thereby revealed, precisely what Socrates understands by "dying and being dead." In doing so, we turn, with Socrates, to seek "the truth of the beings" through "investigation in *logoi*."

Benardete carries on this Socratic turn not only by practicing philosophy through interpretation of the Platonic dialogue. His readings exemplify the Socratic second sailing in a more specific manner, which has to do with the necessity of its being second: they show what it means for philosophic thinking to have to emerge with the breakdown of one's original way of proceeding, followed by recognition of the necessity of that breakdown, but not in a way that would have made possible avoidance of the error from the start.[18] To know that this process must be at work in a dialogue is also to know that one cannot anticipate where it will appear in the course of the argument. This is the core of Plato's verson of *pathei mathos.*

The *hamartia* that the action of a Platonic dialogue sets out to correct is, in its most general form, "Platonism." Not Socrates, but everyone else is a "Platonist." The "ideas" of justice or pleasure are the offspring of Socrates' interlocutors, and it is Socrates' task to disabuse them of the "Platonism" of everyday life, or Plato's task to disabuse us.[19] If political philosophy is the "eccentric core of philosophy,"[20] it is because it devotes itself to the examination of opinion, which is the repository of the "ideas" so understood. Opinion, guided by ordinary language, takes for granted the value of the coin it mints: whatever is under examination in the dialogue—love, death, pleasure, law, courage, moderation, the just, the beautiful—is assumed to be an atomic entity, a monad. The argument of the action of the dialogue undermines this "taking for granted" by uncovering the relations among such entities and the internal structures that make them bound to slip out from our fixed categories and remain resistant to our "ideas."

Benardete succeeds in preserving this slipperiness, or resistance, while revealing the fundamental forms of its artful representation. To give adequate expression to these forms, he has coined his own special vocabulary, speaking of conjunctive and disjunctive twos, of eidetic analysis, of the indeterminate dyad, and of phantom images.[21] In articulating these forms, he is guided by the double character of thinking as a matter of bringing one and one together and of discerning the implicit two in a given one. The *Phaedo* again provides a concrete illustration. At the outset of the conversation, Socrates rubs his leg after the chains have been removed and reflects on his wonder-inspiring experience: that which is called pleasant is naturally related to the painful, which is thought to be its opposite, in such a way that the pursuit of one makes it necessary to take the other with it, as if they were bound in one head. Aesop, Socrates imagines, might have made a myth about a god who, wishing to end the war between the two but being unable, could only join their two heads.[22] This Aesopian myth presents what Benardete calls a "conjunctive two," and he proposes that it provides Plato's model for myth in general. The elements that make up such a pair are assumed to be intelligible independently of one another; if, therefore, they are ever found together in our experience, it looks as if some cause must be responsible for bringing them together. This is precisely what Socrates denies by the first account of pleasure and pain he gives in his own name, according to which the two presumed opposites are naturally bound together "in one head." That account, which illustrates what Benardete calls a "disjunctive two," describes a necessary relation between mutually determining parts of a whole, neither of which can be what it is apart from the other.

In Diotima's myth about the birth of Eros, Benardete again finds these two structures. Diotima begins with a conjunctive two: Poverty, the mother of Eros, and Resource, his father, are presented as two independent beings that must somehow unite with each other to generate their offspring. But once it becomes clear that everything needed to account for Eros can be traced to the resourcefulness of Poverty alone, her self-aware neediness emerges as the disjunctive two of *eros. Eros,* that is, involves ingenuity in the face of need. To represent its dual nature to ourselves we separate its elements and then personify them; but in fact the awareness of our need is never really separable from thoughts of how to alleviate it. To recognize this disjunctive two of *eros* is to correct for the mythical starting point of the analysis.[23]

If fixity, atomicity, and independence are the telling signs of a mythical understanding of things, the Platonic "ideas," each "itself by itself," would be the mythical version of what must finally be understood as internally related elements of a complex structure: the paradigm, which Benardete traces through all the Platonic dialogues, is the triad of the beautiful, the just, and the good. The procedure by which such a structure is opened up in order to discover the relations among its elements is what Benardete calls "eidetic analysis." Eidetic analysis is an account of the being of something that is not meant to be an account of its coming to be. It stands to its alternative—genetic or causal analysis—as the disjunctive two stands to the conjunctive two: in following it, what was at first a part parading as a whole finally shows itself to be part of a whole. The structure that emerges in this process Benardete has termed an "indeterminate dyad."[24] It shows up in a form unique to each inquiry in the course of "collecting" and "separating" what cannot be counted up—a one that splits off part of itself and projects it as something other, or a one that lies hidden behind its fractured appearances.

The elusiveness of the beings that slide from one conceptual net to another, and can therefore be approached only by a fittingly subtle manner of "hunting," becomes thematic in Benardete's account of Plato's search for the sophist. The sophist, as the embodiment of the other, solves the problem of nonbeing he raises, but only to reveal, finally, that being is no less problematic. The sophist is not being sought for his own sake: he and the statesman together are, Socrates proposes, nothing but the split phantom images (a conjunctive two) behind which lies the reality of the single being—the philosopher—who, like a Homeric god, appears to another as what he is not. Socrates wonders whether the Stranger, who has come to take his place, is not just such a god in disguise. Benardete argues that what the Stranger actually sets out to do, in the course of the two conversations he conducts, is to clear away the double phantom image of Socrates—the remarkably influential two-sided figure of Socrates the logic chopper and Socrates the moralist which has come down to us through the centuries.[25] Where Plato's readers have typically identified Socrates with one side or the other—each of which is misleading in its own way and both together incapable of forming a coherent whole—Benardete discloses a complex apparition and sets out to understand what makes it necessary.

The radical revision of received opinion Benardete accomplishes in his readings of the Platonic dialogues is due, in no small part, to his discovery of such a "distorted mirror" of Socrates in all the variety of shapes it assumes throughout the dialogues. In some cases Benardete discloses Plato's representation of misunderstandings or misappropriations of Socratic teachings—the future tyrant Critias, for example, or the general Nicias oblige Socrates to recognize a principle of his own in an alien element.[26] On other occasions, a surprising portrait of Socrates shows itself, under Benardete's examination, to be the alien guise Socrates has deliberately adopted for particular purposes.[27]

The privileged case, perhaps—of which Benardete provides an especially powerful analysis—is the self-presentation at work in the peculiar erotic art Socrates claims to possess, which would enact on a rational level, if it really were an art, what transpires naturally between every lover and beloved. At the heart of this experience, as the soul image of the *Phaedrus* indicates, lies the problem of self-knowledge. Uncovering the hidden dynamic in that image, Benardete shows the white horse to be nothing but the invention of the black horse of the lover's soul which, in its defectiveness and incompleteness, constructs a beautified image of the nature it shares with the beloved, meant to attract the beloved, who is unwittingly in love with himself, for the sake of a shared ascent to engage in contemplation of the beings. The Platonic dialogue, Benardete suggests, is itself such a beautified image, projected from the black horse at its core that is Socratic knowledge of ignorance.[28]

Each Platonic dialogue offers its own access to the discovery of the hidden being of the philosopher. To find it, Benardete looks for that point when the action is taken up in speeches and what we discover turns out to differ from what we thought we were searching for—no longer, say, conduct on the battlefield, but the courage of persistence in inquiry; not a quiet demeanor and sense of shame, but the "hermeneutic *sōphrosunē*" of the interpreter who "does his own thing" by the paradoxical readiness "to question the wisdom of the authority to which one defers."[29] Benardete thinks through what philosophy must be if, as Diotima indicates, it is really the core of *eros,* and how it could be the realization of *eros* in the comprehensive sense, as the desire for happiness; he explores what philosophy must be if it is really "the practice of dying and being dead," and demonstrates the sense of Socrates' arguments once death in the ordinary sense is recognized as nothing but an extension of that primary meaning.[30] The discovery of philosophy, which takes on a distinctive form in each dialogue, begins with turning upside down what was previously assumed to be bedrock reality and its shadowlike derivative.[31]

Benardete's readings disclose the phantom images of the philosopher in speech, while recognizing as essential to the dialogue its presentation of the philosopher in deed. A presentation of the life of the poet, by contrast, does not seem to be essential to the work of the poet. This points to a difference that lies at the heart of the "ancient quarrel between poetry and philosophy." For the philosopher's portrayal of the philosophic life displays implicitly what makes life worth living for a human being, and not out of any illusory optimism about reason, but in full awareness of our essential incompleteness.[32] His self-presentation proves to be nothing less than the presentation of the human soul, "the only part of the whole which is open to the whole and therefore more akin to the whole than anything else is."[33] The poets, on the other hand, at least the tragic poets, do not tell their own story; their paradigmatic subject is the individual guilty of "criminal piety"[34]—above all one whose crimes reveal the sacred foundations of the city.[35] What they depict in connection with such crimes are the tragic passions of fear and shame, which cannot be understood apart from Hades. The shadow world of nonbeing, as Benardete leads us to see, is "the soul of tragedy."[36] Its centrality is inseparable from the perspective the poets portray—even if they do not endorse it—according to which what appears best for a human being is not to be born. Insofar as poetry and philosophy are two, what divides them is nothing less than the question of whether human life can be good: "Poetry's exposition of life does not redeem it; rather, it makes life worth living only to the degree to which poetry has not exposed it."[37]

Tragedy first shows us the meaning of *pathei mathos* in its narrow sense, where depth of learning derives from depth of suffering. And yet, the best of poets, in leading us through progressively deeper understandings of the necessary defects of the characters they represent, show us why the principle *pathei mathos* in its most comprehensive sense belongs at the heart of both poetry and philosophy. Their bond is all the stronger the more the poets have thought through the artful structures that make such representation possible. Hesiod, in any case, suggests as much when his Muses warn him of their ability to "speak lies like the truth." The principle of all Greek poetry, as Benardete sees it, presupposes the philosophic distinction of falsehood from truth and their recombination in *mimesis*.[38] Homer, too, has understood the double character of the beautiful lies by which "the poet divides what is necessarily one and unites what is necessarily two."[39] The poets, it seems, have already reflected on the duplicity of their form and its implication for human wisdom. In opening up this possibility, Benardete shows us how "the *logos* of Plato unveils the *muthos* of poetry for the *logos* it is. Once, however, this is acknowledged, the Socratic revolution in philosophy seems to be coeval with Greek poetry, which had realized from the start, with its principle of telling lies like the truth, the relation of argument and action."[40] In the "poetic dialectic" of image-making, Benardete sees the structures of Socratic philosophizing; in the argument of the action of the Platonic dialogue, he sees the poetic presentation of genuine philosophy. He has made understanding the indeterminacy of this dyad—poetry and philosophy—his life's work.

Notes

1. "Strauss on Plato," 407 below.

2. Ibid., 415. The "double frame" of Greek tragedy is, accordingly, "the political in its innocent autonomy and the sacred in its subversion of that innocence" ("On Greek Tragedy," 103 below).

3. "On Greek Tragedy," 104 below.

4. Socrates' tripartite division of the soul in *Republic,* Book 4, for example, provides a key to the shape of Hesiod's *Theogony* ("The First Crisis in First Philosophy," chap. 1 below). Benardete has suggested other such keys: to the plot of the *Iliad* in Diotima's "ladder of love"; to the character of Odysseus in the analysis of anger and rationality running through the *Republic;* to the *Oedipus Tyrannus* in the account of the tyrant in *Republic,* Book 9; to the structure of Herodotus' *Inquiries* in the divided line of *Republic,* Book 6; to Antigone's burial of her brother's corpse in the *Phaedo*'s account of body and soul. In every case, of course, the Platonic "template" is itself embedded in the dynamic unfolding of the argument of the dialogue as much as it is in the plot of the work to which it provides a key.

5. "On Greek Tragedy," 99 below.

6. The meaning of the formula *pathei mathos* is illustrated by Aeschylus's Prometheus, who, though he knows he will be punished if he disobeys Zeus, cannot understand in advance what he will experience in being punished. Benardete calls upon this model to show us what would be missing from the universal predictive science Socrates works out with Critias in the *Charmides:* by eliminating error, it also rules out altogether any possible philosophical equivalent to tragic wisdom ("On Interpreting Plato's *Charmides,*" chap. 12 below).

7. See *Poetics* 1450a–b for Aristotle's identification of plot as the "soul of tragedy." Benardete's reflections on Greek tragedy lead him to call Hades—*Aïdes* is the poetic form—the "soul of tragedy" ("On Greek Tragedy," 141 below). The two are not as different as they seem at first, for the prominence of plot is the sign of the need to make visible what cannot but be invisible (*aïdes*).

8. See "On Greek Tragedy," chap. 7 below.

9. See "Strauss on Plato," 410 below.

10. In the discussion of *Oedipus Tyrannus* in "On Greek Tragedy" (chap. 7 below), Benardete rethinks with radical consequences his earlier reading of the play (see "Sophocles' *Oedipus Tyrannus,*" chap. 5 below), precisely by attending even more closely to the "obvious" perplexities.

11. See Aristotle's *Poetics,* chapters 10–11.

12. "On Plato's *Sophist,*" 343 below.

13. When Socrates appeals in the *Phaedrus* to the principle of "logographic necessity" as a standard for the written work, it might seem to be just another way of stating the model he holds up of the living animal, whose parts are never superfluous, but all in fitting relation to each other and to the whole (*Phaedrus* 264b–c). For Benardete, however, while the living animal is a model for the structure of the work as a whole of parts, logographic necessity is the principle of the temporal sequence by which one step of the argument follows from another (see his *The Rhetoric of Morality and Philosophy: Plato's "Gorgias" and "Phaedrus"* [Chicago: University of Chicago Press, 1991], 176–77). The relation between them is exemplified in the *Phaedrus* by Socrates' two speeches on *eros:* the second follows after the first as a "recantation" of it, and yet, in this recantation it brings to light the whole of which both speeches together constitute the parts. That this relation may also be at work across dialogues is suggested by Benardete's account of the movement from *Theaetetus* to *Sophist* to *Statesman,* which turns the otherwise independent dialogues into parts of a larger whole (cf. the conclusion of Benardete's discussion of each of these dialogues, chapters 15, 16, and 17 below).

14. These interpretative principles, drawn from Schleiermacher's introduction to his Platonic studies, are presumably among the "five or six extremely important and true remarks about Plato's literary devices" which Strauss attributes to him (see Friedrich Schleiermacher, *Introductions to the Dialogues of Plato* [New York: Arno Press, 1973], 1–19; and Strauss's essay, "Exoteric Teaching," reprinted in *The Rebirth of Classical Political Rationalism: Essays and Lectures by Leo Strauss,* selected and introduced by Thomas Pangle [Chicago: University of Chicago Press, 1989], 67). Yet Schleiermacher assumes only a difference of degree between the understanding of the reader attentive to those devices and that of one who is not; and this assumption, Strauss charges, is a sign of his failure to recognize in the difference among interpretations the kind of radical break that, according to Plato, separates the ordinary understanding of things from that of the philosopher. What sets Benardete's readings apart is his way of tracing the philosophic dynamic of the dialogue which accounts for that radical break.

15. "Strauss on Plato," 409 below.

16. It is the reflection of this action of the argument in the very language of the dialogue that Benardete's linguistic analyses uncover. When Aristophanes ends his speech on eros with the advice to find a beloved *kata noun,* he means "as one likes"; but literally, as Benardete observes, he says "according to mind." Alerted to this double sense, we see that Plato has captured in a phrase Aristophanes' problematic understanding of *eros,* which, in being "divorced from man's rationality," aspires to "a wholeness that lacks intelligibility" ("On Plato's *Symposium,* 175 below). The same expression occurs in the first line of the *Philebus,* where Socrates invites his interlocuter to defend the claim of pleasure to be the cause

of human happiness over against the claim of mind—unless he finds the other view *kata noun:* as soon as Benardete calls our attention to it, we see that language itself, by exhibiting the inextricable mixture of mind and pleasure that the abstractions of hedonism and intellectualism deny, compels us to rethink the argument (see *The Tragedy and Comedy of Life: Plato's "Philebus"* [Chicago: University of Chicago Press, 1993], 1, n. 2).

17. Seth Benardete, *Socrates' Second Sailing: On Plato's "Republic"* (Chicago: University of Chicago Press, 1989), 3.

18. This is a description Benardete offers of the Eleatic Stranger's procedure in the *Sophist* and *Statesman* (see "On Plato's *Lysis*," 211 below).

19. See "On Plato's *Phaedo*," 295, n. 4 below.

20. See Benardete's review of Leo Strauss's *The City and Man,* in *The Political Science Reviewer* 8 (Fall 1978): 4.

21. See, for example, *Socrates' Second Sailing,* 4–5, and notes 22, 24, 25, and 27 below.

22. See "On Plato's *Phaedo*," 282–83 below.

23. See "On Plato's *Symposium*," 180 below.

24. Concerning Aristotle's use of the term, see Benardete's remark on the formula "the more and less" as it appears in the *Philebus* (*The Tragedy and Comedy of Life,* 20, n. 48). Benardete uses the term himself, for example, to capture the Eleatic Stranger's search for the science of the statesman. That science, *politikē,* is originally assigned to the class of theoretical, as opposed to practical, science. But in the course of the analysis, that dichotomy is replaced by a twofold science of measure, where *politikē* comes to light as the architectonic science of the measure of the mean, in contrast to the mathematical measure; yet in this role it applies no more to political practice than to the Stranger's discovery of it, which is some kind of theoretical activity. The gradual slide that produces this "indeterminate dyad" depends on a "deidealization" of the original division: a mutually exclusive dichotomy between theoretical and practical only fits the god of the Stranger's myth, who in one cosmic epoch pilots the universe, in another withdraws in contemplation ("The Plan of Plato's *Statesman*," chap. 17 below).

25. See "On Plato's *Sophist*," 325 below.

26. See "On Interpreting Plato's *Charmides*," chap. 12 below, and "Plato's *Laches:* A Question of Definition," chap. 13 below.

27. While the scholarly tradition questions how the same Socrates could advocate a punitive morality in the *Gorgias* and a hedonistic calculus in the *Protagoras,* Benardete interprets these presentations as the phantom self-images Socrates adopts in the course of his attempt to identify sophistry and rhetoric as phantom images of two genuine arts (see "Protagoras's Myth and Logos," chap. 10 below).

28. This analysis of the chariot image in the *Phaedrus* (See *The Rhetoric of Morality and Philosophy,* 149–51) lies behind Benardete's account of Socrates' par-

ticular interaction with Alcibiades ("On Plato's *Symposium,* chap. 9 below). It furnishes the model for a description of the Platonic dialogue in general, from which Benardete singles out the *Statesman* as a deliberate exception ("The Plan of Plato's *Statesman,*" chap. 17 below.)

29. See "Plato's *Laches:* A Question of Definition," 273 below and "On Interpreting Plato's *Charmides,*" 243 below.

30. See "On Plato's *Phaedo,*" 278 below.

31. Compare this with Aelian's story about the speeches of Socrates, cited in "Strauss on Plato," chap. 20 below. A movement of this sort embedded in language itself becomes thematic in the playful etymologies of the *Cratylus:* by tracing the linguistic extension they represent—from an original, corporeal meaning to a derivative, noncorporeal one—Benardete reconstructs the argument of the dialogue (see, for example, the derivation of "tragedy" from "goat-song," in "Physics and Tragedy: On Plato's *Cratylus,*" 160 below). To understand what the Eleatic Stranger is doing in his "method of division," requires, as Benardete demonstrates, "galvanizing back into life" the original meaning of *methodos* ("The Plan of Plato's *Statesman,*" 364 below).

32. In contrast with the tragic perspective conveyed by the comic poet Aristophanes when he "announces an Eros without hope," since "the human is essentially incomplete and disordered," Socrates sees that precisely "in its incompleteness it is in order and good" ("On Plato's *Symposium,*" 173 below).

33. For this citation of Strauss, see "Strauss on Plato," 416 below.

34. See *Antigone,* 74; *Oedipus at Colonus,* 1410.

35. Tragedy brings before our eyes the meaning of Aristotle's claim that, without the city, man would be more terrible than any animal when it comes to food and sex (*Politics* I, 1253a36–39). Tragedy represents, in Benardete's words, "the offscouring" of the rationalized city in speech that Socrates constructs ("On Greek Tragedy," 100 below).

36. Examining Euripides' presentation of fear in the *Bacchae,* as the counterpart to Sophocles' presentation of shame in the *Oedipus Tyrannus,* Benardete finds an "inextricable involvement with Hades" which marks these tragic passions and explains their "resistance to enlightenment." It is, accordingly, an "antitragic" understanding Aristotle displays when he concludes his account of moral virtue by denying that shame is a virtue, and with that, political courage in the face of fear (see "On Greek Tragedy," 140–41 below).

37. Tragedy's denial of the good in human life is connected with its distance from the real, and that in turn is connected with the way tragedy takes its bearings from the city, that is, from the cave; philosophy affirms life, in contrast, by acknowledging "a divide between man as man and man as political animal that poetry denies" (*The Tragedy and Comedy of Life,* xii).

38. See "The First Crisis in First Philosophy," 4, 7, and 11 below. The playful first line of this discussion—"Virtually everyone knows that Aristotle sometimes

lies"—points to the connection between Benardete's analysis of Hesiod as "first philosopher," in the opening essay in this collection, and his analysis of Aristotle's "first philosophy," in the penultimate essay. In *Metaphysics A,* Aristotle accuses the poets of telling many lies (see chap. 19 below). Of course, as the *Poetics* attests, Aristotle is well aware that there is a truth that can only, or best, be discovered through fiction—that is, through the lies of the poets. In the very context, moreover, of his charge against the poets, he is about to relate a "history" of philosophy, which, in terms of historical accuracy, is full of "lies." Aristotle is in fact displaying a lesson he has learned from the poets: the truth of his account is itself philosophic, conveyed not despite but through his distorted historical presentation.

39. The poet's "lies like the truth" are his systematic construction of what we all do anytime we impersonate someone else, and thus make one into two, or employ nonliteral language, and thus make two into one; the paradigm is the poets' construction of gods, which seems to combine image-making with impersonation (see Seth Benardete, *The Bow and the Lyre: A Platonic Reading of the Odyssey* [Lanham, MD: Rowman and Littlefield, 1997], xi–xiv).

40. "Strauss on Plato," 415–16 below.

THE ARGUMENT OF THE ACTION

ONE

The First Crisis in First Philosophy

VIRTUALLY EVERYONE KNOWS THAT ARISTOTLE sometimes lies. His account of the pre-Socratics in the first book of the *Metaphysics* leaves out of account everything that does not suit his scheme, the gradual disclosure of the four causes, compelled, as he says, by the truth itself. Heraclitus' fire is there, but not Heraclitus' logos. Parmenides' Eros is there, but not Parmenides' mind. This triumphant progress, however, comes abruptly to an end at the end of Book I, and Book II begins the crisis of first philosophy. It is the very triumph of Book I that brings about the crisis of Book II, and it is Book II that is first philosophy: it consists of nothing but questions. These seventeen questions could not have been formulated had not Book I preceded it and confirmed that wisdom was the theoretical knowledge of cause. The knowledge of cause, however, does not establish first philosophy; it merely discloses what still must be known, being. Being emerges as the problem of first philosophy through the nonproblematic status of the four causes. The emergence of being as the problem is not adventitious to the four causes. There lurks within the four causes one cause that is not an answer but a question, and the question is, What is? Formal cause is the only cause that appears among the categorial predicates, and of these it is the only one that is a question, and whose formulation includes in itself that which the question is about. To ask about being is to acknowledge belatedly that it has come to light as a question about which one asks questions. If, then, first philosophy is first only the second time around, where are we to begin? Aristotle has another name for first philosophy. He calls it theology. Theology is a tainted word. It is first used, as far as we know, by Plato, and he puts it in the mouth of Adimantus, whom Socrates is questioning about what myths are to be told the future guardians when young *(Republic).* Theology, then, is theomythy. It precedes any true account of the gods. Socrates' theology is set in opposition to the stories of Homer and Hesiod. It is one set of myths against another. Hesiod's myth, however, is not Hesiod's but the Muses', and the Muses tell Hesiod that they speak *(legein)* lies like the truth and pronounce, whenever they wish, the truth. Before philosophy there are lies like the truth. Before philosophy, we say, there is poetry. Poetry has already divided lies from truth and put them together again. Poetry is not at the beginning but after the beginning, when the speaking about the speaking about things has become part of the speaking. This double speak puts things at a distance from us. The things the Muses speak about are the beginning. We are not at the beginning when we hear the Muses about the beginning. At the beginning are the Muses who sing about the beginning.

Hesiod is the first poet we know of who tells us his name and who writes two works. Not everything he knows, he seems to be saying, is to be found in one poem; but in order that we put together what he has set apart he must give us his name, so that we do not infer from the differences between the two poems that they do not belong together but are of different poets. Hesiod tells us in what order we are to read his poems. The *Works and Days* begins with an admission of a mistake; he now realizes that the goddess Strife is not merely the mother of Bloodshed and Lies but also of rivalry and competition without which there would be no progress in the arts. There is but one Strife in the *Theogony;* she is the offspring of Night and has Nemesis and Old Age as her sisters. But Friendliness, or Philotēs, is also a sister. Could *Philotēs,* then, be the disguised form of Strife as rivalry, and through her complete separation from Strife appear more friendly than she is? Hesiod, in any case, seems to be warning us that his genealogies are mythical precisely because as they divide what are in fact united in a complex structure so they pull apart what is always together. He seems to be saying that his two poems are likewise mythical, and what they have to say is not what is said in either one of them.

We say that Hesiod combined a cosmogony with a theogony, and we mean by that that he combined an account of those things we see and know—heaven and earth—with those things we do not see and do not know—Kronos and Zeus—and for the truth of whose existence we must rely on Muses who do not tell the truth and on their mouthpiece Hesiod, who cannot be more truthful than the Muses want to be. The first things, we say, are subject to a double interpretation; they are the gods of either a "natural" or a conventional religion; but in the case of Hesiod, we can go further: Heaven was once a god, but as soon as he was castrated he became a neutral being and part of the permanent order within which the Olympian gods are effective. Earth is not disposed of as quickly, and not until her last offspring is defeated by Zeus does she too fade into the background. The exhaustion of the generative power of the first things allows for their replacement by gods whose being is not tied up with what they can generate but with what they can make. Becoming is thus split between sexual generation, whose essential nature is that the offspring cannot be predicted or willed by the parents, and artful making, in which the foreknowledge of the plan allows the maker to produce the parts in whatever order he finds convenient. The maker does not have to proceed in order in order for the whole to be in order. From this point of view, the story Hesiod tells is one of the gradual triumph of art and the defeat of generation. Zeus produces Athena out of his own head and Hera by herself produces Hephaestus. The coming of the Olympian gods coincides with the possibility of Hesiod being a poet. The Muses necessarily cannot antedate Zeus. Whereas in Genesis, God is the maker and there is no maker of Genesis, in Hesiod, the gods whom Hesiod celebrates finally become makers and bestow on Hesiod the same gift. The *Theogony* thus looks like the story of the defeat of Eros, who in being the most beautiful of gods overcomes the mind of gods and men alike. The defeat of Eros does not entail his elimination but only his taming. After Zeus, blind coupling is replaced by lawful marriage, and whatever offspring there are can no longer threaten the Olympian establishment.

This first reading of the *Theogony* is paradoxical. The Olympian gods, whose beauty is what most distinguishes them from all earlier and later gods, come to be through the defeat of Eros, whose principle they represent. The demands of reason force the love of the beautiful to become through the mode of production sterile. It would seem, then, that Hesiod prepares the way for Plato, whose innovation consists no less in denying the incompatibility of Eros and mind than in assigning to production a spurious version of Eros. His Socrates is sterile without being a maker. However this may be, the story we have found in Hesiod seems not to be all of Hesiod's story. It has pushed its way through to the end of Hesiod's story and not reflected on how Hesiod got there. It got hold of the intention without attending to the plan of Hesiod.

The model for Hesiod's narrative is supplied by the Muses. Their birth is followed by an account of their function. The being of the goddesses is not separated from their meaning. For the Muses, who do not antedate the order of Zeus, and whose being is to be the conveyors of meaning, such a tight connection between being and meaning is inevitable. In the case, however, of the other gods, the application of this scheme to them upsets the temporal sequence and completes the parts of the whole before there is any whole of which they can be parts. The offspring of Phorcys and Ceto are early in the narrative, but since the role they fill is after Zeus has usurped power, we do not realize at first that these monsters are not primitive residues of an older chaos but the beings Zeus has allowed to be born prior to their destruction through his mortal children. Echidna mates with Typhos, but Typhos was born after the triumph of the Olympians over the Titans, and as soon as he was born Zeus destroyed him, or at least we are led to believe that that is the case since, in accordance with the narrative principle, being and meaning are linked; but in fact Zeus did not defeat Typhos before his offspring were born, all of whom are killed except Cerberus. Heracles kills Geryon's dog Orthus, the Hydra, and the Nemean lion, the last two of whom Hera brought up, and Bellerophon kills the Chimera. Zeus allows these monsters to be born so that the earth can become civilized through heroes. The earth had to be made savage by the will of Zeus before it could be made tame through Zeus.

The way in which Hesiod connects the becoming and the meaning of the Muses is not as simple as we have described. The proem of the *Theogony,* which is devoted to the Muses, is more than one-tenth of the entire poem; indeed, it is longer than any other section of continuous narrative. Hesiod begins by proposing to begin by singing of the Heliconian Muses. They occupy the top of the mountain and sing and dance around the altar of Zeus. This is presented as a habitual practice of theirs. They also habitually descend from the mountain on their usual way, we are led to believe, to Olympus. On their descent, they become invisible and celebrate in song the gods. The gods they celebrate seem to fall into three groups. Zeus and Hera head the first group in which are included many of the Olympians; the second group begins with Themis and ends with Kronos; with one exception, they are all Titans or co-emergent with Titans; and in the last group are the so-called cosmic gods, from the givers of light to black Night. The descent of the Muses involves a song that goes back in time to the beginning; the exception to this smooth regress is Hebe, or Youthfulness, who belongs to the offspring of Zeus's last marriage with Hera but has been put with the Titans. The brother of Hebe is Ares. The Muses, in unrolling the past, suppress the Olympian god of war.

Once the Muses arrive at the foothills of Helicon, we expect them to ascend; and they do indeed ascend after a short digression. In their ascent to Olympus, they habitually sing another song, designed to delight the mind of Zeus. This song too is in three parts; but now the order is from the beginning and not to the beginning. They first sing of Earth and Sky and all their descendants; they then sing of Zeus by himself, the father of gods and men, and how he is the mightiest and strongest of the gods. The third part of their song is devoted to the race of human beings and Giants. This second song prepares the way for an account of their own birth, close to the top of Mount Olympus, and the song they sang as soon as they were born while they went to their father at the peak. This song is about how Zeus is king in heaven, and how he conquered his father Kronos and arranged the laws and honors for the gods. This third song is revealed to be a song only after Hesiod has given it in his own words. It is Hesiod's song before it is declared to be the Muses'.

The movement of the proem is so far the disclosure of the greatness of Zeus along with his justice; but this movement of descent and double ascent, from regular descent and ascent, to a one-time ascent to the top of Olympus, is breached by Hesiod's one-time encounter with the Muses at the foot of Helicon, where he was grazing his sheep. The Muses do not begin their ascent of Olympus before they tell Hesiod what they do and what he is to do. What they do is to tell lies like the truth and, whenever they wish, the truth. What Hesiod is to do is sing of the past and future, celebrate the gods, and begin and end with the Muses. The distinction Hesiod draws between what the Muses do and what he is to do is between direct and indirect speech. Hesiod seems to anticipate the objection of Socrates, who wants the poets in the best city in speech never to assume the guise of anyone but themselves. Hesiod tells us that he could have incorporated what the Muses say into what he says they say; but instead he lets the Muses speak for themselves, or, if we adopt Socrates' view, he becomes for three lines the Muses. As soon as Hesiod moves from narrative to imitation the issue of imitation emerges in the form of lies like the truth. Either in separating himself off from another or in becoming another, Hesiod reveals that there is a speaking that is mixed up with a peculiar form of lying. Whatever else this may mean, it calls attention to the fact that it is only because Hesiod blocks the path of the Muses on their way to the top of Olympus that the Muses must be disclosed as who they are. Without Hesiod the celebration of the might of Zeus would not have included the Muses; and without the Muses there would have been no story of the triumph of Zeus. The disclosure of the Muses through Hesiod forces the celebration of the gods to include the story about the gods. The disclosure of the being of the gods includes the disclosure of the meaning of the gods.

The Muses serve two purposes. They favor either kings or singers. The purpose of singers is to make men forget the evils they endure by recalling the glories of the human past and the blessed gods of Olympus. The purpose of kings, if the Muses look favorably on their birth, is to settle suits in such a way as to reconcile the loser, or him who believes he is the loser, to his losing out. The Muses are not needed for the kings to know what is right; but they are needed to establish right in spite of the opposition to right by those who believe they are in the right. The Muses can fit together right and apparent right. They can do this on earth; Hesiod does not make it clear whether Zeus also needs the Muses to win over those he overthrew to the new order, or he is so powerful that he can dispense with their help among the gods, but he is still not so powerful as not to need them among men. Before Zeus there was Kronos; before Zeus there was the golden age, in which there was neither women nor work. Singers call men back to a time when there was no need of singers, to a time before Zeus, in order to have them forget their troubles and at the same time reconcile men to what is. The belief that once there was paradise now lost and the belief that things are just what they are, or the belief in a cosmogony, are all of a piece. It is the purpose of the Muses to satisfy those beliefs and point the way to their falsity.

Hesiod asks the Muses for help. They are to celebrate the gods and tell their story. They are to begin at the beginning. At the beginning, there is only one god Hesiod knew of before the Muses began; but that god—Earth—is second. The formula used to introduce her as the second is αὐτὰρ ἔπειτα, "then thereafter." This formula, we expect, will at least be repeated whenever the Muses proceed from one class of gods to another; and we are not at first disappointed: the Titans too are presented after the formula αὐτὰρ ἔπειτα. But after this occurrence the formula vanishes only to reappear in a contrafactual at the end—what would have happened "then thereafter" had Zeus not swallowed Metis and been replaced by their son (897). The apparent temporal succession of the poem is replaced by a narrative succession that tempts us into rewriting the poem in accordance with the truth of time, for many parts of the story of Zeus are given before he is born; indeed, his offer to all the gods to overthrow the Titans and his own father is reported in indirect statement long before his mother tricked Kronos into swallowing a stone in place of himself.

At the beginning, in order, are Chaos, Earth, Tartarus, and Eros. All of them came to be. They came to be out of nothing and through nothing. The Muses carry the principle of generation—whatever is, came to be—so far that it becomes nonsense. Let us suppose, then, that the Muses mean that there was no beginning, for what was at the beginning was not cosmogony but theogony. What was at the beginning were not beings but meanings. There were always gods. At the beginning, then, there would be Earth, Tartarus, and Eros. Of these three, Earth dominates the narrative. Tartarus does not enter the story before Zeus finds a use for him as the prison of the Titans. Tartarus is the anticipated home of Right as punishment. As for Eros, though it would seem to be at least meant as an efficient cause, as indeed Aristotle takes it to be, Eros does not reappear except as an attendant of Aphrodite, and in verbal form as the love Zeus conceived for Memory in giving birth to the Muses. Not only, then, is Right an empty form at the beginning but also Eros, who is the most beautiful of the gods. The beautiful and the just are at the beginning but they are virtually fruitless. The third is Earth. She alone immediately produces out of herself Ouranos, "in order that he may hide her completely, so that he may be the ever-safe seat for the blessed gods." The only one of the first beings whom Hesiod knew of beforehand, and who seems therefore to be completely real, has two purpose clauses attached to her first production. The real involves the good. At the beginning, then, are the good, the just, and the beautiful. The story Hesiod tells would seem to be accordingly about the ways in which these kinds were split and combined in the experiences of men: Chaos, or "Gap," would be the difference between any two them. Although the good, the just, and the beautiful are at the beginning, they are not as such at the beginning. What is said about the beginning only dimly reflects the beginning.

Eros seems to be inactive. The possible exception is in the birth of Day out of Night and Erebus, the first act of sexual generation, and it occurred in love *(philotēs)*. The separation into day and night occurs through the most beautiful of the gods. What is to be seen in the light is always at a distance, but the union in love precludes distance and light. At the beginning, the double aspect of Eros is split into day and night: when Ouranos comes to sleep with Earth, he brings night with him. What is to be seen and what is not to be seen in the light are set apart in such a way that they cannot be rejoined. Accordingly, Eros as the separator of night and day is replaced by hatred as the separator of earth and heaven. What orders the cosmos is not Eros the god, but hatred, which is first seen to be effective before we hear of any gods who might be thought to cover the range of meaning in hatred. Hatred emerges as the orderer of the cosmos through an apparent failure of narration. The Muses list the Titans as born before they are really born, for we learn after their birth that their father Ouranos prevented them from being born. To be born means to come into the light. Not to be in the light is not to be born. Ouranos loathed his offspring; he hated becoming or time. The virtual suppression of Day, which is never for always, forced there to be a permanent light into which the gods could be born forever. This new light required the castration of Ouranos, or the permanent separation of the distance and union of Eros.

At the beginning, Day comes from Night and Erebos. The light of day is presumably that of which Ouranos deprived his children; this light, once they are allowed to enter it, will be permanently theirs. When Day and Night return, in the section on the topography of Tartarus, day has become the human day. It is no longer something into which we go and abide, but something into which we go and out of which we pass into night, sleep, death, and Hades. Man has become mortal, and *mortal* is not a neutral term that designates the fact that man dies but a marked term in a pair, whose meaning is determined by its opposite, *immortal.* The shift from the god Death to the god Hades, from a designation of a verb to a subject, signifies the vanishing of being as something we simply know into the experience of being about which we know nothing, and whose meaning is supplied by the gods whom we can never become. The importance of this shift from neutral being to loaded meaning can be measured by Socrates, who in Plato's *Apology* distinguishes himself from all the rest of the Athenians by his ignorance about death and their unshakable conviction that death is an evil. Socrates rests his case for philosophy on the attempt to recover the being of nonbeing from the overlay of its meaning, which is Hades. Hades is not the truth of death but of philosophy, whose constant effort is to discover the invisible and deathless *aïdes.*

The hatred of time, which is created through Eros, leads to the creation of space, into which the Titans can come to be and be in the light. The consequence of this suppression of love in favor of hatred is the coming into being of Aphrodite, who arises from the genitals of Ouranos falling into the sea. At the same time as Aphrodite is born from the foam of the sea, the giants and Furies are born from the drops of blood that fell on the earth. Eros, we may say, is reborn along with vengeance as Aphrodite. Aphrodite is Eros combined with the desire for punishment. The beautiful and the just are now together forever. That this has happened Hesiod indicates by inserting his first pair of speeches. Earth asks who of all her children will punish their father for his crime, and Kronos accepts the challenge, for Ouranos first, he says, devised unseemly deeds. As soon as gods speak, they lie; they interpret necessity in terms of right. Neither mother nor son says that to be born means to go into the light; both falsify the light as right. They color becoming with meaning. Such a coloring means that the Cyclopes and the Hundred-handers, who are equally the children of Earth and Ouranos, do not come into the light with the Titans but are kept imprisoned by Ouranos even after he has been castrated and thus created the distance between heaven and earth into which all his children should have been able to enter. The Cyclopes and the Hundred-handers have their meaning in the story of the Titanomachy and Typhos. What they are and what they signify are separated. They are the only case in which Hesiod allows such a separation. Had he followed his usual practice, the overthrow of the Titans and Typhos would have had to have been given before the Titans had even taken over from Ouranos. Zeus would have been at the beginning, and Tartarus, or the establishment of right, would not have been empty at the beginning. There would have been punishment as soon as there had been crime, and there would never have been time uninfected by the desire for revenge. Hesiod's failure to account for the Cyclopes and the Hundred-handers staying hid once there is light, so that they have to wait for Zeus before they can come into the light, forces us to conclude that Zeus was always, or that a cosmogony that was not from the first a theology is impossible. The recovery of the beings is through the meaning of the beings, for our deepest illusion is that we know the beings as they are in themselves.

It is immediately after the story of the birth of Aphrodite that Hesiod speaks of the gods whose effects we have already seen in that story. There are now Strife, Philotēs, Deception, Speeches *(Logoi)*, and Lies. The same sequence had occurred when Hesiod told the story of the Muses: their names embody the verbs, nouns, and adjectives in the story of their birth. The gods apparently come after what they really are. Hesiod gives us the evidence against his argument in the story he tells. We are forced to use Hesiod against Hesiod in order to understand Hesiod. After the children of Night and Strife come the children of Pontos, or the Sea. The most important of these is Nereus, or Truth (Nemertēs, or Unerringness, is one of his daughters). At the beginning, there were lies and there was truth; they were as separated as the sea from earth and night from day. They were not really separated. There were not at the beginning the Muses who tell lies like the truth. That there are lies and that there is truth is a lie like the truth the Muses tell. The belief that we know the beings apart from meaning is on a par with our belief that lie and truth are apart.

We believe they are apart, say the Muses, because we believe in right: as Horkos, who punishes men when they perjure themselves, is the brother of Speeches and Lies, so Nereus, or Truth, is not forgetful *(lēthetai)* of right and knows the just things and mild counsels. The Muses indulge us in those beliefs while they tell a story that gives the lie to those beliefs.

The difference between Zeus and the older gods first emerges in Hesiod's report on his enlistment of the older gods in his new order. His appeal is based on honor. Whatever god thought he had not received his proper share under the old order could be assured of his place, and no god who already had a place would lose it. The first to enlist was Styx. She brought her children with her. They were Glory and Victory, Might and Force. Zeus distinguished between honor and reward, on the one hand, and, on the other, between disgrace and punishment. For the first time there is knowledge of the difference in natures. Those who do not respond to honor are made to experience punishment. The world splits apart between profit and glory, and the Muses are needed to keep it together, so that those who understand only beating may take pleasure in stories of fame, and those who understand only disgrace may need the others for their fame. The first god who fully exemplifies this principle is Hecate, whose favors according to Hesiod depend solely on her will. These favors are split between men who seek honor in judging, public speaking, war, or contests, and men who seek gain in fishing, farming, or the herding of sheep and cattle. The goddess of the Will,[1] or Hecate, is an innovation of Zeus and Hesiod: she does not correspond except in name to any god known among the Greeks. With Hecate comes appearance; Hesiod mentions it now for the first time: Hecate as easily grants fishermen a large catch as takes it away when it appears. The goddess of the Will follows immediately on Zeus establishing Styx with the power to be a great oath among the gods. The Olympian gods belong to an order based on law. For the first time, immediately after Styx, Hesiod speaks of sacrifices according to law. The law both brings together gods and men and separates them.

It is now possible to sense the shape of Hesiod's poem as a whole. Before Styx, we are in the realm of desire; after Styx and up to and through the Titanomachy and the defeat of Typhos, we are in the realm of the will; and after Zeus is completely in charge, there is the realm of mind. It does not have to be stressed how curiously similar this is to the soul-structure of Plato's *Republic;* but it may be as deceptive as Plato's scheme. In any case, Hecate has prepared the way for Zeus. One of the very first things he does is to replace the separation of heaven and earth, which seemed to be permanent once Ouranos was castrated, by a separation maintained by Atlas: that heaven and earth are separate is now a matter of Zeus's will. The sky may fall at any moment. Zeus introduces terror. The introduction of terror requires its opposite, the promise of the eternal. Woman is due to his making; she is the first being who is nothing but meaning. Her meaning is in both her appearance and her being. In substance she is earth, in appearance she is beautiful. She is a beautiful evil. Woman was made to separate men from gods in reality and reconnect them in appearance. Before Zeus there were no women, and men lived with the gods. Prometheus tried to hoodwink Zeus by offering him two portions from what would be the first sacrificial victim. One portion is covered with skin, the other with fat; under the skin there was meat, under the fat there were bones. Zeus deliberately chose the bones. In his apparent anger at being deceived, Zeus took fire away from men; he either made Prometheus's gift to men unusable or he made men eat raw flesh. Prometheus, however, stole fire back from Zeus and men accepted it. They accepted both Prometheus's apportionment and Prometheus's crime; but they agreed to sacrifice to the gods with fire and leave them the honor and take for themselves the gain. Men always had fire, Hesiod seems to be saying, but only when fire was taken away and stolen back did they really have fire. Fire ceased to be a being in itself and acquired a lawful meaning. In exchange for that fire Zeus had woman made. She too is like the double fire. Hephaestus made her.

The fashioning of woman leads Hesiod to make his first extended simile; it is the first of three. The second occurs in the course of the Titanomachy, and separates what Zeus did from what his helpers did, the Hundred-handers, who really defeated the Titans. It involves a counterfactual and is occasioned by the fire of Zeus proving to be ineffective as a weapon but still full of significance. There is a so-called law of Zielinski which states that epic poetry never goes back in narrative time. Hesiod violates this law twice. He recalls the imprisonment of the Hundred-handers by Ouranos in order to explain how Zeus managed to conquer the Titans. Hesiod goes back in time to give the Hundred-handers a meaning. In doing so, he tells how Zeus used his lightning-bolts to such effect that it seemed to the eyes and ears that he had reproduced what had been the crash when earth and sky had originally come near to one another. Through a simile the first act of cosmic creation has been charged with meaning, the threat Zeus holds out that what is now apart is not in truth apart but is subject to his will. To be together is not the union of love but the union of chaos. The power (δύναμις) of Zeus is the meaning (δύναμις) of Zeus. It naturally comes out in a simile of the Muses.

The third and last simile of the *Theogony* compares the lightning of Zeus in its deployment against Typhos to the melting of iron or tin; it is effective against Typhos, who otherwise would have usurped his rule. Typhos's power consists in his ability to imitate the sounds of all things, including the language of the gods. Typhos is the false god. In his case the simile is true and Zeus's power is real. He is followed by the marriages of Zeus, after all the gods have agreed to his rule. His first marriage was to be with Metis, or Mind, but it did not take place; had it gone forward, and Zeus not swallowed her instead, Zeus would have been overthrown by his son. The name of this unborn god must be Outis, or No-one. Between the anonymity of Mind and the false god Typhos is Zeus. Zeus is the lie like the truth, or, as Heraclitus says, The one is willing and not willing to be called by the name of Zeus. The accusative of Zeus's name is *Dia;* it is indistinguishable from the preposition, which with the genitive divides things and with the accusative designates a cause.

In the whole display of gods and goddesses which is the *Theogony,* only one god does not come to be. His name is Desire, or Himeros. Concealed within Him-eros is the name Eros. Himeros accompanies both the Muses and Aphrodite. On the occasion of the birth of Aphrodite, Hesiod explains why she is called "laughter-loving," *philommeidēs.* She is laughter-loving, he says, because she came to light from genitals, or *mēdea.* The word *mēdea* is in fact two words; one names the genitals, the other wise counsels. Wise counsels belong particularly to Zeus. The movement of the poem is from sex to mind, from *mēdea* to *mēdea.* Could it be, then, that concealed within laughter-loving Aphrodite are not just genitals but wise counsels? Could Φιλομμειδης mean Φιλόσοφος? There is only one occasion, and this I am inclined to believe ends Hesiod's poem, where the plans of the gods are in harmony with golden Aphrodite. It is at the birth of Medeia or Wisdom. She is the granddaughter of the sun, and her mother is *Iduia,* "she who knows."

Note

1. Hesiod underscores the connection between Hecate, whose first syllable is the same as the word "willing" *(hekōn),* by speaking of Hecate's possible willingness six times (429, 430, 432, 439, 443, 447).

TWO

Achilles and the *Iliad*

THE FIRST QUESTION AND ANSWER of Porphyry's *Quaestiones Homericae* run:

> Were anyone to ask, noting the worth and excellence of Achilles, why Homer called his work the *Iliad* and not the *Achilleid*—as he did the *Odyssey* after Odysseus—we would answer that, in one case, the story concerned a single man; while in the other, even if Achilles excelled the rest, yet they too were excellent, and that Homer wished to show us not only Achilles but also, in a way, all heroes, and what sort of men they were: so, unwilling to call it after one man, he used the name of a city, which merely suggested the name of Achilles.

Achilles is a hero in a world of heroes; he is of the same cast as they, though we might call him the first impression that has caught each point more finely than later copies. He holds within himself all the heroic virtues that are given singly to others (he has the swiftness of Oilean and the strength of Telamonian Ajax), but his excellence is still the sum of theirs. We do not need a separate rule to measure his supremacy. But before we can come into the presence of Achilles and take his measure, we must first be presented with the common warrior, who is not just something vaguely but specifically heroic, with whom Achilles shares more in common than he knows. The common warrior is the armature on which Achilles is shaped and the backdrop against which his story is played. Homer assumes our ignorance of what the heroes are, the heroic world from which Achilles withdraws and yet to which he still belongs. And it is our intention here to show how this world circumscribes, though it does not completely define, Achilles.

I. Men and Heroes

When Hector's challenge to a duel found no takers among the Achaeans, "as ashamed to ignore as afraid to accept it," Menelaus, after some time, adopting a rebuke invented by Thersites (2.235), berates them thus: *ō moi, apeilētēres, Achaides, ouket' Achaioi* (7.96, cf. 235–36, 11.389, 23.409). Warriors ought to believe that to be a woman is the worst calamity; and yet Homer seems to mock their belief, in making Menelaus, who warred to recover the most beautiful of women, and Thersites, the ugliest person who came to Troy, the spokesmen for manliness. However this may be, both the Achaeans and Trojans not only insist on being men as opposed to women, but also on being *andres* as distinct from *anthrōpoi.*

Anthrōpoi are men and women collectively, and men or women indifferently, and whatever may be the virtues of an *anthrōpos,* it cannot be martial courage, which is the specific virtue of men. Nestor urges the Achaeans to stand their ground (14.661–63): "Friends, be men *(andres),* and set shame in your heart before other human beings *(anthrōpoi),* and let each of you remember your children and wives, and possessions and parents." The Achaeans themselves must be *andres,* or "he-men"; others, their own children, parents and wives, are *anthrōpoi. Anthrōpoi* are the others, either those who lived before—*proteroi anthrōpoi*—(5.637, 23.332, 790, cf. 1.250, 6.202, 20.217, 220, 233, 24.535)—or those yet to come—*opsigonoi anthrōpoi* (3.287, 353, 460, 6.358, 7.87); and if the heroes employ it of the living, they are careful not to include themselves (cf. 9.134, 276). Others are *anthrōpoi,* but never is another an *anthrōpos.* If you wish to be an individual, you must be either *anēr* or *gunē;* but if you belong to a crowd, indistinguishable from your neighbor, you are both cataloged together under "human beings" (3.402, 9.134, 328, 340, 592, 10.213, 14.662, 16.621, 18.288, 342, 20.204, 357, 24.202). The singular occurs but thrice in the *Iliad,* twice in a general sense and perhaps once of an individual, but in all three cases Homer speaks in his own name, and two of them occur in similes (16.263, 315, 17.572). And not only do human beings in the heroic view lack all uniqueness and belong more to the past or the future than the present, but even Odysseus seems to young Antilochus, as a member of a prior generation, more *anthrōpos* than *anēr* (23.787–91). Old age is as absolute as death, which deprived Hector and Patroclus of their *androtēta kai hēbēn* (17.857, 22.363, cf. 24.6), a heroic manhood that lasts but an instant, and with its end consigns Odysseus to the world of *anthrōpoi* and Hector to Hades.

Achilles in the ninth book is found "pleasing his heart with the clear-toned lyre and singing the famous deeds of men" (*klea andrōn,* 9.189, cf. 524–27); whereas Aeneas, before declaiming his genealogy to Achilles, remarks that "we know each other's lineage and have heard the famous words of mortal human beings" (*prokluta epea thnētōn anthrōpōn* 20.203, cf. 6.490–93 with 6.356–59). Deeds are done by *andres,* words are spoken by *anthrōpoi;* and if human beings do anything, it is only the tillage of the fields (cf. 16.392, 17.549–50, 19.131, but cf. Hesiod *Theogony* 100). The heroes' contempt for speeches is but part of their contempt for *anthrōpoi* (cf. 15.741, 16.620–30, 23.356–68, 248–57), and yet they depend on them for the immortality of their fame (6.357–58, 7.87–91, cf. 8.579–80). *Anthrōpoi* are the descendants of *andres,* the shadows, as it were, that the heroes cast into the future, where these poor copies of themselves live on; and as the adulation they will give would seem to justify their own existence, it is proper that these later generations, extolling the heroes beyond their worth, should look on them as demigods: so the word *hēmitheoi* occurs but once, in a passage on the future destruction of the Achaeans' wall, and not accidentally it is coupled there with *andres (hēmitheōn genos andrōn,* 12.23).[1]

Under one condition are the heroes willing to regard themselves as *anthrōpoi:* if they refer at the same time to the gods. Achilles makes the two heralds, Talthybius and Eurybates, witnesses to his oath: *pros te theōn makarōn pros te thnētōn anthrōpōn* (1.339). The gods are blessed and immortal, while *anthrōpoi* are mortal, and it is only his weakness, when confronted with the power of the gods, that makes a hero resign himself to being human. "Shall there be evil war and dread strife," ask the Achaeans and Trojans, "or does Zeus bind us in friendship, Zeus who dispenses war to *anthrōpoi*" (4.82–84, 19.224). Whenever the heroes feel the oppressive weight of their mortality, they become, in their own opinion, like other men who are always human beings (1.339, 3.279, 4.84, 320, 6.123, 180, 9.[460], 500, 507, 18.107, 19.94, 131, 224, 260, 21.566, 569, 23.788). And the gods also, if they wish to insist on their own superiority, or no longer wish to take care of the heroes, call them in turn *anthrōpoi;* as Athena does, in calming Ares, who has just heard of his son's death (14.139–411, cf. 4.45, 5.442, 21.462–66, 24.49): "Someone better than he has been slain before now or will have been slain hereafter, but it is grievous to save the offspring and generation of all human beings." If anyone had a right to be called a hero, surely this Ascalaphus, a son of Ares, had; but Athena wishes to point out his worthlessness and deprive him of any divine status, so that Ares' regret at his loss might be diminished. For the gods are not concerned with men insofar as they are mortal, but based on their possible divinity.

The word "hero," which Homer identifies with *anēr* (the phase *hērōes andres* thrice occurs, 5.747, 9.525, 13.346, cf. Hesiod *Works and Days* 159), and which clearly has nothing to do with *anthrōpoi,* shows how far apart the Achaeans and Trojans are from ordinary men: even we can feel how jarring the union *hērōes anthrōpoi* would have been (Hesiod, in his five ages of men, never calls the heroes, unlike the other four ages, *anthrōpoi, Works and Days* 109, 137, 143, 180). But in what consists the heroic distinction? First, in lineage: the heroes are either sons of gods or can easily find, within a few generations, a divine ancestor; and second, in providence: the gods are concerned with their fate. Zeus is a father to them—*patēr andrōn te theōn te*—who pities them and saves them from death, while he is not the father but the ruler of human beings, *hos to theoisi kai anthrōpoisi anassei* (2.669). Zeus acts toward the heroes as Odysseus is said to treat his subjects—*patēr hōs ēpios ēen*—and he acts toward us as Agamemnon is toward his men: distant, haughty, indifferent. As the providence extended over human beings is unbenevolent (cf. 6.1, 12–19), Zeus dispenses war to *anthrōpoi,* himself careless of its consequences; but it is a "father Zeus" who, Agamemnon believes, will aid the Achaeans and defeat the perfidious Trojans; and as father Zeus he later pities Agamemnon and sends an eagle for an omen (4.84, 19.224, 4.235, 8.245, cf. 5.33, 8.132, 397, 11.80, 201, 16.250, 17.630).

Andres and *theoi* belong to the same order; they may be built on different scales, but they are commensurate with one another (cf. 19.95–96). Achilles is a *theios anēr* (16.798, cf. 5.184–85, 331–32, 839): *theios anthrōpos* would be unthinkable. The direct intervention of the gods seems to elevate man to *anēr,* whereas the flux of fortune, in which no caring providence can be seen, degrades him to *anthrōpos.* "Of all the things that breathe and move upon the earth," Odysseus tells Amphinomus, "the earth nurtures nothing weaker than a human being *(akidnoteron anthrōpoio);* for as long as the gods grant him virtue and his limbs are strong, he thinks he will meet with no evil in the future; but whenever the blessed gods assign him sorrows, then he bears them, though struck with grief, with a steadfast heart" (18.130–35; cf. 24.49). When, however, Zeus pities the horses of Achilles, who weep for Patroclus, he regrets that he gave to mortal Peleus horses ageless and immortal, for "of all the things that breathe and move upon the earth, nothing is more pitiful than a he-man" (*oïzurōteron andros,* 17.444–45, cf. 21.21). Odysseus talks of *anthrōpoi,* Zeus is concerned only with *andres,* those among us whom the gods favor and try to raise above the common lot of men. It is not the uncertainty in man's life which seems to Zeus man's sorrow; for the gods can put an end to chance and ensure his success; but even the gods are powerless to change his fate, no matter how many gifts they might lavish on him. Mortality and mortality alone makes for the misery of man. Odysseus, on the other hand, did not find man's burden in mortality (already implied in *anthrōpos*) but in his inability to guarantee, as long as he lives, his happiness. Not his necessary death, in spite of the gods' attention, but his necessary helplessness, because of the gods' willful despotism, seems to Odysseus the weakness of man.

Even as the word *anthrōpos* is more frequent in the *Odyssey* than in the *Iliad,* while the word *hērōs* occurs almost twice as often in the *Iliad* (*anthrōpos:* 118 in the *Odyssey,* 70 in the *Iliad: hērōs:* 73 in the *Iliad,* 40 in the *Odyssey;* the same ratios apply to *anēr* (*Iliad* 9.714, 15.478), *phōs* (*Iliad* 9.58, 15.40), *brotos* (*Iliad* 9.415, 15.68)), so Odysseus saw the cities of many human beings, and Achilles cast into Hades the souls of many heroes. The *Odyssey* takes place after the Trojan War, when those upon whom the heroes had relied for their fame are now living and remember in song the deeds of the past (cf. 2.347–52, 8.479–80, 492–93, with 1.358–59, 21.352–53). Phemius among the suitors and Demodocus among the Phaeacians celebrate an almost dead wholly heroic world; and Odysseus also, since he shared in that past but never belonged to it, recounts rather than acts out his own adventures. As Odysseus's deeds are only *muthoi,* so he himself is an *anthrōpos* (1.219, 236, 7.212. 307, 8.552, 11.363–66, 22.414–15), not only as opposed to the gods, which even Achilles might allow to be true of himself, but absolutely so.[2] War is the business of *hērōes andres,* peace, of *anthrōpoi;* and as Odysseus never did quite fit into the *Iliad* and was an obscure figure (his greatest exploit occurred at night, cf. Ovid *Metamorphoses* 13.9–15), he becomes in the *Odyssey* preeminent, while the former great are mere ghosts in Hades, who depend on Odysseus for their power of speech.

The heroes are survivors in the *Odyssey;* they no longer dominate the stage; they are old-fashioned and out of favor. Menelaus is a hero (he often uses the word, 4.268, 312, 423, 617, 15.117, 121), but Telemachus becomes a hero only at his court (4.21, 303, 312, 15.62), where the spell of the past still lingers. Laertes is a hero, or rather "hero-old man" (*gerōn hērōs,* 1.189, 2.99, 19.144, 22.185, 24.134), who putters about in his garden.

Other old men are heroes: Egyptius, Halistherses, Echenus (2.15, 157, 7.155, 11.342, 24.451); and Eumaeus calls Odysseus, when disguised as an old man, hero (14.97). The word has been preserved in the country and remains on the lips of a swineherd—an empty title, without any suggestion of force, nor even an indication of rank; for Mulius, a servant of Amphinomus, can now lay claim to it (18.423, cf. Eustathius *ad loc.*).

II. Achaeans and Trojans

To Agamemnon's demand for an equal prize in return, were he to give Chryseis back to her father, Achilles objects: "Most worthy Atreides—most rapacious of all—how will the magnanimous Achaeans give you a prize?" (1.122–23). The phrase *megathumoi Achaioi* would not at first attract our attention, though we might doubt its suitability, were it not that, after Agamemnon has used it in echoing Achilles (9.135), it never again occurs in the *Iliad* (cf. *Odyssey* 24.57). Not the Achaeans but the Trojans are *megathumoi* (*Iliad* 5.27, 102, 8.155, 10.205, 11.294, 459, 13.456, 737, 17.420, 23.175, 181). Why then did Achilles employ it? As Achilles himself is often *megathumos* (*Iliad* 17.214, 18.226, 19.75, 21.153, 23.168, 498, cf. 9.184, 496), he transfers his own epithet to all the Achaeans, in the hope that, as his anger rises against Agamemnon, the Achaeans, carried along by his rhetoric, will side with him. "High-spirited" is, as the BT Scholiast remarks, demagogic. The Achaeans should also revile Agamemnon's presumptuousness; they should show as much fury as himself, a fury that characterizes the Trojans as a whole without even being persuaded.

The Trojan leaders use *megathumoi* as an exhortation (5.102), even as Hector urges them as *huperthumoi* to fight in his absence, or not to let Achilles frighten them (6.111, 20.366). They are "over-spirited" as well as "high-spirited" in Homer's opinion (9.233, 11.564, 14.15, 15.135, 17.276). Their spirit is not only great but excessive; their exuberance in war turns easily into pure fury (cf. 13.621–39). They are, in the opinion of others, though not in Homer's, *huperphialoi,* "over-proud" and "arrogant" (3.106, 13.621, 21.224, 414, 459), a vice attributed to Penelope's suitors (*Odyssey* 1.134, cf. 20.291–92, 21.289), who are also called *agēnores,* "super-men" or "muscle-bound"; and this the Trojans also are (*Iliad* 10.299, cf. 4.176, *Odyssey* 1.106 passim).[3] Magnanimity may be a vice or a virtue. It contains, for example, the intransigence as well as the fearlessness of Achilles (*Iliad* 9.496, 20.498). It recognizes no obstacles and knows no bounds. It is so high-keyed that the slightest jar untunes it; it has no slack to take up nor any reserve to expend. It is all action and no recoil. Thus the Trojans are "high-spirited" both when they see the blood of Odysseus, and when they see one son of Dares killed and the other in flight (*Iliad* 11.459, 5.26–29). In one case they are spurred to charge and cluster round Odysseus, while in the other they are crestfallen. Men who are high-spirited flourish on success but cannot withstand adversity. "Their courage rises and falls with their animal spirits," to adopt Macaulay's description of Monmouth; "it is sustained on the field of battle by the excitement of action, by the hope of victory, by the strange influence of sympathy"; whereas those more reserved and less outwardly spirited (*menea pneiontes* Homerically, *Iliad* 3.8, 11.508, 24.364, but cf. 2.536, 541) might accomplish less in victory but would not fall off so much in defeat. They would possess a resilience and a steadiness the Trojans lack.[4]

After Menelaus and Paris have finished arming themselves, "they walked into the space between the Achaeans and Trojans, and their glances were fearful—wonder held those who beheld them—Trojans tamers of horses and well-greaved Achaeans" (3.341–43). The Trojans are tamers of horses as the Achaeans are well-greaved; but the epithets are not of the same order. If you see the Trojans, you cannot tell they train horses; if you see the Achaeans, you know they are well-greaved. They appear well-armed but may or may not be brave warriors; but the Trojans, all of them, from Hector to Paris (who shares the same simile of the horse, 6.506, 15.263), are high-spirited in war. The Trojans show more readily their affections than the Achaeans, who can remove their armor and be different in peace than in war; but the Trojans cannot so easily shake off their temper. Their epithets are general and do not particularly belong to an army. If we saw them in peacetime, they would still be "high-spirited" and "tamers of horses." But the Achaeans' epithets describe only their military aspect and offer no clue to their peaceful appearance. We know at once more about the Trojans than about the Achaeans, who are, as it were, many-sided and *polutropoi:* there is no Odysseus among the Trojans. Not only their outward show but the Trojans' inner fiber impress Homer; he sees it immediately. The Achaeans, however, wear long hair, are well-greaved and bronze-clad, and their eyes flash; the Trojans, though no doubt also bronze-clad and shielded, display more of themselves and have a kind of openness in their nature that the Achaeans lack. The Trojans' epithets tell us what they are, those of the Achaeans only hint at what they are.

We learn about the Achaeans—what kind of men they are—before we ever meet the Trojans, whom we first get to know but briefly at the end of the second book; and yet we may say that our knowledge of them both is complete by the tenth; for it is remarkable how seldom their distinctive epithets appear in the later books. Although the most sustained and violent engagements take place in Books 11–17, it is not in these books that the epithets of the Trojans and Achaeans are found most frequently; they abound instead in the early books, of which only the fifth and eighth books include great battles, and cluster round interludes in the war rather than in the war itself. *Eüknēmides,* for example, occurs nineteen times in Books 1–10, but only twelve in 11–24; *chalkochitōnōn* seventeen times in Books 1–10, eight afterward; and *karē komoōntes* twenty-two times in Books 2–4, four later. In the case of the Trojans, whose high and excessive spirit has more of a place in war (hence *megathumoi* and *huperthumoi* occur throughout the *Iliad*), only *hippodamoi* suffers a like decline: seventeen times in Books 2–10, seven afterward. When the epithets have served their purpose—to introduce us to the Achaeans and Trojans—and Homer becomes more concerned with Achilles, they are more sparingly used. Another reason why *hippodamoi* decreases is that Homer assigns to the Trojans many more similes (which both supplement and replace the epithet) after the tenth book than before: they obtain two in the first half (one in Book 3 and one in Book 4), but fourteen from Book 13 to Book 22, and of joint similes—those shared equally with the Achaeans—there are four before Book 10 and nine after. For the Achaeans the opposite holds true: eighteen similes occur in Books 2–9, nine in Books 11–19. The similes complete Homer's description of the Achaeans and Trojans, and as we start from the Achaean side and slowly move across the lines to the Trojan (the plague of the Achaeans turns into the funeral of Hector), so the number of the Achaeans' similes diminishes, while that of the Trojans increases. We must start then, like Homer, with the Achaean host, which is first presented in the second book, where almost half of its similes occur.

When the Achaeans first assemble, at Agamemnon's command, they seem like a mass of bees issuing in a constant stream from a smooth rock and then fly in grapelike clusters to spring flowers: so the Achaeans at first make the earth groan when they come from their tents, and a hum pervades the host, but then, once seated in serious concentration, they are perfectly quiet (2.87–100). But as soon as Agamemnon finishes his disastrous speech, they seem like long waves of the sea that east and south winds agitate—they are disturbed contradictorily—and as thick-set wheat, the shrill west wind shakes them—they are pliant and disordered; and with shouts and cries, whose din reaches up to heaven, they drag their ships down to the sea (2.144–54). In their desire to return home, they forget all discipline and become the riot and chaos of wheat field and sea. So much have they been stirred up, that even after Odysseus has checked them they return to the assembly as they left it, shouting like the tumultuous ocean that breaks against a shore (2.209–10): and later, when they scatter to their tents, their shout is the crash of waves against a high-jutting rock that waves never leave (2.394–97). And yet they are now more singly resolved than before, for only the east wind (not east, south, and west as before) moves them, and they center round one object—Troy's capture—like waves that always drench one rock.[5]

The individuality of the Achaeans, lost after Agamemnon's speech, is slowly restored in the succeeding similes, when they are marshaled and turned once again into disciplined troops. The glint of their arms is like fire, the stamp of their feet like the swelling crash of geese, cranes, and swans; the number of their host like leaves, flowers, and flies in spring (2.455–73, cf. 469 with 87). They reacquire in these animal identities their former status, although they are not yet distinct until the next simile: as shepherds easily order their own flock in a pasture, so the leaders ranked the Achaeans for battle (2.474–77). Then the catalogue is made, which completes their ranking, and they seem like fire spread across the whole plain of the Scamander, and the earth quakes like thunder (2.780–85). The Achaeans are marshaled noiselessly: the necessary clang of their weapons and tramp of their feet alone are heard, as if their high spirits had been purged in the assembly and nothing remained but a quiet resolution. "*Fortissimus in ipso discrimine exercitus est, qui ante discrimen quietissimus*" (Tacitus *Histories* 1.84).

Homer has made all of the second book as a contrast to the Trojans, who as noisily prepare for war as they advance with cries against the silent Achaeans (2.810, 3.1–9, cf. Thucydides 2.89.9). And later when the truce is broken, while the Achaeans, in fear of their commanders, silently move like the continuous roll of waves, and the only sounds are commands, "nor would you say they had speech"; the Trojans shouted, like ewes bleating ceaselessly, "nor was their clamor in concert, for the voices were mixed, as the men had been collected from many lands" (4.422–38, cf. 2.804, 867–68, Aeschylus *Persians* 401–7, Polybius 15.12.8–9, Plutarch *De audiendis poetis* 10, Arrian *Tactica* 31, 5–6). As the Achaeans are silent, they can obey the orders they hear; but the Trojans would drown out in their clamor any command. The simile of the Achaeans is deliberately inexact, for the echoing shore, against which the waves break, has no counterpart in themselves, who, as soon as they are compared to the sea, are distinguished from it. They are—what is inconceivable in nature—an ordered series of silent waves. The Trojans, however, exactly correspond to their similes, myriads of ewes pent up together in confusion. Of the Trojans' other similes in the midst of battle, four single out the clamor they make, as waves, or winds, or storm (13.795–800, 15.381–84, 16.364–66, 17.263–66, cf. 12.138, 16.78, 373, 21.10);[6] but the noise of the Achaeans, even when they do shout (11.50, 18.149), only warrants a simile if the Trojans join in (4.452–56, 14.393–401, 16.736–40), and they are compared but once to water in battle: when their spirit, not any outward sign, shows vexation (9.4–8).

It is not difficult to see how the epithets of the Trojans are connected with their disorder, or how those of the Achaeans indicate their discipline. The high spirit of the Trojans would naturally express itself in cries, and the fine greaves of the Achaeans would indicate a deeper efficiency. The Trojans never equal the Achaeans in the closeness of their ranks, whose spears and shields form a solid wall, and shield and helmet of one rest on helmet and shield of another (13.128–33, 16.212–17); nor do the Achaeans, on the other hand, ever retreat like the Trojans: "Each one peered around to where he was to escape sheer destruction" (14.507, 16.287). They flee, as they attack, in disorder, and more by *thumos* than by *epistēmē* are they warriors (cf. Thucydides 1.49.3, 2.11.8, 87.4–5, 89.5–8). They are, in the later Greek vocabulary, barbarians. Thucydides' Brasidas, in urging his troops to face the Illyrians, could be describing the Trojans; who "by the loudness of their clamor are insupportable, and whose vain brandishing of weapons appears menacing, but are unequal in combat to those who resist them; for, lacking all order, they would not be ashamed, when forced, to desert any position, and a battle, wherein each man is master of himself, would give a fine excuse to all for saving their own skins" (4.126.5, cf. Herodotus 7.211, 3.212.2, 8.86).

How, then, are we to explain the silent efficiency of the Achaeans and the noisy disorder of the Trojans? Has Homer given a reason for this difference? Some one principle whose presence would force the Achaeans into discipline, and whose absence would let the Trojans sink into anarchy? *Aidōs,* "shame," seems to distinguish them. There are two kinds of *aidōs:* one we may call a mutual or military shame, the other an alien or civil shame (cf. Thucydides, where virtue and shame are coupled: 1.37.2, 84.3, 2.51.5, 4.19.3, 5.9.9, 101). The first induces respect for those who are your equals; or, if fear also is present, your superiors (cf. Sophocles *Ajax* 1075–80, Plato *Euthyphro* 12a7–c8); the second is respect for those weaker than yourself. The first is in the domain of *andres,* the second of *anthrōpoi* (cf. Aeschylus *Agamemnon* 937–38). Hector shows civil shame when, in speaking to Andromache, he says, "I am terribly ashamed before the Trojans, men and women both, if I cringe like someone ignoble and shun battle" (6.441–43, cf. 8.147–56, 12.310–21, 17.90–95). And Hector is killed because he would be ashamed to admit his error (of keeping the Trojans in the field after Achilles' reappearance), ashamed lest someone baser than himself might say, "Hector, trusting to his strength, destroyed his people" (22.104–7, cf. Aristotle *Magna Moralia* 1191a5–15, *Eudemian Ethics* 1230a16–26). As commander of his troops, with no one set above him, Hector must either feel the lash of public opinion or become as disobedient as Achilles, who at first lacks all respect for Agamemnon and later all respect for Hector's corpse (24.44).

When, however, the Achaeans silently advance against the Trojans, they show another kind of shame, "desirous in their hearts to defend one another" (3.9, cf. 2.362–63). Their respect is not for others but for themselves. Neither those stronger nor those weaker than themselves urge them to fight, but each wishes to help the other, knowing that in "concerted virtue" resides their own safety (13.237). "Be ashamed before one another," shouts Agamemnon (and later Ajax), "in fierce contentions: when men feel shame, more are saved than killed; but when they flee, neither is fame nor any strength acquired" (5.520–32, 15.562–64). And even when the Achaeans retreat, they do not scatter like the Trojans, but they stay by their tents, held by "shame and fear, for they call to one another continuously" (15.657–58, cf. 8.354–55, 17.357–65). Whatever fear they have before their leaders is tempered by their shame before one another; and as, according to Brasidas, three things make men good soldiers—will, shame, and obedience (Thucydides 5.9.9, cf. 1.84.3)—so the Achaeans show their will in preferring war to peace (2.453–54, 11.13–14), their shame in mutual respect (5.787, 8.228, 13.95, 122, 15.502, 561), and their obedience in the fear of their leaders (4.431, cf. 1.331, 4.402, 24.435).

Agamemnon as a good king and Ajax as a brave warrior appeal to military shame when they incite the Achaeans; but the aged Nestor urges them in the name of civil virtue: "Friends, be men and place in your spirit shame before other human beings, and let each of you remember your children, your wives, possessions, and your parents, whether they still live or now are dead; for the sake of those who are not here I beseech you to stand your ground" (15.661–66, cf. Tacitus *Histories* 4.18.4, *Germania* 7.2–8.1). Even as Nestor has placed his worst troops in the middle, so that they would be forced, though unwilling, to fight (4.297–300, cf. Xenophon *Memorabilia* 3.1.8, Polybius 15.16.1–4), so here he wishes to regard all the

Achaeans as caught between the Trojans in front and their own families behind them; and he hopes by this necessity, of avoiding death at the hands of one and humiliation in the eyes of the other, that they would resist. Nestor leaves nothing to personal courage: it is of a piece to rely on necessity and to appeal to civil shame, for to a man who has outlived two generations the bonds of society seem stronger than those of an army, nor would his own weakness give him any confidence in others' strength. As a very old man he has no peers, and all relations seem to him the relations of the young to the old; so that in making the Achaeans respect their parents he covertly makes them respect himself. Unable to inspire his men by fear of himself and unwilling to trust to military discipline, Nestor falls back on the rehearsal of his own past prowess and on his soldiers' recollection of those absent (cf. 4.303–9).

Military shame never once arouses the Trojans, whom the cry "Be men!" always encourages; and once, when Sarpedon tries to rally the Lycians—"Shame! Lycians. Where are you fleeing? Now be keen!"—the appeal is to civil shame; for as warriors they are urged to be vigorous, and shame is only invoked to check their flight (16.422–30, cf. BT Scholiast 13.95, 15.502). The Trojans rely more on their leaders than on their troops (cf. Tacitus *Germania* 30.2), for we always read of the "Trojans and Hector" attacking (13.1, 129, 15.42, 403, 327, 449 passim), as if the single virtue of Hector more than equaled the mass effort of his men (cf. 13.49–54). If the Trojans act in concert, it is rather by the example of one man than by any bravery in themselves; and Hector himself resembles Xenophon's Proxenus, who "was able to rule those who were noble and brave but was unable to instill shame or fear into his own troops, since he was actually more ashamed before his men than they before him" (*Anabasis* 2.6.19). Aeneas, for example, can rouse Hector and the other captains by an appeal to shame, but it would be unthinkable to employ the same argument before all (17.335–41); and in this Nestor's call to the Achaeans, though it is a kind of civil shame, differs from the Trojan's, which only affects their greatest warriors.

Lessing expressed the difference between the Achaeans and Trojans very precisely in his *Laocoon* (I); and although the passage is well-known, "twice and three the beautiful things":

> Was bei den Barbaren aus Wildheit und Verhärtung entsprang, das wirkten bei ihm (dem Griechen) Grundsätze. Bei ihm war der Heroismus wie die verborgenen Funken im Kiesel, die ruhig schlafen, solange keine äußere Gewalt sie wecket, und dem Steine weder seine Klarheit noch seine Kälte nehmen. Bei dem Barbaren war der Heroismus eine helle fressende Klamme,

die immer tobte, und jede andere gute Eigenschaft in ihm verzehrte, wenigstens schwärzte.—Wenn Homer die Trojaner mit wildem Geschrei, die Griechen hingegen in entschloßner Stille zur Schlacht führet, so merken die Ausleger sehr wohl an, daß der Dichter hierdurch jene als Barbaren, diese als gesittete Völker schildern wolle. Mich wundert, daß sie an einer andern Stelle eine ähnliche charakteristische Entgegensetzung nicht bemerkt haben. Die feindlichen Heere haben einen Waffenstillestand getroffen; sie sind mit Verbrennung ihrer Toten beschäftiget, welches auf beiden Teilen nicht ohne heiße Tränen abgehet; *dakrua therma kheontes.* Aber Priamus verbietet seinen Trojanern zu weinen; *oud' eia klaiein Priamos megas.* Er verbietet ihnen zu weinen, sagt die Dacier, weil er besorgt, sie möchten sich zu sehr erweichen, und morgen mit weniger Mut an den Streit gehen. Wohl; doch frage ich: warum muß nur Priamus dieses besorgen? Warum erteilet nicht auch Agamemnon seinen Griechen das nämliche Verbot? Der Sinn des Dichters geht tiefer. Er will uns lehren, daß nur der gesittete Grieche zugleich weinen und tapfer sein könne; indem der ungesittete Trojaner, um es zu sein, alle Menschlichkeit vorher ersticken müsse. *Nemessoumai ge men ouden klaiein,* läßt er an einem andern Orte den verständigen Sohn des weisen Nestors sagen.

III. Achilles and Agamemnon

Achilles and Hector are heroes, one an Achaean, the other a Trojan; but to know them better, so that even away from their camps we should not mistake them, forces us to find other traits peculiar to themselves. Who then is Achilles? Homer begs a goddess to sing the wrath of "Peleides Achilles."[7] Achilles is the son of Peleus. He is marked off from all other men because of his father; as an only son, without brothers, he was entirely Peleus's heir (24.538–40). And were we to ask, "Who is Peleus?" we would be told, "Aeacides," the son of Aeacus. And if we persisted and wanted to know who he was, Achilles himself boasts it, "Aeacus was from Zeus" (21.189). Achilles then is "Zeus-born," "Zeus-nurtured," or "dear to Zeus." In three generations he goes back to Zeus, and beyond him it would be foolish to go. To ask Achilles who he is means to ask him his lineage; and as he can only define himself in terms of the past, were his ancestors unknown, he would be a nonentity (cf. 6.123 with 145–46, 21.150 with 153). In Achilles' patronymic is summed up part of his own greatness. He is partly the work of generations.

Achilles is not only the son of Peleus but the grandson of Aeacus; and yet to be called "Aeacides" when he is actually "Peleides" means that he has inherited something that was common to all his first ancestors.

Achilles is called the son of Aeacus first in the Trojan catalog: Ennomus and Amphimachus were both killed by Achilles in the guise of "swift-footed Aeacides" (2.860, 874, but cf. A Scholiast). Achilles resembles his grandfather in his ability to kill. As a warrior he is indistinguishable from his forefathers, for killing is a family profession (cf. how each side exhorts their troops in Thucydides, e.g., 4.92.7, 95.3; see also Herodotus 6.14.3, 8.90.4). But during the embassy, when Achilles is most idle, though ironically most Achilles (for his wrath makes up a great part of him), no one calls him the son of Peleus; rather, people point out to him how much he has failed to follow his father's precepts (9.252–59, 438–43). When, however, he returns to the fighting, his father's name is almost as common as his own; and as he assumes his ancestral name, he takes up his father's spear, which no more could be hurled by another than "Peleides" could be said of another (19.387–91, cf. 14.9–11, 16.140–44, 21.174, 178, 20.2). In the last book, however, where his own name occurs more frequently than anywhere else, his patronymic is hardly present, and he is never called to his face the son of Peleus. Somehow he has outlived it.

As Hector has many brothers, to tell us at first that he is the son of Priam would mean little: so Achilles, who first mentions him, calls him "Hector the man-slayer" (1.242). Paris contrariwise does not even deserve his father's name, for his only distinction lies in his theft; he is most of all the "husband of Helen" (3.329; 7.355, 8.82, 13.766), although in his braver moments, which do not last very long, he earns the right that other heroes have without question—to be called "Priamides" (3.356, 6.512).

But were we to ask, "Who is Odysseus?" and turn to the first line of the *Odyssey,* the answer is quite different: "Tell me of the man, Muse, of many wiles who wandered very far." Odysseus is a clever man who wandered very far. He is not made distinct from others because he is the only son of Laertes but because he traveled. His genealogy is contained in what he himself did and not in what his father might have been. Laertes' father is known, but his grandfather is unmentioned; tradition indeed gave him two family stems (cf. *RE* XVII, col. 1918). Homer in the *Iliad* never calls him anything but Odysseus, though other heroes address him as if he were like themselves: "Zeus-born Laertiades, very-crafty Odysseus"; but even here his subtlety belongs to himself, while his divine origins (whatever they may have been) belong to his father. Homer in the *Odyssey* calls him "Laertiades," with one exception (8.18), only after he has returned to Ithaca (16.455, 17.361, 18.348, 20.286, 22.191, 399). For twenty years he is merely Odysseus, but he resumes his lineage as soon as he lays claim to his kingdom. His patrimony gives him back his piety (cf. 24.270). Ovid understood Odysseus when he made him say (*Metamorphoses* 13.140–41):

> nam genus et proavus et quae non fecimus ipsi
> vix ea nostra voco.

He is what Junot said of himself: "Moi je suis mon ancêtre"; cf. Tacitus *Annales* 11.21.

Odysseus's adventures are his lineage, making his very name superfluous. He is a traveler who "saw the cities of many human beings and knew their mind"; and his name, put almost as an afterthought (without his patronymic, 1.21), cannot make clearer his identity nor add much luster to his eminence. He is like Thersites, whose father and country are not given (cf. BT Scholiast 2.212), his deformity and outspokenness being title enough; so that to have Odysseus, his closest rival in anonymity, answer his abuses was a masterstroke. Their resemblance is so close that Sophocles' Neoptolemus, when Philoctetes asks him about a man "clever and skilled in speaking," thinks he must mean Odysseus, whereas he actually means Thersites (*Philoctetes* 440–42). Moreover, Philoctetes, believing it to be a truer lineage, can even call Odysseus the son of Sisyphus; and Odysseus can tell Eumaeus that he is illegitimate (14.202–3).

When Odysseus tells the Cyclops his name, "No-one is my name; my father, mother, and all my companions call me No-one" (9.366–67), he is almost speaking more truthfully than when he tells Alcinous that he is the son of Laertes (9.19, cf. 10.325–30). His anonymity is the result of his guile, for Homer has him pun on the likeness of *outis* and *mētis* (9.414, cf. 408). His wisdom made him no one and cut all his ties with the past.

Although Achilles, if opposed to Odysseus, seems to consist in nothing but his past, yet when opposed to Agamemnon he becomes more unique. Indeed, he stands somewhere in between Agamemnon and Odysseus. Agamemnon does not even appear, at first, as himself but as "Atreides lord of men," while Achilles is "brilliant" or "glorious" in comparison (1.7). Not until he differs from the rest of the Achaeans (who wish to restore Chryseis), although he has been mentioned thrice before, does Homer call him Agamemnon (1.24), even as Achilles calls him "Atreides" after he has convened the assembly (1.59), but "Agamemnon" when he wishes to single him out for his crime (1.90, cf. 94). Agamemnon rises to rebut Achilles, but Homer first clothes him in all possible authority: "Hero Atreides, wide-ruling Agamemnon" (1.102, 7.322, 13.112). This majesty fails to impress Achilles, who, however, begins his reply as if he agreed with him: "Most worthy Atreides," but instead of ending the line, as we later realize he should have, he cruelly inserts, "most rapacious of all" (1.122). The proper end-tag, "lord of men Agamemnon," often occurs, mostly spoken by Nestor, who, old man that he is, knows what loyalty and respect must be shown to a king. When the Achaeans are about to be cataloged, Agamemnon must have full power. He must be not only the "most worthy" because of his lineage, but also the "king of men" in his own name (2.434, but note 2.362). Later, when the fortunes of the Achaeans are lowest, Nestor again bolsters Agamemnon with his titles; and the other kings also, after the embassy to Achilles fails, subscribe in the same way their loyalty (9.96, 163, 677, 697 with which cf. 8.293). Achilles only much later, when he has sloughed off his rage, addresses him properly (19.146, 199, cf. 23.49).

Not until, however, Achilles swears an oath by Agamemnon's scepter (if it is the same as Agamemnon's), does the conflict between them come out in the open: "Yes, by this scepter, which never again shall grow branches or leaves, since it first left its stump on the mountain, nor shall it bloom again, for the bronze blade has stripped it of its leaves and its bark; and now in turn the sons of the Achaeans, the wielders of justice, carry it, those who protect the laws that come from Zeus" (1.234–39). Then he flings down the scepter, "studded with golden nails," the scepter whose true origin we learn much later, just before Agamemnon, doing "what is right" (2.73, cf. B Scholiast [Porphyry]),[8] tries the Achaeans, fearful lest Achilles' refusal to fight and his desire to return home have infected the whole army: "Up stood strong Agamemnon with the scepter, which Hephaestus artfully had made: Hephaestus gave it to Zeus lord Kroniōn, and Zeus gave it to the Treasurer of Riches (who kills with his brilliance), and lord Hermes gave it to Pelops the goader of horses, and Pelops in turn to Atreus the shepherd of his people; and Atreus when he died left it to wealthy Thyestes, and he in turn left it for Agamemnon to wield—to rule over many islands and all Argos" (2.100–108, cf. 453–54). Lessing again in his *Laocoon* (16) has beautifully brought out the reason why the one scepter receives these two descriptions (or if there are two scepters, why there are two):

> Jener, ein Werk des Vulkans; dieser, von einer unbekannten Hand auf den Bergen geschnitten: jener der alte Besitz eines edeln Hauses; dieser bestimmt, die erste die beste Faust zu füllen: jener, von einem Monarchen über viele Inseln und über ganz Argos erstrecket; dieser von einem aus dem Mittel der Griechen geführet, dem man nebst andern die Bewahrung der Gesetze

> anvertrauet hatte. Dieses war wirklich der Abstand, in welchem sich Agamemnon und Achill voneinander befanden; ein Abstand, den Achill selbst, bei allem seinem blinden Zorne, einzugestehen, nicht umhin konnte.

The conflict between them is between authority and power, between the gifts of nature and those of a heritage. Agamemnon's authority consists in mere words (in the spell of his ancestry), and were Achilles to yield to them, as if they were deeds, he would be thought weak and cowardly (1.293–94, cf. 9.32–39). Briseis is only the pretext for his more serious difference, which must always exist whenever power and position do not coincide. The usurper Bolingbroke and King Richard II, for example, work out in smaller compass the dispute between Achilles and Agamemnon; for Richard relies as much on his divine appointment as Agamemnon does; and Bolingbroke, like Achilles, trusts more to "blood and bone" than to ancestral right (cf. *Richard II,* 2, 54–62; 3, 39–53, 73–90).[9]

Achilles swears by the authority of Agamemnon—if his scepter is Agamemnon's—in terms of his own power. He swears by the scepter as he swears by the gods, and only Achilles swears (1.86, 339, 23.43). Agamemnon calls upon the gods more cautiously, as witnesses (as those who know, 3.276–80, 19.258–60), whereas the gods to Achilles are no more than his scepter, which is but the extension of his own power, losing all its force as soon as he casts it aside. Though "studded with golden nails," he holds it in no esteem. Any branch at all would serve him as well. He does not need the past to rally the present. But Agamemnon, who has little confidence in his own strength, must lean upon his scepter, unlike Hector, Achilles' equal, who leans upon a spear while he speaks (2.109, 8.496). Hector's spear is replaceable, while Agamemnon's scepter is unique, and were it broken, he would be doomed to obscurity. He swears neither by scepter nor by gods, but rather he holds up the scepter to all the gods (7.112, cf. Aristotle *Politics* 1285b3–12). His lineage, embodied in the scepter, connects him with the gods. He looks to them. Achilles looks to himself.

Odysseus alone knows how to combine, in the scepter, the rank of Agamemnon with the force of Achilles. He stops the general rout of the Achaeans, which Agamemnon's speech had caused, by making a distinction that Achilles would not, and Agamemnon could not, employ (cf. Xenophon *Memorabilia* 1.2.58, 4.6.13–15). Taking the ancestral scepter in his hand, he speaks to the kings thus: "If you disobey Agamemnon, he shall oppress you; the wrath of a Zeus-nurtured king is great; his honor comes from Zeus and counseling Zeus loves him" (2.185–97, cf. 1.174–75, ABT Scholiast 2.186). He uses the scepter as an emblem of power, threatening the kings, who would be unimpressed by mere lineage, with divine vengeance. Authority lies in power. But against anyone of the rank and file, Agamemnon's scepter turns into a weapon: Odysseus drives them before him with it (2.199, cf. 266–67). He speaks to them quite differently: "Sit down without a murmur, and listen to others who have more authority: many-headed rule is bad; let there be one head, one king, to whom the son of Kronos gave rule." Power lies in authority. As Zeus is Zeus to the kings, but to the common warrior the son of Kronos (cf. 1.175, 9.37, 98, 608), so Agamemnon must appear to the kings as authoritative might, but to the warriors as powerful authority.

The three oppositions we have examined—human beings and heroes, Trojans and Achaeans, Agamemnon and Achilles—dominate the *Iliad* in a double way. We have taken up only one of them—their evident difference; but their underlying sameness is perhaps even more important. It can only be briefly indicated here. Homer gives in each of these contrasted pairs a higher ranking to heroes, Achaeans, and Achilles; but that ranking is only a necessary condition for the *Iliad.* The *Iliad* itself forces us to rethink that ranking, as its plot moves almost contrary to it: from Achilles' wrath to Hector's funeral. Achilles, the Achaean hero, finally yields to his opposites. He acknowledges that his power cannot be a substitute for Agamemnon's authority (23.890–94); he comes to respect his Trojan enemies (24.628–32); and he sees that he is more related as a human being to Peleus and Patroclus than to Thetis and Zeus as a hero (24.511–12). The *Iliad* moves from the apparently higher to the apparently lower, which then comes to sight as something beyond the original distinctions. To clarify that something completely would be to understand the *Iliad.*

Notes

1. Cf. W. Schadewaldt, *Iliasstudien,* Abhandlungen der Sächsischen Akademie der Wissenschaften, Phil.-hist. Klasse (Leipzig, 1938), vol. 43, no. 6.

2. Cf. H. Seiler, "Ἄνθρωποι," *Glotta* 32 (1953): 233, who notes that the expressed opposition of ἄνθρωποι-θεοί is more common in the *Iliad* than in the *Odyssey.*

3. See O. Hoffman, "Ἀλέξανδρος," *Glotta* 28 (1939): 32.

4. Cf. Harvey Cushing, *From a Surgeon's Journal 1915–1918* (Boston: Little, Brown 1936), 132–33: "The Frenchmen of course a brave fellow—gets worked up to a flame heat for a few moments and is then irresistible; but the flame soon

goes out and it takes an exceptional man to kindle it again. British soldiers never flame—only a steady glow all the time."

5. Cf. H. Fränkel, *Die homerischen Gleichnisse* (Göttingen, 1921), 20.

6. Once the Trojans attack without shouting (ἄβρομοι αὐΐαχοι), and only then are they compared to fire (*Iliad* 14.39–41); cf. C. Robert, *Studien zur Ilias* (Berlin, 1901), 124–25; U. von Wilamowitz-Moellendorf, *Die "Ilias" und Homer* (Berlin, 1916), 252, n. 2. Although Hector numerically rivals Achilles in similes of fire, he is often like a storm, river, or sea, to none of which Achilles is compared (11.297, 305, 12.40, 19.161 (storm); 5.597 (river); 5.593, 11.307, 15.624 (waves); cf. 21.273–83, 190–99).

7. Whether "Peleides," "Atreides," etc., are patronymica or gentilicia has been much disputed; cf. K. Meister, *Die Homerische Kunstsprache* (Leipzig, 1921), 148–50; P. Chantraine, *Grammaire Homérique* (Paris, 1948–53), vol. 1, 105–6.

8. F. Jacoby, "Die Einschaltung des Schiffskatalogs in die *Ilias*," *Sitzungsberichte der Bayerischen Akademie der Wissenschaften,* Phil.-hist. Klasse (Munich, 1932), 586–94.

9. It is not accidental that Agamemnon alone calls Odysseus "Laertiades," without adding his proper name (19.184); nor that he bids Menelaus "call each man by his lineage and patronymic, glorifying all" (10.68–69, cf. 4.370–412; 5.635–39, 7.125–28, 8.282–83). Nicias, Thucydides' Agamemnon as it were, does the same (8.69.2; cf. Xenophon, *Oeconomicus,* 7.3). There is in the Catalog of Ships, I suspect, the same contrast between Achilles and Agamemnon. Odysseus is in the center, Achilles and Agamemnon are equally six places away from him; but the number of ships is far greater on Agamemnon's side (732) than on Achilles' (442); and in accordance with that preponderance, the wealth rather than the prowess of those who surround Agamemnon is stressed: place-names are twice as frequent there as on Achilles' side, and even the epithets suggest their prosperity. On Achilles' side the cities the warriors rule are neglected for stories about themselves (641–43, 657–70, 673–75, 687–94, 698–703, 721–25); but on Agamemnon's side little besides their ancestry is said about the commanders.

THREE

The *Aristeia* of Diomedes and the Plot of the *Iliad*

BLUNT AJAX STATES THE PARADOX OF heroic virtue: "Alas, even a fool would know that Zeus himself aids the Trojans: the spears of all, no matter whether good or bad do hurl them, hit their target: Zeus makes all go straight" (17.629–32, cf. 13.222–27, 20.242–43, 434–37, Odyssey 18.132–35). Zeus's partiality makes it almost impossible to practice virtue. Were Ajax to retreat, he would be blameless (cf. 16.119–22, 17.97–101). Zeus can render vain and useless the distinction between good and bad, base and brave. What should prove merit—success—may be wholly undeserved. The javelin cast of Paris, were Zeus to wish it, would go as straight as that of Hector; if the gods had always favored Nireus, he would have equaled Achilles. Were not the providence of the gods inconstant and fitful (cf. 15.139–41, 16.446–47), they would obscure completely any intelligible order of excellence; but as it is, they sometimes withdraw and let the heroes run themselves. Then the world proceeds in the way we know it, and we see the heroes for what they would be among ourselves.

After Achilles set the prizes for the horse-race, and urged the best Achaeans to compete, Homer gives us the order in which they accepted the challenge. First Eumelus, who excelled in horsemanship and had the best horses (23.288–89, 2.763–67); then Diomedes with the horses of Aeneas; third Menelaus with one horse of his own and one of Agamemnon's; and then Antilochus (290–304). Before Homer tells us who came last, Nestor counsels his son on the power of craft. Although Antilochus's horses were swift-footed, they were slower than the three pairs of horses that entered the race before him, yet faster than Meriones', which were the slowest of all (304, 310, 530). Meriones was naturally reluctant to compete; only after Nestor had spoken at length (whose praise of craft gave him a chance) could he bring himself to risk his horses in a contest they could not possibly win.

If we look at the race itself, we see that Homer has presented the horsemen in the order in which they should but do not win (consider the footrace, 754–92). That Eumelus should have been first, although he came in last, Achilles, Homer, and all the Achaeans acknowledge; and were it not that Achilles wished to gratify Antilochus, even in his misfortune he would have taken second prize (535–37, 556). Had not Apollo and Athena interfered, Diomedes would have either come in first or tied Eumelus (382–83); we shall never know which, but in any case he would not have been less than second. Menelaus was due for third place, but the craft of Antilochus upset him; and yet if the course had been longer, he would have outstripped him (526–27). Antilochus, then, should have been fourth, and Meriones, unequal in skill to the others, fifth (530–31).

Two things disturb the order that should have been: art and providence. If Apollo had not wished to help Eumelus, Athena would not have broken his horse's yoke nor given more strength to Diomedes' horses (383–400). The gods made him who was to be first last, and him who was to be second first. And Antilochus's art put him ahead of Menelaus (515): but human art is not eternally superior, for the natural slowness of his horses would have eventually betrayed him (cf. 344–48). Thus providence and art stand very close to one another: both change the order that "nature" sets up and substitutes for it an unpredictable one. The superiority of art is short-lived, and given enough time, "nature" triumphs; whether the gods too are subject to it is a long question.

Homer has also given a third order, the lineup, which the casting of lots determined. Here no one is in his right place except Menelaus: Eumelus is second, Diomedes is last, Antilochus first, Meriones fourth (352–57). Menelaus, who was third in excellence and third in victory, is also third when mere accident assigns him a position. Chance mistakes everyone else but Menelaus: mediocrity is all that you can trust it to find out.

The gods are like chance in depressing the rank of the naturally superior, and they are like art in elevating the rank of the naturally superior; but they are wholly unconcerned with the ordinary and inferior: Zeus is never called the shepherd of men (cf. 12.37).[1] Whether the gods are present or not while the heroes are at war is therefore decisive for the plot of the *Iliad,* for their absence or presence affects the way in which Homer tells his story as much as it affects the heroes themselves. Homer indicates the importance of the gods to him in the description of the first encounter between the Achaeans and Trojans. 4.457–5.83 must be taken as a unit that divides into two parts, 4.457–538 and 5.1–83, while 4.539–44 serves as a transition from the fighting that was equally sponsored by Ares on the Trojan side and Athena on the Achaean (4.439), to the fighting after the withdrawal of both gods at 5.29–36. The *enth' au* of 5.1 points up the balance intended between these two groups of seven killings each, and the near equality in the number of lines (82 and 81, respectively—5.42 and 57 are plus-verses) is hardly needed to confirm it. That 4.457–538, moreover, as the longest sequence in the *Iliad* where a Trojan death alternates with an Achaean, should be Homer's first presentation of war cannot be accidental. War is like that, he seems to be saying; one man dies after another, now on one side, now on the other.[2] All the differences between Achaeans and Trojans (4.422–38) cannot outweigh the mortality they share. And yet the deaths alternate because the gods Athena, Apollo, and Ares interfere. When Athena and Ares retire, six Trojans are killed in succession (5.37–83), and when the gods are entirely absent (6.1), fifteen Trojans, without the loss of a single Achaean, are killed.

Throughout these two sections, the men say nothing. Only the gods speak, once Apollo and once Athena, but on both occasions no one replies (4.507–16, 5.29–36). War is a silent deed, for speech requires perspective, and only the gods have it, Apollo when he shouts encouragement to the Trojans from the city, Athena when she persuades Ares to leave the battlefield and look on from the banks of the Scamander. The man who would not find fault with the *ergon* (4.539), were Athena to lead him unwounded through the midst of the battle, cannot be anyone actively engaged in the war, Achaean or Trojan, for neither would have the impartiality to praise the enemy or the distance to pass any judgment. This man is unique in the *Iliad,* for nowhere else is anyone but Athena and Ares imagined to be in a position to find fault in a battle (13.127–28, 17.398–99). He thus stands closest to the poet himself, who has at the beginning let his interested detachment, which enables him to record the war with exactness, shine through.

In 4.457–538, not only do the men kill without speaking to each other, but they mostly kill or are killed without passion. No one desires or fears to fight (cf. 4.421), no one weeps or laughs, no one feels pain on dying or grief on seeing another die. They retreat but do not tremble (497, 505, 535), they advance but do not rejoice (507). Only Odysseus kills in anger (494, 501), everyone else in cold blood.[3] Odysseus is the first whose feelings Homer sees fit to mention. He alone does not take killing for granted, as something that simply is a part of one's makeup and a necessary consequence of being armed. That Odysseus's anger distinguishes him from the impersonal actions of everyone else, forces one to consider how Homer introduces the various ways of killing and dying that form so large a part of the *Iliad.* Who first dies or first kills in a certain way, what Homer has to say or refrains from saying about each death, and why he puts the deaths in the order he does, are the questions whose answers tie down the plot of the *Iliad* to its episodes.[4] The answers, in turn, all of which point to Homer's understanding of the heroes as mortal human beings, are inseparable from Homer's understanding of the immortal gods, and consequently inseparable from the question with which we began, what effect the gods' presence or absence has on the plot of the *Iliad.*

Of the first seven men killed in the war, three die with the formula *ton de skotos osse kalupse* (4.461, 503, 526), three lose their *thumos* (470, 524, 531, cf. 466, 478), and two fall with a simile (462, 482–87). Only Leukos, at whose death Odysseus gets angry, is killed without adornment (491–93). They all die in silence. Of the next seven killed, no death similes occur, one receives the expanded formula *stugeros d' ara min skotos heile* (5.47), one utters a groan while death covers him (68), another has purple death and mighty fate seize hold of his eyes, a fourth takes the cold bronze in his teeth (75, cf. 4.521), and the three others simply die without anything else being reported but the character of the wound they received. The ways of the killers in the two groups are also different. In the first group no one receives his own simile, though both sides are once likened to wolves (4.471), no one succeeds in stripping a corpse of its armor (460, 492, 532), no one slices off a part of someone's body (cf. 4.525–26), no one spills any blood (cf. 451), and no noneuphemistic or unambiguous word for killing is used. In the second group, however, Diomedes is likened to an autumnal star, the servants of Idomeneus succeed in stripping the armor from Phaestus (5.48), the comrades of Diomedes lead the chariot of Phegeus and Idaeus back to the ships (25–26), Pedasus has his tongue cut out (74), Hypsenor loses his arm, "and the bloody arm fell on the plain" (81–82), and Meges slays *(epephne)* Pedaeus (70, cf. 28, 59).

The explanation for these differences between the two groups can be found in the fact that Athena and Ares are each equally at work in 4.457–538, whereas in 5.1–83 Athena at first unbalances the battle in her desire to make Diomedes conspicuous and brilliant (5.2–3) and then draws Ares out of the war. Athena persuades Ares to stand aside after she sees Hephaestus, the god of fire, rescue one son of Dares, the priest of Hephaestus, whose other son Diomedes kills just after Athena has made him flash with fire. Hephaestus rescued Idaeus so that his priest would not be too sorely grieved, and Athena fears that the other gods too might save their own favorites regardless of which side they are on. The departure of Athena and Ares signals a Trojan rout, in which each Achaean king kills a Trojan. Among those slain Scamandrius was taught to hunt by Artemis; Phereclus, the shipwright of Paris's fleet, was the son of Harmonides, who—the antecedent is unclear—"knew how to make every curious thing, for Pallas Athena loved him"; Pedaeus was the bastard son of Antenor, whose wife Theano—the Trojans had made her priestess of Athena (6.300)—honored him equally with her own sons; and Hypsenor was the son of Dolopion, who served as priest to the river Scamander "and was honored by the people as a god." Neither Artemis, Scamander, nor Athena saved the heroes to whom they were attached; and they are slain along with those who had before been less fortunate and always lacked divine protection. But the gods' withdrawal seems to entail not only the death of those who had some claim on the favor of the gods, but a change as well in the very climate in which the death of everyone, regardless of divine favor, occurs. The darkness that covers the eyes of three men in the providential sequence 4.457–538 becomes loathsome as soon as the gods cease to be concerned. Death, though never named as such as long as the gods were present (cf. 4.517), was mild and sometimes beautiful. Twice doubled in a simile's reflection, it magically lost some of its horror, for the likenesses subsume dying under the larger and hence less terrifying category of falling (cf. 5.558, 560). The simile of the poplar is particularly instructive (4.482–87).[5] It grew in a moist meadow, smooth but for branches at its top, and a chariot-maker cut it down and let it dry out on the banks of a river, "in order that he might bend it into a felloe for a very beautiful chariot." The crest on the helmet of Simoeisios is likened to the standing poplar, but the expansion of the simile leaves him behind and replaces the living tree not with a dead trunk (cf. 4.147) but with its purpose, to be part of something beautiful again. Simoeisios is lost in a work of art. His death becomes less painful. It is transfigured in the presence of Athena and Ares, and both the lack of similes and the death of divine favorites when the gods are absent strongly suggest that it is transfigured because of their presence. The gods, then, would be the artisans or poets of the heroic world and an essential ingredient in Homer's own poetry.

One must digress here to call attention to a strange reticence on Homer's part. It is a digression because the reticence does not directly link up with the plot of the *Iliad* but is still necessary because it points to the ground tone of the *Iliad* that its plot never affects. When the gods are first absent from the battle, someone dies with a groan (5.68), but Homer never goes further than this. We are not told what the groan of a dying man expresses: no one ever dies in pain. Homer never enters into that aspect of death which is not to be grasped by the senses (13.570–73). He omits it neither out of ignorance (cf. 10.325) nor, as Thucydides' Pericles apparently does, in an effort to console: "Cowardice with softness is more painful to a man of pride than the death that occurs insensibly with strength and common hope" (2.43.6).[6] Homer mentions pain only when a hero is not fatally wounded (11.268, 458), and particularly at the moment when the pain is about to be or is being relieved (4.191, 11.398, 848, 15.60, 394, 16.518, 524, 528). The heroes suffer no more than the gods do (5.397, 417, 763), for there is always a cure; indeed, only Hera is exaggeratedly said to have suffered from "incurable pain" (5.394). Homer does mention pain twice in connection with a fatal wound, but once he speaks of the spear itself as being painful and not of the hero's own suffering (5.658), and once he says that the area between the navel and the groin is the most painful to be hit in, but he phrases it indirectly: "where Ares is especially painful for wretched mortals" (13.568–69). The god of war assumes the pain. He takes on what Homer thinks improper to ascribe to the heroes themselves.

The cause of pain, whether spear or Ares, absorbs the pain, in somewhat the same way that the simile of the poplar overshadowed the death it was meant to describe. *Aichmē alegeinē* and *Arēs alegeinos* do not falsify the experience of death; they conceal it as much as they remind us of it, and indicate the underside that cannot be expressed if the world of the heroes is to keep its brightness. Only a horse in its death throes and hit in the most fatal spot (8.81–86) is said to suffer pain; but man's most fatal spot, which the same book describes (8.325–28), does not make Homer say that Teucer felt any pain when Hector hit him there, but rather that his arm grew numb, and the blow itself proved not to be fatal, for Hector threw a stone and not a spear. Virgil, in departing once from this Homeric euphemism, suggests that he understood it. *Duplicat virum transvecta (hasta) dolore* (*Aeneid* 11.645) expands *Iliad* 13.618 *idnōthē de pesōn,* where nothing corresponds to *dolore;* but *idnōthē* occurs twice elsewhere along with *algēsas,* once of Thersites' beating (2.269), and once of an eagle (12.205–6).[7] Virgil, then, deliberately put together two or three Homeric passages in order to connect pain with dying. Homer, on the other hand, in order to keep mortal pain away from the heroes, restricts it to a horse, a weapon, and a god, all of which seem to be ways of clothing the human that lies at the heart of the heroic. In the postheroic world, however, the suitor Eurymachus dies in pain, *aniazōn* (*Odyssey* 22.87), for perhaps the Trojans are only unjust but not wicked, and hence there can be no satisfaction at their death, while the pain of a dying suitor can be regarded as enhancing the justice of his punishment: Polyphemus, too, suffers from his incurable wound (*Odyssey* 9.415, 440). The general absence of moral indignation in the *Iliad* would thus be the other side of Homer's reticence about pain. His dispassionate precision would have been intolerable if he had not known its limits.

To return now to the gods. Athena and Hera return to Olympus at the end of the fifth book, "having stopped baneful Ares from his slaughter of men," and the sixth book announces the departure of all the gods (6.1). Each event will now be unconditioned by the gods: the heroes will act without them and hence will act differently. Diomedes kills Axylus, who was "a friend to human beings, but no one of them warded off his mournful death" (6.11–19). When the gods are absent, it is sadly fitting that a philanthropist, whose kindness benefited other mortals but not the gods, should die. He does not share in a divine providence. He is far more alone than those who were killed in the absence of Athena and Ares at the beginning of the fifth book. Human beings, one might say, now replace the heroes as the subject of the *Iliad*.[8]

Menelaus captures Adrastus alive, whose horses had entangled his chariot and spilled him on the ground (6.37–65, cf. 831–34). As an accident puts him at the mercy of anyone who might find him, Menelaus cannot congratulate himself on his own prowess. He owes everything to chance and nothing to himself; and aware of this, he is willing to accept ransom, until Agamemnon comes up and rebukes him for his leniency, urging him to kill all the Trojans, "even a boy still in his mother's womb." Nothing equals the cruelty of Agamemnon's advice. Though Agamemnon later kills the two sons of Antimachus, who plead for their lives, he at least defends his decision to kill them on a particular ground (11.122–42); and when Achilles rejects Lycaon's supplication, his excuse is his fury which, ever since Patroclus's death, has overtaken him (21.99–106). Here Agamemnon, without offering any excuse, persuades Menelaus that Adrastus should be killed; and, Homer adds, "his words were just" *(aisima pareipōn)*. Not only has Agamemnon become cruel but Homer as well; for the gods, who before had taken sides, are now nowhere to be seen. Their partiality has made the heroic world moral; they set limits to right and wrong, however arbitrary they sometimes may seem; their disapproval, which depended on their affections, had guided Homer in his own judgment. When Achilles refuses to save the life of Tros, who wordlessly grasps his knees, Homer tells us his opinion: "He was not a sweet-tempered man nor mild in spirit" (20.463–69); and when Achilles slays twelve Trojans as an offering to Patroclus, he again blames him: "He resolved evil deeds in his heart" (23.174–77); for Homer, knowing that some gods disapprove of Achilles, can echo their opinion. But now that the gods have lost all interest in human affairs, no one tells the heroes what they ought to do, and without the gods they become bestial. Nestor rallies the Achaeans with the cry, "Let us kill men" (70).

Hector, encouraged by Helenus, charges the Achaeans, who retreat and cease their slaughter: "They thought some one of the immortals had come down from starry heaven to aid the Trojans" (108–9). The Achaeans mistake Hector for a god when no gods are present. As gods and man have never been so far apart, the heroes confound them. Diomedes, whom Athena had so recently favored, cannot tell whether Glaucus is a god or man; he is as uncertain as Odysseus when he confronts Nausicaa (119–29). He asks Glaucus: "Who are you, Oh most mighty power, of mortal human beings?" Only here does a hero call another to his face an *anthrōpos* and not an *anēr* (cf. 9.134 with 276, 21.150). Diomedes reckons in absolutes: Glaucus is either human or divine; he cannot be, what he himself once was, divinely inspired. Critics have been puzzled why Diomedes, who has just wounded Aphrodite and Ares, should now be unwilling to fight Glaucus if he turns out to be a god.[9] But there is no difficulty: the gods have departed and left the heroes, Diomedes along with the rest, alone. His ability to distinguish between human and god depended on Athena's favor (cf. 5.128–32, 827–28). As soon as she withdrew from the battle, he knew no more than the Achaeans, to whom Hector seemed a god.

The burden of their own mortality oppresses Diomedes and Glaucus. One seems at a loss without the gods, the other sees all men as alike and undistinguishable: "as is the generation of leaves, so is that of men." Genealogy is a mere succession of men, *akritophullon,* but Glaucus wishes to gloss over his own sense of smallness and impress Diomedes with his divine lineage. He deals in superlatives: Sisyphus was the craftiest of men, Bellerophon said his battle with the Solymi was the fiercest he had ever entered, and he slew all the best men in Lycia. Glaucus, the son of Sisyphus, fathered blameless Bellerophon, whose beauty and manliness came from the gods, and whom the gods escorted to Lycia and helped to slay the divine Chimera. Providence sponsored his deeds, and even the king of Lycia was forced to believe in his divine descent. But Glaucus knows how fitfully the gods favor men. Bellerophon became hateful to all the gods and wandered alone, "avoiding the track of human beings"; and two of his children fared worse: Ares killed Isandrus, and Artemis in anger slew Laodameia. And yet all their fates were more than human; Glaucus's ancestors were not ordinary mortals. Thus Glaucus himself, in looking back on his past, partly proves that men are like leaves, and partly tries, as he bolsters himself, to astonish Diomedes. If he cannot claim that he is a god, at least he has divine ancestors; and Diomedes, who before had such contempt for the genealogies of Pandarus and Aeneas (5.244–56), now finds an excuse to break off the combat. As his grandfather Oineus entertained and exchanged gifts with Bellerophon, so he and Glaucus should exchange their armor and proclaim themselves "ancestral friends."

Axylus, a friend to strangers, dies; Glaucus and Diomedes, whose grandfathers were friends, agree to separate. Axylus had no divine protection, while Glaucus had its shadow, a divine lineage. The gods leave enough of a trace of themselves to reestablish the sacredness of *xenia. Xenia,* which Paris's rape of Helen had violated, now returns. And yet the war goes on. It can no longer be waged for the sake of vindicating a principle that both sides now acknowledge; it now must depend on something that, as it dispenses with the original cause of the war, is unaffected by, or rather involves, the mutual recognition of enemies: Diomedes offers Glaucus all the Achaeans he can kill (229). The sacred was before a public issue, whether it underlay the crime of Paris or of Pandarus, but now it only serves a private relationship that has no effect beyond itself. The gods, in short, have ceased in any simple moral way to be decisive for the course of the war: Zeus took away Glaucus's wits (234).

When Hector has returned to Troy and bidden his mother pray to Athena, he curses Paris: if the earth swallowed up Paris, and he would see him descending to Hades, Hector would forget his sorrow (280–85). Hector's wish before, though just as vehement, that Paris be without offspring and die unmarried (3.40, cf. 56–57), Paris's cowardice had warranted; but now, whether he shirks or not, Hector longs for his death. Olympius raised Paris as a bane for the Trojans, for Olympius is gone (6.282–83). Everyone feels the absence of the gods. When Helen had heaped scorn on Paris's strength, Paris falsely attributed his defeat to Athena; "Now Menelaus has won a victory with the help of Athena, but at another time I shall be victorious over him; for there are also gods on our side" (3.439–40). He will be victor whenever the gods so wish it. Although he then was wrong about Menelaus, he was right about himself—Aphrodite did save him—so it seemed reasonable to suppose that some god had protected Menelaus. His mistake was justifiable. But now not even he thinks the gods make for victories: *nikē d' epameibetai andras* (6.339). No longer Aphrodite but Fortune is his goddess: Athena has just refused the Trojans' prayer (311–12).

Helen feels despair more deeply than Paris. Priam had kindly received her on the ramparts of Troy; and she, provoked by his kindness, had burst out with: "Would that death had been pleasant to me when I followed your son to Troy" (3.173–74). But now, though Hector has not even spoken to her, her sense of guilt is even greater; on the very day she was born, not on the day she committed her crime, she wishes to have died; but, she adds, the gods decreed otherwise, for the gods no longer protect her (345–49, cf. 3.173 with 6.344).

Hector leaves Helen and Paris and meets his wife Andromache with his son Scamandrius (403–4). They form a beautiful but gloomy scene. Despair finally overtakes Hector; he predicts the fall of Troy: "Well I know this in my mind and spirit, that there will be a day when sacred Ilion will perish, both Priam and his people" (447–49). What Agamemnon had foretold when Pandarus wounded Menelaus, Hector has come to believe, and in the very same words prophesies; but Agamemnon saw Zeus, shaking his dark aegis, as the cause of Troy's capture (4.163–68, cf. 127–29). Hector sees no cause. His convictions that Troy will fall, and that its fall will not be a punishment for any crime, rest on the same basis: the absence of the gods.

The absence of the gods has made the sixth book the darkest in the *Iliad;* and this darkness is essential for bringing about the radical change in the direction of the war. Hector and Paris reenter the battle in the seventh book, appearing like a fair breeze that a god[10] sends to tired rowers; and after some success on their part, Athena and Apollo agree to stop the war for a day and let Hector challenge an Achaean to a duel (7.1–42). The soothsayer Helenus intuits the plan of the gods, who for the first time do not show themselves as anthropomorphic but assume the shape of vultures, and remain, as in the sixth book, invisible to men (43–61). Hector, pleased with his brother's proposal, offers to fight anyone whom the Achaeans might choose as their champion; he also promises, and in this he goes beyond the gods' plan, to give back the corpse for burial, if he should kill his opponent, so that a mound may be built near the Hellespont, "and someone of later times, in sailing by in a large ship over the wine-faced sea, may say, 'That is the tomb of a man who died long ago, whom, excellent though he was, glorious Hector killed'; so someone will say, and my fame shall never die" (87–91). Hector wants immortal fame. Though he believes that Troy will be taken, he wants a monument to be left behind for himself. It shall perish, he shall live on. The gloom of the sixth book, brought on by the gods' absence, is dispelled in the seventh by the light of future glory. Hector finds his way out of a godless present in his fame to come. Fame is despair's remedy. If the gods are gone, if they no longer care, then men must take care of themselves; they must adopt a surrogate for them, and Hector suggests something that Achaeans reluctantly accept, immortal fame. Instead of depending on the gods, they will depend on other men. They will snatch from the very uncertainty of war a permanent gain. No matter who will be victorious, and regardless of the justice of their cause, both sides can win glory. They can share in the success of their enemy and even find a certain satisfaction in being killed.

The difference between the combat of Menelaus and Paris, which took place a few hours before, and the present contest of Ajax and Hector indicates a great change in the character of the war. Menelaus prayed to Zeus that Paris be punished for his crime, while neither Ajax nor Hector prays. Menelaus fought with Paris to settle the war, Ajax and Hector fight in a trial of prowess. They fought to decide the fate of Helen, while Ajax and Hector fight without any regard for Helen, but only to determine who is the better warrior. They exchange threats and boasts, Menelaus and Paris fought in silence. They were in deadly earnest. Hector and Ajax can break off their combat and give each other gifts in parting. Menelaus had wished to accept Hector's challenge, but Agamemnon (with all the other kings) restrained him (7.104–7), for though he was the right opponent against Paris, he would have lost his life to no purpose. He is no longer the champion of his own cause. Had Menelaus killed Paris, he would have recovered Helen; if Hector now wins, the Achaeans would recover Ajax's corpse, which would serve, once it was buried, as a memorial to both Ajax and Hector. Fame and renown would seem to be as precious to Hector as Helen is to Menelaus, and his new ambition so much inflames him that he can refer quite brazenly to the Trojan's perfidy (7.69–72, cf. 351–53). Whatever oaths they may have broken, whatever injustice they may have done, has no relevance now. As long as Helen was at the center of the dispute, the Trojans were in the wrong; but now that she is discarded, and becomes merely a theme for heroic exploits, right and wrong no longer apply. *Publica virtutis per mala facta via est.*

As the cause of the war has changed, so too have the central characters. Helen unleashed a war over which she loses control. The war, having worked loose from its origin, now feeds itself. The desire for Helen generated the desire for fame, but the offspring no longer acknowledges the parent. There can now be no other end to the war than the destruction of Troy. The restitution of Helen will no longer suffice. Diomedes speaks for all of the Achaeans when, in answer to the Trojans' proposal of returning all the stolen goods except Helen, he says: "Now let no one accept either the goods of Alexander or of Helen herself; for even a fool would know that the ends of destruction have already been fixed for the Trojans" (7.400–402). Not even if the Trojans give back Helen would the Achaeans stop fighting. The war has passed out of her hands and become common property. No longer is the war petty. It has transcended the bounds of its original inspiration and assumed the magnificence of heroic ambition. Paris and Menelaus now have minor roles, and Helen is scarcely mentioned (cf. 11.122–42). She was a necessary irritant that has become superfluous, and Helen herself knows this. "Upon myself and on Paris," she tells Hector when the gods are absent, "Zeus has placed an evil fate, so that we might be the theme of song among human beings who shall be" (6.357–58). Not herself but her fame justifies the war: in the perspective of later generations can be found her own raison d'être. What gives purpose to the quarrel is not a present victory but a future fame. In the third book Helen was weaving into a cloak many contests of the Achaeans and Trojans, "who for her sake suffered at the hands of Ares" (3.125–38). As the war had been staged for her benefit, she had gone up on the walls to watch her two husbands fight for her; but now an impersonal fame has overshadowed any personal pleasure, although she may still find some comfort in a future glory. She is the plaything of the future (of her own renown), and no longer manages her own destiny (cf. 6.323–24). She is caught up in a larger issue and concedes her own insignificance. And Menelaus, like Helen, realizes the change that Hector proposes, for he berates the Achaeans and calls them "spiritless and fameless in vain" (7.100), since they are not eager to accept Hector's challenge; for unless they are animated by fame his challenge is meaningless. They must disregard Menelaus and look to themselves. Their own aggrandizement, not Menelaus's vengeance, must become their aim. As their ambition, in becoming more selfish, becomes more grand, so their prowess, in advocating immortal fame as their end, can at last justify itself.

Homer has carefully prepared the shift from Helen to fame as the cause of the war, a shift that the magical disappearance of Paris first indicates. When victory is almost within Menelaus's grasp, as he drags Paris toward the Achaeans, Aphrodite breaks the strap by which Menelaus held him, and "snatching Paris away, she hid him in a great mist, and set him in the sweet-smelling bridal chamber" (3.369–82). Paris is as effectively dead as if he had been killed. Overcome by desire for Helen, he is indifferent to fame: if Athena gave victory now to Menelaus, the Trojans' gods at another time will aid him (3.439–40). He becomes isolated from the war, which now begins again without him. Although his original injustice began the war, it continues by the injustice of Pandarus, which serves as the transition between the recovery of Helen and the desire for fame. Not Paris but Pandarus wounds Menelaus, Paris disappears, and the responsibility for the war spreads among the Trojans, while among the Achaeans Menelaus remains the central figure, about whom they still rally. But he too disappears in the seventh book, when Agamemnon persuades him not to accept Hector's challenge. To transform pettiness into grandeur, a private quarrel into a public war, may require injustice; but once the transformation is completed, once both sides accept the new conditions, the demands of justice no longer apply.

> Were it not glory that we more affected
> Than the performance of our heaving spleens
> I would not wish a drop of Trojan blood
> Spent more in her defense. But, worthy Hector,
> She is a theme of honour and renown;
> A spur to valiant and magnanimous deeds,
> Whose present courage may beat down our foes,
> And fame in time to come canonize us.[11]

The change that takes place among the heroes finds its echo among the gods. Aphrodite saved Paris, but Diomedes in the fifth book wounds her, and she never reappears among men. Even as Paris, a man wholly dominated by desire, disappears, so Aphrodite, the divine principle, as it were, which gives him the most support, retires and leaves the war to Ares and Apollo, Athena and Hera.

After the contest of Ajax and Hector, Nestor proposes that a trench be dug and a wall built as a protection for their ships and themselves (7.337–43). The kings agree, and while they are laboring at the wall, the gods, seated by Zeus, admire their work, and Poseidon speaks among them: "Zeus father, what mortal on the boundless earth shall still disclose his plans for the immortals? Do you not see how the Achaeans have built a wall for their ships and run a trench about it, but they have not offered famous hecatombs to the gods? Its fame will go as far as the dawn scatters light, and they will forget the wall that Phoebus Apollo and I built for the hero Laomedon" (7.446–53). Poseidon fears that the fame of the Achaeans' wall will outstrip the fame of his own wall. He interprets the wall as an insult to the gods. Fame seems not to be in the care of the gods; they can neither hinder nor advance it. Not even the destruction of the wall, which Homer describes (12.10–33), prevents us from hearing of it. As long as the war concerned the quarrel which Hera and Athena had with Paris (4.31–32, 24.27–30), the gods are the ultimate authority; but as soon as the war turns away from Paris and embodies the desire for fame, the gods seem unnecessary. Just as Hector attempted to break loose from them in challenging an Achaean to a duel, so Nestor takes up his suggestion and proposes the building of tomb, trench, and wall. Hector was unsuccessful, for he does not kill Ajax. Nestor succeeds for a time, but even his attempt is thwarted by the gods. The wall would have made the Achaean camp as permanent as Troy; whether they won or lost, it would have remained as a record of their siege. Nestor improved on Hector, for victory was the price of his fame, while Nestor relies on a collective effort that disregards prowess as well as success. The wall is the most glorious attempt to break away from the gods' influence, and it fails. But Zeus helps the Achaeans along in their belief, for he forbids in the eighth book any intervention by the gods in the war (8.7–22). In the fourth book Hera was given carte blanche to do what she wanted, but now that her personal revenge has been transcended, Zeus no longer will brook any interference.[12]

Once the transition has been completed to the second cause of the war, Homer begins to lay the foundations for the third cause. It is now in the eighth book that Zeus outlines the death of Patroclus and Achilles' return to battle (8.473–77). Even as the disappearance of Paris announced the shift to the second cause, so Zeus's prophecy indicates the final cause. Thus three causes underlie the *Iliad:* first Helen (Aphrodite), second fame, which is partly replaced in turn by Achilles' love for Patroclus. From individual revenge to universal ambition and back again to revenge is the *Iliad*'s plot. The third cause thus marks a partial return to the first cause, for Achilles' desire for vengeance seems to have more in common with Menelaus's than with the cause that perpetuates the war in his absence. But what proves to be at stake is entirely different in the two cases. It is not just that Hector's guilt is hardly comparable to Paris's, but that Menelaus wants and finally gets Helen back while Achilles, and this is the shock of the *Iliad,* not unwillingly gives back Hector's corpse.[13] Achilles finds out that he cannot have Patroclus back; his soul slips through his embrace (23.97–101, cf. 24.3–8). Through the abrupt shifting from the soul of a friend to the corpse of an enemy, Homer forces one to consider the possible connection between the second and third phases of the plot. The new conditions laid down for the continuation of the war in the gods' absence must somehow persist throughout the rest of the *Iliad* and thus prepare the way for its ending. The *aristeia* of Diomedes, therefore, as the transition between the first and second phases of the plot, must be examined in more detail.

Why Aphrodite must be wounded has, I think, become clear, but why Ares has to be as well, and in a scene that seems to duplicate Aphrodite's wounding, is still obscure. The explanation rests on two points, the character of Ares and the plot of the *Iliad.* After he has been wounded, Ares, like Aphrodite, never afterward appears among men. He ceases to be active on behalf of the Trojans, and we next see him in his indignation on hearing belatedly of the death of his Achaean son (15.110–42). Ares now becomes solely the god of war, *alloprosallos,* as Athena and Zeus call him (5.831, 889). He is generalized. Only after Diomedes has eliminated him as a Trojan god does Hector's saying hold true, "War is common: he kills the killer" (18.309). The first Achaean to be compared at length with Ares is Ajax, when he advances to confront Hector in a duel (7.208–11); but the first instance Ares can be said to be approaching neutrality occurs when Ares stirs up Menelaus with the aim that he be killed by Aeneas (5.563–64). He shows his partiality for the Trojans by inspiring an Achaean. Homer then effects the transition between Ares the Trojan god and Ares the god of war at the beginning of the sixth book. The battle between the Achaeans and Trojans is then left by itself, and "the warring charged hither and thither through the plain" (6.2). This is the first time Homer himself makes any word for fighting the subject of an active verb (cf. 1.61). *Machē* becomes personified precisely at the moment that Ares departs; and when Ares first returns he is seen controlling the degree of force in the cast of a spear (13.444, cf. Leaf, commentary *ad loc.*). He too becomes a personification. He slips into Hector as *deinos enualios* (17.210–11). His proper name is now a quality that cannot be distinguished from himself. He simply is the essence of total war.[14]

But why must Ares be generalized? Why does the shift from Helen to fame as the motive for war require it? The answer lies in the plan of Zeus. When Zeus first heard Thetis's request, he kept silent for a long time (1.511–12). He kept silent because he knew that Thetis was asking for the death of Achilles. Zeus reviewed in that silence almost everything that later happens in the *Iliad.*[15] He had to weigh Achilles' present wrath against Achilles' fate that automatically would be fulfilled were he to gratify Thetis. It is therefore all the harder to understand why he decided at last to yield to her importunities. The wrath of Achilles causes great loss of life among the Achaeans and Trojans, but it also allows every hero to win as much glory as he can. As long as Achilles was in the field, the Trojans never ventured into the plain (5.788–91, 9.352–55), and as long as Achilles fought, no Achaean could hope to do anything of consequence (cf. 11.104–12), let alone be thought superior to him (6.98–101, 7.289). Achilles' withdrawal is the indispensable condition for the shift in the war, while the shift itself is the justification for Zeus's willingness to honor him. Achilles had undercut the original reasons for the war when he said that the Trojans had done him no injury (1.150–57), and the Trojans' violation of the truce, though it generalized the war, could not by itself adequately compensate for the death of Achaeans. The punishment of the Trojans for an injustice, which Zeus could have accomplished without any war, necessarily looks like a punishment of the Achaeans as well. They pay a very high price to vindicate a sacred principle. Only the possibility of winning immortal fame for themselves can outweigh that price. This is the harsh justice of Zeus.[16] The irony implicit in Achilles' fate is that that which in his own eyes would have justified his fighting the Trojans can only come about through his absence, and hence he must always be out of phase with himself. He must forever long for what he can never obtain (cf. 1.490–93), for when he returns to the war he fights to avenge Patroclus and not to win fame. The plan of Zeus, then, does not start in Book 8 but extends back through Books 5, 6, and 7 to the beginning of 2, and the elimination of Ares the Trojan god is as much a part of this plan as Aphrodite's withdrawal. Ares must be generalized in order that the war be as general as the original motivation for it. The god who presides over the war must cease to be parochial, for only in becoming common to both sides can Ares match the purpose that both sides now share. The fortunes of war must be equal if everyone is to have an equal chance at winning glory. Thus Athena, in effecting the withdrawal of Aphrodite and Ares, as well as in provoking, with Apollo, Hector's challenge, carries out (perhaps without knowing it) the plan of Zeus, just as the heroes die for a cause that is now their own without knowing that thereby they allow Zeus to honor Achilles.

The desire for immortal fame animates the heroes because no higher ambition is open to them. They cannot become immortal (cf. 13.54, 825–28, 7.298, 24.258–59). If Sarpedon the son of Zeus were fated to be immortal and ageless, he would not be among the first in battle; but as the fate of death stands over him, which no mortal can avoid, he must nobly act and die, so that his rank among the Lycians, who now look up to him as a god, will be matched by his deeds (12.310–28). The consciousness of mortality underlies the desire for immortal fame. When Hector proposes a single combat with an Achaean, he stipulates the return of the corpse, either his own so that the Trojans might bury it, or his opponent's so that the Achaeans might erect a tomb and his fame never die (7.77–91). Nothing had been said about the return of the corpse when the conditions for the combat between Paris and Menelaus were laid down. Indeed, the crucial question as to what constituted a victory was left obscure (3.71–72, 92–93, 101–2, 138, 255, 281–87, 308–9, 451).[17] Death is recognized for what it is only in light of immortal fame: the wall that Poseidon interprets as a bid for fame is to be built right next to the funeral mound of all the Achaean dead (7.337). Mortality, in its double aspect of glory and burial, necessarily leads one back again to the *aristeia* of Diomedes, and the *aristeia,* in turn, divided into three sections (the wounding of Aphrodite, the wounding of Ares, and the exchange of armor with Glaucus), shows one how Homer has connected the plot of the *Iliad* with the ways of killing and dying. The order in which these ways appear then helps to explain why Homer begins the *Iliad* with the separation of soul and "body" (1.3–4) and ends it with Patroclus's ghost and Hector's corpse.

The overall and partly symmetric scheme of 4.457–6.237 in terms of the fighting is the following:[18]

a) 4.457–538: 7 killings, Trojans and Achaeans alternate
b) 5.1–83: 7 killings, all by Achaeans
c) 5.84–143: Pandarus wounds Diomedes
d) {5.144–65: 8 killings, 2 at a time, all by Diomedes
{5.166–296: Diomedes kills Pandarus
e) 5.297–310: Diomedes wounds Aeneas
5.311–430: Diomedes wounds Aphrodite
e)′ 5.431–518: Diomedes attacks Aeneas
d)′ 5.519–626: 8 killings, by 2 Trojans and 3 Achaeans alternating
c)′ 5.627–69a: Tlepolemus killed, Sarpedon wounded
b)′ 5.669b–78: 7 killings, all by Odysseus
a)′ {5.679–710: 6 killings, all by Ares and Hector
{5.711–849: Ares kills Periphas
5.850–909: Diomedes wounds Ares
6.1–72: 15 killings by 11 Achaeans
6.73–236: Diomedes and Glaucus

Once one sees that Pandarus's violation of the truce is only a means to establish the second phase of the war, it is not surprising that he must be killed without any mention of his crime.[19] His death is not so much a punishment as a necessity that liberates the war from the question of right and wrong. After eight men have been killed in the presence of the gods and six without them, Homer next deepens our understanding of mortality through what occurs between Pandarus's wounding of Diomedes and Diomedes' killing of Pandarus. Pandarus is the first man to speak since the start of the battle; he boasts to the Trojans of having hit Diomedes (5.102–5). This first nonfatal wound of the battle allows Pandarus time to speak as it forces Diomedes to retire and ask for aid. Although blood shoots up through his tunic when Sthenelus pulls the arrow from his shoulder, Diomedes does not feel any pain. The heroes are still without any nerves (cf. 794–98). Diomedes' prayer to Athena is then answered; she puts new strength into his limbs and grants him the ability to distinguish between a god and a man (128).[20] The distinction is ambiguous, for it can mean either, as no doubt Athena intends it, that Diomedes will now be able to avoid a clash with any other god but Aphrodite, or, as the subsequent events suggest, that Diomedes will learn the ground for the difference between gods and men (cf. 6.128–43). It will prove to be based on a difference in blood (*haima* and *ichōr*), and it is therefore appropriate that Athena lifts the darkness from Diomedes' eyes just after he has been wounded and blood has stained his corselet (100).

Pandarus is the first man to speak, but no one replies; Diomedes' prayer to Athena is the first that is answered (115–32); but not until Aeneas and Pandarus talk is there a conversation among men (171–238). Pandarus's address to Diomedes is the first to an enemy (277–79), but not until he has cast his spear is there anything resembling a conversation between enemies (283–89). A conversation, however, between enemies in which both speak before they try to kill one another does not occur before the meeting between Sarpedon and Tlepolemus, the son and grandson of Zeus (632–54). Their meeting could readily be omitted here were it not that it lays the groundwork for the meeting between Glaucus and Diomedes. The god their ancestry shares lets them recognize one another but does not keep them from trying to kill one another, whereas the man who is the ancestor of Glaucus and was the guest-friend of Diomedes' grandfather does not help to make them known to one another but rather suffices to keep them apart. The movement, then, toward the mutual recognition of enemies as human beings is as follows: (1) Pandarus boasts about Diomedes to the Trojans, (2) Aeneas and Pandarus talk to each other about how to meet Diomedes, (3) Sthenelus and Diomedes talk about Aeneas and Pandarus, (4) Pandarus talks to Diomedes, (5) Pandarus and Diomedes exchange words while fighting, (6) Tlepolemus and Sarpedon talk to one another before fighting, (7) Diomedes and Glaucus talk to one another and consequently do not fight. Diomedes and Glaucus's conversation is the culmination of one way in which Homer has arranged the speeches of his heroes. There are other purposes these same speeches serve that cannot, however, be understood before one goes back to the next series of killings, but one may now remark that the duel between Hector and Ajax, which also results in an exchange of gifts, is unintelligible in terms of the plot without the prior exchange of armor between Glaucus and Diomedes. Hector's challenge resolves the impasse that the Glaucus-Diomedes parting represents: on the new basis of fighting for immortal fame, it becomes possible once again to recognize and to kill one's opponent.

Although Homer has up to now usually stated who was the father of each hero, he has only twice said something about heroes that pertains to the death of their sons. When Ares and Athena are present, he says that Simoeisios did not give back the recompense due to his parents (4.477–78), and when Diomedes, inspired by Athena, has slain one son of Dares, Hephaestus saves the other lest his father be angry with him (5.24). But now that the gods are absent, Homer says of Eurydamas, an interpreter of dreams, that he did not interpret any dreams for his two sons on their going to war (5.150). His sons are killed without any awareness of their fate (cf. 11.328–32). One cannot but be reminded of Achilles, and all the more so on account of the next pair that Diomedes slays (5.152–58). They are the sons of Phaenops, who was worn out by miserable old age *(gērаï lugrōi)* and left no other son to inherit his property; and Diomedes in killing them, "left (imperfect) for their father ritual lamentation *(goon)* and miserable cares *(kēdea lugra)*, since he did not welcome them back alive from the war." The phrase *gēraï lugrōi* is twice used of Nestor (10.79, 23.644), and once by Thetis of Achilles' father (18.434), in which same speech she speaks of her own cares as *kēdea lugra* (430), the only other occurrence of that phrase (cf. 13.346, 24.742). More important, however, than these formulas, whose presence here one can ascribe to chance, is the word *goos,* whose frequency (22 times) prevents this, its first appearance, from being accidental, for only here does Homer himself employ it without referring to Hector, Patroclus, or Achilles; indeed, apart from 17.37–38, it occurs only in speeches of Homer, Achilles, and Priam. Here sorrow first comes to a father. It is the second time since the battle began that Homer has mentioned a passion; the first was Odysseus's anger at the death of a comrade (4.494). Sorrow and anger, the two springs of

Achilles' action in the poem, are now before us as the effects of being killed: anger when the gods are present, sorrow when the gods are absent. It would not be altogether misleading to say that anger is the divine attribute of Achilles (*mēnis* only occurs of Achilles' anger or the gods', cf. 21.523), and sorrow represents his human side. The sorrow the gods have no share in is a certain kind of pity: they never pity a corpse as a corpse (cf. 24.525–26). They only had eyes for the wall and not the tomb that the Achaeans were building. Menelaus is the first to pity (5.561, cf. 610, 17.342, 352), for he sees the sons of Diocleas fall, who came to Troy in their youth to gain honor for himself and Agamemnon (550–53). The gods of course do pity men in their dying (cf. 20.21), but not when they are dead because they are dead: they pity Hector due to Achilles' attempt to disfigure his corpse (24.22–23).

The fourth and last pair of Trojans that Diomedes kills in this part are two sons of Priam, and Homer for the first time assigns a simile to a specific act of killing (5.159–65). It is the first simile that compares the slain to animals: they are the first of whom it is implied that they have a will (*kakōs aekontas,* 164, cf. 366). Homer's gradual disclosing of the heroes' will precedes their own consciousness of themselves as endowed with choice. The first to deliberate, as the first to get angry, in the midst of battle is Odysseus: *maimēse de hoi philon ētor* (5.670). He does not know whether to attack the wounded Sarpedon or kill several of his followers (671–73). It does not occur to him any more than to anyone else that the willingness to kill is shadowed by the willingness to be killed—consider the uninterpreted dreams of Eurydamas's sons. Diomedes "divines" that either Aeneas or Pandarus will be killed; that they might kill him is not a possibility (287–89). Tlepolemus threatens to send Sarpedon to Hades, and Sarpedon in turn threatens to send his soul there, but they do not think of their own lives as at stake (646, 654). Odysseus is again the first, but not until the eleventh book, to accept "kill" and "be killed" as belonging together (11.410); and he does so on the first occasion that anyone talks to his *thumos* (403): he is alone (401). The willingness to kill and be killed emerges in isolation out of a reflection of the heart, and precisely at that moment when *phobos,* which in eleven previous occurrences always meant "flight," slides over into the meaning "fear" (402, cf. 544).[21] Immediately after Odysseus's speech to his heart, the Trojan Sokos admits to Odysseus that he might kill or be killed (430–33). Not until 12.171–72, however, is it acknowledged to be the risk that someone other than oneself has willingly assumed; and not until 12.328 does anyone consider his own death as a matter of glory to another (cf. 13.327, 486); and not until 13.424–26 does Homer describe (in extremely euphemistic language)[22] someone as desirous *(hieto)* of killing or being killed. Odysseus finally sums up this strand in the heroes' awareness of mortality when he rebukes Agamemnon for advising flight: "Zeus has granted us from youth to old age to toil in harsh war, until each of us perishes" (14.85–87).

The fifth pair of charioteer and spearman that Diomedes meets is Aeneas and Pandarus, who go against him only after they have discussed who he is (5.174–87). Sthenelus then tries to restrain Diomedes from attacking them on the ground that Aeneas is the son of Aphrodite, but Diomedes refuses to get up into a chariot, and he advises Sthenelus how he should handle Aeneas's horses if he succeeds in killing them both (243–73). The killing of Pandarus and Aeneas is only a means to win noble fame through capturing horses (273, cf. 435). Although Diomedes had prayed to Athena that she give him Pandarus to kill (118), Aeneas's teaming up with Pandarus has shifted his attention to Aeneas's horses. The goal of punishing Pandarus's guilt, which the Achaeans never learn about, yields to glory as a cause to which everyone can lay claim. The heroes become the agents of their own ends, no longer subservient to an end beyond themselves. "You could not tell," Homer says, "whose side Diomedes was on" (85–86). The self-interest of the heroes, then, however noble it may at first appear, necessarily alters the way in which one understands Achilles' indifference to the Achaean's plight. His indifference is now seen to be by no means unique but merely indicative of what constitutes a hero, for even the civil Hector, when he has the choice to save Troy and tarnish his reputation or destroy it but enhance (or at least not diminish) his own glory, scarcely hesitates to condemn his wife to slavery (22.99–110, cf. 6.441–46).

Pandarus is the first to lose his *psuchē* (5.296). His death is the first to be described with the word whose various senses cluster around the meaning "life." The importance of the *psuchē* for the plot of the *Iliad* can hardly be overestimated, for it decisively separates men from gods: Pandarus loses his soul just prior to Diomedes' wounding of Aphrodite. The gods do not have a *psuchē,* for they can never become corpses (cf. 5.885–87, 15.115–18). They cannot go to Hades (cf. 8.13–16). Hades is as inaccessible to the gods as Olympus to men. The steps, therefore, by which Homer connects these two exclusively human things with one another must be considered. Tlepolemus is the first to threaten someone with Hades (5.646, cf. 190), and Sarpedon in reply is the first to threaten sending a soul to Hades (654); but the first to go under the earth are the philanthropist Axylus and his charioteer (6.19, cf. 18.329–32), and the first who go to Hades are Iphidamas and Koon (11.263). Iphidamas's death is a "brazen sleep" (241), and he himself is "pitiable" *(oiktros)* for having died away from his bride (242, cf. 5.574). Homer's compassion seems to increase as Hades comes more and more to light: Patroclus, whom Homer addresses more often than anyone else, is the first whose *psuchē* goes to Hades (16.856). The soul, however, does not prove to be more than a manner of speaking before Patroclus's soul speaks to Achilles, and Achilles acknowledges that it is, after all, even in Hades something (23.103).[23]

Patroclus's soul reminds Achilles that his corpse still awaits burning and burial. The corpse too is progressively revealed. Although the heroes sometimes view with equanimity the possibility of being killed in battle, no one calmly accepts the possibility of his corpse being left unburied (cf. 22.71–76). Athena is the first to threaten someone (he is just any and every Trojan) with being a prey to birds and dogs (8.379–80, cf. 13.831–82, 11.818), and Homer is the first to say that the slain are potential carrion: "They lay on the earth far dearer to vultures than to wives" (11.162). Homer's compassion that is awakened when Trojans go to Hades is balanced by a sardonic contempt for Trojan corpses. Diomedes later boasts that his spear-cast is always fatal, and whoever is hit rots away, reddening the earth with his blood, "and he has about him more birds than women" (11.391–95). Odysseus, however, is the first to make such a boast wholly particular. He addresses Sokos: "Your father and mother will not close your eyes though you are dead, but flesh-eating birds will pull you apart as they cast their thickset wings over you; but if I should die, the glorious Achaeans will bury me with all the customary rites" (11.452–55). Odysseus tells a dead man that he will deny his corpse burial; it is the first time anyone has spoken to the dead. Odysseus's boast prior to killing Sokos was that his death would give glory to himself and Sokos's soul to Hades; but after the killing he is content, if he should be killed, with receiving a proper burial. The occasion follows closely on Odysseus's speech to his *thumos* (401–4), when he decided that the willingness to be killed belonged as much as the willingness to kill to heroic excellence. A proportion, then, is suggested: as the address to one's own *thumos* is to one's willingness to be killed, so the address to a dead man is to the threat to refuse him burial. To be aware of what is the most honorable course for oneself is connected with an awareness of what constitutes the greatest disgrace. That the greatest disgrace, however, is not simply the reverse of the most honorable course—not flight but lack of burial—points to the peculiarity of the *Iliad*'s conclusion. The *Iliad* does not end with Achilles' resolve to die but with his return of Hector's corpse. Achilles' recognition of what it means to be mortal consists in his willingness to give back a corpse. It is precisely because one can be brave all by oneself but one cannot bury oneself that burial lies at the heart of the human. But the essentially human is not to be separated from the divine: the gods force Achilles' choice. The gods, who are not concerned with the corpse as a corpse, are concerned that it should be a concern to men (cf. 16.453–57, 666–70; Sophocles *Antigone* 1072–73).[24]

Diomedes' wounding of Aeneas prompts Aphrodite to rescue him, and Diomedes, knowing that she was not of the goddesses who hold sway in the wars of men, attacks and wounds her. He senses that Athena's injunction to him means that she has ceased to be central to this war. "The immortal *(ambroton)* blood of the goddess flowed, ichor, the sort that does flow in [the veins of] the blessed gods; for they do not eat bread nor drink sparkling wine, and hence they are bloodless and are called deathless" (5.339–42). M. Leumann has explained this apparently nonsensical passage by pointing to the pair of words *brótos* "gore" and *brotós* "mortal" (124–27). The gods are called deathless *(athanatoi)* because they are bloodless *(anaimones)*, for to be bloodless *(ambrotoi)* is to be immortal *(ambrotoi)*. Men give a name to the gods *(athanatoi)* that replaces an explanation *(ambrotoi)* with a description. They have therefore ceased to be aware of what really makes for the difference between the gods and themselves. Diomedes' wounding of Aphrodite restores that awareness. It is a necessary step in freeing the heroes from the illusion that their likeness to the gods has fostered (441–42). The old men of Troy thought it no matter for indignation that the Achaeans and Trojans suffered so long for a woman's sake, *ainōs athanatēisi theēsi eis ōpa eoiken.* Helen's looks excused and justified the war, but now in the light of the substantial difference between gods and men, they are no longer enough. Something more solid is needed, something that takes into account the blood and fat, flesh and bones of men. Through the wounding of Aphrodite, which makes it impossible for men any longer to compete with the gods, the cause of the war begins to shift to immortal fame. The desire for fame acknowledges what the fighting for Helen does not, the mortality of human beings. The desire for fame, however, is itself only a transition to the complete acknowledgment of mortality, Achilles' return of Hector's corpse. That Paris in Book 3 (six times) and Priam in Book 24 (eight times) are called *theoeidēs* most readily illustrates how far the plot of the *Iliad* moves away from the beauty of Helen (cf. 24.629–32, 3.310, 6.366).

The retirement of Aphrodite leads to the reappearance of Ares,[25] no longer as himself but with the looks of the Thracians' commander Akamas (5.462); and as soon as Ares withdraws for good Akamas is slain (6.5–11). Ares disguises himself as a man just after Apollo has made a likeness *(eidōlon)* of Aeneas (5.449–53).[26] Homer's pointing to the insubstantiality of appearance coincides with his revealing the substantial difference between gods and men. Ares, however, does more than adopt the looks of men: he acts like one. He is the only god who all by himself kills in battle (842–48). He enters so much into the war that he is indistinguishable from any other warrior (cf. 857). He thus unwittingly prepares the way for men taking over his functions: Pylaimenes is the first since the battle began who Homer says is the equal of Ares (576). The merging of the actions of Ares into those of men not only "depersonalizes" Ares but men as well, both the killers and the killed. Homer now presents for the first time a list of those whom Odysseus and Hector killed without saying anything about them except their names; indeed, not one of the men whom Odysseus killed receives either patronymic or epithet (677–78, 705–7, cf. 6.31, 36).[27] This increasing anonymity accompanies the generalizing of Ares, but it does not reach its height until much later, when Antilochus kills the nameless charioteer of Asius (13.385–99, cf. 210–12), and Homer has Patroclus kill twenty-seven men in four words (16.785, cf. 810).

The plot of the *Iliad* depends on Homer's revealing gradually the relations between gods and men, the first of these revelations being contained in the *aristeia* of Diomedes. The next and perhaps more important revelation has the ancient title, "The Docked Battle," Book 8,[28] where Zeus, in disclosing part of his plan to the gods, reveals himself as a cosmic deity. Men are then shown to be not only mortal but earthly beings (cf. 7.99). Here it must suffice to indicate how Homer passes from the opposition between mortal and immortal to that between heaven and earth. The passage is made through the reintroduction of time. That time has elapsed since Agamemnon woke from his dream is first mentioned by the herald Idaeus at 7.282. The combat between Menelaus and Paris, Pandarus's wounding of Menelaus, the *aristeia* of Diomedes, the meeting of Hector and Andromache, and the duel between Ajax and Hector, are all compressed into a single day. The separation of the mortal from the immortal first occurs independently of any demonstration by Homer that one must understand it as existing within a cosmic framework. Nestor's proposal to call a truce to bury the dead first reintroduces time (7.331, 372, 381), and the meeting of the Trojans and Achaeans on the battlefield to distinguish between Trojan and Achaean corpses first presents the sun in its cosmic relations: the rays of the sun strike the earth as it goes up into the sky out of deep-flowing Oceanus (7.421–24, cf. 1.475, 601). And yet time is still not very accurately reckoned; the day of burial passes with hardly a mention (433). The coming of the next night, however, is clearly marked (466), and during that night Zeus for the first time thunders (479). This is a far different Zeus from the Zeus who shook Olympus in pledging himself to Thetis (1.530). Dawn now spreads over the whole earth (8.1), whereas before she was said to have come only to Olympus to herald the light of day to Zeus and the other immortals (2.48–49, cf. 11.1–2). The earth is now part of the cosmic setting, and when the heroes renew the war, they fight within the time-limits that the sun determines (8.66–68, 485–88, 565, cf. 11.84–91). Zeus had referred to the cities of earthly men as being under the sun and the starry sky (4.44–45), but he does not disclose himself as a sky god until now (*ouranos* occurs 15 times in Book 8), as he contrasts his own power with that of all the other gods in terms of the distances between heaven and earth, Tartarus and Hades (8.13–16). He then sends lightning for the first time (75–76, 133–35) and continues to thunder as well (75, 133, 170–71). Zeus is a god of heavenly signs (69–72), whose relation to men is established through sacrifices (48, 203–4, 238–41, 249–50, 548–49, cf. 7.481, 15.370–78). The failure to offer sacrifice is the reason why Apollo and Poseidon destroy the wall of the Achaeans, whose fame would otherwise be as widespread as the dawn (7.450, cf. 8.192). The wall is the first of the links between mortal-immortal and heaven-earth: Zeus helped to destroy it by sending rain (12.25–26). These two pairs of opposites are then linked for the last time in the funeral pyre of Patroclus, which Achilles cannot get to burn before he prays to the winds and promises them sacrifices (23.192–218). Thus the breakdown of the "natural" order, as it makes inseparable the earthiness and the mortality of men, discloses men's dependence on the immortal and heavenly gods (cf. 17.443–47).

Notes

1. This lack of concern is best shown in the way in which Odysseus disregards Athena's advice on how to check the Achaean's flight after Agamemnon had tested them. Athena advised Odysseus, what Hera advised her, to check each man with gentle words (2.180), and Odysseus does speak gently to the kings and outstanding men (189), but harshly to men of the people as he drives them back with Agamemnon's scepter (199). Athena and Hera do not understand the need for force because they have no interest in any man of the people; the ugly Ther-

sites is beneath them. The same mistake ruins Agamemnon's *peira:* under the cover of urging their flight, he makes an appeal for the Achaeans to stay that would only be effective were all the Achaeans noble and capable of shame (110–41). Cf. U. von Wilamowitz-Moellendorf, *Die "Ilias" und Homer* (Berlin, 1916), 267–69; P. von der Mühll, *Kritisches Hypomnema zur "Ilias"* (Basel, 1952), 37; and especially K. Reinhardt, *Die "Ilias" und ihr Dichter* (Göttingen, 1921), 112–13). He too advises that flight be solely checked by words (75; cf. 4.232–33, 240–41).

2. P. Cauer, *Grundfragen der Homerkritik* (Leipzig, 1921), 3:494.

3. Cf. H. Jordan, *Der Erzählungsstil in den Kampfscenen der "Ilias"* (Breslau, 1905), 17.

4. W. F. Friedrich's attempt in *Verwundung und Tod in der "Ilias"* (Göttingen, 1956), to distinguish three major kinds of killing (the grotesque, realistic, and severe styles) that are then to be assigned to different layers, rests on the unstated assumption that the kinds of killing and the order in which they appear have nothing to do with the plot of the *Iliad.* He assumes that poetry is the same as style (8–10).

5. Cf. H. Fränkel, *Die homerischen Gleichnisse* (Göttingen, 1921), 36–37.

6. Cf. L. Strauss, *The City and Man* (Chicago, 1964), 194–95. Winston Churchill is reported to have once said, "The way to die is to pass out fighting when your blood is up and you feel nothing."

7. To judge from G. N. Knauer's lists in *Die "Aeneis" und Homer* (Göttingen, 1964), the source of Virgil's *dolore* has hitherto been unknown.

8. Cf. G. Broccia, "Il motivo della morte nel VI libro dell'*Iliade,*" *Revista di filologia e istruzione classica* 35 (1957): 61–69.

9. But see S. E. Bassett, "On Z 119–236," *Classical Philology* 18 (1923): 178–79.

10. This is the first time that Homer uses the nominative *theos,* which does not refer to a definite god, with an active verb (cf. 5.78).

11. Shakespeare, *Troilus and Cressida,* 2.2.195.

12. It seems to me that Thucydides' mention of the wall as having been built immediately on the Achaeans' landing at Troy does not stand in the way of the genuineness of the second half of *Iliad* Book 7, for one first has to understand how Thucydides read Homer before passing judgment, a consideration that D. L. Page unaccountably fails to mention (*History and the Homeric Iliad* [Berkeley and Los Angeles, 1959], 315–24). Thucydides is perfectly willing to disregard the plot of the *Iliad* for his own purposes. His concern is with the Trojan War and not the *Iliad:* his single mention of Achilles does not even pertain to the Trojan War (1.3.3). He asserts that Agamemnon was able to gather the expedition together not out of *charis* (the oaths of Tyndarus) but through fear (1.9.1, 3). He equally ignores both Paris's rape of Helen and the meaning of the conflict between

Achilles and Agamemnon (*Iliad* 1.158–60). He makes use of Agamemnon's but not Achilles' scepter (1.9.4). Could it be then that he just as deliberately ignores the meaning of the Achaeans' wall, and therefore assigns it, or rather reassigns it to the beginning of the war? If Achilles is not decisive for the course of the war (as Homer makes him out to be) both in his presence and absence, the strategic purpose of the wall, and not Poseidon's interpretation of its purpose, is all that remains; and if its historicity is unquestioned—Thucydides assumes, as most modern scholars do, that artifacts are not part of Homer's inventiveness (cf. 1.10.4)—it must have been built as soon as the Achaeans won their first engagement. That is where it would belong were it not for its meaning. The Trojan War would not be a war fought for honor or fame but for power. It would thus not be the equal of the Peloponnesian War, whose peculiarity is in Thucydides' view that it is the first war fought for honor and glory (1.75.3; cf. Strauss, *The City and Man,* 226–36). What is essential to the plot of the fictional *Iliad,* though it has nothing to do with the Trojan War—it would be an example of Homer's *epi to meizon kosmein* (1.10.3, 21.1)—has now become a true reason for the Peloponnesian War (cf. 2.41.4).

13. Cf. H. Mette, "Homer 1930–1956," *Lustrum* (1956), 72.

14. Cf. Cauer, *Grundfragen der Homerkritik;* von Wilamowitz-Moellendorf, *Die "Ilias" und Homer;* and S. Benardete, "Two Passages in Aeschylus' *Septem,*" *Wiener Studien* NF 1 (1967): 22–30.

15. I owe this fundamental observation to Mr. J. Klein of St. John's College, Annapolis, Maryland.

16. Euripides' Helen says that Zeus caused the Trojan war in order to relieve the earth of an overpopulation, and to make renowned the best men of Greece (*Helen* 36–41). Famine, flood, or fire would have accomplished the first but not the second purpose, which in turn was offered to the Greeks under the guise of fighting for justice; and what Zeus planned was just, but it is not the kind of justice that men would willingly undertake to defend.

17. Cf. von der Mühll, *Kritisches Hypomnema zur "Ilias,"* 66–67. That Menelaus "virtually" won, as von der Mühll expresses it (67, 68), is not sufficient: Eumelus "virtually" won the horse-race, and Ajax the foot-race. That the Trojans may not have broken the truce shows the necessary shifting of the basis of the war from a problematic question of right to fame.

18. See the very different analysis of *Iliad* Book 5 by H. Erbse, "Betrachtungen über das 5. Buch der *Ilias,*" *Rheinisches Museum* 104 (1961): 156–89.

19. C. F. Ameis and C. Hentze, *Odysee* (Leipzig, 1905–32), 2:59–60.

20. Cf. Wilamowitz-Moellendorf, *Die "Ilias" und Homer,* 158.

21. B. Snell's well-known analysis of this passage, it seems to me, does not pay sufficient attention to its context; *Philologus* 85 (1930): 143–45. See also Ch. Voigt, *Überlegung und Entscheidung, Studien zur Selbstauffassung des Menschen bei Homer* (Berlin, 1934), 87–92.

22. Cf. M. Leumann, *Homerische Wörter* (Basel, 1950), 215–18.

23. Cf. Wilamowitz-Moellendorf, *Die "Ilias" und Homer,* 109–10.

24. Cf. Strauss, *The City and Man,* 208, 70. Despite Homer's proem, by which one is led to expect to hear about the souls of many whom Achilles sent to Hades, there are only two, Patroclus's and Hector's; and again, despite the proem, only one corpse becomes a feast, not for dogs and birds, however, but for fish and eels (21.201–4).

25. Cf. Wilamowitz-Moellendorf, *Die "Ilias" und Homer,* 284–85.

26. Cf. E. Bickel, *Homerischer Seelenglaube, Geschichtliche Grundzüge menschlicher Seelenvorstellungen.* Schriften der Königsberger Gelehrten Gesellschaft I, Geisteswissenschaft Klasse 7. (Berlin, 1925), 15–16.

27. Jordan, *Der Erzählungsstil in den Kampfscenen der "Ilias,"* 38.

28. Cf. Wilamowitz-Moellendorf, *Die "Ilias" und Homer,* 26.

FOUR

The Furies of Aeschylus

THE GREEK WORD FOR "RIGHT" is *dikē*. Dikē can mean "punishment," but it never means "acquittal." *Dikastikē*—the science of right—is the art of punishment.[1] "To condemn" is *katadikazō* and very common, "to acquit," *apodikazō*—"to abstain from *dikē*"—and rare. Athena connects the founding of the Athenian system of right with the acquittal of Orestes. She thus goes against the grain of right. The last occurrence of the word "right" in the *Eumenides* is as a preposition *(dikēn)*, and its meaning is "in the manner of" (911). The exaction of right has given way to the inexactness of simile. Athena arranged for the Furies to be deprived of their right to punish Orestes. In the trilogy the Erinys is first mentioned as the divine agent of right; but it is in a simile of the Chorus, who make her stand in reality for the Atreidae (*Agamemnon* 59). Athena seems to have ensured that the Furies, who finally are before us in reality, never leave the level of simile. Now that *antidikos (Agamemnon* 41)—an advocate of right in a lawsuit—will gain its true meaning in the Athenian system of right, there will be no need, it seems, for the Furies to be the agents of right. Athena does say, however, that the Erinys has great power (950–51), and that this means for some men a dim life of tears while for others songs. Indeed, the Furies are often connected with song (*Agamemnon* 645, 992, 1119, 1190; *Eumenides* 331 = 344). They seem to be the tragic Muses whom Athena persuades to settle in Athens (cf. *Eumenides* 308).

The knowledge we are first given of the Furies comes from the *prophētis* of Apollo at Delphi. She is the only character in the trilogy to be in no way connected with its story. She seems to be as superfluous as the entire scene at Delphi, and her only purpose to introduce us to the Furies. No one but Orestes saw them at the end of the *Choephoroi.* They seem to have been his guilty conscience; but now they are twelve and form the Chorus. There is no evident reason why they should be the Chorus. The issue of right could have been presented without the presence of the Furies. Aeschylus could have scrapped the scene at Delphi and made the Chorus from the start Athenians, who would have welcomed Orestes to Athens and then, at Athena's direction, made up the jury. If the Chorus had been the jury, we would have learned why they voted as they did, and whether the bribes of Apollo or the threats of the Furies, both of which could have been imagined by the partisans of either, had any influence. As it is, whether the jury are aware of their own incapacity to reach a decision is unknown to us. We do not know whether they know why Athena has arranged for their incapacity to reach a decision. We do not know whether they realize why their first case must be Orestes', over whom they have no jurisdiction and for whom they cannot devise any sanction. We are thus forced to wonder whether the trial has not been arranged for us. We, however, know much more than the jury is ever told. They do not know that Orestes would have killed his mother even without Apollo's oracle; they do not know that Apollo's oracle was hypothetical, and, as if it were a parody of a law, its threat of dire punishment was the substitute for an argument based on right (*Choephoroi* 298–306; cf. *Eumenides* 84); and, finally, they do not know why Clytemestra killed her husband. Those who vote for the condemnation of Orestes vote for the right of the mother without qualification—she does not have to be in the right; those who vote for the acquittal of Orestes vote for a limited right of the father—the mother must be in the wrong. The jury therefore vote in a way in which we could not have voted; but we do not know whether the jury ever realize the compatibility of their principles. If Iphigeneia's sacrifice had been known to them, they might have condemned Orestes unanimously. Our ignorance of the jury's motives and understanding thus functions as the jury's own ignorance of the facts of the case and their possible failure to understand their own principles and Athena's purpose. Our ignorance of the jury makes the jury be wholly in the dark.

Prior to entering the sanctuary, the *prophētis* divides her address to the gods into two parts. The first she calls a prayer, the second a speech (1, 20, 21). In her prayer she puts Earth first, in her speech Athena. Her prayer is about the temporality of prophetic succession; her speech is about the presence of gods in different places. Apollo is a god in and of time,

Athena in and of place (cf. 65). In her prayer the *prophētis* denies that there has been any conflict between the pre-Olympian and Olympian gods. The transmission of the seat of prophecy to Apollo has been wholly peaceful. In her speech, however, the last of the Olympians, Dionysus, employs violence and kills the Thracian Pentheus "in the manner *(dikēn)* of a hare." The pre-Olympian gods reject force, the Olympians do not. They back a matricide and punish an unbeliever. At Delphi a perfect harmony between the old and the new gods prevails, but not at Athens. Athens knows only of the worship of the Olympian gods. The Athenians are the sons of Hephaestus (13). The Furies are the daughters of Night; they do not share a common ancestry with the Olympian gods through Earth. They do not come from the castration of Ouranos. They are among the oldest gods, but they have never been seen by anyone. The *prophētis* can make only imperfect likenesses of them. Athena's wisdom does not consist in working out a compromise between Olympian gods and gods to whom the Athenians have a prior loyalty; her wisdom consists in introducing the Furies to Athens. She chooses to dilute the worship of the Olympian gods with older gods. Athena effects a transmission of power as peaceful as that at Delphi. The Furies, then, are the newest gods and wholly under the control of Athena. If Apollo had not hinted to them where to find Orestes, the Furies perhaps would never have shown up (224). Wherever else Orestes went, his purification by Apollo was thought to suffice (284–85). Only at Athens is there some doubt as to its efficacy. Athens becomes a holdout through Athena. Athens is another Thebes.

On her return from the shrine, the *prophētis* speaks of her terror. We assume that the Furies frightened her; but the Furies turn out to be asleep, and though her description arouses our loathing, her fear seems groundless. Athena alone testifies to the frightfulness of their faces (990). The only threat in the *prophētis*'s account is posed by Orestes, whom she describes first. He is wide-awake and holds a newly drawn sword (42). We are thus startled into realizing that the *prophētis* is not an intrusion into the story. She must have delivered Apollo's oracle to Orestes. She might reasonably expect no mercy at his hands. Her prayer to Earth in any case was not just pro forma. She must have sensed the need to propitiate Earth.[2] The man she sees seated on Earth's navel was told by her to kill his mother. That she was used by Apollo to suppress the pre-Olympian foundation of Delphi cannot now elude her. The Olympian gods are not squeamish when it comes to having their own way.

The *prophētis* never declares the Furies to be gods; not even Athena recognizes them as gods (411), though she knows their lineage and their names (418). To the *prophētis,* they are and are not women, they are and are not Gorgons; and they recall the Harpies whom she has seen in paintings but they are wingless. The Furies are unknown to painters. According to Pausanias, Aeschylus was the first to put snakes in the hair of the Furies (I.28); and since Orestes mentions the snakes at the end of the *Choephoroi* as that feature which prompts him to liken them to Gorgons (1048–49), it must be the absence of snakes that convinces the *prophētis* that they are not Gorgons (cf. 127–28). The Furies of the *Eumenides* are and are not the Furies of the *Choephoroi.* They are no longer Orestes' Furies. He is no longer mad, and they can fall asleep. When they return to their task, they are unsuccessful. Their binding song fails as much to bind Orestes as Orestes' summons of his father had failed to gain Agamemnon's support.[3] Orestes defends himself before the Furies, but he never refers to them as right in front of him until the Areopagus has acquitted him (761). Indeed, Orestes has long since had the Furies behind him; they never got him to express any regret for his crime. Orestes is remorse-proof. He can be punished as the law but not as conscience understands punishment. If Orestes had refused to obey Apollo, he would have been tortured in body and soul; the Furies were for a time capable of making him mad (cf. 301). Orestes chose body over soul (cf. 137–38, 267). He is the perfect vehicle for establishing law in Athens.

Apollo's purification of Orestes seems to have put a stop to Orestes' imaginings. He now is clean, and the Furies are all his former impurities. They are, however, asleep; they are harmless. In order for them to become agents again, they must be awakened. They are awakened by a dream they have, which we are privileged to see and hear before we hear their waking interpretation of it. We see inside the daughters of Night and know more than they do about themselves. The reality of their dream is the ghost of Clytemestra; we do not have to reconstruct her out of elements that their interpretation has transformed; and we could not have done so anyway, for Clytemestra is not in their interpretation. In their dream the ghost of Clytemestra has become a charioteer—in the manner of *(dikēn)*—whose goad is a reproach to them, and whose lash they feel under their heart and liver. Their viscera are fully human, and they are wracked with guilt. They say the heavy chill that besets them is that of the grim public executioner (155–162). The Furies seem to have come to embody all that they intended Orestes to suffer. Their further persecution of Orestes is therefore no longer on behalf of Clytemestra. Her case has been universalized. Orestes is a source of bitterness to parents (152, cf. 511–15); but he cannot become such a source unless the apparently natural ties between children and parents are thought to be an insufficient constraint on family crimes, and accordingly the law is thought of as the only bond of the family (490–98). The Furies, then, must at this point be perplexed about themselves. They cannot know who they are destined to be. "Their lot," says Athena, "is to manage all things that are within the range of human beings" (930–31, cf. 310–11). We have just witnessed the first step toward that destiny. It is initiated through the soul of the dead Clytemestra becoming a dream.

The Furies first defend themselves before Apollo; their deference to him—they address him as Orestes had (85, 198)—contrasts favorably with his abuse of them. Although Apollo had told Orestes that their dwelling-place was Tartarus below the earth, and gods, men, and beasts find them equally abhorrent, he now casts about for what place would truly suit them on earth. His first suggestion, that they belong where punishments *(dikai)* of Asiatic cruelty are practiced, implies that they are not responsible for man's inhumanity to man. Not all men, then, would find the Furies repulsive. His next suggestion—they should properly dwell in a lion's cave—implies that not all beasts would shun them. Only the Olympian gods truly detest them. The basis of their detestation emerges from the enigma Apollo embeds in his speech. He first threatens them with a bright-quivering winged snake; he then lists a series of punishments whose common element is dismemberment; he then puts them in a lion's cave, and last he orders them out as if they were a flock of goats *(aipoloumenai)* without a herdsman. Apollo hints at the Chimera: a lion before, a snake behind, and in the middle a she-goat. The Furies are loathsome, Apollo suggests, because they are monsters; they consist of parts that do not form a whole; they therefore have no understanding of wholes. Theirs is a partial justice (222–30). The whole to which Apollo appeals is marriage. His example is the "pledges" of Hera and Zeus (cf. *Agamemnon* 879, *Choephoroi* 977). He must have recourse to such a marriage in order to counter the Furies' argument that a wife's murder of her husband is not of kindred blood. The Furies assume the prohibition against incest, and Apollo grants the point by citing a marriage of brother and sister. Since Apollo therefore invokes a whole that is beyond right—and that is all but inevitable if Aphrodite is invoked (215)—he cannot satisfy the longing for wholeness which he has instilled in the Furies. Athena, who is not the offspring of marriage, will have to adjudicate. The city, it seems, is that kind of whole to which the Furies can contribute.

In the binding song, the Furies assert not only that Fate confirmed that they were born for what they do but they chose their task "whenever Ares, being domesticated, kills a dear one." This coincidence between necessity and freedom entails that for the Furies the only reality is moral, and the total ignorance that is madness follows at once upon its violation (377–80). The seemings *(doxai)* of men, no matter how august under the sky, melt to nothing beneath the earth. The Furies, then, identify reality with Hades. Hades, however, is invisible to men. Men cannot help but take this world as the reality. The Furies are amazed to learn from Athena that here there are other than moral necessities (cf. 313–15). They tell her they drive killers of any kind from their homes, and this is what they are doing to Orestes, who deemed it right to be his mother's murderer. Athena wants to know whether it was by some other necessity or in fear of someone's wrath (426). To their startled question—"Where is there so great a goad for matricide?"—Athena replies that only half the speech has been stated: The speech, in order to become a whole, must include Orestes'. The Chorus assert that Orestes would refuse to swear that he committed the crime. Athena comments: "You want to be spoken of as just rather than to act [justly]." The Furies now wish to be instructed; they become aware of Athena's wisdom. Athena instructs them in distinguishing between appearance and reality that is other than the Furies' own, first getting the Furies to acknowledge that there is a difference between who they are—the children of Night—and what they are called—Curses who dwell below earth (416–17). The Furies, too, are seemings; they exist only insofar as they are summoned into existence by men. They now, however, have the chance to be in their own right and no longer subject to individual men. They can act on their own if they become part of the city.

The Furies do not understand the meaning of oaths. They mistake the righteousness of the swearer for the right of that to which he swears (cf. 488–89). Orestes trusted in right in embracing Athena's statue; he did not have to know whether he acted rightly or not (439, 468, cf. 609–13). Half the jury whom Athena herself selected do not believe Apollo, Zeus, or herself; they believe they know what is right better than the Olympian gods whom alone they worship (cf. 621). They are not going to be punished for it. This is Athena's most powerful argument in dissuading the Furies from punishing Athens for their defeat. The right of ignorance must be sacred if juries are to sentence men to death.[4] They must be confident in right without knowing right. Orestes is in a sense the model for the citizen with a clear conscience. His obedience to the lawlike oracle of Apollo is his only justification. His act must be shocking if his obedience is to be pure: at the moment he killed his mother, he obeyed Pylades' reminder of the oracle rather than his own reverent shame

(*Choephoroi* 899–902). Every faction will henceforth be thwarted from enlisting the gods under its own exclusive banner. The right and the holy will no longer be coextensive.[5]

The second stasimon summarizes what the Furies have learned so far. Although they still insist that terror is good and must sit in watch over the mind, they grant that it must not become tyrannical. Such unadulterated enslavement leads to misery, but unadulterated anarchy leads to nothingness. The mean is neither misery nor nothingness: "One will not be without happiness and would not be wholly destroyed (581–82)." Terror, then, must be so softened that one can be just without compulsion (580). Hades cannot be the reality, madness cannot be the punishment. If the text is sound, they put this as follows: "But what city or mortal would still revere right in the same way if he should not bring up his heart in the light (520–24)?" They now recognize seemings. There must be an anarchic principle mixed in with pure terror. This anarchic principle proves to be in Athens the right to vote in ignorance. Blind chance must be acknowledged. The Furies no longer believe that if no wrath comes from them, a man must lead a life without harm (314–15). Defeat, though armed with right, is now possible. In order for Athena's plan to work, it is necessary that Orestes be acquitted, for if the Athenians condemn him, the Furies will not stay; they will not stay if they are not defeated. The votes, however, must be equal if the Furies' dishonor is to be matched by Apollo's (795–96). Their acquiescence in half the vote is to act as an example for the city. The rule of the majority requires the consent without the agreement of the minority. To give in is not to give up one's principles; but they are no longer such certain principles that they can give one the right to get even.

The way in which Apollo and Athena use her motherless origin is not the same. Apollo brings it up after he has argued that murder is unlike any other crime, "since there is no possibility of resurrection, and my father made no incantations for it, for everything else he arranges and turns topsy-turvy, without gasping for breath in his strength (648–51)." It would seem, therefore, that the lack of consanguinity between mother and son, which Apollo argues for next, does not at all meet the point that Clytemestra was murdered. Should not Orestes pay for that? Apollo's inconsequence conceals a threat: Zeus has shown through Athena that mothers are superfluous. If he wants to, Zeus can cancel the role of the Furies altogether by eliminating women. Terror would remain but not love. Athena understands Apollo perfectly: she offers to make the Furies the protectors of marriage (832–36). Athena herself, however, does not use her sexless birth in this way; instead, she cites it as the reason for her vote. She votes her nature (736), and she alone does so. Those who voted with her denied their nature and obeyed hers; those who voted against her followed no less unnaturally the fatherless Furies. Right, as men understand it, is blind to nature. Men believe in absolute right. They believe the gods support them in this belief. Athena denies it, asserting instead that the nature of each human being is double in origin and single in sex. They are therefore too complex to vote their nature. The known requirements of the city must take the place of their own unknowable nature. The male must take precedence. Clytemestra, who comes closest to being male and female at once (*Agamemnon* 11, 351), proves it. She punished Agamemnon for the sacrifice of her daughter, but she never connected that crime with the injustice of the Trojan war. She thus granted implicitly the possibility of its justice, for the perfect vengeance would have been to sacrifice Orestes for the sake of Aegisthus's security (*Agamemnon* 878–85).[6] She could not, however, have sacrificed Orestes without denying her reason for punishing Agamemnon. She knows that the kind of justice to which Agamemnon appealed could not even speciously justify such a sacrifice in Aegisthus's case. Iphigeneia's sacrifice is merely the sign of the city's right to send its young men to death. Mothers must not be given the right to question that. "Let there be foreign war," Athena exclaims; "it is close at hand without trouble, in which there will be a kind of uncanny love *(erōs)* of glory (864–65)." Athena heard Orestes' summons at Troy, where she was taking possession of land that the Achaean commanders had assigned her (397–402). The Trojan War can now take place.

Notes

1. Cf. Plato *Sophist* 229A; *Gorgias* 464B.

2. That no compound with *Pytho-* occurs in the *Eumenides* confirms her guilty conscience (cf. *Choephoroi* 901, 940, 1030), for it alone would have cast doubt on her story of the transmission.

3. The reason why Orestes asks after Clytemestra's dream at the moment when he does is that the failure of Agamemnon to appear implies that Clytemestra's offerings may have succeeded in propitiating him (*Choephoroi* 514–22). The *Choephoroi* is the only extant Greek tragedy in which the word *Hades* does not occur. It is thus left to Clytemestra's ghost to "prove" that Hades is.

4. This argument is all the more telling if it is true, as Demosthenes asserts (*Contra Aristocratem* 66 [642]), that the Areopagus was the only court where no defendant, if convicted, and no prosecutor, if he loses his case, ever complained

that the decision was unjust. Demosthenes later remarks (74 [644]) that the acquittal of Orestes shows that there is holy killing, "for the gods would not have voted what was unjust."

5. Cf. Plato *Euthyphro* 12. We learn from the *Phaedo* (58A–C) that Athens forbade public execution while the sacred ship went to and from Delos every year.

6. Clytemestra must have known that to save Orestes was to guarantee her own death; otherwise, it seems impossible to explain her constant sacrifices to the Furies (*Eumenides* 106–11).

FIVE

Sophocles' *Oedipus Tyrannus*

> Eine Sphinx, das ägyptische Gebilde des Rätsels selbst, sei in Theben erschienen und habe ein Rätsel aufgegeben mit den Worten: "Was ist das, was morgens auf vier Beinen geht, mittags auf zweien und abends auf dreien?" Der Grieche Ödipus habe das Rätsel gelöst und die Sphinx vom Felsen gestürzt, indem er aussprach, dies sei der Mensch. Dies ist richtig; das Rätsel der Ägypter ist der Geist, der Mensch, das Bewußtsein seines eigentümlichen Wesens. Aber mit dieser alten Lösung durch Ödipus, der sich so als Wissender zeigt, ist bei ihm die ungeheuerste Unwissenheit gepaart über sich selbst und über das, was er tut. Der Aufgang geistiger Klarheit in dem alten Königshause ist noch mit Greueln aus Unwissenheit verbunden. Es ist die alte patriarchalische Herrschaft, der das Wissen ein Heterogenes ist und die dadurch aufgelöst wird. Dies Wissen wird erst gereinigt durch politische Gesetze; unmittelbar ist es unheilbringend. Das Selbstbewußtsein muß sich noch, um zu wahren Wissen und sittlicher Klarheit zu werden, durch bürgerliche Gesetze und politische Freiheit gestalten und zum schönen Geiste versöhnen.
>
> —G.W.F. Hegel, *Philosophie der Weltgeschichte*

THE CRIPPLED OEDIPUS, we must imagine, appears before the Thebans leaning on a staff, a staff that indicates as much his present authority as the use he once made of it to kill his father (811, cf. 456). The staff or scepter is thus triply significant: a support for his infirmity, a sign of his political position, and an instrument for patricide. In two of its uses, the staff points to Oedipus's strength, in the other to his weakness; but this weakness no doubt enabled him to solve the riddle of the Sphinx: a man in the prime of life but maimed since childhood and hence "three-footed" before his time saw in himself the riddle's answer. He now, however, appears before a threefold division of his people, whose enigmatic character he fails to see: "Some have not yet the strength to fly far; some are priests, heavy with old age, of whom I am the priest of Zeus; and some are selected from those still unmarried" (16–19). Children incapable of going far, priests weighed down with age, and a group of unmarried men stand before him. Oedipus is the only man *(anēr)*, in the strict sense, who is present. Two of the groups are weak, the other is strong. Together they represent an anomalous and defective answer to the riddle of the Sphinx, for the aged appear as priests, and the two-footed men appear as bachelors. The suppliants for the city are either below or beyond generation: the children have not yet reached puberty, the youths have not yet become fathers, and the priests are presumably impotent. Only Oedipus has been and can be again a father. The absence of women, which in this way is underlined, points to the blight that has now fallen on all generation. A bloody tempest, says the priest of Zeus, threatens to swamp the city: "[The city] wastes away in the unopened fruitful buds of the earth; it wastes away in the herds of grazing cows and in the abortive births of women" (25–27, cf. 171–73, 270–72). The fruit and the cattle perish, and the women abort in giving birth. Thebes has been struck by a plague that exactly fits Oedipus's crimes, for defective offspring is supposed to be the consequence of incest.[1] Oedipus, however, neither understands the meaning of the plague nor sees in the delegation anything defective. His first words—*tekna* ("Oh children")—suggest that he understands himself as father only in a metaphorical sense and is blind to the literal meaning of generation (cf. 1503–6).[2] The play therefore moves from the question of who killed Laius to that of who generated Oedipus. It moves from a political to a family crime, which is, paradoxically, from the less comprehensive to the more comprehensive theme (cf. 635–36). Oedipus's discovery of his parents silently discloses his murder of Laius, but to discover himself as the murderer of Laius would not have disclosed his origins. Sophocles indicates this shift from one theme to the other by the absence of the word *polis* after its twenty-fifth occurrence at 880, the context of which is the denunciation of tyranny.[3] Tyranny links the political with the family crime.

The choral ode in which *polis* last occurs sees the tyrant as the transgressor of "laws that step on high, born in the heavenly ether, whose only father is Olympus, and to which the mortal nature of men did not give birth" (865–70). These laws—there is no other mention of *nomos* in the play—are the prohibitions against incest and patricide, for the tyrant is the paradigm of the illegal, and illegality seems best exemplified in the two crimes that stand closest to the unnatural both in the family and the city. As incest is paradigmatic for illegitimate birth, for no legal ceremony can render incestuous offspring legitimate, so patricide is paradigmatic for illegitimate succession, for it turns regicide into a crime that strikes at the heart of kingship (cf. 1, 58). Patricide, however, is only accidentally, whereas incest is necessarily, a political crime, for the city must be exogamous if the family is not to be self-sufficient and claim a loyalty greater than the city. The movement, therefore, from the question of who killed Laius to that of who generated Oedipus, while it goes more deeply into the family, goes more deeply into the city as well. Oedipus violates equally the public and the private with a single crime. He is the paradigm of the tyrant.

Oedipus is the completely public man. He has an openness and transparency that leave no room for the private and secret. When Creon asks him whether he should report what the oracle replied while the Chorus are present, Oedipus says, "Address it to all, for I bear a grief for these even more than for my soul" (93–94). The city in its public and private aspects alone counts, and Oedipus is a superfluous third: "My soul sorrows together for the city, myself, and you [singular]" (63–64). His own sorrow is neither the city's common nor each citizen's private sorrow; and it is in fact above and beyond either (cf. 1414–15), but Oedipus presents it as if it were only the union of the public and the private: "I know well that all of you are ill, and, though you are ill, there is no one of you who is as equally ill as I am, for your pain comes to one alone by himself and to no one else" (59–63).

Everyone else is ill, but no one is as ill as Oedipus, for all the rest suffer individually, while he alone suffers collectively. He is a one like no other one. As ruler *(archōn)* he is like the one that without being a number is the principle *(archē)* and measure of all numbers.[4] Oedipus's *nosos* ("illness," "disease") is truly unequal to the citizens', for he is the source of theirs, but he regards himself as ill only because his grief is the sum of each partial grief. Oedipus always speaks for the city as a whole. Tiresias refers to himself emphatically as *egō* eight times, but never to the city, whereas Oedipus five times in the same scene refers to the city and only once to himself as *egō:* "But it was I, the know-nothing Oedipus, who came and stopped the Sphinx" (396–97). Oedipus immediately interprets Tiresias's reluctance to speak as a dishonor to the city and just cause for indignation (339–40). Tiresias's silence has nothing lawful *(ennoma)* in it, nor is it an act of kindness to the city that nurtured him (322–23). Oedipus's concern for his own deliverance seems to him to be nothing more than a rhetorical fullness of expression, "Save *(rhusai)* yourself and the city, save *(rhusai)* me, and save *(rhusai)* [us] from the entire taint of the dead" (312–13, cf. 253–55).

The third *rhusai* does not mean the same as the first two; but the deliverance from the pollution is in fact the same as the deliverance of the city from Oedipus. The city must be saved from Oedipus, whose own safety is incompatible with the safety of those with whom he allies himself (cf. 244–45, 253–54). He appeals to the city as though he were the city and no one shared in it except himself (626–30, cf. 643). His utter publicity, his being only what he is as ruler of Thebes (cf. 443), makes him think the charges of Tiresias are prompted by private gain (380–89, cf. 393–94, cf. 540–42). He received the kingship as a gift but had no desire for it, for he solved the riddle of the Sphinx with complete disinterest (383–84, 393–94, cf. 540–42). As a stranger but lately enrolled in the city, he stands above all factional interests (219–22). His incorruptibility is the most evident sign that he lacks a private component; but the deepest sign is identifiable as his crimes. The tyrant, says Socrates, commits those crimes (among which is incest) that most men only dream about (cf. 980–83). The dreams of others are the deeds of Oedipus. "For those awake," Heraclitus says, "there is a single and common order, but each one turns when asleep into his own" (fr. 89). Oedipus is always awake and a member of the common order (cf. 65). All the illegal desires of dreams, by being fulfilled in him, leave him empty of everything that is not public knowledge. He consists entirely of *doxa,* or "seeming" (cf. 1186–96).

Seeming and likeness are opposed to what does not seem and resemble but is. In the case of Oedipus, however, seeming and likeness always turn out to be true. He will seek the criminal, he says, as though he were fighting for the sake of his own father (264–65), because he holds the kingship Laius had before, "having the marriage bed and woman of the same seedbed" (260). His wife is indeed *homosporos,* not in the transferred sense that Laius and Oedipus share the same wife, but in the sense that Oedipus is literally kindred with her and sows the same seedbed where he himself was sown (cf. 460, 1210–12). And what Oedipus then put potentially—that if Laius had had children, they would be in common with his own—is now true of himself (261–62, cf. 249–51). And finally, in calling Laius's murderer *autocheir* (231, 266), he points to the murderer as one who killed in his own family.[5] The ordinary imprecision of speech always betrays Oedipus. Speech in his presence becomes literal and as univocal as mathematical definitions. Although "tyranny" and "tyrant" are loosely used throughout the play for "kingship" and "king," they prove in the end to be strictly true of Oedipus in his crimes.[6] If Creon uses the singular *oikos* (house) three lines after Oedipus had used the plural, the change apparently has no significance (112, 115); but when Oedipus changes Creon's *lēistai* (highwaymen) into the singular, he has unwittingly pointed to the truth (122, 124, cf. 292–93). He asks Creon what prevented the Thebans from finding out who killed Laius (128–29). The Sphinx or "Constrictor" that asked about the four-footed, two-footed, and three-footed animal was in the way of their feet (*empodōn,* cf. 445) and enticed them to look at what was at their feet *(to pros posi)* and neglect the obscure and invisible (*taphanē,* 130–31). Oedipus solved what was at their feet and now he is called upon to solve the invisible. He does not know that this distinction between the near and the distant is no longer applicable. "I shall make it *(aut'),*" he says, "evident once more from the beginning"; and while he means *taphanē,* it is equally true of *to pros posi,* for his crippled feet finally identify him as the son of Laius and his murderer. The truth of Oedipus is right in front of him. There is nothing latent in him. He is the wholly unpoetic man, and hence it seems not accidental that in *Oedipus Tyrannus* alone of the seven plays we have of Sophocles the word *muthos* (speech, tale, false tale) never occurs.[7]

The name of Oedipus perhaps most clearly shows that the surface truth of Oedipus is the sign of his depths as well. To be crippled was considered to be a sign of tyrannical ambitions (cf. 878), and the very name of the royal family, Labdacidae, contains within it *labda* or lambda, the letter that resembles an uneven gait.[8] Oedipus's name, then, as a sign of his defect, shows that the general truth expressed in the riddle of the Sphinx does not apply to himself. The answer "man" fails to cover the particular case of Oedipus. His defect, however, by placing him outside the species-characteristic of man, allowed him to see the species-characteristic. Oedipus has never reflected on his divergence from the species, nor understood why he alone could solve the riddle. The solution to the riddle depends on seeing that only one of the three kinds of feet literally holds. Oedipus saw the heterogeneity that underlies an artificial homogeneity, but he does not see his own disparity. Oedipus never fits the groups in which he puts himself as a third element. The public, the private, and Oedipus do not make a genuine triad, any more than do the altars of Apollo, Athena, and Oedipus at which the Thebans sit (2, 16, 19–21, cf. 31); the alliance of Apollo, Laius, and Oedipus (244–45); or the joint rule of Jocasta, Creon, and Oedipus (577–81).[9] The speciousness of the riddle's triad conceals a doubleness in man himself. He is a biped but an upright biped (cf. 419, 528, 1385), and his uprightness, which is shared by neither the baby nor the three-footed aged, indicates his ability to look up and know;[10] and Oedipus, we learn, in spite of a lameness that would direct his glance downward to his feet, guided his flight from Corinth by looking at the stars (794–96).

Man is endowed with self-motion and awareness (cf. 6–7, 396–97).[11]

He is an *oide-pous* (knows-a foot) or *Oidipous,* a pun the messenger from Corinth unknowingly makes when he asks the Chorus: "Would I learn from you, strangers, where *(mathoimi hopou)* the palace of the tyrant *Oedipus* is? And, most of all, say whether you know where *(katisth' hopou)* he himself is" (924–26, cf. 43, 1128).[12] Oedipus, who can see man in his motion, cannot see where *(pou)* and on what basis he himself rests (cf. 367–68, 413). The distant perspective his defect afforded him to see man in his three ages kept him from seeing the ground on which he himself stood. Oedipus's knowledge is divorced from his own body, but the crimes he committed are bodily crimes. His crimes have their origin in the privacy of the body (*his* mother and *his* father), and they are detected through his body; but his own lack of privacy, which perfectly accords with the absence of all desires in Oedipus, leads him to look away from the body. He seems to stand at an Archimedean point. He somehow is pure mind.

Human knowledge, however, unlike divine or divinely inspired knowledge, does not have the purity and openness that Oedipus thinks it has. The Chorus suggest to Oedipus that Apollo should properly disclose who killed Laius, but Oedipus reminds them that no one can compel the gods against their will (278–81). The Chorus have another suggestion, and Oedipus allows them even a third (282–83). Tiresias is the second possibility, and though Tiresias is provoked by anger into speaking, the truth that he tells is completely useless. Tiresias does not offer, perhaps because he cannot, any evidence for what he says. He is as enigmatic and teasing as was the drunken Corinthian who started Oedipus on his quest for his origins (779–86). The one clue there is (cf. 118–21)—the third suggestion of the Chorus—is the "dumb and ancient tale" that some wayfarers slew Laius (290): false, but still a clue. Human error, like the defective feet of Oedipus, leads to the truth, while divine knowledge is either unavailable or enigmatic.[13] The lone survivor of Laius's retinue had out of fear exaggerated the number of attackers (cf. 118–19); but if he had not, "one could never prove equal to many" (845, cf. 120), and Oedipus would not be the murderer. The clue is a false arithmetic. Jocasta is certain that there were many, for the city heard it, and not she alone (848–50). What is publicly made manifest cannot be untrue. Both Jocasta and Oedipus identify the evident with the city, but the city lies wrapped in opinion that only parades as knowledge. And yet Oedipus can test this falsehood, while he finds the truth, which is naturally inborn in Tiresias (299), refractory to testing (cf. 498–511). Tiresias's blindness prevents him from ever knowing where he is, but the sacredness that keeps him detached from human and political things allows him to be unconcerned with the ground of his knowledge. Oedipus mockingly asks Tiresias why he did not solve the riddle of the Sphinx (390–94). The answer is plain: the riddle has a wholly human answer, and Tiresias knows about man only in his relation to the gods. Oedipus, unsupported by any extrahuman knowledge—"the know-nothing Oedipus" (397)—solves it because he is himself the paradigm (1193–96). Oedipus represents the human attempt to replace the sacred—his failure to return to Corinth is his denial of oracles—[14] by the purely human. He is to be the third element alongside the public and the private (cf. 16, 31–34). The purely human, however, seems to entail not only the destruction of the sacred, but the collapse of any distinction between the public and the private. The purely human, at least as far as Oedipus reveals it, will prove to be the monstrous.

The Chorus are outraged that anyone should disobey the oracles (883–910). The oracles are three in number: One foretold that Laius would be killed by his own son, another that Oedipus would kill his father and marry his mother, and the third said that the presence in Thebes of Laius's murderer caused the plague. The Chorus want all three oracles to turn out to be true, but they also want their own lot *(moira)* to be such that they do not break the sacred prohibitions against patricide and incest (862–72). Oedipus, on the other hand, wants the oracle addressed to himself to prove false, so that human morality will be maintained; but the gods want the authority of all the oracles, i.e., their own authority, maintained even at the expense of human morality. Human morality, however, was not brought about by human nature: Olympus alone was its father. It is the nature of Oedipus, then, to break these laws, but he does not know that it is his nature. He believes it to be the work of Apollo (1329–30, cf. 376–77). Oedipus, who thinks himself the manifestation of the city, turns out to be the manifestation of human nature itself, and the fate of human nature by itself is to violate the divine laws of the city. *Hubris* is the natural in man, and man is naturally a tyrant (873). *Hubris* makes man rise to heights he cannot maintain and hence plunges him into sheer compulsion, "where he wields a useless foot" (873–79). The swollen foot that is Oedipus finally trips him up.

Even if Oedipus lacks any secret desires, he still is not free from all passions. His overriding passion is anger. He first shows it when Tiresias refuses to speak. "You would enrage," he tells him, "the nature of a stone," so unmoved does he think Tiresias (334–36). "You blame my temper," Tiresias replies, "but do not see your own that dwells with you." Tiresias's *orgē* (temper, anger) is his indifference to the city, Oedipus's *orgē,* which is all of Oedipus, is his concern for the city. "Who would not become enraged on hearing such words as yours," he answers Tiresias, "in which you dishonor the city?" Oedipus's anger is entirely at the service of the city. His anger now expresses his private devotion to public justice, though the same anger once brought him to kill Laius and his retinue (807). Oedipus cannot stand opposition. He must overcome everything that resists him (cf. 1522–23). He fails to see any difference between his indignation at an injury to himself and one to the city (629, 642–43). His indignation is a passion for homogeneity (cf. 408–9). Everything must be reduced to the same level or eliminated until he alone as the city remains.[15] The sacred in the person of Tiresias and the private in that of Creon must go (cf. 577–82). He is opposed to the Chorus's wish that god never dissolve noble contention and rivalry in the city (879–81). His belief that he is a unique one in the city is rooted in his total public-spiritedness, but the passion he brings to that role also looks toward his crimes against the city.

Anger as the leveler of distinctions resembles the homogeneity of law—there can be no exceptions to Oedipus's decree, not even himself (816–20)—but this extreme reductionism in Oedipus's anger duplicates another kind of homogeneity that comes from his crimes. "Now I am without god and the son of unholy [parents], but I alas am of the same kind as those from whom I myself was born" (1360-61). Oedipus is of the same kind as those from whom he was born. He is equally husband and son of Jocasta, father and brother of Antigone, and killer of Laius who gave him life (457–60, cf. 1402–7). By killing his father and marrying his mother, he has destroyed the triad of father, mother, and son. He is not a third one over and beyond his origins, but he is at one with them (cf. 425). In his being he is the reduction that he tries to carry out with his anger. The law against incest that forbids homogeneity in the family emerges in his violation of it as the homogeneity of anger. Oedipus's anger is the surface expression of his incest. They share in common the exclusive care and defense of his own without concern for anything alien; and this exclusiveness is characteristic of the city that Oedipus has made his own. His public anger and his private incest therefore come together in the Thebans' belief in their autochthony. Autochthony would give the earth to everyone as a common mother and hence make incest inevitable; but it would also best justify a city's exclusive possession of its land and hence most inspire the citizens to defend it.[16] The Chorus divine that Oedipus will share with Cithaeron a common fatherland—it will be his *patriōtēs*—and that Cithaeron will prove to be his nurse and mother as well (1086–92). Oedipus, however, turns out to be autochthonous in another nonmetaphorical sense. "How, how could the father's furrows, alas, bear to keep silence for so long?" (1211–12). His father's furrows are Jocasta's loins and not Theban territory (cf. 1482–85, 1497–99, 1502). What would have been the complete vindication of Oedipus as the city if the *patrōiai alokes* had been the *patrōia gaia* (earth, or land), signifies instead his greatest crime against the city.[17] Oedipus, then, in destroying the ground of the private, reveals the ground of the public. In his violation of the unwritten law, he is the truth of civil law. But Oedipus is also the nature of man as it appears in itself without the restraint of divine law. Thus the monstrousness of Oedipus consists in his being together the ultimately natural (the private) and the ultimately lawful (the public) in man.

Oedipus believes that Jocasta, ashamed of his base birth, does not want the herdsman to be questioned; but he insists on discovering his origins even if they are small. "I count myself the son of beneficent chance," he says. "She is my natural mother, and the months that are my congeners made me small and great" (1080–83, cf. 1090). Oedipus is the son of chance and the sport of time. Jocasta had asked him, "Why should a human being be afraid, for whom the ways of chance are sovereign, and there is clear foreknowing of nothing? It is best to live at random" (977–79). If chance controls Oedipus because he is its offspring, he has nothing to fear from any disclosures that time might bring (1213–15, cf. 917). They would all be as indifferent to him as they are to chance. The lack of discrimination in chance, its randomness, necessarily leads to the loss in Oedipus of any distinctions, and that is his crime. Chance is the ground of his apparent unconditionality, for his crimes have uprooted his own origins and made him his own *archē* (origin, principle). He is completely free. The one condition attached to his freedom is his swollen feet, but they are literally Oedipus himself. He stands in the way of his own nature (cf. 674–75). Oedipus says that he met Laius at a triple road, but Jocasta calls the meeting of the ways from Daulia and Delphi a split road (733, 800–801, cf. 1399). A *triplē hodos* (triple way) is the same as a *schistē hodos* (split way). Two is the same as three. If one is walking a road and comes to a branching of it, there are only two ways that one can go, for the third way has already been traversed. If, however, one is not walking but simply looking at a map of such a branching, there appears to be three ways to take. Action sees two where contemplation sees three. Oedipus places himself in the camp of *theōria,* but it is a naive *theōria.* He thinks he has one more degree of freedom than he has. If his swollen feet are the sign of this double perspective, his crimes, one might say, are its truth. He has, in committing incest, made literal the metaphor of political theory. Even as dreaming and waking are for him one and the same (cf. 980–83), so he is blind to the difference between theory and practice. The distant and the near view are in him merged: *taphanes* (the invisible) is *to pros posin* (that which is at the feet).

Oedipus wants to become invisible to mortals before the double guilt of incest and patricide overtakes him (830–33). And he later effects his invisibility by blinding himself, for he lives so entirely in the realm of *doxa* (seeming, opinion, and reputation)—the famous Oedipus is the know-nothing Oedipus (7, 397)—that his inability to see is equivalent to his not being seen (cf. 1371–74). "This day," Tiresias had told him, "shall bring you to birth and destroy you" (438). The day that brings Oedipus into the light takes away his light (cf. 375, 1375–76). His blindness has made him who was completely transparent opaque. He is now *skoteinos* (1326). In thus turning away from the sham clarity of *doxa* into himself (1317–18, 1347–48), Oedipus restores the private that he had destroyed. He recovers his shame. "If you no longer feel ashamed before the generations of mortals," Creon tells him, "at least feel shame before the all-nourishing light of the sun, to show unhidden such a taint that not earth, not sacred rain, not light will welcome. Go into the house at once: it is holy only for those who are kin to see and hear kindred evils" (1424–31).[18] Not just the city, but the world itself turns its back on Oedipus. He had forbidden any citizen from receiving or addressing the murderer of Laius, from sharing with him the prayers or sacrifices to the gods, and from granting him the use of lustral waters (238–40); but now the crime of incest has withdrawn Oedipus from things that are beyond the civil order. He must return to the private. And yet Oedipus does not need the seclusion of a house in order to retire from the world; the blinding of himself has already done it for him. His one concern is for his banishment from the city, whose physical presence *(astu)*, whose towers, whose sacred statues of the gods he no longer dares to look upon (1377–83). The restoration of the private must be accompanied by the restoration of the public that he had equally destroyed. He therefore is at the end what he was at the beginning, a superfluous third.

As the report *(phēmē* or *phatis)* of oracles has been confirmed in the light *(phōs)* of truth (151–58, 1440); (the two words share linguistically the same root [cf. 472–76]),[19] so the unseeable Oedipus is also the unspeakable Oedipus: "Oh, my abominable cloud of darkness hovering, unspeakable" (1313–14). He is surrounded by silence and darkness (1337–39). If there had been some way to stop his ears, he says, he would not have held back from closing off his body (1386–89). He would no longer hear, as he no longer sees, his crimes. He would deprive himself of sense, as he was once deprived of motion.[20] He would cut off the knowing as he was cut off from the walking in his name. He had abused Tiresias as blind in his ears, his mind, and his eyes (371); but he himself now wants to hear and see nothing: "For thought to dwell outside of evils is sweet" (1389–90).

Oedipus forgets to put out his mind. He does not regard *nous* as a third faculty distinct from hearing and sight. He is like Plato's Theaetetus, whose mathematical knowledge rests on his thinking, but who believes that knowledge is sensation. The Chorus call Oedipus equally wretched for his calamities as for his reflection *(nous)* on them (1347), and Oedipus himself, when he cannot see, reflects on the wretched future of his daughters (1486–88). In spite of his own practice, he does not consider that thinking is irreducible to sense, just as he did not understand that his ability to solve the riddle of the Sphinx revealed more about man than did his answer. Man is the being that solves riddles. The difference between man as two-footed and man as three- or four-footed does not consist in his being literally a biped—the *dipous* in Oedipus's name—and only metaphorically three- and four-footed, but in his thinking. The homogeneity Oedipus discovered in his origins has made him blind to this heterogeneous element. Oedipus discovered the speciousness of the triad in the riddle, but he then found that the heterogeneity of mother, father, and son concealed in his case a sameness. He distinguished a difference in what the riddle had presented as a sameness, only to discover a sameness beneath an apparent difference. His thinking as differentiating found itself confronted with the undifferentiable. The single night in which his blindness has cast him seems to be truer than the daylight of his understanding (cf. 374–75). His anger in finally turning on himself condemns him to live the homogeneity of his crimes.

The first indication that Laius might be Oedipus's father occurs when Oedipus asks Jocasta what the nature *(phusis)* of Laius was, and she says that he did not differ much from the shape *(morphē)* of Oedipus (740–43). They look alike because Oedipus is the son of Laius, but Oedipus, in killing his father and marrying his mother, points to a deeper sameness in generation itself. He is not different from his origins. He is the same as that from which he came. He is the son of chance. Not the *eidos* of man, which the Sphinx had posed as a riddle, but his *genesis* is the riddle of man. An artificial riddle yields to a natural riddle, and Oedipus is thrice characterized by his nature. He says himself that Tiresias's silence would anger the nature even of a stone (334–35), and the nature of stone is to be without sex and human shape;[21] while Creon says that Oedipus's nature is his *thumos* (spirit, anger, heart), which makes itself almost too painful to be borne (674–75, cf. 914, 975); and Jocasta says that Oedipus's nature or shape was close to Laius's. Oedipus has a threefold nature: his potential shapelessness, his *thumos,* his generated shape. His *thumos* is unbearable because it shows through his crimes that his generated shape only hides his potential shapelessness. Oedipus's crimes seem to have uncovered the undifferentiated beginnings of man. They point to his nonanthropomorphic *archai.* As violation of divine law they point to the *archai* that lie behind the anthropomorphic gods. If the Olympian gods gave men their own shape (cf. 1097–1109), the prohibitions against incest and patricide would mean that man was not to search into the shapeless elements beyond these gods. If he did he would find Chaos with its offspring Night and all things mixed together. He would find Ouranos as the son and husband of Earth—the prime example of incest in the Greek theogony—and Ouranos castrated by his own son.[22] Oedipus, then, who discovered what man is in his *eidos,* seems to have discovered in his *hubris* the nonhuman *genesis* of man. The whole of earth, sacred rain, and light, of which Creon forbids Oedipus to be a part, must be informed by the sacred if it is justly to exclude Oedipus (1424–28, cf. 238–40, 1378–83). The sacred must bind together and keep apart the public (light) and the private (earth).[23] If the whole does not have this bond of Olympian sacredness, which guarantees the human in man, then Oedipus, whose *thumos* points jointly to the homogeneity of law and the homogeneity of nature, is truly the inhuman paradigm of man. This is the question that the three particles that most nearly make up the name of Oedipus, *ou dē pou* ("Surely not?"), can be said to introduce—a question raised in utter disbelief, but sometimes answered affirmatively (cf. 1042, 1472).[24]

In *Oedipus at Colonus,* we learn that Oedipus, toward the end of his life, came to the bronze-stepped threshold rooted in the earth (1590–91), where Hesiod says grow the roots, the beginnings, and the ends of the earth, sea, and sky;[25] and that just after his disappearance Theseus was seen reverencing together in a single speech Earth and the Olympus of the gods (1653–55).

Notes

An earlier version of this chapter appeared in J. Cropsey, *Ancients and Moderns,* copyright © 1964 by Basic Books, Inc. Reprinted by permission of Basic Books, a member of Perseus Books, L.L.C.

1. Xenophon *Memorabilia* 4.4.20–23.

2. Perhaps, then, one should read at 1505, *mē sphe, pater, idēis* (Do not overlook them, father) with J. Jackson, *Marginalia Scaenica* (London: Oxford University Press, 1955), 139–40.

3. *Apoptolis* (without a city) occurs at 1000 of Oedipus, *astu* (city as buildings, walls, etc.) twice in the second half (1378, 1450). Jocasta addresses the chorus after the last mention of *polis* as *chōras anaktes* (lords of the land) (911, cf. 631); Oedipus

is called *anax* (lord) fourteen times, only twice after 852, and both times by servants (1002, 1173).

4. Aristotle *Metaphysics* 1016b17–21; 1021a12–13; *Physics* 220a27.

5. Cf. Sophocles *Antigone* 172, 1175–76.

6. *Basileus* (king) is used only twice in the play, once of Laius and once of Oedipus (257, 202), but *turannos,* etc. (tyrant) occurs fifteen times.

7. In *Philoctetes, muthos* does not occur before the appearance of Heracles (1410, 1417, 1447).

8. Cf. Herodotus 5.92b1; Xenophon *Hellenica* 3.3.3.

9. The first triad is in Oedipus's first speech, "The city is altogether full of incense, paeans, and groans" (4–5, cf. 64, 913–15). Plutarch thrice quotes these lines as revealing of the soul, once likening them to Theophrastus's view of the triple source of music: enthusiasm, pleasure, and pain (*Quaestiones conviviales* I. 5 [623C-D]; cf. *De superstitione* 9 [169D]; *De virtute morali* 6 [445D]; also Plato *Republic* 573a4–5).

10. Plato *Cratylus* 399c1–6.

11. Cf. Plato *Charmides* 159b2–5.

12. Cf. B. Knox, *Oedipus at Thebes* (New Haven: 1957), 183–84.

13. The tribrach *phonea* (murderer) occurs three times as the first foot in the line (362, 703, 721), twice of Oedipus as the murderer of Laius, and the third time in Jocasta's denial that Laius's son killed him; but what Jocasta says starts "a wandering of the soul and agitation of the wits" in Oedipus (727), which is also the third and last time that Oedipus refers to his soul (64, 94). And again *poteron* (whether) occurs three times at the beginning of the line (112, 750, 960)—twice of Laius and once of Polybus, Oedipus's supposed father.

14. 794–97, cf. 855–59, 897–910, 964–72.

15. Cf. Herodotus 5.92.

16. Cf. Plato *Republic* 414d1–e6.

17. Cf. Herodotus 6. 107.1–2.

18. Cf. Euripides *Phoenissae* 63–66; frs. 553, 683.

19. *Anecdota Graeca,* ed. J. A. Cramer (Oxford: 1839–41), vol. I, 428, 19–23.

20. *Arthra,* which literally means "joints," occurs three times, twice of Oedipus's pinned ankles, and once of his eyes that he blinded with Jocasta's pins (718, 1032, 1270).

21. Cf. *Odyssey* 19.163.

22. Hesiod *Theogony* 116–36, 176–81.

23. Cf. Sophocles *Antigone* 1066–73.

24. Cf. Sophocles *Antigone* 380–81.

25. *Theogony* 726–28, 736–41, 811–13.

SIX

Euripides' *Hippolytus*

ONE CANNOT PRAISE TOO HIGHLY Euripides' understanding and his ability to represent his understanding of the casual moods that suddenly open up into deeper problems. The nurse brings Phaedra out into the open air; she complains of Phaedra's inconstancy—whatever is absent Phaedra believes more dear—and then in her temporary exasperation she declares that the whole of human life is painful and toil never stops. Whatever truth there might be in this view is immediately balanced by a more general reflection of the Nurse: "But whatever is dearer than life darkness envelops in clouds: we are passionately and irrationally in love with the here and now whatever it is that gleams on the earth; and thus through our ignorance of another life and the non-showing forth of what is below the earth, we are vainly carried this way and that by stories." We cannot help being attached and attracted to this life, she says; but the meaning of this attraction and this life, precisely because of its brilliance and our own infatuation, is entirely unknown to us; and as a consequence we attend to stories, which, though they speak of what is not evident, have the advantage of offering a meaning to human life. We are torn between the brilliance of the unmeaning and the darkness of the meaningful. The Nurse believes that Phaedra is starving herself to death in order to discover the ultimate meaning of life; against this she can only urge Phaedra to be noble and bear what is a necessity for mortals; but when Phaedra speaks, and her longing turns out to be simply crazy—she wants to be an Amazon, and thus (we add) a worthy companion of Hippolytus—the Nurse realizes that Phaedra's problem is of a different order. Phaedra's contemplation of suicide has nothing to do with ultimate things: the advice of the wise—nothing too much—suffices for both the Nurse and Phaedra. Phaedra can be handled within the horizon of the proverbial; she does not require that the Nurse go beyond her competence. Perhaps Euripides is telling us through the Nurse that this play does not touch on the more serious things.

The *Hippolytus* falls into two equal parts, the first part female, the second male: Hippolytus, with his virginal soul, overlaps both parts. The link between the two parts is the second stasimon, almost literally in the center, in which the Chorus express the wish to become birds; for as birds they could fly beyond the Adriatic, where the sisters of Phaethon were turned into black poplars and now weep tears of amber in pity for him. The link between the two parts is the Chorus's wish to feel no pity. Why is such a wish the proper center of the play?

Aphrodite says that she is a goddess of overwhelming power among mortals and gods; she does not regard herself as the cause of sexual desire among the other animals. She presents her power as coordinate with knowledge of her name: she seems to limit herself to the Mediterranean, for only those who dwell between the Black Sea and the Atlantic experience her graciousness or her enmity. Hippolytus, we know, is punished; but whom of her votaries does she favor? Is it Phaedra? It is Aphrodite who tells us that Phaedra will die with glory; it is her excuse for killing her; and Phaedra does share with Aphrodite a no-holds-barred pursuit of honor and glory. Hippolytus, according to Aphrodite, says that she is the worst and Artemis the greatest of the gods. Elsewhere in Euripides, Eros and Dionysus are said to be the greatest of the gods *for men;* but the only gods who are called greatest without qualification are Earth and Zeus. On this ground alone, Aphrodite would seem to have a case against Hippolytus; but there is more: Hippolytus refuses to get *married.* This Aphrodite is not the goddess of love or of sexual license. She is the goddess of lawful wedlock; and Hippolytus's denial of Aphrodite exposes him to the just punishment of the law that enjoins marriage on every citizen. The necessary attribute of a lawful Aphrodite is punishment; there is no conflict here in the personification of love as a nonloving goddess. The extent to which Aphrodite works within the law is shown by the following: Phaedra fell in love with Hippolytus at Athens; but in order that her love grow into something deadly, it was necessary that Theseus voluntarily impose upon himself a year's exile in Trozen for his justified killing of the Pallantidae. Theseus's scrupulous regard for the law, beyond the minimum requirements, is due to Aphrodite, just as the necessity for Theseus to be away three days from Trozen in order to consult an oracle on some minor business must equally be due to her. Aphrodite uses only the most lawful of means to destroy Hippolytus.

But does not this Aphrodite also inspire Phaedra with an adulterous and quasi-incestuous love? She does; but Phaedra cannot fall, for she loves the chaste Hippolytus. Hippolytus guarantees that Phaedra's love is not a crime punishable under law. The unseduceable Hippolytus works in perfect harmony with Aphrodite in upholding the law.

Before Hippolytus rudely dismisses his old servant, who has urged him to comply with the honors due Aphrodite, he tells his servants to prepare his dinner, "for a full table after the chase is delightful"; and once he has "sated himself with food" *(boras korestheis)*, he will go to exercise his horses. The phrase *boras korestheis* is shocking, for one expects that sexual abstinence on principle follow upon abstinence in general. For Hippolytus this is not the case; if it were, one could at once understand why there are explicit references to a statue of Aphrodite but none to a statue of Artemis. Hippolytus hears only the human voice of Artemis; he never sees her face. Asceticism would then go hand in hand with the incorporeality of the gods; but since Hippolytus is not ascetic, there must be another reason for the absence of Artemis's statue. The *Hippolytus* was produced in 428 B.C., long before one had a nude Aphrodite; and one wonders how one could tell the difference between an idealized Aphrodite and an idealized Artemis without their respective attributes. Not despite it but because Hippolytus never sees Artemis, does he call her the most beautiful of virgins and the most beautiful of Olympian gods. The phrase *boras korestheis* is shocking for a second reason; it is so crude: the verb "to eat" *(esthio)* occurs only in Euripides' *Cyclops.* What then does this departure from tragic decorum mean? The parodos begins in a high-flown way: "There is a rock that drips, they say, the water of Ocean, and it sends out from its sheer face a running stream in which pitchers are steeped." But the Chorus are only describing the place where Trozen does its laundry. If the Chorus can turn the everyday into a mythical event, could not Hippolytus have done the same with his dinner, especially since the Chorus are even able to poeticize Phaedra's starving herself: "she keeps her holy body away from Demeter's grain"? One can eat alone but one cannot love alone; and though love lends itself to poetry—the deeds of golden Aphrodite—eating as opposed to drinking can neither inspire nor be glorified. The Nurse later insists on calling a spade a spade and thereby misunderstands Phaedra's love; Hippolytus says *boras korestheis* because nothing else can be said. The lone Hippolytus has no share in either the Graces or the Muses. His conversations with Artemis must have been about the hazards of the chase and how much game he had killed.

The Nurse pries out Phaedra's secret in the following way: "Know this: If you die, you betray your children; they will not inherit their paternal estate. I swear the truth of this by the lady horsewoman Amazon, who bore a master to your children, a bastard who thinks legitimately, you know him, Hippolytus." The Nurse then misinterprets Phaedra's cry of despair; but she used an argument that on the face of it is absurd. Why should the illegitimate Hippolytus be favored over Phaedra's legitimate children? Her death cannot be the cause; rather, Theseus must already have decided to make Hippolytus his heir, and only if Phaedra stays alive could he possibly be dissuaded. Here we have a Theseus who exiles himself for the sake of ritual purity, who consults an oracle for nothing serious, and yet who does not scruple to ignore legitimacy. If Aphrodite is the goddess of lawful wedlock, one wonders whether Theseus and not Hippolytus is the real victim of her wrath, and Hippolytus, like Phaedra, no more than a means to bring about his father's suffering. It is the possibility of Theseus's adultery that the Chorus offer as the central reason for Phaedra's silent suffering; he had, after all, already committed adultery with Ariadne, Dionysus's wife and Phaedra's sister. In the prologue Aphrodite says, "I shall make the matter known to Theseus." Her words are true only if the appearance of Artemis, who actually informs Theseus, is part of Aphrodite's plan. The Chorus, at any rate, herald the appearance of Artemis with a hymn to Aphrodite, and the last words of the play are Theseus's: "How much, Cyprian, shall I remember the evils you have caused." Aphrodite's vengeance can only be satisfied by the destruction of the bastard Hippolytus and the grief of the adulterous Theseus; but that does not mean that Theseus's punishment, in being the main thrust of Aphrodite's plan, is also the theme of the play: Hippolytus still remains the protagonist despite his insignificance for the play's moral. Theme and moral are not the same.

When Phaedra has managed to have the Nurse bring out Hippolytus's name—Phaedra herself utters it just at the moment that she ceases to love Hippolytus—the Nurse becomes frantic. She wants to die at once; she cannot stand being alive. The Chorus go even further; they want to die even before they conceived a thought like Phaedra's. Everyone assumes at once that Phaedra's course is the right one; suicide is the only way out.

No one tries to help Phaedra: that time will cure her, that Hippolytus is unattainable, that Hippolytus is not that attractive anyway, and all the other pieces of proverbial advice that might conceivably console Phaedra are missing. The thought of adultery can only be expunged by death. The atmosphere in which Phaedra's death is inevitable is moralistic to the extreme: what Hippolytus later wishes upon the Nurse and Phaedra is the same as what they have already wished upon themselves. It is this moralism that forces Phaedra to assimilate herself to her mother and sister and regard adultery—not with Hippolytus but just adultery—as her fate. It is this moralism that makes her say, when the nurse has said that human love is most pleasant and at the same time painful, that she has experienced the pain; for by denying her pleasure in it she conceals from herself what makes it so hard to overcome: if love were only painful, Phaedra would have had no trouble in resisting it. It is this moralism that makes the Nurse say that she can no longer live since the chaste willingly love the bad, as though Phaedra were in love with adultery and not with Hippolytus. And again it is this moralism that makes the Nurse declare that Aphrodite is not a goddess but greater than a goddess: the Nurse had assumed that Aphrodite was solely the inspirer of lawful love.

Phaedra's defense of her suicide must be understood in the same light. The premise from which she starts is that virtue is rewarded and vice punished; her problem is that she is not rewarded and adulteresses are not punished. In spite of this, Phaedra has found a way of getting the adulteresses punished and herself rewarded. Mortal life is not ruined by lack of understanding, she says; we know the good but do not take the trouble to achieve it. *Eu phronein* does not mean "to be prudent or wise" in any exceptional sense; good judgment is the same as having been told what is good. Phaedra assumes that there is no difficulty in knowing the human good; she cannot conceive of a circumstance that would make her doubt what everyone knows. There is no conflict among the goods: in her account, pleasure is not chosen because it is thought to be good, any more than anyone thinks that the moral is pleasurable. Men fall into evil; they do not labor at it for the sake of something they hold to be good. Men drift into evil through consequences of actions and behavior that are, if reprehensible, not punishable: idleness and other kinds of pleasure—long chats, lack of busywork, and shame. Shame is a pleasure because it forces one to think about doing what is bad even as it prevents one from both speaking about it and doing it. Phaedra seems to attach the pleasure of love to the pleasure of shame. Not love but shame has corrupted her. There is the shame of speaking out (this keeps her silent) and there is the shame of action (this keeps her from adultery). The second shame is good, but the first entails an ignominious death, for Phaedra cannot die gloriously unless she reveals the reason for her death, and she cannot reveal the reason without shaming her death. Suicide will restore her reputation only after she has lost it. Phaedra starved herself for three days in order to solve this problem. She is now weak enough to appear to have succumbed to the Nurse's entreaties; and being under the compulsion to comply with the sacredness of supplication she can piously speak what cannot be decently said. Piety permits what shame forbids: the Chorus, we recall, presented her starving herself as a religious fasting.

And yet why does Phaedra choose suicide in the first place? There are two good reasons for this. Phaedra does not think she can get away with committing adultery—to do it without speaking of it—and yet not to do it without speaking of it is intolerable, for it would then be unknown; she does not believe that the gods would know of her restraint. Neither men nor gods praise one for not committing adultery. Women are hated as such, even before they commit any crime; they are thought to be criminal in intent; so Phaedra cannot keep her reputation intact by being chaste, for women are suspected even if they are chaste. Since a woman is never praised for having the virtue she is supposed to have, a woman has to commit suicide in order to be praised.

The second reason is this. Phaedra presents her decision to die as the last of three stages. First she kept silent about it; next she planned to bear her folly by *sōphronein;* and last, she resolved to die when she found she could not prevail against Aphrodite. Phaedra recognizes love as Aphrodite only when she finds it too strong for her: the resolution to die emerges with the recognition of Aphrodite: the moralistic and the demonic are in perfect agreement. But we are puzzled by the first two stages: surely Phaedra should have tried *sōphrosunē* first, and then, when she could not prevail, decided to keep silent? The actual sequence shows that we do not know what Phaedra understands by *sōphronein.* Aphrodite, however, has already told us: Phaedra in Athens dedicated a temple to Aphrodite. Her anonymous gift was her way of appeasing the goddess, as if Aphrodite were like any other god, for example, Artemis, who the Chorus had supposed now punishes Phaedra for her failure to sacrifice to her. *Sōphrosunē* for Phaedra is nothing but ritualistic piety, and the shame that kept her silent had long before yielded to the silent speaking of piety: she must have then prayed to Aphrodite. It is, however, this act of piety that at once guarantees Phaedra's future glory and future shame: men will later speak of the temple as founded for Hippolytus. Aphrodite's honor demands that men know who dedicated a temple to her and for what reason. At the moment, Phaedra believes that Aphrodite has failed her; she has not cured her and what is worse has not made known all adulteresses. Phaedra is powerless to punish them and unable to join them. And yet only if it is inevitable that they get punished is it inevitable that she punish herself. "Time," she says, "reveals the bad, just like a mirror set before a young girl; among them might I not be seen." Time is like a mirror because it reveals decay: Phaedra cannot die at a more appropriate time; to be old and in love is ridiculous. So time, which supposedly reveals the bad, in fact reveals the ugly. Love has made Phaedra aware of her mortality, and this is the only sure punishment for adulteresses.

A first reading of the Nurse's speech suggests that she urges Phaedra to accept *(per impossible)* Hippolytus as her lover because love is as universal as it is irresistible. All living beings from fish to gods are under Aphrodite's spell. But a second reading shows that this is an impossible interpretation. First, the Nurse says, "You love? What's astonishing about that? You do so with *many* mortals." She is not thinking of Hippolytus in saying "many" rather than "all"; and second, she mentions no terrestrial being except man. One must begin again. The Nurse says that the *wrath* of the goddess has struck Phaedra. She thus connects Phaedra's initial silence, which applied to love the remedy appropriate for a fit of anger, with Phaedra's later realization that Aphrodite was the cause. Love then becomes a punishment: What then is the crime? The crime, I should suggest, is the castration of Ouranos by Kronos, from whose genitals when they fell into the sea Aphrodite was born. The castration of Ouranos entailed the dethronement of the cosmic gods and the worship of the Olympians. Aphrodite thus punishes gods and men on behalf of her father. This is not the Aphrodite of the prologue who presented herself as the upholder of the Olympian law; and yet Aphrodite never tells us her genealogy—in this she differs from Artemis. The only epithet she receives in the play is *pontia* (of or belonging to the sea)—and the Nurse understands Phaedra's submission to love as an obedience to law. The strongest evidence that love is a punishment is to be found in Phaedra's experience, for she suffers from unrequited love. It is within the context of unrequited love that the Nurse distinguishes between those who submit to their punishment and those who resist it; the gods are wise because they submit to it—they rape those mortals whom they are driven to love. No love, the Nurse implies, survives union. In order to have avoided her fate, Phaedra ought to have been born either on different conditions or with different, i.e., pre-Olympian, gods who are not subject to the law; but as it is she cannot possibly free herself from love. The wisdom of mortals, therefore, consists in hiding the ugliness of this punishment: husbands pretend not to see the adultery of their wives, and fathers help their sons get away with committing adultery, for their transgression is only apparent; it is in fact a painful obedience to the law. Phaedra, however, cannot do what the gods do: they not only submit, they practice adultery in the open. Since the equivalent to human suicide would be divine shame, the equivalent to divine shamelessness is human shame: human shame is likened to not finishing perfectly accurately what cannot be seen. The recognition of human defectiveness—this is the subjective side of love as punishment—is like a carpenter's carelessness; it is something casual, not worth eliminating since it can be neutralized. The remedy for one's own shame is mutual love. Since love is a punishment, the Nurse proposes that Phaedra punish Hippolytus; her own casual love is cured by deliberately punishing Hippolytus with love, for love would make Hippolytus see his own defectiveness. This is the one advantage lovers gain from their obedience to the law.

The Nurse, however, does not herself entirely believe her own argument. If Phaedra's life were not in danger, she later says, she would never have suggested this cure for the sake of her sexual pleasure. The Nurse tried to make sexual pleasure attractive to Phaedra by presenting it as a punishment. Her authority for doing so was not just the experience of unrequited love but her reading in the ancient poets, from whose silence about it she deduced that the gods are without shame and content to submit to their punishment. The Nurse has not listened to folktales but studied the writings of poets. They are authoritative not only because they are old but because they write: they are old and civilized poets. Phaedra learns from the Nurse. Not only does she punish Hippolytus but she writes. The folktale of stepmother and stepson is thereby transformed into a plot that can only happen in a literate society. And Theseus in fact will later unwittingly denounce the disproportion between the progress in the arts and the decline in morality, of which Phaedra's letter-writing is a perfect example.

The Chorus react to the ambiguous proposal of the Nurse with a hymn to Eros. In form, the hymn is traditional but in content it is not, a sign of which is this: Eros in the first strophic pair is four times put where its short epsilon occupies a place normally reserved for a long syllable. From the second strophic pair, we learn that Aphrodite delights in human sacrifice: she is not an Olympian god. The Chorus, therefore, propose an innovation: we are mistaken to worship Aphrodite in the way that Phaedra had, by founding a temple and treating her as if she were the sort to be so appeased. Rather, Eros, whom the Chorus on their own authority make the son of Zeus, should be worshipped; perhaps he will be appeased by animal sacrifices. Eros is the tyrant of men, and it is vain to sacrifice to the other gods if we do not sacrifice to him as well. Eros can be civilized, Aphrodite cannot. The Chorus accept the Nurse's view that Aphrodite is pre-Olympian, and then in the guise of the traditional enlarge the traditional pantheon. If madness is controlled by Dionysus, and the thunderbolt by Zeus, why should not Aphrodite be controllable through this new Olympian god? The cult-god Eros is the last stage of civilization. The Chorus's new poetry improves on the old poetry. The Chorus's solution, however, is no more adequate than that of the Nurse, who pretends that she can magically control Aphrodite.

Even before they hear Hippolytus's denunciation of all women, the Chorus are on Phaedra's side: they do not now regard their own knowledge of Phaedra's secret as a disclosure of her secret. The Chorus will later swear to keep silent; and their oath is so sacred that it never occurs to them to break it. Hippolytus does not break his oath either, but he considers breaking it; and he is only checked by the consideration that he would need witnesses; he would need the Chorus. Hippolytus does not ask them—he has no knowledge of their oath—because he believes they will lie. Hippolytus's low opinion of women joins with the piety of the Chorus in destroying him. However non-manly Hippolytus may appear, he is still a man; he can never be as instinctively pious as women. All the men in the second half of the play are doubters: Hippolytus's servant, who reports the miraculous destruction of Hippolytus, which Theseus properly takes to be confirmation of Hippolytus's guilt, draws no such lesson from it. And Theseus himself earlier, when Hippolytus begs him to consult oracles before he condemns him—Theseus after all had just returned from consulting an oracle—dismisses the proposal with exactly the same words with which Hippolytus had dismissed Aphrodite: *poll' ego chairein lego,* "Good riddance!" Artemis praises Hippolytus for keeping his oath; but that the Chorus keep theirs is so much to be expected as to warrant no praise. The Chorus had sworn—without being asked to—by Artemis; and if Artemis were not in secret agreement with Aphrodite, the Chorus would surely offer a perfect target for her wrath. She reserves her greatest wrath for Theseus, who did not believe that the evidence of his eyes needed to be confirmed by divine means. Perhaps, however, the most subtle means Euripides employs to distinguish between male and female is this: the Chorus in the third stasimon use the masculine singular participle to speak of themselves when they express doubts about divine providence.

That Hippolytus denounces women should not be taken for granted. We think of misogynists as men who have been crossed in love; Hippolytus has had no experience of women, and yet his hatred of them extends to virgin daughters, who are under the protection of his own tutelary goddess Artemis. In order to understand his speech, one must reflect on the frequency of the imperfect *chrēn* in unreal conditions in this play (more than in any other play), and the sixfold occurrence of *eithe* in wishes, four of which are in Hippolytus's mouth. Hippolytus's speech is in two parts, of 23 lines each. In the first part he tells Zeus how, if he wished to have a race of mortals, he could have arranged it without the help of women. Men would deposit in Zeus's temples a sum of property proportionate to their several class assessments, and men would thus live free without women. Some of the consequences of Hippolytus's proposal are these: children would be a kind of private property; there would be no city, since there would be nothing exchanged among families except goods; no child would be illegitimate; everyone would be as chaste as Hippolytus, and he would no longer worship Artemis; and finally, in contrast to the spurious coinage of women, there would only be genuine money. Hippolytus does not ask why Zeus did not make women better; if there are women, the violation of the law by them is inevitable. Hippolytus, moreover, judges nature in light of the law rather than law in light of nature. His scheme depends on keeping the law of private property: the abolition of nature is better than any cancellation of the law. So important is the legitimacy of private property to Hippolytus that he cites the fact that fathers give away their daughters in marriage as a proof of the innate wickedness of women, for he thereby forgets that the prohibition against incest rather than paternal hatred dictates exogamy. His standard for the law is money, the most conventional manifestation of law, and not the deepest roots of laws, nothing in any case that could be called natural law.

Hippolytus's reformist zeal cannot stop here, for he cannot but sense that if women are as bad as he says they are, Zeus could have meant them only as a punishment for men—the Hesiodic account—and that in his avoidance of marriage he is evading divine punishment. His sense of this makes him wish to have a stupid wife if marry he must, and then that wives should have voiceless beasts for servants in order to limit their wickedness. Although marriage is bad, adultery is worse; and as a defender of the law Hippolytus does not view nature as an obstacle. Hippolytus's reverence for the law, one might say, does not even yield to the impossible, but rather to his reverence for the divine law—his oath, which at the moment prevents him from unjustly denouncing Phaedra to Theseus. Hippolytus's oath keeps him from needlessly paining Theseus and ruining Phaedra for a crime that has not been committed. It keeps him from the meanness that always attends the exact execution of private law. The gods make Hippolytus act more charitably than he would have on his own.

After hearing Hippolytus, Phaedra bewails the misfortune of women. Chance *(tuchē)* is a calamity for women because they are punished for what they are thought to have planned with as much severity as for their unjust deeds. To get one's deserts follows at once from having the thought. So Phaedra decides that Hippolytus should suffer exactly the same punishment. He should suffer not for what he has done but for what he will be thought to have done. If he wants to show up women by proving to be their superior in the virtue women must have, he will have to experience the same hatred and suspicion that all women know. Phaedra, however, fails. No one except Theseus believes her. Hippolytus's chastity has nothing in common with female chastity.

In the second stasimon the Chorus wash their hands of Phaedra: when they later hear the Nurse's cry for help, they decide to ignore it. The oath that prevents them from helping Hippolytus is balanced by their conviction that suicide is the only way out for Phaedra. They never have any qualms about maintaining the strictest morality; but the price they willingly pay for such a stance is pitilessness. This is their wish, to pass as birds beyond pity to the land of the Hesperidae, which lies beyond the gates of Heracles. There Zeus married his sister Hera and the happiness of the gods is increased. Only where lawful Aphrodite no longer holds sway can Phaedra find solace; her love they now call an unholy love; and the Chorus are as loath to save Phaedra against the law as they are willing to destroy Hippolytus with it. They resign themselves to Phaedra's death by imagining that her departure from Crete and arrival in Athens were equally ill-omened. The law works with the inexorableness of fate: the law stops at nothing in preventing whatever it forbids.

Hippolytus's defense could not be worse. In the first half he lists his virtues, the first of which is a wisdom that has nothing to do with the rest of his virtues and which, he claims, makes him incompetent to speak before the unwise. Hippolytus correctly recognizes that he is *amousos,* without any of the ways to charm a crowd or persuade a father. (That he is unlovable Phaedra's love for him proves, for it is the work of Aphrodite.) His charmless wisdom has nothing to do with *sōphrosunē,* under which he includes his piety, his justice, and his chastity. There is nothing sensible about his moderation or moderate about his wisdom. He knows nothing of prudence. He therefore defends himself against a charge of which he is not accused. Since he believes that all women are bad, he does not believe that rape is possible, and since Theseus never in his presence tells him what Phaedra wrote, Hippolytus argues the case of why he would never have seduced her. Against the charge of rape, Hippolytus's defense could have been irrefutable: no rapist lets his victim live if he believes he can be identified, to say nothing of the palace servants who should have heard her cries. Hippolytus's rational defense, however, does contain one point that, had Theseus been listening, would have by itself convinced him of his son's innocence. "Was Phaedra's body," he asks, "more beautiful than any other woman's?" Hippolytus thus supposes that to fall short of perfect chastity is to engage in libertinism. He knows nothing of the fateful individuality of love, which makes the beloved so inexplicable a choice to everyone, including the lover. Hippolytus can speak of Aphrodite but never of Eros: the one time he uses the cognate verb, he calls for his sword: *amphitomou lonchas eramai.* In Hippolytus, then, there is a strange coincidence of lack of eros with lack of prudence. His unloveliness works against his sobriety.

It is only for a moment that Hippolytus knows himself. It is when Theseus scorns his wish that the house itself bear witness for him. "Alas," he says, "Would that I could weep for the evils we suffer." Hippolytus recognizes that there is no one to pity him, for only another Hippolytus could, and there cannot be another, for he does not want a friend—another *I*—but his very self. He is entirely alone; he conversed with Artemis; but Artemis is not another Hippolytus—she is female and the goddess of childbirth. Hippolytus saw his uniqueness but he was not able to accept it; he looked around for a god who was like him, someone he could claim he imitated; but he does not imitate Artemis—he is naturally chaste—and he cannot worship Artemis, for he does not need her. It is for this reason that he can so readily propose to Zeus a situation that would dispense with Artemis. Hippolytus does not need anyone. He is not a human type in any sense; he is not devoted to an ideal against which he measures himself and of which he falls short; rather, he is perhaps the only individual, literally understood, that any poet has ever presented. We therefore cannot either fear for him or pity him. Hippolytus does not practice at being chaste; he does not come close to innocence, beset on all sides by temptations that he must strive to avoid. He is by nature perfect innocence. He certainly does not belong to a sect like the Orphics for whom asceticism is the means for salvation. He is not a monk. Hippolytus's mistake, however, is his piety. It leads him to set Artemis against Aphrodite, who are in cult not enemies at all: the virgin, devoted first to Artemis, prays after her marriage to Aphrodite.

When we first hear Hippolytus, we think that Euripides means us to understand the contrast between Aphrodite and Artemis as that between a religion in which the gods tell men what to do and a religion in which men do what the gods do. But Hippolytus's way is not the way of imitation. An old servant of his asks him whether he knows the law established among men to hate the proud and unfriendly; Hippolytus agrees that he should abide by such a law and convention. The servant then asks whether he expects the same to hold among the gods. "Yes," says Hippolytus, "provided we mortals use the laws of the gods." The servant meant to draw a parallel between the way men want to be greeted by one another and the way the gods want to be greeted by men; but Hippolytus understands him differently: human conventions of politeness have their source in the conventions of the gods; we adopt the laws that dictate the behavior of the gods. Imitation for Hippolytus is obedience. It is, accordingly, not completely true that Hippolytus is entirely without love; but what he loves is as alien as he himself is. After wishing that he could pity himself, and Theseus having accused him of self-worship rather than justice toward his parents, Hippolytus bursts out: "Oh miserable mother! Oh bitter birth: may no friend of mine be a bastard." Legitimacy, he believes, is the indispensable basis for love. So Hippolytus *is* in love; *he is in love with the law.* When Theseus later praises his nobility (calling him *gennaios*), he tells him to pray to have his legitimate children *(gnēsioi)* like himself. This love of Hippolytus cannot be requited, for he is outside the law both by birth and by nature, and therefore in his uniqueness he longs for the universality of the law. His hatred of women is thus not a direct function of his chastity but his way of being useful to the law from which he is forever excluded.

Euripides won first prize with the *Hippolytus;* but if what we are saying is true, that we do not and cannot pity Hippolytus, it would seem that such a triumph is hardly plausible. But the last part of the play presents Hippolytus in a different light. It is the joint effort of Artemis and the Chorus. On Hippolytus's departure, the Chorus express their doubts about divine providence; but since Hippolytus directly owes his exile to their silence, the stasimon seems to be the rankest hypocrisy. But it is here that the Chorus most show their piety: first, they did not expect the oath they had sworn to lead to trouble, and then they expected that Theseus would believe Hippolytus's most solemn oath; and when he did not, they thought a miracle would resolve the crisis. Their present inability to see any pattern in human affairs arises from their perplexity as to how the gods can allow oaths to be sworn, for oaths presuppose a certain constancy in human life. In the antistrophe they solve this problem: they will no longer try to understand the gods' ways; they will pray for their fortune to be unchanging but they will no longer act as if they expected it to be; instead, within limits, they will adapt themselves to chance. This means in context a song in praise of Hippolytus, as if they were his partisans; but look how ill it suits Hippolytus. They praise him for his being *mousikos;* they address the Graces as if they were the natural champions of Hippolytus—the Graces who, according to Hesiod, pour forth love from their eyes; and what is most absurd, they say that the girls of Trozen will no longer be able to run after Hippolytus, the most eligible bachelor in town.

This is not the Hippolytus we know; this is the Hippolytus of Artemis's cult, in which virgins before their marriage cut their hair and sing a dirge for him. The Chorus on their own begin the rehabilitation of Hippolytus and his transformation into someone pitiable. Only by reinterpreting Hippolytus so that he becomes a representative of a certain stage in life can they pity him. The unique Hippolytus becomes the representative of the common and thus becomes part of the law. He who manifests the essence of love's illusion, that whom we love is an irreplaceably unique individual, becomes completed by and absorbed into the law, but only after his death. The Chorus mourn Hippolytus while he is absent; when he returns half-dead there can be no *kommos,* and Hippolytus must pity himself. He is not very good at it. The pitiable Hippolytus cannot help holding forth in a comic vein. He calls himself *ton kakodaimona kai kataraton; kakodaimōn,* which is not the opposite of *eudaimōn,* but rather an expression of vulgar contempt, occurs nowhere else in tragedy, never in the historians, once in the orators, and thrice in Plato, but it is very common in comedy. Hippolytus cannot pity himself without despising himself. His saying *kakodaimōn* is like his saying *boras koresthesis* at the beginning of the play. He is beneath our concern. And yet Hippolytus finally does elicit our compassion; his last words are to Theseus: he asks him to cover his face. Only when Hippolytus is a corpse does he need anyone.

SEVEN

On Greek Tragedy

I

OF ALL LITERARY FORMS, tragedy and comedy alone seem to make a natural pair. They are natural in that they designate something not merely in letters but in life, and they are a pair in that, taken together, they seem to comprehend the whole of life, not just some aspect of it. We recognize as much when we speak of "the tragedy and comedy of life," which is a phrase as old as Plato.[1] At the same time, tragedy seems to raise a claim that by itself it is the truth of life. Aristophanic comedy, at any rate, is parasitic on tragedy, and Plato suggested that the artful tragic poet is a comic poet as well, but not the other way round.[2] Yet tragedy's claim to be the truth of human life does not mean that this truth is wholly sad. As we know, there is also gaiety in human life, which is neither outweighed nor subsumed by its sadness: we laugh at least as much as we weep, and it would be a severe moralist who would trace all our laughter to pain. While tears are the natural ground of tragedy, from which tragedy can never wholly cut itself loose, tears by themselves seem to be inadequate as a sign for the whole of human life. Tears, one might say, have to become synecdochal if they are to signify so much; and they cannot become synecdochal unless they are informed by art. "The tragic sense of life" stands in need of tragic poetry.

The universality at which tragedy aims holds especially for Greek tragedy. Unlike Old Comedy, Greek tragedy is presented as if it had no author; its illusoriness is complete. Thus its perspective appears to be absolute, that is, without perspective. No one represents unequivocally the wisdom of the poet in Greek tragedy; everything that might detract from its absoluteness is usually suppressed, and this is done so systematically that some effort is required to notice what has been suppressed. Although the stories of tragedy, like its language, are taken from heroic epic, the word *hero* in the Homeric sense does not occur in the extant plays. The legends of tragedy are not legendary; its representation of the past is shadowless. Monarchical rule had long ceased in Athens (the word *king* survived as the name for a magistrate who no longer ruled the city), yet tragedy has nothing but kings and queens for its protagonists; the people are hardly more conspicuous in tragedy than they are in Homer.[3] Its women move as freely in the open as do its men; and there is hardly a line in Aeschylus or Sophocles to remind the audience that their own women are confined strictly to the home. Again, whatever its origin might be, tragedy as we know it is Athenian; but the stuff of tragedy is not. Thebes looms larger than Athens; when Aristophanes has Aeschylus boast that his *Seven Against Thebes* once filled the audience with martial spirit, he is sharply reminded that the Thebans are his beneficiaries.[4] The greatest single event in Athenian history, in which the Athenians would legitimately take pride and to which we ourselves can hardly be indifferent—the defeat of the Persians at Salamis is shown to them as a Persian catastrophe, and in order to make it all the more unrelieved, Aeschylus has the Chorus pretend that Darius never mounted an expedition against Greece and Marathon did not take place. On the other hand, Sophocles must have seemed as enigmatic as the Sphinx when he attributed to Oedipus's grave an eternal power to defend Athens from attack, for the audience would have been hard put to remember any such occasion. Were they to believe that at some future time Sophocles would be vindicated? If, finally, the role of the Areopagus were a political issue at the time of the *Oresteia* (458 B.C.), what political lesson could Aeschylus have conveyed in revealing that its first trial ended in a hung jury and that Athena spoke for the acquittal of someone who pleaded guilty to the charge of matricide?

The placelessness and timelessness of Greek tragedy remind one of Plato's *Republic,* in which Socrates presents the best city in speech. There, not only does the ever-present urgency of the problem of justice occasion the best city in speech, its utopian nature is readily granted to be a consequence of its beauty. The beauty of Greek tragedy, however, is a nightmare, in which the terrible is not abstracted from but distilled. Greek tragedy is, as it were, the offscouring of Socrates' city. The criminality against which the city has devised its strongest prohibitions is the setting for tragedy's celebration of its protagonists. Tragedy prosecutes as it praises. It crosses the beautiful of epideictic oratory with the justice of forensic oratory, but it wholly fails to join them with the good of deliberation.[5] Tragedy simply suspends the political good, even while its horizon is the city's. Aeschylus's Clytemestra could have swung the Chorus of elders to her side had she but seen fit to link Agamemnon's injustice in his killing of their daughter with the general injustice of the Argive suffering at Troy, for which the Chorus are convinced Agamemnon deserves punishment. But she refuses to condemn the war, despite the fact that her enticement of Agamemnon to walk on rich embroideries can only be designed to provoke the people's resentment at his impious and barbaric squandering of the royal wealth. Clytemestra muffs her chance to found a regime that would combine authority with consent. The killing of Agamemnon exhausts her (1568–76); it serves Aegisthus but neither herself nor the people she has ruled for ten years. She lets Cassandra divert the Chorus from the political issue of the war to the inherited fate of the Atreidae, even though this entails that Iphigeneia's sacrifice, about which Cassandra knows nothing, be forgotten and Clytemestra herself appear to be a common adulteress.[6]

Cassandra's diversion of the *Agamemnon*'s initial theme seems to be typical of tragedy. The plague that affects all of Thebes is due, we are told, to the murder of its former king; but Oedipus becomes so enthralled, as are we, by the riddle of his origins that he never learns from the sole eyewitness of Laius's death whether in fact he is guilty of regicide. The city would have been satisfied if Oedipus's discovery had been so limited but, as matters turn out, it has only his inference to rely on, and even at the end we do not know whether his exile is still needed as a civic purification. We realize here, as elsewhere, that we have become estranged from the city's primary concerns, and that what has estranged us is the sacred. The sacred loses its political place in tragedy. "First and Fifth," Aristotle says, is the care of the divine;[7] it is fifth for the city and first for tragedy. Prior to its admission into the city, the city attenuates the sacred. In the *Antigone,* where there is a conflict between divine and human laws, Tiresias reaffirms the sacredness of burial without vindicating Antigone (1016–22, 1070–71). He interprets the divine law as applicable to each and every corpse; he does not limit the obligation to the family, ignoring the fact that Antigone would not have done what she did if Polyneices had not been her brother. The first stasimon of the play allows for civility to be part of the uncanniness of man; but to be devoted to the sacred strikes the Chorus, when they first catch sight of Antigone, as a demonic monstrousness, and, after they have heard her defend the sacred, they detect in her her father's bestial savagery (376, 471–72); she is, of course, the daughter of Oedipus. Aristotle distinguishes between moral and heroic virtue, and their respective opposites, vice and bestiality.[8] Tragedy looks away from moral virtue—the pairs of vicious extremes are the subject of comedy—and toward heroic virtue, which, without the mean of moral virtue, ceases to be the opposite of bestiality. Antigone herself speaks of her criminal piety; she says she stops at nothing in the performance of holy things (74). Antigone shatters the single limit which the first stasimon ascribes to man (death), and she shatters it by becoming at one with the sacred. The sacred shines through Antigone not despite the fact that she is the offspring of an incestuous union but because of it. Out of the family that violates the family comes the defender of the family's inviolability. *Antigone* means "antigeneration."

At the beginning of his *History,* Herodotus identifies human happiness with political freedom and greatness (1.5.3–4). He goes on to indicate that justice is incompatible with such happiness (1.6.2, 14.4), and he then illustrates their incompatibility with the story of Croesus. After having made Lydia into an imperial power, Croesus invited the Athenian Solon to inspect his treasury and then asked him whom of those he had seen did he judge to be the happiest. Solon's answer was Tellus the Athenian: Athens was well-off, his sons were beautiful and good, they had made him a grandfather, he himself was well-off by Athenian standards, and his end was most brilliant, for in an engagement with Athens's neighbors he routed the enemy and died most beautifully, in return for which the Athenians buried him at public expense at the spot where he fell and honored him greatly. In this judgment the private goods depend on the public good and are fully in harmony with it: the sacred is absent. Croesus, however, is not satisfied and asks Solon whom of those he had seen he would put in second place. Solon does not answer this question, for he now does not speak as an eyewitness but reports a story, one in which the beautiful and the political good are absent. The story concerns Cleobis and Biton, two Argive brothers whose livelihood was adequate and whose bodily strength was such that they had both won contests. It is not said that Argos, where they lived, was well-off, nor that they were beautiful. On a day sacred to Hera, their mother—she must have been a priestess—had to be conveyed to the sanctuary, but since the oxen could not be found and time was running out, Cleobis and Biton yoked themselves to the cart and dragged it forty-five stades. "Observed by the festival gathering," Solon relates, "the best end of life befell them, and the god showed in their case that it is better for a human being to be dead than to live." These verbs of seeing and showing are deceptive, for just as the story is only hearsay, the cause of what follows is speech and what follows is itself ambiguous. The Argive men blessed the strength of the Argive youths, the Argive women blessed their mother for having such sons, and she, overjoyed by their deed and its acclaim, stood before the statue of Hera and prayed to the goddess to grant her sons whatever is best for a human being to obtain. The brothers lay down in the temple and never got up again, and the Argives, on the grounds that they had proved to be best, made statues of them and dedicated them at Delphi (1.31).

Solon tells these two stories as if the moral common to them both—no one is to be judged happy before he is dead—could conceal their differences. These differences constitute the double frame of Greek tragedy: the political in its innocent autonomy and the sacred in its subversion of that innocence. The last words of Aeschylus's *Seven against Thebes,* which are the last words of the trilogy (the first two plays are lost), give perfect expression to this doubleness but do not resolve it. The Chorus of maidens divides between those who side with Antigone in her resolution to bury Polyneices and those who side with the city that prohibits it. The first group says: "Let the city injure or not the mourners of Polyneices; we shall go and join in his burial, we his escorters; for this is a grief common to the [human] race, and the city praises the just things differently at different times." The second group replies: "But we shall side with him (Eteocles), as the city and the just jointly praise. For after the god and the strength of Zeus he checked the city of Cadmeans from being overturned and being swamped altogether by a wave of foreigners." Nothing better indicates the difficulty if not the impossibility of any resolution than that the partisans of the city speak of the gods while the others are silent about them, yet the sacred still lurks in their appeal to a common humanity.

Herodotus's Solon did not leave it simply at distinguishing two kinds of happiness; he went on to warn Croesus not to believe that their combination was possible (1.32.8–9). Croesus failed to heed Solon; confronted with the growing power of the Persians, he consulted the Delphic oracle as if his own political greatness could concern Apollo. When Croesus later tells Cyrus that he wants to charge Apollo with deception, Cyrus laughs (1.90.3). Croesus, however, though his happiness was not unalloyed even before he met Solon (one of his sons was mute), so much identified happiness with empire and freedom that even the subsequent loss of his other son, for whom he mourned in idleness for two years, did not force him to acknowledge his misery (1.46.1). Only after the capture of Sardis, when he was about to be burned alive, did he remember Solon. Croesus was immune to tragedy. Its elements were at hand but not the recognition of them. That the same men are not always prosperous was all he learned from Solon (1.207.1).

Croesus's immunity to the tragic is all the more surprising because he had a part in a complete tragedy. Adrastus, the son of the Phrygian king, accidentally killed his own brother. Banished, he came to Croesus to ask for purification according to law (Lydian law, Herodotus says, is in this respect close to Greek law); and once purified, he lived at Croesus's expense. The inescapable, however, which was latent in his own name (Adrastus means just that), overtakes him in the guise of Croesus's son Atys, whose name signifies "Doom." A wild boar was devastating the fields of the Mysians; they requested Croesus to send them his son along with hunters and hounds. Croesus granted the rest but denied them his son, for a dream had warned him that an iron spear would kill Atys. As a consequence of that dream, Atys's marriage had been hastened, all iron weapons in the palace had been transferred to the women's quarters, and he himself was forbidden to join in any military expedition. Informed of the dream, Atys argued that a boar's tusks were not of iron and that his enforced detention shamed him in the eyes of his bride and fellow citizens. Croesus then relented, but he insisted that Adrastus accompany his son to guard him against highwaymen. Adrastus agreed reluctantly to repay the kindness of Croesus, and when the boar was cornered, he aimed at it, missed, and hit Atys instead. Croesus then called upon Zeus the god of purification to witness what he had suffered at the hands of Adrastus, and he called upon the same Zeus as the god of the hearth and of comradeship, since the stranger whom he had welcomed he had cherished only to become his son's murderer and had sent him as a bodyguard only to discover in him his greatest enemy. Adrastus himself appeared before Croesus and surrendered to him, urging him to slay him over the corpse of Atys, recounting his double misfortune and concluding that life was not worth living. Croesus took pity on Adrastus and forgave him; "but Adrastus, the son of Gordias the son of Midas, he who was the murderer of his own brother, and the murderer of his purifier, when the grave site of Atys was deserted, in recognition of the fact that he was the most weighed down of all the men he knew slew himself over it" (1.45).

The specifically tragic element in this story is the law's incompetence to absolve Adrastus of the double guilt he experiences despite his innocence. Greek tragedy is concerned with those experiences of the soul that are situated on the other side of the frontier of the law. Although Oedipus tells the men of Colonus that he is "pure by law" (548) and beats back

Creon's attempt to fasten guilt upon him, yet when Theseus returns his daughters to him, and Oedipus in his gratitude asks him to extend his hand so that he can touch and kiss his head, "if it is sanctioned," he checks himself and says, "What am I saying? How could I in my misery be willing to touch a man with whom no stain of evil dwells?"[9] Tragedy is not possible if the law is experienced as asserting the complete coincidence between Ought and Is.[10] The Persians, Herodotus says, deny that anyone has yet killed his own father or mother, but as often as such as event has occurred, they say there is an absolute necessity that if the matter is examined thoroughly it will always be discovered that the offspring was either supposititious or the consequence of adultery, for everything that Persians are forbidden to do they are forbidden to say (1.138).[11] Or as the Roman jurist Papinian puts it: "Any acts which offend against pious reverence, reputation, or our shame, and to speak generally are done in contravention of morality, must be believed to be acts which we not only ought not, but cannot, do."[12] And if neither Persia nor Rome admits of tragedy, Christianity no less precludes it. The pagan historian Zosimus tells us—his accuracy is not in question here—that Constantine murdered his son Crispus on suspicion of his having committed adultery with his stepmother Fausta, and when Helen, the mother of Constantine, took this hard, Constantine consoled her by having Fausta burned in her bath; but when he asked the priests for purification of his crimes and was told that no rite of purification was capable of cleansing him, an Egyptian from Spain informed him that Christianity absolved any crime, and the impious who converted were at once free of sin (2.29.3). The tragic consists in what is both impossible for morality and forgivable by a religion of salvation.[13] Tragedy discloses the inevitability of the morally impossible for which there cannot be any expiation.

The Egyptian king Psammenitus, Herodotus tells us, had ruled for six months when Cambyses took him captive and made trial of his soul. He had his daughter dressed as a slave and sent to carry water along with other noblemen's daughters; and while they passed by their fathers with wails and cries, which were echoed by those who saw them, Psammenitus looked, understood, and bowed his head to the ground. When they had passed by, the king's son with two thousand other boys of the same age, with their necks in halters and their mouths bridled, were likewise exhibited on the way to their death; and though the rest of the Egyptians wept at the sight, Psmmenitus behaved as he had with his daughter. But when one of his drinking companions, now reduced to a life of beggary, happened to pass by—he was not part of Cambyses' experiment—Psammenitus shouted aloud, called him by name, and struck himself on his head. Called upon to explain his actions, the king said, "Son of Cyrus, the evils that are my own were greater than lamentation, but the sorrows of a friend deserved my tears: he has fallen from great happiness to beggary on the threshold of old age."[14]

If silence is the proper form of private grief, tragedy is not only paradoxical because it imitates action in speech but—and particularly—because it gives voice to silence. Aeschylus managed at least twice to keep his protagonists silent for an entire play within a trilogy.[15] The *logos* of silence is the rhetorical equivalent in tragedy to its thematic transgression of the law. Their equivalence can be shown by means of a passage in Plato's *Philebus.* Socrates cites seven occasions when the soul experiences by itself a mixture of pleasure and pain. They are anger, fear, longing, *thrēnos,* love, envy, and jealousy (47e1–2). *Thrēnos* is plainly out of place, for whereas the others are all unmediated passions of the soul, *thrēnos* is the expression of a passion. It is not grief at the death of someone—that is *penthos*—but a song sung at a funeral. A *thrēnos* is no less conventional than is the occasion of its utterance, but as the phrase "to be in mourning" suggests, the conventional face of grief is inseparable from whatever is in fact experienced. The tragic poet can neither strip grief of its conventions without having it fall silent altogether nor leave it to its conventions without failing to articulate it. Grief, however, not only baffles the poet, it attracts him, and in just the way Socrates indicates: the pleasure that accompanies its expression betrays the pain of the original grief. The *thrēnos* induces in us an innocent guiltiness that deepens the experience from which it relieves us. Poetry thus assumes the task of purification which the law itself can neither do nor acknowledge the need to do.

Poetry, according to Aristotle, has a double base in our nature.[16] We learn by imitating others and take pleasure in images as images. We impersonate and keep our distance, are both actors and spectators. Our sociality is a function of our emulation, and our delight in images of our curiosity. The imitative arts thus bring together without truly uniting them man's natural desire to know and his nature as a political animal. That from which the morality of the city makes him avert his eyes is brought before his eyes in an image. The image transgresses the moral and yet pleases. Aristotle's two examples are paintings of loathsome animals and corpses; they correspond respectively to comedy and tragedy, of which in turn there is the dung beetle of Aristophanes' *Peace* and Sophocles' Antigone, who in scorning her sister's offer to die with her says, "My soul has long been dead" (559–60). How the image succeeds in preserving the law while cancelling it is not easy to say. Aristotle suggests that this is due to the illusory equation it effects between the artfulness of the image and the purposiveness of the imaged. The image is the image of a natural teleology.[17] Antigone, accordingly, would be the *telos,* the artful perfection, of the corpse. The guard who brings Antigone before Creon, who has forbidden burial to her brother, likens her to a bird that on seeing her bed bereft of its nestlings bursts out with a piercing cry of lamentation (423–27). Polyneices' corpse stripped of its ritual dust affects Antigone in the way in which the loss of her brood affects the mother bird. As Sophocles develops this figure, the corpse is Antigone's nest, the dust her young. The corpse now stands tenantless; it was occupied when Antigone clothed it in dust. The corpse is lifeless, now that it no longer houses the dust. The life of the corpse is the dust, and the dust is Antigone's. It was her life that the guards brushed off Polyneices. She alone was not affected by the stench of his rotting corpse.[18]

The beautiful image of the ugly is but one aspect of tragic poetry; the other is the beautiful image of the beautiful, or the praise of the noble. Tragic poetry reserves its praise for those whose nobility appears to be without calculation. The self-evident impossibility of joining the good with the noble—the prudence of Ismene or Chrysothemis with the nobility of Antigone or Electra—seems to be the unexamined premise of tragedy. Perhaps, however, tragedy only starts from that premise in order to question it without incurring the suspicion that its questioning is due to rancor. Goethe's criticism of Antigone's last defense, in which she narrows the grounds of her action, suggests as much.[19] Aristotle, in any case, seems to imply that though tragedy is the proper form for those poets whose natures are noble, the manner of their praise does not issue in admiration but in pity and fear. Pity and fear are the truth of praise. When Caesar entered Rome, his sole opponent was Quintus Metellus, who barred his access to the public treasury. Metellus stood his ground, even when Caesar threatened to kill him on the spot; but he yielded when Caesar added, "Young man, it was harder for me to say it than to do it." Bacon characterizes this as "a speech compounded of the greatest terror and greatest clemency that could proceed out of the mouth of man."[20] Our experience of tragedy is not unlike that compound. The fear of Metellus is in a sense the pity of Caesar.

Pity is for those who do not deserve their suffering, whose suffering is sensed to be in excess of what they did and who they are. Pity thus assumes a moral universe—Ought and Is are in agreement—in which an exception has occurred. The exception, moreover, is experienced not as a sign of the difference between "for the most part" and "necessity" but rather as no less deliberate than the presumed coincidence of virtue and happiness. The suffering is understood to be punishment. There are gods. To interpret the punishment as disproportionate, however, is to presuppose that all that has happened is separable from him to whom it has happened, whereas in tragedy it is shown that no such separation is possible; to undo the one is to undo the other. Where suffering and being fully match, there is the experience of fate, of which the most superficial sign, and consequently the deepest one as well, is the significance of tragic names. The victim of fate can *be* if and only if he suffers what he ought not to suffer. Our pity ends in our own terror. At the very moment that Oedipus at Colonus has had confirmed his new-found security—Theseus has just restored his daughters to him—the Chorus say, "Not to be born surpasses every account."[21]

This saying of the Chorus is a hard-won acquisition for them. Through their experience they are forced to coin the proverbial. And what holds for the Chorus holds for tragedy in general. It too renews the ancient. It brings to light those experiences that no longer seem to be possible as experiences. It must therefore transport us. The here and now must drop away. We experience this displacement—this *ekstasis*—as enthusiasm, the indwelling of a god, of which the fundamental moods are pity and fear.[22] The condition for the possibility of tragedy is post-Promethean, but what it presents is pre-Promethean man, for whom death is before his eyes and there is neither art nor hope. In taking us outside ourselves, tragedy makes us experience our total dependence on gods. The abyss over which they suspend us reveals our need of them.[23] Tragedy unfolds the significance of Athena seizing Achilles by the hair when he draws his sword to kill Agamemnon;[24] it does not concern itself with Odysseus, who, trapped in the cave of the Cyclops, draws his sword but checks himself.[25]

We may recall the nursery rhyme, "Hush-a-bye, baby." Its recitation is meant to accompany an imitative performance of itself. The baby is first rocked as if he were in a cradle on the top of a swaying tree; he is then dropped at the very moment at which the song presents hypothetically the breaking of the tree's branches; but since the baby's fall is then checked, the song's hypothesis is at the last minute denied to be possible. The nurse who induces the terror relieves the terror. The terror is induced presumably out of a sense of the baby's unfocused anxiety that can only be soothed if it is first translated into a terror whose source is made known.[26]

The enchantment of tragedy works something like that. It gives a name to the nameless. Man's mortality gets paired with and yet separated from the immortality of the gods. Death thus ceases to be the negation of life without entirely ceasing to be what it is. It is both willing and unwilling to be called by the name of Hades. The Chorus who declare that not to be born is best do so immediately after they assert that death is an ally who exacts at last the same from all, "when the hymnless, lyreless, danceless fate of Hades comes to light"; and in the next stasimon they invoke and revere, "if it is sanctioned," Persephone, "the nonevident goddess" and Hades, whose very name means "unseen" (1556–78).

II

These remarks on the general conditions for Greek tragedy are very far from comprehending its variety, let alone the particular ways in which a tragedy arrives at the revelation of the tragic. The individual tragedy shapes the universally tragic. If the *Antigone* represents a conflict between state and individual, it first represents the conflict between a city's decree and a divine law; and it further represents the city's decree as an arbitrary decision of its ruler and the divine law in a specific interpretation of it; and finally the ruler is Creon, who proves to have modeled his understanding of the city on the family, and the defender of the divine law is Antigone, who is in love with death. Thus the closer one looks at the action and actors of a tragedy, the less manifest the tragic as such becomes. We are forced therefore to look at anything within a tragedy that sounds like the universally tragic in light of the action that has prompted its utterance. Our nearest example is the Chorus's saying, in *Oedipus at Colonus,* "Not to be born surpasses every account." Their interpretation of Oedipus's experience is not neutral to his experience; it has been refracted through their own experience, which images but does not duplicate exactly his experience. Oedipus, after all, has stated at the beginning of this play that his sufferings, along with time and the noble, have taught him to be content (7–8). His contentment seems to be an acceptance of his experience: he would not now choose not to have been born. Perhaps, then, the Chorus need time before they can echo Oedipus's contentment, and if they are deficient in nobility, they may never be able to bring themselves to affirm it.

The Oedipus of *Oedipus Tyrannus* is a riddle to himself; the Oedipus of *Oedipus at Colonus* is a riddle to everyone else. The first scene of the play contains so many mysteries that almost in desperation one concludes that Oedipus has become his own oracle. Oedipus's first words are a question: "Daughter of a blind old man. Antigone, to what region have we come, or the city of what men?" Does Antigone not know that her father is old and blind (cf. 21–22)? Is there a signpost that Antigone has just read? Could they have come to a region that is not a city of men, or to a city that is not a region? Oedipus does not wait for an answer but asks another question: "*Tis,*" he begins. It might mean "Who?" or "What region?" or "What city?" "Who/What," he asks, "will welcome the wanderer Oedipus today with meager gifts—he asks for little, receives still less, and this suffices me?" Does Oedipus always identify himself by name when he begs? Does the "Who" have to be human, and the "meager gifts" food and lodging (cf. 104)? And of whom does he ask this question? Antigone cannot know any more than he does. Does he abruptly turn to talk to himself? Why does he ask for more than he finds sufficient? Is the still proud Oedipus trying out the role of humility? The "we" of his first question has become "Oedipus" at the beginning of his second question and "me" at the end. When he turns back to his daughter, he deepens his mysteriousness. "If, daughter, you see any seat, either at profane places or at the groves of the gods, set and establish me, so that we may learn by inquiry where we are." If it makes no difference where he is seated, why does Oedipus note the difference? Why should his being seated make it possible to find out where they are? He has not yet asked whether the place is inhabited (27–28). Does he mean that if it is a profane place it is not the place he has been looking for, and if it is sacred it might be?

"We have come as strangers," he says, "to learn from citizens, and to practice whatever we are told." And yet, despite this admission of ignorance, no sooner does Antigone inform him that she knows by sight that a city is far off and by conjecture that they are in a sacred place—the place they are in is less plain than the place they are not in—than Oedipus asks her, "Can you tell me where we are?" Antigone, to our surprise, knows the answer: "Athens, at least, I know, but not the place." And then to turn our surprise to bewilderment, Oedipus says, "Well, every wayfarer told us that much." Oedipus knew all along that he was in Attic territory. Why, then, did he ask at the beginning what city they had come to if his ignorance extended only to the place? And, finally, if he is so willing to do what he is told, why does he at once defy the first inhabitant he meets? Indeed, he has already planned to defy the citizens, for of the alternative—profane places or groves of the gods—"profane" *(bebēla)* means literally "that on which one is permitted to walk," and hence "sacred groves of gods" must mean a place whose access is forbidden. Oedipus is now prepared to violate the sacred knowingly.

The riddles of the opening cluster around the knowledge of place, and the knowledge of place is embedded in Oedipus's own name—"Know-where." Can Oedipus himself have been the place he was looking for (cf. 1520–23)? We learn at the end of this play that the place of his disappearance is not to be known to anyone, for though Theseus presumably knows—how, if he covered his eyes at the last minute and Oedipus disappeared without a trace?—and transmitted his knowledge to his successor, Athens is now, in the time of the audience for whom the play was written, a democracy and no longer can have a custodian of this secret. "Know-where" has become "Nowhere" (cf. 1649).

The riddles continue. The native of Colonus forbids Oedipus to ask any more questions before he leaves the place where he is, "for you occupy a place not sanctioned for trespass." Is there a connection between out-of-placeness and questioning? Oedipus complies by asking two questions: "What is the place? To whom of the gods is it held to belong?" The stranger then ignores his own prohibition and answers both questions: "A place untouchable and uninhabited. The goddesses in whom terror dwells occupy it, daughters of Earth and Darkness." Antigone was mistaken; the place is not inhabited. Could there be two places? Oedipus then asks what the awesome *(semnon)* name of the goddesses is; plainly, he is eliciting the name he wants to hear—*Semnai*—the distinctive epithet of the Furies at Athens and their name in the oracle he has (89); but, he is told, "The people *(leōs)* here would call them the all-seeing Eumenides; elsewhere, different names are beautiful." Oedipus must have come to the wrong place; but Oedipus decides otherwise: "Well, may they graciously *(hileō)* welcome the suppliant, since I would no longer depart from this place." Oedipus is going to stay regardless of whether the Furies are gracious or not, for whereas the name Eumenides points directly to the word *eumeneis* (kindly disposed), Oedipus chooses to substitute an equivalent word of the same metrical shape that puns on "people" (cf. 486). Does Oedipus need the graciousness of the people more than the kindness of the gods? It is striking, in any case, that Theseus does not need to consult an oracle to confirm Oedipus's interpretation; indeed, neither Theseus nor anyone at Colonus is ever told the oracle. Oedipus's defiance now shakes the native's confidence; he decides not to expel Oedipus "apart from the city." What city? It cannot be Athens, for the inhabitants of Colonus have total control over this place (78). Is Colonus then a city too? If it is, then the situation into which Oedipus has stumbled must occur shortly after Theseus had consolidated all of Attica under the sovereignty of Athens, when the country towns were stripped of their political independence but their sacred places were left intact.[27] Oedipus, however, has now violated the sacred, and since we never learn whether Ismene managed to perform the elaborate rites of purification before Creon seized her, Oedipus might remain polluted to the end: during the interval in which Ismene would be performing the ceremony, the Chorus learn of Oedipus's crimes (510–48). We are made to wonder, in any event, whether Theseus needs the violation of the sacred, for if, on the one hand, the place of Oedipus's disappearance is not to be approached (1760–63), and, on the other, that place is not to be known, transgression is inevitable. Oedipus, "pure by law," brings to Athens the permanence of guilt.

We are not yet done with Oedipus the riddle. After the native of Colonus has allowed him to stay where he is, Oedipus asks him, "What is the place in which we have come?" (52). Had not Oedipus already asked this question (38)? Is this yet another place? The native, in any case, does not repeat himself: "The whole place is sacred. Awesome Poseidon occupies it. The Titan god, the fire-bringer Prometheus, dwells in it; and the place you tread upon is called the bronze-footed threshold of this land, the bulwark of Athens. The neighboring fields claim the horseman Colonus as their founder, and all in common have his name." "This land" does not refer to Colonus; it is not even clear whether it includes Colonus. The root of Athens is not in Athens; the root of Athens, it turns out, is in Hades (1590–91). Colonus is many together bound in name to, and apart in being from, Athens: the native distinguishes between what the place is called and its *sunousia.* "It is this sort of place, stranger, not honored in speeches but more in a being together *(sunousia).*"

Oedipus, in staying in this place and refusing to go to Athens, grants Athens "the greatest gift of his *sunousia*" (647). Oedipus seems to be needed in order to weaken the apartness of Colonus without fully assimilating Colonus to Athens. He says he is sacred (287). The togetherness and apartness of Colonus are expressed in the first stasimon in which Oedipus, on the authority of Theseus, is finally welcomed by the Chorus. The first strophic pair is devoted to Colonus, the second to Athens. Their connection is only made at the beginning. "You have come, stranger, to the best dwelling on earth of this land of good horses, gleaming-white Colonus" (cf. 694, 700). The difference between "earth" and "this land" recalls Socrates' noble lie: the warriors of his best city are to believe that the earth is their mother, and they must, "as about their mother and nurse, deliberate about the land in which they are and defend it if anyone attacks it, and on behalf of the rest of their fellow citizens think of them as brothers and earthborn."[28] The earth is literally their mother, the land is *as if* it is their mother. The land is an image of the earth. Yet the image prevails over the imaged as soon as it is a question of war. Oedipus had come as well in order to be an eternal defense against the attack of strangers. The stranger-citizen (cf. 637–38), who becomes the sacred place that is nowhere, is the link between Colonus and Athens. "Pity," he says to Athens, "this wretched image of Oedipus the man" (109–10).

The native has explained to Oedipus the place or places where he is. Oedipus asks, "Does anyone dwell in these places?" "Of course. They are named after this god." Do we not know this already? But Oedipus has listened better than we have. The neighbor said only that the neighboring fields bear the name of Colonus; and Oedipus, who saw through the metaphor of the riddle, is now inclined to interpret everything literally. The demesmen of Colonus are at one with their deme; in some sense, they are already what Oedipus is going to become. According to the first stasimon, Dionysus, the Muses, and Aphrodite inhabit Colonus, and there are no men. Colonus the god is Colonus the place: Colonus means "Hill." When Antigone descries Creon, she says: "O plain, well-endowed with praises, now it is your task to make manifest these so-brilliant words" (720–21). She too realizes that Colonus is its people; what she does not realize is that Oedipus set out from the start to separate them, for without separation there can be no unity of Athens. As soon as the native had left, Oedipus disobeyed him once more. Told to remain where he had come to light (77), Oedipus ordered Antigone to conceal him.[29] Oedipus now goes out of his way to compound his original transgression. When the Chorus enter and cannot find him, Sophocles makes them speak as if he could not avoid violating verisimilitude; they say they must neither look nor speak when they pass by the grove. But they are speaking, and they are looking; and they are doing both because Oedipus, by concealing himself, has made them commit his crime. Not only that, but on their entrance they say, "Look! Who was he? Where does he dwell? Where has the out-of-place one darted, the most insatiate of all? Look! Seek him out! Search everywhere! The old man is a wanderer, a wanderer, not of this place, for otherwise he would not have entered the not-to-be-trodden grove." Oedipus, they say, is guilty of trespass and reveres nothing (134), and Oedipus, they say, is innocent, for he must be ignorant. Oedipus's concealment has made the Chorus rehearse the twofold experience of his own crimes, and they are made to do so while they commit knowingly a crime of their own. When Oedipus pops up at them, it would not be surprising if they took him to be at first one of the Furies. Oedipus beseeches them in these words: "Do not behold me the lawless."[30] To behold Oedipus is to see reflected their own impiety.

We are now in a position to answer our original question. Why do the Chorus assert that not to be born is best just after Theseus has proved by deed that Oedipus is henceforth secure? The Chorus do not leave it at what is truly best; there is a second-best: "And, once one has come to light, to go there quickly from where one has come is by far the second best, since as soon as youth has passed, youth that brings airy thoughtlessness, what labor wanders far outside? What toil is not there within?" The Chorus find youth tolerable because of youth's ignorance; they identify knowledge with evil: "murder, civil factions, strife, battles, and jealous resentment." Knowledge brings with it the city; it is what Oedipus brought them when he took away their innocence. "Not to be born surpasses every account *(logos)*" because nonbeing is without *logos;* and *logos,* they have learned from Oedipus, goes with being. The stranger brings *logos.*[31] The being-together *(sunousia)* of themselves with Colonus is no longer possible without *logos.* In the first stasimon, their praise of Athens, unlike that of Colonus, calls attention to their own speaking and their knowledge of the difference between hearsay and autopsy. Their praise of Athens includes her arts.

III

The Chorus's praise of Athens points back to the anomalous place of Prometheus the fire god in the sacred setting of Colonus (54–56). Colonus is not quite as artless and prepolitical as is suggested by the unhewn and natural rock upon which Oedipus first sits (19, 192). How the arts affect the human condition is the theme of Aeschylus's *Prometheus Bound,* in which we find Prometheus chained to a rock by Zeus as a punishment for his service to men. The gift of arts is but one of Prometheus's three crimes; the other two are his rescue of men from their annihilation and his cure of their despair. The relation that obtains among his three crimes is not at once clear, even though Prometheus puts them together in his talk with the Chorus (228–58). We are given to understand that as soon as Zeus usurped his father's throne he distributed among the gods who had sided with him various offices and honors, but he assigned no special role to men and planned to destroy them entirely before he produced a new race. Prometheus does not explain what lay behind the plan of Zeus, but on the basis of what Prometheus himself tells us about man's pre-Promethean misery, Zeus's plan does not seem to be altogether unreasonable. Prometheus's pity should not dissuade us from looking at ourselves pitilessly. To be pitiless is to be, according to the Chorus, "iron-hearted" (242), and iron is a Promethean gift. The Chorus, at any rate, do not praise Prometheus for his rescue of men; they do, however, praise him for his second crime.

> Prometheus. I stopped mortals from seeing death as their lot in front of them.
> Chorus. What remedy did you find for this disease?
> Prometheus. I settled blind hope in them.
> Chorus. You gifted mortals with a great benefaction.
> Prometheus. Besides this, I gave them fire.
> Chorus. And now mortals who live for a day have flame-faced fire?
> Prometheus. Yes, and from it they will learn many arts.

Mortals once saw death as their lot in front of them; they could not have simply foreseen the day of their death (as it is usually translated), for then Prometheus would not have been compelled to give them blind hopes; he would have only had to take this faculty away. Prometheus made death invisible (Hades). The pre-Promethean situation of men was the constant awareness of death, and as this made any activity based on future expectations impossible, which is the presumption of any productive art, Prometheus had to remove men's oppressive sense of their own mortality before the arts could become useful. Mortals are ephemeral *(ephēmeroi),* according to the Chorus; they live in the light of day in which they once saw themselves as only mortal. But Prometheus's gift of fire, coupled with blind hopes, means the replacement of this natural light by artificial light, whose purpose is precisely to conceal the original horizon within which men live. The price paid for the arts is blindness.

The Chorus believe that to see death before one's eyes is a disease, and that Prometheus benefited men in setting blind hopes in them. On the other hand, the Chorus ask in wonder whether men have fire, but they seem not to regard it as a great benefit to them; only Io, for whom the arts are of no use, will address Prometheus as though she thought it is (612–13). The Chorus are immortal, and it would not be strange if they thought fire was primarily a benefit to the gods. Without fire, men could not have sacrificed to Olympian gods; if they sacrificed at all, they could have only poured libations and offered first fruits. And if one thinks of the technical expression "fireless sacrifices," which are sacrifices to the Fates and Furies, it is fitting that a pre-Promethean man, haunted by his own mortality, should appeal to the only gods who as far as men knew controlled his life and death. In any case, such fireless sacrifices would necessarily assign a higher if not exclusive position to the chthonic gods: even the immortal gods would have made men think of death. No wonder, then, that Zeus when he assumed power had no regard for those who could neither please nor displease him.

Prometheus's three crimes change radically not only the condition of men but also the relation of men to the gods. Prometheus's reflection on this latter change is embodied in his description of the arts; but before we turn to that, we must consider how Prometheus viewed his effect on simply human life. The order in which he has presented the arts is not at first clear (450–503), for the fact that number, though the "chief of contrivances," is third in his list shows that it is not a self-evident position. Men originally lived in the dark; their caves were sunless and they did not know how to make houses whose windows faced the sun. Their emergence from caves into the sun naturally leads Prometheus to describe the art of distinguishing the seasons. The night sky gave them clear signs for discrimination, but since the risings and the settings of the stars are sometimes still "hard to discern," Prometheus gave them numbers, which are the only sure way of marking the seasons; and as numbering is useless unless one remembers accurately, it is joined with the invention of letters. Thus the first four arts form a whole: (1) openness (houses); (2) the seeing of the sky in its differences (astronomy); (3) the precise discrimination of the stars' movements (number); (4) the precise recording of these movements (letters). The fifth and central art is the taming of animals, which partly is necessary for agriculture and hence depends on the preceding three arts. The mention of horses suggests ships, the horses of the sea, and Prometheus then reflects on his own situation in which he has no device to release himself from his pains; for if Prometheus saved men from the flood sent by Zeus by advising Deucalion to build a ship, his own helplessness would now especially come home to him.

The Chorus next interpose and compare Prometheus to a bad physician who cannot cure himself. Prometheus is thus provoked into describing medicine. Medicine deals with symptoms, which are the predictive signs of disease, and hence Prometheus couples it with prophecy, also an art of interpreting signs which can be either good or bad. The phrase that closes his account of prophecy—"These are the sort of things"—would seem to indicate that metals, the ninth and last invention, are on a completely different plane. The connection with what preceded seems at first purely verbal: "the signs that arise in fire" were previously dark, and just as Prometheus gave men eyes by which to see them, so he showed them the benefits hidden in the earth. But if one considers that metallurgy is the only art mentioned that essentially needs fire (apart from certain kinds of divination), and that "the signs that arise in fire" could equally well describe the way in which one judges in smelting the state of a molten batch, metals are the fitting climax to the Promethean arts of prophecy. The last four arts, however, are much harder to see in their inner unity than the first four. Taming of animals might have led Prometheus to reflect on mastery in general, and from the mastery of the sea he might have got to the mastery of disease, and that in turn may have led him to the mastery of chance through divination. The discovery of metals, then, would be related to the previous three arts somewhat as housebuilding was related to astronomy, numbers, and letters. As housebuilding meant the coming out into the open of men which entailed in turn the arts of discrimination and accuracy, so metallurgy, as the art of bringing out into the open things that are not naturally out in the open, would entail the three preceding arts that make use of hidden characteristics of the sea, the earth (herbs), and fire (sacrifices).

Prometheus first described men as clear-sighted in the face of death, and his own activity as one of blinding; but in the account of the arts he presents men as originally blind and the arts as means to bring them out into the light. The contradiction is traceable to Prometheus's failure to state what he believes to be the nature of man. Men were previously *nēpioi,* he says, and he made them sensible and in control of their arts. If we take *nēpioi* literally, Prometheus claims that men were originally unspeaking; but beings without speech and sense can hardly be considered men at all, and Prometheus says that he showed them how to write and not how to speak. If, however, *nēpioi* means only "foolish," as it usually does, then his claim to have given men those arts they are capable of finding out for themselves seems unfounded. The art of astronomy is altogether different from the gift of fire. Men might never be so favored as to find out how to make a fire (cf. 367–69), but as long as they can see and reason they can discover the order in the movement of the stars. And again, if men can speak and thus make distinctions, they can count, and no Prometheus would be necessary to instruct them.

What the silence of Prometheus about the nature of man implies is revealed in a remark that at first looks like a merely grammatical curiosity. Among the ways of divination is ornithoscopy: "I discriminated for them accurately the flights of crooked-taloned birds, whichever are on the right by nature and those on the left" (488–90). The last phrase is constructed in such a way that "by nature" cannot be taken to refer to the birds on the left. "On the right" means by extension propitious, but "on the left" literally means "of good name," and only because one recognizes it as a euphemism for "unpropitious" does it mean "on the left." The words for "left" and "right" are themselves signs that have to be interpreted. The right is right by nature, but the left is only sinister by name; but since they are correlative terms, right and left as propitious and unpropitious have suppressed the distinction between nature and convention. That distinction is not operative for men, for it has been replaced by art; consequently, the distinction between speech and language cannot be drawn. Prometheus does not distinguish between the natural numbers and the conventional sign of letters. The fourth art (letters) and the eighth (divination) equally show that Prometheus, in bringing men into the light, has not revealed all the distinctions to be found in the light, and that the ambiguous status of speech and reason in his account is founded on the blindness he first gave to men. It is impossible to reconcile his giving men blind hopes as well as the art of divination unless their belief that they accurately know this art is in fact the basis of their blind hopes. Men first lived in chaos and were like the shapes of dreams (448–50), but Prometheus showed them how to tell which dreams were fated to turn out true. Men do not altogether awaken under Prometheus's guidance but still live in a twilight. They now believe they can tell apart "reality" from "dream," but "reality" is only the reality of dreams. "I opened the eyes of mortals," Prometheus says, but only so that they could see the signs concealed in fire and not the light of the sun. For Prometheus makes no distinction between the "hard to discern" risings and settings of the stars and the "hard to discern" cries of birds (458, 486). But men as surely lack the complete art of divination as Prometheus possesses it. The arts that illuminate the human world are embedded in an all-encompassing darkness.

The list of the arts begins with man's emergence into the open and ends with the bringing to light of metals. Within this framework of light, the central art is something of an anomaly. The verbs Prometheus uses to describe his ways of giving each art are those of showing, distinguishing, and discovering (altogether thirteen times); but in the case of taming, the verbs are surprisingly direct: "I yoked" and "I led" (462, 465). Taming is apparently not an art that can be taught in speech; Prometheus has to show it in deed. And what holds for the tamer holds for the tamed: it must learn by suffering. Prometheus thus alludes as fastidiously as he can to the need for force and compulsion in taming, for even in his medicine there are only "gentle remedies" (482). The taming of Prometheus himself, which is constantly described in terms of subduing a horse, is sufficient proof that persuasion does not suffice. Prometheus, who pities even the fate of the monstrous Typhon (352), is inclined to discount and reject compulsion—he calls horses "lovers of the reins" (465)—but his tacit admission of its necessity raises the question of whether the same relation that holds between men and beasts should not also obtain between gods and men. The gods, as beings of a different order, may have to rule by force. It is "the bit of Zeus" that compelled Inachus to eject "by force" his daughter Io from the house and country (671–72). That the gods need to use force would be perhaps the major concession Prometheus will later make in being reconciled with Zeus. The very condition of his release—the continuation of the reign of Zeus—means that he can no longer simply please Io and by implication the rest of mankind (cf. 756–70). "Violence" is here as a silent actor in the first scene, because Prometheus does not yet understand it. Prometheus now, however, regards not men but the new gods as savage, and the gods are shown to be at best indifferent; Oceanus never mentions men. The tyranny of Zeus must be moderated if human life is to become tolerable, and Prometheus offers a way to make the gods as philanthropic as himself. Sacrifices are a way to tame the gods, for they give the gods a reason for taking an interest in them. The first effect that sacrifices had, one can imagine, was to persuade Zeus to abandon his plan of destroying the race, for Prometheus, though he saved it once from a flood, surely could not have saved it from the onslaught of thunderbolts.

These implications behind Prometheus's list of the arts do not suffice to explain its dramatic function. Why does it occur between the Oceanus-scene and the arrival of Io? Just prior to Oceanus's coming, Prometheus told the Chorus to stop bewailing his present troubles and hear the future that awaited him (271–73), yet Oceanus's arrival not only delays this relation for the moment but puts it off until Io comes. Oceanus must somehow have made Prometheus meditate on the past and remember the arts he gave to men. "Do not think," he tells the Chorus, "that I am silent out of willful pride and disdain, but I devour my heart in deep reflection to behold myself thus outraged" (436–38). Prometheus's thoughts are on the arts, and if not thoughts of remorse they are almost of despair. To the Chorus's confident belief that once released he will be as strong as Zeus (508–10), he replies that he is not thus fated to lose his chains, "for art is far weaker than necessity" (511–14). This looks at first as if it only meant, "my art is weaker than the compulsion of Zeus" (cf. 107), and hence Prometheus's list of the arts would be his way of acknowledging his own weakness; but were this its primary sense, it would not have led the Chorus to ask, "Who then is the helmsman of necessity?" The general form of Prometheus's assertion makes it applicable to Zeus as well: "His art too (these chains) is weaker than necessity." The Chorus phrase their question personally; they do not ask, "What then is master of (stronger than) necessity?" They sense at once that art no more than necessity is a purely abstract noun. The Fates and Furies are necessity; and since Zeus is weaker than they, the conclusion seems plain: not Prometheus but Zeus essentially is art.

The ordering of human life through the arts parallels the ordering of the world that Prometheus accomplished on Zeus's accession to the throne. The empire of Zeus would also have been surrounded by darkness. Indeed, this empire, in which each god has a specific task, is presented in the first scene, where Zeus is shown to control both the art of metal-working (Hephaestus) and the art of taming (Force and Violence). But Zeus, who has assigned a share to every god, turns out to have only a share on his own. There is something for which he has no art. The three Fates and their executive arm, the Furies, have no part in the arts of Zeus. Zeus's defect consists in his ignorance of generation. He does not know that if he marries Thetis she will have a son who will overthrow him. Zeus, then, lacks the art of the Fates or generation. Their art is weaving. Of the three human needs—food, clothing, shelter—Prometheus mentions arts that satisfy the first and third but not the art of weaving. As the only female art does not appear among the arts of mortals, so it is not counted in the technocracy of Zeus. When Zeus did learn Prometheus's secret, he generated Athena nonsexually, the goddess of weaving. The perfect product of art, who solves the problem of generation among the gods, solves it also for men: by virtue of her being motherless, she later tips the scales in favor of Orestes.[32]

IV

The tragic poets are masters of presenting deadly thoughts in the garb of innocence. Their words float long before they sink and terrify. They seem to have learned how to do this from Homer. When Hector returns to Troy and goes to upbraid Paris at home, Helen says to him: "Come, enter, brother-in-law, and sit upon this seat, since especially the toil of war has occupied your heart on account of myself a bitch and the original offense of Paris, upon whom Zeus did place an evil fate, in order that hereafter we may be the subject of song for men who will be."[33] Homer lets Helen divine that the Trojan war, which had its ground in the Achaeans' vindication of sacred right, finds its ultimate end not in the heroes' glory, but in Homer himself.[34] Aeschylus's *Oresteia* likewise begins with the Trojan War and the issue of right; the evils it has caused puzzle the *Agamemnon*'s Chorus; but those evils seem to be overcome through the establishment of right at Athens, until we hear Athena say, "Let there be foreign war! It is at hand with no effort at all. Therein will be some dread love of glory."[35] Has matricide been condoned just to have Athens no longer be aware of the issue of right? The Furies have not vanished; they have gone underground. "Surely, the grace of the gods is violent."[36]

One of the means by which the terrible beauty of tragedy is indicated without actually speaking out is the incoherent. Be it by a word out of place, a sentence, an argument, or an entire scene, suddenly we are startled and filled with unease. In the course of her third defense, Antigone says, "If I had been the mother of children, or my husband died and wasted away, never would I have undertaken this toil despite the citizens. On account of what law do I say this? If my husband died, I would have had another husband, and a son from another man, if I had lost my husband." This speech is doubly incoherent, for not only does it seem to mar Antigone's nobility, it presupposes that the death of a hypothetical son requires the death of a hypothetical husband; but that could only hold if her husband were her son. Antigone can imagine herself to be, against the meaning of her name, a mother; but she cannot imagine any family other than her own. Similarly Hippolytus, in Euripides' play of that name, appears to argue brilliantly for his innocence when he perceives that his outraged father has just read Phaedra's letter traducing him, until we realize that he does not know the charge against him is rape and he is proving that he could not have been a seducer. Hippolytus's misogyny has betrayed him, for it has made him believe that rape is impossible.

Euripides' Medea has long been planning the murder of her children; Aegeus, the king of Athens, arrives, and first in learning from him that men consult oracles for the sake of having heirs, and then in gaining from him the promise of Athens as a place of refuge, she resolves to execute her plan. Medea takes the motiveless appearance of Aegeus as a divine confirmation of her justice. Chance looks like providence. How else can one explain the perfect coincidence between her own safety and the meaning of her crime? A barbarian takes it upon herself to exemplify for the Greeks their own belief that the punishment for perjury is the annihilation of one's family.[37] The Chorus in *Antigone* remark on Haemon's entrance that he is Creon's younger son and thus obliquely refer to Megareus (1303), whose sacrificial death in appeasing the wrath of Ares has just now helped to save Thebes.[38] It would seem, then, that Creon has already shown that he rules in accordance with his own laws: he has given up his son for the sake of his fatherland. Yet he has decided not to glorify Megareus's death but has strangely chosen Eteocles' as the highest form of patriotism. His fall would surely gain in poignancy if the loss of his elder son underlay his hatred of Polyneices and Antigone. Creon, however, never refers to Megareus, and he gives no indication that he has ever experienced suffering. If the death of Megareus meant nothing to him, the death of Haemon and Eurydice will not either; and what looks like the fitting punishment for his crimes will altogether miss its mark.

Perhaps the most beautiful of all choral odes is the parodos of the *Agamemnon.* Twelve Argive elders begin by singing of the expedition against Troy and their own age that exempted them from military service; they then recount Calchas's interpretation of an omen that occurred at Argos prior to the setting sail of Agamemnon and Menelaus; his interpretation foretold the sacrifice of Iphigeneia and the sack of Troy. The rest of their song describes vividly the sacrifice of Iphigeneia at Aulis, but they insert between the omen and the sacrifice an account of Zeus's justice that begins, "Zeus whoever he is." At first we are swept along by the Chorus, but we are soon nagged by a strange omission on their part: they fail to state what crime Agamemnon committed in punishment for which he had to sacrifice his daughter. They move directly from a sign to that of which it is a sign without speaking of a cause. Do they believe that a sign can double as a cause? We then notice that the Chorus cut off their description of Iphigeneia's sacrifice just before her throat was slit: "What happened next I neither saw nor shall I say (247)." Contrary to our own reasonable surmise that the Chorus never left Argos, they now inform us that they were at Aulis and averted their eyes at the last minute; but if they were there and yet not part of the army, it seems necessary to conclude that the Chorus escorted Iphigeneia from Argos to Aulis. In the insert, between the omen and the sacrifice, they ascribe to Zeus the establishment of the law, "By our suffering understanding." Understanding is guilt: "There drips instead of sleep before the heart a distress that remembers the pain" (179–80).

At the same time, then, that we learn of the Chorus's complicity, we learn that they put no trust in anything but what they can see with their own eyes. They are acutely sensitive in regard to morality and extremely skeptical in regard to evidence. They doubt everything they hear but do not see.[39] They do not believe Clytemestra when she reports the fall of Troy; they find the perfectly plain visions of Cassandra very hard to follow;

and they decide not to help Agamemnon, when they hear his cries, because at least half the Chorus are not certain what they mean (1346–71). Their skepticism, however, is at odds with their morality, for hardly anything they see conforms self-evidently with their morality. Their morality needs to be grounded in knowledge of cause, but all they know of Zeus is his name; he is only a likeness (cf. 160–65, 1486). Their silence, then, about what caused Agamemnon to sacrifice Iphigeneia embodies their probity and distress. This does not mean, however, that the Chorus cannot see how detestable Aegisthus is, and they are prepared to fight him (1651); but Clytemestra, despite Cassandra's best effort to blacken her, baffles them to the end (1560–61).

The disparity between the Chorus's morality and their reliance on eyesight alone seems to be resolved, if not for them then for us, in the *Choephoroi,* where Orestes sees before his eyes the Furies, and guilt thus becomes visible. Its visibility, however, seems to entail a diminution of its power; it is no longer an experience of the soul that the law cannot reach.[40] The Furies terrify Orestes, but they do not succeed in bringing about his remorse. Orestes never regrets what he did. Guilt made visible separates the fear of future punishment from the impossible wish to undo one's crime. The Furies' manifestation is thus indispensable for Athena's establishment of right in the form of law. The Furies become Kindly Ones in becoming pure instruments of punishment. Law deters through its sanctions; it is indifferent to the curative power of remorse. Law has nothing to do with the tragic. It cannot care less whether or not Clytemestra has bad dreams. The Chorus of the *Choephoroi* are the first to anticipate the conclusion of the *Oresteia.* Sent by Clytemestra to appease with libations those below the earth, they are afraid that they *will* be appeased and that she will not have to pay for her crime (21–83). Guilt cannot redeem; it is the luxury of the successful criminal (cf. 841–43). Orestes too is disturbed lest Clytemestra has managed to appease his father, for he, Electra, and the Chorus have conjured Agamemnon to come into the light and join with them against his enemies (459–60), but Agamemnon has failed to appear. Accordingly, Orestes, even after he has resolved to act (514), hesitates. He has to know what prompted Clytemestra to send libations; that they are, as he says, "less than her fault" (519), does not entail that they did not suffice to turn aside Agamemnon's wrath and baffle his epiphany (cf. 461). The dream cannot mean what the dream-interpreters, who engaged themselves to speak "from god" (39–42), made it out to mean. And when we hear the dream, we are puzzled as to how it could have admitted of any other interpretation than Orestes' (527–50). Clytemestra dreamed that she gave birth to a snake and when she offered it suck it bit her on the breast and drew blood. Who else could the snake be than Orestes? The sole wrinkle in Orestes' straightforward interpretation is one line, which is ordinarily taken to say—it assumes an unexampled hyperbaton—that she anchored the snake like *(dikēn)* a child in swaddling clothes but could possibly mean that in the swaddling clothes of a child she anchored just punishment *(dikēn).* The child, then would not be Orestes but Iphigeneia, and the interpreters would have told Clytemestra that the sacrifice of Iphigeneia does not now sanction her father's murder. It is, in any case, remarkable that Clytemestra, when she defends herself before Orestes, does not mention Iphigeneia (cf. 242).

Orestes has no qualms about having killed Aegisthus; he believes he had the law behind him (989–90), but he does not believe that Apollo's oracle is as compelling as the law; his reasons for obeying the oracle are not unmixed (298–305). The Athenian jury too did not find Apollo's case altogether convincing. This is truly astonishing. There stood before them the ugliest and the most beautiful gods, and they could not make their verdict unanimous. The attraction men have to the ugliness of punishment has never been more vividly conveyed.[41] Athena arranged for a contest in which it was shown that the Olympian gods could never wholly gain the worship of men. In persuading the Furies to become part of the new political order of Athens, Athena placed within that order a reminder that men do not have the capacity to recognize fully the justice of Zeus.[42] Athena's wisdom thus partly consists in the admission that mortals cannot know her wisdom as wisdom. This admission lies behind her persuasion of the Furies. The Olympian gods will not punish Athens for its failure to reverence them with all its heart, with all its might, with all its soul. She asks the Furies to make the same concession (795–96). The visible gods of the city relax their grip on the soul, for the human undecidability of Orestes' case signifies the inevitability of human error—the acquittal of the unjust and the condemnation of the just— for which there is to be no punishment. The city that subsequently condemned Socrates postponed his execution until the sacred ship *Salaminia* could return from Delos. It purified itself *hosiou heneka,* which literally means "for the sake of the holy" but came to mean "for form's sake." By the same token, once the gods have sanctioned public error within the city, the city can obviously kill its foreign enemies without any qualms. The Trojan War can now take place. All that the city perhaps still needs is the supplement of tragedy.

The *Choephoroi* is divided into two unequal parts, a high and a low.

The high part goes up through the first stasimon (652), the low contains the killing of Aegisthus and Clytemestra. The first part looks at matricide in the element of divine command and moral duty, the second part presents matricide as it is. Orestes needs his friend Pylades to remind him of Apollo's oracle (900–904). The disjunction between the two parts cannot be missed if one keeps together the last words of the first stasimon—"deep-counseling Fury"—with Orestes' first words in the execution of his plan—"Boy! Boy!"(653). The Chorus say that deep-counseling Fury is introducing Orestes into the palace, but Orestes has to shout and knock like any figure on the comic stage in order to be admitted.[43] Not even Euripides, as far as we know, ever went this far in violating tragic decorum. Tragic decorum simply does not suit the brutal business of a mother's murder: the urine and feces of the infant Orestes are more consonant with it (749–60). So are slaves. The Nurse who speaks about the mindless beast that Orestes was is but one of three such who between them make possible Orestes' actions. The Chorus of slave women persuade the Nurse, in as miraculous a way as Athena does the Furies, to suppress part of Clytemestra's order in repeating it to Aegisthus; and the cries of the slave who discovers Aegisthus's corpse get Clytemestra to come out of the women's quarters unarmed and unescorted (877–84). The house of Atreus is freed by slaves. Orestes did not anticipate any of the difficulties they manage to overcome; indeed, the very phrase, "where is the stranger from?" which he had imagined would die in Aegisthus's throat before he could utter it, is spoken by the slave doorkeeper (575, 657). Orestes, moreover, did not even expect to be welcomed, "since the house is inspired by evils" (570), let alone be welcomed by his mother. In the entire rehearsal of his contingency plans, he never mentioned Clytemestra. "Mother" never crosses his lips until he says, "Pylades, what shall I do? Shall I shrink from killing my mother?"(899).

Perhaps, however, what most distinguishes the second from the first part of the play is the absence of Electra. She does not speak after Orestes asks the Chorus about the dream; she has no part in the murder (554). Orestes spares Electra against her will and the expectation of the Chorus (473, 481–82; cf. 279). The incoherence of his plan seems to be a way of freeing her from even the charge of conspiracy.[44] Orestes faces the Furies alone because he has arranged to face his mother alone. If, however, he had strictly complied with the oracle, he would never have faced his mother at all; he would have killed her as he had Aegisthus (and as Clytemestra had killed Agamemnon), without ever revealing why she was to be killed and who he was (cf. 555–59, 831–32). Orestes, however, cannot bring himself to act as if he is the pure executor of the law, any more than he can let Electra participate in the killing. That Apollo defends him anyway, despite his disobedience, is a sign perhaps of the violent grace of the Olympian gods.

V

Sophocles' *Oedipus Tyrannus* seems to be the most systematically ambiguous of all Greek tragedies. It admits of two entirely different interpretations, neither of which seems to be a deeper version of the other. The first interpretation takes its bearings from Oedipus, the second from the plot. For the first the plot is nothing but an instrument of disclosure; and whatever difficulties there are in it do not detract from the showing of Oedipus. The second interpretation refuses to ignore the knots that complicate the plot unnecessarily. We begin to wonder whether Sophoclean irony truly consists in our knowledge and Oedipus's ignorance, or rather in our own ignorance of which we never become aware. Each interpretation has to be worked out separately from the other before they can be joined together to illuminate what is darker than either Oedipus or the plot—the gods.

Any interpretation of Oedipus has to face this riddle: What is the necessary connection between Oedipus's solution to the riddle of the Sphinx and Oedipus's two crimes? This riddle, to which Oedipus gave the answer "man," was, What walks on four legs in the morning, two at midday, and on three at evening? Is the answer that Oedipus gave the cognitive equivalent to the actions of patricide and incest? That Oedipus is, as the Chorus say, the paradigm of man—he shows that beneath all the show man is nothing but show (1186–96)—does not seem to require that he know what walks on four feet in the morning, two feet in the afternoon, and three in the evening. The universality that Oedipus supposedly represents sits awkwardly with his uniqueness; *he* never crawled on four feet or walked on two. A sign, however, of their connection is his name. His name means either "Swollen Foot " or "Know-Where."[45] Inasmuch as it identifies him either as his body or his mind, it identifies him as both: the two identifications might be the same. When Oedipus explains his self-blinding, he adds that had there been a way of closing off his hearing, he would have done that too. "For the mind to dwell outside of evils is sweet" (1389–90). Oedipus assumes that his mind would vanish with his seeing and hearing; indeed, he has already identified

Tiresias's blindness with his deafness and his mindlessness (371). Oedipus, therefore, through his denial of any separation between body and mind, can identify happiness with ignorance and knowledge with misery. His wish to be a Lucretian "blind body" agrees not only with Jocasta's assertion that to live at random is best but with his own boast that he is the son of Chance (977–79, 1080). To see through seeming—the riddle—is to discover that there is nothing but seeming: the king is his father, his wife, his mother. Oedipus saw through the riddle but not through the form of the riddle, in which man's distinguishing feature was a corporeal one that changed in number but not in kind.

Oedipus is first challenged to reflect on the connection between the Sphinx and the plague in the first scene. A priest describes his petitioners: "You see what ages we are who sit at your altars: some do not yet have the strength to fly far, others are priests heavy with age—I am of Zeus—and others are a chosen band of still unmarried men" (15–19). Oedipus is here confronted with a divergent solution to the riddle, whereby aged priests replace the aged and bachelors replace man the biped. The sacred and the sexual, neither of which was in either the riddle or its solution, are now in front of him. Not only, then, is the prohibition against incest encoded here in its inconspicuousness and thereby imitated, but by contrast a link is hinted at between the solution "man" and the asexual and the nonsacred. The link is made explicit in the first stasimon of the *Antigone,* where the gods do not pose any limit for man and man in his uncanniness is a neuter "this" (334). It would seem that Oedipus does not know what his solution means, which is that man as he understands him is independent throughout his life; the sacred involved in his beginning (incest-prohibition) and the sacred involved in his end (burial) do not pertain to man as man. Oedipus, in any case, does not now reflect on the absence of any women before him, let alone the nature of the plague: "The city is wasting away in the earth's seedpods of fruit, it is wasting away in the herds of cattle, and the aborted birth of women (25–27, 171–73)." That barrenness is the way in which the city is being punished for harboring a regicide does not puzzle him. It is as if he had never heard of the old wives' tale that links incest and degenerate offspring. As the son of chance, coincidence is for him without significance. In his first speech he called all of those assembled before him, despite the disparity in their ages, children (1, 6).

Oedipus soon defines himself: "Children to be pitied, you have approached me desiring what is known and not unknown to me. I know well that all of you are ill, and though you are ill there is not one among you who is as ill as I am, for your distress comes to you alone and by yourself, but my soul groans together for the city, for me, and for each one of you" (58–64). Oedipus takes it for granted that he is unique; he is the only one who can bridge the gap between the city and the individual: he inserts "me" between "the city" and "you" (singular). He thereby implies that he is different from both the extremes that he joins together. He comprehends both the public and the private, while remaining a separate one. Asked by Creon whether he is to report the oracle to Oedipus alone inside or to the assembly, he replies,"Announce it to all. I bear a grief for them more than for my own soul" (93–94). The soul of Oedipus discounts the soul of Oedipus. He is the uniquely selfless self. He alone has nothing to hide.

The objectivity of his solution to the riddle is of a piece with the disinterestedness with which he accepted the city's gift of the monarchy and the queen (383–84). His indignation at Tiresias's silence is the result of Tiresias's refusal to help the city—Tiresias never says "city," Oedipus speaks of it five times—and the old man's harping on himself: Tiresias says "I" eight times to Oedipus's once (396). The sacred is indifferent if not hostile to the city. Tiresias pretends that had he known why Oedipus summoned him he would not have come (316–18). Oedipus, on the other hand, is devoted wholly to the city. His chance success of solving the riddle, Tiresias tells him, destroyed him. "It's no concern of mine," Oedipus replies, "if I saved this city" (443). His open anger testifies to the purity of his public-spiritedness; he does not stop to calculate, as Creon does, how to combine the profitable with the noble (595). There is for him only the city, since he *is* the city (625–30).

Oedipus's transparency extends even to his language. He speaks all the time as if he knew from the start what he set out to discover. Creon says that Laius was killed by highwaymen, Oedipus picks it up with "highwayman" (122, 124). "Since I now have," he tells the Chorus, "the rule that he had before, and have his bed and wife, in whom we both did sow, common would be the offspring of common children if his family had not been unfortunate; but as it is, chance swooped upon his head; but in exchange for this, just as if for my own father, I shall fight on his behalf" (258–65). Oedipus cannot speak metaphorically; everything he says is literally true. Such literalness would seem not only to do away with poetry but with dreams. The imaginary would be reality. That which Jocasta tells him has already happened to many—in their dreams they slept with their mother—has already happened to him without dreaming (981–82). Oedipus has nothing private to turn to, away from others. His destruction of the family is therefore the indispensable means for grounding his own self-understanding. Oedipus did unwittingly what he would have had to do knowingly if he was going to be what he says he is. He finds, however, that he cannot will retroactively the condition that defines him. His self-blinding seems to be an attempt on his part to restore the private condition he destroyed: Creon granted him his wish to be allowed to touch his daughters (1466–77). "It is holy," Creon had told him, "only for those in the family to see and hear the evils of the family" (1430–31). Oedipus has become opaque (1326).

This interpretation of Oedipus's fate makes him out to be a root of the city that the city needs but cannot afford to have represented. Thebes is autochthonous. Its present generation is the offspring of the dragon teeth that Cadmus once sowed (1). The Thebans as Thebans have only one mother; they are therefore fraternally bound with one another and isolated from everyone else. Oedipus's son Eteocles, in Aeschylus's *Seven Against Thebes,* appeals to the citizens to defend their "dearest nurse, Mother Earth" (16; cf. 422–26, 476); he does not ask them to defend their "natural" parents. The fraternity of the Thebans, however, necessarily entails incest, for any weakening in the sense of mother weakens the justice of their claim to Theban territory. And yet to treat their claim literally is to accept Oedipus's criminality: "How in the world, how in the world, could your father's furrows have put up with you in silence for so long?" (1210–12). The Chorus's question admits of an answer if his father's furrows are not Jocasta, but insofar as they are Jocasta, Oedipus has violated the indispensable condition for the existence of the city, the prohibition against endogamous marriages. That prohibition allows for the bonding of the city's families *qua* families, but not for the bonding of the citizens *qua* citizens, which can only be effected if the prohibition against incest that holds for each family does not hold for the city as a whole. Oedipus's identification of himself with the city cancels of necessity that prohibition, and that cancellation in turn makes Oedipus the one true citizen of Thebes. Oedipus is the tyrant (873–82) whose illegitimacy legitimates the city.

Oedipus's blindness seems to be set off against a neutral background of Theban awareness. He alone does not know where he stands; everyone else is in place. His way is solely a way of self-discovery, for no one else needs to be exposed. We are first compelled to question this when Creon tells Oedipus that Laius was the former king: "I know by hearsay, for I have not yet seen him" (105). We are so bemused by our being one up on Oedipus that we fail to weigh carefully Creon's reply: "[The oracle] now plainly orders us to punish by force his murderers" (106–7). Oedipus is told for the first time that Laius was murdered;[46] and if Creon is reporting accurately, the oracle uses the plural "murderers." The plural is for the moment not troublesome, but Oedipus's ignorance of Laius's murder is. Since only the sequence—Laius's murder, Oedipus's arrival at Thebes—is necessary to the plot, not the interval between them, Oedipus could have taken the road to Daulia after the killing rather than have continued on his way to Thebes. A lapse of a year or so would not have altered anything essential, and it would have made the Thebans' silence, to say nothing of Jocasta's and Creon's, much more plausible; as it is, the squeeze on time brings in its train a more serious awkwardness. Laius left Thebes in order to consult the oracle at Delphi (115); he told no one of the purpose of his journey, but it is easy enough to suspect that he wanted to have it confirmed that he had indeed thwarted the oracle. His action on the road strengthens this suspicion, for, according to Oedipus, when Oedipus was passing by the cart, after he had struck in anger the driver, Laius (if it was he) without provocation aimed a blow at Oedipus's head. Laius, it seems, was taking no chances that this young man might be his son.

However this may be, Laius left Thebes prior to the coming of the Sphinx, and Oedipus arrived at Thebes just after the coming of the Sphinx. Oedipus only now learns of this sequence. Creon agrees that if highwaymen or a highwayman killed Laius, the assassination must have been planned at Thebes; no one would have dared such a crime unless he had been bribed (124–26). Laius's assassination must have had a political purpose, and only Oedipus's timely solution of the riddle forestalled a coup d'état. Since Creon alone stood to gain by Laius's death, and since Creon had suggested that the king tell him in secret of the oracle, Oedipus's accusation against Creon is not a sign of his ungovernable temper but a display of his shrewdness. Oedipus is rightly puzzled by the Thebans' failure to investigate Laius's murder. Creon's excuse would only deepen his suspicions. "The complex-singing Sphinx led us to forego what was not evident and examine what was at our feet" (130–31). In itself, the excuse is plausible; but in the given time-span it almost suffices to convict Creon (cf. 566–67). Within days if not hours of the posing of the riddle, the riddle was solved (736). The allusion in Creon's words to Oedipus's condition has distracted us; it would not have distracted Oedipus, who would not understand why the Thebans had not put him to this second test. "Even if the master was not divinely ordained," he tells the Chorus, "it was not proper for you to let it go unpurified" (255–56). That Oedipus did not connect the killing of Laius with the availability of the Theban throne should not surprise us, given that he was ignorant of the former; but that the Thebans were never puzzled by the coincidence of his arrival with the report of Laius's death should surprise us. If Oedipus had to conclude either that the Thebans were incapable of putting two and two together, or that he must have stumbled on a conspiracy, who but a madman would not have chosen to err on the side of reason?

Sophocles has combined an ironic linguistic surface that holds no riddles for us with an ironic structure of actions for which we have no guide. He has made us experience the collapse of the coherence of seeming: the dreamworld is not Oedipus's but our own. We are turned into Thebans, for whom nothing has to make any sense. Jocasta must have long noted the close resemblance Oedipus bears to Laius (743), but she casually mentions it as if it were of no significance. There is no necessity, after all, that resemblance entail consanguinity. The servant who escaped from Laius's retinue saw no reason why he should denounce Oedipus. He was so afraid apparently that his lie would be exposed—there was no band of highwaymen—that he preferred to let a regicide be king; indeed, since he must have known that the baby he declined to kill had grown up to be a prince of the royal house of Corinth, it must be said that he preferred to allow Oedipus to commit incest rather than to be known as a liar. As the sole survivor from Laius's retinue, he would have been no doubt reluctant to tell the truth, for the suspicion would have been strong that he had abetted a single assassin; but in the face of the alternative—an incestuous regicide on the throne at Thebes—his silence seems inexcusable. He must have convinced himself that the violation of the law, no matter how sacred the law is, does not count as long as it is not publicly known. He asked leave of Jocasta so that he would not have to face Oedipus with his guilty knowledge (758–62); but he believed, as does Oedipus, that even here the saying holds good, "Out of sight, out of mind."

"It is best to live at random, as much as one can. Don't fear marriage with your mother. Many mortals have already even in dreams slept with their mother. But to whomever these things are as nothing, he bears his life most easily" (979–83). This principle, which Jocasta lays down, presumably only to cajole Oedipus out of his terror of the oracle, simply formulates the universal practice among the Thebans. Since the events of the play seem to refute the principle, Sophocles has checked us from wondering whether or not the Thebans have any evidence for their adherence to it.

Of the three ways of access to the truth, two are divine, one human.

Apollo cannot be compelled, Oedipus says, to yield up any more than he has; Tiresias knows the truth but cannot or will not offer any way of verifying it; the servant who was an eyewitness lies. That "many" cannot be equal to "one" is Oedipus's ultimate refuge (843). As long as that inequality holds, Oedipus is not guilty of regicide. Jocasta's confidence in its truthfulness seems to be grounded on nothing more than her equation of public knowledge with truth: "Know that this was expressly said, and he cannot cast it out again: the city heard it, not I alone" (848–50). Oedipus's confidence, on the other hand, is grounded more firmly. His own account cannot possibly be squared with his guilt, for he states that at the crossroads he slew them all (813). No one escaped, for if one had escaped, the coincidence of the five in Laius's retinue and the five in Oedipus's story, with one fugitive from each group, could not but have convinced Oedipus that he had indeed slain Laius. Jocasta, moreover, gives two versions of the crucial sequence. The first conforms with our belief: the city was informed of Laius's murder shortly before Oedipus was declared king (736–38). But twenty lines later, Jocasta inverts the sequence: "When [the servant] returned from there (i.e., the place where Laius was murdered) and saw that you had the throne and Laius was dead, he took me by the hand and begged me to send him to the fields and pastures of the flocks" (758–61). Oedipus, then, had already solved the riddle, won the throne, and married the queen before the city knew that Laius had been murdered.

This sequence certainly saves the morality of the servant, who might well believe that no harm is done if both mother and son remain ignorant. But his morality is saved at a preposterous cost. Laius's murder would now have to be proclaimed to everyone but Oedipus. And yet, is this more difficult to believe than the accepted version, that with nothing to hide, no one at Thebes ever hinted at Laius's murder? We know that Jocasta did not wear mourning at her wedding. But, the objection runs, this alternate sequence means that in the course of a single day two retinues of five men each, each with one mule-cart and one herald, passed the same spot on the road to Delphi. Is *this* more difficult to believe than that the servant who fled from the scene just happened to be the servant to whom Laius had entrusted the baby Oedipus? And that the Corinthian messenger who came to report Polybus's death just happened to be the shepherd to whom Laius's servant handed over the baby Oedipus? Once coincidences are accepted, one more or less cannot matter. It would not have troubled either Jocasta or the city that with Laius still alive she was committing bigamy. Jocasta certainly feels no guilt that, if the oracle delivered to Laius were false, she and Laius were guilty of the gratuitous murder of their son.

Either Oedipus killed his father and married his mother, or he married his mother but did not kill his father. In the former case, the oracle is vindicated, in the latter it is not. In the former case, the gods would seem to be malevolent, ready to have a man violate their own sacred laws in order to prove that their oracles are true. Oedipus had assumed that the prophecy was conditional: if he went back to Corinth, he would fulfill the oracle. And the gods surely cannot believe that the clarity of divine prohibition is less revealing of themselves than the obscurity of oracular pronouncements. Even if one grants that the more the law becomes "second nature" the less its author is recognized, there still seems to be no necessity that the revelation of the legislator be at the expense of the authority of the legislation. Oedipus, at any rate, does not need to be punished in order to know that the prohibition against incest is sacred: "Never, never, O holy majesty of the gods, might I see that day, but might I vanish before I see the taint of such a calamity upon me" (830–33; cf. 863–73).

If, on the other hand, Oedipus did not kill Laius, there would be no actual connection between the oracle that limited the cause of the plague to Laius's murder and Oedipus's detective work. The gods would thus have let Oedipus make that connection on his own. He alone would be responsible, through error, for discovering his crimes. It seems at first that Tiresias's presence argues against this, but Tiresias, for all the effect he has, could just as well have remained silent about both Oedipus's patricide and incest. Neither Oedipus nor the Chorus ever mention that part of the prophecy, Oedipus because he believes it agrees with the oracle he had already construed, the Chorus because, being Thebans, they never notice anything. Tiresias, of course, could not have anticipated that he would be so ignored, but Tiresias contradicts himself. He states on his entrance that had he known why he was summoned he would not have come; and he states on his exit that he has said all that he had come to say (447).

Tiresias apparently provoked Oedipus so that he could pretend to blurt out in anger what he had planned to say all along. If so, his plan backfired; Jocasta and Jocasta alone made Oedipus afraid through her wish to prove to him the unreliability of oracles. Oedipus himself, moreover, initiated his own fate by believing a drunkard rather than his putative parents. If Oedipus had been a true Theban, he would have shrugged off the drunkard's remark; and if Corinth had been a Thebes, a rumor about his illegitimacy would never have spread (779–86). The threat that the rumor posed to the Corinthian monarchy reinforced Oedipus's own unease. The gods, it seems, use simply human experiences as such in order to accomplish their end. These experiences are enthusiastic: they have the gods within them and are wholly independent of the truth or falsity of oracles and divines.

Admittedly, the story of Oedipus does not seem to deal with the human at all; rather, it seems to present man with an inhuman choice. Either everything happens by chance and nothing is intelligible, or nothing happens by chance and everything is intelligible, but with this proviso: the possibility of discovering the pattern is remote, for it too depends on chance, and the pattern once discovered is sure to make life unlivable. There are either no gods or gods whose graciousness solely consists in guaranteeing that we shall never find out that they exist.

To believe in chance is to be inspired by grace. We must wish for the Theban condition. This wish, however, can not only never be granted us, for Oedipus has destroyed its possibility once and for all, but the disenchantment of the Thebans cannot be a matter of regret. One wonders, then, whether Oedipus is altogether disenchanting: he does not kill himself. The Chorus do not know why Oedipus chose a life of blindness rather than death. Oedipus explains: "Had I gone to Hades, I do not know with what eyes I would in seeing have beheld my father, nor in turn my miserable mother, to both of whom I have done things that deserve more than hanging (1371–74)." Oedipus's unwilled crimes uncover in him an autonomous element of shame. Shame is the human experience that reveals the gods. Oedipus now knows that Hades exists. Hades is the god of whom a man like Oedipus alone can never have any experience (cf. 972, 987). It needs crimes as terrible as his to infuse human shame with divinity.

Oedipus can now enlighten the Thebans. The Chorus had told us, though no one, not even Tiresias or the priest of Zeus had remarked on it, that the corpses of the plague's victims were being left unburied 180–89; cf. 29–30). The Theban's disregard of this divine law is of a piece with the rest of their practice; the Chorus make it plain that only women—wives and aged mothers—bewailed the absence of due burial rites. Faced, then, with the Thebans' invincible ignorance and undefiant impiety, the gods found that Oedipus was indispensable: he charged Creon with the task of burying Jocasta (1446–48). That the divine law of burial is the underground theme of the Oedipus story is suggested both by his daughter's sacrificial defense of it and his own peculiar end. Oedipus, who believed he was his own origin, is the only man who ever buried himself.[47]

Oedipus's shame is that which distinguishes him from the virtuous man *(epieikēs),* who Aristotle says should not be the subject of tragedy.[48] At the end of his analysis of the moral virtues (apart from justice and prudence), the last one of which is wittiness or "educated insolence," Aristotle denies that shame belongs to the virtuous *(epieikēs),* regardless of whether some things are truly shameful and others are only thought to be shameful. The virtuous man will not do either because he ought not to do either; and even if he does, he will not have willed it, and shame can only be for what is willed.[49] Oedipus's shame, on the other hand, is for what he neither willed nor can will; it can only be ascribed to his imaginative experience of that which puts an inviolable limit to his seeing. Hades the invisible recovers the nakedness of his parents. The prohibition against incest thus comes together with the command to bury the dead. They are united in Hades, through Hades, and by Hades, for without Hades, parents cease to be anything but sexual beings and corpses cease to be anything but carrion. In guarding man against man's possible bestialization (through incest and cannibalism), Hades sanctifies the so-called humanity of man. This function of Hades is due almost entirely to the poets; it is their gift to the city and its laws.[50] Homer has Achilles say, after he has seen a perfect likeness of the dead Patroclus, "So even in the house of Hades soul and image are, after all, something."[51] Hades is the locus of the reality of the image; it is the natural home of the poet.

VI

Of the four philosophers who have discussed tragedy, two are ancient, two modern. For Plato and Aristotle, *Oedipus Tyrannus* was the paradigmatic tragedy, for Hegel it was *Antigone,* and for Nietzsche, Euripides' *Bacchae.* Plato and Hegel agree at least in setting tragedy against the background of the city, for both detect in the sacred an unassimilable albeit indispensable element of the city, and Aristotle too, insofar as his morally virtuous man is to be proof against the tragic experience of Oedipus, can be grouped with them; but Nietzsche's account of tragedy does not seem to take its bearings by the sacred city. His theme is rather the poet than the poem. Accordingly, the *Bacchae* is his play, for it is in a sense the same Dionysus who schemes to reveal himself to the Thebans and is the god of the Attic theater. The *Bacchae* is almost a tragedy about tragedy: it begins with the god's explanation of his human disguise. Unless the god of the theater goes masked, he cannot reveal himself to be the god he is.

The paradox of a concealed god attempting to become manifest shows up in the various formulations that Dionysus gives of his purpose. "I have come," he begins, "the son of Zeus, Dionysus, to the land of the Thebans" (1–2); but two lines later he says, "Transformed from a god into a mortal shape I am here at the stream of Dirce and the water of Ismenus." He then tells us that Thebes is the first Greek city he has come to, after he had established his dances and rites throughout Asia Minor, "in order that I might be a god manifest to mortals" (22).

Now, either the cult itself or the initiatory rites of the cult sufficed elsewhere to reveal Dionysus, whereas Thebes must learn not only that it is uninitiated in his rites but that his defense of his mother consists in his coming to light for mortals as a god she bore to Zeus (39–42). The Dionysian creed has a codicil at Thebes: Dionysus is a god born from a mortal woman. But the action of the *Bacchae* is that Pentheus, the king of Thebes, is at war with Dionysus; he excludes him from his libations and prayers, "on account of which I shall point out to him and all the Thebans that I am born a god" (47). Dionysus does not want any special worship at Thebes, but he cannot gain acceptance there unless he treats it as a special case. Once he has settled things at Thebes, he will move on, "showing myself," as he says; "but if the city of Thebans in anger seeks with arms to drive the bacchants from the mountains, I shall join forces with the maenads: it is for this purpose I have altered into a mortal form and changed my shape into the nature of a man" (50–54). Pentheus's war against Dionysus, then, requires the disclosure of Dionysus; Pentheus's war against his crazed followers requires the concealment of Dionysus. Since, however, Dionysus's own actions abort the second possibility and yet do not strip him of his disguise, Pentheus seems to be punished for not seeing through what was designed to be opaque. Pentheus suffers for Dionysus's frustration of his own plan.

The worship of Dionysus cannot consist with the recognition of Dionysus. The Chorus worship Dionysus according to convention (430–33, 712, 890–96); they hear but never see Dionysus (577, 590). Pentheus comes to obey Dionysus, but he then sees him as a bull (920–22); he does not submit to him as Dionysus. Belief and knowledge are of different orders; their inconvertibility is a lesson that Dionysus too has to learn. Although he sees the smoldering ruins near the palace, which bear witness to his mother's vain attempt to see Zeus as he is in himself, he does not realize their application to himself (6–9).[52] Tempted by Hera to confirm by autopsy that Zeus was truly her lover, and thus to confute her sister's claim that she had imputed Zeus to her own disgrace, Semele prevailed on Zeus to show himself and was burned to a crisp for her presumption. The gods, however native, are forever strangers; they can cease to be strangers if they are willing to give up their being for their being believed. Dionysus testifies to the primacy of the latter in the course of his report to the Chorus on how he eluded Pentheus: "Thinking he was binding me, [Pentheus] could not touch me, but, fed on hopes, he found a bull in the stall, where he had led me, and tried to shackle its knees and hooves, breathing out his anger, dripping sweat from his body, and biting his lips; and I sat by and quietly looked on. At that moment Dionysus came and rattled the palace and lit a fire at the tomb of his mother; and Pentheus when he saw it, thinking the palace was on fire, rushed about in distraction, ordering his servants to bring water, and every slave was engaged but all in vain; but Pentheus, dropping this task, seized a sword and rushed into the palace—as if I had escaped—and then Dionysus, as it appears to me, I speak only belief, made an apparition in the courtyard; and Pentheus rushed at that and stabbed the brilliant air, as though he were slaying me" (616–31).

There are altogether four gods in this account: (1) the god who speaks, (2) the god who certainly rattled the palace, (3) the god who apparently made (4) an apparition of (1). Pentheus confounded the first with the fourth Dionysus, but the first is a disguise of the second; the fourth too, then, in being no more an illusion than the first, must be indistinguishable from it. Did Pentheus go after the real apparition of Dionysus, and is the Dionysus who now speaks its illusory double (cf. 286–97)? Perhaps Dionysus himself cannot tell; his words, "as it appears to me, I speak only belief," could express his own uncertainty as to whether he really did make an image of an image; but possibly the fourth Dionysus, no less than the third, is only in speech: the first Dionysus would have had to invent him in any case if he were going to remain incognito to the Chorus.

The puzzle Dionysus has set for himself, trying to do what Zeus could not, comes out clearly in his first confrontation with Pentheus. Dionysus asserts that his own initiation occurred face-to-face with Dionysus. Pentheus asks what visible aspect the rites (or instruments) of initiation have. Dionysus replies, "The uninitiated are not to know what cannot be said" (472). Pentheus then asks what benefit is conferred on those who sacrifice. Dionysus replies, "It is not allowed for you to hear, but it deserves to be known" (474). Pentheus cannot know before he is initiated; he refuses to be initiated before he knows. He must have belief prior to knowledge; his conversion cannot be grounded on either present evidence or promised good.

The stubbornness of Pentheus is amazing. Not one miracle opens his eyes. His servant reports that the bacchants bound in a public prison had had their shackles loosened of their own accord, "and keys unlocked the door without mortal hand" (488). This first miracle Pentheus does not even comment on; the second miracle—his bound prisoner escapes—puzzles him enough to ask how he did it, but not enough to wait for an answer (642–46). The third miracle—the burning of his palace and the collapse of some of its beams—gets him to call his servants, but he himself soon loses any interest in it. The fourth miracle, again a report—that one bacchant when she struck a rock with the thyrsus opened up a gushing spring, another produced a fountain of wine, still others scratched the soil and got milk, and honey dripped from ivy-covered thyrsi—all this provokes his servant to say, "If you had been there, the god you now blame, you would have approached with prayers" (711–12); but Pentheus does not even bother to argue him out of his delusion. The fifth miracle hardly has a parallel in Greek literature. "At the appointed time the bacchants shook their thyrsi for bacchic rites, invoking Iacchus with collective voice the son of Zeus; and the whole mountain joined in bacchic revelry and every beast, and nothing was not in motion" (723–27). A mountain dances; Pentheus is unaffected. The sixth miracle consists in the rout of his men, and the seventh in the utter destruction of a village (728–64). These last two events only serve to convince Pentheus that the women could not resist heavy-armed troops (780–86); they do not convince him that a god is behind them.

Euripides did not assign such stubbornness to Pentheus merely to comment on miracles; he also wanted to present through Pentheus our own condition as audience. We are asked to imagine Pentheus as a spectator who comes to the theater after *The Bacchae* has begun; he has not heard the prologue but must still try to figure out the plot without Dionysus's help. We are further asked to imagine that Pentheus comes without a program; indeed, he has never been to the theater before. The collapse of the palace is for him neither a miracle nor its image; it is crushed cardboard. A stagehand pulled some strings, he does not know exactly how, but if he wanted he could learn the trick too. We, however, without even thinking about it, see triple: there is Dionysus, there is Dionysus disguised as a man, there is a man playing the disguised Dionysus. The play does not work unless we believe in exactly this way, but we must be very hard put to persuade the naive Pentheus we have imagined that he must believe as we do. That is the difficulty Dionysus solves: he persuades the reluctant spectator Pentheus to become part of his drama. He gets him to imitate a bacchant, and once caught up in his role he is ripe for conversion. The conversion of Pentheus is the paradigm of the willing suspension of disbelief.

Dionysus deters Pentheus from sending armed troops against the Theban women. It is not clear why he should prefer to destroy Pentheus alone and unarmed; the effect is to diminish the miraculousness of Pentheus's destruction and therefore to suggest either that Pentheus armed is proof against conversion or that Pentheus, unmoved by ostentatious miracles, must be converted in another way. Pentheus promises the stranger he will sacrifice all the women, "as they deserve" (796); the stranger predicts a shameful rout; Pentheus gets exasperated and will not listen any longer; the stranger proposes another way, whereby he will bring back the women without arms; once more Pentheus scorns the stranger and calls for his arms. Pentheus's arms act as almost a magical charm against enchantment, and inasmuch as Pentheus is presented as if he were the only active male citizen of Thebes—Cadmus and Tiresias sound like doddering drunkards—his armor can be said to stand in for the city. The enchantment of the city is his sole protection against the enchantment of the stranger.

Pentheus begins to be disarmed when Dionysus asks whether he would not want to see the women sitting together in the mountains (811). Over and above the latent prurience of Pentheus, to which Dionysus appeals, the pleasure Pentheus would obtain from the painful sight of drunk women is due to his quietly contemplating their future punishment. Dionysus objects that they will track him down if he goes in secret; Pentheus sees at once that secrecy belongs to the kind of rites that the stranger is introducing and is not consonant with the openness of the politically noble; but he forgets that punishment, no matter how just, is not necessarily noble. Dionysus appears to go along with Pentheus's revised plan, but he orders him to dress up in women's clothes. Pentheus is shocked. After having been reminded of the noble, he is urged to be shameless. Dionysus explains, "lest they kill you if you are seen there as a man." Pentheus accepts the explanation; despite his armor, he is suddenly afraid of being killed. Pentheus panics. The cause of panic was the fourth of the seven attributes that Tiresias assigned to Dionysus: "He has a share as well in Ares: terror flusters an army under arms and at its station before it touches a spear" (302–4).

Panic is groundless fear. It is itself the cause of the result that it fears. It makes inevitable the possible and brings about the conviction of fate: *The Bacchae* is the only extant play of Euripides in which the word "chance" does not occur. But to say that Dionysus is the cause of causeless fear is to say no more than that the disguised Dionysus is the cause of Pentheus's panic. Pentheus panics through the stranger's recommendation of extreme caution. Terror parading as unmanly moderation is Dionysus's specialty: the true miracle of the bacchants is their chastity, sobriety, and decency (686–88, 940). Pentheus experiences his fear as reasonableness (826); what still holds him back is shame (828); even as he enters the palace, he still hesitates to follow Dionysus's counsel. Euripides has brought Pentheus to the point of conversion and stopped; even though Dionysus promises the Chorus that Pentheus will be punished, he still has to invoke himself in order to make Pentheus senseless, "for if he is of sound mind, he will never be willing to put on female dress" (851–52). Since the next scene shows Pentheus fully converted, Euripides seems to have denied us the very moment of conversion;[53] all we see and hear is the result: "Bring me through the middle of Thebes: I am the only man among them who dares this" (961–62). Prior to his conversion, Pentheus had to be assured that Dionysus would lead him through Thebes unobserved (840–42); now he boasts that he has achieved the peak of manliness. Pentheus comes to terms with his panic by representing his adoption of female dress as courage. He is now too manly to need the trappings of manliness. To be unafraid of disgrace covers the formula for both shamelessness and courage, but while the formula seems to sponsor the defiance of convention, it conceals death under convention. Death is a kind of bashfulness that Pentheus has outgrown. He is now too noble to prevail over women by force (953). This is now his sober interpretation of his former fear that they would kill him.

Euripides' showing of fear is the pendant to Sophocles' showing of shame; and just as shame is the passion with which Aristotle ends his account of the moral virtues, so fear is the passion with which he begins: the blush of shame and the paleness of fear comprehend the moral virtues. Courage, however, unlike shame, is for Aristotle a virtue, but it gives him the most trouble. Courage is the only virtue that he admits can also be spoken of in five spurious ways.[54] Political courage, which shame partly constitutes, is the highest form of these phantoms. But what is true courage is left unexplained. It must be in the service of the noble, but what the noble could be that on the field of battle transcends the sacred fatherland and yet is not an "ideal" seems to resist definition. Not only does courage alone fail to bear the sign of virtue—its performance must be with pleasure (1117b15–16)—but courage is shadowed by Hades, and Aristotle allows that Hades' existence might affect the way in which human happiness is judged (1100a10–30, 1101a22–b9). Fear and shame, then, are a kind of residue in virtue as virtue is ordinarily understood; they are accordingly the tragic passions. Their resistance to enlightenment is a function of their inextricable involvement with Hades, and Hades is the soul of tragedy.

Agathias in his *Histories* (2.30–31) tells the following story. Seven Greek philosophers, dissatisfied with the prevailing opinion about God (i.e., Christianity), and falsely informed about the state of Persia, that its people were just and its ruler Plato's philosopher-king, decided to leave the place where the laws forbade them from living without fear and to settle in Persia, despite its alien and incompatible customs. Although they were royally entertained, they found that neither the Persians nor their king lived up to what they had heard; and on their journey back—the Persian king stipulating in his treaty with Byzantium that they were to be left alone regardless of their opinions—they came across the corpse of a man lately dead, tossed aside, in accordance with Persian customs, without burial. Out of compassion for the lawlessness of the barbarian law, and in the belief that it was not holy to allow, as far as it lay in their power, nature to be wronged, they had their attendants prepare the body for burial and then bury it in a mound of earth. That night one of the philosophers had a dream: a man whom he did not know and who bore no resemblance to anyone he knew, but for all of that with an august countenance and the beard and dress of a philosopher, seemed to address him with the following injunction: "Do not bury the unburiable; let him be prey to dogs. Earth, mother of all, does not accept the mother-corrupting man." Neither the dreamer nor his comrades could make anything of the dream; but on continuing their journey, and the lay of the land being such that they were compelled to retrace their steps, they came across the corpse they had buried the day before lying naked on the ground, "as though the earth of its own accord had cast it up and refused to save it from being eaten." Thunderstruck at the sight, the philosophers made no further attempt to perform any of the burial rites. They concluded that the Persians remain unburied as a punishment for their committing incest with their mothers and are justly torn apart by dogs.

This story measures the distance between us and Greek tragedy. When Gibbon retold it, he followed Agathias in all particulars but one: he omitted any mention of what befell the philosophers on their journey back. The sacred did not fit readily into his opposition between superstition and enlightenment.

Notes

1. *Philebus* 50b3.

2. *Symposium* 223d3–6.

3. Euripides experimented in his last play, *Iphigenia at Aulis,* with having the protagonist wholly invisible: the army with its demagogic leader never appears, but nonetheless determines the action. The army is the locus of morality: they need to punish Paris in order to deter other wives from following the way of Helen (543–57).

4. *Frogs* 1023–24.

5. Cf. *Republic* 604c1–d2.

6. Even more striking than this mistake of Clytemestra is her acceptance of the role in which Cassandra has imaginatively cast her (*Agamemnon* 1497–1504). She needs the support of the divine in order to ground her sense of right, even though the right supported by the divine (Thyestes' curse) does not ground her right (Iphigeneia's sacrifice).

7. *Politics* 1328b11–12; cf. *Nicomachean Ethics* 1145a10–11.

8. *Nicomachean Ethics* 1145a15–33.

9. Sophocles *Oedipus at Colonus* 1132–34.

10. Cf. Plato *Republic* 378c7.

11. Cf. Sophocles *Oedipus Tyrannus* 1409.

12. *Digest* 28.7.15.

13. Racine indicates this in the following way: Although he follows closely either Seneca or Euripides in his *Phèdre,* he departs from both in adding to Théramène's account of Hippolyte's death the fact that when the monster came out of the sea, everyone else took refuge in a neighboring temple and was saved, "without arming themselves with a useless courage" (5.6), but Hippolyte went out and faced it. This departure from his sources is connected with another, apparently formal change: Hippolyte is no longer chaste but secretly in love with Aricie, who has been forbidden by Thésée to have any suitors. Hippolyte's horror at Phèdre's confession of love for him arises from his recognition that he too has broken the law no less than she: the decree of his father and the prohibition against incest are equivalent. *Phèdre* is the last play on a pagan theme that Racine wrote; he retired shortly afterward to Port-Royal and drew his inspiration for his dramas from the Bible.

14. Herodotus 3.14.10.

15. Aristophanes *Frogs* 911–20.

16. *Poetics,* chapter 4.

17. *On the Parts of Animals,* 644b22–645a36.

18. 409–12; cf. Euripides *Suppliants* 760–68, 941–47.

19. "There is a passage in *Antigone* which I always look upon as a blemish, and I would give a great deal for an apt philologist to prove that it is interpolated or spurious. After the heroine has, in the course of the piece, shown the noble motives for her action, and displayed the elevated purity of her soul, she at last, when she is led to death, brings forward a motive that is quite unworthy and almost borders upon the comic." Goethe then summarizes the passage, 905–12. "This is, at least, the bare sense of the passage, which in my opinion, when placed in the mouth of a heroine going to her death, disturbs the tragic tone, and appears to me to be very far-fetched—to savor too much of dialectical calculation." *Conversations with Eckermann,* 227–28 (London, 1901).

20. *Of the Advancement of Learning,* 1.7.28.

21. Sophocles *Oedipus at Colonus* 1224.

22. Plato *Ion* 535b1–c8; Aristotle *Politics* 1342a7.

23. Cf. Plato *Symposium* 215c1–6; *Minos* 318b5–c1.

24. *Iliad* 1.188–222.

25. *Odyssey* 9.299–305.

26. Cf. Plato *Laws* 672b3–c5.

27. Cf. Thucydides 2.15–16.

28. *Republic* 414e2–6.

29. The obscurity of the Greek seems justified only if Oedipus wants to pun on his own name: "out of the way foot"—*ex hodou poda*—sounds like *Oidipodā.*

30. The usual translation assumes an unexampled construction: "Do not behold me as lawless."

31. Herodotus's second book is devoted to Egypt. Although it contains many stories, there are only three (they all involve Greeks) told in dialogic form. The first story concerns Paris and Helen—his violation of the sacred; the second concerns Amasis, a usurper, who acts in an unroyal manner; and the third also concerns Amasis, who is moved to speak because, he believes, a Greek woman from Cyrene has bewitched him (2.112–15, 173.2–4, 181). Speech comes with the departure from law: the Egyptians are excessively pious, according to Herodotus, and avoid the adoption of foreign customs (2.37.1, 9.1).

32. *Eumenides* 657–66, 736–38.

33. *Iliad* 6.354–58; cf. *Odyssey* 8.578–80.

34. Cf. Euripides *Helen* 35–41.

35. *Eumenides* 864–65.

36. *Agamemnon* 182, cf. 1206.

37. Hesiod *Works and Days* 282–85.

38. *Antigone* 626–27.

39. Cf. 475–98, 988–93.

40. This effect is acknowledged indirectly by Cicero: "Do not believe, Senators, that, as you see on the stage, wicked men by the onslaught of the gods are terrified by the burning torches of the Furies. His own deceitfulness, his own criminality, his own wickedness, his own recklessness put his mind in disarray. These are the furies, these the flames, these the torches." (*In Pisonem* 20 [46]): In Euripides *Orestes,* the difference between "conscience" and "god" appears in the following way: Menelaus is shocked to find a filthy and unkempt Orestes after the murder of his mother. He asks him, "What illness is destroying you?" Orestes replies, "Intelligence (or conscience), because I know the terrible deeds I have done." Menelaus is perplexed, partly no doubt by the use of "intelligence" to explicate illness. "What are you saying? Clarity, you know, is wisdom, not obscurity." Orestes replies, "Pain is dreadful but all the same curable" (395–99). The goddess Pain is both manageable and intelligible; "intelligence" is neither.

41. Cf. Plato *Republic* 439e6–440a3.

42. *Eumenides* 616–21.

43. Cf. Aristophanes *Acharnians* 395, *Clouds* 1145.

44. Orestes is consistent on this point. His delay in revealing himself to Electra makes sense only if he never had any intention to reveal himself. His placing a lock of hair on his father's tomb almost betrayed him (he did not suspect that Clytemestra and Aegisthus had forbidden anyone to pay his due respects to the corpse (cf. 429–50); but Electra concluded (fortunately for Orestes) that the lock meant that Orestes would not or could not return (cf. 167, 179–84); but the two sets of footprints that she then noticed forced her to realize that Orestes must have come himself and not just sent a messenger. This forced Orestes to show himself, though Electra does not recognize him (211). Why Aeschylus crossed the perfectly correct reasoning of Electra with false imaginings is a question that goes to the heart of tragic poetry.

45. The messenger from Corinth (924–26) end his first line with *mathoim' hopou* (I would learn where), his second with *Oidipou* (of Oedipus), and his last with *katisth' hopou* (you know where), all of which point to "Oedipus" as meaning "Know Where" *(Oida pou)* (cf. 1036).

46. Cf. Aristotle *Poetics* 1460a27–31.

47. Cf. *Oedipus at Colonus* 1520–21, 1599.

48. *Poetics* 1452b34–36.

49. *Nicomachean Ethics* 1128b10–33.

50. Horace says, "Sacred Orpheus, the interpreter of the gods, deterred savage men by terror from slaughter and loathsome food (i.e., cannibalism); he is said on account of this to soothe tigers and fierce lions" (*Art of Poetry* 391–93). Horace

points to the complete coincidence in the highest poetry between the useful ("deterred by terror") and the pleasant ("soothe"); cf. 333–43.

51. *Iliad* 23.103–4.

52. Euripides' *Alcestis* presents a not dissimilar lesson for Apollo. He gave his son Asclepius the power of resurrection; Zeus killed him; Apollo in anger killed the Cyclopes, in punishment for which he had to serve Admetus as a slave. Apollo rewarded the friendly treatment he received at the hands of Admetus by getting the Fates to postpone his death if he could find someone willing to die in his place. His father and mother refuse the privilege, his wife Alcestis accepts. Apollo did not understand why Zeus had disapproved of his gift of immortality; consequently, he tried to get around what he took to be Zeus's jealousy. Zeus lets him learn by a demonstration that the relations men have with one another cannot bear this kind of divine interference. Alcestis no sooner makes an offer that loses its grace if she demands recompense than she manages to make Admetus's future life intolerable (347). The demand for justice is on the part of men stronger than love with no strings attached (cf. 299–302, 336–39). The abuse that Admetus heaps on his father for his unwillingness to die for him loses all its cogency as soon as one imagines that he was addressing his mother. Zeus adds another lesson: not Apollo's son Asclepius but his own son Heracles resolves the difficulty into which Apollo has fallen.

53. Euripides does vouchsafe us something: the choral ode that intervenes between Pentheus's entrance into and exit out of the palace is devoted to punishment and happiness (862–911): the satisfaction that the punishment of enemies gives fills up the gap between the complete freedom from need that men want (and Dionysus promises) and the median contentment that is granted to them. We learn after Pentheus's death that Cadmus's one regret at the outcome is that Pentheus will no longer address him affectionately as he asks, "Who wrongs you, old man? Who dishonors you? Who disturbs and troubles your heart? Speak, so that I may punish, Father, the one who wrongs you" (1320–22).

54. *Nicomachean Ethics* 1116a15–17.

EIGHT

Physics and Tragedy: On Plato's *Cratylus*

THE *CRATYLUS* SEEMS TO BE a caricature of a Platonic dialogue. It gives us Socrates as seen in the distorting mirror of an alien inspiration. It begins as a farce and ends as a tragedy: Socrates finally invokes the "ideas" like so many *dei ex machina* in order to be saved from the perplexities of the Heraclitean flux. The suddenness of their invocation merely underlines the difficulty we experience throughout the dialogue of gauging its tone correctly. The dialogue seems to shift constantly between the playful and the serious; and though such a mixture no doubt characterizes every Platonic dialogue, the units with which it deals, names, are so small that it seems to be composed of nothing but a jumble of minute tesserae, some of which are in themselves as brilliant as any argument in Plato, while most are as desperately forced as the patter of a standup comic. The *Cratylus* has the look of a Platonic dictionary. It throws light on every other dialogue and leaves itself in the dark. Socrates' question to Polus, All the beautiful things—colors, for example, and figures, sounds, and pursuits—are you looking at nothing on each occasion that you call *(kaleis)* them beautiful *(kala)?*" (*Gorgias* 474d3–5), gets deepened if one recalls Socrates' etymology here of *kalon* (416b6–d11); but this etymology like all the rest seems to do nothing to deepen the argument of the *Cratylus.* It is, however, the thesis of this paper that not only does the profusion of etymologies deepen the argument but that in doing so it adumbrates the Platonic understanding of tragedy. The problematic relation between "goatsong" and "tragedy" is the paradigm for the linguistic as well as the nonlinguistic problem of the original and the derivative.

In order to see what is going on in the etymological section, it is necessary to start at the beginning—Hermogenes' invitation to Socrates to interpret the oracular and ironical Cratylus. Cratylus's irony consists in his saying that though Cratylus is his name, and Socrates is Socrates', Hermogenes is not Hermogenes' name, not even if all human beings call him that. Socrates at once explains the joke to Hermogenes; but it takes him most of the dialogue to figure out Cratylus the oracle. "Cratylus asserts," Hermogenes tells Socrates, "that there is a natural rightness of name for each of the beings, and a name is not whatever some have set down together to call (something), uttering a part of their own language, but there is naturally a certain rightness of names for both Greeks and barbarians, the same for all." Socrates sets out to interpret this assertion without consulting Cratylus; once the oracle has spoken, no more help can be expected from it.

If one takes Cratylus's joke as the guide to his general statement, "each of the beings" would mean each individual, and the statement would imply that the only correct name for each and every being is a proper name, and nothing is by nature a member of any class. The connection between the denial of the existence of natural classes and the thesis of Heraclitean flux is obvious; it underlies the argument that Socrates develops in the first half of the *Theaetetus.* Whatever the merits are of the Heraclitean thesis, Cratylus's joke does point to a feature of proper names. Proper names are that part of each language which are most liable to survive intact when uttered in any other language. Tacitus does not become Silent in English, nor Cicero Chickpea. The proper names of men are not in need of translation. Their invariance across all languages, despite the mispronunciation they might undergo in an alien tongue, seems to give them a natural status, not because an account can be rendered of them but because each man presents himself through his name as something that resists universalization. Our names seem to be a sign of our refusal to be explained and explained away.

Proper names are the most opaque part of any language, for not only are they left untranslated from one language to another, but even within their own language they are without meaning, regardless of how plain their meaning is. Only if A. Comfort writes a book entitled *The Joy of Sex* does meaning show through. It is therefore possible for a language to have an entirely opaque vocabulary, in which each word would be a foreign word with no known or imagined connection with any other word: Socrates suggests that "fire," "water," "dog," and "evil" are barbarian words imported into Greek (409e10–410a6, 416a1–7, 421c12–d6). Since it seems, however, most improbable that there was, is, or will be any such language, the question arises whether there is a natural way in which all languages extend their vocabularies from a number of original roots. Hermogenes, for example, employs the word *sumbalein,* which literally means "to throw together," for "to interpret" (384a5). (The extension is exactly parallel to "conjecture.") The example suggests a generalization: for human beings the corporeal is primary and the noncorporeal derivative. All languages, one might guess, are in principle anti-Platonic; but because the literal core of noncorporeal meanings tends to fade over time, all languages are more or less at any given time Platonic, for the independence of the noncorporeal is tacitly assumed. It thus seems to be impossible either to separate entirely or to collapse entirely corporeal roots and their noncorporeal extensions. Puns might be one way a language has of acknowledging this twofold impossibility. A university bookstore once put the mathematics textbook *Rings and Ideals* in its marriage section.

These two possible ways of interpreting Cratylus the oracle—the invariance of proper names and the uniformity all languages exhibit in extending their primary vocabularies—can be supplemented by a third. It is perhaps the one that would first come to mind if one heard it said that there was a natural rightness of names. A nameless Greek poet wrote the line, "I am a countryman and call a spade a spade." To call a spade a spade is literally a tautology and figuratively the sign of either boorishness or frankness. It implies that "spade" is the right word for things whose name is "spade." The saying enjoins us not to disguise low things with highfalutin names. A set of opinions is not to be called "a philosophy." Insofar as the saying favors simplicity, it seems to condemn Socrates for saying "the things within his cloak" and to praise the man who asked the old Sophocles whether he could still have intercourse with a woman.[1] The saying implies that either nothing is by nature shameful or the naturally shameful is not what most men hold to be shameful. In either case the saying is an attack on the reticences of law and convention; but it thereby assumes that a language is not so tied up with law and convention as to lack the words to call a spade a spade.[2] The namegiver is apparently closer to nature than the law-giver. If, however, language neither is nor can be entirely free of the law, the right name for everything could never be expressed. Only the unpronounceable ideal language would be by nature.

We have begun with these three ways of interpreting Cratylus's hypothesis in order to make it somewhat plausible that Socrates is willing to consider the dispute between Cratylus and Hermogenes at all and not just declare Hermogenes in the right. While the *Cratylus* argues for a natural correctness of names, its argument is composed of names correct only by convention, for otherwise we would necessarily misread both medium and message. Socrates, however, seems to know at once that if the argument runs counter to Hermogenes' stated position, Hermogenes will not be altogether displeased. Hermogenes has long been obsessed with the possibility of the natural correctness of names (427d3–7), for he takes everything seriously and never sees the joke in anything. Hermogenes wants the world as he knows it to be full of meaning. He would like to believe that the world is providentially a Platonic dialogue in which there is no other cause than "logographic necessity." That "Polemarchus" means "Warlord" and Polemarchus is not polemarch in Athens are significant for the *Republic* (cf. 332e3–5); but Hermogenes is not content with such fictions. He wants being always to follow in truth on meaning, and nothing to be by chance. The action of the *Cratylus* consists in Socrates' attempts to persuade Hermogenes that the world is not a book, and to accept a less than perfect coincidence between meaning and being.

Hermogenes finds it particularly distressing that Cratylus should make an exception in his case and deny that Hermogenes is his name. Socrates' interpretation of Cratylus's joke is twofold. At first he suggests that since Hermogenes desires money *(chrēmata)* but always fails in its acquisition, "Born of Hermes" is not a suitable name. Hermogenes makes no comment on this suggestion; but later, when Socrates proposes that Hermes means "Provider of Speech," Hermogenes exclaims, "By Zeus! That I am not Hermogenes is, I think, a good saying of Cratylus after all; I am not at any rate well-provided with speech" (408b6–7). Hermogenes has not lived up to his name; if his parents gave him his name as a form of prayer, it has gone unanswered (cf. 397b1–6). If it had been answered, Hermogenes would have been both wealthy and eloquent; he would have been a rhetorician or a sophist and fleeced his brother Callias of the inheritance he did not control (391b11–c4). "Money talks" is literally the truth of Hermogenes' name. Socrates condenses this *logos* of "Hermes" into the single word *agorastikos* (408a1), for the agora is indifferently the place for public speaking and the place for buying and selling. Money is altogether by convention, as the name *nomisma* (currency) indicates; and the service it performs is not unlike names: both make it possible to avoid handling things directly. Money is to barter as names are to things; and just as money allows for perfect exchange independent of immediate needs, so names allow for perfect exchange independent of present perceptions. The freedom from immediacy that money gives allows for usury: and the coining of noncorporeal meanings out of corporeal roots likewise becomes possible by names. Concepts seem to be the unearned interest on names. There are no doubt several other resemblances between money and names; the devaluation of money and the debasement of language are perhaps the most obvious, but they are chiefly linked through the notions of exchange and communication. The money-hungry and tongue-tied Hermogenes thus incorporates the problem of communication, both human and divine. It was very lucky of Socrates to have found him.

Hermogenes' way of exemplifying the conventional thesis—"We change the names of our domestic slaves"—indicates that he is thinking of law from the legislator's viewpoint (cf. 385d9). The slave cannot complain that his master addresses him incorrectly, for all the other masters would turn a deaf ear to his appeal. The masters agree among themselves that each of them has the right to name whatever is his own. Socrates' initial questioning is meant to test Hermogenes' understanding of "one's own." He does this by translating the apparently neutral word *chrēmata* of Protagoras's saying—"Man is the measure of all things *(chrēmatōn)*—into its presumed Attic equivalent, *pragmata* (386a2). The translation suppresses the monetary meaning of *chrēmata* and presents things as things done rather than as things needful. *Pragmata* are the beings with which we deal and are of interest and concern to us; they are not the beings as they are in themselves (cf. 386e7–8). For *pragmata,* a reasonable sense can be made out for the natural correctness of names. If, for example, the unit of the family in a tribe or city is "nuclear"—father, mother, children—every name of a relation beyond this group is likely to be transparent, i.e., a compound name whose meaning can be read off from its elements (e.g., father-in-law); but if, on the other hand, the family were to extend, say, to the cousins on the mother's side (Latin *sobrinus*), the names of all relations within that range are likely to be opaque, i.e., nonderivable lexical items.[3] An opaque name for a relation of no importance would probably be a survival. Natural correctness of names in this sense would merely be the linguistic equivalent to Montesquieu's spirit of the laws; it would not entail that the ratio between linguistic opacity and transparency was fixed, but only that *pragmata,* however they are understood, dictate the names of *pragmata.* The nameless is the insignificant.

Once Socrates gets Hermogenes to accept a certain stability in *pragmata,* for otherwise Hermogenes could not hold on to his experience that there are very many, very wicked human beings, Socrates asks after actions or doings *(praxeis).* "If, for example," he asks Hermogenes, "we were to try to cut any of the beings, must we cut each (thing) in whatever way we want and with whatever we want, or if we want to cut each according to the nature of cutting and being cut and with that which is by nature (fit to do so), shall we cut and will it be to our advantage, and shall we do this correctly, but if contrary to nature, shall we not fail and do nothing (be unsuccessful)?" Socrates follows up the example of cutting with that of burning; as a pair they can mean either surgery and cautery or the ravaging of a countryside by fire and sword. The two verbs of action are neutral to kill or cure; but once we choose either end, and thus transform the beings into *pragmata,* the ways and means are no longer arbitrary. A scalpel is not made for cutting down men or a torch for cauterizing a wound; but it does not follow that their abuse spells failure. If names are instruments, as Socrates is beginning to argue, they might always be more or less clumsy, and yet, employed with enough skill, still do their job. Socrates, after all, has just done quite well without either "cautery" or "surgery"; and if he has selected his examples with his usual care, he has suggested that there is a therapeutic as well as a punitive kind of name. A more precise vocabulary could have suggested only the punitive—"sin" and "damnation" to the exclusion of "mercy" and "redemption"; whereas the ambiguity of "cutting and burning" points to the inseparability of such therapy from its experience as punishment: corrective punishment is still punishment (cf. *Gorgias* 476a7–477a4). Socrates, then, connects *praxis* with what has come to be called affective words. He thus alludes at the start to a major theme of the *Cratylus*—the psychopathology of naming. "Sticks and stones may break my bones but names can never harm me" is a saying that pretends that there is only body while it itself is an incantation to protect the soul.

Names tell things apart. Socrates implies that speeches put things together. Some of us are crazy, most of us get angry. The comic poet Philemon has someone say, "We are all crazy when we get angry." This insight, which brings together a condition and a passion of the soul, seems to be an easy acquisition for us: "mad" has already put them together. Usage, however, plainly distinguishes them; there is "mad mad" and "mad crazy"; and so we are no more aware, without reflection, of the connection between them than a foreigner is. Names must be translated even in one's own language. On the other hand, names that are not proper names seem as if they must be put together; but in fact names in themselves are always proper names. Collecting is a part of speaking and not naming. That "animal" ranges over a many is not inherent in "animal." Only names in the plural would entail a plurality. The first name in the plural which Socrates analyzes is "gods"; it is also the first name analyzed which is not a proper name.

Socrates' line of argument leads to a paradox. If names are instruments, they can be used beautifully by the expert teacher; and either the rest of us have usurped them for our own use illegitimately, or all of us are equally expert. The knowledge of how to use names seems to be like the knowledge we are supposed to have of the law; we ourselves know its major provisions but consult lawyers for the interpretation of doubtful cases. Two nonexperts in conversing with one another are bound to err. Hermogenes speaks of the "bronze-worker" *(chalkeus)* as the maker of an iron drill (338d3, 389c7); but Socrates understands him perfectly. Greek, it seems, belongs to the bronze age, but its names were extended to keep up with innovations. Like our obedience to the law, the intelligibility of names depends on their stability; but imperfect discrimination is its inevitable accompaniment. Names come down to us; insofar as they preserve the past, they are more like customs and rituals that are still practiced but whose meaning has been forgotten than like written laws whose purpose can be questioned. The power of law seems to be a function of our unawareness; the prohibition against incest is almost as opaque as a proper name. Socrates can bring law and name together because Hermogenes is unable to say who makes the names that the expert teacher uses. Law is the substitute for Hermogenes' lack of *logos;* it hands over to him the answer he could not supply by himself. If he had followed the argument, he would have had to make up a name for the maker of names and thus shortcircuited the argument. Socrates' own answer—"namemaker" *(onomatourgos)*—is merely Socrates' question all over again in the transparent disguise of a compound name.

Since Hermogenes does not understand the import of Socrates' analysis, that names reveal most by what they do not name of the *pragmata,* he is not content with it; he wants Socrates to demonstrate the natural rightness of names. Socrates' demonstration consists of seven different lines of inquiry: 1) the language of gods and men; 2) the language of men and women; 3) the names in a mythical genealogy; 4) the names of natural beings; 5) the names of Greek gods; 6) the names of celestial things; 7) the names of moral and intellectual virtues and vices. For our purposes, the first, second, fifth, and seventh of these are the most important. Homer is the authority for the first two, Euthyphro, a contemporary mystic, for most of the other five, with the Heraclitean thesis supplying the formula for the last three but especially the seventh. The interest that each etymology has is inversely proportional to the use that Socrates makes of the Heraclitean formula. Systematization makes the answer known even before the question is posed. The most enigmatic of theses proves to be without surprises. The *Cratylus* thus illustrates the error of what Socrates called in the *Philebus* making the many too quickly into one (16e4–17a5). It is this error that connects the apparently disparate themes of law and tragedy with Heracliteanism.

All but one of the divine names that Homer mentions are transparent; all their human equivalents are opaque. Xanthos (Tawny) is the gods' name for the river men call Scamander; *chalkis* (brazen) is for the bird men called *kumindis;* Planktai means "Wanderers," Briareos "Brawny," and what for men is a hill called Batieia, is for the gods the tomb of Myrine; and the word for tomb *(sēma)* literally means "sign." Socrates refers to three of these names and quotes two. The first is from the twentieth book of the *Iliad.* The passage in which it occurs describes the opposing lineups of Greek and Trojan gods: "A great, deep-swirling river (stood) against Hephaestus; the gods call him Xanthos, men Scamander." The gods know that the river is a fellow god, and as much the son of Zeus as Hephaestus is. "Xanthos" seems to be their nickname for him. If he is a god, it is a correct name, just as Hephaestus is a correct name on the same condition. "Fire burns" and "Hephaestus burns" do not say the same unless "Hephaestus" names no more than "fire," and "Hephaestus prevails over Xanthos" is equivalent to "Fire is more powerful than water." That which we might call, then, the simple poetry of the gods' naming might not be poetry at all. Either the north wind pushed Oreithyia off some rocks, or Boreas raped her (*Phaedrus* 229b4–d2). The name Boreas can be read either way; sleep, we might suppose, cannot. But Sleep, too, is a god, the brother of Death; he is bribed by Hera to put Zeus asleep, and in order that Zeus might not detect his presence he makes himself look like the bird gods call *chalkis* and men *kumindis* (*Iliad* 14.286–91). So *chalkis* is not the correct name for this bird; it is "Sleep." "Brazen sleep" is not a way of naming death (*Iliad* 11.241), but the truth of bird and god together. Metaphor is impossible if being is this mysterious. Not only is everything full of gods, and a proper name the only correct name, but the world is wholly hieroglyphical. What seems to be plain text is in fact in code, and only revelation can crack it.

Socrates, accordingly, no sooner starts than stops his inquiry into divine and human naming; he turns instead to the more human, the distinction between the names men and women call the same thing. Whether the exclusive use of certain oaths by women suggested it, or he had heard of a language like Japanese in which there are male and female vocabularies, Socrates tortures a passage out of Homer to yield the distinction. Whereas Homer says that Hector called his son Scamandrius and the rest

Astyanax (*Iliad* 6.402–3), Socrates gets Hermogenes to agree that if the Trojans called him Astyanax the women must have called him Scamandrius. Socrates implies that either Hector was exceptionally uxorious or women would adopt Hector's private name for his son. The private is opaque, the public transparent ("Lord of the City"). The son gets the title that the father, as long as Priam is alive, cannot have, and that, after the fall of Troy, can be at best only a reminder of past glory (*Iliad* 22.477–514). Socrates guesses that Hector's name too is Greek, given to him by Homer himself, and signifies just about the same as "Astyanax." "Hector" is shorthand for "Astyanax"; but even on the most generous interpretation "Hector" covers no more than *ana* (lord); it does not say what Hector rules, possesses, and has. The forced equation of "Hector" and "Astyanax" sinks both of them into the class of royal names and denies any difference between father and son. Socrates' preference for transparent names is his way of denying "individuality," of which the specious opacity of proper names is a sign. To recover the meaning of a proper name is not, as it might seem, to enhance the importance of the bearer, but just the opposite, to demote him. He is nothing more than an example of a common type. Socrates, then, associates the masculine through the political and the transparent with the generic (cf. 392c6–8), and the feminine through the private and the opaque with the individual (cf. 410a5). In the genealogies that follow, Socrates is silent about the mothers.

If a member of a kind breeds true, its offspring is to be called by the name of the kind. This rule seems to condemn the usage of "human being" *(anthrōpos)* in Greek, which in the singular, and particularly in the vocative, carries with it the notion of contempt. The shift from a sexual to a generic designation of human excellence is perhaps the most obvious indication of the philosophic turn. Socrates' use of the oath "By Hera," which belongs to Athenian women, points in the same direction. Plato speaks of "divine human beings" (*Laws* 951b5, *Minos* 318e9); "divine man" *(anēr)* is common from Homer on. In compensation for the self-denigration as a kind, men give themselves proper names; but these proper names, in their meaning, are still class-names—royal, martial, medical, or whatever—to which one is entitled only if one's nature is in accord with it. Nature alone legitimates the patronymic. Among men, however, prodigies or monsters *(terata)* are so frequent that patronymics are rarely appropriate. Man is by generation a deviant animal; the opacity of class-names testifies to it, and their opacity is the inevitable consequence. At this point, Socrates introduces the word *dunamis* (power or capacity) to express "meaning." He is thus able to make an analogy between the apparent differences of proper names and their equivalent generic meaning, on the one hand, and the apparent differences in color and smell of drugs and their equivalent power, on the other. Syllabic differences among names are insignificant as long as the names signify the same. Socrates contrasts the four vowels in Greek which do not need names in order to be spoken (E, Υ, O, Ω) with the name *bēta* for which the addition of eta, tau, and alpha does not interfere with the declaration of "B"; indeed, they are the "noise" which alone makes its declaration possible. The soundless "B" is the *eidos* of "B"; BA, BE, BI, BO, BU are, as written, some of the dimensional patterns which show up in infinite variations in our speaking the names "bat," "bet," "bit," "boot," and "butt." Whatever application this might have to a Platonic physics (B's resemblance to a "quark" is probably deceptive), Socrates argues that men are taken in by the evident difference between, say, "King" and "Roy" and thus fail to discern the sameness of their power or meaning. Individual human beings are mostly made up of meaningless noise through which there shine for the expert knower of kinds the silent consonants that are alone significant. Men believe in their own individual mysteriousness because they mistake opacity for profundity; they do not know that "personality" is a disguise, however indispensable it might be for the manifestation of a kind.

If body is at the root of individuality, the multiplicity of meanings that Socrates finds in its name would both reflect that fact and point to the illusion to which it gives rise. "Body" is as equivocal as body is divisible. One possible root of "body" has a double meaning: *sēma* signifies either "tomb" or "sign." So the body is either the tomb of soul or that by means of which soul signifies whatever it signifies. If body is the instrument of significance, or meaning, it cannot be a perfect instrument unless it is itself without significance. A tombstone marks the place where a body has been buried; it points to the place where it is itself placed as if something else were there in place. But Homer says that men call a hill Batieia which the gods call the tomb of Murine. Men forgot that the hill was a sign and gave it a name of its own. A place-name is a sign that does not point elsewhere; likewise, the name of body, now that it is distinct from sign, points simply to body. Since "body" is now neutral, it admits multiple meanings; but as long as "body" was *sēma,* one could not name it without pointing beyond it, and hence body, strictly speaking, was then nameless. The modern name of body supplies the ground for the ancient meanings of "body"; the opaque makes its own transparency possible. But if the opaque modern name has its source in a former name of body which was meaningful, then a meaning, which is yet to be grounded, is the ultimate ground for the present meaningless name. Socrates' etymology of "body" recognizes that body is both itself and not itself; as itself it is what one can point at and name "body"; but as the universal instrument of meaning, it is never itself, always of another, and its name is "sign." It seems as if the gods' name "tomb of Murine" and the human name Batieia were both correct.

With the alternative root of "body," Socrates appeals explicitly to image for the first time. "Body" is an Orphic name; the soul is kept safe *(sōzetai)* in the body *(sōma)* until it has paid the penalty for its crimes in full, for the body is an "image of prison." Hermogenes was not being severe enough when he said that there were very many, very wicked human beings; everyone alive is unjust and undergoing punishment. Even though there could not be a more terrifying reading of human life, the Orphics chose not to convey its terror in their name for body. The name of body is not "prison" but "salvation"; its name is therapeutic rather than punitive. The name itself saves men from the truth; they now utter a sound that, while it preserves without the distortion of a single letter its root, conceals the doctrine that explains the root. "Body" is a euphemism. Its account precedes immediately Socrates' interpretation of the names of Greek gods. Their manifest beauty and hidden terribleness seem to be the framework within which each of the gods will be understood. Socrates' interpretation culminates in Pan, the emblem of the tragic life.

The most beautiful way of examining the names of the gods is, according to Socrates, to start with a confession of ignorance: "We know nothing about gods, either about themselves or in their names, whatever they call themselves." Socrates confirms this with an oath; it is his first. He calls upon Zeus to bear witness to his ignorance about Zeus. "By Zeus" is, we say, just an expression; it does not mean anything (cf. 410a5, 411b3). "By Zeus" is usually no more to be interpreted than a proper name; but it becomes transparent like a proper name whenever its context galvanizes it into significance. Socrates has done that; so confident is he that he is not committing perjury that he is willing for Zeus to punish him if he knows anything about Zeus. If Socrates does not know whether Zeus is and cares, he knows that Zeus does not care whether he knows it or not, for he would be foolish to swear otherwise; but then Socrates does know something about gods, and he asks for a punishment he knows he will not receive. Socrates has managed to perjure himself with impunity; he has restored meaning to a meaningless expression only to render it meaningless. But, it can be objected, "by Zeus" is not meaningless; though everyone now says it in the spirit of Hippolytus's "My tongue has sworn, not my mind," it still is a way of conveying the degree of one's sincerity and concern. One's listeners are to believe not that Zeus but that one's very life and soul are bearing witness. Religion has become rhetoric. The beautiful has overlaid the terrible.

A second way of nominal correctness is the way of the law. It commands us to address the gods in our prayers with a saving clause—"whoever they are and with whatever name they are pleased to be called, this we too call them." The law does not doubt that the gods are and care, but it admits our inability to name them correctly. Zeus may not be "Zeus." The gods are one group of speakers whose names are not authoritative for other groups; they are like slaves whose names we change at will. The gods are always one's own gods. Socrates begins according to the law with Hestia, the goddess of hearth and home. He begins with that god to whom one first sacrifices. What ones does is the guide to what one believes. "Hestia" is "the being *(ousia)* of all *pragmata,*" for the essence of what one does and is concerned with is one's own. *Ousia* originally meant "property," especially wealth, even though etymologically it means "being." In keeping with the localized sense of Hestia, Socrates appeals to a dialectal form of "being" *(essia)* in order to establish the etymology. The meaning of Hestia appears in present-day Attic only in the third person singular of the verb "be" *(esti).* One's own is in Athens no longer the essence of things but only that which partakes of the essence of things. One's own has become alien in Attic. Attic is an enlightened language; the primary has drifted out of the language without ceasing to be primary in fact. Its neutrality is an illusion.

Hestia is the only god in the *Phaedrus* myth who always stays at home and never beholds the "hyperuranian" ideas (247a1–2). Socrates here, however, deliberately ignores the obvious connection between the verb "stand" *(histēmi)* and Hestia; he suggests instead that another dialectal form of "being" *(osia)* is from the verb "push" *(ōtheō),* and its speakers were Heracliteans, who believed that the beings move and nothing abides, and *osia* is their cause and principle. The root of "Hestia" is "being"; but "being" seems to admit of two irreconcilable interpretations. Since, however, being as one's own necessarily allows for its meaning to vary from place to place, the Heraclitean interpretation is the truth of being as one's own, for it alone comprehends the changeableness of one's own. Hestia as mover is the universal principle of the local. Accordingly, Timaeus can call the "wandering cause" place *(chōra);* indeed, "place" and the verb "move" *(chōreō)* look like cognates (cf. 402a8). The law says, Begin with Hestia; it says, Begin with one's own. This law is both a particular law and the characteristic of all law in general. For those who obey this law, there is nothing but all that the laws have laid down as one's own; but those who reflect on this law recognize in its injunction a statement about law itself. Whether the Heracliteans, however, in grasping the nature of law have also grasped the nature of nature, or somehow being still remains their being, and "one's own" still clings to it, proves to be the chief issue of the *Cratylus.*

It is with "Poseidon" that Socrates first resorts to the beautiful to illuminate the apparent opacity of names. In this dialogue, the beautiful is another name for the tragic. The name-giver named the sea in terms of its effect on himself—it was a bond to his feet *(posi desmos);* but for the sake of beauty and decency *(euprepeia)* perhaps he inserted an epsilon *(Poseidon).* As soon as the nature of something is interpreted from the perspective of one's experience of its nature, the beautiful is introduced. Socrates at once proposes two other etymologies, one of which would make the sigma spurious, the other pi and delta, while both would accept the epsilon as genuine. If the first etymology is sound, beauty would lure one into attributing knowledge to the sea: "Poseidon" looks like "knowing so many (definite) things." Knowledge seems to be the accidental by-product of beautification: a more concise formula for stating the historical relation between Greek poetry and philosophy could not be made. One cannot help noticing, moreover, that a combination of Socrates' first two etymologies turns *Poseidon* into an anagram of *Oidipous,* or "Know-foot." The paradigm of man is a god spelled inside out. The tragic figure par excellence arises from the union of a primary and a secondary meaning; but that which binds the feet of Oedipus and puts him into a state of perplexity or *aporia* is not the sea but himself. An alien element frustrated the name-giver of Poseidon; the riddle of Oedipus frustrates Oedipus. Socrates seems to hint that once the knowledge of things is equated with the experience of things, tragic self-knowledge will be its inevitable fulfillment. Oedipus is the truth of the beings as *pragmata.*

"Pluto" is the first transparent name of a god which Socrates considers; it is one of two names of the god. Its transparency is due to the fear that the other name, equally transparent, induces in the many. The many give Hades a name that refers to this world—"Wealth *(ploutos)* is sent up out of the earth from below"—for they mistake *toutou tou theou tēs dunameōs,* which can be translated as either "the meaning of Hades" or "the power of Hades" (403b3). The power of Hades consists in the meaning of Hades. "Hades," the many believe, means "invisible" *(aïdēs),* and invisibility connotes for them two things: Hades is our eternal abode when we are dead, and the soul stripped of the body goes away to Hades. Hades is both a place and a god. As a place, Hades is where we go as ourselves; as a god *(ekeinon),* Hades is he to whom soul alone goes off. Not to be here is as terrifying as to be without body. Our attachment to our place in this world and our own bodies is so strong that not even Hades, who seems preferable to annihilation, can console; what truly consoles is wealth. Wealth gives meaning to death; one's substance *(ousia)* is thereby preserved.

What comfort Hermogenes, the impoverished heir of great wealth, would draw from this is hard to say; perhaps he would take it as another sign that he is not the offspring of Hermes the psychopomp. "Pluto" is not sufficient to remove the fear of death from born losers like Hermogenes; and so Socrates goes on to make Hades truly enchanting in his eyes. He begins by asking Hermogenes whether desire is a stronger bond than necessity to keep any animal anywhere. Hermogenes replies that desire far surpasses necessity. Since necessity cannot, strictly speaking, be weaker than anything, either "necessity" must be one of those names that have lost their original force, or Hermogenes believes that all necessity is pseudo-necessity (cf. 420d7–9). Perhaps such a belief would be the indispensable condition for the meaning of "necessity" to weaken. To hold such a belief, in any case, is to be enchanted, for enchantment is grounded in the denial of necessity. The spokesmen for the denial of necessity are the sophists, whose beautiful speeches admit no obstacle to the fulfillment of desire; but since beautiful speeches are still just speeches unless necessity is in truth nonexistent, only the disappearance of the body guarantees that necessity would not prove to be refractory to speeches however beautiful. Hades is thus the perfect sophist; and Socrates enchants Hermogenes with the prospect that he will in death surpass his brother in wealth (Pluto sends up just a fraction of his riches), and without spending a cent be instructed by the arch-sophist Hades. Hermogenes' two incapacities will be cured together. Hermogenes will finally prove to be "Hermogenes." So the absence of necessity turns out to be the condition for the coincidence of being and meaning. But since body is that by means of which soul signifies, and Hades cannot bind if the body's desires still hold, the enchantment of Hades is nothing but sophistry. There can be no significance without body; but if there is necessity, being and meaning cannot coincide.

Of the fourteen gods whom Socrates now discusses, and who fall into six groups, Hermogenes asks about nine of them, and Socrates interpolates six names: Athena, like Hades, has two names. Four of Hermogenes' gods and all but one of Socrates' are female. Socrates follows Hermogenes' order with two exceptions: he inserts Persephone between Hera and Apollo, and the Muses, Leto, and Artemis between Apollo and Dionysus. These insertions postpone the explanation of Athena, Hephaestus, and Ares and make Hermogenes suspect that Socrates has forgotten the gods of his own city; the female, we recall, represented the private, the opaque, and the individual. These insertions also make Hermogenes forget his own list for a moment and ask instead about Dionysus and Aphrodite. "Aphrodite" is the only name whose etymology is traditional: Hesiod is Socrates' authority. Socrates says that for "Aphrodite," as well as for "Dionysus," he can only give the playful account; Hermogenes will have to ask others for the serious. That "Aphrodite" comes from foam *(aphros)* conceals her terrible origin; she comes from the genitals of Ouranos that Kronos cut off. Her sisters are the Furies. Aphrodite is a goddess of revenge whose name makes her charming. Her name therefore is both like and unlike the names of Persephone and Apollo, both of which are beautiful and yet inspire fear. Apollo's name was deliberately altered in order to prevent it from looking like "Destroyer," but the alteration was not wholly successful. Some saw through the change and concluded that it was meant to hide the truth of Apollo the destroyer. In the case of "Persephone," too, beautification only led to the suspicion that its true significance was terrible. Socrates, on the other hand, in recovering the originally attractive meanings of "Apollo" and "Persephone," cannot show that they are beautiful. Truth and Beauty do not go together. Beauty and Terror do.

The meaning of that conjunction becomes clearer if two of Socrates' etymologies are compared. The badly concealed meaning of Apollo is "he who ranges over all things at once" *(ho polōn hama panta);* and the meaning of "Pan goatherd" *(aipolos)* is "he who reveals everything and ranges over everything always" *(ho pan mēnuōn kai aei polōn)*. "Apollo" also indicates simplicity *(haploun)* and truth. Pan is double *(diplous),* true and false. Now the image of Pan is smooth and divine above, rough and *tragikon* (i.e., goatish) below. *Tragikon,* however, no longer means "goatish" but "tragic"; it has been smoothed over (cf. 414c5). The divine smoothness of Pan therefore is ambiguous; it is indistinguishable from the terrible beauty of "Apollo" in its false interpretation. Apollo is tragedy's own view of itself. Pan is Socrates'. Tragedy interprets Pan's smoothness as a gloss on the god's terribleness, and his roughness as that which tragedy has as its task to conceal. The goatishness of Pan is the laughably human about which tragedy sings its myths and lies. Pan is the root of the tragic Apollo. But since Pan is the son of Hermes, the deviser of speech, he is *logos* or kin *(adelphos)* to *logos;* and the formula, "Everything *(pan)* is logos," is the claim of the sophists. Sophistry and tragedy, it seems, are twins, for the equivalence of "Pan is *logos*" and "Everything is *logos*" implies that the individual loses nothing of himself in attaining significance. Now this implication, which is the essence of tragedy, was shown to obtain *per impossible* only in the realm of the arch-sophist Hades. "It surpasses every *logos,*" the Chorus of *Oedipus at Colonus* sing, "not to be born."

Hermogenes asks about the beautiful names that pertain to virtue; we do not know whether he suspects that the virtues are nothing but fine names. According to Socrates, "the beautiful things" *(ta kala)* were originally "the so-called things" *(ta kaloumena),* and "name" was "a being of which there is searching"; so Hermogenes' phrase, "beautiful names," signifies "so-called questions of being." The key to the meaning of this oxymoron is now supplied by Socrates in the single most important statement of the *Cratylus.* It is both a summary and a prospectus. "By the dog! I believe my divination was not a bad one, which I just now understand, that the men of long, long ago, just like many of the wise nowadays, suffered vertigo from their constant whirling in their search to find out in what way the beings *(ta onta)* are, and so it looked to them as if the things *(ta pragmata)* were revolving and moving totally. So they charged *(aitiontai)* not their own inner experience *(pathos)* as the cause *(aition)* of their opinion, but the things themselves *(auta ta pragmata)* were by nature in this state, and none of them abided or was stable, but everything always flowed, moved, and was full of every kind of motion and generation." The ancients mistook the state of perplexity for the state of knowledge. Although they identified the dizziness of questioning with the dizziness of things, they did not know that that was what they were doing. They did not conclude that being was enigmatic because they found it so, but rather that their search had finally put them in touch with the beings, and the beings without mediation disclosed what they were. They must, then, have reflected on their own inner experience and yet lost sight of its significance. It must have seemed to them impossible for their own soul to be a cause: the dispassionateness of their searching was proof against the soul's self-infection. Even these assumptions, however, do not by themselves explain their mistake. Socrates implies that the corporeal character of the language for noncorporeal things was due to a theory that there was only body; so what now looks like the extension of names for the sake of economy was originally a doctrine of the identity of inner experience with corporeal motion. In the beginning there were no metaphors, and to be in a whirl was literally true. So the union of corporealism with the probity of disinterest issued, by way of perplexity, into the thesis that to know was to be disoriented. Not to be at home was to be in contact with the beings. Hestia was not their model but Persephone, the wife of Hades, whose name, like the name of wisdom, means "to be in touch with motion." Since to be in touch with motion, however, is to be in motion, and hence to know the being is to be or act the being, what they finally knew was their own. So Hestia, the goddess to whom one first sacrifices according to the law, was their model after all. The premise of the law was thus their own misunderstood assumption, for it is not understanding but belief that follows on behaving.

One of the words for "meaning" in Greek is *boulēsis,* or "will." The imagined omnipotence of the will can take two forms, triumphant defiance or acquiescence. Tragedy seems to adopt the first, Heracliteanism the second. The first senses its owns deceptiveness, the second is self-deceived, for it believes that it is letting the beings speak for themselves while in fact it is misreading the condition of its consciousness. Wisdom is selfless knowledge of the self-absorbed self, or mysticism. The only difference such a wisdom can allow are differences of degree. "The good" *(t'agathon),* therefore, is the admirable part of speed *(tou thoou to agaston),* and "the just" *(to dikaion),* insofar as it is that which goes through everything *(diaion),* must be both the subtlest, in order that nothing can keep it out, and the swiftest, in order that it can use everything else as if this quantity were standing still. The just controls all becoming instrumentally; as the subtlest of instruments, it makes the most refined discriminations, and as the swiftest it communicates with everything. Now Socrates had begun the discussion of names with Hermogenes by arguing that a name was an instructional and discriminatory instrument. The just, then, is the name of names or the *eidos* of name: "just" and "justly" are used by Socrates throughout to signify nominal correctness. Since, however, names are the work of the legislating name-giver, the just is the lawful itself, and all names are more or less crude approximations of the lawful; even *to dikaion* is not exact, for the kappa has been added for euphony. The homogeneity of the beings, which was the original insight of the name-giver, thus finds its complete expression in the law, which admits no exception to its rules. The law's uniformity, however, is grounded in the individual will misunderstood as self-denial. The total self-denial of the will is acquiescence in the flow of things; but if this mystical union is proclaimed as law, wisdom becomes indistinguishable from obedience. Obedience to the law is the opaque translation of the transparent original that stated wisdom to consist in the imitation of things. Euthyphro's role in Socrates' inspiration is now clear. Euthyphro did not scruple to prosecute his father for murder on the grounds that he was merely doing what Zeus had done to his father. To do what the gods do is the pious, just as to be indifferent to individuals is the legal version of Heracliteanism. They are united in Euthyphro.

For Heracliteanism injustice and cowardice are indistinguishable, and the riddles of tragedy nothing but the willful beautifications of vice. The thirteen names from "courage" to "virtue" form a group (413d7–415el); "art" and "device" are intrusive elements in this group. "Art" is particularly recalcitrant to interpretation; so much so that Hermogenes protests and says that Socrates is really reaching. Socrates' defense is that those who "want to tragedize" names have confused them as they were first laid down, and for the sake of euphony, to which end time has no less contributed, they have brought it about that "not a single human being can understand *(suneinai)* what a name wants to be." The tragedians, he implies, have had their greatest impact on the names that pertain to mind. Socrates' example of a tragedized name is "Sphinx," in which the original form "phix" is now concealed completely. Its tragic alteration has made an originally opaque name transparent. "Sphinx" means "Binder."[4] Now since to be bound is, literally, to be incapable of movement, and figuratively, to be in a perplexity *(aporia),* Oedipus's condition should epitomize injustice and cowardice (or vice in general), for injustice is an impediment *(empodisma)* to the transit *(to diaion)* of the just, cowardice is a strong bond on the soul's motion, and evil is whatever is before the feet *(empodōn)* and stands in the way.

Tragedy, however, seems to deny Oedipus's viciousness while accepting the injustice of his acts, for at neither the beginning nor the end does it recognize the incompatibility of Oedipus the bound with Oedipus the knower. Unwittingly, tragedy puts together in Oedipus complete virtue and complete vice. Oedipus solved the riddle of the Sphinx; he figured out that man was the being which went on four feet in the morning, two feet in the afternoon, and three in the evening. Oedipus is a partial Heraclitean. He discovered man in his motion, but failed to carry that discovery through and realize that his motion was the way of wisdom itself, for the three ways of locomotion characterized for him only man in time. There are gods. The knowledge of man's mortality is the knowledge of universal motion made tragic. Furthermore, if to be in motion is to come into contact with the principle of all things, and hence to be at one with one's own origins, the incest of Oedipus is not a crime but knowledge: the aorist infinitive of the verb "understand" *(suneinai),* which

Socrates has already interpreted as "go with" *(sunienai),* is the same as the infinitive of the verb "be with," sexually or otherwise. Cognation and cognition are the same. Tragedy refuses to face up to the identity of Oedipus's crime with Oedipus's understanding. At the very moment when Oedipus's self-knowledge should have liberated him, tragedy bound him again: his self-punishment made him incapable of moving on his own. The perplexity in which Oedipus was then caught, of suffering for what he had not willed, could only be resolved by the immortal gods. The gods stand over against motion. They are tragedy's device for getting out of the riddles it itself has devised. Socrates discusses the name for "device" *(mēchanē)* and will soon refer to its use by the tragic poets (425d1–8), immediately after "art." He prefaces his discussion with a half-line from the *Iliad,* which Hector speaks to his mother when he asks her to pray to Athena. Her prayer goes unanswered.

It almost goes without saying that this critique of tragedy as half-hearted Heracliteanism is not Socrates' own; but that tragedy somewhat compromises with the morality and the gods of the city is not inconsistent with his own suggestion that tragedy mixes primary and secondary meanings together and rests on a misinterpretation of the first things. His suggestion can be combined with a non-Heraclitean form of the Heraclitean critique of tragedy in the following way. *Nomoi* can just as easily be translated by "songs" as by "laws." In Plato's *Minos,* Socrates distinguishes between the songs for oboe of Marsyas and Olympus, which "alone move and reveal those who are in need of gods," and the most ancient laws of Minos and Rhadymanthus, which "even now still abide inasmuch as they are divine" (318b1-c3; cf. *Symposium* 215c). This distinction implies that law, in spite (or even because) of its need of the gods for its own authority, insists on its own self-sufficiency, and, in denying that its subjects have any needs it cannot satisfy, is essentially anti-theistic. Nothing is higher than itself. Law wants nothing better than to restrict the human horizon to the familiar and routine; but the city still needs the supplement of the outstanding—those men and women the city admires and looks up to. The city needs to instill emulation no less than obedience. It is around the outstanding that stories grow. Through the law's denial of any access through itself to the outstanding, these stories tend to be about transgressions of the law. Criminality is thus the element in which the higher necessity comes to light, even if, as in the case of Antigone, the higher seems to be fully in accord with the law. Tragedy, however, is not just antinomian; rather, its psychagogic power consists in its apparent success in bringing about a coincidence between the needs of the soul and the life-denying homogeneity of the law. This coincidence is the excessive punishment the gods inflict on the protagonists of tragedy.

Socrates makes the connection between tragedy and punishment in the course of completing his systematic etymologizing. Thirty-four names fall into six groups: I. Profit and Loss; II. Pleasure and Pain; III. Desire; IV. Belief and Will; V. The Necessary and the Voluntary; VI. Name, Truth, and Being. There are no surprise etymologies among them, unless the implicit identification of pleasure, the good, and knowledge can be so counted, since hedonism seems to be a self-contradictory basis for any legislation. Socrates implies, perhaps, not only that there is an element subversive of the law in any language, but that the picture of a paradise or a golden age, which often accompanies the equation of the good with the ancestral, is essentially hedonistic. The law recognizes its own painfulness and promises, on the basis of an original freedom, an ultimate release. The tragic form, then, of modern names would express the harshness of modern legislation. The moral is now the binding *(to deon);* originally, it was that which passes through *(diion);* and "day" in its most ancient form meant "that which men desire after darkness," but now that it has been made tragic it seems to mean "that which makes things tame." Tameness and obligation are contemporary. People must now submit to what they once desired: society is due to constraint. There are at least two indications of the extent to which harshness now dominates political life. Despite the apparent corporeality of the original names, their etymologies are with one exception always in terms of the soul's experiences: body is mentioned only in relation to one of the names for pain (419c2, 3). It is as if the moderns took literally the images of the ancients. The second indication seems to confirm this. Socrates claims that the original form of *zēmiōdes* (ruinous) was *dēmiōdes;* but in present-day Attic *dēmiōdes* could only mean that which pertains to the public executioner *(ho dēmios).*

Notes

1. *Charmides* 155d3; *Republic* 329c1–2.

2. See Cicero's letter to L. Paetus on obscene language (*Ad familiares* 9.22); and cf. Maimonides *Guide of the Perplexed* (tr. Pines [Chicago, 1963]): "I can also give the reason why this our language is called the holy language. It should not be thought that this, on our part, is an empty appellation or a mistake; in fact it is indicative of true reality. For in this holy language no word at all has been laid down in order to designate either the male or the female organ of copulation, nor are there words designating this act itself that brings generation, the sperm,

the urine, or the excrements. No word at all designating, according to its first meaning, any of these things has been laid down in the Hebrew language, they being signified by terms used in a figurative sense and by allusions. It was intended thereby to indicate that no terms designating them ought to be coined. For these are things about which one ought to be silent; however, when necessity impels mentioning them, a device should be found to do it by means of expressions deriving from other words, just as the most diligent endeavor should be made to be hidden when necessity impels doing these things.

3. Lucan's persistence throughout his *Bellum civile* to call Caesar the *socer* (father-in-law) of Pompey is attributable not just to the resemblance between the strife within a family and civil war but to the nontransparency of *socer* within Latin, so that the transgressiveness of the sacred can be seen. *Socer,* moreover, reflects a change in the family structure: *socrus,* mother-in-law, was originally the more important member of the family into which the bride entered; v. Ernout-Meillet, *Dictionaire étymologique de la langue latine* (Paris 1959), *s.v. socer.*

4. V. Sophocles *Oedipus Tyrannus* 128–31.

NINE

On Plato's *Symposium*

SOME PLATONIC DIALOGUES ARE BOUND closely to the life and times of Socrates, and some are set at a particular time of day. The *Phaedo* and *Symposium* satisfy both criteria; they are also non-Socratically reported dialogues, and both contain Socrates' own account of his early thought. The *Phaedo* tells of the last hours of Socrates, from the early morning to the setting of the sun, when Socrates remembers at the last moment that he owes a cock to Asclepius; the *Symposium* tells of an evening party that ended when the cock began to crow, and Socrates left the poets Agathon and Aristophanes asleep and went about his usual business. The *Phaedo* and *Symposium* between them occupy a full day. In prison Socrates identifies philosophy with the practice of dying and being dead; at Agathon's house he identifies philosophy with eros. If each definition is as partial as their temporal setting, the whole of philosophy is somehow comprehended by these two dialogues. As the practice of dying and being dead is the practice of separating body and soul and in its dialogic counterpart the exercise of separating an argument from its conditions, so eros should be the practice of putting body and soul together and its dialogic counterpart, the practice of unifying argument and conditions. Ultimately, of course, the disjunctive and conjunctive modes of interpretation should yield to an understanding of the double practice of *(sunkrisis* and *diakrisis)*—of collection and division—whose single name is dialectic; but it would be well to start, in the case of the *Symposium,* with the peculiar difficulties we face if we accept the invitation to put its six or seven praises of eros back into a unified whole.

To put the *Symposium* together is not easy; it is not a normal dialogue but consists for the most part of a set of six speeches on Eros, each one of which seems as if it could be spoken at any time and any place, since they severally express what the speakers understand of Eros, or more exactly how they experience eros. They are almost all speeches of lovers who are reflecting on their own experience; they are not speeches addressed to a beloved, designed to have the beloved undergo through speech the experience the lovers themselves did not have through speech. The dialogue devoted to erotic speech of that kind is the *Phaedrus,* where the issue of persuasion naturally opens up into its relation with reason and dialectic; but in the *Symposium,* we have speaker after speaker declare his experience of eros in such a way as to defy the possibility of unifying that manifold and thus to deny to philosophy any way to turn experience into argument. Socrates is left the task to preserve the truth of the experiences of the previous speakers and to refute their interpretation of their own experience, without anyone except Agathon being brought to see his error. Agathon's error initiates Socrates' speech because, Socrates confesses, it was his own youthful error before Diotima set him straight. That the refutation of everyone else occurs without anyone being shown his error reveals the power of Eros to convince each lover that his interpretation of his experience is necessarily the truth of his experience.

How we come to read the *Symposium* is as peculiar as is its nondialogic form. Apollodorus, who will be found crying uncontrollably throughout the *Phaedo,* is its narrator. He had given a recital of the *Symposium,* though perhaps less full, two days before; and he is all too eager to go through it once more for a group of businessmen, for whom he has the utmost contempt; but this contempt is mitigated somewhat by his own self-contempt, for he knows he is despicable along with everyone else, and only Socrates is exempt from reproach. The *Symposium* is for Apollodorus a kind of mantra, which confirms at each recital his own worthlessness. He follows Socrates around like a puppydog and can easily be distracted into a denunciation of everyone. The time of his latest recital is, I believe, a few years after the end of the Peloponnesian War and thus a few years before Socrates' death. He is *the* fanatic. His devotion to Socrates has soured him on everything else; suicide is the only way out for him once Socrates dies and he can no longer lash himself into a frenzy of self-abnegation by comparing his own nothingness with Socrates who alone is a somebody. Apollodorus seems to be the third of slavish followers of Socrates; the second was Aristodemus, a shoeless atheist from whom Apollodorus heard the story of Agathon's party; and the first was Alcibiades, whose speech at the end of the *Symposium* reveals his own dependence on Socrates and how, he believes, he broke the spell. The report, then, we get of the *Symposium* concerns the quasi-religious atmosphere Socrates created around himself from the time he first met Alcibiades to the day of his death, when his disciples demand that he enchant them with reason. This cult of personality raises the question of what conditions would have to be met in order to transform it into a true cult with its own god. The *Symposium*'s answer seems to be if and only if Eros were a god and Socrates his first worshiper. Through Diotima Socrates sets out to prove that Eros is not a god and no religion can form around him. Socrates thus answers Phaedrus's original question, which prompted this famous night of speeches, why no poet ever praised Eros. Eros is not a god, Socrates is not his prophet, and Plato not the poet for whom Phaedrus is waiting.

Agathon threw a party the day after he won his first victory in the tragic contest. The year was 416 B.C., during which, in Thucydides' *History* there is the only dialogue of a political kind, in which the Athenian ambassadors at Melos frankly declare the divine ground for imperialism. It is one year before the Sicilian expedition, on which occasion, Thucydides tells us, eros swooped down upon all the Athenians; and before the fleet departed Hermae throughout Athens were defaced, which so terrified the Athenians, as if the defacement were a signal for a tyrannical conspiracy, that they disregarded all legal safeguards and executed numerous Athenians on rumor, and summoned Alcibiades back from Sicily to face the charge of chief instigator of the mutilation as well as of profaning the Eleusinian mysteries at the same time. This suggestive juxtaposition of eros and tyranny, laced by superstition and religious longing, puts a political cast on the *Symposium.* It is as if Plato intended us to read the *Symposium* in light of Thucydides and take Socrates' radical account of eros as having its distorted and fragmentary echo in Athenian imperialistic designs. The *Republic* in a way confirms this, for there Socrates asserts the tyrant is Eros incarnate and the offspring of radical democracy. It is in any case in this heavily charged atmosphere, in which Alcibiades is at the peak of his influence, and who carried Eros with a thunderbolt as emblem on his shield, that Plato has Socrates vindicate eros for philosophy and draw it back from its imminent misinterpretation and misuse. Socrates sets out to purify eros from the dross of the political and theological in which it is necessarily found in its natural, unreflective state.

Although the political-theological dimension of the *Symposium* first becomes explicit with Aristophanes, it is first hinted at by Phaedrus. What puzzles Phaedrus the most about Eros is self-sacrifice. The lover gives up his own life for the sake of another, even though the other might be totally worthless. Alcestis is his chief example of this spirit, Orpheus his chief counter-example. Phaedrus interprets the backward glance of Orpheus, when he is leading Eurydice out of Hades, as a sign of the poet's self-regard: he refuses to give up everything for nothing. Alcestis, on the other hand, radicalizes his suggestion for an army of lovers and beloveds, who out of mutual shame would imitate natural virtue. Shame before the noble or beautiful, which in itself is superior to the grounds of patriotism, vanishes in Alcestis's case. Alcestis therefore needs the gods if she is to get anything out of her sacrifice; but if there are no gods to support the lover, the beloved alone gets the good. Love, therefore, must be a god if it is powerful enough to overcome self-interest. The beloved, one might say, in becoming a god for the moment in the eyes of the lover, gathers all the good into himself and lives at the expense of the lover. Phaedrus, then, sees that the Olympian gods, who compensate the lover, cannot be combined with the real thrust of Eros, which serves the good of the beloved. The problem of the relation between the beautiful and the good, or between the lover's sacrifice and the beloved's advantage, is first set out by Phaedrus. The problem is solved by Socrates in reversing Phaedrus. In his solution, the lover gets the good and the beloved keeps the beautiful.

Now that the beautiful has come to light in our discussion, it ought to be remarked on how indifferent all the speakers are prior to Socrates to the initiating experience of eros: the sight of the beautiful in the beloved. Eros primarily means for them "being with" and not "looking at." Accordingly, the speakers are inclined to assimilate love to friendship and to disregard the equal need for contemplative distance in eros. The cognitive element in eros is at a discount. A willfulness therefore pervades their several accounts in their attempt to stamp eros with a single trait and consequently in their refusal to acknowledge that the conjunctive impulse in eros is no stronger than the disjunctive, and eros ceases to be itself if either is given up, and nothing can resolve the tension between them. The praise of Eros, as the speakers understand it, involves the praise of satisfaction. Eros is not for them, as it is for Socrates, an in-between, but a fulfillment. The beloved therefore tends to be identified with eros, for in not starting at the beginning of eros—the sight of the beloved—they overlook the possibility that the beloved too is but a pointer to something beyond. The presence of the beautiful in the beloved does not entail that the lover's good is present there as well. They pin their hopes on the beloved, but the beloved is as displaced as eros is homeless.

The next two speakers after Phaedrus, Pausanias and Eryximachus, are a pair. Not only do they both subscribe to the view that Eros is double, but they both attempt to adjust the higher to the lower Eros, or they attempt to conceal sexual pleasure under the veneer of the beautiful. They also complement one another. For Pausanias the veneer is at different parts of his speech, Greekness, freedom, philosophy, and morality; for Eryximachus it is either on a universal scale theoretical physics or humanly a neutral diagnostics or theoretical medicine. Between them law and nature are covered. What they share is the notion of the neutrality of action and natural process. No action, Pausanias says, is in itself beautiful or ugly, whether it be drinking, singing, or talking. What refutes him is the fact that he cannot call a spade a spade and must use euphemisms for sexual acts. Conventional language asserts that these actions are not in themselves as indifferent as he claims, so that only the manner of doing them ennobles or debases them. Pausanias, then, would have to propose a revision of language itself; instead, he expresses a wish that the law had been different so that even philosophy would be respectable. The combination of education and philosophy cannot but remind us of the *Republic;* but Pausanias, because he wishes there to be no tension between philosophy and the city, must allow philosophy to be only a plausible cover for seduction. There is to be no penalty if he does not live up to his promises. Pausanias, one might say, is how Socrates appears to Athenian fathers. Pausanias offers the same patter, and the law is incapable of distinguishing between the genuine and the spurious versions of Socrates.

Eryximachus presents the same problem of discrimination within philosophy itself. In extending eros into a natural principle, Eryximachus grants that the cosmic order, over which uranian eros presides, operates in a regular manner that precludes the good of man. Men can only gain their good, which is pleasure, at the expense of that order; and the greatest art is therefore needed to go against nature without proceeding too far and suffering self-destruction. Eryximachus proposes, then, a set of theoretical sciences that would guide our exploitation of nature and tell us how much we could get away with in our tinkering. Precisely because pleasure is the sole human good, there is nothing in the discovery and contemplation of the cosmic order that answers to anything in the human soul. Eryximachus represents a version of the *Timaeus* as much as Pausanias represents a version of the *Republic.* They both point to Socrates.

The next two speakers, Aristophanes and Agathon, also form a pair, not only because they are tragic and comic representatives of Eros, but also because they too split apart something in Socrates that Socrates manages to keep together. The two foci of the *Symposium* are Phaedrus and Socrates. Phaedrus's challenge to Pausanias and Eryximachus is to find some good for the lover without the help of the gods. Pausanias's answer is law and Eryximachus's is art. Agathon, who is Pausanias's long-standing beloved, celebrates the unity of the beautiful and good in Eros, and Aristophanes, whose place Eryximachus took, denies that the present order, without which Eros cannot be, allows any room for adjustment to human needs. Man was once in harmony with the cosmic order; but now it is an impossible ideal, for any return to it, if *per impossible* it occurred, would demand the total elimination of man as man. Agathon and Aristophanes deepen between them the speeches respectively of Pausanias and Eryximachus. They thus become the way into their own overcoming by Socrates.

Before we turn to Aristophanes' speech, we should consider the occasion that brings about the order of the *Symposium* that groups the comic and tragic poets together with Socrates. A bad case of the hiccups on Aristophanes' part forces Eryximachus to speak before the comic poet and allows him to complement Pausanias, who also maintained that Eros was double. A disorder for which Eryximachus prescribes several remedies rearranges the order of the speakers. It is a funny noise whose cure consists in the funny noises of gargling and sneezing. Aristophanes finds it funny that funny noises heal funny disorders; but Eryximachus does not find it funny; we certainly must find it strange at least that bodily disorders establish the harmonious structure of the speeches of the *Symposium.* Had the hiccup not occurred, Eryximachus would have spoken over Aristophanes' speech to Pausanias's, and Aristophanes' proposal for a new religion would have been an awkward insertion between Pausanias and Eryximachus. It seems, however, that the juxtaposition of Pausanias and Aristophanes would have made a new connection: that the solution Pausanias sought in the law was found by Aristophanes in the nature of the city itself. Eryximachus, on the other hand, makes use of the disturbance in the order in the same way as his account proposes a disordering of the cosmic order for the sake of human pleasure; but he cannot account for the coincidence of disorder and the good of reason. Aristophanes, however, in denying the doubleness of Eros, accounts for why both Pausanias and Eryximachus required Eros to be double even though they had no explanation for it. Aristophanes heals their double Eros and makes it one whole at the same time that he supplies the ground for their belief. Aristophanes, in unifying Eros, accounts for the diremption in the cosmic and the human order. This diremption is incurable by either art or law. In completing both Pausanias's and Eryximachus's speeches, he announces an Eros without hope. The human as such is essentially incomplete and disordered. Socrates agrees that it is incomplete, but he asserts that in its incompleteness it is in order and good.

Aristophanes, one might say, starts from two common expressions we employ—"They were made for each other" and "I don't see what she or he sees in him or her." The mysterious fatefulness of love experientially has its source in the radical rearrangement man underwent in altering from a being of cosmic origins to a being who must submit to the Olympian gods. This alteration is presented entirely in terms of the body, but it gains its significance only if it is translated into the soul. Human beings were originally spherical, with two heads that faced in opposite directions, four legs, four arms, and two sets of genitals. They took after the sun if they were all male, after the earth if they were all female, and after the moon if they were male and female. What they all had in common were proud thoughts. As a punishment for their attempt to scale heaven, they were split in two by Zeus and their heads were turned around to face the cut in order that they might be humbled; Apollo at the same time straightened out the hemispheres in order to make them look like the Olympian gods. Man owes his shape to the Olympian gods, but his soul belongs to an older order. These slices of men immediately sought out their counterparts and clung to each other unto death. Zeus accordingly had to turn their genitals forward so that in the sexual embrace they might satisfy their longing to be wholes and at the same time perpetuate the race. Man is an experiment of the gods. He has been so twisted about and rearranged that nothing can heal him. There lives on in the soul a longing for something that never can be figured out, let alone achieved. Aristophanes expresses this by distinguishing between being a whole and being one. Hephaestus, who occupies the role of the physician in Eryximachus's speech, offers to melt two lovers together, but he does not offer to untwist them and put them back the way they were. Indeed, the unity Hephaestus holds out would obtain only in Hades where only ghosts and shadows are and there is no embrace.

Aristophanes sees the essence of eros not in sexual pleasure but in the embrace. The embrace is a vain reaching out for one's other half, which is not the other that is ever embraced. Our wish, he implies, in facing one another is to recapture our original natures in which we were back to back, when there was no possibility for one spherical whole to come close to, let alone embrace, another. Recognition is for the sake of communion without cognition. Eros is an unintended result of the double reshaping the Olympian gods performed on us, first by way of punishment and then by way of survival so that we could continue to serve them. There is now a generic adequation of partial selves, when male comes together with male, female with female, or male with female, but there is no possibility of discovering the other half of our individuality. That is forever lost, either at the time of the original punishment or diluted through sexual generation over the course of time. Since the division in the self is presented corporeally, it is not possible to translate it entirely into psychic terms; but Aristophanes seems to assign the soul two layers, an original pride and a subsequent shame, that cannot but remind us of the biblical Fall. Pride made man scale heaven, shame made him realize his defectiveness. Eros, then, is an ever-to-be-thwarted longing for a second try on heaven. We turn to each other in lieu of our rebellion against the gods. For the best of us, the all-male descendants of the sun, gratification of our pride is found in political life. The city replaces the whole, and its rulers retain vestiges of man's former ambition. Within the constraint of the laws of the city smolders a defiance of the gods that is too weak to succeed. Perhaps the most serious defect in Aristophanes' account is his failure to propose an intermediary between the individual and the genus to which the individual belongs. Everyone seeks his other half, but he is condemned never to find it; for even if one posits a split soul, which never alters in the course of generations, there is nothing unique about the fracture line in it that would match up with only one other soul with its corresponding edge. Aristophanes seems to imply, therefore, that this feeling that out there somewhere there is our soul-mate is an illusion. Aristophanes, then, would have told a story that accounts for this feeling and showed it up as an illusion. Because there is no cognitive element in eros for Aristophanes, he cannot offer a typology of souls, which would stand in between sexual difference and individuality. Since the ultimate goal is dissolution of our fragmentary selves, there is no speaking to one another in Aristophanes. The complete silence which his perfect beings would have to maintain toward themselves is foreshadowed by his own hiccup that kept him from speaking in the first place. When he later wishes to criticize something in Socrates' speech, he is again forced to keep silent.

In the biblical account, man and woman experience shame after they eat of the Tree of Knowledge because they realize that neither is in the image of God, who is neither male nor female; in Aristophanes' account, man's shame before his defectiveness is a reminder that he is subject to gods into whose likeness he has been remade. Out of this shame, or at least simultaneously with it, arose eros, a desire to bypass the gods of the law and recover the strength of one's original nature. That nature essentially consists in proud thoughts. Eros blindly serves our claim to be somebody, and the sole purpose of that claim is to be powerful enough to be without constraints. The satisfaction of eros is on the way to the will for power, of which there is still a mutilated version in the devotion of pure males to political life. The city on earth is a poor substitute for our original assault on heaven.

That assault signified the right to be oneself, to be one's own man; but as long as there are gods, the city, and the law, man must put up with love of his own, which is always an arbitrary construction on man's deepest longing. If we ask what basis there is for man's will to be himself, the answer seems to require another Aristophanic story, how man's great thoughts owed their origin to his sense that he was superior to the Olympian gods who somehow or other managed to gain control of the cosmic elements and along with them first subjugated and then punished man. There was once a harmony between man and the cosmos, but the dissolution of that order left man so permanently damaged that even what he thinks would cure him could not restore him. This allows us to formulate the deepest difficulty in Aristophanes' account. It is not that the complete freedom of man would be worse than his present condition, but that the strict individuality that he detects to be the secret spring of eros is not of the same order as man's cosmic origin. Because eros is for Aristophanes not original with man it is divorced from man's rationality. Eros therefore can aspire to a wholeness that lacks intelligibility. To be and to be known are radically separate. When Aristophanes uses the phrase *kata noun,* which literally would mean "according to reason," he intends it to mean "as one likes it." The literalism of Aristophanes, from which his comic inventiveness stems, deserts him at this crucial point. The joke is finally on him.

Insofar as Aristophanes tells a funny story with a tragic message, there would seem to be no place for Agathon, since, though one could say he gives the silliest speech, it is not to be understood in either comic or tragic terms. That Aristophanes' speech suggests both comedy and tragedy throws some light on Socrates' argument at the end, to which both Agathon and Aristophanes put up some resistance, that the artful tragic poet is a comic poet as well. Whatever Socrates may mean—it is striking that neither Aristodemus nor Apollodorus has any interest in asking Socrates for a summary of the argument (neither, it seems, believes that that discussion is part of the *Symposium* or its theme)—Aristophanes' speech is apparently not to be taken as an example of such a synthesis, or Agathon's speech would be unnecessary. Agathon's speech is the only conspicuously well ordered speech in the *Symposium.* It is not only perfectly arranged, but it also states what it intends to do in a clear manner. In this preface Agathon for the first time distinguishes between the god Eros and the effects of which he is the cause. If anything makes Agathon a representative of tragedy it is the focusing on the being of a god. The being of the god is in his beauty, the causality of the god is in his virtue or goodness. The beautiful and the good are thus for the first time separated. The separation between the fourfold character of the beautiful and the fourfold character of the good which Agathon attributes to Eros—on the one hand, youthfulness, softness, liquid form, and beautiful color, on the other, justice, moderation, courage, and wisdom—amounts to a distinction between the beloved and the lover. The beauty of Eros is manifest in the beloved, the goodness of Eros is conferred on the lover. This twofold immanence of Eros is so complete that the god disappears into his human counterparts. Eros, which begins as subject, ends up as a predicate. Eros is simply the verb, "to love." Agathon, in being the first to celebrate the god, is also the first to eliminate the god.

Agathon's speech turns completely on verbal equivocations. Eros, he says, is the most recent (*neotatos*) and always resides in the young *(neoi).* What is young in human time reflects what is youngest in cosmological time. Agathon infers an identity between two orders of time through their identity in language. He uses the homogeneity of language in order to gather unlike things together. His poetic art operates from the beginning in order to bring about the phenomena he claims to interpret. Eros is fully manifest only in poetry; it cannot be fully experienced except in and through poetry, so that rather than poetry and eros being linked phenomena, Eros becomes the invention of poetry. It is wholly non-natural. The issue of poetry becomes explicit in his account of Eros's second trait. Homer is needed, he says, to show the softness, tenderness, and mildness of Eros. Without a poet of the caliber of Homer, what is manifest is not manifest. Agathon needs Homer so that he can model Eros on what Homer said of Ate. Through the tender feet of Ate, Eros obtains feet, too, and thereby a body. No figuration of Eros is possible unless a poet shows the way; but the poet Agathon is not poet enough to work out a human shape for Eros. The form of Eros is so much dependent on its function that Eros ends up completely amorphous, or, if you will, polymorphous. Eros assumes the shape of that in which he resides: on the one hand, the body of the beloved, and the soul of the lover, on the other. Eros, he says, dwells among flowers; his beautiful complexion can be deduced from this. Eros is an allegorical figure; he always points elsewhere and never to himself. Eros is a trope, or, more exactly, he is the essence of all tropes. He is poetry.

The inner nerve of Agathon's speech emerges at two points, first when he assigns to Eros the wisdom of production. Eros is the cause of the coming into being of new beings, both sexually and poetically. Here once again Agathon exploits the language, so that the making of children and the making of poems fall under the same cause. Without realizing it perhaps, Agathon implies that just as a child is not a rational production of his parents, the poet too does not know what the truth is in his poems. What is unknown to Agathon in what he says gives Socrates the opportunity to tie Agathon's speech to his own. Agathon concludes his speech with an extraordinary display of Gorgianic jingles, at the end of which he says, "Eros is the best and most beautiful guide whom every man must follow in hymning him beautifully, partaking in the song that Eros sings in enchanting the thought of all gods and men." Eros's song of enchantment is a song that celebrates as it causes the overcoming of necessity. The essence of necessity is in the difference between the lover and the beloved. The identity of the lover and the beloved, or the disappearance of the alien as such, which was the impossible dream of Aristophanes' speech, occurs through and in song. It is the song of Eros that survives the fusion of the Aristophanic whole.

Socrates begins by attacking all the previous speakers. He does not accuse them of ignorance of the truth about Eros, but rather that they know the truth and consequently could not find anything in Eros to praise. The truth about Eros is terrifying, and only by decking Eros out with spurious beauties and excellencies was praise possible. They were all tragic speeches, Socrates implies, and whistlings in the dark. Socrates himself knows how to praise; one takes the beautiful parts of the truth and arranges them becomingly. Socrates announces that he is going to suppress the ugly elements in Eros; we can say that that ugliness is what all the previous speakers saw and tried to cover up. It is not clear what happens to the whole truth about Eros if Socrates is prepared to present only the beautiful truth; but we can make the suggestion that even in the beautiful truth Socrates manages to insert the whole truth, or that the beauty of Eros comprehends its ugliness. Socrates in fact identifies eros with a certain kind of neediness. He is going to praise the defective. He is going to render the good of the lover beautiful. He is going to praise himself, the ugliest man in Athens.

In the argument with Agathon, Socrates first establishes that Eros is essentially relational. It is always in a relation; it does not enter into a relation. This relation is of a fully determined structure. It is not personal—"I love you" is not its chief characteristic, nor does its object represent a completion of itself. Aristophanic self-love is not of its essence. Socrates uses Agathon's Eros as a god to assign it a structure that is independent of whatever human being it vanishes into, and therefore operative in itself regardless of how anyone believes he experiences it. Eros is fully at work with its own deep structure apart from whatever superficial syntax anyone of us attributes to it in our utterances. Eros as a god is the common acknowledgment that Eros has this structure. Eros, then, is determined to be relational prior to any determination of what it is in relation to and how it is in that relation. Eros, moreover, once it is settled that it is eros or love of something, retains that "of" even after the nominal predicate is translated into a verb. It is supposed to follow from the fact that Eros is eros of something that Eros desires something, even though it does not follow from sight being of color that sight sees color unless one adds, "whenever it does see"; but it is precisely that condition which Socrates omits in the case of Eros. Eros is always desiring something regardless of whatever its human subject thinks or believes.

A peculiarity of Socrates' argument ought to be stressed. His argument is couched in terms of a hypothetical argument with a hypothetical interlocutor. It is through the skillful questioning of Socrates, who forces the interlocutor to bring out into the open what he means, that the conclusion Socrates draws follows. Desire is subject to a dialogic examination so that there is no possibility of self-ignorance. In this brief hypothetical dialogue, Socrates indicates a possible connection between eros and philosophy and suggests how the speeches we have already heard would have disintegrated had Socrates been able to take their speakers through a version of this dialectic exercise.

Socrates brings Agathon to the conclusion that Eros cannot be either beautiful or good; but he does not take him to the next step, that Eros cannot be a god. That next step belongs to a report of Socrates' instruction in erotic things by Diotima. This instruction constitutes the last of three stages in Socrates' philosophic education. The first stage Socrates gives in the *Phaedo.* There he tells his disciples about his conversion from thinking of cause in an Ionian manner to his discovery of the ideas and his turn to speeches; the second phase is in the first half of the *Parmenides,* where Parmenides proves the impossibility of his ideas. According to Parmenides, the most telling objection to them is that even if they exist they cannot be known by us, for there must be a complete separation between divine and human knowledge. It seems to be Diotima, with her notion of the in-between or the demonic, who offered Socrates a way out of the impasse Parmenides left him in. Diotima's solution is not easy to follow, not only because Socrates compresses what must have been a series of lessons into one but because in the course of these lessons she wavers between the beautiful and the good as the primary object of eros. The clearest way to structure Diotima's speech is to divide it between the first part, which concerns Eros as an in-between or *daimonion,* and the second, which concerns the human experience of eros. This division turns out to be equivalent, on the one hand, to a split between the good and the beautiful, and, on the other, to a split between philosophy and pederasty. The division of Diotima's speech into two also proves to be a division between the truth about Eros and the truth about the false beliefs about Eros that all the previous speakers had.

Before we turn to Diotima's complex argument, we should touch on Diotima herself. Socrates presents her as a witch with powers that extended far beyond erotic knowledge. Socrates mentions one disturbing thing about her: she somehow foresaw the coming of the plague to Athens and postponed it for ten years. Rather than the plague exhausting itself in an uncrowded city, Diotima's action served to multiply its virulence when all the country people had been jammed into Athens at the start of the Peloponnesian War in 432 B.C. If Diotima had not interfered and everything else had remained the same, Athens would have almost completely recovered from the plague by the start of the war, and its outcome would fairly certainly have been an Athenian victory. Socrates reports this in the year before the Sicilian expedition and Athens's greatest defeat. That the truth about Eros should be connected, however remotely, with these terrible events seems strange, especially since an Athenian victory in the war would in all probability have saved Alcibiades from exile and Socrates from death. The postponement of the plague recalls the postponement of the report of Agathon's party. Could both be connected alike with the fate of Athens? Apollodorus's postponement of his report would make sense if there were a delay in the confirmation of something Socrates accomplished, which can only now be recognized. If there is anything to this suggestion, it should have to do with Alcibiades, whose political actions turn out to have a Socratic element recognizable only in retrospect.

After assigning Eros to the in-between, Diotima tells the story of his birth, which is meant to show what traits he got from his father Resource and his mother Poverty. What first startles us in the story is that Eros has nothing essentially to do with Aphrodite; he is conceived on her birthday but otherwise they have nothing in common, except insofar as Aphrodite in being a goddess is beautiful and Eros attends her as he does anything else that is beautiful. At the party Resource got drunk on nectar and lay down to sleep it off; but Poverty, who was not invited, hung around the doors like a beggar and plotted like a thief to conceive a child from Resource because of her own resourcelessness. Poverty is both resourceful and resourceless; she already contains within herself everything Eros is supposed to inherit from his father. Eros, then, is poverty, for poverty is split between need and neediness, or self-aware desire. The story is a story—a *muthos* and not a *logos*—because it splits a single entity with an internal structure into two separate entities that then have to be recombined to recover the original. And I would suggest that what characterizes Platonic myths in general is precisely this: a principle is sundered in such a way that a two emerges from a one before it is reabsorbed into something that looks but no longer is one. The procedure, then, for interpreting a Platonic myth would be to reinsert into its negative or dark side a negative version of the positive. If Poverty is negatively resourceless or *aporos,* positively she is *aporia* or perplexity. However this may be, the genealogy of Eros has the advantage of allowing Diotima to spell out all the attributes of Eros as Poverty. On the basis of the presumed identity of the beautiful and the good, Socrates had gotten Agathon to agree that eros is not the good; but among the traits Eros has from his mother in her impoverishment are several that are good without being attractive. He is tough, shoeless, and homeless. Socrates shares in the first two characteristics; but the third—his homelessness—is the most significant. If homelessness is as double as poverty, the lack of a home does not necessarily entail, as Aristophanes believed, that man once had a home from which he was expelled and for which he is forever seeking. Rather, Diotima implies, Eros is completely at home in his homelessness. He is ever at home with neediness. He is indifferent to comfort. Eros, then, never mistakes the local for the universal. Love of country is not part of his makeup. Aristophanes is again mistaken: the city is not his second-best home.

As Diotima presents it, Eros on his mother's side is a being and has a personality, but on his father's side he seems to be colorless and equivalent to what the verbs, nouns, and adjectives that describe him suggest: sophist, enchanter, magician, hunter, etc. Such a distinction reminds us of Socrates, whose irony would seem to dissolve his uniqueness and leave nothing but the philosopher as such. Diotima implies that Eros is in fact the philosopher, for the only thing he desires is wisdom *(phronēsis),* and the only thing he does throughout his life is philosophize. We can then say that Socrates offers through Diotima a self-portrait, which Alcibiades recognizes but misunderstands and gives a completely false account of. Alcibiades is impressed by the features in Socrates of Eros's mother Poverty, but Socrates the philosopher is all-beautiful to him. Alcibiades cannot but acknowledge the ugliness of Socrates, but he believes it can be stripped away entirely and a god within be exposed. Alcibiades delivers a speech that underlines the importance of the in-between, of resisting the temptation to separate and combine mythically or nondialectically. Like Eros, Socrates is not a solution wrapped in an enigma. The enigmatic wrapping is the solution.

Immediately after Diotima establishes the in-betweenness of philosophy—that the midpoint between ignorance and wisdom is not half-ignorance and half-wisdom but the knowledge of ignorance—she turns to the issue of the beautiful and the good in relation to eros. She begins with the dictionary definition of eros—eros is of the beautiful things; but when Socrates cannot answer her question—What does one desire to get in desiring the beautiful?—she switches to the goods, and then Socrates has no trouble in saying that the desire for the good is for one's own happiness. He further admits that everyone wants to be happy; but he is stumped by the question, If all human beings are lovers of the good, why do we not call everyone a lover? The rest of Diotima's account is designed to answer this question. What is left obscure is the relation between Eros as philosopher and happiness or the good. Initially, the identification of the beautiful and the good in Socrates' argument with Agathon denied happiness to Eros; but now that they are no longer the same, it would be possible for Eros still to be not beautiful and yet good, but only if philosophy makes for happiness, or, more precisely, only if knowledge of ignorance is the cause of good. It looks as if this is an issue Diotima left Socrates to decide for himself.

Diotima, as I have said, has to explain how the universal desire for the good, which is eros, has been universally limited to a certain kind of eros, which involves the beautiful. In her account the transition is made through a slide from eros always being of the good for oneself to eros being of the good for oneself always. The shift from the eternity that belongs to eros to the eternity that one desires for oneself grounds the distinction between the good and the beautiful. The beautiful is the reification of desire, not as the beloved but as the production in the beautiful of one's own. Through such a formula Diotima comprehends and corrects Aristophanes, who had seen that eros was of one's own but not that it was productive or generative and effective as such in the beautiful. Self-perpetuation thus becomes the characteristic of eros, first through children and ultimately through glory. Diotima, then, reinterprets Aristophanes in two ways. The desire for oneself, which Aristophanes had seen was impossible, is in fact an illusion, for it always requires a dilution of the self in another. This other represents the beautiful, in which the eternity of the beautiful and the eternity of the self are mutually annihilated in the birth of an illusory self. On the lowest level, this is the mortal offspring; on the next level it is the speech of the lover in which is embodied a version of himself and the beloved. On the highest level, this speech is freed from the individual beloved and is generated in the beauty of the moral; it produces in the first place the heroes of poetry and in the last place the apparently eternal glory of the poet. The poet's fame is the closest to the immortal that the individual can come.

It thus turns out to be no accident that Diotima compared the restriction of the word "lovers," which in the comprehensive sense includes all men, to the restriction of the word "poets," which in the comprehensive sense includes all makers. Diotima denies that Eros as the philosopher is the core of the core of the restrictive term "lover;" rather, Eros as the philosopher is the core of the comprehensive term, while the poets in the broad sense of inventors, makers, and generators are the "lovers" in the restrictive sense, and the core of "lovers" in this restrictive sense are nothing but the poets themselves. The poets exploit the moral for the sake of their own nominal perpetuation. Diotima, then, manages to combine the tragic poet Agathon's stress on production and the beautiful as characteristic of Eros with Aristophanes' stress on the recovery of the eternal self as the forlorn desire of Eros. By this interpretation Diotima is able to account for the sudden awareness of mortality which always accompanies the experience of eros. The feeling of the transience of the self, of body, soul, and every excellence, is the starting point for the variety of attempts to preserve the self, which, though not one of them can ever be successful, achieves its most dazzling effect in the poem, where the beautiful is the vehicle of the good in the form of the poet's renown. Aristophanes' story, one might say, was a vain attempt to get rid of the beautiful entirely and try to win the eternal for the self by itself.

Diotima's account of the connection between lovers and poets is complicated by an interpolation about pederasty, which seems as if it belongs to the next and last section of her speech. Between those who believe they perpetuate themselves corporeally and the poets and legislators who lay down quasi-eternal memorials of themselves, Diotima speaks of the pregnancy of noble youths; but it turns out that what these noble youths are pregnant with are the conceptions of the poets. These conceptions include not only the political virtues but most importantly the Olympian gods, who, Diotima implies, following Herodotus, are the highest offspring of Homer and Hesiod. They are the beings that the noble young absorb and then attempt to reproduce in the beloved through speeches. They are the phantom images of the eternal that always appears in the mode of production. The *daimonion* Eros, on the other hand, is, like Socrates himself, completely sterile.

In the final section, Diotima rehearses the previous section in a pederastic mode. It is addressed as an exhortation to Socrates. Because it is pederastic, eros is no longer productive but visionary. It is not therefore an account of the poet as self-perpetuator in the element of the moral, but an appeal to the young Socrates to give up the pettiness of individuality, which holds no less for the ordinary lover than for the poet who conceals it, and to ascend to the beautiful in itself. Diotima exploits the beautiful in itself against the particular beautiful for the sake of—and this is as truly astonishing as it is bold—eliminating eros entirely. In the ascent of eros, as soon as the lover passes beyond human beings and contemplates the beauty in laws and practices, he ceases to be a lover and becomes solely a spectator. Diotima goes the poet-inventor-legislator one better. She attempts to wean Socrates away from pederasty by setting before him a unitary beauty that the poets never even dreamed of; or rather, it is the unitary beauty that Agathon's praise of Eros pointed to and could not reach, so infected was he by the anthropomorphism of Homer. Diotima surpasses Agathon's Eros by having the beautiful and the good collapse and failing to preserve the difference between seeing and being with, so that the beautiful gives birth to true virtue. The individual returns in the form of a nonpoetic deathlessness. Diotima first explicates Aristophanes and then explodes Agathon. The key word in her contest with the poets is "imagination." The ultimate beauty, she tells Socrates, will not be imagined *(phantasthēsetai)* to be corporeal but will be imagined to be always alone by itself, and everything else to be a participant in it. Since she fails to account for the manner of participation, she admits by her previous argument that this ultimate vision is right opinion and not knowledge. Diotima has managed, then, to give her own version of the double Socrates, the embodiment of Eros the philosopher and Socrates the moralist. It only remains to be seen what Alcibiades makes of it.

Alcibiades says that Socrates does not allow any god or man to be praised when he is present. Alcibiades' speech is in fact the first Greek speech we have which praises in prose a living human being. The possibility of there being such praise seems to depend on the denial that Eros is a god. Whether or not Alcibiades is aware that this is so, and that according to Diotima there cannot be anything that can properly be called religious experience, would be irrelevant, if we can accept for writing the principle *post hoc ergo propter hoc.* Something Socratic would be at work in Alcibiades despite the fact that Alcibiades speaks of his experience of Socrates as a form of religious conversion and comparable to old songs that reveal those who are in need of gods. Alcibiades' speech is an extravagant praise of Socrates' moderation; it makes chastity, temperance, and endurance central to Socrates and denies him wisdom. Alcibiades never takes back, at any rate, his crowning of Agathon for being the wisest and most beautiful. At the beginning of the *Symposium,* Agathon had proposed a contest between Socrates' wisdom and his own tragic wisdom with Dionysus as the judge; at the end, Alcibiades, crowned with violets and ivy, and looking very much like a drunk Dionysus supported by his acolytes, gave the prize to Agathon. Socrates receives as recompense a drunken praise of his sobriety. This sobriety of Socrates, which Alcibiades identifies with his insolence, is said to be the inner truth of Socrates. Socrates' declaration in the *Phaedrus* that the highest form of eros is moderation should not be confused with Alcibiades' caricature, for Alcibiades does not connect his understanding of Socrates' moderation with philosophy. Alcibiades asserts that everything he says is true but at the same time he admits that his speech will not be coherent. The separation he effects between truth and coherence is of the same order as his failure to connect the outer Satyr mask of Socrates with the beautiful image of a god within. Alcibiades does indeed find something in Socrates, but it is not what he believes it is.

In most of his speech, Alcibiades speaks of Socrates in the third person, but in one section he addresses him directly. That section is about Socrates' speeches, whose power does not depend on Socrates being the speaker of them, but regardless of how poor their delivery is they affect Alcibiades in the same way. We know already that Apollodorus's reaction also did not depend on a dialogic encounter with Socrates. In the case, then, of Apollodorus and Alcibiades, the nondialogic character of the *Symposium* suits them. They both revel in self-abasement whenever they hear the Call in Socrates' words. For Apollodorus, the Call is for philosophy; for Alcibiades, the Call is moral. Socrates for him is fundamentally a preacher, whose exhortations to repentance cannot but give Alcibiades pleasure as he wallows in self-contempt. But for all his power, which does not require his presence, Socrates is still nothing but a Sunday preacher. All that Alcibiades retains is the hum of a bad conscience. He does not change his ways. What baffles him about Socrates is the universality of his message and the extraordinary uniqueness. He therefore denigrates the common things Socrates always talks about—shoemakers and blacksmiths—in favor of golden words about morality. In other words, Alcibiades discards philosophy along with the Aristophanic absurdity of Socrates' outer shell and keeps the beautiful god of Agathon. It is this god of moralism which he links up with Socrates the individual through his experience of the unseduceability of Socrates. Socrates merges into his speeches through the insolent treatment of Alcibiades' beauty; and Alcibiades concludes from Socrates' resistance to his charms that Socrates is the real thing, a most moral moralist. On the other hand, Alcibiades senses that Socrates is playing the coy lover, and that his self-control is a device to turn the tables on him and convert him into a lover; but what he is wholly unaware of is that, as a lover, he has reprojected onto Socrates the beloved the image of himself. Alcibiades fell in love with and, as the guests believe, is still in love with, an image of Socrates that reflects himself. This is the mechanism, according to Socrates in the *Phaedrus,* by means of which the lover doubles himself in the beloved, so that in complete self-ignorance the beloved loves himself. This is the final twist on Aristophanes' myth.

It seems, of course, quite fantastic that Alcibiades' image should be of moderation and that Socrates should have implanted in him something that bears so little relation to the Alcibiades we believe we know, especially on the eve of the Sicilian expedition, which, with its fantastic hopes, was the very antithesis of sobriety and moderation. But Alcibiades, as we learn from Thucydides, after he had gone into exile and escaped certain death, and had helped the Spartans both strategically and diplomatically, returned to Athens as its sole salvation, which consisted in winning Athens over to a course of moderation. It is Plato's conceit that this act of moderation was due to Alcibiades' failure to understand Socrates, and thus the enactment in himself of his false image. It is through this long-delayed effect that Socrates came that close to saving Athens. Now that Alcibiades is dead—he died in 404 B.C.—the crazy Apollodorus can tell the true story. Alcibiades will never know.

TEN

Protagoras's Myth and Logos

IN GENERAL, A SPEAKER SHOULD NOT promise more than he can deliver, nor should he present conclusions as the setting for his argument; but in this case, where a part of a Platonic dialogue is to be examined, it is necessary to say something about the way in which Socrates has reported his discussion with Protagoras. Socrates' narration gives a mythical setting to a nonmythical event. Protagoras is another Orpheus who by his voice alone arranges his followers into a disciplined chorus; the house of Callias, whose butler is a very Cerberus, is itself Hades where Socrates as Odysseus sees Hippias as Heracles and Prodicus as Tantalus. Protagoras, then, who chooses to tell first a myth and then a logos, though he could have told a logos from the beginning, is set inside a myth from which we are to extract a logos. The difference between Socrates and Protagoras involves from the first the difference between the Socratic claim that the logos can never be told apart from the myth, and the Protagorean claim that it can. For Socrates, the presentation of *philosophia* is always *muthologia.* Socrates' myth has as its logos the proof that Protagoras is mistaken about the possibility of an immediate access to the logos, and hence Protagoras's myth must remain a myth and never emerge as a logos. Protagoras's myth stands in for a logos that would embrace man in a complete cosmology. That virtue is teachable would be a strict deduction from the nature of all things. The incoherence of Protagoras's myth and logos is a direct outcome of Protagoras's implicit claim. The *Protagoras* as a whole is Socrates' attempt to get at the essential incoherencies in Protagoras's myth and logos and account for them. The *Protagoras* shows that sophistry represents in a ghostly way the city to the city in its essential incoherence. Sophistry encapsulates what it claims to have understood and mastered.

Socrates gets Protagoras to agree that he teaches good counsel *(euboulia),* and that this is the political art that instructs one in how to manage one's own household best and how to be most capable in doing the affairs of the city and speaking of them. Socrates doubts whether good counsel is teachable and cites as evidence the Athenians themselves as likewise not believing it. As evidence, Socrates distinguishes between technical and political matters: the assembly allows only the competent to speak about the former but allows anyone to speak about the latter. Protagoras's myth attempts to ground this distinction; he thus accepts it fully; he does not raise the objection Gorgias does that the proposals for technical matters are in the hands of the politicians. Protagoras distinguishes between Promethean and Jovian gifts and implies that Hippias is to himself as Prometheus was to Zeus. Protagoras has come to complete what Zeus started. That project, Socrates will prove, cannot be completed by Protagoras or anyone else; it cannot even be completed by the union of Hippian and Protagorean knowledge in the form of a hedonistic calculus.

Protagoras begins by distinguishing between gods, on the one hand, and Prometheus-Epimetheus, on the other. He hints that the gods were not, any more than mortal animal was, at the beginning. Gods and Epimetheus both work in the dark. The gods fashion the shape of mortal animals and Epimetheus assigns them the various powers to survive; all these powers are natural and instinctive; but Epimetheus worked out an "eco-system" by adapting fertility to mode of eating, size to habitat, and strength to speed. Epimetheus had three considerations: 1) protection of the animals from each other; 2) protection from the weather; 3) food. Since the first and the last go together, Protagoras seems to have split them in order to indicate the difficulty of juggling several factors simultaneously. Now the distinction between shapes supplied by the gods and powers supplied by Epimetheus certainly reminds us of Hades, or the region of powerless phantoms. If Hades is the workshop of the gods, it is Protagoras himself who suggested to Socrates the notion of representing Callias's house as Hades and the sophists as so many ghosts: Socrates brings the sophists into the light and gives them life. Socrates makes sense of them. Orpheus, for all his enchanting music, failed to bring Eurydice back.

Now man is an intrusion into the perfectly balanced eco-system of Epimetheus. The intrusiveness of man is due to his lack of instincts, a lack to be made up for by art and law. More particularly, man's intrusiveness is due to his lack of cohesiveness as a genus: it is striking that women are not mentioned in the myth. Protagoras implies that had Epimetheus been wise, man would have been a beast without either reason or political life. Rationality is a compensatory mechanism for man's failure to have the right makeup from the start. (One may note that if Protagoras's story is slightly altered, and we say that man was a latecomer in a system in which all niches were already occupied, then a theory of evolution can readily be sketched in.)

Since there was not enough time for a redistribution of powers to be carried out before the appointed hour came when all animals had to come into the light, Protagoras makes Prometheus's action the model of good counsel. Good counsel is needed when the pressure of events precludes perfect solutions. Man became rational because reason was not in control from the start. Since man was going to come into the light as completely helpless, had not Prometheus intervened, and since it seems that Epimetheus must have given the shapes as well as the powers to the other animals, man was in his original state nothing but life itself or the mortal itself. Man is the mortal being in himself; his rationality and sociality are adventitious accretions on that essence.

In order to compensate for Epimetheus's failure to leave some combination of powers for man, Prometheus had to violate the original distribution between mortal and divine and steal from one to make up for a defect in the other. The consequence of this violation was that Prometheus ruined Epimetheus's system as well. Prometheus made each and every man perfectly and completely artful and as a consequence self-sufficient and isolated from other men. There were houses but no families, there was language but no neighbors, there was religion but no cities. The strangeness of this slips into the absurd when Protagoras asserts that men had to found cities in order to protect themselves from wild beasts, as if the houses he does grant them afforded no protection and the arts Prometheus stole from Pallas Athena and Hephaestus did not include the art of making weapons. Furthermore, since man now becomes the prey of wild beasts, Prometheus prevented Epimetheus's system from working: man was so tempting a morsel that the beasts ceased to eat one another and turned en masse on man.

Before some account of this can be given, it must be observed that Prometheus grafts *technē* onto mortal life as such without giving man a distinctive shape. Man is all brains but no body. It is therefore worth pondering that everyone who makes a speech on Eros in the *Symposium* is present in the *Protagoras* with the exception of Aristophanes, and Aristophanes' speech gives an account of man's shape along with his relation to political life and eros, but Aristophanes is completely silent about art and mind. The Platonic understanding of man is the proper mean between the Aristophanic and Protagorean accounts. How such a mean is to be understood is hinted at by Socrates prior to his meeting with Protagoras: the laugh and the blush, he suggests, were the true contribution of Zeus to man's makeup.

But back to our story. We must, however, make still another detour. It is clear that Protagoras is reworking older stories; the possibility of his coming forward publicly as a sophist depends in part on his ability to be a critic of poetry; in particular, his list of Promethean arts bears comparison to two other lists, the first in Aeschylus's *Prometheus Bound*, the second in Sophocles' *Antigone:*

Prometheus Bound	*Antigone*	Protagoras
1. housing	ships	gods
2. astronomy	farming	altars
3. number	hunting	statues
4. letters	taming	speech
5. taming	speech	housing
6. ships	thought	dress
7. medicine	civility	shoes
8. divination	housing	bedding
9. metallurgy	medicine	farming

[In the first list, the second, third, eighth, and ninth items are in opposition to the drift of the second list; the third and seventh items in the second list are in opposition to Protagoras, and the first three items of Protagoras's list are opposed to the drift of the second list, and its sixth, seventh, and eighth items are opposed to the first list.]

Several things jump to the eye. Protagoras's distinction between the Promethean and Jovian phases implies his awareness of the failure on the part of Aeschylus's Prometheus to understand rule and political life, while failing himself to notice the problem that taming raises; and in the case of the *Antigone,* that he noticed, on the one hand, the difference between the second antistrophe about divine law and the rest of the stasimon, and, on the other, the anomaly of *autonomoi orgai* or civility in a list of man's uncanniness, which implied that civility was possible without gods, and so Protagoras reversed it and first gave man gods without civility and then civility in a second distribution. As prominent as gods and things of the gods are on Protagoras's list, so are clothing and other kinds of bodily protection. (He must have noticed the absence of weaving in the *Prometheus Bound* list.) "Gods and clothing" look as if they are the Promethean version of the Jovian distribution of justice and shame. We are therefore forced to wonder why clothing is divorced from shame.

Protagoras does not allow man to be armed against beasts individually, and he does not allow the first city of Promethean man to be armed against one another. Protagoras, then, has given a peculiar version of Socrates' true city of the *Republic* in which the collective life of artful man involves religion but no rule. Protagoras, however, has not made man when isolated a jack of all trades and when social a specialist; rather, he has started from omnicompetent individuals in isolation who on coming together become specialists without, however, working justly together. Plato, we may say, lets Protagoras observe the defects in Socrates' true city and try to solve them in a way that does not involve any intervention on the part of the interlocutors: Protagoras appeals over the heads of those he is addressing to the character of Athenian democracy as a corrective to the radical isolation of Promethean man. This appeal allows for the introduction of sociality but still without a ruling element. Whereas in the *Republic* Glaucon's objection to the true city ultimately allows for the rule of the philosopher-king, Protagoras's adjustment of his story to fit Athenian democracy does not allow for the rule of the sophists. In light of the later argument, in which Socrates asks Protagoras how the five virtues are related to one another, Protagoras should not have said that each was a part of the face but rather that moderation and justice correspond to the face as a whole and thus represent their indispensability as habits for the possibility of the rule of wisdom or good counsel.

Protagoras says that completely self-sufficient men first came together to protect themselves against beasts; but they dispersed when they proved to be unjust to one another. He seems to imply that man's injustice to man did greater harm or was experienced as greater harm than whatever beasts inflicted on them; but he has taken away the possibility of any economic basis for their injustice by making each man self-sufficient. Man, then, is by art radically separate and by nature radically unjust. Man, then, cannot be mortal life; he must be essentially willful over against others. Protagoras seems to be in need of something like *to thumoeides* in order to ground man's injustice. Protagoras has certainly seen that artful man is wholly unerotic and asocial; the specialization of arts forces men to be together but it does not make them live together; but Protagoras is altogether silent about the domineering nature of man over man; for had he admitted it, he would have had to acknowledge its social character and therefore the impossibility of there ever being pre-Promethean man. A sign of the difficulty is this: Protagoras speaks metaphorically of the war beasts waged against men, but though he grants that *polemikē* is part of *politikē,* he never speaks of wars between cities. Promethean men have internal and external enemies; Jovian man ceases to have internal enemies and by a kind of miracle his external enemies have disappeared. Protagoras's error, one might say, arises from his moving too quickly from the city of arts to the democratic city without reflecting on patriotism.

When Zeus finally interferes with the Promethean scheme, he learns from Hermes that in cities the arts are assigned in accordance with the Socratic principle of one man one job. How Promethean man lost his omnicompetence is not explained; it was certainly due neither to justice nor the principle of justice, for if it were, then Zeus or Prometheus before him would have distributed justice in the same way, and either Promethean man would have been perfectly just and perfectly self-sufficient or Jovian men would have had among them men who by possession of the political art would be the rulers of other men. There lies concealed, then, in Protagoras's story the outline of the *Republic:* the just man is the philosopher and the true ruler of the city. Protagoras therefore is being represented as a figure transitional between the deeper wisdom of Aeschylus and Sophocles and the Socrates of the *Republic.* Indeed, Protagoras shares one feature with the Chorus of the *Antigone:* like that Chorus, everything Protagoras says is very profound while he himself remains a man of extraordinary thoughtlessness. Protagoras, in his extreme incoherence, parodies the circumstantiality of prudence. Protagoras makes it clear that "political art" is his name for what Zeus calls justice and shame (322b8). He thus implies that a range between amateur and professional could have been introduced by Zeus, so that whereas Zeus is needed to distribute noncognitive justice and shame throughout the city, Protagoras himself is needed to transform the habits of civility into the knowledge of rule. Protagoras, however, cannot avail himself of this range without coming forward as the subverter of democracy and contradicting his claim to distinction, that for the first time with him sophistry has presented itself publicly as sophistry without his incurring any risks.

Protagoras regards the range within the city of amateur-professional as less decisive than the difference between civility and savagery. That difference is established by Zeus in the form of a law that orders cities to execute those men who are incapable of partaking in justice and shame. The gods of the city differ from the Promethean gods by being punitive.

Zeus is needed in order to sanction the execution of criminals. This is not something that Promethean man could figure out for himself: he could not figure out, on the basis of the difference between art and non-art, that criminals are not the ignorant. Protagoras implies, therefore, that the political art is teachable but is not art. This massive contradiction explains why the structure of the *Protagoras* is so complex: if the political art is virtue and is teachable, every argument that Socrates mounts that purports to prove that virtue is knowledge should meet with Protagoras's immediate acceptance; but Protagoras balks at accepting every one of Socrates' arguments, which are all designed to refute Socrates and confirm Protagoras's claim. To understand why Protagoras does not let his own claim be vindicated by Socrates is at the heart of the mystery of the *Protagoras.*

Socrates had said that the Athenians do not believe that everyone has political virtue; to prove, to the contrary, that everyone partakes of justice and the rest of political virtue, Protagoras offers the following. If someone says he is a skilled flute player and is not, everyone laughs or gets angry, and his relatives try to put sense into him as if he were crazy; but if someone whom everyone knows is unjust denounces himself in front of the many, everyone says this is madness and not moderation; and everyone ought to say he is just regardless, and everyone who does not pretend to it is crazy. This proof is not easy to understand: how does it prove that everyone really believes that men partake of justice and moderation and not that everyone must pretend to partake? Protagoras seems to be saying that the distinction between moderation in technical knowledge and moderation in morality shows that moderation is not just habit but rational and evidence of the presence of good counsel in all men. More cautiously, one can say, everyone knows that one must tell lies, and the city of Promethean man is the city of truth-telling, or, in Socrates' language, the true city, and that justice is not possible without falsehood. The city, then, does not rest on a myth, as Socrates would have it, but on the universal knowledge of the use of myths. There are two requirements of political life, justice and sanity (knowing when to lie and when not). Zeus arranges for justice by allowing men to execute the justice-incompetent; the human equivalent for moderation is to agree that the truthful unjust man is crazy. The crazy, however, cannot be justly killed; the city kills only the sane; they kill those who lay claim to justice; they kill those whom Zeus forbade them to kill, for the savage are those outside the city who do not know enough about justice to lie about it. Protagoras, then, can get everyone sensible and moderate but not simultaneously just; and in the argument with Socrates later he creates a diversion before he would have been forced to identify justice and moderation and reaffirm the unity of virtue. If, moreover, one puts together Protagoras's argument about the universal distribution of moderation with real justice, one gets Socrates' counter-example before Cephalus, from which it would follow of necessity that not everyone has good counsel, for otherwise one would not need to lie because no one would be crazy.

Protagoras's evidence for the teachability of virtue is punishment. No one unless he is like a beast punishes irrationally. Protagoras assumes that this image *qua* image is always an effective deterrent; otherwise, he would have to admit that it would be possible to punish bestially and irrationally, and so it would be possible to institute a city of quasi-beasts. As Protagoras develops his argument, it turns out that the city can punish rationally if it punishes on each occasion for the sake of those who witness the punishment and who are thus deterred from injustice. So regardless of whether the city punishes rationally or not, it punishes rationally if the desired effect is achieved. Protagoras confuses rationality with the teaching of a lesson. He takes the literal meaning of *noutheteō*—to put mind into someone—as the true meaning of "knocking sense into someone" by beating him up. Punishment is rational because what one says one is doing is what one is doing. It is the collective justice of the city that matches the individual's sensible refusal to admit that he is unjust.

The essence of irrational punishment or vengeance is to try to undo the done. No man in the city is unaware of the irreversibility of action, and in this sense everyone in the Jovian city is rational. Promethean man, then, was apparently unaware of the noncancellability of time. The arts because they are synthetic do not contain this knowledge. Promethean man did not know that he would die, or he believed in resurrection. So Zeus brought man through Hermes the psychopomp the knowledge that death is final. Man then became sober. The Jovian law of execution revealed the minimum condition for sobriety. "Kill the unjust!" meant "Know that you are mortal." Now it is remarkable that in Aeschylus's account, pre-Promethean man did have knowledge of his own death while Prometheus removed it and put in blind hopes instead. Protagoras has apparently taken this to mean that the universal opinion that man is mortal is a post-Promethean gift of Zeus. (In any case, one should consider in light of this, Pindar's *Olympian* II, where the overthrow of Kronos by Zeus is taken to entail the cancellation of time through the invention of the soul. The Zeus of Pindar acknowledges man's irrational resentment against time and tries to mollify us with the hope of an afterlife.) If, then,

Protagoras is connecting the awareness of time with Zeus, the unintelligible sequence of Promethean man's arts would reflect his unawareness of time.

The parade of irrationality in the guise of rationality in Protagoras's myth emerges in two ways. He says the Athenians punish those they believe are unjust; they thus violate Zeus's commandment to punish the justice-incompetent, for that commandment depends on knowledge and not opinion. Protagoras will later say that the most unjust within the city is just if compared to the savages outside the city. He thereby implies that none of these can be punished in conformity with Zeus's commandment. Protagoras's silence, moreover, about war once the Promethean city dissolves is explicable if one draws the consequence of his argument: the enemy are killed because they are incapable of partaking in justice. Thus the war against beasts in the Promethean city becomes realized in the Jovian city because the enemies are beasts. The bestialization of man belongs together with the civilization of man, and it is not true that the savages do not partake of justice. Protagoras has to cite a comedy in order to show whom he means by savages. Savages are an invention of the poets designed to conceal the savagery of the city.

So much for Protagoras's myth; when he comes to answer Socrates' question, why the good do not teach their own sons to be good, Protagoras calls it a logos. This distinction should reflect the difference between the minimal justice and moderation all citizens must have and the good counsel reserved for the good. It should reflect the difference between the justice and shame Zeus distributed and the good counsel Zeus himself had in so distributing them. So the myth and the logos sections ought to correspond to a distinction between morality and prudence and fit more or less with the movement of the *Republic.* It is not at once obvious that this is the case: if Protagoras had wanted to do so, he could have dropped all mention of piety in the logos-section. Piety, however, belonged to Promethean man and was separate from justice and shame. It could not be dropped without dropping every connection between art and morality and thus admitting that the political art cannot be taught. "Belief in gods" at the beginning implies that in time it can become knowledge.

Perhaps the most remarkable feature of Protagoras's logos is the resemblance of its stages to those of the *Republic* 2–3 together with an extraordinary emphasis on beating. Protagoras's education is both musical and unmusical; it is as if he maintained the identity of the philosopher and the dog, with which Socrates starts out as a serviceable image, and preserved it throughout, whereas Socrates gradually moves from the presentation of education as the musical education of the thumoeidetic to its truth as the education of the erotic. Such a movement does not take place in Protagoras's account. This Orpheus is the enchanting preacher of punishment and revenge.

Protagoras divides education into two stages, private and political. Private education is itself divided into a preliterate and a literate stage. The family has its biggest role at the first stage, when the noble, the just, and the holy are taught. Protagoras, however, is silent about the good; indeed, he never speaks of the good as a piece of instruction by anyone, even though he claimed that good counsel or advice about the good was his own art and the city's knowledge. A sign of this is the ellipsis of the apodosis at 325d5, where he does not say what the consequence is if one obeys or is persuaded by one's earliest teachers. Protagoras is much more explicit about the consequence of disobedience: the child is bent and twisted like a piece of wood until he is straightened out by threats and beatings. If, however, the boy is so straightened out, how come he does not keep his acquired shape? How come at the end the city has to straighten him out again after he has finished his private education? In the second stage, the central lesson comes from good poets in whose poems there are models of emulation. Protagoras says not a word about the gods. What Protagoras presents so casually, the praise of good men, is the hard-earned result of nine books of the *Republic,* where in the tenth book the possibility of such encomia is granted alongside the hymns to the gods. In the third stage, which belongs to good lyric poets, Protagoras moves, just as Socrates does in Book 3 of the *Republic,* from speech to rhythm and harmony. But perhaps what is more astonishing, the training in courage is entirely given over to gymnastics; but this reassignment, which portrays courage as entirely corporeal, is the culmination of the movement in the separation of courage and moderation in Socrates' account so that they finally emerge as problematic objects of inquiry. Protagoras does all this with the left hand.

It looks, then, at this point that justice and piety are learned in nursery school, moderation and courage in grammar and high school, and Protagoras of course is the graduate dean. But where is the college of wisdom? The answer is, the laws of the city. The city compels the young to learn the laws and live in conformity with them so that they may not act at random. As far as the city goes, all that expensive education is a waste, for whatever the young have been taught and however they have been whipped into shape are wholly inadequate for instilling obedience to the law. What has happened? The laws of the city are the legislation of the ancient good legislators. The good legislators are not the good poets, for if they were, Protagoras could not have said that the former poets concealed their sophistry under the guise of poetry; but it is now revealed that the secret sophists who were poets are openly used for education in private. Protagoras thus admits that education in poetry is in fundamental violation of the city and its laws. He admits in short with Socrates that ancient poetry cannot be the proper education if the standard is virtue as the city understands virtue. Protagoras admits, then, that poetry does not teach political virtue and that political virtue is nothing but the result of terror and pain. Insofar as the city teaches anything, it teaches one not to get caught. That Protagoras knows or at least comes to know that this is the consequence of his argument comes out later when, in abandoning the main argument that virtue is a whole of parts, Protagoras criticizes Simonides for having a contradiction in a short lyric poem. Protagoras calls such criticism a large part of education. He thus implies that education in poetry is not political virtue and is incompatible with it. In criticizing Simonides, he sides with all men who believe that to keep virtue in one's possession is the hardest of all things, whereas the poets are at one in saying that once it has been acquired it is easy to retain. The poets say virtue suits man, Protagoras says it is troublesome. Protagoras, in attacking poetry, in the name of universal opinion, urges the city to abandon music education and rely entirely on punishment and threats. Protagoras the rationalist urges the brutalization of man.

Later in the dialogue there is a discussion of the word *deinos,* which literally means "terrifying" and comes to mean "skilled and clever." It is the word used at the beginning of the first stasimon of the *Antigone*—πολλὰ τὰ δεινὰ κοὐδὲν ἀνθρώπου δεινότερον πέλει: the uncanniness of man turns out to be behind Protagoras's myth. Protagoras claims that the teachability of virtue is the same as the hidden unity in the double meaning of *deinos:* To teach is to terrify. Now such a forced mating of Beating with the Muses amounts to the theme of the *Gorgias,* where Socrates explores the possibility of a punitive rhetoric. The *Protagoras* and the *Gorgias* are a paired set of dialogues that take the *Republic* apart. The *Gorgias* examines the soul-structure of the *Republic* apart from the city, and the *Protagoras* examines the city-structure of the *Republic* apart from the soul. The two dialogues thus fulfill Socrates' claim that the relation between rhetoric and sophistry is analogous to that between the art of justice and the art of legislation, which he sketches at the beginning of the *Gorgias.* There he asserts that as cosmetics is to cookery so sophistry is to rhetoric, and as gymnastics is to medicine so legislation is to justice.

Sophistry and rhetoric are the phantom images of two genuine arts. They are phantoms because they pass off the irrational as rational, Gorgias in starting from the so-called Socratic thesis that virtue is knowledge, and Protagoras from the rationality of punishment. The movement of the two dialogues is thus reversed. In the *Gorgias,* Socrates passes from the epistemic-high of the Gorgias section, through the rationality of just punishment, to an attack on pleasure, whereas in the *Protagoras,* Protagoras begins with the rationality of punishment, and Socrates separates them through his Spartan myth, where Spartan courage is the mask of wisdom, only to end up with a pseudo-science of pleasure. Socratic politics in its truth is as alien from harshness as it is from hedonism, but this does not preclude it from playing at both as genuine displays of its own good counsel; rather, it is all but compelled toward these.

ELEVEN

On Plato's *Lysis*

> [Professor James Gordley] had asserted that within limits a word can be applied to different particulars, but still have an invariable meaning. Thus, one can make a "friend" of a multiplicity of human beings—though not of a kangaroo. Professor Daube replied, "Perhaps in staid Berkeley, a sincere and lasting friendship with a kangaroo is beyond the pale, but in San Francisco, where I live, it is regarded as entirely normal."[1]

IN THE *LYSIS* PLATO HAS SOCRATES present himself at his sleaziest. He reports how he undertook to pimp for the silly Hippothales and succeeded first in smashing the false pride of Lysis and then in breaking down the distinction between love and friendship, so that Lysis could not but accept Hippothales into the same association he shared with Menexenos. The puzzle, Who is a friend? served as a cover for the display of Socrates' erotic technique. That he did it for free seems to make it all the more reprehensible, since he did not have the excuse of his own advantage for disillusioning Lysis about his family and advancing Hippothales' interests. If we disregard the frame and consider the arguments about the friend in themselves, we imitate Socrates, who argues for the neutrality of body, soul, and other things, if each is taken by itself, as if there ever were a living body that was neither sick nor healthy. The theoretical attitude that Socrates exemplifies, in urging the perspective of neutral being, is as false to the nature of things as is the detachment of the perplexities of friendship from a setting that determined from the start the triumphant assimilation of *philein* to *eran.*

This harsh indictment of Socrates is delivered by Socrates himself. He makes himself look bad without offering any defense. His account, which confirms the worst nightmares of Athenian fathers, supplies his auditors with far more information about what really happened than anyone within the dialogue could know. There is, in the first place, the difference between the circle of young men, whom Socrates meets outside Mikkos's palaestra, and the boys within, who do not know the purpose of

Socrates' questioning. The boys are naive theoreticians of friendship, the young men have already lost their innocence. Among the boys, moreover, Lysis shares with the young men an argument that Menexenos does not know; Lysis shares with Socrates a conversation that the young men are not privy to; and we share with Socrates his interpretation of events no one knew at the time. We know in particular of a mistake Socrates almost made. Even if, however, we are more privileged than anyone else, we still have not been fully taken into Socrates' confidence. We are not his most intimate friends before whom Socrates lets down his hair and from whom he holds nothing back. Socrates' shamelessness, in allowing us, on the basis of evidence he himself supplied, to look at him in the worst possible light, cannot be construed as candor. Socrates has left things out. He does not explain, in general, why he retells the story, and, in particular, why he decided to help Hippothales out and not continue on his way to the Lyceum. Although he is not unattracted by Hippothales' invitation to join him and enter the palaestra, he still resists before he finds out whether there is anything in it for him. In the interval between Socrates' question—"On what condition shall I enter?"—and the arrangement that guaranteed the ensnarement of Lysis, Socrates heard something that made up his mind to enter. We are left to puzzle out for ourselves what finally induced Socrates to show off his skills and blacken his name.

The complete trust we associate with friendship, Socrates assigns to knowledge. It is through wisdom, Socrates tells Lysis, that Lysis could be universally loved and at the same time gain the freedom to do as he liked. Just as whoever is trusted to be an expert cook can add to the soup all the salt he wants, and whoever is trusted to be an expert physician can pour ashes into the eyes of the son of the Persian king, so Socrates, who proves to Hippothales his own competence in erotic things, can delude any forlorn lover, who puts himself entirely in his hands, and carry out any whimsical enterprise he has in mind. On this occasion Socrates' whim is to declare his lack of friends and bafflement before the question, "Who is a friend?" Within the claim to be wise in erotic things, Socrates discusses his own ignorance. While he pretends to know in an instant who is lover and who beloved, he pretends not to know who is the friend. If we assume that the lover wants to become a friend, or, at least as Hippothales puts it, wants to become friendly *(prosphilēs)* to the beloved, Socrates' knowledge stops at inequalities, but if and when an equality is realized, his ignorance begins. Socrates knows everything there is to know about the imbalance and instability of relations, but when it comes to harmony and what the proverb *koina ta philōn* means, Socrates is at a loss. Philosophy,

Socrates seems to be saying, is what he knows, but wisdom, in which the knower and the known would be as one, eludes him, not only in the sense that he does not have it but also by way of Meno's paradox that he would not know what it was even if he did have it. If this is the drift of Socrates' argument, then the grafting of Hippothales onto the friendship of Lysis and Menexenos was not designed to promote the lover but to demote the friend and introduce longing and desire into what the lover believes he wants and the friend believes he has achieved.

Such a conclusion, however, is not altogether satisfactory. In the dialogue, philosophy belongs, as its name indicates, to what Socrates does not know; it is not assigned to the outer frame, in which the issue is eros and Socrates' knowledge. The setting of the dialogue thus seems to put into question the relation between Socrates' erotics and Socrates as philosopher, which in other dialogues, where they are treated as the same, cannot even be raised as a problem. If the question were to be put linguistically, one would ask whether it was just an accident that *philosophia* had not been designated *erōtosophia* (wisdom of love), and if Socrates had been in charge from the first, whether philosophy would have been stamped with his own understanding of it. If Socrates is necessarily a secondary development within philosophy, is the emergence of eros as philosophy likewise secondary? Parmenides' own chariot is urged on by *thumos,* but when Parmenides is a Platonic character he speaks at least metaphorically of *erōs.*[2] It might be thought, alternatively, that Socrates is perfectly satisfied with "philosophy," and nothing is at stake in the apparent difference between *philein* and *eran.* The peculiar structure of the *Lysis,* in which everything turns on keeping friendship and love distinct, argues against Socrates' acquiescence in "philosophy." If, however, *erōs* does bear on philosophy, we seem to be invited by the *Lysis* to infer that as Socrates' knowledge is to Socrates' ignorance as *erōs* is to *philia,* so the breaking of the barrier between the outer and the inner frame, which is symbolically represented by the occasion of the Hermaia that allows young men and boys to mingle, would involve the emergence of philosophy as Socrates' knowledge of ignorance. Socrates would thus be recounting in the *Lysis* how he came to understand the relation between the two primary constituents of his makeup, the gift from god to recognize lover and beloved and his constant search from childhood for friends. Socrates has already worked up the first into an art and the second into a conundrum. The conundrum is that he must in some sense know what a friend is but does not know how to go about finding one, and the art is that he knows what something is that no one else who ever experienced it knows. There is, on the one hand, the opacity of an experience, and, on the other, the obscurity of a way. Socrates figured out what it means for the ideal to be experienced as the real, but he still does not know whether his own postulated goal is real. He is possibly under a delusion himself while he has seen through the illusions of everyone else. If the *Lysis* represents Socrates' relation to philosophy, then it should indicate how Socrates combined his erotic science with his erotic disposition toward the acquisition of friends.

If we take Socrates at his word, his desire to have friends is no more explicable for than another's love of horses or quails.[3] There is no "theory" to explain his taste, any more than a preference for redheads has a deep significance. Socrates the pederast goes to the heart of things, Socrates the *philetairos* is just the way he is. It is neither good nor bad, neither grand nor base. Socrates seems to be the paradigm of neutral being, on which his account of friendship turns. Socrates' individuality, which resists logos and metaphysics, seems to be equally true of friends. Lovers talk about their love, and that is what makes them philosophically interesting—"truly" and "always" are never far from their lips; but friends do not talk about their friendship, and that is what makes them devoid of interest. The lover Hippothales cannot shut up about Lysis, the friends Lysis and Menexenos have never discussed in all their quarrels what the proverb *koina ta philōn* means. *Erōs* is experienced as a god, *Philia* or *Philotēs* is a fiction of poets. Diotima has to demythologize *erōs* against experience and make its verbal cognate central, but no one is needed to do the same for "Friend." Gods show up as strangers and not friends. Just as there is nothing theologically at stake in the friend, so there is a range in *philos* that resists an exact determination. Whoever or whatever one is attached to in whatever degree or manner is *philos.* If Helen is the ultimately desirable, for whom not even Trojan elders are distressed to fight, Briseis is not, even though Achilles uses her as an excuse to quarrel with Agamemnon. Briseis is but part of Achilles' measly reward for merit, *oligon te philon te,* of which "a small thing but my own" is not an entirely incorrect translation.[4]

Everything unfathomable about friendship shows up in the relation between Hippothales and Ktesippos. Granted that Ktesippos is particularly insolent and sharp,[5] it is surprising how scornful and mocking he can be of Hippothales and still remain his friend. If he were not a good friend and very understanding, he would not have put up with the drunk and sober Hippothales singing and reciting day and night his compositions in praise of Lysis. Even if he exaggerates and Hippothales does not harp on Lysis as much as he claims, or his poems are not as bad as he says they are, Hippothales, if he had to put up with this kind of abuse, would have broken with him long ago were not there something he valued in his friendship with Ktesippos, unless of course we are to suppose that he tolerates this side of Ktesippos only to gain access to Lysis through his cousin Menexenos (206d3); but if this were the case, Ktesippos is surely clever enough to have figured it out and broken with him for that reason alone. There is, then, already in the outer frame enough matter for reflection on the friend, and it would have been unnecessary to confront a milder version of the same tensions in Lysis and Menexenos. Lysis has already detected in Menexenos the eristical training of Ktesippos and feels himself to be enough at a disadvantage to want Socrates to knock the stuffing out of him and make him feel the lash of denigration as much as he had just experienced it from Socrates. Socrates, however, seems not be interested in these aspects of friendship. He records them but does not treat them. He seems to be after the alphabet, or better perhaps the syntax, of friendship that can afford to assign things of this order to the unlimited of individual experience. Whereas we might be inclined to suppose that that was all there was to friendship, Socrates, by making philosophy central to his understanding of it, thinks he discerns a structure in it that can be formulated precisely and dispense with all the variety of its expression. This structure, however, for all its comprehensiveness does have a core of individuality. It is Socrates the philosopher who stands at the center of "the friend."

The Hermaia was a festival that allowed some loosening of the rules that governed palaestras but not as much, if we can trust Aeschines, as Socrates represents in the *Lysis.* The *neaniskoi* could mingle with the *paides,* and the slaves could get drunk on the job, but Socrates should still have not accepted Hippothales' invitation.[6] We must suppose either that the regulations were not at all times strictly maintained or that Socrates deliberately flouts them and courts trouble for himself and Mikkos. To discuss friendship is to challenge the authorities. In deed, Socrates has not let the corrupting talk about seduction intrude on the more innocent discussion of friendship and in this sense has obeyed the intent of the law; but since the earlier talk sets up the later, we cannot say that Socrates is as moral as he might appear at first to Lysis and Menexenos in carrying on so high-minded a discussion. Lysis certainly seems to see through him at the end, even if he did not notice Hippothales' face changing into all the colors of the rainbow. Lysis's disenchantment, however, does not happen early enough to spoil the structure of Socrates' argument. It is timed exactly right. The license of the Hermaia, of which Socrates takes advantage, imposes certain constraints as well. The occasion separates Lysis from Menexenos for a crucial moment, as Menexenos goes off to attend to some sacrifices, and Socrates manages to complete in the interval the master argument for the subsequent discussion: Socrates returns to it at the end. The subsequent discussion, in which Menexenos is the main interlocutor, is under a time constraint. It can last no longer than the time available before Lysis has to go home (211b5); and again Socrates manages to come in under the wire, but perhaps only because the slave *paidagōgoi* delayed as long as they dared to gather up their charges. The situation recalls the *Republic,* where Cephalus's withdrawal to attend the sacrifices allows Socrates to dismiss any obligation of ours to the gods as part of justice. Cephalus's withdrawal also weakens the obligation Polemarchus might otherwise have felt to defend his father's position. In the *Lysis* Socrates exploits Lysis's isolation from his friend to destroy any confidence Lysis might have had in the unconditioned love of his mother and father. The family, as the primary experience of *philia* and one's own, goes by the board under the auspices of Hermes. The sacred works in harmony with Socrates to overthrow the sacred. The slaves return as *daimones* at the end too late to repair the damage.

Socrates' argument with Hippothales, which convinces him of his expertise and encourages him to enlist Socrates in making Lysis more amenable, bears directly on the first argument with Lysis. Socrates convinces Lysis that knowledge alone makes for right; so that even his own is not his own unless he can show he knows how to use it, and once he has that knowledge his own is no more his own than his neighbor's is his own since knowledge knows no boundaries between "mine" and "thine." In light of this argument, Hippothales' celebration of Lysis's family is doubly absurd. In supposing that what belonged to members of Lysis's family belongs to Lysis—it is all in the family—Hippothales betrayed his belief that if Lysis became his all the glory of Lysis's family would descend on him as well. Just as the beautiful blond on the arm of her escort is presumed to shed her beauty on him (even if it is only a proof of his power), so Hippothales, in crowing before he won, was laying claim to goods that, Socrates proves, not even Lysis has. Hippothales cannot have a share in what is not Lysis's to offer. Hippothales had put Lysis out of reach and made himself absurd by writing a poem in which he declared that he was in love with a descendant of Zeus. Indeed, had he put together the victories of Lysis's father and grandfather with the origin of the family in the offspring of Zeus and the daughter of the founder of the deme Aixone, and then coupled them with the entertainment this offspring gave to Heracles on the basis of their kinship, Hippothales would have written an old-fashioned Pindaric epinikion.

We can easily reconstruct on a Pindaric model the general plan of such a poem. It would have begun with the parallel between Hippothales winning Lysis and his family winning chariot races. There would then have been an account of the relation between the universal and the local, between Zeus and the daughter of the hero-founder of an Attic deme, and how this relation led to the bestowal of a hereditary priesthood of the Heraclidae on the family of Lysis.[7] Hippothales' love-poem and victory ode in one would also put side by side a story of love and a story of friendship *(xenismos).* A mythical connection would have been made between *erōs* and *philia.* The Pindaric Hippothales would be saying that the heroic contains within itself both the beauty of *erōs* and the sacred bond of friendship, and the latter is an offspring of the former. One's own is erotically divine in origin, but genealogically it is preserved through the sacred. All this would then be renewed in the mutual love of Lysis and Hippothales, of which the poem itself would be the new offspring.

Socrates dismantles this entire fairy tale. It may do as poetry, but it does not answer Hippothales' needs. Ktesippos saw that Hippothales had lost sight of Lysis in writing up family history and myth. Despite the attention he must have given to Lysis, Hippothales could not come up with anything that was both properly Lysis's and lovable. Lysis's beauty, which made him known to Socrates, was in the form of *eidos* (204e5)—it manifested the class—and everything else Hippothales collected had nothing peculiar *(idion)* to Lysis in it. It is, I think, this remark of Ktesippos that settles the issue for Socrates whether he is to interrupt his journey or not. The *idion,* which is good and does not become universal once there is knowledge, determines Socrates' inquiry into the friend. In taking away from Lysis any ground for his pride, Socrates offers simultaneously the exhilaration of omnicompetence or wisdom that would give back to Lysis even more than was taken away. But what happens to Socrates, who knows that wisdom is impossible? How can he keep anything his own in light of his ignorance? Socrates can knock Lysis down while he sets him up, but is not Socrates already down and out for the count? The picture he paints for Lysis—the freedom to do whatever he likes while usurping through his wisdom what is really his—cannot even be a dream for Socrates. Within the domain of his erotic science, Socrates can of course become everyone's friend and do with them what he likes, but this partial science is as nothing to what Socrates does not know; and besides, even within the erotic domain, Socrates does not have anything that is his own, for by his knowledge his own returns to him as a universal. It is precisely because the wise Lysis would have nothing of his own that Socrates has to offer him the freedom of whimsicality. The indifference of velleity survives total wisdom, and nothing else. It is the counterpart to Socrates' personal taste for friends in light of his erotic wisdom.

Lysis's peculiar good, which Hippothales failed to spot, is discovered by Socrates. An outburst of Lysis against his express promise not to be more than a listener elicits Socrates' pleasure at his *philosophia* (213d7). Philosophy seems to be that which can be one's own despite one's ignorance. A blush immediately followed Lysis's outburst. He realized that he had erred and against his will confessed it. This involuntary expression of shame, which publicly displays something one wishes to keep private, is at the opening of the *Lysis*. Hippothales first blushes when Socrates sees through his carefully neutral and philosophic answer to Socrates' question, "Who is the beauty?" "One of us thinks one is, another another." By his wording, Hippothales wanted to forestall Socrates' question, but instead he left an opening. He wanted Socrates to enter without declaring his interest. His wording expresses the same indifference as Socrates does when he puts his love of friends on a par with any other acquisitive preference (204b3, 211d7–8). Hippothales blushes a second time and even more after Socrates tells him about his peculiar gift. Socrates' gift seems to be nothing more than the capacity to understand the blush. That the blush occurs exclusively in Socratically narrated dialogues—and nowhere more frequently is there the verb for it *(eruthrian)* than in the *Lysis*[8]—suggests that it is of some importance for philosophy and Socrates' need to retain his own without knowledge. The *Lysis* also contains the only occasion when Socrates admits he almost made a mistake. After he has humiliated Lysis, he was about to point out triumphantly to Hippothales that this is how one goes about cutting a beloved down to size, but he checks himself at the last moment when he notices the anguish in Hippothales' face and remembers that he had not wanted to make his presence known to Lysis (210e5–7). Socrates' pride almost got the better of him and ruined Hippothales' prospects while trumpeting his own skill. Had Socrates blurted out what he had intended to say, he would apparently have blushed a second later when he realized that he had betrayed his role and thereby aborted any further discussion of the friend. Socrates' account of his almost-error and quick recovery cannot but remind us of his sudden inflammation on catching sight of what was within Charmides' cloak and his regaining self-control with some effort.[9] Both episodes seem to point to the issue of self-knowledge and its impossibility: When Charmides blushes after Socrates urges him to look within and report what he perceives his moderation to be, he does not say that it is shame (157c5–d6).

The erotic diagnostics of Socrates seems to be as trivial and useless as Socrates says he is in all other respects (204b8–c1). It is trivial because it consists of an easy inference from a blush, and it is useless because nothing can be done with such an inference. It is as certain as it is vain. If, of course, it were the same as the detection of philosophic natures, and Lysis's blush were as indispensable for its detection as his ejaculation, then the display of a defect, which through its very display reveals the defect to oneself, would have some weight for Socrates' understanding of the connection between his well-known interest in beautiful boys and philosophy proper.[10] This possible connection makes Socrates' examination of the friend all the more puzzling. A large range of the blush belongs to *erōs;* the blush seems to have no place in friendship. Hippothales pestered Ktesippos and others shamelessly about Lysis; but as soon as he met someone outside the circle of his intimates, he blushed. Ktesippos does not have as nice a sense of the difference between the private and the public as Hippothales does; or else he believes that Socrates is to be included among Hippothales' friends, though even so he thinks he has to justify the treachery by saying that Socrates would have learned of Lysis soon enough. On the basis, then, of the opening scene, we can say that Socrates is looking for someone to whom he can say anything and everything, and before whom he will not have to blush: the auditor of the *Charmides* might be thought to fit the bill. It would thus seem that Socrates' search for a friend is a search for the unblushing philosopher, the philosopher without shame, the philosopher who has overcome his radical defectiveness or is not aware of it. In either case, for Socrates to gain the friend would be to give up eros.

Socrates criticizes Hippothales' approach to Lysis by way of two images. He is as poor a hunter as he is a poet (206a6–b8). Hunter and poet immediately recall the *Sophist,* in which the Stranger, after an elaborate series of divisions, has to abandon the sophist as hunter and reclassify him instead with the poet. But in the *Lysis,* Socrates gives no hint that the two models may be incompatible, though it is not easy even here to harmonize them with the lover. The task of the poet is to enchant and not bestialize, and the task of the hunter is to not scare off his quarry. Since Hippothales' mistake was to use his poetry to puff Lysis up, and in this sense enchant him, Socrates must mean by enchantment its very opposite:

the humiliation of Lysis involves his disenchantment. He must lose confidence in everything he believed he could count on; but at the same time, he must not be frightened off. He must be disenchanted without falling into despair. Socrates admits in the *Theaetetus* that he himself was not always successful in checking the savagery of those he had relieved of their false opinions (151c4–7); but in Lysis's case, he does manage to bring about both disillusionment and hope. He enlarges the horizon of Lysis's ambition, so that even to rule the entire world is not precluded, while he destroys the foundation of all security in his home and family. The disenchantment of Lysis goes along with his enchantment. To sacrifice the local, the neighborhood, and the private—everything, in short, summed up in the word *oikeion*—for the sake of the universal, seems to be the same as to replace *philein* with *eran.* Such a replacement, however, is only possible for Lysis because he is taken in by Socrates' picture of the ease with which Lysis's wisdom would be accepted worldwide. Not even in the *Republic* does Socrates imagine that the philosopher-king could put an end to evils in more than one cave. What happens, then, when Lysis discovers that neither the Athenians nor his neighbors, and perhaps not even his father, are willing to entrust him with their things just because he is competent? Will he settle for Gorgianic rhetoric and give up true knowledge? And finally, in the best case, when Lysis dismisses the enchantment with a shrug and keeps the disenchantment, will he not be thoroughly frightened and like a cornered beast turn savage? Even before such a reaction sets in, Lysis's first move is to urge Socrates to punish Menexenos, his friend.

The proverb *koina ta philōn,* were it expressed by the friends themselves, would simply be *hēmetera,* "ours." Lysis speaks of his *paidagōgos* as "ours" (208c4), when he vainly tries to maintain his freedom even while he is being ruled by a slave; but by the end of the argument he agrees with Socrates that everything will be "ours"—his and Socrates'—once they prove their competence (210b5). This second "ours" is misleading. What they would have in common would be knowledge, but what they had of others would belong to each separately; "all mine" would be as true for either as "all ours." Socrates, then, initiates the issue of friendship by arguing that knowledge dissolves any community, whether it be our country, our family, or our friends, and in its imperialistic takeover turns each of them into its slaves and playthings. If, moreover, the friend is another self or another I, Socrates' first argument with Lysis proves its impossibility, since the total alienation of the self is the necessary consequence of wisdom. Lysis's father will turn over to Lysis both himself and his own things *(kai hauton kai ta hautou)* on the very day he believes Lysis is wiser than himself (209c4–6). Lysis's father will then love Lysis completely, but he will be just the opposite of another self of Lysis. If we then suppose that this self-alienation is as impossible as it is repulsive, and we put ignorance at the core of the self, we still do not make it any easier to understand what another ignorant self would mean. We would not care to say, I believe, that friendship was a *folie à deux.*

Before Menexenos left, Socrates was going to ask the two friends who is wiser and who more just; but the argument with Lysis alone makes wisdom the enemy of justice, for the friends Lysis would acquire from his knowledge would all be at the mercy of his will. If friendship were designed to be the bond between wisdom and justice, it would have to be, as in the *Republic,* entirely mythical.[11] This purely hypothetical conflict between justice and wisdom takes a more serious turn when the argument Socrates mounted against Lysis's freedom and happiness is reapplied to Socrates. Lysis's mother and father prevent him—for his own good—from doing whatever he likes with what is his; and were he allowed to compete in a chariot race with his father's horses or beat his father's mule-team, Lysis would be in some danger; but when it comes to his mother's wool-working tools, which he could handle without risk, Lysis admits with a laugh that his mother would not just prevent him but, "I would be beaten should I touch them." According to Socrates, the principle involved is, "Do not tamper with things you don't know." Socrates, then, deserves a beating every time he starts an inquiry, for if he cannot come to an understanding he leaves everything he touches in shambles. The philosopher who lurks behind the argument with Lysis has virtually nothing he can call his own and seems, in his practice, to be exercising the freedom to do whatever he likes that, according to Socrates, would be rightly granted him if he were believed to know what he was doing. The childish view of happiness—the license to do whatever one likes—that Socrates promises Lysis he can realize once he becomes wise has already been gained by Socrates, and he does not know anything. It is no wonder, then, that the philosopher lives only in a democracy.[12] That Lysis's heroic ancestry included a grandfather whose name was "Democrat" is a nice touch.

The question "Who is the friend?" was already at issue in Socrates' first questioning of Lysis and Menexenos, for there seemed to be in principle nothing that could not have initiated a dispute between them and ultimately sown the seed of their enmity; but the interruption of this line of questioning, after they had allowed that the question which of them was richer could never be debated—the concession had been easy since they have no money of their own—seemed to force the issue underground, once Socrates began to represent Lysis to himself as an unhappy slave. The starting point of the interrupted conversation was the dual substantive *philō* (207c8), "a couple of friends;" but the starting point of the argument with Lysis by himself is the verb *philein:* "Surely, Lysis, your father and your mother love you very much (207d5–6)?" The reciprocity of the substantive is lost in the verb; the verb goes only one way, regardless of whether it is active or passive. Socrates later raises this difficulty with Menexenos; but at the moment one should notice how impossible it would be to say that Lysis's mother and father are his friends.[13] One can say that Lysis is dear *(philos)* to them, and they to him, but not even this mutual love would turn them into friends. *Ho erastēs* and *eran* have their counterpart in *ho philos* and *philein,* and it would seem that Socrates undertakes in the *Lysis* to do for friendship what Diotima did for love—to shift to the verb and treat the substantive as derivative. Such a shift not only ceases to make *philosophein,* where there can be no question of reciprocity, as marginal as it otherwise would be, but it also makes the promotion of the good an essential part of loving. Lysis's parents want him to be happy, and despite or rather because of this they check him at every turn. It is difficult to imagine, on the other hand, that Lysis's wish for Socrates to chastise Menexenos has anything to do, in his own mind, with Menexenos's good.

What underlies Socrates' shift from substantive to verb is the following consideration. The expression "We're friends" conceals in its grammar the speaker. Lysis's and Menexenos's response to Socrates' question "You're a couple of friends, aren't you?" is *panu ge* (207c9). This narrative representation, coupled as it is with the dual *ephatēn* (The pair affirmed it), covers over the fact that *panu ge* was spoken twice, once by Lysis and once by Menexenos. Although Socrates' report, "Then they both laughed" *(egelasatēn oun amphō)*—Socrates had asked whether they would also dispute who was better-looking—is narratively true, it is not true to the facts at ground level. The substantive "friends" adopts a theoretical perspective to the phenomena as experienced; as experienced, the friend is necessarily either the subject or the object of the verb (cf. 212a2–3). That Lysis's father and mother love him—particularly since Socrates keeps the verb in the singular *(philei)* despite the plural subject—and are not his friends, does not necessarily mean that the friend is a ghost of narration, but it is noteworthy how Socrates sends off Lysis and Menexenos at the end. The bystanders, he tells them, *will say* as they depart that *we (hēmeis)* believe we are friends of one another." It is through a report of a belief that they are friends.

It would seem to follow from Socrates' argument with Lysis, in which the blind trust of another's love is a guaranteed consequence of one's own wisdom, that that is not the kind of friend Socrates has been looking for, or else, in knowing that wisdom is not available to him at least, the quest for such a friend is nothing but the quest for wisdom. If, however, the latter possibility were the case, philosophy would not be for the sake of wisdom but for the sake of universal love, which would be, in turn, nothing but universal tyranny. The criminal prospects Socrates dangled before Lysis came about through a radical split between the selflessness of art and the selfishness of the artisan. Socrates had Hippothales eating out of his hand, but there was nothing in it for him if he did not find his reward in Hippothales' gratitude, which Hippothales himself might of course mistake for love.[14] If, on the other hand, the good friend Socrates is looking for is of a different order, it is not easy to say who he could be. Lysis's action, however, that intervenes between the end of the first argument and the beginning of Socrates' account of his own makeup, suggests that the friend is to be understood over against the enemy. It is always "us against them." Lysis is impelled to draw Socrates into a conspiracy directed against Menexenos. Just as Hippothales had engaged Socrates to humiliate Lysis, so Lysis engages Socrates to punish Menexenos; and we certainly have to reckon with the possibility, at least for a moment, that we are meant to interpret the discussion of the friend as the chastisement of Menexenos, and what Hippothales takes to be the breaking down of Lysis's resistance is taken by Lysis as teaching Menexenos a lesson. Lysis's desire for Socrates to punish Menexenos is at first all the more astonishing because when Socrates refuses to repeat the argument to Menexenos and urges Lysis to do so on his own, Lysis seems not to realize that the argument in his own mouth would no longer humiliate Menexenos but serve to exhilarate them both—"Together we'll rule the world!"; but perhaps Lysis does realize this and therefore requires another kind of putdown for Menexenos. Lysis's conspiracy, however, does not extend beyond the first argument with Menexenos. Lysis's outburst sucks him into the argument, and his wish to "get" Menexenos vanishes in their shared perplexity. The venom of revenge is drawn out of Lysis through the discussion about the friend. His blush acknowledges how much he gave up in speaking out.

Socrates understands a friend as a kind of possession *(ktēma ti).* If the argument with Lysis is not to hold, he wants something that is his own despite his ignorance. Since, moreover, he understands what he is on the model of *philippos* and *philortux,* he is a *philophilos,* or, as he phrases it in order, perhaps, to lessen the paradox, a *philetairos* (211e8);[15] but in the ordinary understanding of a friend, Lysis has Menexenos as his friend, he does not have someone who is nothing but a friend. A horse or quail exists in itself, and then one acquires it; but Socrates wants to acquire what is before his acquisition of it a friend. The friend, then, must be from the start his own; but if he does not have it, it must be alienated from him, and what he wants is for his own to be restored to him. Socrates says he has lived in this radical form of self-alienation since childhood. It is as if he had directed early on the argument with Lysis against himself and discovered what was his own was not his own. The primary form of this experience is to doubt the legitimacy of one's birth; we may call it the Telemachean experience in honor of the one who first expressed it in Greek literature.[16] According to Socrates himself, the young experience philosophy just as if they realized they were adopted: they no longer consider as true anything the law tells them.[17] Socrates, then, would have just delivered this shock-treatment to Lysis; and in order to set him on the right course represents himself as permanently in this condition. What is this condition? If we replace Socrates' *philetairos* with *philophilos* and thereby make the second element as verbal as the first, Socrates' *philein* is of a *philein.* Since it is hard to imagine what that second *philein* could be except philosophy, Socrates would be a lover of philosophy from childhood. In order for this to make sense, it would have to be the case that philosophy was elusive, and not every time Socrates engaged in a philosophic issue was Socrates engaged in philosophy. Socrates would necessarily be aware of what constituted philosophy, but philosophy would not automatically be before him once he started asking about what he did not know. A physicist is doing physics while he is looking for the answer to some problem; but the philosopher does not have available to him a way of going about philosophy. He falls into philosophy.[18] What the Stranger shows in the *Sophist* and *Statesman* is that philosophy comes with the breakdown of one's way and the subsequent awareness of the necessity of its breaking down, but that one cannot anticipate the breakdown and start with the correction of error built in (cf. *Lysis* 213e2–3). Socrates' own name for this is a second sailing.

That Socrates has philosophy in mind as his elusive friend is not obvious; but in surveying the arguments one cannot help noticing that Socrates leaves behind the poets and those who talked and wrote about nature and the whole as soon as he starts over again with the unprecedented notion of the neither/nor. The plan of the eight arguments about the friend is as follows:

1. Argument with Lysis:	the destruction of the *oikos* and the *oikeion* of Lysis (207d5–210d8).
2. Argument with Menexenos:	*ho philos tou philou* (211d6–213d5).
3. Argument with Lysis:	*to homoion* (213d6–215c2).
4. Argument with Menexenos:	*to enantion* (215c3–216b9).
5. Argument with Menexenos:	*oute agathon oute kakon* (216c1–217a2).
6. Argument with Menexenos:	two kinds of *parousia* (217a3–218c3).
7. Argument with Menexenos:	*heneka* and *dia* (218d6–220b5).
8. Argument with Menexenos:	*oikeion* and *epithumia* (220b6–222b2).

The last four arguments turn back on the first four, and at least on paper a restoration of the *oikeion* is attempted without any recourse to the wisdom Lysis had been assured would bring him back home.

It would seem to follow from Socrates' first argument with Menexenos that there are three kinds of "friends," and nothing can bring them under a unitary idea. There are lovers, who imagine, correctly or not, that their love is not returned or even that they are loathed (Hippothales is one); there are others, like Socrates, who do not even expect that their affection is to be returned; and finally there is Lysis, whose loathing of his parents after their exposure by Socrates does not affect the intense love they have for him. The central difficulty might be thought to consist in Socrates' failure to distinguish, on the one hand, momentary feelings of hatred from permanent states of enmity, and, on the other, apparent from true friends. In saying that some lovers suspect their love is not returned, Socrates points to the imaginary character of the transitivity of *erōs.* The lover believes that the beloved is automatically established through his loving; but as Socrates hinted to Hippothales, since the lover is in love no less than he loves someone (204b6–8), the stative form of the verb makes it unclear whether anything happens outside the sphere of the lover. Lovers tend to make the same mistake as Polus does, who believes that, if one punishes, another is punished; but the will to get through to the other is no guarantee that it is effective. Socrates therefore expresses doubt whether he has understood correctly his erotic disposition as a form of *philein.* He had interpreted "horse-lover" not as an *energeia,* in which the fondness for horses is complete in itself, but as involving an action that aimed at a certain result, the acquisition of horses; but it now appears that *philein* results in *philein.* If one takes a later example of Socrates, the *philogumnastēs* (222d7), whatever the exercise-lover acquires as a consequence of his training might be a byproduct and not of much importance to him. The dance-lover loves to dance. In dancing he finds that which enhances his own being. The X of the X-lover is that in which the lover is realized. Accordingly, the child who when beaten hates his mother is still the apple of her eye, since it is in him that she is fulfilled. In light of this, the philosopher would be like the wine-lover who has no head for it,[19] and the practice in which he finds his end is that in which he stumbles badly and is always falling over his own feet. But still he dances.

In order to reinforce the view that reciprocity is not essential for the friend, Socrates quotes two lines of Solon, which, if Socrates' argument did not deny it, we would understand as saying that he is happy who has dear (or his own)—*philoi*—children, single-hoofed horses, hunting dogs, and a guest-friend from elsewhere; but we are required instead to read *philoi* as a predicate and take happiness to consist not in possessions but in friendships. In Socrates' reading, Solon begins with the home and ends with the stranger. He encompasses the range Socrates had offered to Lysis once he acquired wisdom. The most striking item is the *xenos allodapos,* the stranger from elsewhere, for not only does it recall the *xenismos* Hippothales celebrated between Heracles and Lysis's ancestor, but it brings into the field of the friend the nonfriend or stranger, whomever one does not know and is not acquainted with. Through some kind of bond, however, the stranger has been pulled into our orbit and yet remains in his own. He is at a distance but close. This alien intimacy seems not to be unconnected with philosophy, which cannot be understood as either friend or enemy. Now of the three kinds of examples Socrates gives, lovers, philosophers, and parents, the simplest to understand would be the last. One loves what one makes.[20] If one then considers the lover in this light, especially with Hippothales in mind, whose poetry, Socrates has shown, is a celebration of himself (cf. 214a1), the philosopher seems in danger of mistaking making for doing and the extension of himself in the beings for the disclosure of the beings in themselves. Even if the philosopher acknowledges the nonreciprocity of his love, must he still not assume that the beings are user-friendly and not hostile to their being known? The expression *xenos allodapos* cannot but remind us of the gods, who according to one of Penelope's suitors take on this disguise as they wander among men to survey their insolence or obedience to the law.[21] The suitor implies that the gods never become our acquaintances *(gnōrimoi)* and are in a state of permanent estrangement from us. If we let the gods stand for the highest beings, are they, as Parmenides argued with young Socrates, cut off from us completely,[22] and, insofar as they are related, is it our justice rather than our knowledge that is at stake? Socrates had certainly argued with Lysis for knowledge rather than justice.

The attempt to interpret "friend" in terms of itself fails. "Friend," one can say, has been shown not to be an irreducible category. Friends, then, are not what friends sometimes believe they are, loved for themselves alone. When Socrates resumes this discussion, in argument 7, he gets as close as he can to the friend in himself, but with a difference: the enemy is now part of the inner structure of the friend (219b2–3). The enemy was an outsider in argument 2 and threatened to prove the impossible—that there could be an enemy to the friend or a friend to the enemy; but, in the Socratic arguments, causal accounts are put together with the formal account of the first argument with Menexenos. This difference can be generalized to mark the difference between the first four and the last four arguments. The first four are categorial arguments, the last four are dynamical. Despite the fact that Socrates raised the question in terms of becoming—How does another become the friend of another (212a5–6)?—there is no discussion of becoming prior to the introduction of the neither/nor. Only then does time become a factor to be taken into account.

In both arguments 3 and 4, a cosmological theory is introduced into what up to now had seemed to be a strictly human phenomenon; but it would perhaps be more accurate to say that nothing in the account of the friend, under the principle of either "They were made for each other" or "Opposites attract" stands in the way of the friend losing his human face and falling under a comprehensive account of nature. As long as nothing peculiar marks off the friend from a general theory of "magnetism"—there is desire but no soul (215e4)—the friend ceases to be of any interest in itself unless one can claim for it that it offers an exceptionally easy way into the general theory and merely exemplifies what can be observed throughout nature. The ontological counterpart to the epistemological tyranny that Socrates offered Lysis would be the denial of distinct natures to things. Such a denial would entail, in Socrates' description of his predecessors, the collapse of the phrase *peri phuseōs te kai holou* into a hendiadys "about the whole of nature." Socrates' resistance to such a collapse is no more at the moment than his peculiar thing, which may either be too eccentric to affect the general theory or only an apparent exception to it. If the Socratic turn begins at argument 5, it might be thought strange, if the objection to the prior arguments is their unrestricted range, that this turn involves a general ontology of the neither/nor; but it turns out to be precisely the virtue of the neither/nor to allow for the search of the manifold of natures without the postulation of a general theory or cosmology. It is "us" and "our things" that primarily belong to the neither/nor (cf. 220d5–6).

Although both speak of the like, the poet has "the god himself" bring the like to the like, and the physicists speak of the necessity that like be a friend to like. In both cases, the two alikes are not from the start together. There is some obstacle that stands in the way of the ideal condition of the physicist being realized, and for the poet no human enterprise would ever overcome the apparent disparity between Odysseus, the master now disguised as a stranger, and Eumaeus, the former prince now a swineherd. On the surface, Socrates wrenches the line from the *Odyssey* out of context, for whereas Socrates wants to restrict its meaning to the good, the actual speaker of the line, Melanthius, uses it of the bad: "It really is peculiarly apposite: bad is leading bad."[23] Socrates, however, can be defended; without Melanthius knowing it, they really are the good guys. But if they are the good, they have been put together by Athena to carry out justice and punish the suitors. Indeed, Odysseus and Eumaeus can be conceived of as alike only in terms of their common enemy. Without the evil they are to wipe out, they would have remained apart. By this reflection on the passage from which the line is cited, there is a direct link with Socrates' associating the bad with the unjust, although he does not say that the good are the just. The drift of Socrates' argument does not allow for the good to be in a relation with the bad. They are autonomous, all of a piece, and self-sufficient. The thought that underlies this idealized situation comes to light later, but it is not even then formulated explicitly. It is this. The difference between anger and hatred, Aristotle says,[24] is that the angry man wants to retaliate and inflict pain, but in the case of hatred one wants the enemy to cease to exist. There is behind the pair "friend-enemy" an ideal that if realized would make the friend fall away. So what looks like a false abstraction represents in fact the degree to which friends refuse to acknowledge their dependence on their contrary. The friendship of Odysseus and Eumaeus culminates in Eumaeus and Telemachus chopping Melanthius up and feeding him to the dogs.[25] The meaning of Odysseus's name, Homer tells us, is Enmity.[26]

In the first argument with Menexenos, the treatment of *philein* led to an unstable relation between the active and the passive voice. In the second argument with Lysis, Socrates, in order to show Lysis what he dislikes about their conclusion, that the good alone are friends, decouples the like and the good and treats the like in terms of patiency and the good in terms of agency. The conclusion of the like-argument, "How is it a friend if it should not be cherished *(agapōito)?*" and the conclusion of the good-argument, "Whatever should not cherish *(agapōiē)* would not even love (215a3, b2)," puts the problem squarely. Some kind of difference is needed within the like in order for patient and agent to operate, and some kind of lack is needed within the good in order for its presence to be felt and its absence to be missed. There must be a shading of the self-consistent so that it can be affected, and there must be a shading of the self-sufficient so that it can be effective, and these two defective modes must be together in the friend as the effectively needy. However suggestive this may be of Socrates' capacity to bring about *aporia,* there still seems to be no way to determine how much off from the good and the like the friend must be if the only restriction is that one must avoid the total instability and incompetence of the bad. Whatever ratios prove to be appropriate must, as the physicists say, be fed in by hand, and the problem of the friend not admit of any but ad hoc solutions. We knew from the start that the circumstantial was of overwhelming importance when it came to the friend.

The sequence of results up to now is this: In Socrates' first argument with Lysis, the wise who wants friends can make anyone he wants a friend but cannot be a friend himself; in Socrates' first argument with Menexenos, the befriended could be a friend and yet be an enemy, and likewise the one befriending could cherish an enemy. In Socrates' second argument with Lysis, where the like and the good come in, there is, *qua* like, no possibility of the befriended, and, *qua* good, no possibility of befriending. Now Socrates, to achieve this last result, had to force the meaning of "like" and not accept the proverbial sense of Melanthius's utterance: "Birds of a feather . . ." He now does so in citing Hesiod. The poet shows the way to the literal. Socrates again, however, reverses the plain meaning of Hesiod. Hesiod is speaking of a mistake he made in the *Theogony,* where Eris was only the cause of evil; but here in the *Works and Days,* he begins with an admission that Eris is two, and the state of war Socrates' source asserted to hold for those of the same kind is to be traced to the *Theogony*'s Eris. Hesiod, then, was right the first time. Competition and war are inseparable. Indeed, according to Hesiod, Friendliness *(Philotēs)* is the sister of Eris.[27] If Hesiod's second thoughts are separated from the grandiose theory to which Socrates attaches them, then the like of Socrates' own account, which was so much all of a piece as to be ineffective, is now different enough to resume its power in the rivalry of friends. Differentials of this kind were already at work in the friendship of Lysis and Menexenos. What makes this solution inadequate is the third pair of rivals Hesiod cites: beggar against beggar. The first two pairs are artisans, potter and singer, and they can stand for the like as the good; but the lack the beggar represents had to belong to the good, insofar as it was not the same as the like, if the good were going to be loving. Thus Hesiod's lines merely pose in themselves the difficulty Socrates had already worked out by himself on the basis of his eccentric interpretation of the like. A fully artful neediness once more emerges as the general formula for the friend; and once more it seems that Eros as the offspring of Poverty and Resource is Socrates' own mythological solution to it.

The eloquence of the spokesman whom Socrates heard (he reminds one of Eryximachus) for a quasi-Heraclitean, quasi-Empedoclean theory seems to have carried him away into nonsense. There are at least two pairs in his list of contraries—bitter/sweet and sharp/blunt—that evidently do not fit.[28] The blunt may well need sharpening, but the sharp gets blunted against its will. If, however, we take our bearings by these pairs, the theory would not be about contraries in themselves but about the actual determination of one member in each apparent pair of contraries by the other. The sharp is the less blunt, the sweet the less bitter. Health, then, would be a lesser degree of sickness, and friendship a slackening of hostility. Differences in magnitude would be experienced as differences in kind. Knowledge too would be ignorance, but not as much. Consequently, the objection the professional contradictors make, and which Menexenos believes is decisive, that friendship would have to be friends with enmity, would not hold, since the language of things is more absolute than the nature of things. Hesiod's error, then, would not have been just in differentiating Eris herself the second time around, but in having first made Eris and Philotēs sisters, though in fact Philotēs is but the spurious offspring of Eris; she is only experienced as distinct. It would now seem that the shading of the good, which Socrates' prior account needed, was misconceived. A shading of the bad is what is wanted. Such a demand could not be met as long as the bad and the unjust were identified. Accordingly, the issue of justice vanishes from the dialogue once Socrates cuts himself loose from his predecessors and is on his own. What might be thought to take its place and had been absent so far is the beautiful. Socrates, at any rate, had not said a word about its monstrousness if the ugly were a friend of the beautiful. He must have been thinking of himself all along.

If we now survey the arguments about the like and the contrary, we have, on the one hand, the *homoion* split between a union and division of *homoia,* and, on the other, the *enantion* split between a union and division of *enantia.* Such a double split recalls the structure of the diacritical-syncritical way that the Stranger practices and discusses in the *Sophist* and *Statesman.* In the *Sophist,* the cutting apart of same from same is paired with the separation of good from bad, and in the *Statesman* the putting together of same and same is paired with the reluctant putting together of good and bad. One would perhaps just leave it at this remarkable resemblance between the ways in which the friend shows up and the ways of dialectic, were it not that Socrates, when he tries to break out of their present impasse, notices that, as an old proverb has it, "The beautiful is a friend" has been confirmed not through any new insight into the friend in itself but through the slipperiness with which the friend has eluded them in the argument (216c4–d2). What the friend is comes to light through a reflection on how it failed to come to light. Somehow the way of the argument about the friend has become associated with the friend. In a way typical of Socrates' second sailing, the speeches about a being take over from the being itself; and again, not untypically, this rerouting involves an image. When Menexenos asks Socrates what he means by his proposal about the neither/nor, Socrates says, "Well, by Zeus, I do not know, but really and truly I myself am dizzy by the perplexity of the argument, and it's probable, in conformity with the ancient saying, that the beautiful is *philon.* It bears a likeness, at any rate, to something soft, smooth, and sleek; and accordingly perhaps, because it is of this kind, it easily gives us the slip and slides away." Socrates experiences a disorientation and ascribes it to the friend. The beauty of the friend shows up in its making itself known through its literal elusiveness. Socrates thus admits that the friend is not a possible possession: he could not tell Diotima what he would get were he to get the beautiful.[29] The friend remains attractive and out of reach. If, then, we were to follow Socrates and apply the ways in which the friend came to light to the friend itself, the friend would be whatever there is in which the fourfold way of dialectic is to be found. The friend would be the beauty of being insofar as it was ready for philosophy.

Socrates recovers his footing by accepting that there must be a difference between the active and the passive of *philein.* The previous arguments have convinced him that it is hopeless to find the friend in mirror-structures. Perhaps he recalls the literal meaning of *enantion* as "in face of," for whereas one's own mirror image would not reverse left and right, "another I" would. In any case, for the new definition, the friend is clearly the subject, and it is the friend of the beautiful and good. It is the friend of whatever benefits as it makes itself known (cf. 217a3). Socrates' divination, that the neither good nor bad—simplified throughout as the neither/nor—is the friend of the good, turns out to be a *reductio.* A canvasing of all other possibilities shows that it alone is left, but there is neither any human meaning nor causal account yet attached to it. It first falls out of the *logos* and does not emerge as the result of a division among the things that are. It seems to entail two radical disjunctions, one between neutral beings and the good, the other between neutral beings and whatever is becoming either good or bad. Socrates even speaks at one point of the neither/nors as being such *auta kath' hauta* (220c4–5). One might infer that this is a consequence of Socrates flooding the friend with the argument about the friend, so that what seems to be a recovery of his balance is merely his accommodation to the dictates of the *logos.* Socrates himself suggests that the neither/nor, and everything that followed from it, was nonsense and put together like a long poem without any point (221d4–6).

The neither/nor is a slippery class, and Socrates treats it in an odd way. He does not allow the body as being neither/nor to be the friend of health on the grounds that in itself it follows some natural way toward health and puts up a natural resistance to disease, but he separates what it is in itself from what it is on account of the presence of evil, as if the sick who is a friend to the doctor is not the same as the body that is neither/nor. Socrates' procedure allows him to have a subject of the verb *philein* that is not the same as what causes it to love the doctor. All love is conscious and rational. It does not acknowledge any way to health except through knowledge: the first argument with Lysis is still having its effect. As Socrates phrases it, the neither/nor would slide over into the bad and cease to love the good at the moment the doctor would declare that the case is hopeless; otherwise, the body would be bad only a moment before death and not a minute sooner. One would complicate things further were one to assign desire exclusively to the soul and take into consideration the will to live, for when the soul gives up on a cure, are we then to say that the body is bad? Socrates, moreover, by inserting the medical art as the friend, makes the neither/nor depend on the possibility of a cure. Philosophy, then, which Socrates is about to mention as an illustration of the neither/nor, would have to be considered bad unless the wise were in principle available. The utter hopelessness of the philosophic state may not leave the philosopher helpless.

In order to clarify the neither/nor, Socrates introduces a distinction between two kinds of presence, in appearance and in reality, which does not apparently make it any easier to understand the difference, if there is one, between those who do and those who do not befriend the doctor. If Socrates means that the body is fundamentally sound and suffers from some surface lesions, then the body is not neither/nor but both good and bad, and it is "both/and" in the sense that either the bad is separable from the good (one can draw it off or cut it out), or there is a blending of the two which defeats the best efforts of the doctor to disentangle them. Socrates speaks of the progressive spread of the bad and not of a possibly stable but not necessarily static mixture of the two. Socrates' own example is hard to apply. He distinguishes between a white-lead coating on top of Menexenos's blond hair and the white that old age will bring. No one, however, would say of a house painted white that it was apparently white, any more than that Socrates' ignorance was an artificial dye smeared over perfect wisdom, however much it might appear that he was putting us on and really knew all the answers. It would be truer to say that Lysis's confession of ignorance was a temporary coloring of a perfectly healthy pride, and the older Socrates gets the greater his ignorance grows: his present self-deprecation is a sign of what the future holds in store.[30] If, then, the example of hair-dye is to fit the foolish and ignorant, they are not those who are all of a piece, but those whose appearance is the contrary of what is already fully present. They are the *doxosophoi,* who have succeeded in changing colors and looking like gods. Perhaps, however, the sophists never lose the suspicion that they do not know what they say they know, and for all the show ignorance ultimately peeps through.[31]

Apart from the general difficulties the notion of a neutral soul poses, Socrates' own desire for friends is hard to formulate in terms of apparent and real presence. Socrates is friendless, but he does not say he has enemies, whose presence would cause the desire for friends. He could of course be anticipating the future, particularly if the dramatic date of the *Lysis* is after the *Clouds,* and the potential for trouble is already in Strepsiades' wish to draw up an indictment.[32] However that may be, the presence of the absence of friends seems not to fit very well the model of white-lead, unless the point of the model lies not so much in the mere presence of white-lead as in the self-evident fact of its presence—no one would mistake it for anything else than for what it is—and accordingly what is decisive is Socrates' awareness of the absence of friends, just as in the case of philosophy it is the knowledge of ignorance that, in corresponding to the presence of evil, makes for desire. The presence of evil, then, that cancels the desire must be its nonmanifestation as evil, either in not showing itself at all or in declaring itself to be the opposite. If, however, philosophy as knowledge of ignorance is never fully present as itself to the philosopher, only the symptoms of ignorance could be present and manifest. These symptoms seem to be the equivalent of the blush. They are equally involuntary and at the start perhaps only manifest to another. The friend would thus be indispensable for the philosopher. He would either have to notice the other's blush or induce it. This friend must be of a peculiar kind. Hippothales never blushed in the presence of Ktesippos alone.

In speaking of Menexenos's hair, Socrates carefully distinguishes between "whiteness" and "white." "Whiteness" is used only of the unreal presence of white, and "white" only of the white old age imparts. So we have a simple linguistic differentiation. If we can speak "Platonically" of the presence of something, it is an appearance; if we cannot, it is real. This seems neat but not helpful. Utter shamelessness, after all, does not have to show up in a constant flush.[33] In the case of the unwise, Socrates assigns the same *agnoia* to philosophers and fools alike but calls only the latter *agnōmones.* To be *agnōmōn* is either to be ignorant and without judgment or to be cruel and unforgiving. Ignorance, then, would be a wholly negative state when it expresses itself in the desire to punish another. Lysis's first reaction to his own proven senselessness was to lash out at Menexenos. Lysis's recovery toward the neither/nor was signified by a blush. Lysis's blush was an unwilled sign of error. Socrates then told us of his delight in Lysis's *philosophia.* If *philosophia* follows the rule Socrates set up for "whiteness" and "white," Socrates detected in Lysis the sign of a good but not the good itself. The language of Platonism, one might say, is the language of modesty. In refusing to take the appearance of things for the truth of things, it is always returning us to the appearance of things. Seen in this light, the neither/nor would not be, as it first appeared, an arbitrary abstraction from the things that are, but, quite the contrary, the expression of the way these things. "Good" and "bad," on the other hand, would hardly ever be strictly applicable. The example of white-lead hinted that even "healthy" has to be put against the scale of time.

The neither/nor has its payoff in the philosopher. At first flush, this means the philosopher has neither the good of wisdom nor the bad of ignorance. The bad of ignorance, however, is a peculiar ignorance; it is to believe one knows what one does not know. The philosopher, then, has one kind of bad and lacks another kind of bad. His hold, moreover, on what he lacks is tenuous: "he still believes he does not know what he does not know." He does not strictly have the good of the bad, namely, knowledge of ignorance; but his belief gives him the appearance at best of knowledge of ignorance, and at worst of ignorance of ignorance, and in this sense he is a neither/nor; but he must also realize that it is bad to be a neither/nor; otherwise, he would not desire to know. But what he desires to know cannot be wisdom, if he knows that is impossible, but knowledge of ignorance. He wants to know what it is he believes he does not know; he does not want to be in the exhausted state Socrates left Theaetetus, who had no answers left to the question what is knowledge but was still unaware of what the problem of knowledge is.[34] The good of the philosopher is poised very precariously between a bad that cannot be eliminated and a bad that possibly can be ameliorated. Socrates tells us how he experienced this state after Lysis and Menexenos supported completely the conclusion that the neither/nor is friend of the good on account of the presence of bad. "I myself," he says, "was very pleased too in barely *(agapētōs)* holding on, like a hunter, to what I was hunting (218c4–5)." *Agapētōs* is the adverbial form of the verb *agapan,* which Socrates has used throughout as the equivalent of *philein;* and were it not for the context, the adverb could have its usual meaning, "gladly" or "contentedly." Perhaps, however, as Socrates' joy attests, "barely" and "gladly" are indistinguishable.

Before Socrates can explain to Menexenos why he suspects they have gained phantom wealth, he has to complete the definition of the friend through the addition of final cause to the efficient cause he has so far been content with. *Heneka* (for the sake of) is put at the front of the definition and *dia* (on account of) at the end: "For the sake of the friend the friend is friend of the friend on account of the enemy (219b2–3)." Socrates has managed to revert to a form that does not use any other terms than those he introduced in his first round with Menexenos; but the uniformity of the language conceals differences. The friend who is friend of the friend is a neither/nor; and neither the object, whose friend the neither/nor is, nor the friend, for the sake of which the subject is a friend, is a neither/nor; both rather are good, one as the means, the other as the end. Socrates, then, for the sake of his understanding, is a friend of philosophy on account of his ignorance. If, however, this plugs the proper values into the general formula, then it would seem that "neither/nor" could in some sense hold throughout, since the means, the end, and the efficient cause are all versions of the neither/nor. As philosophy represents the completeness of this defective mode, so Socrates' own future understanding would be superior only to his prior state of putative ignorance (cf. 218e2). Even if the means is not philosophy but a friend of philosophy, whether it be Lysis, Menexenos, or Ktesippos, the neither/nor would still prevail throughout the formula. Granted, this is a special case, and it is remarkable that philosophy disappears as an issue once "for the sake of which" is introduced. Its disappearance, however, might be deceptive. The drinking of hemlock proves to be the key example.

Socrates wants to distinguish between phantom images of the friend and whatever is really and truly the friend; and he forces Menexenos to concede the distinction on the grounds that the never-ending series "for the sake of the friend" would wear them out unless there were a first friend. He wins this concession, however, by doubtful means. Health is the only friend Socrates designates; the second friend for the sake of which health is a friend is left blank, and so is the third. Socrates warns Protarchus that it is a contemporary mistake to go so quickly from the one to the many without counting the kinds in between.[35] Suppose we follow Glaucon and say the second good is sight and the third thinking.[36] It is not immediately obvious that these three goods arrange themselves hierarchically, or if they do whether Menexenos knows the conditions attached to each. Socrates would have been more sensible had he taken the friends of the "that for the sake of which"-clause for the structured constellation of goods, all of which we may cherish without having any precise understanding of how they are related to one another. Socrates himself cites an example that ruins his case. He assures Menexenos that though we say we make much of gold and silver, gold and silver really are for the sake of whatever we hold in the highest esteem (220a1–6), as if we did not know of misers and self-made millionaires whose horizon does not extend any further than the preservation or accumulation of their wealth. It is clear in any case that none of the goods in a constellation of goods is a phantom image of another, or if any of them are, Menexenos knows which they are. By failing to fill in the blanks, Socrates can glide into an example whose jerry-built structure is altogether different from that which would obtain for the permanent set of goods.

We must remember that the sick was a friend of medicine for the sake of health; but in the case before us, in which a father believes that wine is an antidote to the hemlock his son has drunk and accordingly cherishes the wine and the cup, the physician has not been consulted or if consulted not believed, and we are confronted with a crisis where the father will find his son dead in minutes. Socrates finally gives an example where one has ceased to be a friend of the doctor either rationally at the moment one drinks the hemlock or shortly afterward; but the father is out of his mind with fear and latches onto a nostrum he cherishes only because he cherishes his son. The dearness of the son irradiates with dearness the specious means of his survival, and once he was lost, the wine and the cup would soon sink back into indifference. Now prior to the crisis, the son like all of us was a neither/nor; and if his father were like Lysis's, he wanted him to be happy; and if he fell sick, he would be a friend to the doctor but would not be so foolish as to cherish the pills or the scalpel the doctor was going to use. The father, then, wanted his son to be good; that is, he wanted him to have all the goods that constitute the constellation of goods that make up happiness for him. In the crisis, however, any consideration of this kind disappears; and unless his son drank the poison by accident, it would have vanished at the moment the Athenian court condemned him to death on some criminal charge. The son, then, gets to be the real friend, insofar as he is either neutral or bad, only through the crisis. It is the imminent risk the son is incurring that alters the father's evaluation and puts him at the top of the scale. It might be of course that the father has only one son, and his anxiety about his son's survival runs in tandem with an anxiety about his own; but even if this were not the case, the father's grasping at straws cannot be separated from what the occasion induced in the son. Had Lysis threatened suicide, his mother would surely have allowed him to tamper with her things.

Once we see that the friend exists within two different horizons, one in which he is patient of good and bad, in conformity with some structure of goods, and the other in which the friend in itself is ranked temporarily at the top of cherished things without any assumption that it is good, it is possible to understand why Socrates formulates the true and real friend in terms of an opinion that cannot be translated into knowledge. Whereas it is perfectly possible that all the goods in the first structure of the friend are understood and supplied by arts, there is nothing in the father's making much of the son *(peri pollou poieisthai)* to which any epistemic equivalent corresponds. Socrates had convinced Lysis earlier that it was his knowledge that made him dear to his parents. Lysis was good at certain things because he knew them; he was not in these respects a neither/nor. For the father now, however, there is no connection whatsoever between the reality and truth of the first friend and the father's knowledge. Indeed, as Socrates phrases it, the father makes much of the son "for the sake of holding the son of the highest importance" *(peri pantos hēgeisthai)*. Antigone, in risking her life for her brother, risked everything for the sake of burying her brother; she acted, according to Socrates, for the sake of making the most of her brother, for without her action her brother would be nothing. The father, then, shows and sets out to show the importance he attaches to the son; had he befriended the doctor with a secret antidote, he would not have proved anything.

What, then, of Socrates? We know the formula for him within the horizon of goods; but, when he is in prison, and proposes treating the hemlock as if it were wine, and claims to know that death is good for him, the formula would have to be revised to read: "For the sake of philosophy, Socrates was the friend of hemlock on account of the enmity of the Athenians." If, however, the *hou heneka* clause must be altered to conform with the father's "for the sake of," it would read, "For the sake of showing the high importance he attached to philosophy, Socrates etc." It is only in the crisis brought on by his trial and condemnation that the purpose clause shifts away from his own advantage, and the immediate friend ceases to be philosophy or the philosophical young. Socrates, however, does not distinguish the two cases, one of which concerns the continued existence of philosophy and the other his own good; but it was Socrates himself who had put philosophy at continuous risk by his reinterpretation of it. This reinterpretation by way of political philosophy necessarily affected the way in which every so-called philosophical question was raised. These questions could no longer be put by themselves; they had to be encountered through and in light of the urgency that gave rise to them. The perspective of the urgent, however, is nothing else than the perspective of crisis, however disengaged from a particular crisis others may be. Cephalus laughs off the issue of justice and leaves. It would therefore follow that only for Socrates do the two horizons tend to fall together, and Socrates is always on trial and making a defense of philosophy while he minds his own business (cf. 222e2).[37]

If we set aside the possible coincidence in Socrates' case of the neither/nor which can become either good or bad and the neither/nor whose existence is on the line, it is possible to offer a solution to Socrates' apparently inadvertent confusion of *heneka* and *dia* at the point where he should have maintained the difference most carefully. The real friend, he says, if evil should depart and no longer affect the neither/nors, would obviously have a nature contrary to the so-called friends, for, while they are for the sake of the friend, it comes to light as for the sake of the enemy (220e2–4). "For the sake of the enemy" should obviously be "on account of the enemy"; but perhaps Socrates means what he says. The enemy for whose sake the true friend exists can only be the true friend itself. In the case before us, the paradigmatic structure of the good, which the father hoped would apply to his son, falls away and is replaced by the circumstantial structure of the friend, which, while it is becoming more precious by the second, resists any predication of the good. It is this resistance that makes the true friend the enemy. It is against the nature of a neither/nor to jump its class and be treated as if to be not-good were to be good. If existence itself were a good and nonexistence a bad, Socrates' class of neither/nors, which he now calls the betweens (2206), would already be good and would never become bad as long as they were. If, on the other hand, it were not existence as such that was good but the existence of one's own, then Socrates' first argument with Lysis goes into effect: the son ceased to be the father's own once his recourse to false belief revealed that he did not know how to use him. If this argument is sound, one has to stress that the "for the sake of the enemy"-clause can apply only to the circumstantial and not to the paradigmatic structure; and, indeed, Socrates separates once again the discussion about the real friend from the discussion about the good. In appealing back to "that friend in which all the rest ended," Socrates gives up the good that had no place in the former discussion either (220d8–e5).

The thought-experiment Socrates proposes has its ultimate purpose in the isolation of desire from need; but its proximate aim is to determine whether the neither/nor loves the good on account of the bad. Socrates does not set up the experiment with all possible precision. If the bad were to vanish, the neither/nor should become the not-good; but Socrates does not alter the class of the neither/nors. We remain what we were. It thus seems that the bad does not perish but simply no longer affects us nor does us any harm; and in his first formulation, Socrates goes no further than this (220c1–7). We would, then, still have evils but they would be as if they did not exist. We would not treat them as evils. Socrates said he did not know whether death was an evil; and insofar as he identified it with philosophizing he seemed to be saying it was good. So death was either a good or a neither/nor even when no thought-experiment had banished the bad. If, moreover, the philosophers are neither/nors, the *doxosophoi* would still be ignorant of their ignorance and pretenders to knowledge regardless of whether ignorance had ceased to be an evil or not, for even now they do not know that ignorance is an evil.[38] If the city itself is the sophist of sophists, as both Socrates and the Stranger agree,[39] then the city would not be unjust to Socrates, for though it would retain its ignorance, the trial of Socrates would be an occasion of mockery and laughter.[40] The more serious question is whether knowledge of ignorance would be possible under these conditions. The Eleatic Stranger, who did not just imagine the absence of evils but elaborated a world complete with the reversal of time (Menexenos would be born with white hair and die a blond), in which there were no evils, professed not to know whether Socrates was then possible.[41] What seems to settle the issue is this consideration: Socrates' proposal amounts to treating ourselves indifferently. We would be like sticks and stones, which are just what they are. The theoretical attitude, which we had thought at first characterized the neither/nor, is really in effect when everything is not-good, for the neither/nor was for the philosopher good and bad and could not possibly remain good if it ceased to be bad. Just as those ignorant of their ignorance would not be unjust, so those who knew or believed they were ignorant would not be benefited by a knowledge, let alone a belief, about something that was not bad. It is not surprising, then, that Theodorus, the theoretician par excellence, dreams of the end of the evils and has to be told by Socrates that it is impossible.[42]

If we revert to Socrates' distinction between artificial and natural hair-color, or what we thought were the same, the blush and the unflushed complexion, if the blush still occurred, what would it signify? It could not be the acknowledgment to oneself or another of a defect. Surely Socrates would be able to know that Hippothales was in love and in love with someone; but would he then be useless in pointing out the mistake Hippothales had made in wooing Lysis? Hippothales would presumably not regard as an evil his failure to catch Lysis; and for all we know, it might be good were he not to succeed; but Hippothales would in any case not ask Socrates for help. Socrates' erotic science, then, would never be called on, though his diagnostic ability would be as unerring as ever. The Eleatic Stranger's myth anticipated this result. As long as the god has not withdrawn from his providential care, there is no *erōs.* What is still left open perhaps is whether Socrates' desire for friends would survive.

What Socrates has been driving at does not become clear until he makes a surprising move. He blocks off any answer to the question whether there will be unharmful hunger and thirst when there are no evils—"The question, What will be or won't be? is absurd: Who knows?"—and comes back to what we do know, that all of these desires can be harmful, helpful, or neither, and then uses the survival of neither/nor desires in the absence of evils to show that desire is the cause of friendship. Now the emergence of desire as the cause simply rephrases Socrates' original formulation of the neither/nor. Not only did he identify the neither/nor with the friend (219a6–b3), but that friend had been the subject of *philein.* Socrates' *to epithumoun* is merely the merging of noun and verb into the participle. *To epithumoun,* however, has undergone a change. As a neither/nor, it desired the good; now it desires the neither/nor that is truly neutral. It desires what is missing, but what is missing is the not-good; it is simply one's own *(oikeion).* Socrates has taken a long way around to confront Aristophanes, who had in the *Symposium* told a story about how we were once whole and, on account of our assault on heaven, had been cut in two and rearranged so that we would be ashamed of our defectiveness and in sexual satisfaction perpetuate the race and find some recompense for the irrecoverability of our original selves. Aristophanes, however, had argued for *erōs* as the desire and pursuit of the whole under the condition of evil: our partial selves were due to divine punishment. Socrates gets rid of the evil and keeps the desire. He questions whether there is any necessary connection between the two, since Aristophanes did not equate the original whole with good. If he had, then the evil would causally be related to the good, and the problem Socrates' account faced would return. As it is, the very longing to go back to one's own might be thought to depend on the constraints the present order has imposed. Socrates himself had offered a parody of Aristophanes in his treatment of Lysis. By taking away his own, he had cut him down to size, and he blew him up again by offering its return through wisdom, which would finally give him the freedom to do whatever he liked. He could once again have proud thoughts. Socrates' version had the disadvantage that "his own," which Lysis got in return, was no longer restricted to what had been his own; Aristophanes' version has the disadvantage that the return is equally impossible and what one gets instead is anything one likes, and the proud thoughts one has are confined to one's own city.[43] The issue between them thus turns on the status of philosophy as another kind of neither/nor, for without mind the good of good and bad vanishes.

If the Aristophanic *oikeion* were what belonged to us in accordance with mind, it would be the cosmos of intelligible beings; and Aristophanes' denial that our own can be restored to us would, under this translation, be equivalent to a declaration of the permanent fragmentation of the beings as they are for us. This fragmentation would make the beings appear to be not parts of a whole. They would be beings alone by themselves *(auta kath' hauta)* and detached from each other and the good. Such was indeed Socrates' description of ourselves and our parts, but strikingly none of them was treated as a part, and accordingly there was no whole of which they were the parts. We could well apply, then, to these beings the expression "phantom images" *(eidōla)*, which Socrates had used for those things over which the real friend casts its own character. These phantom images would be, like the wine and the cup, the presumed means for getting the philosopher back to the real. He would have to prize them highly and take them seriously in light of an ignorance as profound as the father's as to whether or not they are fated or not to serve the true and the real; but they do serve his own good in the constant life of thinking. His own thoughts, which are as private as his body but more liable to alienation, whenever he or another comes to know, are these so-called friends. They are literally *(rhēmati)* in speech. Through the *oikeion,* then, there is a way back to the cosmological speculation that Socrates had abandoned when he had turned to the human dimension of the friend; but we must remember that with this turn to the neither/nor philosophy became central.

Socrates allows the issue of the *oikeion* as what is missing *(endees)* to be glimpsed only for a moment; it is quickly replaced by the *oikeion* as whatever is "on one's own wavelength" *(kata,* 222a2–3). This necessary condition for the possibility that what is lacking fit that which desires it, obviously does not suffice to characterize a missing part. If and only if there were no whole of parts but *to epithumoun* were homogeneous throughout would the necessary and the sufficient collapse into one. Socrates thus anticipates his own argument that establishes first the identity of the *oikeion* with the *homoion* and then its equal uselessness. The one possibility he does not examine, that the good is *oikeion* to the neither/nor, could be thought perhaps as either equivalent to the first Socratic thesis, that the neither/nor is the friend of the good, or too paradoxical, if the good were found to be at home with what is neither good nor bad. Yet Socrates might still have intended to make up for this omission in questioning the older boys (223a1–2), had not tipsy and solecistic slaves forced Lysis and Menexenos to go home with their brothers. They were after all in the right (223a5).

Notes

1. M. E. Smith, *Essays on Law and Religion. The Berkeley and Oxford Symposia in honour of David Daube* (Berkeley, 1993), xi.

2. *Parmenides* 137a4.

3. Cf. *Odyssey* 14.224–28.

4. *Iliad* 1.167.

5. *Euthydemus* 273a7–b1.

6. Aeschines *Contra Timarchum* 10.

7. J. K. Davies, *Athenian Propertied Families 600–300 B.C.* (Oxford 1971), 359–61.

8. *Rivales* 134b4, *Charmides* 158c5, *Euthydemus* 273d6, 297a8, *Protagoras* 312a2, *Republic* 350d5, *Lysis* 204b5, c3, 4, d8, 213d3.

9. *Charmides* 155d3–4.

10. *Charmides* 153d2–5, *Lysis* 204e5–6.

11. *Republic* 412d2–8.

12. *Republic* 561c6–d1.

13. Cf. the *sphodra* at 207d6 with that at 212a4.

14. Cf. Xenophon *Oeconomicus* 20.29.

15. Aristotle *Nicomachean Ethics* 1159a34 uses *philophilos* in the context of an argument for the primacy of loving in friendship.

16. *Odyssey* 1.215–16.

17. *Republic* 537e1–539a4.

18. *Sophist* 253c6–9.

19. *Symposium* 176c2–3.

20. *Republic* 330b8–c6.

21. *Odyssey* 17.485–87.

22. *Parmenides* 134d9–e6.

23. *Odyssey* 17.217.

24. *Rhetoric* 1382a14–15.

25. *Odyssey* 22.474–77. In the *Gorgias* 510b4, there is an allusion to the same line Socrates quotes here; it helps to explain what "friend of the regime" means: to be protected from the injustice, on the one hand, and, on the other, to partake in the injustice, of the regime.

26. *Odyssey* 19.406–9.

27. *Theogony* 224.

28. Cf. *Symposium* 186d6–e1.

29. *Symposium* 204d8–11.

30. Cf. *Sophist* 216b3–6.

31. *Sophist* 268a1–4.

32. *Clouds* 1481–82.

33. Tacitus *Agricola* 45.2.

34. *Theaetetus* 210c3.

35. *Philebus* 16e4–17a5.

36. *Republic* 357c2.

37. The late Leo Strauss once suggested that the meaning of the title *Apology of Socrates* was that all the dialogues had the same purpose.

38. *Symposium* 204a4–7.

39. *Republic* 492a1–e1; *Statesman* 303b8–c5.

40. *Euthyphro* 2c2–7.

41. *Statesman* 272b8–d4.

42. *Theaetetus* 176a3–8.

43. *Symposium* 192a6–7, 193c5–d2.

TWELVE

On Interpreting Plato's *Charmides*

THE *CHARMIDES* IS ABOUT *sōphrosunē,* "moderation and self-knowledge"; but part of Socrates' original question in the dialogue is about the state of philosophy in Athens; and since self-knowledge is presumably the mark of Socrates' philosophizing, the *Charmides* is about Socrates' own understanding of his kind of philosophizing; it is the self-knowing philosopher Socrates confronting his own teaching about self-knowledge. The *Charmides,* therefore, is a Socratically narrated dialogue (one of four), for narration of dialogue is the most obvious way to represent reflexivity.

The auditor of Socrates' narration is anonymous, but unlike the other three narrated dialogues, he is addressed by Socrates (three times): in order for reflexivity not to be lost on the narrative level, it is necessary that it too be given a perspective. That perspective consists of two things: (1) ignorance of (and therefore indifference to) political matters—the auditor has not heard about the battle of Potidaea, the start of the Peloponnesian War; so the auditor must be a foreigner; and (2) a certain priggishness in sexual matters; so Socrates addresses him twice in a row when he speaks of the erection he suffered when he saw the things within Charmides' cloak. A man, then, who does not know his way to the marketplace and is embarrassed by sex can only be a Theodorus. In the Platonic corpus, Theodorus is the representative of pre-Socratic science. (Perhaps science is necessarily always pre-Socratic.) Socrates, then, presents his own reflection on himself before someone who is as oblivious of the political as he is reluctant to face eros: Socrates' account of self-knowledge is somehow the link between Socrates as the discoverer of political philosophy and Socrates' *erōtikē technē.*

The dialogue is in three parts. The first is mostly narrative. Socrates' arrival, his greeting by Chaerephon, Socrates' question, the arrival of Charmides, and Socrates' question about him; the second is the examination of Charmides; the third of Critias. Not only is the setting political—Potidaea—but it contains the democrat Chaerephon and the future tyrants Critias and Charmides. Chaerephon is said by Socrates to be *manikos* and the bloodthirsty Critias is hardly moderate. The setting is of political extremes, but they are in the future; in the present it is the extreme reaction of everyone—including Socrates—to Charmides: the transgressive character of eros—Charmides affects even little boys—foreshadows political extremism. And yet the argument of the *Charmides* never touches upon moderation in the Aristotelian sense (and of the *Republic* too)—food, drink, and sex. This ordinary kind of *sōphrosunē* is present only on the narrative level, and in a way behind the back of Socrates himself, insofar as the fates of Chaerephon, Charmides, and Critias lie in the future. This displacement seems to be the condition for the radical proposal of Critias—*sōphrosunē* is the science of science—and the no less radical critique by Socrates of Charmides' sensible definitions—quietness, shame, and minding one's own business.

The frame embodies Socrates' self-knowledge; but within the frame a distinction must be drawn between the examination of Charmides and Critias. Socrates suggests to Charmides that the definition he proposes for *sōphrosunē* comes from an examination of himself (i.e., he suggests that Charmides by self-knowledge discover that *sōphrosunē* is self-knowledge), but when Charmides gives up, and Critias takes over, the linkage of the question of what *sōphrosunē* is with the one who is being questioned seems to be abandoned, since Critias comes forward to defend a position regardless of whether or not that position expresses his own state; and yet it is only when introspection is not an ingredient in the discussion that *sōphrosunē* is defined as self-knowledge. Argument and action cannot be together, but only if they are together can there be philosophy.

Socrates begins by saying that he has been away from Athens for some time; and this interval is long enough to have transformed Charmides from a boy to a youth, and for Charmides to remember that Critias once associated with Socrates. Socrates' questions furthermore—who are the new beauties and wise, and what is the state of philosophy in Athens—imply that sufficient time has passed to make a difference. On the other hand, ancient campaigns usually last but a season; so it is hard to believe that Socrates was away for more than a year or two. Socrates, then, has exaggerated the length of his absence. He has done so perhaps in order to represent a situation comparable to what the Eleatic Stranger describes in the *Statesman:* if a statesman had to go abroad for a length of time and left written laws, what would he do if he returned sooner than expected and found changed conditions? Would he abide by his own laws? Socrates, then, represents himself as returning to Athens after sufficient time has passed for his way of philosophizing to have been passed on to Charmides by Critias, the direct disciple of Socrates. The question of *sōphrosunē* is a question about the transmissibility of philosophy as self-knowledge. It is tackled first through the question of its presence or absence in Charmides, and then in the case of Critias, the manner in which he has understood and therefore can transmit the Socratic teaching. Socrates' self-knowledge comes to light across the examination of Socratic self-knowledge as it comes to light in others. Charmides and Critias are found wanting, and despite both being poets neither is capable of transmitting philosophy. Socrates will have to wait for Plato, a member of the same family who has not yet been born.

That *sōphrosunē* as moderation has been taken up to the narrative level is first indicated at 153d2, when Socrates sums up the talk they had about Potidaea by saying, "When we had had enough of this sort of thing . . . " The imminent life and death struggle of Athens, the deaths and woundings of their friends and acquaintances, all this they turn away from as if we could limit our concern as we restrict our diet. Moderation, then, shows itself as indifference to simply human concerns;[1] and Socrates takes over by asking about "the things here." Since this expression is not on the dialogic level, we cannot gauge the degree to which Socrates' actual question contrasted, with the arrogance of the ivory tower, their concern with Athens and their friends with his concern: Socrates had the nerve to identify Athenian affairs with the state of philosophy. Indeed, we do not know whether "philosophy" occurred on the dialogic level at all, or whether the issue of philosophy was Socrates' interpretation to the auditor of what he asked his acquaintances, whether among them there had proved to be young men outstanding in wisdom, beauty, or both. Socrates' threefold question at any rate gets only a partial answer, for Critias restricts himself to the question of the beauties; and when Socrates gets hold of the discussion again, the issue has become Charmides' nature with respect to his soul, and that in turn becomes the question of his *sōphrosunē*. That *sōphrosunē* might be the equivalent of philosophy, and that a good nature with respect to soul might in turn be the equivalent of *sōphrosunē* is one thing, but that philosophy could be the equivalent of a good nature with respect to soul is quite another, especially since Socrates comes forward with the claim that he has at his command beautiful speeches that induce *sōphrosunē*. Could beautiful speeches replace, in the case of soul, nature? Such a possibility seems tantamount to the claim that Socrates' *erōtikē technē* wholly breaks down the distinction between art and nature. One sees at any rate that philosophy is transmissible if and only if such a breakdown is possible.

If courage means minimally "not easily frightened," and *sōphrosunē* minimally "not easily tempted," then perfect *sōphrosunē* might be unseduceability, and Socrates remarks that if Charmides has in addition to beauty of form goodness of soul he is unbeatable; but at the end he concedes that he will not oppose Charmides if Charmides is prepared to use force. Charmides, then, is not unbeatable; and Socrates finds once more that he can resist. Socrates' resistance means that he cannot be taken over, and Charmides' deficiency, that he is not his own man; he is the creature of Critias, like an actor, says Socrates, who has muffed his lines. Philosophy, then, is transmissible only if the receiver is wholly resistant to a takeover. Socrates the philosopher is on the lookout for someone who matches him in autonomy. Natural goodness of soul consists in a resistance to enchantment that has not been bought at the price of the experience of disenchantment.

It is not at once clear that Charmides is defective. Far from there being a new crop of beauties in Athens, as Socrates' question had implied, there is only one. Charmides has attracted everyone; no one, with the exception at first of Socrates who applies his mind to everyone else, can look on anyone else but Charmides. Everyone is either his lover or loves him; this distinction refers to their public acknowledgment of their love or their experience of it. To be the object of universal desire is to overwhelm the differences among men: Charmides cancels natural types. Chaerephon expresses this by distinguishing between Charmides' appearing *euprosōpos* and his seeming *aprosōpos* should he strip, so *to eidos pankalos* is he. Charmides' own individuality would disappear with the uncovering of his *eidos.* The *eidos* in itself, it seems, does not allow for the co-presence of the face—Socrates had already indicated this in saying that everyone gazed on him as if he were an *agalma* (i.e., without life)—and so the lovability of Charmides as Charmides would vanish with the full display of his form. The occlusion of the beings is for the recognition of the beings indispensable. Socrates diverts them from Charmides' form by asking about his soul. Charmides' beauty with respect to *eidos* is as

Charmides' possibly good nature with respect to soul. Critias says that Charmides is beautiful and good in this respect too; and Socrates proposes to strip "this very thing of his" and look at it before the *eidos.* Socrates implies that Critias was praising Charmides' soul with its outer covering, but that he wants to see the soul naked. The soul, then, seems to have a face-like part and an *eidos*-like part. The soul has its own individuality, and this does not interest Socrates; he wants to see whether the soul of Charmides exhibits soul with natural goodness and nothing else. Socrates will identify such a state of soul as the health of soul, or *sōphrosunē.* If *sōphrosunē* were the beauty of soul, the parallel between Charmides' naked body and naked soul would be exact; but we know that this skewed relation is deliberate, for *sōphrosunē* is never called a virtue in the *Charmides,* and "virtue" indeed is only mentioned once, as one of the outstanding traits on the father's side of his family.

Two suggestions can already be made. The first is that *sōphrosunē* as self-knowledge cannot mean knowledge of the self, as a unique bundle of particular features, but it must refer to a class-knowledge. Self-knowledge as class-knowledge seems to be hinted at already in Socrates' claim to his auditor that when it comes to the beauties he is *atechnōs* white on white: almost the entire class of the young appear beautiful to him. Socrates cannot be a lover of Charmides because he is for him nothing but a representative of a type. Charmides is already, without stripping, faceless to him. But Socrates says *atechnōs:* he is without knowledge precisely because he cannot tell the beautiful from the not. Self-knowledge as class-knowledge is not knowledge at all, for if Socrates is white on white, his belief that the young are beautiful is nothing but his belief that he is beautiful, and he is the ugliest man in Athens. Perhaps the second suggestion might help here: if Charmides had stripped, he would have exposed his sexual parts: the things within his cloak, as Socrates delicately says, his *aidoia* as Greek says. Does the soul when likewise stripped reveal its *aidoia* too? Whatever that might mean, it indicates a possibly necessary connection between *sōphrosunē* and *aidōs,* and this highlights the importance of Charmides' identification of the two in his second definition. In any case, these two suggestions yield one question: can self-knowledge as class-knowledge be rescued from its own illusiveness through the notion of the shame of soul?

The meeting between Charmides and Socrates is arranged through Critias, who sets out to put Socrates in a false position and keep himself in charge. Critias's ploy, however, to have Socrates pretend to be a doctor, is justified on the grounds that Socrates' proposal to strip Charmides requires that Charmides not be ashamed of exposing himself to a stranger, and the easiest way to arrange that, Critias believes, is to make the relation a professional one between doctor and patient: Doctor Socrates has automatic access to the secrets of Charmides.[2] Knowledge makes shame vanish. It is the psychic equivalent to the public display of nakedness that, established by custom, distinguishes Greeks from barbarians.

Critias tells Socrates that Charmides has been waking up each morning with a headache. "The headache is," to quote a medical manual for the family, "without a doubt the most common symptom of man: almost any disorder can initiate an attack." The headache is a universal sign, manifest in a part, that some part or other is not in its proper condition. Charmides' headache is no more than suggestive of the doctrine Socrates ascribes to Thracian doctors, that the good condition of the part depends on the good condition of the whole, for the headache is a general sign, it is not a sign of the general. The experience of disorder in a part that by itself points directly to the plausibility of a disorder in the whole as being causally related to it, is left to Socrates. When Charmides has come over and sat down, his direct glance at Socrates forces him to look away and down; Socrates thereupon sees *ta entos* and has an erection, which he describes to the auditor in suitably veiled language. It is not Charmides' headache but Socrates' own experience, to which no one present is privy, that initiates the elaborate tale of Thracian medicine with its incantations and drugs. We have then a split between the basis of the dialogue and the basis of the narrative. Charmides' experience of immoderation is the occasion for the form in which the question of *sōphrosunē* arises; but it is Socrates' immoderation that experientially grounds the Thracian teaching. What is theory for Charmides is fact for Socrates. The examination of Charmides' *sōphrosunē* serves Socrates' self-knowledge.

The auditor learns that Socrates at this moment was no longer in himself *(en emautou)*; he learns this when Socrates is fully in control: as narrator he can say and not say what he wants about himself and everyone else. Self-control in the strict sense seems to be possible only if there is complete control of everyone else. Narration is the retrospective equivalent of what in the present would be universal tyranny. Socrates had returned to his customary haunts with all the confidence that the routine brings; his being white on white had assured him that he would not be forced to depart from his ways by anyone. Socrates could always adapt to any circumstance and play the role it called for. Charmides was no challenge. Nothing could surprise Socrates. He is incapable of wonder. He cannot philosophize, for philosophy ceases to be itself if it becomes routine. It is not possible to think philosophically if what one thinks is a tradition, in which thought has become belief. Thus the issue of the transmissibility of philosophy is the same as the issue of Socrates' self-knowledge. To be outside oneself is the necessary condition for philosophy, and to be outside oneself is to be wholly lacking in moderation and self-knowledge.

Socrates says that the approach of Charmides caused much laughter. Everyone, in trying to make room for him next to himself, pushed his neighbor, and they succeeded in knocking one man at one end sideways, and another at the other end was forced to stand up. The expression Socrates uses, *epoiēse gelōta polun,* makes it unclear whether anyone actually laughed when they were pushing in earnest *(spoudēi)*; and it is perfectly possible that the laughter belongs to the narrative level: the auditor should find it funny. The funny indeed is the only way in which philosophy can be transmitted intact, for only it by nature contains within itself the necessary distance between surface and insight. What then was funny about the situation Socrates describes? Since everyone had heard what the arrangement was, that Socrates was to converse with Charmides, and that accordingly the only proper place for him was between Critias and Socrates, it is hard to see why room was not made for him at once. Only if everyone was no less excited than Socrates and hence embarrassed to stand up does their pushing make sense. The auditor is thus forced to experience in the form of laughter the intrusion of the unexpected that Socrates himself underwent. The wholly particular character of eros is transmitted in the universal form of the laughable. *Technē* and *aporia,* "art" and "perplexity," cease to be opposed to one another.

Socrates informs Charmides that the drug for the head is of no use without a prior incantation. Charmides says, "Then I shall copy it from you." The incantation is a universal formula that allows for the name of the patient to be inserted in the appropriate slots. The incantation is in the form of any successful transmission: Charmides can recite it where and when he wants to without the presence of Socrates or any other witness. The stripping of his soul is either unnecessary or it can be done by himself in private without shame. Socrates' question seems to grant Charmides' assumption: "If you persuade or even if you do not?" There is nothing intrinsically impossible in transcribing the incantation, regardless of whether Socrates himself has written it down or not: Socrates could be forced to hand it over. It turns out, however, that the incantation is not necessary; the drug by itself could cure Charmides' headache, but the Thracian doctor strictly enjoined Socrates not to give the drug without first applying the incantation. Without *sōphrosunē* it is of no use for Charmides to be without a headache. Charmides cannot become healthy in his body until he is sound as a whole. The particular good must wait on the common good; and if the common good is the beautiful condition of the whole, Charmides will have to wait forever if, as Socrates demands, the beautiful condition of the whole cannot be induced before one knows in what such a condition consists. *Sōphrosunē* cannot be handed on unless one knows what *sōphrosunē* is, and yet it might be present without one's knowing what it is. *Sōphrosunē* does not entail self-knowledge.

The risk for the Thracian doctor was for Socrates to give the drug without the incantation, persuaded by either wealth, nobility, or beauty; but the risk for Socrates himself was Charmides' dispensing with Socrates as the sole enchanter. Socrates implies that not even the health of the whole is any good unless one knows what it is. Whatever else *sōphrosunē* is, it cannot include either knowledge of itself or knowledge of its own goodness, for otherwise Socrates could have sung the incantation over Charmides and then tested whether Charmides knew what it was and what good it was. This leads to a further difficulty. Did Socrates learn the incantation without being *sōphrōn* himself? If he did, it is possible for the incantation to be passed along without any effect: enchantment can be had without the recipient being enchanted. Philosophy can survive a nonphilosophic transmission. If, on the other hand, Socrates did have *sōphrosunē* induced, it was not enough by itself to inure him against all blandishments, for otherwise he would not have had to swear to the Thracian to abide by the sequence of first the incantation and then the drug. The oath Socrates swore seems to be as good as *sōphrosunē.* It suffices to guarantee that he will not be seduced. The oath is a formula in terms of which one binds oneself to stick to certain conditions regardless of circumstances. The lack of confidence oneself or another has in one's resistance is made up by an appeal to a god or gods who will make sure that, however sorely tempted, one will not give in. Surely an oath is a kind of beautiful speech—one invents a perfect version of oneself which one is ashamed and afraid to betray—but it is not the sort of beautiful speech that Socrates learned at Potidaea from Thracians who are said to make themselves immortal.

Since Charmides never does get the incantation, one is inclined to ask whether the beautiful speeches that induce *sōphrosunē* are not in fact the set of arguments of the dialogue. Is this possible? Can speeches about *sōphrosunē* as to what it is induce by themselves *sōphrosunē?* Can *sōphrosunē* be the same as perplexity? Philosophy then would be misological skepticism and as dogmatic as any teaching, for just because Charmides and

Critias cannot get out of the difficulties they land in means as little as if Socrates found them no less insuperable. Philosophy cannot despair. If, moreover, the question of *sōphrosunē* were *sōphrosunē,* there would be no something about which one asked questions, and a self-reflexive question would be as empty as Socrates proves Critias's science of science to be. What is what is *sōphrosunē*? may be a way of asking what it means to ask the question, What is X in general? but it cannot be such a way if X itself is a question. Socratic ignorance must be informed by knowledge.

The Greek teaching on medicine stops at the body; it is a whole with parts, and doctors try to treat and cure the part with the whole; but the Thracian teaching says that one should not cure even the body without soul. Soul seems to be both the whole of which body is a part and a part of what Socrates calls the entire human being. As a part it is the source of all good and bad for the body and the entire human being; but Socrates does not say what it is as the whole. Perhaps the soul as the whole is that element in the Thracian teaching that Socrates does not accept, for it would certainly seem that if an incantation could order the soul perfectly, the immortality the Thracians are said to produce would necessarily follow. Either, then, there cannot be a flawless health of soul, a flawless health of soul does not suffice for immortality, and the Thracian teaching is mistaken that all good and bad proceed from soul, or a flawless health of soul is the necessary condition for mortality, for it is good that man dies. This last possibility seems to be the teaching of the *Phaedo,* in which Socrates preposterously claims that he alone dies, for the practice of dying and being dead is philosophy. However this may be, the Thracian teaching seems to preclude philosophy, for it is hard to conceive of how perfect order could be compatible with wonder, laughter, and eros. Socrates himself only laughs on the day he dies.

Socrates gets to the question of what *sōphrosunē* is by suggesting that Charmides might already have it and hence can dispense with the incantation. Critias says that Charmides is exceptionally *sōphrōn;* he is thought the most moderate of his contemporaries, and Socrates asks Charmides whether he agrees with his cousin and partakes of *sōphrosunē* adequately or is wanting. If Charmides asserts his own moderation, he will seem immodest; if he denies it, he will show that he has it and does not need it. The presence of moderation will check one from claiming it; the denial of moderation will make everyone believe that one has it regardless of its presence or not (176b6). If moderation is self-knowledge, it is unlike any other kind of knowledge, for its publicity cancels it. Self-knowledge and dialogue do not go together. Socrates can insist all he wants that he knows nothing but no one believes him. His *sōphrosunē* is labeled irony. Now Charmides offers a version of this argument but not before he blushes, which made him, Socrates says, "appear still more beautiful, for bashfulness *(to aischyntēlon)* suits his age." Charmides' blush is the counterpart to Socrates' own experience, for it too is an unwilled sign of some disturbance. It enhances, however, the beauty of Charmides' face and indicates by itself the presence of *sōphrosunē* in some sense but not of genuine *sōphrosunē.* It is not clear whether blushing is capable of being present together with genuine *sōphrosunē,* but if it is not, we would know already that Charmides does not have genuine *sōphrosunē,* and he would, precisely because he has a version of it, be incapable of knowing that he lacks the genuine article. If blushing disappears with time, without anything but the weight of unreflective experiences checking its possibility, then *sōphrosunē* can never become fully rational in the way in which Critias will claim. Something that we on our own can neither induce nor suppress is the ground for self-knowledge.

Charmides' blush precedes his answer; but is his answer the interpretation of his blush? Does his blush say, "If I deny I am *sōphrōn,* it is strange to say something of the sort against oneself and I shall show up Critias as false and many others in whose eyes I seem *sōphrōn,* as he says; and if in turn I assert it and praise myself, it will perhaps appear annoying. So I do not know what I am to reply to you." Charmides' speech is concerned with the shamelessness of either answer; but the blush is not shameless; it is a sign of Charmides' simultaneous pleasure in being praised for moderation, and his anxiety that such pleasure betrays a lack of moderation. It thereby signifies that he has not yet differentiated between the pleasure in moderation and the pleasure of immoderation. His blush in itself shows that he does not know himself. Its true interpretation is not in Charmides' direct speech but in the reported speech, "He said it was not easy at the moment either to agree or deny what was asked." Since Socrates has put this speech into his narrative frame, we cannot tell whether we can reconstruct from it Charmides' original speech or Socrates has given his own interpretation of the now-unrecoverable speech of Charmides. In either case the direct speech we are given, though it purports to explain Charmides' dilemma, does not fully account for the state he is in.

Socrates proposes to get out of Charmides' difficulty by examining with him whether he has *sōphrosunē* or not. "Clearly," he says, "if *sōphrosunē* is present to you, you can opine something about it, for it is surely a necessity that if it is in you that it supply some awareness *(aisthēsis),* from which you would have some opinion about it as to what *sōphrosunē* is and what sort it is." Socrates is referring to Charmides' blush, the heat of which should make Charmides aware of its cause and identify *sōphrosunē* with shame. Charmides does make it his second answer but not his first. His first, quietness *(hēsuchiotēs),* does not require either that he have it or that it supply him with a perception of it; his definition is merely, as Socrates says, something that people say. In order to distinguish between a transmitted opinion about *sōphrosunē* and its actual presence, Socrates had interposed the notion of *aisthēsis.* An *aisthēsis* of *sōphrosunē* must be of *sōphrosunē;* something of *sōphrosunē* must show up in the perception of it and yet not be *sōphrosunē*—*sōphrosunē* must be a kind or class of which one senses some individual, like the face of Charmides and unlike his form. If *sōphrosunē* is present, it must appear in a passion or an action. If it is not in Charmides' blush, it seems as if it must be in his hesitation and unwillingness to answer the question, whose generalization Charmides sums up as quietness and Socrates interprets as slowness. Socrates' "slowness" is closer to Charmides' experience than Charmides' expression of his experience, which he has adapted to fit a common opinion. Charmides' slowness, though it occurs on the occasion of the question of *sōphrosunē,* does not necessarily have anything to do with *sōphrosunē.* Charmides' error is based on the reasonable inference from what Socrates has said, that *sōphrosunē* must show up in everything one does, and hence his present slowness must testify to its presence or not. The manifestation of the state of the whole is an adverbial qualification of the working of a part.

Socrates shows by implication that no adverb that is restrictive enough to constitute an explanation of what a beautiful order is can cover the range of all our actions of body and soul. Charmides can hardly be blamed for not knowing of the indeterminate dyad of the beautiful which the Eleatic Stranger presents as a solution to Socrates' question. It is precisely the generality of the condition that is the ground for any virtue, so that *sōphrosunē* cannot be a virtue among virtues, that baffles Charmides and Critias and precludes the Stranger's solution. Socrates hints at the Stranger's solution when he urges Charmides to apply his mind more, look at himself, realize what sort of person *sōphrosunē* by its presence makes him and by being of what sort itself it would make him of that sort. "Figure out all this," he says, "and then say well and bravely what it appears to you." Charmides then paused, took a look at himself in a manly or brave way, and said *sōphrosunē* was shame. Socrates thus makes Charmides disassociate the manner needed to discover and express *sōphrosunē* from what he discovers *sōphrosunē* to be. He therefore cannot be noticing the state he is in while he is examining what state the presence of *sōphrosunē* would put him in. He lacks self-knowledge, but he knows enough to refrain from saying that courage is moderation. *Sōphrosunē* must necessarily be elusive if the intensity and effort needed to lay it bare cannot consist with the delicacy and gentleness that make the man of moderation imperturbable. Charmides imitates in this respect the pre-Socratic philosopher, whose blind devotion to the truth makes him blind to himself. It was Socrates, who in turning away from looking at Charmides, applied his mind to the spectators.

Socrates began to question Charmides' first definition of *sōphrosunē* as "quietness" by having him agree that *sōphrosunē* is beautiful—it can never fail to be beautiful, it cannot alter in light of circumstances. The moderate life, Socrates concluded, is not the quiet life. There is nothing beautiful about being deliberate. Lightning judgment is usually suspect, not because it would not be as good or better than its opposite, but because it is usually the case that what we have to decide upon is recalcitrant to speed. Socrates' argument is not based on any reflection about our nature, the power of our passions, or the fragmentary character of our knowledge. Charmides fails to define *sōphrosunē* because Socrates abstracts from human nature and the nature of our circumstances: *sōphrosunē* would not be good if we were not what we are. It therefore can be beautiful and deserving of praise only if it is not like Charmides' blush, which enhances him only in light of a limitation of his nature. It is a question of time. Socrates began to question Charmides' second definition by having him agree that *sōphrosunē* is good: *sōphrosunē* is good if and only if it is the cause of good. Socrates' argument has a gap in it: he never gets Charmides to agree that if something is bad it can never cause good. This gap links the beautiful and the good: to say that *sōphrosunē* is beautiful is to assert that bad cannot produce good. Socrates thus makes use of the connection between shame and innocence in order to get Charmides to conclude that shame is not *sōphrosunē*. Charmides would have had to have been no longer innocent (i.e., incapable of blushing), in order to maintain that the nongoodness of shame does not prevent it from being productive of good. Charmides' own state, which is an acknowledged defectiveness, forces him to assume that defectiveness cannot make for good, even though in his case it makes for good and made him more beautiful.

Just as Socrates' refutation of Charmides' "slowness" is itself refuted by Socrates' slow refutation of it, so Socrates' refutation of shame as *sōphrosunē* is refuted by Charmides' acceptance of the authority of Homer who denies the goodness of respect. Socrates gets Charmides to oppose authority in general on the authority of an authority. That authority is Homer; but Socrates can only make Homer an authority by ascribing to him a line that Telemachus in fact speaks. Socrates is not exactly lying. Even if Telemachus spoke it, it is not untrue to say that Homer said it, just as every word in the *Charmides* is said by Socrates. If Socrates had asked Charmides whether he thought Telemachus spoke beautifully when he uttered this line, Charmides would have been asked to give up his own opinion for that of another young man. So Charmides is shamed into denying that *sōphrosunē* is shame. Once more he is shown to lack self-knowledge. The first consequence of this denial is to put forward a definition he once heard from someone. He does not claim as his own view that minding one's business is moderation. He no longer is minding his own business, which was to look at himself and report on his own state. He defers to Homer and ceases to defer to Socrates. Socrates is outraged. Charmides, he suspects, has heard the definition from Critias or someone else who is wise. Critias of course had heard it from Socrates and passed it off as his own. Charmides inadvertently asks Socrates to examine his own definition. Can Socrates bring himself to look at his own as if it were not his own? Charmides sees no difficulty. "What difference does it make, Socrates, from whom I heard it?" It is not the speaker but the speech that counts. There are now no authorities for Charmides. Socrates has done his work well, so well in fact that he is told to forget himself while seeking self-knowledge.

Charmides' principle, however, though it certainly puts Socrates in a quandary, is of no use to Charmides, for as soon as Socrates shows him how enigmatic the definition is, Charmides frankly confesses his ignorance and adds, "But perhaps nothing prevents even its speaker from not knowing what he had in mind." Charmides has no stake in the definition; he thus gives the strongest argument for trust in authority, for no one will have an incentive to face up to the enigmatic unless he can believe that it is worth the effort to unravel it. Deference to authority is indispensable for the possibility of interpretation. Hermeneutical *sōphrosunē* consists in questioning the wisdom of the authority to which one defers. One transgresses on the basis of obedience, and one can only be forced to transgress if the wise authority looks crazy. Hermeneutical *sōphrosunē* means to look hard at another's; but it is also *sōphrosunē* to defend one's own. One has to surrender oneself to another while fighting every inch of the way. *Sōphrosunē* is the orderly and quiet harmony of doing one's thing and deferring to another. Charmides' failure to harmonize them expels him from the discussion.

A character in a Platonic dialogue says there is no need for Platonic dialogues. He immediately refutes himself by abandoning the search for the meaning of something precisely because he knows who said it and wants to put him down. He discounts the possibility that the saying is enigmatic. Socrates' claim, however, that it is enigmatic, that a distinction has to be made between the verbal utterance and the speaker's intent, is only possible because Socrates does not lay claim to his own definition. It ceases to be enigmatic and becomes merely obscure as soon as it becomes Socrates' own. The enigmatic only makes sense as a form for the transmission of philosophy: it keeps out the legion of Charmideses and Critiases, the former because they cannot take it seriously and the latter because they cannot defend what they claim as their own. The Platonic dialogue, then, is the perfect vehicle for the transmission of philosophy. It contains its own defense, and when it is not funny it is enigmatic.

Ta hautou prattein, if translated as "to know one's place," connects not only Critias's definition of *sōphrosunē* as "self-knowledge" with his defense of *ta hautou prattein,* but it also links up with Charmides' second definition. Shame, one might say, is the consequence of one's not being fully certain as to what one's place is and therefore confining oneself more than the true extent of one's place allows. Socrates' puzzle about it arises from the fact that the knowledge of knowing one's place is a knowledge of what class one belongs to and not a knowledge of how to do or make at all. Socrates interprets the formula as wholly empty of content in itself with each of its parts, *prattein* and *ta hautou,* as a rubric for any action and any object of that action respectively. He thus points to the difference between the parts and the formula as a syllabic whole. As a syllabic whole or idiom, it appears not to allow for substitutions. The difference, then, between its literal and idiomatic meanings is the basis for the parallelism and lack of parallelism between the structure of the city and the structure of the soul in the *Republic.* The shoemaker by art makes shoes; he does not by art mind his own business, though in making shoes by art he is minding his own business. Minding one's own business does not belong to the level of action and dialogue but to that of narration: "I was minding my own business when . . ." The task of the philosopher, then, is to mind his own business by art; this is self-knowledge. Ordinarily, however, *ta hautou prattein* is determined negatively. There is always another over against which one's own is defined. For man, it is beast and god; for the city, other cities; for the citizens, other citizens (not being nosy); for the artisan, other arts ("stick to your last"); for me, you. As a principle, it requires a prior determination of what pair is involved. It is a principle and not a way of finding out what is one's own. In some cases the determination is not given but has to be discovered—a prior meddling is necessary if the principle is to be employable; in other cases, the determination is given but it can be imagined to be canceled—Aristophanic comedy exemplifies this. Through the nondetermination of things, a moral principle becomes equivalent to philosophy as the determination of the nature of things. The nondetermination of man establishes the need to determine the nature of at least three things. Philosophy therefore is always placeless, and the philosopher always a Stranger.

Socrates' erection was succeeded by Charmides' blush; Charmides' blush in turn is succeeded by Critias's visible "agony." Critias has been "running" Charmides and letting him be his mouthpiece; his anger when Charmides botches his poem shows that he lacks the *sōphrosunē* of writing, which requires that one let go once one has published. Indifference to one's own plaything is the acknowledgment of the difference between words and their meaning. Mind as such can never be passed on; the possibility of misunderstanding belongs of necessity to transmission. Critias, however, steps in because he wants no one to think him a fool, and that is clearly impossible unless one is either a god or a tyrant. Critias's anger, which recalls the occasion on which Thrasymachus got angry, forces him to tell Charmides in effect, "Mind your own business—You lack *sōphrosunē.*" This is the counterpart to Charmides' mockery of Critias, which without Charmides being aware of it implies that Critias did not know what he was talking about when he praised him for his *sōphrosunē.* Charmides shows his moderation by his indifference to what is not his own; Critias shows his moderation by caring for his own. Charmides' indifference led to his denying even the authority of his cousin and guardian Critias; Critias's concern will lead him to speak without clarity out of shame of revealing his ignorance. Critias's shame, however, is superior to Charmides' indifference. Socrates abandons Charmides as soon as he does not care; he forces the discussion forward when Critias refuses to admit that he does not know.

All of the following arguments with Critias are fueled by grammar. Syntactical ambiguities and errors are either exploited or ignored. The reflexivity of thought, it seems, does not show up clearly in speech. Critias begins by distinguishing between *prattein* and *poiein,* not in the Aristotelian way of action and production, but by claiming for *prattein* the noble and beneficial part of *poiein.* This division within making is not balanced by a comparable division within *ta hautou;* there is not the class of one's own of which a part consists of noble and good things; rather, one's own things are only the good things. *Sōphrosunē,* then, is to do the good things; but to do is itself to do the good things. Critias thus counters Socrates' argument that had split the idiom into its elements by unifying the syllabic whole of the formula to the point that it has nothing but redundant parts. *Sōphrosunē* is now entirely self-enclosed and immune to analysis. One's own, then, ceases not only to be in opposition to anyone else (justice toward others becomes total selfishness), but it ceases as well to allow any access to itself. Self-knowledge is neither possible nor necessary for *sōphrosunē.* Socrates concludes this argument as follows: "Sometimes, then, the doctor though he acted beneficially or harmfully does not know himself how he acted/fared" *(ou gignōskei heauton hōs epraxen).* Socrates introduces casually the theme of the rest of the dialogue by making use of the so-called binary construction: the reflexive *heauton* as the direct object of the verb *gignōskei* is also in sense the subject of *epraxen.* The self of self-knowledge is a virtual object of knowledge.

The Delphic inscription "Know thyself" *(gnōthi sauton)* is not in intention a command; it is a concealed assertion: "You are not a god." Critias moves to *sōphrosunē* as science of science by denying that "Know thyself" assigns the addressee to the class of humans in opposition to the class of gods, just as he had turned the formula of justice, "Mind one's own business," to the formula for imperialism by denying any implicit opposition between one's own and another's. If, however, we combine the original meaning of "Know thyself"—"You are not a god"—with Critias's insistence on the formula's self-containment, we get the philosophical command, "Know what a god is." To examine the speech means to examine the speaker, for the speaker is the being to be known. The *Charmides* has consistently directed us to this way of interpretation. Hermeneutical *sōphrosunē* thus consists in putting the meaning of an utterence back into the surface sentence. On this reading the Sphinx asks, "What is man?" and Socrates' proof of the immortality of the soul in the *Phaedo* runs, "Soul will never accept the separation of body and soul."

Critias, in shifting from *ta hautou prattein* to *gignōskein heauton,* makes a break between action and knowledge that lets *sōphrosunē* slip through his argument. He asserts that one could never be *sōphrōn* and not know it. He thereby denies that Charmides is *sōphrōn;* but does he imply that he is? He surely thinks of himself as being moderate in not insisting that he was right about *ta hautou prattein;* and he implicitly urges Socrates to concede that he (Critias) might be right; but if his new definition is right, and he claims to conform with it, he already has confirmed Socrates' later point that if one has self-knowledge one does not know anything, even about *sōphrosunē,* since Critias now grants that *ta hautou prattein* might be *sōphrosunē.* If that were true, there would be two equivalent definitions parading as different, while the man who holds both is *sōphrōn* without knowing that he is. Critias, moreover, says that he would not be ashamed to say that he misspoke. *Sōphrosunē* means not to have false pride; but Critias thus admits that he does not know *what* the mistake was in the previous argument any more than he knows *that* there has been a mistake. Critias is certainly now deferring to Socrates' authority, to the extent that Socrates has uncovered Critias's true belief about *sōphrosunē* which Critias did not know he had. So regardless of what might hold about knowing one's own *sōphrosunē,* one does not know on the basis of self-knowledge that one has self-knowledge as one's definition of *sōphrosunē.* "Self-knowledge" is like a bird in Socrates' image of the dovecote: it is not linked up with the bird "*sōphrosunē*" that is also flying about somewhere.

Critias's interpretation of "Know thyself" is not easy to make out, for he seems both to agree with Charmides that the speech and not the speaker is to be taken into account, and to disagree with Charmides, since he speaks of the intention of the dedicator; but he also speaks as if the god too is the speaker of the letters, and in turn as if the letters themselves are speaking. Critias, in any case, admits that there is an enigma here. "Know thyself" looks like a piece of advice; before him it was never understood as the preferred alternative to the greeting *chaire* (Rejoice). The god is not saying to his worshipers as they enter the temple, "I am addressing you in a way different from the way you greet one another because I am a god," but he is saying that his way is the right way for men to greet one another. Men are now to say what a god says, but to say it as they now say *chaire.* One man is to greet another with *gnōthi sauton,* and the other is to reply, *kai su ge* (You too). *Gnōthi sauton* is not a piece of advice, for there is perfect equality between addressor and addressee. The imperative form is, on the one hand, to be doubled—the god says, "Say, 'know thyself,' "—and, on the other hand, it is not a command at all but the expression of a wish, "I hope you know yourself." It is purely formal and does not require one to do anything more than echo it when one hears it. It is just a polite version of "Mind your own business." Critias has to formalize the Delphic inscription in order to guarantee that one cannot be ignorant of one's own doing and still be moderate. The shadow-sentence that accompanies *gnōthi sauton* and makes it an example of an ellipsed binary construction *(hōs ouk ei theos)* does not associate being with doing. It therefore has to be cut away from the audible sentence. The god who said it is none other than the man who wrote it down.

Critias denies that *mēden agan* is the equivalent of *gnōthi sauton.* Moderation has nothing to do with *sōphrosunē.* Critias has so radicalized *sōphrosunē* that it no longer can cover its ordinary meaning. It is as if Socrates' identification of justice as an art in *Republic* I were never modified in the course of the discussion and justice as will never taken into account. The dialogic level of the *Charmides* is Critias's, who as Socrates' disciple has pushed his teacher's doctrine to the point that the inner core of things has become the whole of things. *Ta hautou* of *ta prattein* lends an element of unclarity and indistinctness to minding one's own business, for it allows for an indeterminate expansion and contraction of one's own things, while its complete contraction in knowing oneself seems to make for the greatest clarity. The reflexive pronoun points to self-identity. Critias will not allow for *sōphrosunē* to have a structure like justice, with both a comprehensive and precise sense, whose duality can be kept together only in thought. Critias had right from the start identified soul and mind and implied that the beautiful speeches of Thracian medicine would make Charmides better in thought. Health of soul, then, is knowledge and the knowledge of health of soul the knowledge of knowledge, both comprehensive as the science of science and precisely as the science of itself. "Know thyself" originally meant "Know what you are"; in Critias's version it means "Be knowledge." Critias ends up with the pure mind of Aristotle, which has nothing to think but itself; and just as the world falls away from Aristotelian mind, the self of *gnōthi sauton* vanishes into the self of *epistēmē heautēs.*

The emergence of science as its own object happens in the seemingly most casual way. Socrates replaces the verb for knowledge by acquaintance (*gignōskein*) with the noun for scientific knowledge *(epistēmē).* The noun, of course, can no longer take a reflexive personal pronoun, though Critias at first lets it; but the science would strictly have to be of the *egō* or, if the reflexive from the verbal phrase is to be preserved, it would have to be of itself. What astonishes us in the grammatical legerdemain is that Socrates proposes it on his own; but it ceases to astonish when we notice that Critias is really controlling the argument and Socrates is feeding him the lines. That Critias is in control shows in the way he hints in the first phase of the argument that he has already prepared the second (165e4). He first opposes mathematics to Socrates' example of medicine in order to distinguish between those sciences that have some product apart from themselves and those that do not; and he then claims *sōphrosunē* is unique because it is of itself and all the other sciences. Critias, then, first denies that *sōphrosunē* is good and then asserts that it is the whole without being the good. He begins in short by displaying the science of science, since he divides the sciences according to their several natures and criticizes

Socrates for failing to discern differences in similar things. If Critias knew what he was doing, he would be proposing that division in the *Sophist* in which the Eleatic Stranger puts together and separates his own diacritical way and the cathartics of Socrates. Critias would then be saying that *sōphrosunē* is the science that distinguishes between product-sciences and measure-sciences, good-related and non-good-related sciences, how they are related to themselves and one another. Critias, however, does not know what he is saying; he consistently fails to connect the argument with what either he or Socrates says, even though by his own definition, it would seem that *sōphrosunē* should equip one to follow one's following of an argument.

Despite Critias's control of the argument up to this point, Critias without provocation turns on Socrates: "You are far from being unaware *(lelēthenai)* of this, but as a matter of fact I believe you are doing what you just denied you do: you are trying to refute *me,* with the dismissal of what the speech is about." Socrates does not deny the charge but rather links the refutation of Critias with the examination of the argument: "Think of what you are doing if you believe that if it is granted that I am refuting you I am refuting for the sake of anything else than for the sake of which I would examine myself as to what I say, in fear that without being aware of it *(lathein)* I believe I know something and do not know it!" All Socratic examination of others is self-examination, and self-examination is examination of what he says. Self-knowledge is once again binary. To test Critias is to test a piece of Socratic opinion that is parading as knowledge. Critias is the unawareness *(lathein)* of Socrates. *Sōphrosunē* is the science of truth *(a-lētheia);* but it cannot be such a science unless there is unawareness or latency *(lanthanein)* in truth and it is the alpha-privatizing of not-noticing, for the latent in itself resists its own negation. Knowing and belief are in themselves distinct; they can overlap and seem the same only in the would-be knower. *Sōphrosunē,* then, is of necessity a continual *praxis* and cannot but disappear and contradict itself should it ever come to believe—it would never know—that it has reached its goal. If *sōphrosunē* is a virtue, it is not knowledge; and if virtue is knowledge, it is not a virtue. Immediately after this, Socrates gets Critias to agree that *sōphrosunē* is also knowledge of ignorance.

Socrates divides the first phase of the discussion into the uniqueness of *sōphrosunē* if it is the science of itself and the possible existence of *sōphrosunē* if it must have the being relative to which it has the power. At the beginning he summarizes the issue of its possibility, if we adhere to the reading of the major manuscripts, as follows: *to ha oiden kai ha mē oiden eidenai hoti ouk oiden*—"the knowing of what one knows and does not know that one does not know." The phrase *to . . . eidenai* looks complete, and the supplement *hoti ouk oiden* seems to stand outside it and undercut the distinction between what one knows and what one does not; i.e., the knowledge that one does not know is a consequence of what one knows and does not know. The binary construction is thus exploited in order to reveal that Knowing What and Knowing That are united in knowledge of ignorance, and what are apart in the first element of the construction are together in the second. The knowledge of indirect question (I know what) and the knowledge of indirect statement (I know that) coincide only if what one knows is a question. The form of soul as self-moving motion has the cognitive structure of questions. This is *sōphrosunē.*

Socrates offers Critias a list of cognitive and appetitive faculties of soul and asks in various ways, "Have you noticed . . . ?" This faculty of noticing is not on Socrates' list, for it notices not only all other faculties as well as itself, but it also does not have any range to which it is restricted; we can call it the surveying or enumerating faculty. There is nothing infallible about this faculty. Desire *(epithumia),* Wanting *(boulēsis),* and Love *(erōs)* are in Socrates' presentation lexically distinct; the first has pleasure, the second the good, the third the beautiful for its proper object. The denial of reflexivity to them is thus restricted to these objects. It is therefore possible for eros to be a good and a kind of pleasure and thus to be itself the object of wanting and desire respectively; and if eros is in truth a desire for the good and a wanting it to be one's own, then eros could be of itself across Socrates' mistaken division. Elasticity of reference would be the minimal condition for reflexivity. This elasticity would be satisfied for anything imperfect that has the capacity to be itself. Anything, in short, that can be a class-member without being identical with the virtue of the class to which it belongs can be said to have such a reflexive capacity. Knowledge of knowledge therefore is possible only if such knowledge can belong to the class of knowledge without being the virtue of the class. Knowledge must not be disqualified as knowledge if it turns out to be nonknowledge too, any more than self-knowledge requires that he who knows that he is a man be the perfection of man. Critias is too exacting to be moderate.

In his enumeration of faculties, Socrates, it seems, misplaces *doxa* (opinion); it follows fear and should follow perception. Socrates, moreover, fails to say what *doxa* is of, but simply asks, "[Have you observed] a *doxa* that was *doxa* of *doxai* and of itself, but what all other opinions opine about opines nothing?" Critias answers, *oudamōs.* It is strictly an answer to "Have you noticed?" and not directly about opinion of opinions and of itself, for if it were, he would be mistaken, since *oudamōs* is certainly an expression of an opinion about opinion, and it is false; indeed, it could not possibly not be false. Critias in fact has knowledge that there is opinion about opinion; he therefore has a false opinion about his false opinion. Critias's mistake is necessary for him; otherwise, one could have a true opinion about knowledge of knowledge and be *sōphrōn* without being *sōphrōn* in Critias's sense of knowing that one was *sōphrōn.* If Critias, moreover, now has a true or false opinion about knowledge of knowledge, he certainly has an opinion about it; and yet he does not notice that knowledge of knowledge must be of itself, and if Critias cannot prove that it is possible, he was asking Socrates to agree to something he himself does not know.

Socrates distinguishes between the manifest impossibility that relative measures could be self-reflexive and the intense distrust that nonmeasurelike things could ever have such a power. He seems to imply that it could be settled if all nonmeasurelike things could be shown to be in fact measurelike; but even this proof, that their difference was only apparent, would fail to solve the problem, since once this science in charge of this proof were in place, it would have to examine itself and find accordingly that it was baffled as to which class it should assign itself. A complete Pythagoreanism seems impossible, and a science of science necessarily incomplete. Only a nonscience of nonscience is possible. Socrates' perplexity at this point is the manifestation of its existence. "When Critias heard me and saw that I was perplexed, I thought that he too, just as those who see yawning people facing them, experience along with them this same thing, was compelled by my being perplexed to be caught by perplexity." That Critias's next speech is obscure without being enigmatic shows that he is merely imitating Socrates' perplexity. Critias does see Socrates perplexed, but he does not see that this is knowledge of ignorance and Socrates has refuted himself. His failure to see that the disproof of Socrates' argument supervenes on Socrates' argument is due in part to his truly acting in accordance with his original assertion—no *sōphrosunē* without self-knowledge—for he can only see through Socrates' argument if he gives up his thesis, which requires the thematizability of knowledge of knowledge. His thesis stands in the way of his seeing and thus refutes itself, since he cannot know himself either, inasmuch as he does not recognize what he should according to his thesis. His shame dominated his pseudo-*sōphrosunē* and therefore confirmed Socrates' pseudo-proof that it is not good; but this pride—this reluctance to call it quits—is the basis for the logos continuing. It is Critias's holding onto something not good which is his own and which enables him to go on. Critias's impure care for his thesis is good. It is no wonder, then, that Socrates can now only divine that *sōphrosunē* is good; when he was speaking with Charmides, he was certain that it was good and therefore not shame.

Critias's stubbornness lets Socrates formulate the difference between knowing that and knowing what. Without any knowledge of whatever an art or science deals with, knowledge of knowledge is reduced to knowing that here is knowledge and here not. This is not altogether trivial, since it implies that one can know something without knowing that one knows it. Critias's restriction, however, of knowledge of knowledge to the arts and sciences makes it trivial, for the man with medical knowledge invariably says, "I am a doctor." Latent knowledge, which Critias needs, seems more to characterize Theaetetus, who on Socrates' telling him the cause of his bewilderment says, "I do not know." Theaetetus thus declares that he knows knowledge is knowledge of cause. Nonsystematic knowledge, then, could be the proper field of the exercise of *sōphrosunē,* but Critias cannot by definition avail himself of this. Knowledge of knowledge is a diacritical power designed to separate things known from things unknown; but Critias has to deny that it is anything more than the recognition of that separation and not the separating itself, for the latter implies that the known and the unknown were initially confused and knowledge of knowledge would have to know and not know the beings. Socrates illustrates what he means by saying that political science is of the just. Political science knows the just and unjust. The city is the locus of the set of all possible opinions about justice. Political science, then, is the science of the just and of opinions of the just; but opinions of the just are the same as varieties of pseudo-political science. Political science is of the images of political science. It is of itself across nonpolitical science; and if the locus of nonpolitical science is the city, it is itself the locus of justice. The knowledge of justice is of its cognitive and noncognitive character; in its cognitive character it is philosophy, and in its noncognitive character it is the city. Political science is of soul and city, of itself and not itself.

Once the question of knowledge of knowledge is broached, it might surprise that the *Theaetetus* question is not raised, What is knowledge? Suppose Critias had said that *sōphrosunē* is the name for the answer to that question, and just as there impurity was ineradicable through our knowing while not knowing, so here the answer would be impure through our not knowing while knowing. At the end of the *Theaetetus,* Theaetetus knows that he does not know what knowledge is; he knows his nonknowledge of knowledge; and Socrates says that he is in the position he claims to be possible for Critias's knowledge of knowledge if it is limited to knowing that. Since Socrates' maieutic science, with which he never tested Theaetetus's mathematical competence, brought Theaetetus to this knowledge, Critias seems to be given the opportunity to identify it with a partial science of science. Socrates, however, does not allow Critias to examine Socratic knowledge because Critias shows that he does not have the knowledge to examine Socrates. Critias lacks the maieutic science; but if the holder of the maieutic science generates nothing, can the maieutic science examine itself? Can "nothing" be examined? The issue of nonbeing in the *Sophist* follows directly from this puzzle. If Critias is the *lathein* of Socrates, he cannot be his own *lathein;* Socrates would have to be his *lathein,* and his self-knowledge be across Socrates' ignorance. Critias had in fact tried to arrange for this, for he assigned to Socrates the role of the sham-doctor and thus believed he had automatic knowledge of Socrates' nonknowledge; but Socrates eluded him by presenting a doctrine that, in arguing for the partiality of the art of medicine as the Greeks understand it, defied Critias to prove that Socrates' knowledge was spurious. Socrates indeed lets Critias draw that conclusion, for he gets him to agree that each science minds its own business. Critias's science of science is *sōphrōn* because it acknowledges the *sōphrosunē* of each science. The pretender with his sham-knowledge always shows up in his violation of the boundary conditions of each science. Socrates is the transgressor who has Critias accept the inviolability of class-distinctions.

Having reduced *sōphrosunē* to a knowing that, Socrates outlines the good they expected would have accrued to them had *sōphrosunē* been also a knowing what. His outline consists of the true city of the *Republic,* in which everyone is in his proper place and that place is determined solely by knowledge. Everyone leads an error-free life. *Sōphrosunē,* however, because it governs everything, does not have to be yours in order for you to reap exactly the same benefits as you would should you possess it yourself. If you do only what you know, and someone else decides what of yours you should hand over to others who know, you will lead a life in conformity with *sōphrosunē* without being yourself guided by it. Even if you know nothing and hand yourself over entirely to others in the strictest obedience, you would be in the same condition as anyone who was individually as well-organized. An error-free life is a life in which inside and outside causation are indistinguishable. So if Charmides were as beautiful on the inside as on the outside, he would be faceless and have no inside.

Hiding, then, seems to be compatible only with error, the range of which extends from Charmides' blush to Socrates *lathein.* Soul cannot be beautiful. In the *Phaedrus* it is a monster in love with the beautiful.

That *sōphrosunē* might be knowledge of what one knows and what one does not know is a concession against the logos that did not allow *sōphrosunē* to be that if it were *sōphrosunē* in Critias's sense; but nothing stands in the way of there being such a knowledge as long as it is not *sōphrosunē.* It is a part of political science. Socrates thus proves that even with this political science we would not be happy. It is not the true and healthy city but the false and unhealthy city that is good. Socrates thus looks at *sōphrosunē*'s usurpation of political science and discovers that in its pretension it is not good. The concessions made against the logos are in fact nothing but the sham disguises of *sōphrosunē. Sōphrosunē* as the science of science is sophistry, the indispensable shadow of philosophy.

Socrates first gave a contrafactual argument for the goodness of Critias's science of science in the full sense; he then asks whether science of science has not a more limited scope, to make one's own learning easier and the examination of others more beautiful; and though we are expecting an examination of this possibility, Socrates instead goes back to the contrafactual and proceeds to prove that the seemingly impossible is not good. This proof dispenses with the need to wait for some great man, as Socrates puts it, to determine whether any of the beings has its own power relative to itself. The philosopher is without hope. The structure of the argument suggests that the more modest function of *sōphrosunē* was precisely to discover that the scientific life was not good. *Sōphrosunē* makes learning easier because, on the one hand, it puts up resistance to the drift of an argument on the grounds that something is too good to be impossible; and because, on the other, it resists the attraction of the impossible good. Socrates thus suggests that one of the highest themes of philosophy would be to consider whether anything impossible is good or whether every good is in principle realizable. If the first is true, philosophy ends in despair; if the second, that the good is the cause of the being of the beings would be more than a divination.

The strange consequence that now appears before Socrates, if to live scientifically is not to live happily, consists in this: Their supposition had been that an error-free life was good. This was an error. They would not have made this error if they had had the error-free science of *sōphrosunē.* They would have known at once that it was not good. Why, then, was the error better than the truth? Why was Critias's failure to admit his perplexity better than Charmides' confession of ignorance? His failure allowed Socrates to formulate the difference between knowing what and knowing that. This difference in turn leads Socrates to suppose that someone has knowledge of all that has been, all that is, and all that will be. This comprehensive divinatory knowledge is a knowing that. Aeschylus's Prometheus knows that if he disobeys Zeus he will be punished; but his poet reveals that his knowledge cannot extend to the knowledge of what he will experience in meeting his fate. Prometheus cannot anticipate his experience and know beforehand what his punishment will do to him. The tragic formula for this is *pathei mathos.* The universal predictive science suffers from the same fault as Promethean knowledge. Its elimination of error eliminates the possibility of, as it eliminates the motive for, asking about the what of things, for such a science must begin with what there is and cannot ask the Socratic question about what there is. The *Republic* rests on three points: no understanding of justice without an understanding of the city; no understanding of the city without an understanding of the soul; no understanding of the soul under these conditions. "What is X?" cannot be properly formulated unless it is erroneously formulated. This constitutes the philosophical equivalent of tragic wisdom and its name, too, is *sōphrosunē.*

Socrates justifies his examination of his strange vision by saying, "It is necessary to look at what appears before one and not dismiss it idly, if at least one cares for oneself even a little." No one else cares for another's dream. The dream alone escapes control because it escapes the interest of whoever rules with the political science of science. Socrates opposes what is his own, regardless of its truth or falsity, to the perfect security that an error-free life would bring. He thus raises the same question as the Eleatic Stranger does when he doubts whether any philosophy superior to materialism would have been possible in the golden age when the god ruled in the only manner compatible with rule in the true city. The Stranger's myth had entailed that Socrates was impossible as long as there was such rule; and Socrates here implies that the human equivalent to this kind of divine providence is the technological society, whose ruler would be the tyrant Critias. Socrates represents the small but unconquerable bulwark against the realization of this project. He has come back just in time to thwart Critias, who has reflected not inconsequentially on the implications of some parts of the Socratic teaching. His deepest reflection is this: Critias, in admitting that knowledge of good and bad especially makes us happy, admits that in the absence of this knowledge the benefits of medicine, shoemaking, weaving, piloting, and generalship will have deserted us. Knowledge of good does not just determine the good; there is no good unless there is knowledge that there is good. There is no unexamined good and therefore no happiness without knowledge of happiness. Perhaps, then, it is in this way that the good as the cause of the knowability of the beings can be understood to fall together with the good as the cause of the being of the beings. In any case, the disjoining and conjoining bond in the compound name *philosophia,* between the knowledge of the beings that is wisdom and the desire to have that knowledge as one's own good, is *sōphrosunē.*

Critias wonders why the science of science could not rule the science of good while still being benefited by the science of good. The science of science cannot be subordinate to any science. It totals but does not complete. In order for it to complete the sciences, the science of science would have to rearticulate the sciences in a way different from the self-conception of each science. It would have to look at the sciences in light of a whole unknown to any other science and hence transgress the self-imposed boundaries of each science. Critias is not criminal enough to undertake this enterprise; his science of science requires that everything be in place prior to his rule, for otherwise the science of science would have to know something besides rule. Rule, however, also turns out to be superfluous. Critias's interpretation of Socrates' teaching amounts to the replacement of the good with the beautiful as the highest principle. The faceless *eidos* of Charmides symbolized that principle; and the teaching of the Thracian doctor was Socrates' proleptic interpretation of it. Critias accordingly could not figure out whether that teaching was genuine or not, for Thracian medicine offered perfect order unaccompanied by any understanding of what perfect order is. That understanding is in the beautiful speech of Socrates, the *Charmides* itself. It is his alone and cannot be copied by the likes of Charmides and Critias. Socrates comes back to Athens and takes back his own.

Notes

1. Cf. *Iliad* 21.462–69.
2. Cf. Herodotus 3.133.1.

THIRTEEN

Plato's *Laches:* A Question of Definition

THE *LACHES* RECORDS THE MEETING between Socrates and the inglorious sons of Thucydides and Aristides, on the one hand, and, on the other, the now-famous generals Laches and Nicias. They meet sometime after 424 B.C., the battle of Delium, and before 418 B.C., the battle of Mantineia, where Laches lost his life (Thucydides 5.74.3). The meeting cannot be said to have been a complete success. No definition of courage is arrived at, and Socrates' proposal, that they all go back to school, was not, it seems, followed up. The last words of the dialogue are Socrates'—*ean theos thelēi*—and they show him to be cautious even about tomorrow in Athens. This caution could not have been very different from that which he displayed at the battle of Delium itself, which impressed both Alcibiades and Laches (*Symposium* 220e7–221c1). According to Thucydides, the left wing of the Boeotians was defeated by the Athenians, but the Athenians, on seeing two cavalry detachments that Pagondas had sent to their rear, panicked and ran in the belief that another army was about to attack them (4.96.5). If we imagine that Socrates was stationed on the initially victorious right wing—Laches' praise of him would not be as suitable if he were in retreat from the start—then Socrates' precaution, his being more *emphrōn* than Laches, would have consisted in his not taking anything except for what it is, with no false imaginings allowed, which would have earlier prevented him from killing his fellow Athenians when the enemy line bent into a circle and some of the Athenians lost their heads and failed to recognize their own (4.96.3). Socrates' caution seems to be a species of prudence, and hardly a matter of courage as either

Laches or Nicias think of it. His prudence seems to be halfway between the fully epistemic character Nicias impresses on courage and the natural force Laches believes the lion, leopard, and wild boar share with brave men.[1] The essence of bravery is to be found in a beast, and a female one at that, for it is impossible to tell apart the predicate adjective in Socrates' remark to Nicias, *oude tēn Krommuōnian hun pisteueis su ge andreian gegonenai* (196e1–2), from the substantive *andreia* in which one would say that Socrates and Laches share (193e3). The bestiality of Laches' courage is at the opposite pole from Nicias's divinization of courage, so that, as Laches believes, only a god could possess it (196a6).[2] Socrates' middling position, which covers both his actions on the battlefield and in a friendly conversation, certainly seems to be of a human sort; but it wins this position at a price: the human *(to anthrōpeion)* takes over from the manly *(to andreion),* and Socrates becomes a whole by letting slip out of sight the half he really is.

This internal opposition between the human and the manly is noted by Nicias: "That's good, Laches, . . . and it will no longer make any difference to you, it seems, if you along with me know nothing of those things whose exact knowledge *(epistēmē)* it is fitting for a man who believes he is something to have. Now you in fact seem to me to be doing a truly human *(anthrōpeion)* thing" (200a4–b1); but for Nicias the human all-too-human is despicable, common though it is, or, better perhaps, because it is so common, and this is what Laches is doing, seeing Nicias's discomfiture as a vindication of his own, while what he should be doing is looking to himself, since he believes he is a real man and a somebody.[3] It might be thought strange that Nicias of all people should appeal to Laches' manhood, since he could not have forgotten Cleon's jeer in the Pylos campaign, that the situation could have been resolved "provided the generals were real men *(andres)*" (Thucydides 4.27.3). To be a man, then, carries with it so immediate a recognition that Laches, when he is forced to admit that thoughtful daring is less manly than thoughtless, falls back on his intuition, which, he acknowledges, he cannot express, but it still remains undamaged by Socrates' argument: "I am really distressed if I am not able to say just what I am thinking" (194a8–b7).[4] The hardheaded Laches has a mystical faith in his inexpressible conception, and nothing Socrates can say could dislodge this conviction. Nicias too is still filled at the end of the dialogue with the view Socrates elicited from him, but his error of confusing a part with the whole is corrigible, and he has complete confidence that he will work out the wrinkles before too long. Socrates, then, does not make too much of a dent in either Nicias's belief in his own progressive perfection or Laches' ineffable mind.

If we discount the sons of Lysimachus and Melesias, who speak one line in unison (181a3), the dialogue consists of two nobodies and two somebodies, with Socrates belonging to neither or both groups. For Nicias and Laches, Socrates is clearly a somebody, but for Lysimachus and Melesias Socrates is not much, since it did not occur to them to invite him to the hoplite-show of Stesilaos, though Lysimachus knows of him through his father Sophroniscus, but he lost touch with him since Socrates was a boy, or so Nicias infers (187d6–e4). Socrates, in any case, whatever his standing is in the eyes of Nicias and Laches, did not have the public position that could have excited Lysimachus's interest. Lysimachus and Melesias are concerned with their own lack of exploits with which to regale their sons, and in some sense they want to learn the formula for political success; but this concern, though it seems to be the spring of their joint action in inviting Laches and Nicias, is overlaid with a more meritorious impulse, to make sure their own sons who are somewhere between 15 and 20 might be the best possible (179d7; cf. b2). If political success were their real concern, a reflection on their fathers' careers would have given them a more immediate insight into what was needed; but since they say nothing about how their grandfathers brought up Aristides and Thucydides, they cannot believe that the old formula, if there were one—it seems to be represented in not an entirely false light by "Just Speech" in the *Clouds*—would now be effective (cf. *Laws* 698b4–6, 700a3–c7). Education in some kind of knowledge seems to be the key to the way up, for they do not even ask Nicias and Laches how they made it to the top.

"Science," now a magic word in Athens, seems to characterize the Athenian way. In Thucydides, in all cases but one, *andreia* is opposed to *epistēmē* or *empeiria,* and in all cases but one *andreia* is not an Athenian trait;[5] and in the dialogue, Nicias, who believes he has learned it from Socrates, is the representative of Athenian know-how. According to the Corinthians of Thucydides, technical innovation, or *epitechnēsis,* is the hallmark of the Athenians (1.71.3); but perhaps what is truer of them is that Laches is as much an Athenian as Nicias and yet stands for the Spartan way. Athenians are not all of a piece, and there are more exceptions in Athens to the Athenian way than there are exceptions like Brasidas in Sparta (cf. Thucydides 2.41.1, 4.84.2; *Laws* 642c4–d1). Within Athens, in any case, Laches stands to Nicias as Sparta to Athens.[6] It is not only that Laches cites at first only hoplite tactics—naval strategy is never mentioned by anyone (even though Laches' illustration of Stesilaos's absurdity involves it)—in his characterization of courage,[7] but he suspects anything that smacks of innovation and sophistry, appeals to the failure of teachers of hoplite-fighting to make any inroads in Sparta, speaks of the Dorian mode as the only truly Hellenic one, and clearly despises the esteem in which Athens holds tragedy (182e6–b6, 188d2–8). At the same time, however, Laches clearly does not regard himself as devoted to war to the same extent he believes the Spartans are, and Nicias deliberately gets his goat by citing the *philopolemos* Lamachus as no less wise than he (197c5–7).[8] What best shows off perhaps his Attic strain is his catachresis of *mousikos* and *dōristi* (188d3, 6). *Mousikos* does not mean for Laches "skilled in music," which it still does for Socrates when he says in the *Republic* that Glaucon, Adimantus, and he will not be *mousikoi* before they are thoroughly acquainted with the species of moderation and courage in themselves and their images (402b9–c8); but Laches' *mousikos* has taken on a novel sense that, while drained of *technē,* does not preserve any connection with the performance of music either, even though Laches has to borrow the musical term *dōristi,* but again it is unrelated to any scale. In spite, however, of these noncognitive extensions of *mousikos* and *harmonia,* Laches is saying that the real man (*hōs alēthōs anēr ōn,* 188c8) is not as reticent as a Spartan but has speeches to match his deeds. He may be claiming, it is true, a love of speeches only to accommodate Socrates, from whom he seems to expect an eloquence that he can then borrow as his own and thus live up to the really *(tōi onti)* harmonized man he has postulated; but Laches' admiration for Socrates saves him from being entirely Socrates' timocratic man, who is more willful and slightly less musical than Glaucon (*Republic* 548e4–549a1).[9]

There is more to Laches than he can express; but there is also more in what he says than we find in his words on courage. His view of courage is much narrower than what he indicates he believes constitutes a real man. Although it would seem that a phrase like "a man truly a man" should be no different from the nature of manliness, Laches never connects the virtue courage with what he takes to be the *anēr mousikos.* That Laches senses a connection is shown particularly in his confrontation with Nicias, where he plainly appeals to himself and others as proof positive that Nicias could not be more mistaken. Perhaps what stands in the way of Laches' thematizing the connection is his agreement with Socrates that *andreia* is a part of virtue, whereas he surely does not suppose a true man is defective in any way. Laches, then, fails to grasp courage because he feels compelled to restrict it to a part while what he esteems is a man who is a whole and all of a piece. If Nicias stumbles because he expands a part into a whole, Laches misses the mark the other way around: he has a whole in mind that courage as a part cannot measure up to. The loose language of contempt—like Cleon's "If the generals were men"—which

Laches fully expresses and somewhat understands, resists guiding or even being taken into account once Socrates raises the formal question, What is courage? Not only the language but the opinions generally held have drifted away from the reality of what it means to be a man. The shift from substantive *anēr* to possessive adjective *andreios,* and the second shift to a resubstantized *andreia* have left behind the being that Laches still divines is the real issue. Laches, in short, does say what he thinks, but he does not know it.

It is easy enough to connect Lysimachus' question, How can his sons become as good as possible? with Socrates' question, What is courage? if one recalls the original meaning of *agathos* as "brave."[10] The connection cannot have been entirely lost on Lysimachus either if he believes that Nicias's and Laches' assessment of hoplite-instruction provides a test of their advice about the more general question he poses. The Megillus of the *Laws* would perhaps have joined the two questions at once with some citations from Tyrtaeus that proved their essential equivalence. Laches too must have retained something of the original meaning of *agathos* if he separates, as he does, wisdom so entirely from virtue, even though he does not disparage wisdom and believes the wise man too can be in a Doric harmony (188c7). To be a man, then, has also moved beyond its original sense and taken in more than *andreia* can. *Andreia* seems to be stuck between a concrete and global past, when it characterized all that a man could be, a Socratic present, in which its scope has been restricted, and the future where its very existence is precarious if it is nothing but a human excellence in which anyone can share regardless of whether one has a natural basis for it or not. Nicias, one can say, represents a flawed version of that future, and the question would be whether it has to be flawed if nature is so ruthlessly banished.[11]

In order to get a handle on what Laches wants to have Socrates advocate, it is necessary to go back to his advice about hoplite-instruction. In the course of arguing against the worth or even the existence of such an art, Laches tells an anecdote about Stesilaos, in which his novel weapon of spear plus pruning hook got him into trouble. The anecdote in itself shows that Stesilaos's invention was not well thought out; it proves neither that Stesilaos was a cowardly man nor that his training gave him a false sense of confidence; indeed, Stesilaos did not lose his head when his spear-pruning-hook got stuck in the rigging of a freighter, and he held on as long as he could. What Laches cites as the most telling objection to Stesilaos is that his behavior provoked laughter first among the sailors on board the freighter, and then among his fellow marines. That the show he put on, complete with applause, probably saved Stesilaos's life does not impress Laches; the fact that he became the object of ridicule in the first place settles the issue for him. To be a real man, then, is to be laughter-proof, never to slip on the proverbial banana peel and be shown up as claiming more than one can prove (cf. *Philebus.* 48e8–49c5). This is a hard test to pass;[12] but it is particularly significant if we recall that, one year after the battle of Delium, Aristophanes in the first version of the *Clouds* held Socrates up to universal mockery and cut him down to size. The *Clouds* seems to narrow the time in which we are meant to imagine the dialogue we are reading occurred. Even if Lysimachus and Melesias stay mostly at home, it is hard to believe that a report about Socrates and his reflectory would not have made the rounds and reached even them; and it is even more impossible to believe that Laches would not be looking at Socrates askance, despite Delium, if he had known that Socrates was not immune to ridicule. He might have protested and argued against Aristophanes' Socrates that that was not the Socrates he knew, but he certainly would have thought twice about associating with someone as tainted with sophistry as Aristophanes made Socrates out to be. If it is safe, then, to assume that the *Laches* is to be dated before the first *Clouds*—the publication of the second version as long as it was not produced would not have immediately damaged Socrates' reputation—then we have the striking situation in which Plato presents Socrates with his own reputation intact while showing up two illustrious generals as absurd. It is this kind of humiliation that Laches believed a real man could not be subject to; but here he is being exposed to scorn, and as there is nothing he can do against the agent who brought him low he turns against his fellow general, who he realizes is curiously unaffected by the devastating criticism of Socrates. Nicias turns out to be immune to ridicule, because he is not aware that he is ridiculous. Self-assurance is not what Laches means by being a real man; one has to be one's own man with the complete approval of one's neighbors. The stubbornness of invincible ignorance is not enough.

If this argument is right, Plato chose the moment before the fall to show Socrates in the best possible light before the powers that be in Athens. Socrates passes with flying colors. Ghosts from a glorious past choose him as their spokesman, and those who are soon to negotiate peace with Sparta—Thucydides puts the names of Laches and Nicias side by side among the signatories to the treaty (5.19.2; cf. 24.1)—cannot but acknowledge their inferiority to him. That Socrates now reveals some kind of crisis of self-understanding among the Athenian leadership has not brought about any enmity on their part, even though one can imagine that Lysimachus's and Melesias's sons were not slow to spread the word among their contemporaries about the surprising defeat Nicias and Laches experienced at the hands of Socrates. Just before his trial, Socrates singles out for mention Lysimachus's son Aristides as one of those who left him too soon, before his midwifery could have its full effect, and thus aborted everything Socrates had previously assisted to see the light at his lying-in (*Theaetetus* 150e1–151a2); and in the *Theages,* Socrates tells how Aristides realized that Thucydides, Melesias's son, was preening himself as being a somebody and forgetting that before he consorted with Socrates he was no better than a slave (130a8–b8). Socrates, then, has some disappointments in store for him, but at the moment he is riding high and could easily be imagined to be strutting in his usual way in his total defeat of know-nothing politicians. There is something delicious in Plato's conjuring up Socrates' imaginary triumph, but also something absurd in taking this kind of revenge on Aristophanes. It is possible, however, that a moment or two later, after the gathering broke up, Laches and Nicias came to their senses and realized who was responsible for showing them up and putting them down, and the *Laches,* far from recording a contrafactual Socratic victory, documents the origins of the enmity Socrates incurred among the politicians of Athens.

Socrates is very artful in the way he diverts the interlocutors away from an immediately practical question—should the sons of Lysimachus and Melesias be instructed in hoplite-fighting—to his own kind of question, What is courage? whose only practical consequence is his own impractical suggestion that the old men, the generals, and he go back to school and disregard the ridicule they will probably incur. His suggestion gains support only from Lysimachus, who cannot lose any more face than he already has, and neither Laches nor Nicias—though the former would be willing to entrust his sons to Socrates if they were of age, and the latter is all for Socrates taking charge of his son—has any interest in consulting Socrates further on his own behalf. Nicias promises to go back to Damon and others to correct his partially flawed definition of courage, and Laches is not prepared to fulfill his ambition to track down courage, once he is secure in the knowledge that Nicias knows as little as he. The impracticality toward which Socrates slants the discussion does not hold throughout. No one can read Socrates' remark to Nicias, which Laches alone is made to confirm, that Nicias and Laches as generals can bear witness that generalship best takes care of the things within its domain, and the art of divination must serve the art of the general, just as the law also ordains, without feeling that Socrates is warning Nicias, ten years before the fact, that he is destined to yield fatally to soothsayers (Thucydides 7.50.4).[13] Not only is the *Laches* a monument to the cloudless days of Socrates but also to the terrible disasters that await Athens through the incompetence and timidity of Nicias. The *Laches,* then, represents an occasion on which the philosopher might have had an effect on the politics and life of his own city. Although this practical effect lies outside the dialogue, it must color our reading of it. Such a perspective raises two questions: Was it just an accident that Nicias was incapable of heeding Socrates' advice, or does Nicias represent or point to something in the city that philosophy cannot budge? The second question is this: Does Plato's reconstruction of the premises for the Sicilian disaster contribute something of an entirely different kind from what we find in Thucydides? Is not Nicias done to a turn by the historian without any help from philosophy, and does he not give us material as rich for reflection as any that Plato made up?

If, for a moment, one has to conceive of a typical sequence in Thucydides, one could say that it consists of a speech or speeches that propose some course of action, followed by a deed or deeds that show the consequences of the advice taken or not taken. Every speech, no matter how focused on a single action, tends to be couched in universal terms: Cleon and Diodotus have to give a wide-ranging account of Athenian democracy from which it is supposed to follow that the Mytilenean decree is to be put into effect or rescinded. The first part of the *Laches* somewhat resembles this Thucydidean practice. Nicias and Laches each give a speech, with one recommending and the other urging the rejection of hoplite-instruction. Both present their arguments in universal terms and thus contain in embryo the issue about the nature of courage, to which Socrates then turns the discussion. Indeed, the resemblance of Nicias's and Laches' speeches to a Thucydidean debate is strengthened through the intervention of Melesias, who suggests that that advice should prevail with which Socrates casts his vote, and thus turns Lysimachus and himself into an assembly of two, who go with the majority of the *dēmēgoroi.* In blocking this way out, Socrates arranges for his deed, in which he takes on Laches and Nicias and pins them both in record time. This divergence to a higher level of universality than any in Thucydides, seems to be the Platonic response to Thucydides: only with the Socratic turn can the truth of the particular emerge. There is, however, at least one occasion in Thucydides when the universal is wholly in the particular, and that is the curious discussion between the Boeotians and the Athenians that immediately follows the battle of Delium. A small force of Athenians is still holed up in the temple of Apollo at Delium, and when an Athenian herald comes to ask permission to pick up the dead from that battle, the Boeotians refuse to grant it on the grounds that the Athenians had violated the customs of the Greeks, which prohibit the use of temples and sacred precincts for ordinary purposes (4.97–99). The Athenians in reply give two answers: One involves another Greek law that hands over to the conqueror the absolute use of whatever land he controls no matter how small. The Athenians' second answer turns on the issue of compulsion, and whatever guilt they have incurred through misapplication of sacral waters is involuntary, and the gods are the paradigm of forgiveness in the face of necessity. Here is a case where the actions of the two antagonists draw their support from the highest of grounds, the law and the gods.[14] The sacred is that issue in which universal and particular are always bound together, for a ritual practice *(nomizein)* always carries with it a belief *(nomizein einai),* however buried it might be in the details of the practice itself. I should suggest, then, that the odd angle at which the sacred intrudes into Thucydidean deeds is the point of contact with the Socratic investigation of the *Laches.* Just as Laches detects in Nicias's assertion that courage is wisdom the implicit claim that its knower is a god, so Socrates concludes that Nicias's courage as knowledge contains both justice and holiness and is the provider of all goods (199d7–e1).[15]

In order to see how the gods and courage are connected, it is merely necessary to recall Ajax. His remark in the *Iliad*—"Even a fool would know that father Zeus helps the Trojans: the darts of all hit their targets, whoever hurls them, whether bad or good; Zeus makes them all go straight" (17.629–32)—is the starting point of Sophocles' *Ajax,*[16] where Ajax's claim to be the best after Achilles conceals the boast to be Achilles' superior, since Achilles needed the gods and he does not: "Even a nobody would acquire superiority with the help of the gods; but I, even apart from them, am confident to win this glory" (767–69). "Nobodies" *(outidanoi)* are *anthrōpoi,* and they need gods; *andres* do not.[17] To be an *anēr* is to be strictly self-reliant; it is to be as sure of oneself as of one's ability to tell friend from foe and human from beast.[18] When, in Sophocles' drama, Athena interferes and prevents Ajax from seeing things as they are—Odysseus admits that no one was *pronousteros* than Ajax (119)—Ajax resolves to kill himself. Athena, he implies, cannot get between himself and himself so as for him to fail to know at least who he himself is, although everything around him might be unreal. Ajax, however, changes his mind; although he first intended to commit suicide on top of the cattle he had tortured and slaughtered in his tent, he has to go outside to carry out his resolve. The change of scene points to Ajax's refusal to see his dead body as carrion; he wants it to be a *nekros,* the man-specific form of a dead animal.[19] To be a corpse, however, means to accept the intrusion of the sacred into the makeup of being a man. Ajax needs Hades (cf. 865). If we apply, then, this tragedy to the *Laches,* we can say that Laches is Ajax before the fall, who, given the choice, goes with the beasts in his defiance of Nicias, and Nicias represents the total disappearance of the manly in light of the gods. One of the actions of Nicias that Thucydides records was his willingness to give up a trophy to signify his victory on the field of battle for the sake of burying two missing dead, even though Athenian law allowed for burial in honor of the unrecovered dead (4.44.3–6; cf. 2.34.3; Plutarch *Nicias* 6[527b]).

To be one's own man *(heautou einai)* and to keep one's cool *(emphrōn einai)* have both an unreflective natural side and a reflective element that knows what it means to look to oneself. To look to himself is precisely what Nicias asserts Laches refuses to do (200b1). Laches is all reaction. He is best when he argues against Nicias and worst when he is on his own. In his first attempt at a definition, Laches goes no further than the word *amunesthai* to characterize the brave man; it is Socrates who has to introduce the word *machesthai* (190e5, 191a2,a6;cf. b6). If one were to put Laches' view in terms that never come up in the dialogue, Laches understands courage as primarily the willingness to be killed, but not with its necessary counterpart, the willingness to kill. Not only does he fail to see at first that there can be steadiness in flight—despite his admiration for Socrates in retreat—as well as in maintaining one's post, but he holds out against pursuit as part and parcel of bravery.[20] When the dialogue takes a sudden turn—Socrates proposes that Laches' second definition, persistence, has a dialogic equivalent in their keeping up their search for courage—Laches immediately translates it into the nearest thing to standing still: "I, for my part, Socrates, am ready to be not the first to stand away *(proaphistasthai)*" (194a6).

Laches' failure to comprehend Socrates' behavior at the battle of Delium into his definition of courage seems to belong to a more general failure on his part to link manliness with bravery. Laches' praise of Socrates is worth looking at not only for its intrinsic interest but for what he omits in his definition. The language of his praise is supplied by Lysimachus, who exclaims after hearing Nicias's and Laches' recommendation of Socrates, and his son's and Melesias's confirmation that the Socrates they are always talking about is indeed the son of his old friend, "That's good, Socrates, that you hold upright *(orthois)* your father" (181a3–4). *Orthoun* is an odd word for Lysimachus to use so metaphorically—"to exalt" covers it only if one thinks of its original sense—but Laches' play on it astonishes: "I observed you holding *upright* not only your father but your fatherland; for in the retreat from Delium he was withdrawing along with me, and I tell you that were all the rest willing to be like him, the city would now be *upright* and would not then have fallen in the fall it did" (181a7–b4). "Fatherland" and "the city" are missing from Laches' definition: the enemy can be equally brave. It is one thing, moreover, to extend "father" into "fatherland," but it is quite another to keep *orthoun* in presumably Lysimachus's sense and then revert to its original sense in resorting to its literal contrary, "to fall" and "fall." This is in the style of ancient poetry, to stretch a word and compress it at the same time, so that it is impossible to give up the literal while one is still being forced to give it up in order to accommodate its extension. It is perhaps not surprising that this should occur in a dialogue in which *andreia* cannot and must be kept together with *anēr*. That the puns should be Laches' suggests that his incapacity to say what he thinks has something to do with the resistance poetry puts up to translation, and that in courage there lurk images that cannot be brought into the light of day. If *polis* reduces *patris* into a nonimagistic form,[21] what happens to Socrates' father in that reduction? And if that is all that *patris* really means, why does the city then suffer a fall and contrafactually be upright? Creon rings changes on *orthoun* and *orthos* when he first reports his decree to the Chorus: the gods righted the affairs of the city, Oedipus once kept the city upright, and we make our friends on condition of the city's sailing right side up (Sophocles *Antigone* 162, 167, 190), but it would be hard to find anything comparable in the orators.[22] Socrates exalts his fatherland as a fact, and his city is upright as a hypothesis. *Orthoun* belongs to the language of praise, *orthos* belongs to the language of fact. Laches seems to show himself as *mousikos* in a rather ingenious way: there is harmony between the exaltation Socrates bestows on his fatherland as a matter of its praise and the success the city would have experienced had everyone been willing to be like Socrates. Before he gets to say whom he admires, Laches comes forward as a composer of something in the Doric mode. Socrates is made all of a piece by Laches fitting *patris* to *polis* and speech *(orthoun)* to deed *(orthē—ptōma)*. Laches forces the matchup through the imaginary; he is incapable of showing the matchup in the real.

Socrates is a puzzle to Laches; to Nicias he is an open book. In the first part of the dialogue, Nicias knows from experience that Socrates is the expert adviser (180c8–d3); in the second part he explains Socrates to

Lysimachus and claims that he knew from the start how Socrates would turn the conversation into a personal rendering of accounts (187d6–e4). In the language of the *Gorgias,* Nicias joyfully submits to corrective punishment at the hands of Socrates and thereby proves that to anticipate with pleasure the reform of one's errors makes it certain that one will only sink more deeply into self-ignorance and folly. Nicias has two elements of the genuine Socratic teaching: to be good is to know oneself and to be good is to be wise, and yet he gets them all wrong. He recalls the Critias of the *Charmides,* who took Socrates' *ta hautou prattein* and pushed it to the incoherent extreme of knowledge of knowledge. That both dialogues end up with the admission that neither moderation for Critias nor courage for Nicias can be the knowledge of good and evil, and that this is the highest knowledge, should make one wonder why Socrates gets encapsulated in so empty a formula once his teaching spreads among politicians or potential politicians. Plato is trying his hand at the sociology of knowledge when he ruminates on Socrates and his effect on politicians in Athens.[23]

The difference between Socrates the true politician and all his phantoms is not just a theoretical difference, in which Plato sets Socrates as a foil over against an imaginary character like Callicles, but he also involves him with men who have been affected by him in one way or another. Nicias is in a sense the most curious; if we follow the manuscripts, he claims to be on the level of speech as close to Socrates as if he were family. In his trying to be Periclean and steering a middle course, Nicias should be expected to be least prone to the extremism philosophy necessarily breeds in the young (cf. *Republic* 537d7–539a4; *Philebus* 15d4–16a3). Nicias is perfectly satisfied with himself. It did not occur to him to suggest that Socrates would be a better consultant than himself when it came to the matter at hand; he seconds Laches' recommendation, but he is not at all surprised, as Laches was, that Lysimachus and Melesias did not approach Socrates first. And yet Nicias does seem to be given to extremes: his understanding of both hoplite-fighting and courage have all the earmarks of the abstract reasoning practical men presumably most despise. Is it possible that this extremism only seems to be the same kind as philosophic reasoning but in fact has a far different source?[24] Such a possibility would go some way in explaining, in general, why political philosophy is so large a part of Socratic philosophy, and, in particular, why Socrates incorporates Laches into himself when he takes on Nicias (194b8–c1; 196c5–7). Laches does not have the wit to refute Nicias on his own; all he can do is splutter and fall silent, but there still is something in him that though silent Socrates thinks deserves to be allied with himself against Nicias. We know at any rate that Socrates did not ask Nicias to join with him while he talked with Laches.

Nicias makes seven points in his recommendation of *hoplitikē* (181d8–182d2). He begins and ends with the body. The body in its inner strength and the body in its outward display of form, which can induce terror in the enemy, enclose, as it were, the contributions of the art to the soul.[25] It seems as if Nicias has devised a program for the complete man, of which the first step would be the art of the hoplite and the last *stratēgia* (182c1). It is not surprising, then, that courage should also turn out to be equivalent to the whole of virtue if even at the start, in the discussion of a test case, Nicias thinks big. What is most curious, however, in Nicias's speech is his separation between the benefit he promises from *hoplitikē* on the occasion of a breakup in the battle-line and the greater confidence and courage that, he says, come with such knowledge. Nicias knows that whoever knows it "would suffer nothing at the hands of one, and perhaps not even by several" (182b2–3); but this science, he says, "would not by a little make every man in war both more confident and more manly than himself *(auton hautou)* (182c5–7).[26] The artful hoplite has greater confidence and courage, but Nicias knows that he is almost immune in certain circumstances. Nicias does not have the nerve to say that *hoplitikē* gives one the knowledge he has. The confidence one has in one's own survival is of a different order from the knowledge Nicias has of one's survival. For a hoplite to say to himself, "Should I have this scientific knowledge I would suffer nothing at the hands of anyone," would pass for boasting and not knowledge (cf. 184c1–4). Nicias's knowledge would be in general of those things that make for confidence in another, one of which is *hoplitikē;* but his knowledge is not yet the same as that which gives him confidence. Nicias is still looking at courage from a distance. His perspective recalls the very first words of the dialogue: "Have you seen the man fighting in armor?" (178a1). There is not a hint in Lysimachus's words that this is not for real, and they have not taken up an observation post of some skirmish (cf. *Republic* 467c1–e8); indeed, we never do find out whether Stesilaos had a partner, or he was fighting no one even in play. That anyone could have drawn any conclusions from a mock exhibition of fighting, where nothing is at stake and there is no element of chance, is past belief; but Nicias, without any appeal to his own experience, draws an entire set of conclusions as if theater were real life. There seems to be a deep connection between Laches' mention of tragedy as that which is most highly esteemed in Athens and Nicias's theory of *hoplitikē.* Nicias is involved in a play of which he is at first the spectator and finally the protagonist.

Nicias and Laches seem at first to be totally unlike. Nicias is speculative, Laches is factual when it comes to an assessment of Stesilaos's kind of instruction. Laches looks to the man, Nicias to the ways in which a whole cluster of sciences would arrange the events of one's life. This difference about *hoplitikē* is then expanded and developed into the deeper issue of courage. The natural beast-man of Laches is opposed to the knowledge of Nicias, which knows the good and evil of every past, present, and future event. Laches tries to get Nicias to say that Nicias himself is the courageous man in his sense (195e3–4); but Nicias will not be drawn and persists in developing an argument that is wholly divorced from any known carrier of the knowledge. If we label Laches' understanding of courage "character" and Nicias's "plot," we have the two elements that make up any tragedy. Pulled apart, as they are in the dialogue, plot overwhelms character. Nicias devises a plot of inescapable necessity, in which everything unfolds in the future in accord with a causal nexus that stretches far back into the past and far forward into the future. This plot is wholly indifferent to character and, curiously enough, it sweeps Nicias up into its net and displays him to us ten years before the denouement as already fated to act out his historical future. Plato, in other words, by inserting the *Laches* into time, allows us to watch the beginning of the catastrophe we read in Thucydides. We become spectators of a man fighting in armor, who ties himself up in such a way that the solution is the outcome we already know. Nicias, Thucydides says, least deserved the degree of misfortune he met with (7.86.5); but Plato has Nicias himself draw up the theory that predetermines that end. Nicias lives a peculiarly Athenian tragedy.

As Socrates leads Nicias to explicate his understanding of courage, a certain brutality comes to light in Nicias and Laches that could pass for either the ruthlessness of reason or the indifference indispensable to the general who must send men to their deaths. It is again the split between plot and character, so that one should not take the agreement between Nicias and Laches on this point as necessarily having the same source and admitting of the same rationale. In answer to Laches' objection that neither the doctor nor the farmer is courageous because he has knowledge of the terrible and encouraging things, Nicias gets him to admit that just as it is not better *(ameinon)* for all to live so it is preferable *(kreitton)* for many to be dead (195d1–3). That Laches does not think at once of the general as the one who has this knowledge shows that he does not take the estimation of battle-losses to be a judgment on the worth of those who are going to be killed. What, however, about Nicias? Of whom is he thinking when he denies that the soothsayer knows whether or not it is better to suffer death, defeat, disease, or loss of money? Laches dismisses the possibility that Nicias could mean a god—immortals have nothing to fear—and assails Nicias for his insincere elusiveness. He grants that if they were on trial, Nicias's tactics would be in order (196a4–b7); but he does not see that Nicias's model is the judge, who passes sentence in light of the good and evil the accused should undergo. Nicias's judge, however, must be divine, and his knowledge be a theodicy in accordance with which everything turns out in conformity with right.[27]

That Nicias himself believes that he is in possession of such a teleological horoscope emerges from his actions in Sicily. Just prior to the moon's eclipse, and subsequent to a disastrous night battle, Demosthenes recommends withdrawal; but Nicias refuses, and the first reason he gives is that on their return they will face a hostile court and be condemned by the very soldiers who are now complaining so vociferously about the dreadfulness of their present circumstances, and that he at least prefers to be killed by the enemy—he does not speak of death on the battlefield—rather than to perish unjustly on so base a charge at the hands of the Athenians (7.48.3–4). The eclipse of the moon gives Nicias the chance to bring about a coincidence between his judgment that his army would be better off dead in Sicily than unjust and alive in Athens and the interval needed to insure that result. Nicias saves the Athenians from themselves without lifting a finger: he merely follows divine guidance. The salvation he grants them agrees to the letter with the theory Plato assigns him. To condemn so many men for the sake of holding them back from an error their nature would otherwise make them commit, surely requires nerves of steel. This is a grace under pressure Hemingway never dreamed of. Nicias's knowledge of the terrible is terrible.[28]

If a theodicy stands in the background of Nicias's understanding of courage, what stands in the foreground? The knowledge of *ta deina kai ta mē* is usually formulated in a speech that is designed to give others confidence in the policy one proposes. Demosthenes, for example, at Pylos makes such a speech (4.10), just as Phormion does before the second naval battle of the war (2.89); but it seems strange to identify the confidence Demosthenes or Phormion might have had in his own speech with knowledge. If, however, one's proposal were framed in terms of greater and lesser risks, then knowledge is courage if one always were to choose the lesser risks and to run away from the greater dangers. In the *Phaedo* Socrates says that this is his understanding of vulgar courage (68d9–10), and

Nicias seems to exemplify it perfectly. He preferred peace to war, Thucydides says, because he thought he would be less likely then to lose his reputation or mar the string of his continuous successes (5.16.1). In terms of the *Laches,* then, Nicias stands for always running away and Laches for always staying,[29] and whereas always to run away can look like knowledge, always to stay has an absoluteness in it that can never pass for knowledge. Laches wants courage to mean "to stand one's ground no matter what," either behaviorally as *en taxei menein* or psychically as *karteria;* but whenever Nicias would stay put, even if he were in line with Laches, he would be running away from something else. The vividness of Nicias's imagination, by painting in darker hues whatever he wants to avoid, replaces knowledge and passes for it. Nicias objectifies his fears and hopes and then calculates their value on the scale of good and evil. He does not have to fight against his pains and pleasures, as Socrates had suggested (191d6–7), for they are his version of self-knowledge. The ultimate objectification of fears and hopes would of course be the gods. The gods, in their assignment of good and evil, which is theodicy, are at one with Nicias's knowledge of *ta deina te kai ta tharralea,* which are rooted unknowingly in the passions of the soul.

The argument with Nicias revolves around the good and bad, the argument with Laches involves the beautiful and ugly, or the laughter-proof and the ridiculous. The *kalos kagathos* is split between them. The good is always calculated in terms of the bottom line, the beautiful is something in itself. Although Socrates argues that thoughtless daring is harmful and shameful, Laches is stumped because he asserted courage was one of the most beautiful things and not that it was one of the best (192c7). That persistence can be good is due to its alliance with thoughtfulness, but thoughtfulness does not naturally inhere in it; and once thoughtfulness is subtracted daring ceases to be grand. If one starts with Laches' experience of Socrates, his withdrawal is prudent; but if one goes back a moment, his withdrawal is due to his having advanced into Boeotia as part of Demosthenes' daring plan to distract the enemy with a two-pronged attack at two points so far apart from one another that no coordinated counteroffensive could be mounted (Thucydides 4.89). Socrates was a cipher in a grandiose scheme that bears all the earmarks of thoughtful daring without the drawbacks of unlovely calculation. Socrates, however, did not originate the "beauty-part" but merely went along with it; on his own he executed the good part that returned Laches and himself to safety.

It seems that only a mixture of an advance with too many imponderables to calculate and a retreat that minimizes risk could reunite Laches and Nicias. Socrates offers Laches such a mixture, and though Laches accepts it in principle he neither carries it out in practice nor reflects on the possibility of its satisfying the beautiful and the good at once. Socrates' offer comes about in the following way: He suggests that they adopt in deed their own speech (193e4), *Karteria* is to be the motto of their search for courage, "in order that *andreia* herself may not laugh us to scorn, because we are seeking her not manfully *(andreiōs),* if after all persistence herself is *andreia*" (194a2–5). Socrates implies that the argument he just used against the identification of courage and persistence might not be sound. They overlooked themselves in their pursuit of courage (cf. *Charmides* 160d8–e2): they themselves exhibit Laches' definition, they are being thoughtful, and they do not know. To search for courage is already an act of persistence; it cannot be done at all if there is no persistence. Socrates has thus inserted Laches' definition of courage into a verb; and this verb contains within it thoughtfulness, for one is not moving aimlessly when one is searching. Socrates then picks up Laches' language about the flight *(diephugen)* of courage and his failure to seize it *(sullabein)* in order to give to their search a character that is both epistemic and empirical: "The good hunter must run in pursuit and not let up" (194b5–6; cf. *Sophist* 235b–c6). The hunter's persistence is there from the start and at one with his art. The hunter pursues either elusive or hostile beings, and possibly both. Courage is the being that now eludes them; the hostility is not in it but in their passions against which one must fight if courage is not to disappear. Laches admits that *philonikia* has gripped him (194a8); but it turns out to be easily satisfied by his discovery that his fellow hunter is as ignorant as he. His *philonikia* turns out to be hatred of Nicias.

At the end of the dialogue, Socrates suggests that they all go to school if they can find a teacher; he suggests that they join in search of a teacher. This suggestion amounts to a denial that the first part of the dialogue, which has as its question, Who is good at giving advice?, has a satisfactory answer. There is no possibility of expert advice, except in the form of disregarding any advice that does not advise extreme caution (185a9; cf. 188b1, 198e3). What is left, then, is the second part, cautious and daring at once: the asking of the question, What is? This question is Socrates' action, which results from the failure of "Thucydidean" advice. Socrates' action, however, is nothing but speeches (cf. *Apology of Socrates* 38a1–5). It is always on the way to being a "Thucydidean" action. To be always on the way is to be out hunting the beings.[30] One of the beings to be hunted is man, the most elusive and hostile of the beings. To be a man is to be something in asking what that something is. It is to be *deinos.*

Notes

1. Cicero splits versions of Nicias and Laches—*maioris omnino est consili providere ne quid tale accidat* (as what Trebonius suffered), *animi non minoris fortiter ferre, si evenerit*—just after he has united them—*est enim sapientis, quicquid homini accidere possit, id praemeditari ferendum modice esse* (*Phil.* 11.7). What is *sōphrosunē* in the wise man is *andreia* by itself.

2. The difficulty of reconciling them is beautifully expressed by Socrates' juxtaposition of a proverb—*ouk an pasa hus gnoiē*—that supports Nicias's position and a myth—*hē Krommuōnia hus*—that supports Laches' (196d4–e1).

3. For the equivalence of these two expressions, compare Aristophanes *Equites* 177–79.

4. Cf. how similarly Euthyphro speaks of his understanding of the holy and the unholy (*Euthphro* 11b6).

5. 2.87.4 (Athenians); 5.72.2 (battle of Mantineia); 6.69.1 (Syracusans); 6.72.2 (Hermocrates; cf. 6.72.4 Hermocrates again). In the funeral speech, Pericles opposes Athenian *rhathumia* and *tropoi andreias* to Spartan *ponōn meletē meta nomōn* (2.39.4).

6. Cf. J. de Romilly, "Réflexions sur le courage chez Thucydide et Platon," *Revue des Etudes Grecques* 93 (1980):309.

7. Thucydides' remark that hoplites in formation always veer on their exposed side away from the enemy's left suggests that there is an element of self-deception in Laches' confining courage to hoplites, for Thucydides assigns fear as the cause of this maneuver and does not allow of any exceptions (5.71.1).

8. If either Bergk's or Kock's corrections are right, Aristophanes put Laches and Lamachus together in the *Agricolae* (106), to be dated around 424.

9. There is an excellent presentation of Laches in Th. de Laguna's "The Problem of the *Laches*," *Mind* 43 (1934):170–80, but Nicias is mishandled.

10. Eteocles praises Amphiaraus as a "moderate, just, good *(agathos)*, pious man" (A. *Th.* 610), where it is as clear that *agathos* means "brave" as it is significant for the *Laches* that prior to philosophy "pious" is the alternative to "wise."

11. There is a curious parallelism between the gender of *hus* as a matter of language and a matter of fact and the gradual etiolation of *anēr* in *andreia*, so that in both cases the strict reference is there for the taking even though the language as spoken resists such an appeal. The masculine as a grammatical category shows up in Socrates' interpretation of Nicias: *kai moi dokei anēr sophian tina tēn andreian legein* (194d8–9).

12. Cf. Custis, G.W.P., *Recollections and Private Memoir of Washington* (New York, 1860), 175n: "It is related of the Honorable Gouverneur Morris, who was remarkable for his freedom of deportment toward his friends, that on one occasion he offered a wager that he could treat General Washington with the same

familiarity as he did others. This challenge was accepted, and the performance tried. Mr. Morris slapped Washington familiarly on the shoulder, and said, 'How are you, this morning, general?' Washington made no reply, but turned his eyes upon Mr. Morris with a glance that fairly withered him. He afterwards acknowledged that nothing could induce him to attempt the same thing again."

13. In Montaigne's *Essais,* the eleventh chapter of Book I, *Des prognostications,* begins with a discussion of ancient divination and ends with Socrates' *daimonion;* and the twelth chapter, *De la constance,* summarizes at the beginning Socrates' refutation of Laches' first definition of courage. This sequence certainly suggests a careful reading of the *Laches* on Montaigne's part, as well as a general reflection on its relation to Socrates' *daimonion.*

14. Immediately after this dispute, Thucydides tells how the Boeotians invented a novel way to burn the Athenians' wall at Delium (4.100.2–4). War makes even the Boeotians, of all people, technically ingenious, while the Athenians innovate on the higher level of divine law.

15. Cf. Nicias's remark: *kaitoi men es theous nomima dediēitēmai, polla de es anthrōpous dikaia kai anepiphthona* (Thucydides 7.77.2).

16. For a fuller discussion of what follows, see M. Davis, *Ancient Tragedy and the Origin of Modern Science* (Carbondale, IL, 1988), 14–33; an earlier version is in J. Peter Euben, *Greek Tragedy and Political Theory* (Berkeley, 1986), 142–61.

17. Cf 1 Epistle to the Corinthians 1.28.

18. Caesar, immediately after saying *hic subitam commutationem fortunae videre licuit* (*Bellum Civile.* 3.27.1), says *hic cognosci licuit, quantum esset hominibus praesidii in animi firmitudine* (28.4), and recounts the fate of two of his ships. Both anchored over against Lissus, which was held by Pompey's forces; one ship was filled with raw recruits and in trusting to an oath that if they surrendered they would be unharmed were at once cut down, *contra religionem iurisiurandi;* but the ship of veterans, though they received the same offer under oath, held out—*neque ex pristina virtute remittendum aliguid putaverunt.* Although Caesar at the beginning offers to swear an oath (1.9.6), he never does; all oaths are sworn by Pompey and his lieutenants (1.76.2–5; 2.18.5; 3.10.9, 13.3–4; 87.5–6, 102.2). Consider 3.87.7: once the Pompeian forces had sworn, *iam animo victoriam praecipiebant.* Pompey is Caesar's Nicias.

19. Cf. *Gorgias* 524c1–3. The catachresis of *nekros* at *Ajax* 309 is remarkable.

20. Unlike Megillus (*Laws* 638a1–2).

21. That *polis* and *patris* are not the same, Thucydides shows by having Pericles not speak of the fatherland until he turns away from the praise of Athens to the praise of the dead (2.42.3), and Plato by having Socrates not speak of the fatherland before he discusses the tyrant (*Republic* 575d5, 7).

22. When Demosthenes 19.248–50 uses similar language, he is alluding to Creon's speech.

23. For a sketch of this area of inquiry, see P. Vidal-Naquet, *La Dēmocratie grecque vue d'ailleurs* (Paris, 1990), chapter 4, "La Société platonicienne des dialogues," 95–119.

24. Cf. H. G. Ingenkamp, "Laches, Nikias und platonische Lehre," *Rheinishes Museum* 110 (1967):247.

25. Nicias alone mentions the body (181e4). Nicias's point about terror through show recalls his suggestion of what the Athenians should do with their armada in Sicilian waters (Th. 6.47; cf. 11.4).

26. Observe how this idiomatic expression confirms Laches' view that a coward, should he believe he had *hoplitikē epistēmē,* would in becoming rasher *(thrasuteros)* expose him for what he was (184b4–6).

27. The best evidence for this is Nicias's remark to his troops (Thucydides 7.77.4). This theodicy is to be compared with what the Melians maintain and the Athenian ambassadors urge them to abandon (5.104–5).

28. Socrates prepares us for this pun by speaking to Laches first of all of those who *pros lupas andreioi eisin ē phobous* and then of those who *pros epithumias ē hēdonas deinoi machesthai* (191d6–e1); cf. 192c3–5.

29. Cf. S. Umphrey "Plato's *Laches* on Courage," *Apeiron* 10, no. 2 (1976): 19.

30. For this notion, see *Phaedo* 66a3; *Sophist* 221d13; *Statesman* 285d9–10; *Euthydemus* 290c1–4.

FOURTEEN

On Plato's *Phaedo*

I WISH TO DISCUSS FOUR THINGS in Plato's *Phaedo.*[1] First, the intention of the dialogue as a whole; second, the plan or structure of the *Phaedo;* third, some arguments of the *Phaedo;* and fourth, the reason for the structure of the dialogue.

Of Plato's narrated dialogues, three are not narrated by Socrates. The three Platonic dialogues that are narrated by someone other than Socrates—*Phaedo, Symposium,* and *Parmenides*—all include an account of the early thought of Socrates. Their chronological order puts the *Phaedo* first, where Socrates himself gives an autobiography of his early thinking; followed by the *Parmenides;* and, last, by the *Symposium.* Of these three accounts, only the *Phaedo* contains a picture of the wholly pre-Socratic Socrates, and that account, consequently, is the only one that is nondialogic in form.

Now the question that confronts us in the *Phaedo* is that Socrates, in this autobiographical part, talks about his second sailing, or his recourse to speeches. The context of the *Phaedo* is the last day of Socrates' life, and the issue is the immortality of the soul. There would therefore seem to be a connection, not immediately obvious, between man's mortality and Socrates' recourse to speeches. (Would it be too facile to say that underneath these two themes—man's mortality and Socrates' recourse to speeches—there lurks Aristotle's definition of man as *logikon zōon*?) In order to bring out the problem in terms of the way the issue is presented, one immediately turns to the parallel in the Platonic corpus, namely the *Symposium.* The *Phaedo* begins in the morning—early in the morning—

and ends with the setting of the sun, when Socrates drinks the poison and dies. The *Symposium* begins in the evening and ends when Socrates leaves the dinner party after he has drunk everyone under the table and can still go about his business. So the *Phaedo* and *Symposium* together clearly represent the philosophical life accomplished in one whole day, which in turn suggests that the connection between them is presented as a total opposition. On the one hand, in the *Symposium* philosophy is described as a kind of eros. In the *Phaedo* philosophy is described as a kind of dying and being dead. What links them is clearly that the experience of eros is the way in which we experience our own mortality, while we do not have any experience of death though we undergo it. Consequently, one should not take for granted what the connection is—what the parallelism between these two dialogues means. If eros is primarily understood as love of the beautiful, the parallel for the *Phaedo* should be an analysis of the fear of death. But there is not really an account of fear, but rather of death. In order to show that eros in its inner core is philosophy, it was necessary for Socrates to show that the ordinary understanding of eros was somehow the general setting in which that core was revealed. Death does not seem to fit this criterion, of an inner core that we can identify with philosophy and an outer shell that everybody experiences. So Socrates' task in the *Phaedo* seems on the surface both more paradoxical and more difficult to carry out. Death seems to exemplify an instance that does not compel Socrates to have a second sailing and have recourse to speeches.

Everybody can immediately recognize in the *Phaedo* a perfect fit between the circumstances in which the discussion takes place and the discussion itself. Not only is this our own impression, but it is also asserted by Socrates in the dialogue: "No one will say that I am talking about an irrelevant issue on this day." The interlocutors also perceive a connection between the circumstances and the discussion. Though the *Phaedo* presents itself as a dialogue in which it seems to be impossible to separate the argument—if there is an argument that runs through it—from the situation in which that argument is presented, as interpreters of the dialogue, we wish to make such a separation in order to see how the argument would stand up if the situation in which it occurred were removed. This interpretive procedure of our own turns out to be identical with Socrates' own procedure in the dialogue where he attempts to interpret the circumstances that will lead to the separation between the circumstances of his death and the argument itself. That happens in all dialogues more or less, but most strictly in the *Phaedo*. So, in following Socrates, we are in fact pursuing our own interpretive enterprise. He calls this interpretive enterprise the practice of dying and being dead—the separation of the argument from the situation. I shall try to show how he went about it and to what extent he succeeded.

The dialogue begins with Phaedo, the narrator, being asked a question by a man named Echecrates, as follows. In the Greek, the first word is *autos.* In the sentence it means, "Were you present *yourself,* Phaedo, on the day in which Socrates died and drank the poison?" That word suggests that the *Phaedo,* insofar as it is an account of the soul, must be about the relation between the self—understood as the union of body and soul—and body and soul. At the end of the dialogue we are left, through Socrates' contrivance, with his friends compelled to watch him turn into a corpse. Though it begins with Phaedo being asked to report, on the basis of his own presence, about the separation between the body and the soul, it ends with Socrates being present to us in the dialogue only as a corpse. This movement, from the self of Phaedo to the corpse of Socrates, is reminiscent of the beginning of the *Iliad,* where Homer tells us that the wrath of Achilles sent the souls of many heroes into Hades and left *them*—*autous*—as prey to dogs and food for birds. So in Plato, "*autos*"—the co-presence of body and soul—is understood as the corpse in Homer. That is an indication of the way in which the dialogue is going to proceed.

Now the opening part of the *Phaedo* consists of four main sections, which are then repeated in each of three more parts, each consisting of four sections. So there are sixteen sections altogether, in each part a group of four. Here is the structure of the *Phaedo:*

Part I
1. Purification of Athens—no killing: Separation
2. Phaedo's mixture of pleasure and pain: Together (soul)
3. Socrates' pleasure and pain: Together (body)
4. Purification of Socrates—mythmaking: Separation

Part II
1. Philosophy as the practice of dying and being dead
2. Proof of necessary sequence of opposites generated out of one another
3. Doctrine of recollection as proof
4. Aesopian ghost story

Part III
1. Simmias's objection
2. Cebes' objection
3. Socrates talks to Phaedo about the character of logos
4. Refutation of Simmias

Part IV
1. Socrates' autobiography to refute Cebes
2. Refutation of Cebes
3. Myth
4. Socrates' death

Jacob Klein has observed that the context of the *Phaedo* is mythical because, when Phaedo has to explain to Echecrates the reason for the delay in Socrates' execution—between the time he was condemned and the time he drank the poison—he has to tell the story of how Theseus saved fourteen Athenian youths from the Minotaur, which was the yearly contribution that Minos, the king of Crete, required from Athens. And in Phaedo's description of those who were present on this last day, he mentions fourteen names. At the end of the dialogue, Socrates is referred to as looking like a bull—looking somewhat like a Minotaur. A wholly mythical structure is imposed upon Socrates; it is not something he devises. It is the labyrinth out of which he will have to lead his fourteen companions and save them from the fear of death. Now the consequence of this story about Theseus is that every year the Athenians send a ship to Delos, during which time the law prohibits public executions. According to Phaedo, this constitutes a purification of the city. So the occasion of the *Phaedo,* which is now coming to an end, is that the city, Athens, has suspended its right to execute criminals it has lawfully condemned to death. And this is said to be a purification. During this time, then, Athens has given up its own identity, therefore allowing for the possibility that the city itself is based upon an unrighteous foundation. The purification turns out to have led Socrates to revise his interpretation of his recurring dream about what he should do. The dream kept on telling him that he was to practice music, and he had interpreted this to signify the practice of philosophy. Because the city has suspended its own nature, Socrates has wondered whether he, too, is guilty of misunderstanding the dream. He has turned to his own form of purification in writing poetry. The purification of Athens and the purification of Socrates are the topics of the first and last sections of the opening part of the *Phaedo.* When Socrates is engaged in his own activity, namely philosophy, the city is engaged in its own activity. And these two activities are in direct conflict with one another. When the city, on the other hand, suspends its own activity, Socrates suspends his also. So the normal understanding of the relation between Athens, in doing what it does, and Socrates, in doing what he does, is a situation of two intersecting activities leading to his condemnation. When however, the city suspends itself and Socrates suspends himself, they meet in the realm of poetry and myth:

Each doing their own thing

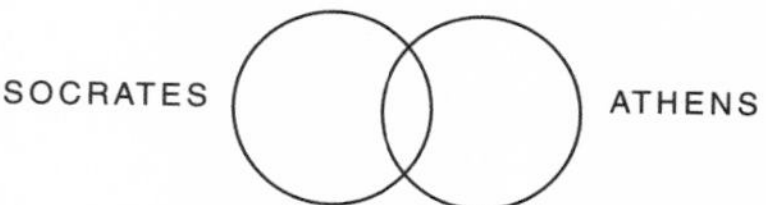

Each abandoning their own thing

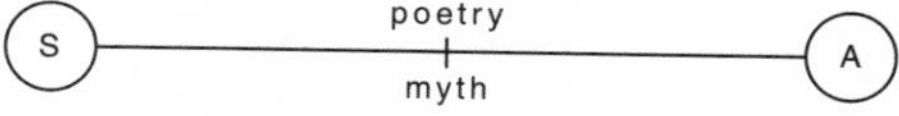

Phaedo then tells Echecrates about his unusual experience on this last day of Socrates' life. He says that it was an unfamiliar mixture of the pleasure of philosophy with a pain due to his realization that this was Socrates' last day. In his presentation of this mixture, Phaedo reveals his own belief in the purity of philosophical activity, insofar as pleasure is concerned, and also in the purity of the pain he would feel if he had been present at the death of anybody else but Socrates. He presents his own experience in this form: "I did not have pity, which I would ordinarily have had when a friend of mine was going to die, because I thought that Socrates was going to go off and be happy." In other words, Phaedo is put in the very remarkable position of resenting the fact that Socrates is getting what he deserves. But apart from Phaedo's possible misunderstanding of his own experience, more remarkably, Phaedo becomes conscious, for the first time, of a possible relation between the argument and the setting. So what we as readers know about every Platonic dialogue—that an adjustment is taking place between the circumstantial and the argument—Phaedo now experiences without necessarily understanding that his experience of the circumstances might be determined by his understanding of the argument. Phaedo feels a mixture of pleasure and pain, which comes from two totally opposite sources, he believes, that admit of no connection with one another.[2]

Immediately after, Phaedo's focus shifts to Socrates, who has just been released from the shackles in which he was held and is rubbing his leg. I quote the passage in which Socrates proposes—although no one who listens to him understands what he is proposing—the topic of the *Phaedo.* The interlocutors take a long time to catch up, and I am not sure they entirely understand what he has done: that Socrates is proposing for discussion an account of his own experience. Socrates bends his leg and begins to rub it with his hand, and as he is rubbing it he says this:

> "How strange, gentlemen, seems to be that which human beings call pleasant. And how wonderfully is it naturally related to that which is thought to be its opposite, the painful, for though the two are unwilling to be present simultaneously to a man, still, if one pursues one of them and takes hold of it, one is just about compelled always to take hold of the other, just as if they were two that were bound together from one head. And it seems to me," he said, "if Aesop had understood this he would have composed a myth that the god, wishing to reconcile them that were at war with one another, since he was not able to do so, joined their heads into the same. And because of this, to whomever one of them is present there later follows also the other." (60b3–c5)

Socrates gives a twofold account of his own experience: the first account in terms of nature, the second in terms of a god's attempted production, which fails. The thing one immediately notices is that the first, nonmythical account refers to what people call pleasant and what is thought to be its opposite. In the mythical Aesopian account, on the other hand, the union of pleasure and pain is a matter of their succeeding one another, with no revision in the understanding of what pleasure and pain might be after one has removed the fact that they are what people say is pleasant and what people call pain. The first account, which is based merely on an analysis of the experience, emphasizes that this is a human opinion and totally sidesteps the issue of cause. Only the mythical account introduces cause. Now in Socrates' autobiography, he explains how and why he had to turn from a pre-Socratic account, understanding things in terms of cause, to his second sailing. This difference is already present in the two accounts Socrates gives of his own experience of pleasure and pain. These two accounts exemplify two ways in which one is to understand "two," and the difference between them determines the entire structure and intention of the dialogue. I call the two represented by the nonmythical account—where pleasure and pain are bound together in a single head—a disjunctive two, and that represented by the myth—where pleasure is presented as one head and pain as another, which then must be bound together—a conjunctive two.

Conjunctive two Disjunctive two

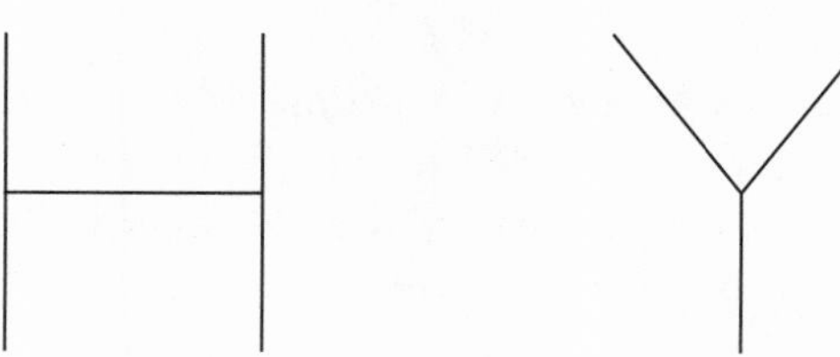

The *Phaedo*'s concern is with unraveling or explicating the logos (the disjunctive two) as opposed to the myth (the conjunctive two). In the *Phaedo* this activity is called *mythologein,* or "rational enchantment." What that means is that it is not possible to start with the disjunctive two. It is necessary to start on the mythical level with the conjunctive two. The structure of the *Phaedo* consists in moving the main interlocutors—Simmias and Cebes—from understanding things pre-Socratically, in terms of the conjunctive two, to a Socratic understanding in terms of the disjunctive two. That one has to begin incorrectly is a sign of the Platonic principle that the way is always the obstacle.

Now this pattern of the beginning of the dialogue is then reproduced three times. I shall first sketch in how that goes and then examine certain parts of it in detail. In the first section of part II of the dialogue, the definition of philosophy is given as the practice of dying and being dead. That issue comes up because Simmias and Cebes want to know why Socrates is committing suicide. They take it for granted that he is, and Socrates does not at any point deny this. It becomes more complicated later, but initially he accepts that. The second section is a proof that there is a necessary sequence of opposites that are generated out of another. There follows a section that Cebes introduces by being reminded about the so-called recollection theory that he has often heard from Socrates, which, presumably, ends with a proof that the soul does not die. The fourth section of part II is what I call the Aesopian ghost story told by Socrates, occasioned after the third section, where Socrates gets Cebes and Simmias to admit that they are afraid of death. Although they did not initially object to arguments 2 and 3, they now want to be enchanted: a little child that is within them wants to be soothed. So Socrates obliges with a ghost story. The consequence, however, works to awaken the reasoning of Cebes and Simmias. The enchantment of the fear of death leads to disenchantment with that enchantment. It marks the beginning of the second half of the dialogue, parts III and IV, which are concerned with Socrates' second sailing.

The first section of part III begins with Simmias's objection to Socrates' account. The second begins with Cebes' objection. The third comes about in the following way: it turns out that the enchantment of the fourth section of part II, followed by the apparent refutation of what Socrates had said in its second and third sections, leads the entire audience of young men to be extremely perturbed that they were taken in by this specious treatment of Socrates. In order to rally them, Socrates talks to the narrator, Phaedo, about the character of logos. He points out that their pain at hearing a refutation of Socrates convinces them of the truth of the refutation. After having rallied them, the fourth section consists of his refutation of Simmias. In order to refute Cebes, Socrates has to give his autobiography, which is the first section of the last part (IV). This is followed by the refutation of Cebes. Another myth follows,[3] then Socrates' death—what happens when he has to drink the poison.

This is, as far as I know, the most highly organized, symmetrical dialogue that Plato ever wrote. I will try to account for this tight structure. The key parts of the dialogue are parts II and IV, but the whole thing, I think, is clear. Parts I and II have to do with philosophy understood as a direct dealing with things. And the second half—namely parts III and IV—has to do with the logos. The separation, then, between the two halves reproduces our own interpretive activity, while representing Socrates' own move from pre-Socratic to Socratic thought.

A word about Simmias and Cebes. Their concerns initially are not the same. Simmias's concern arises from the problematic meaning of the divine prohibition against suicide; it becomes the issue of Socrates' justice: What right does Socrates have to abandon his care for them? His justice should consist in continuing to tend them. Cebes' concern is with Socrates' prudence: Is it wise for Socrates to die, that is, is it for his own good? So Socrates must prove both his justice and his prudence, that is, he must show that what is good for him is good for them. It is good for them that he die, and it is good for him that he die. The movement of the dialogue consists in Simmias—who is concerned with the issue of justice—coming to understand the issue of Socrates' prudence, and Cebes—who is concerned with the issue of prudence—being made to see the issue of Socrates' justice through the moving of both interlocutors in opposite directions from where they have started out. This criss-cross movement is reminiscent of the pair of dialogues in which, just before his trial, Socrates listens to an Eleatic Stranger coverse with two mathematicians, Theaetetus and young Socrates: in the *Sophist,* Theaetetus, who is rather on the moderate side, is made to be bold and get some of the trappings of courage, while in the *Statesman,* and young Socrates, who is rather courageous and bold, is made to take on some of the trappings of moderation. Now, one sees immediately that by combining the *Sophist,* the *Statesman,* and the *Phaedo,* we get the four classical virtues. So the *Phaedo* reproduces, on the level of justice and prudence, what Socrates had heard the Eleatic Stranger do before his trial on the level of moderation and courage.

The relation between justice and prudence, in the *Phaedo,* is the same as that between the two aspects of soul that have to be put together in order for it to be understood—soul as the source of life, and soul as the source of knowledge or awareness. In the first part of the dialogue, what incites Simmias, and particularly Cebes, to rebellion is that Socrates gives an argument for his prudence that leads to the conclusion that only he, Socrates, dies, and no one else. Man's mortality is a pseudo-universal; it applies only to Socrates. The evidence in the dialogue for this is Crito's question, "How shall we bury you?" and Socrates' answer. In the second half of the dialogue, Cebes is made to undergo the opposite movement, in which he comes to see that the common characteristic of soul—namely that it is the cause of life to body—is what makes every soul like every other soul. And no soul is more soul than any other. The relation between the cognitive character of soul and the life character of soul introduces a structure into soul which is parallel to the account that Diotima gives to Socrates in the *Symposium* about the double aspect of eros, namely, as it is ordinarily understood in terms of generation, and as philosophy. What again unites the *Symposium* and the *Phaedo* is this: neither eros nor death can be understood physiologically.

It might surprise us that when Socrates first asks whether death is something, he does not add, "Or is it nothing?" Not only would the answer, "Death is nothing," seem to imply its insignificance, but on the basis of the sentence's plausible translation into "Death is not," it would entail a conclusion that could not possibly be our first answer. Death thus partakes of all the difficulties of nonbeing itself, which makes it the appropriate problematic link between the soul and the beings. Socrates first speaks of the beings as deathless; and Cebes first identifies Socrates' argument with the thesis that the soul is deathless. It is the "ideas," whose existence is never proved but accepted, that are the obstacle to proving that the soul is immortal.

Nowhere in the dialogue does Socrates say that the body dies. His own definition of death is silent on the identity of that which undergoes the dying, as well as indifferent to the fate of the soul and the body in death. He says, "[Do we believe death is] anything other than the release of the soul from the body? And this is to be in the state of death, the body to have become (*gegonenai*) alone by itself and apart (*chōris*) once it is released from the soul, and the soul to be (*einai*) alone by itself and apart (*chōris*) once it is released from the body?" (64c5–8). The apparently redundant *chōris* points to the need for a double bonding of body with soul and soul with body if there is to be life. It points to the possibility that life is only thought to be the opposite of death, but in truth it is always together with dying, and the soul is that which makes us mortal.

Socrates' final argument, in any case, which is designed to show that the soul is deathless, proves to mean something other than what "deathless" is thought to mean, for the soul as the transmitter of life to body is held to be that which does not admit death. Thus the soul does not admit the double separation of soul and body. (Socrates reinterprets "deathless" is such a way as to bring it into line with the Eleatic Stranger's understanding of nonbeing.) The soul proves to be a part of a disjunctive two, while it was presented at first as capable of the apartness of the conjunctive two.[4]

Inasmuch as Socrates' definition of death is nonphysiological, the significance of Socrates' account of the generation from opposites is likely to share this feature. So if the cognitive equivalent of life, or the reunion of body and soul, is perception, and that of death is the intellection of separated beings, then the cognitive meaning of dying is separating, and of reliving is combining; but separating and combining are together in dialectics no less than in life, for the argument for cyclical generation implies that there cannot be a separation of body and soul unless their union also exists. The defect in Socrates' argument for such a cycle—he fails to keep to his own example in which there cannot be a "before" unless there is already an "after" (i.e., he speaks conjunctively rather than disjunctively)—ceases to count dialectically where the necessary copresence of opposites is independent of space and time.

The second sailing latent in Socrates' argument of section II.2, so that its difficulties as physiology are canceled as dialectics, is even more vividly suggested in his Aesopian story (II.4). There, in arguing that one becomes what one practices, and the likenesses of one's practices are wholly confirmed in reincarnation, Socrates shifts from the language of place to the language of kind (82a–b). Kind is the dianoetic equivalent of place. So all Socrates' talk of his death as a "going" would have to be translated into its "eidetic" truth. What would emerge after such a translation occupies the second half of the *Phaedo.*

Socrates' autobiography shows that even as a pre-Socratic he was primarily interested in man—in the relation between man as thinking being and man as living being. When he has set out his original questions—they turn out to be four—he mentions four things he thought he knew prior to turning toward philosophy. These four things, when confronted with his pre-Socratic questions, generate another set of four questions that make everything he thought he knew totally unintelligible. This set of four questions turns out to be the problem of the number two. What Socrates sees causes his recourse to speeches, his second sailing: that any account of coming into being or of going out of being must necessarily be translatable into some kind of numerical account. Therefore, all questions of becoming can be reinterpreted as questions about addition. Now any causal account whatsoever must necessarily admit this: opposite causes cannot have the same effect. What Socrates realizes is that a naive understanding of the operations of numbers—of counting—leads to a contradiction because opposite processes do have the same effect. How is it, Socrates asks, that one gets two from two ones? The naive presentation of that is to say a "one" has come near to another "one" so that the joining together makes them two. But if that is the case, Socrates goes on, how come when one separates something, which is the opposite of joining together, one also gets two? We now have the following schema:

Bringing near leads to two: definition of life	Separation leads to one (implicit)
Separating leads to two: definition of death	Bringing near leads to one (explicit)

We have: "Bringing near leads to two." "Separating leads to two." But it is even worse. If bringing near leads to two, then its opposite must lead to one. So "separating leads to one." But if separating leads to two, then "bringing near leads to one." We have a fourfold schema of the problem as Socrates understands it.

It is clear from what we have said so far that Socrates' definition of death has been of this kind, and the definition of life would be its contrary. Immediately after he says he does not understand this at all, he goes on to describe having heard somebody reading from a book of Anaxagoras about how mind is that which accounts for everything. Without hearing any more, Socrates begins to think to himself what exactly that would mean. He concludes that what Anaxagoras ought to say in his book is that any account of cause would have to be an account of the good, because mind as cause can only be distinguished as a cause in terms of its being a rational good. He is surprised, however, to discover that Anaxagoras does not understand cause—using mind as a cause—in terms of the good but only in terms of the making of something into a pattern or a plan, and this plan itself cannot be understood as being good. Socrates then says that his inability to find anybody else, and his own inability to bring about what he thought the Anaxagorean project would consist in—that is, a complete teleological cosmology—forces him to move to speeches. Now the immediate question is, Why does Socrates' account of his despair go from the problem about number to a problem about mind to a problem about good to a problem about speeches? The answer is that the problem about the relation between mechanical causation and teleological causation is not the only one. There is a problem concerning an opposition within mind itself: the problem of numbers that Socrates raised could only be understood in terms of mind—of Anaxagorean mind—but mathematics cannot be understood in terms of the good.

Two things emerge from this: one sees that these problems about what it means to make two—in terms of either separating or dividing—are all based on the understanding of space. If there is an apple on the moon and an apple on earth, no one is going to say, "That's a couple of apples." Presumably they have to be together. But once one understands numbers in terms of their being together, this Socratic problem develops. It follows that Anaxagoras's error, in asserting that before the operation of mind all things were together, and after the operation of mind things were divided, was in not seeing—and this is absolutely crucial for understanding the *Phaedo*—that things can only be together if they are understood as being so through an operation of mind. The failure of the first half of the dialogue results from the way space and time are understood as the substructure underlying all processes: all the arguments in the first half are based on false images, reflecting our ordinary understanding of how two comes to be. Once one sees that "apart" and "together" can be understood only in terms of the operation of logos itself, one sees also that Socrates' definition of death does not encompass physiological death but rather defines philosophy as a process of separation. The spuriousness of the arguments in the *Phaedo* consists in his interlocutors' unawareness that Socrates is forcing them constantly to jump to logos away from fact—from what he calls *pragmata,* "the things," for the things themselves do not lend themselves to the kind of direct analysis that these people have in fact undertaken. Socrates alerts them to this.

The extraordinary consequence of the analysis of the *Phaedo* is that any understanding of body is necessarily mythical. That is a great shock because one would think it should be the opposite: any understanding of soul should be mythical. The definition of death in terms of separation was understood by Socrates' interlocutors to be a characterization of body and soul as two separate substances; when Socrates returns to it, he shows that what is called death is in fact philosophy. So it turns out that the ordinary understanding of death has as its true meaning the practice of dying and being dead as philosophizing, not the other way around. Now this raises more than one puzzle. But part of the movement of the dialogue consists in this: Socrates argues for dying and being dead as the aim of philosophy and of the philosopher on the grounds that the philosopher wants to be removed from his body in order that the pure soul by itself might be in contact with the pure beings. And he shows that this is based on a misunderstanding of the character of knowledge because it does not preserve the necessary twoness of the relation between mind and its object, but leads to a union, which makes knowledge, in fact, impossible.[5] Now, after Socrates has laid this down, Cebes is reminded of the recollection theory in which he remembers Socrates' assertion that everytime we learn, we are really remembering what we once knew before we were born. What Cebes sees, and what Simmias is made to see once this theory is accepted, is that if the recollection theory is true, then the grounds for saying that philosophy is the practice of dying and being dead—one has to die in order to come in contact with the beings—are totally destroyed. Because apparently now, through the recollection theory, one is able to have knowledge in this life, whereas the whole understanding of death implied that one can only have knowledge when the soul is separated from body. So the recollection theory brings in a new assertion that one cannot have thinking *unless* one has perceiving, i.e., they belong together: the disjunctive two as opposed to the original conjunctive two.[6]

Simmias and Cebes come up with two different kinds of objections to what Socrates has been saying. Simmias's objection occurs in two parts. He argues, first, that everything Socrates says could also be said of the harmony produced by a lyre when it is in tune, and no one would conclude that the harmony survives the lyre. The second part of Simmias's thesis is that the soul is in fact a harmony. Cebes comes up with another objection: granted that the soul exists prior to its taking on the body, what guarantee is there that it does not wear out a number of bodies and then finally die? Now the fantastic thing that happens is this. Simmias has reduced soul to body. Soul no longer exists except as a superfluous term; it turns out to mean nothing but harmonized body—hence one can dispense with it. Cebes' objection turns out to mean, As long as the soul is not incorporated, it never dies. He gets rid of body. So Cebes' question is, Why is there becoming rather than being? Between them, Simmias and Cebes have accomplished just what Socrates wanted: they have made a separation of body and soul. One has found body, the other soul. Unbeknownst to themselves, they have followed Socrates' definition of death, not as they thought it was to be understood, but according to their own logos. Socrates then tries to show in the second half of the dialogue that this is a false understanding of the relation of body and soul, in terms of the conjunctive two, and that one has to understand them rather as a disjunctive two.

He proceeds to tackle this as follows. Let me go back to Socrates' autobiography. After having mentioned the problem of cause in the question of how two comes to be, and the problem of cause in Anaxagoras's failure to carry out the project of mind, Socrates gives the following illustration of what a teleological account requires: "It would be just as if one said that nothing that I [Socrates] do is done without mind, and then, while claiming to explain why I am sitting here in this prison, talked about nothing but my bones and sinews. Such an account would neglect the true causes." Now I have to read you the passage because it is an extraordinary thing Socrates goes on to say about these true causes. Since the Athenians "thought that it was better to condemn me to death—because of that—I in turn thought that it was better to sit here and that it was more just in remaining to undergo whatever punishment they command, since, by the dog, as I believe, these bones and sinews would long ago be around Megara or among the Boeotians, carried away by the opinion of that which is best, unless I thought that it was more just and more noble to undergo the punishment, whatever the city enjoins, prior to fleeing and running away." Now the first thing one notices is that opposite causes have the same effect. The city thinks that Socrates is unjust. Socrates thinks that what he is doing is just. But they both have the effect of making him stay in prison. It would seem, then, that any teleological account, starting with human experience, leads to the same paradox with regard to the principal question of physics. Not only that, but it is rather odd that whereas it can plausibly be said that what Socrates does is by mind, one cannot possibly say that what the Athenians do is by mind, in the sense of an understanding of the true good. So it is rather strange that where he gives a teleological example, the example is put not in terms of knowledge, but simply in terms of opinion, i.e., this is not the operation of mind but the operation of apparently irrational principles, at least on one side or the other. Not only that, but one sees that a teleological account of man, which Socrates at this point abandons, would require an account of the relation between mechanical causation and teleological causation, that is, an account of the relation between body and soul *being added together* and making one. This is one of the four arithmetic operations Socrates articulated. But it is unintelligible precisely because the same operation leads to exactly the opposite result. The marriages of these two causes is the same as their divorce. So it turns out that the problem of arithmetic is in fact embedded in the problem of teleological causation. When Socrates talks about the good as a cause after this passage, he talks about the good as the *binder*.

In terms of the specific content of the *Phaedo,* the reason why any kind of teleological causation has to be abandoned is that the premise of the dialogue as a whole has been that it is better to be dead, i.e., for there to be a separation between body and soul. But if that is the case, no teleology—which would have to be concerned with the union of mechanical and teleological causation in a living being, that is, a being with a body—could possibly provide the account. But there is a deeper difficulty with regard to the problem of number that also causes Socrates to abandon teleology. He is forced to resort to speeches. What does this recourse to speeches consist in? Socrates emphasizes that in order to account for why he is sitting in prison it is no longer possible to operate with a unitary concept of the just; rather, the just has to be split open and articulated in relation to the good and the noble. This is the dialectical examination of the ideas, i.e., it has exactly the same structure as what Socrates had proposed at the beginning with regard to the question of what is said to be pleasant and what is thought to be its opposite. As long as one thinks of them as being totally divorced, one can make no progress. It is only when one sees their overlapping structure that one can move. And this is primarily what is happening in the *Phaedo.*

When body and soul are together, soul is concerned with the preservation of life in the body (91a1–8). So there is a perfect union between the operation of body and soul. One is combining conditions for the operation of a higher end, and that is making a two into a one. But one immediately thinks of it in terms of space: "Here we have the end, here we have the sinews. And we have to make an adjustment between the two by bringing them together." Socrates shows in this particular case that in order to account for why he is sitting in prison one has to explain why the Athenians have the opinions they do and why *he* has his opinion. To go on to what the relation is between those causes, that is, the articulation of the relation of these three things—the noble, the good, and the just—with reference to how they operate on the living being, would require an account of the physiology of persuasion. We are no longer on the level of the combination of mechanical and teleological causation. Not in the *Phaedo,* but in the *Phaedrus,* Socrates calls attention to this problem of causality—that people are moved by speeches to act in a certain way. The explanation of how that happens, which is very mysterious, is, I think, the account Socrates gives in the *Phaedrus;* but to what extent it can be understood from physics is another question. That effort has to be abandoned once one sees what the real problem is. Death, however, looks like a matter of fact, to which Socrates' turn to speeches would seem not to apply.

Let me go back a step. Socrates says he abandoned the investigation of the beings because he found them blinding. So, just as when one wants to watch an eclipse, one looks at it in an image—in water or in something else, for otherwise one cannot see it—so he looks at the beings through the medium of speeches. Now the one counterexample in the context of the *Phaedo* is the corpse itself. What is so blinding about it? It is just there. What is blinding must be fear, but that seems to be something irrational, something therefore that wishes to be soothed. Since reason is not involved, once one gets over the fear, why not just look directly? Socrates then has to show that death turns out not to be a matter of fact but something that is in itself a matter of logos. That is a remarkable feat. Death does not seem to be of that order. Another way of putting it, though this might be too paradoxical: Socrates decides that it is better for him to be dead. So he undergoes the trial and the punishment. Aside from the question of the immortality of the soul, this is very hard to understand teleologically, because, if there is a good, it has to be good for someone or something. How can there be a good for somebody who is dead? The ordinary understanding of teleological explanation in this case makes no sense. In other words, it turns out that our own mortality cannot be understood. It comes out most clearly in this particular case, but even if one says that it is better for so-and-so to die under certain circumstances, that cannot be understood in ordinary terms as being good for someone. Now this paradox might ultimately be resolvable somehow, but at least initially there is a problem.

In conclusion, I want to go back to our original question: Why does the *Phaedo* have this structure? Well, in the *Parmenides,* Parmenides proposes to the very young Socrates a gymnastic of hypothetical examination. That consists of taking any notion, hypothesizing it, and examining that notion in the following way: (1) If the hypothesis holds, what is the relation of the thing one is examining to itself? (2) What is its relation to something else? (3) What is the relation of that other thing to what one is examining? and (4) What is the relation of that other thing to itself? That turns out to be identical with parts II and IV of the *Phaedo.* The hypothesis in part II is that soul is separable from body. First: What is the relationship of soul in respect to itself? The practice of dying and being dead. What is the relationship of soul in relation to body? Generation from opposites. What is the relationship of body in respect to soul? Recollection. Finally, what is the relation of body to body? The Aesopian ghost story. The hypothesis in part IV is that soul is not separable from body. What is the relationship of soul to itself? Socrates' autobiography.

What is the relationship of soul to body? Socrates' refutation of Cebes. What is the relationship of body to soul? The myth. And what is the relationship, finally, of body to body? Socrates becomes a corpse. It would take a further analysis, which I will not do at the moment, to show how parts I and III fit in. But primarily one sees that when Socrates at the end of his autobiography proposes a hypothetical procedure of his own, it is in fact what he accomplished in the *Phaedo* itself. At the end of his life, Socrates fulfills the promise Parmenides divined in him when he was very young.

Notes

1. This chapter is a revised transcript of a lecture given at Catholic University, Washington, D.C., on 30 January 1981. Answers from the question period are added as notes.

2. While Xanthippe has at her disposal habitual ways of handling death, nothing of the kind is available to the men. And the conventional practice which she indulges in exactly illustrates the necessary relation between pleasure and pain. But the men who remain after she leaves do not understand that precisely because she is a woman. They feel superior to her, so they cannot understand their experience of the same thing. One of the remarkable features of the dialogue is Phaedo's presentation of everything in terms of either habit or non-habit. Socrates looked like a bull; that is how he habitually looked. He did this as he habitually did. We philosophized as we habitually did. On the other hand, there is that which is completely non-habit—death. Socrates proposes a very funny thing: Philosophy as the practice of dying and being dead precisely consists in the habituation to non-habituation. No habits. Habitually. It is as if the interlocutors in the *Phaedo* were readers of Platonic dialogues. That is, they have been forced to step back and see that somehow the argument and the situation belong together. They had never realized that had been happening all along, whenever they talked to Socrates. They thought all of the arguments were pure and they were disembodied souls, with Socrates, also a disembodied soul, talking to them on the pure level of logos. This, therefore, is their first philosophical experience, the death of Socrates, and they do not know what is happening. We see them trying to orient themselves in relation to what is going on in the argument and what is going on before their eyes, which happens only once. Is this what it means to preserve the life of the logos, which Socrates wants Phaedo to do? Socrates was never more ironical than at his death. There is humor when Socrates sets out to account for the practice of dying and being dead as philosophy and asserts that the philosopher is somebody who has nothing to do with drink, or food, or sex; Xanthippe, of course, has just gone out holding his baby.

3. The refutation of Cebes—namely, section IV.2—in fact accomplishes the analysis of the character of soul totally in terms of the so-called ideas. And the myth is a presentation of soul as body. In other words, total separation of body and soul. It is another way of doing what Socrates said death consists in. So the myth is in one sense merely a blown up version of the internal structure of the human body presented as the structure of the earth. It is all body, nothing but body. (One sees that very clearly if one looks at Timaeus' account of the internal physiology of the human body.) As a consequence, when Socrates comes in this myth to the abode of the philosophers—or the life of the philosophers—he says, "Well, somewhere else. I cannot tell you about that now." In other words, the original reason for what he is doing and what he has done is totally abandoned. But the myth is more interesting. It consists in two parts. The first occurs entirely in indirect statement; it is all infinitives and accusatives. Somewhere in the middle, at exactly the point where Socrates introduces nature, it turns into direct discourse. And there he talks about cause. The kind of cause that he is talking about does not seem to be comprehensible, either mechanically or teleologically. This very peculiar account of cause corresponds to nothing except perhaps the principle of sufficient reason. Why does the earth oscillate in this way? The answer: Well, it cannot do anything else. Presumably this is something like an application of the theory of logos to the question of cause.

Let me put it this way. The whole dialogue begins with an account of the ship that Theseus went on to Crete, and then the ship that the Athenians send to Delos every year. Phaedo implies that both ships referred to are one and the same, a sameness that resembles the self of Phaedo and what the dialogue really should deal with. But what does it mean to combine body and soul into a self? At no point in the dialogue is that question raised directly, although in fact it lies behind Simmias's and Cebes' questions, but they are not able to formulate it properly. When Socrates talks about his reason for turning to poetry, he makes the following remarkable statement: "Often the same dream came to me in my past life, at one time appearing in one kind of dream, at another time appearing in another, but saying the same things." The sameness of the dream is identified with the speech that the dream makes in its various forms. So Socrates implies that the self is a dream, whose logos is the same. Now it turns out that what Socrates makes his interlocutors finally fear is, not death, but *self-contradiction.* Cebes laughs when he is told that he will be afraid that his speech will contradict his own speech. That is the *Phaedo.* So the movement of the dialogue is to show that the false understanding of the union of body and soul has to be replaced by an account in terms of logos and self-contradiction.

4. Socrates shows that in some sense the philosopher practices death. But his interlocutors are puzzled. It seems to lead to the conclusion that you become what you practice. The consequence is that only the philosopher's soul becomes deathless. In other words, deathlessness is not an attribute of the soul itself, but something you work at. This puzzles them. So the other view comes in, that no soul is more soul than any other soul, and as a consequence, soul can be under-

stood only as the giver of life. But what happens to mind? It somehow vanishes. The reconciliation between what I call the just and the prudential, or between the class and the class goal, is necessarily dialectical. It must be understood in terms of the disjunctive two or it will lead to a paradox one can never solve.

I would suggest that every time a myth appears in Plato, one of the terms in the account is superfluous, based on a false separation of something that had an internal structure. The *Timaeus* provides a very good example. Timaeus can never arrive at the correct number he needs for the causal account, and this relates back to his initial assertion that he is going to give a mythical account. In the *Symposium,* Diotima's story about the parents of Eros is a striking example in which one can see very clearly the parallels with the Aesopian myth Socrates tells in the *Phaedo.* Socrates asks Diotima, "Who are Eros's parents?" The story she tells is that on Aphrodite's birthday, all of the gods came together, including a god named Resource, but some being named Poverty was not invited. Poverty, however, desired to have a child from Resource. So when Resource got drunk, she slept with him, and Eros came about. As the union of Poverty and Resource, Eros has a double nature. This is a mythical account precisely because it splits the double nature of Poverty into two opposite principles and then brings them together. The double nature of Poverty consists in not only the state but the recognition of the state of being poor. That is, poverty is in fact both resourcelessness and the awareness of resourcelessness. Once one sees that, it turns out that Eros is identical with his mother Poverty. The myth consists in the presentation of Eros as a conjunction of two opposite principles. The true understanding of Eros consists in what I call its dialectical understanding.

In the *Phaedo,* Socrates himself makes this mistake when, in the middle of the dialogue, Simmias and Cebes think about whether objections would be proper. Socrates says, "You must have the false understanding people have about the swan song. They believe that swans sing loudest just before their death because they are in pain. But no bird sings when it is in pain." This presupposes that when one sings a song of mourning there is only pain. But a song of mourning in fact necessarily mixes pleasure and pain. The dialogue had begun precisely with Phaedo and everybody else unaware that pleasure and pain are related, as though they are totally opposed and then conjoined. But inside pleasure there is pain; it is not something in addition. Socrates shows that at great length in the *Philebus.*

What Plato's myths show is how much all ordinary understanding is to an extraordinary degree based on what everybody attributes to a Platonic theory of the ideas. The most obvious example of that is in the *Philebus,* where it turns out that Philebus, as a hedonist, believes in the idea of pleasure. And Socrates goes out of his way to prove that it is not an idea. In the *Republic,* Glaucon believes that justice is an idea. He is the first one to mention such a thing, and he asks Socrates to prove that justice *is* an idea. The reason for this is what one might call the systematically misleading character of language itself, which necessarily leads to the pseudo-Platonic theory of the ideas. Socrates has to charm us away from that.

5. One encounters difficulty if one believes one has identified prior to the analysis what is going to be put together, i.e., if one believes that in fact one element is totally self-evident and only the other has to be examined. What Socrates saw was that the thing one is combining with mind has to be examined on the level of mind. It too has a logos that has to be considered prior to looking at the problem of causation. The mistake he is correcting is a very understandable one, because these things appear to be exactly what they are. That is why Socrates gives the example about pleasure mixed with pain. It does not seem to be problematic and therefore in need of an account. So in the same way life seems not to need an account.

6. In *Metaphysics* Λ, Aristotle's account of the nature of mind has nothing to do with mind as cause. So the being of mind and the causal character of mind are totally separable. That is equivalent to an extreme version of the structure of the *Phaedo.* What mind wants—what soul wants—is to know the beings. But what soul is, is that which gives life to body: consequently, suicide. Soul wants, for the sake of its own being, to give up what it is as cause. So the problem is to try to show that soul is the beneficiary of itself when it operates as cause, and that these two characters of soul belong together out of necessity. And that is what Socrates tries to do in the *Phaedo.* He tries to show, not how they are internally related to one another, but that, in attempting to separate them, one is not going to get what one thinks. When he says that the good is the binding at the end of his account of teleology, what I think he is pointing to is this: a true understanding of the good would be in terms of parts and wholes. This is connected with the duality of Eros in the *Symposium*—the longing to be with plus the longing to contemplate. What Diotima shows there is that these two aspects of Eros are totally at odds with one another, and that the desire within eros itself is therefore self-contradictory. The contemplative aspect of desire is a disjunctive two; the union aspect of desire is a conjunctive two. But desire as it is originally postulated evades the fact that these two aspects cannot in fact be reconciled. Aristophanes, in his speech in the *Symposium,* gives up contemplation for the sake of union and he gets nothing but his own body in an "ideal" form.

FIFTEEN

Plato's *Theaetetus:* On the Way of the Logos

THE OPENING OF THE *Theaetetus* is curious. The report we have of another opening of nearly the same length indicates that it was always a curiosity.[1] If both openings are Plato's, and the rest of the dialogue they preface were not different, then Plato changed his mind about how to start off the trilogy to which the *Theaetetus* belongs; if the second version is spurious, someone thought he could surpass Plato and make a more sensible introduction; but if ours is spurious, then we cannot hope to interpret it. If we assume its genuineness and that it represents Plato's only or final recension—the other one is said to be spurious and rather frigid—then the *Theaetetus* opens with our listening in on a recital of the conversation Socrates had with Theaetetus and Theodorus shortly before his death: we are supposedly hearing it in Megara many years after the conversation occurred. The temporal and spatial layers are these: 1) the original conversation; 2) Socrates' report of it to Euclides, in which every speech, explicitly or not, had a parenthetical "I said" or "He said"; 3) Euclides' notes on Socrates' report which Euclides corrected after his frequent returns to Athens; 4) Euclides' retranslation of Socrates' report into non-narrated dialogue; 5) Plato's eavesdropping on Euclides and Terpsion in Megara, and his subsequent transcription of the slaveboy's reading of the dialogue after their return to Euclides' house; 6) our reading or hearing the dialogue at another time and another place. It is possible to ticket each of these layers, but it seems impossible to do anything with our careful discrimination of them. We are left with a logos whose indexes of space and time alter while it itself presumably remains the same. It carries a reminder of the irrecoverable particularity of the original setting no less than of its subsequent transpositions, but the logos stands clear of what occasioned it and remains to be viewed without distortion under strata of illusory transparency.

The publication of the logos is due to Plato; Euclides was content to render an illusion of the original conversation, in conformity with Socrates' recommendation in the *Phaedrus,* as his own private reminder, though one might suppose that he would not have gone to so much trouble had he not intended to publish it at some time or other. Had not Plato intervened, and Euclides got around to bringing it into the light, we might have had a non-Platonic Socratic dialogue, which would have had a purely accidental link with Plato's *Sophist* and *Statesman.* They could still be taking up where the *Theaetetus* left off, but the difference in authorship would have hindered us from reading the *Theaetetus* in light of Plato's twins. The *Theaetetus* would not be standing at the head of the seven dialogues that now constitute a single logos about the trial and death of Socrates. It seems, then, that Plato has imagined what the transmission of Socrates' teaching would have been like had his illness at the time of Socrates' death been fatal *(Phaedo* 59b10), and Socrates had had to rely on Euclides for getting out his message. The extreme skepticism of the Megarian school, with its reliance on nothing but logos, would have received its imprimatur in Euclides' *Theaetetus.* The solution to such a radical skepticism that we now find in the *Sophist* and the *Statesman* would have been missing. The *Theaetetus* of course would not have been entirely free of the circumstantial. Socrates implies in his first speech to Theodorus that he is tied down to the local more than Theodorus is, and he does not fail to bring the dialogue down to earth by mentioning at the end that he must go to the stoa of the King Archon to face the indictment Meletus has drawn up against him. Socrates the gossip, who knows all about Theaetetus's father, cannot possibly be the philosopher whom Socrates describes to Theodorus, whose body alone remains in the city but whose thought flies above and below the earth. Theodorus would call such a theoretical man a philosopher but not apparently Socrates (175e1–2). This high-flying philosopher, however, who does not know whether his neighbor is a beast or not, devotes himself to Socratic questions: What is man? What is human happiness and misery? What is kingship? (175c2–8). The perspective of this Socratic pre-Socratic seems to be the perspective in light of which we are being made to read the *Theaetetus.* We are forced to abandon Theodorus's image of Socrates as another Antaeus, who weakens if he is raised above the earth but grows stronger whenever he renews contact with it (169b2–4) and adopt a perspective, against the Socratic understanding of things, which Plato reproduced in the structure of the *Theaetetus* itself, of the universality of logos. The *Theaetetus* spells out defiantly the paradox of the *Phaedrus.* Its logos invites us, despite its built-in warning against our doing what we cannot help ourselves from doing, to read Socrates out of the dialogue and replace him with Theodorus's understanding of the philosopher, for whom the Eleatic Stranger and not Socrates is divine *(Sophist* 216b8–c1). This end run around Socrates has the consequence that we are led to discount Socrates' maieutic knowledge, which resists the notion of the universality of science and elevates a private eccentricity into a principle.

If we resist the temptation Plato set in our way and try to insert Socrates' knowledge into the issue of knowledge, we are faced with the paradox that Socrates seems to prove conclusively that it is as impossible to know what one does not know as either not to know what one knows or to mistake what one knows for what one does not know. Theaetetus, however, seems to be the evidence to the contrary of the latter impossibility and Socrates himself of the former. The dialogue thus seems to be a knockdown proof that Socrates cannot have the knowledge he says he has and Theaetetus cannot have made the mistakes he acknowledges he has made. The logos of *Theaetetus* sweeps the board of every answer it examines and then cancels itself and denies that what Theaetetus experiences could ever occur. Such a conclusion must have prompted Theaetetus, Theodorus, and young Socrates to ask the Eleatic Stranger about Socrates: What could possibly explain the sophistry of Socrates that parades as philosophy? According to Socrates, such an apparition is a necessary consequence of the position from which the philosopher is viewed, but, according to the Stranger, Socrates the sophist can be accounted for without grounding him in the reality of the philosopher (*Sophist* 216c4–217b3). Socrates belongs to a distinct species that can be comprehended by itself. This Parmenidean claim must have been a consolation to Theaetetus and Theodorus. Speeches stripped of everything are going to be shown for what they are.

If that was what they expected, the company was bound to be disappointed by the Stranger's own logos. Rather than adopting the experiential mode of Socrates, who had likened perplexity to the labor pains of women, he will assure Theaetetus that he can be brought closer to the beings without ever experiencing the disenchantment of innocent youth (*Sophist* 234e3–6; cf. *Theaetetus* 207e7–9) and urge him to assume, since Theaetetus has never seen a sophist, that the sophist he is addressing is blind

(*Sophist* 239e1–240a2). The *Theaetetus* and the *Sophist* thus seem to stand together and deny us any easy way to restore to the *Theaetetus* a revindication of Socrates' insistence that the arguments of Theaetetus cannot be separated from the mode in which he delivered them from him. Since Theaetetus seems to say on his own no more than "Knowledge is perception," "Knowledge is true opinion," and "Knowledge is true opinion with logos," while the elaboration of each of these propositions belongs exclusively to Socrates' doing, Socrates seems to refute himself. There is no science of midwifery. It is just a way of encouraging Theaetetus after the failure of his first answer, but there really is nothing to it, and Socrates' claim to be barren in point of wisdom stands refuted by the variety of his wise inventions that he falsely attributes to Theaetetus's conceptions. The refutation that Socrates anticipates the Eleatic Stranger as a refutative god will inflict upon him for his poorness in speeches has already been inflicted by himself. Socrates is willing, it seems, to endure a second beating (169b6–8).

The problem Theaetetus is called upon to solve has been stated emblematically even prior to Socrates' formal questioning of Theaetetus about knowledge. He puts the emblematic question on the basis of Theodorus's praise of Theaetetus's nature. Theodorus's praise has nothing to do with Theaetetus's particular aptitude for mathematics, about which Socrates could never have cast doubt, and which Theaetetus later displays on his own when he shows how he classified irrational square roots. Socrates, by speaking of "geometry and the rest of philosophy," had allowed Theodorus to stick to his special knowledge in his praise of Theaetetus (143d3); but Theodorus, rather than mentioning Theaetetus's ingenious procedure, chooses to stray into Socrates' field of expertise and give an account of Theaetetus's soul—he never mentions the word—that, if true, would put at the beginning of the trilogy the union of moderation and courage which the Eleatic Stranger discusses at the end with young Socrates. The phrase "geometry and the rest of philosophy" seems to imply that either philosophy is a science or philosophy and science are all of a piece (cf. 172c5), and Theodorus's praise of Theaetetus is a praise of his philosophic nature, which is the indispensable basis for his purely mathematical skills. Theodorus, one might say, comes forward as one of the guardians of Kallipolis and declares Theaetetus to be fit for the higher training in dialectic. He seems, at any rate, to be challenging Socrates. Socrates, to be sure, does not let on that Theodorus has poached on his knowledge; instead, he gets Theaetetus's assent to the view that whoever is praised should be as eager to display his excellence as the listener of the praise should be eager to test its truth.

Socrates' question about knowledge naturally follows from the apparent impossibility of putting together Socrates' knowledge with Theodorus's, even though Theodorus's general remarks about the disparate natures of the bold and the temperate seem within the competence of any experienced teacher, and his praise of Theaetetus as an exception to the rule also seems to be well within what Theodorus could have picked up in a long career. Theodorus thus has scientific knowledge about a number of subjects and ordinary human understanding of his students; but Socrates cannot compete with him scientifically, and he is simply absurd to come forward with the claim that he has replaced Theodorus's experience with a science that in his own case did not need any experience to precede his acquisition of it. What seems to have rankled Socrates was Theodorus's preliminary remark that Theaetetus was almost as ugly as Socrates, and therefore his praise of him could not possibly be construed as due to any desire for Theaetetus on his part. In his conversation with Theaetetus, Socrates began by casting doubt on Theodorus's credentials: he could not say that Theaetetus was ugly unless he were a skilled painter (144e8–145a4). Socrates left it open at that point whether he was so competent; but when Theaetetus finally comes around to assigning to "soul by itself" certain functions, Socrates triumphantly declares that Theaetetus is beautiful, "for he who speaks beautifully is beautiful and good." Socrates' knowledge discounts the senses, and just as Theodorus had to disclaim any erotic attachment to Theaetetus, so Socrates has to claim to be barren in order that his attachment to his own might not interfere with his delivery of Theaetetus. Socrates is on a par with Artemis, and unlike her human surrogates, he never had to have put the age of childbearing behind him in order to turn to the delivery and examination of another's offspring.

The implausibility of Socrates' pretensions seems to make the emblematic confrontation between Theaetetus's knowledge and Socrates' a nonstarter. Theaetetus certainly does not see that if two such radically different types of science are involved, the possibility of a comprehensive characterization of science seems precluded. Once, however, Theaetetus supplies a series of mathematical sciences, along with their productive counterparts, as his first answer, and Socrates later gives an account of maieutics, we cannot help but believe that Socrates has asked Theaetetus to put together the apparently irrational science of soul, of which he is the sole master, with the rational sciences of number and measure.

Theaetetus first offers Socrates an indeterminate number of sciences as science; but once Socrates shows him that he did not answer the question properly, Theaetetus abandons everything he knows and declare his incapacity to say what science is. Just as Meno's first answer to Socrates' question, What is virtue? allows for a simple answer that would comprehend all the examples Meno gave—virtue consists in doing one's own job well—so Theaetetus's list is just as easy to stamp with a single sign: science is the knowledge of how to count and measure. After Theaetetus has told Socrates how he understands the question—it is comparable to the question he and young Socrates raised, how to characterize irrational square roots positively—he does not even try to do the same for knowledge. Had Theaetetus given the answer we expect, he would have shown his daring in extending what he knows into all that he does not know and claiming thereby that whatever is not countable or measurable is not knowledge. Theodorus's knowledge of Theaetetus would have been demoted and put in a field that resists any scientific account, though for all practical purposes it may be good enough; indeed, Socrates could even say he was superior to Theodorus in this regard without ever advancing the claim that he was just as much an expert in souls as Theodorus was in numbers and measure. Theaetetus's innate modesty, it seems, checked him from extending the domain of mathematics. He is more moderate than Theodorus, who, according to Socrates, naturally pulled into the field of relative measures what was not susceptible to geometrical proportions *(Statesman* 257a6–b7).

Socrates does assign moderation to Theaetetus, but only at the end of the dialogue when he is completely empty (210c3); but if he had indeed been moderate, he would have refused to give any answer at all once he was persuaded to give up mathematical knowledge. Socrates persuaded him that he could not mention any art or science unless he knew what science was; and since he had just listed the arts and sciences, he was convinced he could not give any answer in light of what he knew. Socrates emptied Theaetetus of everything Theodorus had taught him. His first essay as midwife was to cast out from Theaetetus whatever he had thought was a science. He cauterized Theaetetus's womb and then encouraged him to give birth. So whereas mathematics looks to be a rival to maieutics, and indeed is if one steps back from the *Theaetetus* and looks at the pieces as they are laid out, still from the temporal perspective of Theaetetus, who does not learn about maieutics until after mathematics has been set aside, there is only one science on the board that is supposed to be accounted for, and that is Socrates' midwifery. From the moment midwifery is described until the very end of the dialogue, when Socrates allows Theaetetus to have once again the arithmetical art (198a5), *maieutikē* is the only *technē* Socrates mentions while talking with Theaetetus. Even with Theodorus only rhetoric is mentioned by name (177b6). Theaetetus is challenged to account for Socrates' speciality, something he does not know, and which, like his characterization of irrational square roots, has to rely on an image to make it plain.

Theaetetus's second answer, perception, is the answer of one who has just been born (186b11–c2). It puts Socrates' art in its place. Midwifery is nothing but a knack, slowly acquired through the course of a long life; it is no more than that which lay behind Theodorus's praise of Theaetetus. Theaetetus himself may not have intended his answer to be so interpreted. He might have thought that if everything Theodorus taught him could not be the characteristic of science, Socrates must have wanted a prescientific answer, that without which we would not know anything. It is not until later in the dialogue that Socrates reveals to him the necessity of conversing impurely, and that means, in the context, to speak about knowing and not knowing while trying to answer the question, What is knowledge? The impurity of conversation is nowhere more clearly hinted at than in Theaetetus's response to Socrates' assertion that the dizziness he has felt is not due to his emptiness but to his pregnancy: "I do not know, Socrates, but I say what I have experienced." Theaetetus distinguishes perception from knowledge and implies that knowledge is always knowledge of cause. Socrates indeed goes on to confirm this when he reports that people say of him that he is most strange and makes them perplexed. He then asks whether he should tell Theaetetus the cause, which is that they do not know that he has the same art as his mother, but he does not maintain that they are mistaken in attributing to him the power to perplex them. Socrates not only forestalls Theaetetus's answer, but he hints at an understanding of knowledge that does not come up again in the *Theaetetus.*

If, however, we turn to the *Sophist* and *Statesman,* and look to the highest sciences of each, the *Sophist*'s answer seems to be the divine knowledge of making, and the *Statesman*'s answer, insofar as the ruler is the knower of the order of ends, seems to be knowledge of the good. The union of these two knowledges would be a teleological physics, or precisely that science Socrates once figured out should have been contained in Anaxagoras's book if he maintained correctly that mind was the highest cause (*Phaedo* 97b8–d5). There is embedded, then, at the start of the *Theaetetus* the problem that prompted Socrates from the start. Perhaps it would have been too much to expect Socrates' look-alike to renew the issue, even though the shadow of the problem came out of himself and did not require any teasing on Socrates' part. His first answer had already suggested that wisdom would consist in a science that would combine the mathematical sciences with the causal knowledge implicit in shoemaking and the like. That Theaetetus was on the edge of renewing Socrates' earliest speculation shows that the barrenness of Socrates, upon which his claim to disinterested authority rests, cannot be genuine. Even if we do not count the "ideas" as his second birth and identify them instead with a comprehensive structure of questions, Socrates' own autobiography contradicts the premise of his maieutics. Socrates decided to release through Euclides a version of himself that discounts his own experience. Socrates relies on nothing but logos. He was always young and beautiful.

If, moreover, Theaetetus had simply listened to Socrates' description of his own art, he could easily have put the problem of knowledge in terms of what he knew and what Socrates knows. Socrates' knowledge seems to amount to self-knowledge. He knows through his art that knowledge of soul is not wisdom, and no other art knows through itself that it is necessarily limited in its possible range. Theaetetus could then have asked whether it was possible to put scientific knowledge and self-knowledge together into a single science, for scientific knowledge, once it has comprehended everything, cannot comprehend scientific knowledge itself, and whatever knowledge does comprehend scientific knowledge cannot be scientific. Socrates' knowledge also seems to differ from any other known science in one important respect; unlike every other science it cannot as self-knowledge be written down. It cannot be taught. It thus seems not to be knowledge at all but at best a kind of virtue. What holds for Socrates also holds for those he delivers. Their wisdom must be *their* wisdom; it too cannot be found in a book, but it must have their individual signatures upon it; otherwise, it would become Socrates' own wisdom as soon as he brought it into the light. The identification, then, of wisdom and knowledge, with which Socrates begins his question (145d12–e7), cannot be right. The offspring he delivers must necessarily be so many instances of pseudo-wisdom or sophistry. Whatever knowledge his pregnant charges have must produce by itself a completion of itself that is necessarily a phantom image of wisdom. Sophistry is the inevitable consequence of the contact of soul with science.

There were, then, several ways in which Theaetetus could have got hold of the question Socrates put to him, but he takes none of them. He gives an answer that confirms his bafflement once Socrates has blocked the only way open to him to approach the problem. Socrates finds it relatively easy to refute the answer once he has gotten rid of his spontaneous variations on a theme supplied by Theaetetus, just as he later finds it no less easy to refute Theaetetus's second answer, true opinion, once he returns from his unsolved puzzle about false opinion. The *Theaetetus,* then, has a remarkably symmetric structure: the first part is dominated by Socrates' Heraclitean-Protagorean thesis, which he simply foists on Theaetetus, and the second part is dominated by the intrusion of Socrates' own perplexity about false opinion. The theme of the first part is that there is neither true nor false opinion but there is wisdom of a certain kind; the theme of the second part is that false opinion is impossible. These two theses amount to a concealed assault on Socrates' midwifery—he has no wisdom on his own and he can tell infallibly true from false opinion. The *Theaetetus,* then, has a single theme, Socrates' maieutics and why it cannot be a science. Insofar as one believes that the attack Socrates mounts against his own knowledge is successful, one has to conclude that the *Theaetetus* restores to Theaetetus all the knowledges he was persuaded to set aside at the beginning of the dialogue, and that accordingly mathematics does not have to share its claim to knowledge with anything else: Socrates' problem is not a problem. Socrates' suicidal mission also gives Theaetetus a model of what philosophical courage is. It is not a model he has the guts to follow. He does, however, practice a phantom image of Socrates' daring: for a time he gives up what he knows.

It would be easy enough to assimilate Socrates' midwifery to what he claims elsewhere to be his sole knowledge, competence in erotic things; but it would require the sacrifice of what is central to erotics—the generation of beautiful speeches on the beautiful *(Symposium* 208e5–209c7), for Theaetetus is not beautiful. Since, moreover, maieutics demands that Socrates share with his mother the art of the go-between, which cannot publicly be distinguished from the art of the pimp, it might seem that maieutics becomes fully artful at the expense of the spontaneity of eros; but one could suppose that Socrates' erotic art is just another name for this original sorting of natures, and Socrates' mistake is to jump over this initial stage with Theaetetus—he had seen him before but had not been attracted to him—and try to exercise his art on a nature that did not fit his own. Socrates does indeed speak of beautiful offspring as the possible outcome of his technique (150d7), but since he says they are not his, are we allowed to suppose that Theaetetus inspired in him a phantom image of Theaetetus that he generously imputed to Theaetetus himself? It certainly looks as if the account of Theaetetus's definition is Socrates' alone, and Theaetetus falls for an alien falsification that fits himself. What is fatal, however, to such an association of erotics and maieutics, is that Theaetetus's four offspring are not viable, and once they are brought into the light they cannot survive Socrates' examination. Rather than offering Theaetetus something he can live with or live by, Socrates does his best to make Theaetetus as perplexed as himself. The Eleatic Stranger, on the other hand, does hold out to Theaetetus something beautiful: he gives him a proleptic vision of his own future self in which his nature will finally fit his own opinion that a god made everything *(Sophist* 265d5–e2). This completion of Theaetetus's nature stands at the opposite pole from Socrates' suggestion that he (Socrates) no less than the Stranger is a god.

Socrates' science knows how to induce labor pains and soothe them. These labor pains are perplexities. "Protagoras" will later argue that it is impossible to live in the element of perplexity: everyone is forced to come up with a solution, which is neither true nor false but strong or weak. Even apart from this "Nietzschean" criticism of Socrates, Socrates' presentation of his art, however, is deeply flawed. He admits that his delivery of conceptions can be fully understood in light of his mother's art, but he grants that her art has nothing that corresponds to his infallible testing of truth and falsehood. If, then, the testing of the offspring does not match anything in female maieutics, Socrates cannot appeal to it in order to make good his claim that his critical knowledge is part of midwifery. Socrates may well have such an art, but unless he can show that it coheres with the art of delivery as much as the art of the go-between must belong no less to his mother than to himself, he comes forward with two arts, the unity of which is far more puzzling than the unity of Theaetetus's list of arts and sciences. The twoness of Socrates' singular art is mapped onto and enlarged in the two parts of the *Theaetetus;* and this largescale display of Socrates' maieutics drives home the point that each part can be treated separately and does not necessarily belong to the other. The two offspring of Theaetetus's soul that control severally the two parts of the dialogue—perception and true opinion—refute the unity of Socrates' art.

Each part of the *Theaetetus* has a controlling principle. For the first part it is that nothing is one by itself, but every apparent one is a two (152d2–3; 153e4–5); for the second part the principle is that there are nothing but ones, whether they be the ones of pure arithmetic, elements, or individuals like Socrates, Theaetetus, or Theodorus. The first principle is the Heraclitean ground for the Protagorean principle that man is the measure of all things. It supplies the physics for relativism. Socrates builds up the Protagorean-Heraclitean theory from 151e4 to 160e4. This interval corresponds to the gestation and labor pains of pregnancy, after which Theaetetus's offspring is finally brought forth. The initial offspring is, as it were, a disembodied logos; it gets a life only through the ministrations of Socrates, who has had to cajole Theaetetus to allow it to be shaped and not drop stillborn at every possible objection. Theaetetus's definition, which appeared as one, now comes to light as having concealed a two—Protagoras and Heraclitus—who have come together to produce Theaetetus's definition. It now contains a causal account; but insofar as it is a causal account, it contradicts the definition of knowledge. The causal account, then, must be spurious; it cannot possibly be true but only a product of another two that are thought to be separable and each to be a one apart. This illusory two is Socrates and Theaetetus, who in contact with one another play the role of agent and patient, respectively, and have engendered together Theaetetus's thesis. The Protagorean-Heraclitean theory, as Socrates formulates it, requires a version of Socrates' maieutics, in which Socrates is no longer the neutral helper and inspector but a co-producer of what Theaetetus is told is his alone. Socrates, then, works out a way in which his maieutics could be understood as fully in conformity with Protagoras's understanding of wisdom.

The Protagorean thesis has two anchors. The first is relatively trivial. The bitterness or sweetness of wine depends on the condition of the drinker. At the other end is the plausible thesis that cities are likewise either healthy or sick, but the set of authoritative opinions of each city, which are called laws, determine what is beautiful and just or what is ugly and unjust. We can call the beautiful and just together morality. Morality is the way in which the city expresses as a symptom its condition. It is the equivalent of a plant's perceptions—its turning to the light, for example, or its sending out roots in search of moisture—that reveals to the farmer its underlying state, which the plant knows no more about than the city knows about itself. Each city holds its morality to be true, but morality is not true or false but a way of life grounded in conditions or states that are neither true nor false but good or bad. A city is in a good condition if it can either resist being absorbed by another city or absorb another city. Health is the power to expand or defend, sickness is its contrary. Between the individual's bodily state and the city's condition, Socrates comes forward with a theory about the soul, which, insofar as it speaks of pregnancy and barrenness, supplies an account comparable to talk of health and sickness. Socrates cannot but admit that if wisdom must be one's own wisdom, everyone says what he is, and the individual's logos is but a symptom of his underlying condition. It is therefore absurd for him to claim that he can speak of true or false symptoms, any more than he can determine whether Theaetetus's assertions are true or false. He has been the agent and Theaetetus the patient. As patient, Theaetetus believes he has produced something verifiable; but that belief is merely a sign of his patiency. The wise public speaker does not try to enlighten the city and replace morality with health; instead, he presents to the city a version of its morality that fits what is to its good. Socrates is urged to follow the same procedure: he is to show his wisdom by reproducing on the level of symptoms his own health, so that nothing remains in Theaetetus of his former perplexities but he copies the agency of Socrates in a passive reflection (167e3–168a7). This is a very powerful condemnation of Socrates: the city will ultimately prove to be healthier than he could ever be by killing him. If we follow Protagoras, we can say that every city established through what it holds to be the highest beings—the gods—the symptomatic network of its condition, and it is forced to live within the horizon of putative truth while it undergoes whatever the real power relations among cities determine. On Protagoras's interpretation, Athens takes out on Socrates its defeat by Sparta: it naturally believes that its weakness is Socrates' falseness.

Theaetetus's second irrational answer—knowledge is perception—seems to represent the soul's answer, once its scientific superstructure has been dismantled. The soul, however, cannot possibly see that its answer contradicts itself in its very formulation, for it must be blind to the nonperceptibility of such an equation. Socrates' elaboration of Theaetetus's answer attempts to derive it from the union of two theories, Protagoras's "Man the measure" and Heraclitean motion. Heraclitean motion is given a mathematical structure, and Protagoras's measure poses a counterclaim to Socrates' knowledge. Together they produce a total wisdom that claims to solve the problem that Socrates had put first to Theaetetus in casting doubt on Theodorus's competence and that he had then let us formulate for ourselves in setting up the contrast between mathematics and maieutics. Socrates' version of wisdom is designed to show Theaetetus what it would mean to have a grasp of science prior to the understanding of any particular science. It offers, for example, an understanding of power *(dunamis)* that lends itself very naturally to its mathematical sense. Power as agency and patiency easily fits the multiplication of numbers and magnitudes, where the equivalence of 4×3 and 3×4 points simultaneously to the nonfixability of agent and patient and the need to fix temporarily one number or the other as the patient of the other's agency. The more special use of *dunamis* as root is connected with Theaetetus's imagistic translation of all numbers into magnitudes, so that as magnitudes they can represent motions of any size.

Protagoras's sentence does not lend itself to an interpretation that readily fits Theaetetus's definition. In itself it seems to be a clever way of saying what part of the Chorus in Aeschylus's *Seven* say: "Even the city praises the just things differently at different times" (1070–71). Their saying could be further generalized: "Different tribes believe in different gods"; and in this form it seems to bear a not too distant relation to the implication of Socrates' maieutics. The gods are those beings that complete the individual's particular knowledge, and such completions are of necessity nonscientific, however indispensable they are for understanding the way in which the individual understands his own knowledge. In the spin that Socrates puts upon it, Protagoras is made to bestow divinity on Theaetetus himself, but if one replaces this identification with a somewhat weaker version, that what Theaetetus generates out of himself is an ideal of total wisdom, which Socrates implies is always an idol of total wisdom, then the political or conventional interpretation of Protagoras and its radically subjective interpretation, with which Socrates starts, acquire a middle position that is hard to distinguish from Socrates' own.

Theaetetus had originally said, *ouk allo ti estin epistēmē ē aisthēsis* (151e2–3). Socrates had rephrased it without "is": *aisthēsis, phēis, epistēmē?* (151e6). *Phēis,* "you say," the bond between "knowledge" and "perception"; but *phēis* is Theaetetus: he puts the two together. He is the "man" of Protagoras's general formula. Theaetetus is the place where knowledge and perception meet. Such a meeting involves the replacement of both with *ta phainomena;* but *ta phainomena* seems to be paired with *ta onta.* In order, then, for *ta phainomena* and *ta onta* to be in turn fused together, *ta onta* must be replaced with *ta gignomena,* and then again with *ta kekinēmena.* The things in motion are then to be distributed between *ta poiounta* and *ta paschonta,* agent and patient motions. Socrates, however, does not go as quickly as this to his suggested mathematical physics. He first appeals to Homer as the propounder of the view that Ocean stands for motion and then that the sun in its revolution stands for motion. In the second interpretation, motion is the cause of good and rest, of decay and nonbeing. If one cancels the difference between water and fire, Socrates seems to be appealing to an anti-entropic principle, to which we can assign, following the *Phaedo* and *Phaedrus,* the name "soul." There lurks under the Heracliteanism Socrates uncovers the indispensable ground he himself needs if soul is to be something nonderivative. Heraclitean motion and Protagorean relativism thus turn out to be a not bad copy of Socrates' teaching in the *Phaedrus,* where soul as self-motion has its counterpart here no less than do the Olympian gods. What seems to be missing, the hyperuranian beings, has been supplied by numbers, which, though officially eliminated through Socrates' refutation of Theaetetus's first answer, recur in the disguised form of fast and slow motions.

The principle of Socrates' interpretation of Theaetetus is not that nothing is one, but nothing is one by itself. Every apparent 1 is a 2, and this apparent 1 is such through the imaginative connector soul, but there is nothing there. The soul is that which puts the line between numerator and denominator and interprets the ratio as greater or less than some constant, but this constant is an illusion, for to say that Theaetetus is greater than he was a year ago identifies the Theaetetus of a year ago as the real Theaetetus, for if one says that Theaetetus and the measured Theaetetus are the same, it is impossible to say that Theaetetus becomes taller than himself, for "himself" is not apart from whatever size he is. We want to believe that Theaetetus the measure is not the same as Theaetetus the measured. We do not want to trust our mathematics. This conflict between mathematics and the hallucinations of becoming is nothing other than the apparent conflict between Theaetetus's first and second answers, but his second answer turns out to be fully in accord with his first, provided one replaces becoming with motion. All three *phasmata* of becoming share at their base an assumption about counting: the first states that nothing becomes greater or less as long as it is equal to itself, the second that what is not added to or subtracted from is always equal, and the third that whatever it was not before but is later cannot occur without becoming. Nothing, then, alters in time unless there is the equivalent of an arithmetical operation; but $1 \pm 1/2$ is only $1\frac{1}{2}$ or $1/2$, it is not $1\frac{1}{2}$ and 1 or 1 and $1/2$; but unless it is both at once, 1 has not become $1\frac{1}{2}$ or $1/2$. Every magnitude is just what it is, for there is no real becoming in number. Number therefore allows us to handle change while denying change.[2] Theaetetus had felt dizzy because his experience was not in accord with his mathematics, but Socrates has shown him how they could be reconciled without giving up either what he felt or what he knew. The rational and the irrational are in perfect harmony, and Theaetetus is all of a piece. It is a consequence of this that when Theaetetus says "I don't know" a second time, he means that he does not know his own experience, for Socrates has not yet molded him completely to his taste (157c4).

At the very moment Socrates has completed delivery of Theaetetus's offspring, he seems to admit that he has delivered his own as well: "Well, this, it seems, whatever it is exactly, we at last generated *(egennēsamen)* with difficulty" (160e5; cf. 150c8). Socrates then goes on to speak of the offspring as *to gignomenon,* and they must consider whether it deserves to be brought up or is a wind-egg and false (160e8–9). The offspring is to be considered simultaneously under two different aspects: Is it viable? and, Is it true? If the issue is viability, Socrates' maieutics is exactly parallel to his mother's, who would likewise have examined the offspring for signs of life. But if the issue is truth, the equivalent for Phaenarete would be whether it was suppositious, and again for Socrates whether Theaetetus had genuinely given birth or it was all due to Socrates' spoonfeeding. Socrates, however, not only denied from the start that his art could be interpreted in this way, but he reasserts it now when Theodorus expresses astonishment that the offspring could possibly be false (161b1–3): "You don't get *(ennoeis)* what's happening *(to gignomenon),* that none of the speeches comes from me but always from my interlocutor *(para tou emoi prosdialegomenou).*" Socrates implicitly distinguishes between *to gignomenon*$_1$, which exclusively is the thought of Theaetetus, and *to gignomenon*$_2$, which is the course of the conversation he and Theaetetus are having. Now Socrates has just developed a teaching that denies that these two *gignomena* can be separated, for one is due to him and the other to Theaetetus, but the one due to him is the combined result of himself and Theaetetus and cannot accordingly be told apart from *to gignomenon*$_1$, as Socrates' own *egennēsamen* had already indicated. This argument is not directly refuted by Socrates. Instead, he allows it to remain while he dismantles its components into three separate arguments that came together in it. Theodorus confronts the Protagorean and Heraclitean arguments, and Theaetetus confronts his own thesis apart from that double support. Each collapses quite easily. Their refutation therefore shows the power of the combination in which Socrates' own science is at stake. It shows that, contrary to what Theaetetus comes to believe, a whole is not a sum.

"Protagoras's" radical criticism of Socrates' knowledge allows one to formulate more precisely what must be involved in Socrates' practice of delivery and verification. If his double practice involves a distinction between soul and mind *(nous)* or thought *(dianoia),* and if that distinction entails in turn a difference between the excellence of soul and mind, or a difference between virtue and wisdom (145b1–2, 176c4–5), then the denial of the possibility of complete knowledge or wisdom entails the corresponding elevation of the moral virtues of moderation and courage into nonscientific or philosophic equivalents, one of which goes by the name of self-knowledge, while the other is more elusive, since the daringness of thought or *deinotēs* is commonly pejorative and to be devalued as mere cleverness. Socrates implies, however, that there is a true and not seeming *deinotēs* (176c3–6). Socrates' insistence, through his reliance on the model of midwifery, on private experience and private wisdom, underlines the resemblance between Socrates' "Protagoras" and himself and the need to separate the Protagorean thesis that soul is to the speech of soul as condition is to symptom from the Socratic thesis, that soul, without philosophy, necessarily completes what it knows with a phantom image of what it knows. Soundness of soul or strength of soul has to be separated from "Protagoras's" understanding of health or sickness in terms of the power to affect or be affected. Theodorus had originally posed the problem by his praise of Theaetetus's virtue, which he had associated with his knowledge in a not altogether clear manner. He had implied that Theaetetus's virtues were indispensable for his learning whatever Theodorus could teach him, but once he gained this knowledge his virtues could fall away. He certainly did not imply that his knowledge would override his virtues and produce ghosts of wisdom.

In order to slip out from under his own critique, Socrates appeals to Theodorus. He thus reproduces himself again in a second phantom. By dragging Theodorus into the argument, he gets him to concede to Protagoras the relativism of *praxis* and assign to philosophers like himself an immunity from the Heracliteanism of the waterclock. The good of life and death belongs to the city, the beautiful and the just are divorced from it and relegated to a higher region. Theodorus is led to believe that this relegation also applies to Socrates, but it does not, either in general or on this occasion, when Socrates does not have the leisure both Theaetetus and Theodorus believe he has (172c2, 187d10–11). The innocence of Theodorus makes him as unaware of the threat Socrates now faces as of the applicability of the revised Protagorean argument to Socrates. Even were he made to see its applicability, it would not disturb him; it would only go to show the absurdity of Socrates' claim to an art that simultaneously depends on his knowing the way to the marketplace and on his detachment from the city.

Theodorus does not notice, and he would not think it matters if he did, that Socrates' flattering portrait of him does not involve any mention of the soul. He has *dianoia* (173e3); the pettifoggers have a paltry soul and are engaged in a battle for their life or soul (172e7, 175d1; cf. 173a3, 6, 175b4). Theodorus, however, for all of the purity of his attitude, is not unattracted by Protagoras; he is infuriated by the slippery answers of the Heracliteans, but he is very reluctant to criticize Protagoras. There is something that attaches Theodorus to Protagoras that goes beyond friendship. After all, Protagoras is already dead. The first hint of that attraction shows up in Theodorus's understanding of speeches as his slaves, over which he has complete power (173b8–c5); but its hidden ground emerges once Socrates has finished with his account of the Theodoran philosopher and his opposite. The Theodoran philosopher has nothing but an attitude to sustain him. His remoteness from ordinary life is not grounded in anything but a highminded snobbery: he looks down on everyone else, but he has made no reflection on his own aerie. He therefore is tempted to treat evils as only a matter of opinion and inclined accordingly to hope that with a change of opinion more in conformity with his own opinion evils would cease. Socrates separates himself from Theodorus on precisely this point.

"If you should persuade all," Theodorus tells Socrates, "of what you are saying, just as you persuaded me, peace would be more extensive and evils less among men (176a3–4)." Socrates first separates Theodorus's sentence into two propositions. He treats the question of evil apart from the issue of persuasion. He implies that evils are not exclusively a question of what convictions men have or might have. Evils will persist regardless of whether Socrates succeeds in persuading everyone or not. Theodorus has accepted, then, the Protagorean understanding of power: Socrates could in principle effect a universal change in public opinion. Socrates denies not only that evils can perish but asserts that "god" (θεός) is most just. God's justice consists in his knowledge that evils cannot perish. He therefore is not tempted to eliminate them: what seems to be god's injustice, in not exercising his power to do away with evils entirely, is in fact his wisdom. Human wisdom consists in a comparable awareness of the necessity for this limitation on divine power: "The understanding of this is wisdom and true virtue, and ignorance [of it] folly and manifest vice (176c4–5)." It consists in an awareness of the reasons for abstaining from political life.

Theodorus, however, does not know this. He believes that it is possible to combine the theoretical sciences with Protagorean power. Such a combination would be nothing but a version of what we call technology, whose very name betrays the union of science with the productive arts. Theaetetus had already suggested such a union in his very first answer, where he had added to what he had learned from Theodorus the Socratic example of shoemaking. "Shoemaking" stood for all the productive arts, and in itself could be understood, in accordance with Socrates' suggestion in the *Philebus* (55d5–57a5), as implying no more than that its strictly scientific part consists in its dependence on an applied mathematics, and the remainder is to be dismissed as the flair of experience. If, however, the theoretical sciences can be fused with the productive arts, then the increase in power such a fusion would engender seems to offer the prospect of the total relief of man's estate. Socrates seems to imply that Theodorus could never have dreamed of this prospect had not he come along and first refashioned Protagoras into a more formidable opponent than he actually was and then shown Theodorus to himself, who does not know that he does not know what he does not know (173e1, cf. 174a3). Such a refashioning was made necessary once Socrates' maieutics was subject to examination in light of Theodorus and Theaetetus's knowledge; and such a showing of Theodorus to himself freed him from his troublesome relations with other men and suggested his triumphant return to political life with almost infinite power. Socrates, with an uncharacteristic dogmatism, simply stated the vanity of Theodorus's hope; but we may see in the myth of the *Statesman* the reasoning behind Socrates' statement: the world that the demiurgic god rules is not only ugly but lacks the good of philosophy. The only consolation Socrates offers Theodorus is a punishment of the unjust that consists in their ignorance of their own misery. If one of them is to become aware, he must be manly and not run away from his confutation: Callicles is to be left off the hook. This too is part of god's justice.

Any dissatisfaction we may feel with the first part of the *Theaetetus* is nothing compared to our unease after we finish reading the second part. Socrates gets Theaetetus to acknowledge the need for a single form *(mia tis idea)* or soul to coordinate the manifold of perceptions; but he does not get him to see that that which the soul by itself deals with, which ranges from the being of number to the being of good (186c3), encapsulates the very problem Socrates had posed at the beginning. Once Theaetetus has admitted that there is knowledge only in reflection on aesthetic experience, he should have said that knowledge consists in a comprehensive *sullogismos* about all aesthetic experiences as well as about the categories the soul by itself uses and discovers in its survey of them. Theaetetus admits that he thinks "is," "both," "same" and "other," "one" and "two," when he thinks about sound and color, and he grants that it might be possible to go on to examine the likeness and unlikeness of them (185b4–6). He thus admits that the aesthetic and the dianoetic might be comparable, as Socrates' use of "touch" for "understand" suggests (186d4; cf. 186a4, 187b1), and therefore knowledge would consist in an account that separated and combined the aesthetic and the noetic beings. Such an answer would have been the equivalent of Aristotle's "The soul is somehow all things." Would, then, anything be missing? Socrates already implied that what would be missing would be the Parmenidean whole that cannot be understood as the equivalent of soul: the one that Parmenides is, is not the one of his teaching (183e5). The Parmenidean one eludes the soul regardless of how extensive the soul's range is presumed to be. We can say if we wish that the unexamined Parmenidean one is doing double duty in the *Theaetetus:* it stands for the unknown unity of knowledge of number and knowledge of good, and for the unknown unity of the cause of being and being known, neither of which is to be found in the unity of soul by itself.

Theaetetus's answer—knowledge is true opinion—must be seen as a disappointment in light of all that Theaetetus himself has admitted. It is also disappointing in a more limited sense inasmuch as Theaetetus refused to assign to soul any instrument comparable to the sense-organs. Whereas the answer "the soul through speeches" seems to be strongly hinted at by Socrates' way of phrasing the question, Theaetetus's "soul by itself" cannot handle errors of thought, since it is too inflexible within itself to make mistakes. Theaetetus's third answer is as self-opaque as his second. It is the answer of one who has not yet lost his innocence and still has confidence in the good and the beautiful of opinion (200e5–6; cf. *Sophist* 234d2–e3). True opinion cannot confirm its own truth and experientially does not have a different feel from false opinion. Experientially, then, a false opinion is no less an opinion than a true opinion (cf. 187d3). Opinion *(doxa)* is according to Socrates a logos (190a5); but this logos differs from that which the soul conducts before itself in silence when it asks and answers questions (189e6). To ask or answer a question is presumably not in some sense to speak or opine; it is only when one stops asking questions and decides the questioning is finished that one has an opinion. Socrates implicitly separates the logos of *dialegesthai* or *dianoeisthai,* which is the soul's instrument, from the logos that is *doxa.* It is not easy to discern the difference except in terms of the conviction behind doxastic logos, that this logos is unqualifiedly true.

If we revert to Socrates' maieutics, Socrates now pulls apart *ōdinein* from *tiktein.* To give birth is to utter an opinion, to suffer labor pains is to go on questioning. Socrates now formalizes what was implicit in his account of maieutics. Opinion is always false opinion, the phantom image of complete wisdom. There is, then, no true opinion, not because there is no false opinion, but because opinion is merely the offspring of the soul that has lost its connection with the dialogic character of thinking. Theaetetus is not saying what knowledge is, he is saying what the character is of whatever offspring Socrates' maieutics examines. We are being shown what Socrates deals with; he deals not only with the offspring of the soul—the first part of the *Theaetetus*—but also with the belief that accompanies the offspring. At the very moment Theaetetus had given his second answer—knowledge is perception—he had begun by saying, "It's my opinion" (151e1). Accordingly, Socrates' digression on false opinion is not a digression at all, but rather an account of what is involved in the soul's pronouncement on its own phantom image, "True."

It seems, however, that when the issue of the speech, which either silently or not accompanies any offspring of the soul, is treated by itself, the speech is always true: it is impossible that Theaetetus could ever have made a mistake in thought. Whereas in the first part of the dialogue there could be no truth, for everyone says what they are—whether they be the "streamers" *(hoi rheontes)* or "the stoppers of the whole" *(hoi tou holou stasiōtai)*—in the second part everyone says what is. If Socrates' maieutics is to be saved, it is necessary that the two parts of the *Theaetetus* be put together over against their manifest separation. It is not easy to say how this can be done. Socrates first offers three possible ways in which false opinion could be possible: 1) the mistaking of what one knows or does not know for what one knows or does not know; 2) the mistaking of what is not for what is or what is for what is not; 3) the mistaking of the other for the same or the same for the other. Socrates does not consider the possibility that mistaking occurs when all three propositions are combined: The one who has a false opinion believes that those things which are not are not those things which he knows are not but some other things which he knows are, or "Zeus is not Osiris but heaven," "Eros is not Aphrodite but love," "Homer's Hades is not Milton's Beelzebub but death."

Since it is possible for someone to maintain any or all three of these propositions and be mistaken, why does Socrates fail to examine the combination of his three kinds of mistaking and thus reproduce here a parallel to the combination of Protagoras, Heraclitus, and Theaetetus that proved to be so fatal to his maieutics in the first part? In the first part, the principle of patiency and agency was that nothing is together what it is apart; in the second part the principle is that everything is just what it is and nothing else. This principle requires the identification of part with element and whole with sum. Such an identification, however, has the consequence that Theaetetus must deny that the soul is some single form (*mia tis idea;* 203c5–6, e4), in which the manifold of perceptions come together. Theaetetus is made to give up that which made him beautiful in order that he can recover his mathematics. The atomicity of things, which runs through the second part of the *Theaetetus,* seems to be more in accordance with what Theaetetus knows than the doubleness of things, which Theaetetus was induced to accept from Socrates' delivery of his phantom image. Theaetetus, however, does not see that he must sacrifice the principle of arithmetic in order to keep his arithmetic. He sacrifices the principle when he admits that the soul in thinking converses with itself—a one is therefore a two—and again when Socrates asked about seven itself and five itself (196a2; cf. *Philebus* 56d9–e3)—indistinguishable ones are many. The sacrifice of the principle thus reproduces within Theaetetus's own expertise Socrates' problem, for however the one that is two of soul is to be understood, it is of a different order from the manifold of ones with which arithmetic deals. Socrates has pulled off within the restriction of a false principle a kind of miracle: a genuine image of his own question about the unity of his knowledge and Theaetetus's. What makes this image so miraculous is that it occurs despite Theaetetus's sacrifice, for Theaetetus does not know that he made the sacrifice when he could not hold onto the notion of a whole.

In the course of the analysis of Theaetetus's third definition of knowledge, Socrates offers two images of the soul, wax and birds. Neither solves the problem of false opinion. Theaetetus does not see, however, that these two images are images of a science of soul; they are not the science of soul. They are images of the science Theaetetus does not know and Socrates claims for himself. Of the two images, one is more materialistic than the other, and together they point to the difference between aesthetic soul and dianoetic soul, which Socrates hinted at when he moved so abruptly from the single form of soul, which must be there if the senses are not to be lodged in us as if they were soldiers in the wooden horse, to the variety of functions soul undertakes when it reflects on its aesthetic experiences (184d1–6). One image fits us from the moment we are born (186b11–c2), the other corresponds to our learning the sciences (197e2–3). When Socrates gives the arithmetical art back to Theaetetus, he characterizes it as a hunting for the knowledges *(epistēmai)* of every odd and even number (198a7–8). "Hunting" *(thēra)* implies that arithmetic as a science is not a complete science; it is out in the wild and demands the virtues of patience and daring if the hunter is to snare his prey. If, moreover, the number-hunter fails to catch anything, he does not cease to be a number-hunter. He is not a complete or perfect arithmetician who has domesticated all that he knows, but he is still an arithmetician (cf. 198b9). There is no reason to suppose that this model cannot be extended to the scientist in general: he is the hunter for the knowledges of the beings (cf. *Euthydemus* 290b1–c6). Socrates implies that the dialectical art, too, can be called a hunting. The dialectical art is the hunting of the various huntings of the arts and sciences. It is the hunting of perplexity itself.

When Socrates had admitted he was going to be shameless in defining *epistasthai* before defining *epistēmē,* Theaetetus did not know what he was talking about (196d6). "We have long been infected with conversing impurely," Socrates tells him, "We have said thousands of times 'We know' *(gignōuskomen),* 'we don't know,' and 'we have scientific knowledge' *(epistametha),* and 'we don't have scientific knowledge,' as if we were understanding *(sunientes)* one another while we still are ignorant *(agnooumen)* of science *(epistēmēn)* (196e1–5)." As a matter of fact, not one of these verbs has occurred at all in their conversation; and Socrates implies as much when he now calls attention to his use of *sunienai* and *agnoein* (196e5–7).[3] What Socrates is referring to, though Theaetetus does not understand, is their conversation. Every time Theaetetus or Socrates has asked a question, he has said, "I do not know this or that in your speech"; and every time either has asked a question, he has also implied, "I know this or that in your speech." The same goes for every answer they have given. As long as the continuity of question and answer is not broken, there has been a mixture of knowledge and ignorance. Socrates' second image tries to formalize the impurity in dialectical knowledge; but it fails to do so because the double state of knowing the image postulates—between use and possession—is not the same as the impurity of simultaneously knowing and not knowing that belongs in the image to "art" and not "science." "Art" denotes the field of some expertise, "science" denotes each and every thing know within that field.[4] It is not surprising, then, that once a number is captured no false opinion proves to be possible, but while a number is being hunted it is. Socrates does not discuss the arithmetician as hunter but the arithmetician as knower. Socrates thus allows for a kind of partial knowing while forbidding it to Theaetetus. How is this possible? Socrates had called one logos the logos of the soul's conversation with itself or the soul's asking and answering questions; and he had called another logos opinion when any answer had separated itself from question and answer. Theaetetus called any true answer, apart from question and answer, science. Socrates implies that anytime any art or science ceases to be a hunting and becomes complete it becomes a false opinion. It becomes a part that parades as a whole. It is phantom wisdom.

When Theaetetus recalls that he heard someone say that knowledge was true opinion with logos, it is almost as if Theaetetus were recalling Socrates' own identification of opinion with logos. By the end of the first argument about this definition, Socrates has shown not only that the elements must be as knowable as the compounds,[5] but that there cannot be a whole that is different from the sum of the parts; but since he has not shown that the parts of a whole are the same as the elements in a whole (i.e., though one is an element in five it is not as one a part of five), he has allowed the soul to be a whole of parts in a sense that eludes Theaetetus. Accordingly, the first account of logos is equivalent to the problem posed by Socrates' own maieutics, that it must handle the soul as a whole if its matter is not to be reduced to speeches in themselves. Socrates then says there are three other possible meanings that logos could have in Theaetetus's definition. The second possible meaning is that logos is that which makes clear one's thought through sound with words and phrases (206d1–2); but though Socrates seems to prove that everyone who has an opinion makes it plain, whether he does it slowly or quickly, he does not argue that everyone can do this with his thought *(dianoia)*, for thought was silent *dialegesthai,* and *dialegesthai* is subject to an art and involves the knowledge of soul, speech, and being.[6] So far from trivial is this capacity to express one's thought that whoever spoke the opinion Theaetetus heard did not make his thought clear (206e6), to say nothing of Socrates' failure to understand what Parmenides said, let alone what he thought (184a1–3; cf. *Sophist* 243a6–b7). Indeed, when Socrates turns to the third possible meaning of "logos," he implies it is in a conversation, since to go through the elements is to answer a question that someone else has put (206e6–207a1). If, then, we insert this correction into the second possible meaning of "logos," "logos" now means either "knowledge of soul" or "knowledge of conversation," and the first two senses of "logos" then sum up the first part of Socrates' maieutics.[7]

The third possible meaning of "logos" is the knowledge of how to put together all the elements of something. We may call this, following the Eleatic Stranger, *sunkritikē.* It consists in the knowledge of how to put together like with like and worse with better. The fourth possible meaning of "logos" is the knowledge of how to give the one differential by means of which one thing is told apart from everything else. We may call this, again following the Eleatic Stranger, *diakritikē.* It consists in the knowledge of how to divide like from like and better from worse. Socrates' cathartics of soul is meant to exemplify a form of this diacritical task; but in fact the fourfold form of the diacritical-syncritical art is nothing but Socrates' presumed knowledge of how to tell true speech from false speech. The four meanings of "logos" thus comprehend the range of Socrates' maieutics. What is the difficulty, then, that Socrates saw which prevented him from claiming to have total wisdom? The difficulty was that within diacritics and syncritics there is the art of arithmetic, and arithmetic and everything that goes along with arithmetic do not fit Socrates' knowledge.

The *Theaetetus* thus ends with a double conclusion. On the one hand, there is lurking within Theaetetus's understanding of arithmetic a double dilution of his own principle, and, on the other, there is lurking within Socrates' maieutics a science that does not need his science even though its way is partly his own way of division and collection. Theaetetus himself had started on this way when he collected numbers into two separate kinds and put a distinctive mark on each; but he could not put a mark on his knowledge and Socrates', any more than Socrates could combine their knowledges even though he could collect and divide them.

Theaetetus had given the following case as an example of false opinion (191b3–6): "Sometimes I, in being acquainted with *(gignōskōn)* Socrates, but seeing at a distance another with whom I am not acquainted, believed him to be Socrates whom I know *(oida)*." This example can readily be applied to what happened in the first part of the dialogue: "The science one knows makes one believe that the science one does not know is the science one knows." It might seem strange, however, that the examples chosen are always of perception and do not rise to the level of science until Socrates and Theaetetus are far into an examination of the third definition, and that Socrates reverts to perception to prove conclusively that true opinion is not knowledge. His counter-example concerns a jury, who on the basis of mere speeches come to a just decision with regard to a matter that requires firsthand evidence. Socrates is about to go on trial. Those who will acquit him do not know Socrates firsthand; they do not know he has an art, which is the cause of the common opinion about his strangeness. Theaetetus had been told the cause and experienced its effect in his own perplexity; but he does not know Socrates the knower, for he has given birth to four phantom images of what Socrates knows: he has given birth to pseudo-wisdoms that image Socrates' knowledge of his own ignorance. Socrates' knowledge arises from a comprehensive reflection on the *doxosophiai* of those he delivers. Once, however, Theaetetus's opinion is separated from himself and treated apart from its cause, it seems that he could never have conceived such an opinion. The very form of the *Theaetetus,* in which conception and delivery are split from opinion and logos, acts as a barrier against solving the issue of false opinion. The conjunctive two of its form stands in the way of the disjunctive two of Socrates' dialectic, in which Socrates and Theaetetus are a couple and question and answer are together. This is the logos of an action.

Within the Platonic corpus, Theaetetus is the only character who is examined twice by two different philosophers. Socrates questions him through Theaetetus's own experiences, the Eleatic Stranger questions him without disillusioning him. Socrates' maieutic art seems designed to induce in Theaetetus moderation; the Eleatic Stranger's image of hunting is designed to induce in Theaetetus courage. The *Theaetetus* ends with the restoration of Theaetetus's mathematical knowledge to himself without his knowing what he does not know; the *Sophist* ends with the problem of sophistry solved through the Stranger's bestowal onto Theaetetus of his future self or that which will fulfill his nature. The *Theaetetus* is concerned with the discovery of what knowledge or wisdom is; the *Sophist* has as its premise that wisdom for man is impossible *(Sophist* 232e6–233a7). The problem Socrates puts to Theaetetus in the *Theaetetus* is assumed to be insoluble in the *Sophist.* The effect of the *Theaetetus* has been to convince Theaetetus that any solution to the problem of knowledge is pseudo-wisdom, but he has been convinced without ever gaining anything but a phantom image of the true problem and by taking Socrates for the sophist. The *Theaetetus* seems to suggest that Theaetetus's ignorance of the true problem and his mistaking Socrates for a sophist are one and the same.

Notes

1. *Anonymer Kommentar zu Platons Theaetet,* ed. H. Diels and W. Schubart (Berlin, 1905), 3.28–35 (p. 4, column 2).

2. This recalls the equivalence of Newton's dynamical equation $F = ma$ to its static representation $F - ma = 0$.

3. In the very first argument with Theaetetus, *sunienai* occurs four times (147a7, b2, 4, 7): they had started off conversing impurely; cf. 208e8. Before Socrates meets Theaetetus, he and Theodorus each use *gignōskein* once (144c4, 5).

4. At 146c7–d1 Theaetetus seems to distinguish *epistēmē* and *technē,* as Aristotle will, by assigning the former to what he learns from Theodorus and the latter to shoemaking and the like; after that, *technē* occurs eighteen times, seven of them in Socrates' discussion of maieutics; at 207c2 *epistēmōn* and *technikos* occur together. Socrates never calls maieutics a science. The suffix *-ikē* occurs eleven times, once of arithmetic and once of music (206b2).

5. *Grammatikē* illustrates perfectly how an art, as a hunting, becomes as science false opinion, if one remarks that the Greek alphabet represents the results of an incomplete science of Greek, let alone of language in general. Since the bonding that occurs after alphabetization occurs only perceptually, Socrates implicitly raises the question whether there is a dianoetic bond of the smear: the *Philebus* is meant to answer this question. *Grammatikē* also illustrates Socrates' observation about *skiagraphēma* (208e8). Our knowledge of *grammatikē* informs

us at what distance we are to stand from Euclides' writing; without such knowledge it becomes a blur of signs that make no sense; but at the "right" distance it gives us the illusion of individuality; it is in fact an atomic species of logographic necessity.

6. Although Socrates begins by speaking of thought *(dianoia)*, by the end of the sentence thought has become opinion *(doxa):* the transformation has been accomplished through an image (206d1–4).

7. At 161e5, immediately after he refers to his own maieutic art, Socrates speaks of the entire business of conversing *(sumpasa hē tou dialegesthai pragmateia).*

SIXTEEN

On Plato's *Sophist*

ONCE THE STRANGER TAKES OVER the discussion at the beginning of the *Sophist* and agrees to discuss the sophist, the statesman, and the philosopher, it is hard to remember that Socrates had arranged to meet with Theodorus, Theaetetus, and young Socrates once more, even after he had left Theaetetus completely barren, at least temporarily, and had encountered resistance from Theodorus to his further participation in any argument that the interval of a single day could not, it seems, have overcome (*Theaetetus* 169c6–7, 183c5–d5). The Stranger's intrusion thus makes us fail to notice that Socrates' only possible interest in the same group would have been in young Socrates, about whom he knows only that he developed with Theaetetus a way of classifying two kinds of number, those with integral square or cube roots and those without. If Socrates had engaged young Socrates in a discussion, and informed Euclides about it in the same way as he had reported his discussion with Theodorus and Theaetetus, we know that Euclides could not have transposed Socrates' report into direct discourse and omitted Socrates' "I said" and "He said." A transposition of the kind Euclides practiced in the *Theaetetus* would have led to the indiscernability of the two Socrateses, since each would have addressed the other as Socrates, and there is no reason to believe that the wiser answers would have consistently belonged to only one of them.

The dialogue between the two Socrateses, which does not occur at dawn on the day after Socrates' appearance before the king-archon, would not perhaps be of any interest if it did not call attention to the characterization of thinking, on which Socrates and the Stranger both agree: Thinking is the silent conversation of the soul with itself (*Theaetetus* 189e4–190a7; *Sophist* 263e3–264a3). A double negation is assigned to thinking; thinking depends in its presentation on the denial of two things that are indispensable for conversation: it must be before another, and it must be spoken. To strip speaking, on the one hand, of its vocalic character is to assign it consonants by themselves and thus to deny it the possibility of any combination of elements, even though the combination of consonants with vowels is that which alone makes it possible to overcome the problem of nonbeing and falsehood (253a4–6), and to strip speaking, on the other, of a second participant in the conversation, is to transform the single speaker into a double thinker, who retains in his doubleness the singular identity of the speaker, and who in going by the same name cannot control the split he needs in himself so that whatever thought one self gives birth to the other self can test "objectively" and not succumb, as fathers do, to favoring his own thoughts because they are his own.

The Stranger's intrusion thus looks like a godsend for both Socrates and Plato. It is a godsend for Plato, since a philosopher of the same caliber as Socrates can continue the discussion in a form that Plato has no trouble transcribing, and it is a godsend for Socrates, since he is not forced to face the true difficulty his own revision of Protagoras had raised, How is thinking possible if the thinker in becoming a double agent becomes thereby a double patient, and whatever he thinks experiences a multiplicative effect that is in no time completely out of his control? Socrates proposes at the beginning of the *Statesman* to examine young Socrates as a means toward his own self-knowledge (257d1–258a6). Whether or not he could have succeeded in such a task, we know that Plato could not have shown him in either his success or failure if he had continued to preserve the non-narrated form of the *Sophist* and the *Statesman.* The missing dialogue *Philosopher,* which would have been the truth of which the *Sophist* and *Statesman* are two phantom images, can never have been written without Plato's reversion to Socrates' or Theodorus's narration of it. If it is hard to conceive of Theodorus as narrator, we are back with a Socratically narrated dialogue, in which the representation of young Socrates through and by Socrates would have effectively concealed the true difficulty. This difficulty has two aspects: the impossibility on the part of Plato of presenting nonimagistically the reality of the philosopher, and the paradox for Socrates that his own thinking necessarily takes an imagistic form as soon as he begins to think about it. Socrates can think in a genuine way as long as he does not think about thinking. Socrates, then, cannot have self-knowledge. Socrates therefore cannot be a philosopher, and the missing *Philosopher* represents not an impossibility for Plato the poet but an impossibility simply. The death of Socrates thus looks like the suicide of philosophy itself.

Plato has so arranged his story that through two divergent paths it ends in silence. One path of silence is that not taken—the conversation between Socrates and young Socrates immediately after Theodorus's return with the two mathematicians. The other path of silence is taken but only partway. The Stranger proposes three discourses, but he delivers only two of them. The third would have been either a speech by himself, in which he would have given the Eleatic version of the philosopher and concealed his own view, or it would have been a speech about the philosopher without being the direct presentation of the philosopher since his discourse would be before others and as audible as any other speech. As an image of thinking (cf. *Theaetetus* 206d1–6), it would have been incapable of getting around itself. It seems, then, that something happens during the *Sophist* that makes the Stranger abandon his original plan and allows Socrates to take over from him and complete his intention of the day before to talk with young Socrates. The Stranger succeeded in clearing the way for the silent return of Socrates by getting rid of the two phantom images of Socrates, the logic-chopper and the moralist, to which he assigns the names "sophist" and "statesman." The *Sophist* and the *Statesman* are two portraits of the Socrates we know, a Socrates who harnesses the quibble in the service of morality. That we do not recognize at once Socrates in his split form testifies to the persuasiveness of Plato, who does not let the seams show. Once, however, Socrates is split, it seems impossible to put him together again, for there is nothing real beyond his double image. As Socrates himself had inadvertently revealed in his self-portrait as midwife, he has the art to assist the young in aborting or giving birth to their thoughts, and he has the art to test the truth of their progeny, but these two arts cannot be one, since no woman gives birth to phantom offspring. The singular Socrates is refuted by his own image. It is only natural, therefore, for Socrates to suggest at the beginning of the *Sophist* that the Stranger has come as a god to punish him. He is finished.

This gloomy reading of the setting of the *Sophist* matches the mood of Theaetetus, who is only saved from despair by looking into the Stranger's face and seeing, according to the Stranger, his own destiny (265d1–e2). Theaetetus reads his own nature in the Stranger's face and thus accepts without argument what he will come to maintain. His reading thus reproduces the problem of thinking, for in his unthinking acceptance of the

Stranger as another while the Stranger is in fact nothing but his future self, Theaetetus reproduces in time the problem of thinking. As the Stranger presents it, the problem is particularly acute, since it is immediately after he opposes irrational nature to rational creation that the Stranger asserts that Theaetetus's nature will on its own accept the creativity of mind. This irrational path to reason seems to be the climax of the unreasonable procedure of the Stranger, who is going to lead Theaetetus without experience to a rational account of nonbeing (234e5–6). Theaetetus is supposed to come to an understanding of the sophist without ever having seen a sophist (239e1). The sophist is going to be deduced by reason. The sophist, we can only guess, is going to be deduced out of reason, and the nonbeing he represents is to be reason's own.

In the first half of the *Sophist,* the Stranger presents himself as a hunter of the hunter sophist; and if the Stranger has an art of hunting, it too must belong to the class of acquisitive arts. Once, however, the sophist is reassigned to the art of making, which the Stranger had originally opposed to that of acquisition, it would seem that the Stranger is the original of which the sophist is the copy (265a4–10). The sophist duplicates in the mode of nonbeing the real acquisitor, the Stranger. Far from being a copycat of the acquisitive ways of the sophist, the Stranger is himself the model for the sophist. This turnaround, however, is not exact. The Stranger's way seems to diverge from the sophist's at the division between the hunting of lifeless things and the hunting of animals (219e4–7). Hunting in itself is the hidden hunting for the hidden or elusive beings and applies across the board to what the philosopher as ontologist does; but the hunting by the sophist of rich young men has nothing to do with what the Stranger does but everything to do with what Socrates does. The divergence between the Stranger and the sophist at this point conceals the divergence between the Stranger and Socrates: Socrates is the hidden quarry of the Stranger's pursuit. If, however, Socrates is a philosopher, the Stranger is in pursuit of one of his own kind, who not only does not imitate the Stranger's way but practices the Stranger's hunting of the beings in the hunting of men. Socrates seems to have a double name for this twofold pursuit. The first he calls dialectic, the second erotic. Socrates often leads us to believe that they are mysteriously the same; but if they are the same for Socrates, they are not the same for the Stranger. Socrates flits from genus to genus in the four or five varieties of acquisition, but the Stranger does not accompany him. He is not seeking himself in his double search for Socrates and the sophist. There would thus be a split in philosophy itself that is represented by the Stranger and Socrates. The

Parmenidean Stranger catches Socrates and sets him before the royal speech (235b10–c2). Socrates is to be disposed of by a more comprehensive and less idiosyncratic art.

The way of the Stranger seems to lead to two conclusions. On the one hand, it is not so certain a way as not to mistake the apparitional manifold of the sophist's art for the sophist's art and to get the sophist's art right only on the second try and even then at the high price of bewilderment before the problem of nonbeing, which the Stranger had not recognized when he noticed the resemblance of the sophist to the angler; and, on the other hand, the Stranger's way leaves Socrates behind in fragments, since if he cannot be unified through the notion of production, the philosopher shows up in a genuine manifold within the art of acquisition. This unsatisfactory conclusion would seem to require a critique of the Stranger's way which the Stranger cannot give. His initial success at catching Socrates is worse than his initial failure to catch the sophist. The nonbeing that lurked in his failure coincides with the being that showed up in his success. The Stranger is not prepared for either.

The fifth or sixth division that sits uneasily between his original insight into the sophist as acquisitor and his second view of the sophist as maker has no standing in his almost *(schedon)* perfect division of the arts in two (219a8). In the sixth division he finds in the last cut Socrates, but he puts himself in the first cut. The sixth division thus has at the top the Stranger as the separator *kat' exochēn* and at the bottom Socrates as the purifier. The divider of the beings discovers at the end the cleanser of souls. A diacritical ontology subsumes under itself a psychology. This distinction cannot but remind us of the *Sophist* and *Statesman* respectively: the Stranger is the philosopher and Socrates the statesman. There is, then, no need for the third dialogue, since as the Stranger remarks to Theaetetus they have already fallen into philosophy in the course of their examination of the sophist (253a6–9). Such an interpretation would entail the demotion of Socrates and the elevation of the Stranger: the Stranger adopts Aristotle's view of Socrates before the fact (*Metaphysics* 987b1–4).

The Stranger's subordination of Socrates to himself along with the implicit claim that his diacritical ontology is the unity of acquisition and production makes one wonder whether the alternative does not lie in the thwarted conversation between Socrates and young Socrates, in which Socrates could have found his true successor in his namesake, who despite his reality would have eluded any representation. The triumph of the Stranger would not be a true triumph, but only the triumph that is compatible with writing and institutions. Socrates would live over against the

Academy. This possibility suggests that the Stranger has not got Socrates dead to rights, but that Socrates slipped away from the final trap. The Stranger admits to Theaetetus that insofar as Theaetetus cannot tell Socrates apart from a sophist the Stranger's sixth division vindicates the view of Socrates (231a4–b2), that the sophist is a phantom image of the true philosopher, and Theaetetus's mistake is necessary. Indeed, if at any point the Stranger can isolate the sophist from the philosopher for the nonphilosopher Theaetetus, then and only then is Socrates refuted. It looks, then, as if the confinement of the sophist to the mode of production must give way to the establishment of the being of nonbeing, that is, to the necessity of the intertwining of being with nonbeing.

Since Theaetetus has never seen a sophist and nevertheless believes that the description of soul-cathartics resembles the sophistic art, Theaetetus must have taken Socrates for a sophist, for not only does Socrates' maieutics correspond fairly closely to soul-cathartics, but Theaetetus's own experience of his ignorance through Socrates agrees with the Stranger's account, particularly since Theaetetus's attribution of the highest state of moderation to one so purified echoes Socrates' claim about Theaetetus's moderate condition at the end of the *Theaetetus* (*Sophist* 230d5; *Theaetetus* 210c3). The *Theaetetus,* then, parallels to some extent the *Sophist,* and if the philosopher would have been discussed by Socrates and young Socrates, then the Stranger's third discourse in its absence is the same as Socrates' second conversation in its absence. The situation, then, is this:

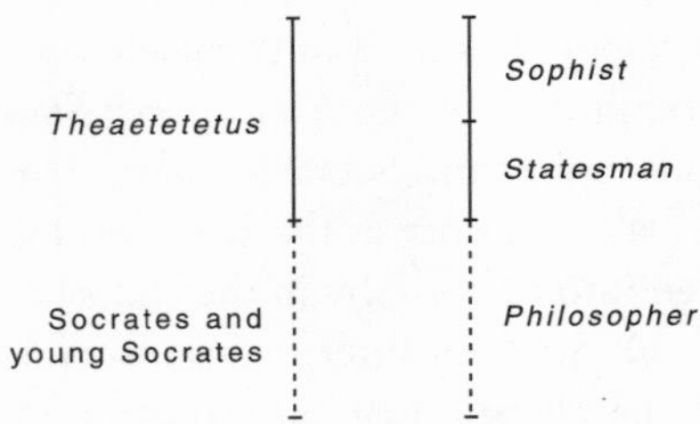

If this scheme is right, the Stranger must have split through his diacritical ontology the unity of Socratic dialectic (maieutic-erotic) of the *Theaetetus.* The *Sophist* and *Statesman* are the two *phantasmata* of the *Theaetetus.* What, then, is the *Theaetetus*? Why is it not the missing *Philosopher* all by itself? If it is not the *Philosopher,* but as much an image of it as Theaetetus is of Socrates, how does it differ as an image from its twofold image, the *Sophist* and *Statesman*? If Socrates is sitting for his portrait in the *Sophist* and *Statesman,* what is missing from the portrait in the *Theaetetus*? If Euclides had preserved Socrates' original narrative, the *Theaetetus* would have been something like a self-portrait. Do the *Sophist* and *Statesman* make up for Euclides' decision to get rid of Socrates' perspective? If they do, why do "I said" and "He said" undergo the transformation into different dialogues with two different interlocutors? If the *Sophist* is to the *Statesman* as rationalism is to empiricism, in the sense that the sophist is to be deduced in the former without the intervention of experiences, particularly of sight, and the statesman is to be induced in the latter in young Socrates' endurance of political practice, there is obviously a way in which Theaetetus's experience of false births in the context of the discovery of logos as that which sets apart knowledge from true opinion reproduces the duality of the *Statesman* and the *Sophist.*

If the philosopher cannot thematize himself but must be thematized by another, the Stranger seems initially to disagree with Socrates as to how this can be done. Socrates says that his own thematization must show up in two separated apparitions; the Stranger says that the school of Parmenides holds that a separate account of the philosopher is possible. The evidence Plato left us tells us that the Stranger is mistaken. If he realized his mistake, he must have done so during the discussion of either the sophist or the statesman; but on the basis of his admission that he is about to commit philosophical patricide (241d3–8), he realizes his mistake at the point where Theaetetus cannot tell Socrates apart from the sophist, and therefore nonbeing must be if Theaetetus' error is to be grounded in something more than an accidental inadvertence. It is hard to believe, however, that the Stranger had not foreseen this crisis from the start, since he declares that he had long broken with the Parmenidean doctrine of his youth (239b1–3, 242a7–8). The Stranger, then, is deliberately set on a path of illusion; he knew that his *diairesis* would not give a logos of the sophist. The Stranger proceeds deliberately into error. He makes error an indispensable part of the way of truth. This way of truth consists in the apparent borrowing of the thematized term "hunting," so that it necessarily appears as parasitic while it is in fact the original host. As apparently parasitic it cannot, as apparently nonparasitic it can, be thematized. Is this, however, a special case of the inversion of priority, or do such inversions hold everywhere? If they do, then the Stranger's schematism—simple paradigm and complex copy—must be the paradigm for any philosophical procedure: the paradigm must break down, and only after it has broken down does "true" philosophy begin. "True" must be bracketed because if such a procedure is necessary, the "false" paradigmatic beginning is part of philosophy. The *Sophist,* then, if it approaches as closely as possible to the thematization of philosophy, must do so very late in its examination. The true beginning of philosophy is precisely at that point where the Stranger ends his discussion of pre-Socratic philosophers and begins again with the problem of logos (251e7). It is at that point where the Stranger and Socrates merge and proceed from thence forward in step until the end of the *Statesman.*

The actual conditions for the conversation between the two Socrateses precludes its being written up; but the alternative, that Theodorus did not bring the Stranger with him, seems to allow for a Socratically narrated dialogue in which philosophy would be the subject. If we should then ask what occasion would have led to such a topic, it would seem at first as if we cannot dictate whatever Plato would have found most appropriate; but on reflection the germ from which Socrates could most plainly start would have been a discussion of Theaetetus's errors in the *Theaetetus,* of which the two most conspicuous were his failure to see how to generalize his first answer—knowledge is knowledge of whatever is measurable and numerable—and his failure to see that "through speeches" is the answer to Socrates' question, Through what does the soul handle being and non-being? (185c9–e2). Theaetetus's first failure blinded him to the issue behind Socrates' description of soul-maieutics—how can knowledge of number and measure be put together with knowledge of soul?—and his second failure blinded him to the manner in which the discussion of speech omitted the kind of speech Socrates and Theaetetus were employing in the discussion. A conversation, then, between Socrates and young Socrates, if it had begun with the failure of the *Theaetetus,* would have thematized philosophy. This thematization had in fact already occurred, since Socrates, in narrating the dialogue he had with Theodorus and Theaetetus, would have thematized philosophy, inasmuch as his representation of Theaetetus through himself had put Theaetetus in the proper perspective. Euclides had wiped out that perspective as soon as he wiped away all traces of perspective: Euclides cut himself out of the picture and thus claimed for himself a position outside of space and time from which he could survey everyone else and cast no shadow of his own. If this argument is found plausible, then the missing dialogue *Philosopher* is as latent in the *Theaetetus* as it is in all other dialogues. This latency cannot be developed in the light directly; it must undergo a split along the lines of the *Sophist* and *Statesman,* which are in turn present at least in every other dialogue. Whether they are present in each other is another question.

Perhaps the most perplexing omission in the *Sophist* occurs at this point: the Stranger gives an account of the painter's art, by means of which all things are imitated and in being exhibited to the foolish young at a distance deceive them into the belief that the paintings are the beings and the painter competent to make the beings themselves. The Stranger then gets Theaetetus to agree that there could be a parallel art in speech, so that the sophist, in showing spoken phantoms *(eidōla legomena)* to the young, who are still at a distance from the truth of things *(ta pragmata)*, would be believed to be speaking the truth and be the wisest in everything (234c2–e4). Even apart from the puzzle of the inversion in the parallel, whereby the distance of the young from the paintings becomes the distance of the young from the truth of things, and Theaetetus has to agree that he is the believer in the phantom speeches of the sophist before becoming disillusioned by direct contact with the beings, the Stranger gets Theaetetus to agree on a possible art of imitation through speeches without ever exemplifying what a spoken phantom is. When, moreover, the Stranger proceeds to divide the art of image-making into eikastics and phantastics, he does so again on the basis of painting and does not stop, before he plunges into the problem of being and nonbeing, to illustrate the difference between an eikastic and phantastic speech. We seem to be left on our own to devise a sense for *eidōla legomena* that would ground the Stranger's argument. Our task is in a sense made easy by the existence of the *Sophist.* That is obviously a case of phantom speech, but we have no way of knowing whether it was produced by eikastics or phantastics unless we can determine what we mean by calling it an imitation. If, however, Plato emerges as the master sophist, how is not the whole argument of the Stranger undermined, if the philosopher Plato shows up apparitionally as the nonphilosopher and the philosopher Stranger as his finest product? In looking outside the dialogue, we detect the *phantastikos* Plato; in looking into the dialogue, we find the philosopher pure and simple. Once, however, we incorporate the perspective we gained from the outside into the inside, the Stranger is a phantom philosopher or sophist, who catches the pseudo-sophist, that is, the sophist who is not an apparition of the philosopher. Theaetetus at any rate declares the sophist to be the impersonator of the wise (268b10), and whoever the wise is, whether god the maker or the wise simply, he is not the philosopher.

The difficult position into which Plato put the Stranger seems to prove that philosophy cannot be thematized without undergoing a transformation into an apparition of itself. Plato thereby vindicates Socrates' view of the relation between the philosopher and the sophist and denies any validity to the Parmenidean view the Stranger was asked to expound.

Before, however, we claim to find the truth about the sophist solely in the form of the *Sophist,* Plato has not left the Stranger without his own way of exemplifying the problem of spoken phantoms, even if Theaetetus is put in the funny position of following an argument he cannot follow except in the image of spoken phantoms—images in deed. Up to the point where the Stranger turns to the analysis of image-making, hunting and pursuit dominate his language and align what he is doing with what the sophist does. Of words with *-thēr-* in the *Sophist,* forty-seven occur before 235a11 and two afterward, first when the Stranger recalls his remark that the sophist was hard to catch *(dusthēreuton),* and then when he summarizes the kinds of acquisitive arts they had first assigned to the sophist (261a5, 265a7). What happens then in the course of the *Sophist* is a reflection on its starting point in the doubling of the image of hunting in the action of the sophist and the Stranger. His controlling paradigm is thus subject to a double critique: what grounds his discovery of the kinship between angler and sophist, and what grounds his understanding of what he is doing in the same terms? Theaetetus is at first reluctant to admit that there is a hunting of men (222b6), but he does not notice that while the sophist hunts men, he and the Stranger hunt the beast sophist. The image of hunting is more literal on the level of the Stranger's method than on the sophist's. The Stranger thus denies what Theaetetus had accepted—men are tame and there is a hunting of them—by making the sophist a wild animal that they are to turn over to the royal speech.

If, then, a spoken phantom is exemplified by the sophist and the Stranger as hunters, the Stranger is asking, in generalizing the issue of his own language, whether images in speech necessarily involve deception, or the nonbeing of spoken images entails falsehood, and whether it is not possible to proceed in one's understanding without any recourse to images. When the Stranger began by saying that the sophist was not the easiest to grasp *(sullabein),* that he believed the genus of the sophist was hard to hunt down *(dusthēreuton),* and that he knew of no easier way *(hodos)* than to practice the sophist's pursuit *(methodos)* on an easier subject (218c6, d3, 6–7), there was no reason for Theaetetus to galvanize his language back into life and anticipate the Stranger's exploitation of expressions that he could have as easily let fade away in the course of the discussion. Phantom images in speech thus seem to be a difficulty of the Stranger's own creation, so that whereas he has to face the problem of image-making in speech, the sophist does not, since the sophist after all does not have to accept the Stranger's picture of himself. The sophist can go about his business without ever entangling himself in an image. He would thus argue that his own spuriousness arises from the invention of the Stranger, and the Stranger has to account for himself without a shred of evidence that the sophist ever resorts to images in speech.

How easy it would have been to dispense with the Stranger's language can be seen if one reflects on the structure of his first example, the art of angling. The division falls into three sections, with three items in each. The first section establishes the manner of the art—it is a kind of hunting; the second establishes the object of the art—fish; and the third establishes the means employed to catch the fish—hook and line. The Stranger's example, then, could have been generalized at once, and the sophist's art determined by its manner, object, and means, and there would have been no need to bring hunting to bear on either the sophist's or the Stranger's activity. The paradigm of the angler allowed for the scaffolding on which the Stranger's image-making to be dismantled without any loss to the inquiry or any distraction from it.

If, then, the sophist had been confronted straight-on with this threefold question—how, what, and by what means—he could have been said to lure young men by means of speeches. To be sure, he could not have been distinguished thereby from Socrates, but that, according to Socrates, is as it should be. Why, then, does the Stranger get himself involved in a series of definitions that, he claims, cannot be unified except through the notion of phantom speeches? A possible explanation can be found in the observation that Theaetetus has never seen a sophist and has no experience of the disillusionment that comes from experience after living in the world of phantom speeches. Through the Stranger's literalization of language, he represents to Theaetetus a world of phantom speeches, which Theaetetus recognizes as such when he realizes the impossibility of discovering the sophist's unity in the manifold of his different arts. Within the dialogue and through experience in speech alone, the Stranger gives Theaetetus an image in speech of what is entailed in the experience of things. The disillusionment of reality is presented in an image. The Stranger thus implies that the fundamental experience of the beings which most men undergo after their initial distance from them is the discovery of this principle: Everything is just what it is and nothing else. This principle is enshrined in the formula, a being is that which does not stand in need of another. The ones of phantom speech are shown to be phantoms as soon as they submit to analysis. This atomism, whether material or ideal, has as its corollary that to be is to be countable. It thus links up with the implicit definition of knowledge, at least in part, which Theaetetus first offered Socrates.

The starting point of the Stranger thus reaches back to the beginning of the *Theaetetus* and goes forward to his examination of the philosophers who count the beings. The problem of nonbeing, which comes to light through a manifold that can be shown to be one only if nonbeing is, leads to the problem of being, in which it turns out that there can be no stable counting of the beings, regardless of whether there is to be only one or more than one. Initially, every manifold that was designated by a single name betrayed the presence of appearance and the failure to get at what something is; but the impossibility of keeping to the original count in the case of the beings entailed that it was not appearance that multiplied unity but being itself was infected with the same multiplicative virus. The Stranger's solution to this ontological crisis is to incorporate nonbeing into being as the other. The other is designed to cure three things simultaneously. Being is no longer countable, or nothing is just what it is and nothing else; appearances are a reflection of nonunitary being; and false speech still consists in saying what is not, even though it is always speaking of that which is. Whether in fact the other does solve all three problems, it puts the Stranger's artificial phantom image in speech of the sophist in a new light. The discovery of the manifold beneath the illusory one of the sophistic art, where each art is just what it is, is the inverse of the truth. The sophist, in his being always the other, is the mark of what is. The Stranger had prepared us for this inversion by speaking of the truth of things *(ta pragmata),* and not the truth of the beings *(ta onta),* as that from which the young stand far removed (234c4). To grasp the beings in all their vividness through experiences is not necessarily to grasp the truth of the beings.

If the sophist is the sign of being as the other, and therefore it is not inappropriate for the Stranger to be the philosopher in being his hunter, he still is not the only other in the *Sophist.* The threefold question Socrates raises happens to coincide not only with three discourses the Stranger can recite off the top of his head but the question Theodorus, Theaetetus, and young Socrates asked the Stranger sometime between the end of the *Theaetetus* and their meeting with Socrates (217b4–8). Whatever we may think of this coincidence—Theodorus's distress at the going-over he received from Socrates (*Theaetetus* 169a6–c6), reinforced as it was by Theaetetus's futile answers, might well have prompted him to question an authority about Socrates—we know that neither the Stranger nor Theodorus came to the question in the same way as Socrates did. Socrates' way into the question began with his tweaking Theodorus for his possible failure to recognize the Stranger as a god in disguise. In reply Theodorus distinguished between "godlike" *(theios)* and "god," or between philosopher and god (216b9–c1). Philosopher and god are not two of a kind. Socrates replied that the philosopher too has his apparitions, or that "philosopherlike" applies no less to sophist than to statesman. Since, however, Socrates continued to employ his Homeric citations even after Theodorus's denial, he implied that "philosopher" and "god" are the same, or, to follow Socrates more exactly, the philosopher belongs to the genus to which god belongs.[1]

Socrates was led to this possibility by Theodorus's introduction of a philosopher as a nameless stranger. He turned a typical piece of indifference to the human-all-too-human on Theodorus's part into a general question—Who could possibly be of necessity forever nameless and a stranger?—and gave the answer, "A god." Gods can never become our acquaintances *(gnōrimoi);* they must always remain outside whatever group, large or small, we belong to. "God," then, is the other as such. As the other, he is not merely something else *(allo ti),* but he is attached to that of which he is the other because he is the other. As the other, god is not subject to a wholly negative theology; man too is the other, for he is the other of that other. The indeterminate pair that god and man constitute makes one wonder whether the *Sophist* and the *Statesman* are not the same pair in its apparitional form. The *Statesman* cannot determine the politician without separating him from god the ruler and from man the political animal; and the *Sophist* puts the sophist in his place only through the notion of god the rational maker. Mind as efficient cause thus emerges as the apparition of god as the other. God sets the structure of making but is divorced from the structure of acquisition, at the head of which would be the knowing ignorance of the philosopher. God, then, is as apparitional as the sophist, and he is other than the philosopher when he appears as maker. Socrates had opposed the Stranger as a punishing god to himself. The Stranger asserts in the myth of the *Statesman* that there cannot be a punishing god; indeed, he denies that Zeus is a name for god, since the age of Zeus stands for the time when the god has let go of the universe and it is on its own. Zeus is a concealed negation; it means "not-god" or "without god." God with a name designates "not-god." He is the other of the other.

The Stranger and the sophist compete for the title of the other, one as god, one as beast. Both are outside the circle and yet they are not apart from man. Indeed, if man as such is not a third between beast and god, then the Stranger and the sophist cover all that man is. Man, then, would emerge as the other *kat' exochēn:* he is the primary piece of evidence for the denial that there is anything which is just what it is. Man becomes exemplary of being once the highest being is a defective being, and, as the Stranger later says, there is no part of nonbeing that is any less than any being (258a7–b3). That man is an issue, and perhaps even the issue, behind Socrates' question is already foreshadowed in the *Theaetetus.* Socrates there tried to get at the question of philosophy through the question, What is knowledge? The necessity for philosophy emerges if it can be shown that knowledge or wisdom is impossible (*Theaetetus* 145e5); and it can be shown to be impossible if there is an obstacle to wisdom for man as man. This obstacle must take the following form: knowledge consists of two or more kinds that cannot be understood as an apparitional manifold. Each is just what it is even though each is knowledge. Protagoras's "Man the measure" is not an answer to the question of knowledge but its enigmatic representation. Socrates with his knowledge and Theaetetus with his are together the same enigma; but they cannot be together because there is no "vocalic" bond between them. When Socrates first formulates a version of the Protagorean thesis, he asks two questions about its meaning—"Does it state that what sort each several thing appears to me such are they for me, and what sort to you, such in turn for you, and you and I [are] man?"—Theaetetus answers the first question and does not notice the second (152a6–9). In particular Theaetetus does not notice that in Socrates' second question a plural subject has a singular predicate, and there is no copula. Socrates and Theaetetus are severally man, but they are not anything together. The determination of man as the vocalic bond between beast and god can be said to be the theme of the *Sophist* and the *Statesman.*

In the course of his setting out his model for definition, the Stranger consistently presents the undivided class as suffixed with *-ikon* but never with *-ikē,* with which *technē* is either expressed or implied. The *-ikē* suffix occurs only after a class has been divided. The Stranger's language thus duplicates the historical development of the suffix from being an ethnic to a skill, which we know occurred very rapidly toward the end of the fifth century.[2] The Stranger indicates thereby that there is no art for the undivided species but only for the atomic class. There is no art of hooking *(asgkistreutikon),* but only of its two species, *triodontia* and *aspalieutikē.* Art implies specialization, and until one gets to the smallest division of labor there is an element of inexpertness that lurks in any general action. The Stranger's starting-point, "art," is misleading, for if one looks to the man who could possibly do all the things the manifold of arts do, one would not find the artisan but the jack-of-all-trades. "Sophist" or "Mr.

Know-it-all" necessarily looks spurious once the arts have developed in the way that Socrates assumes in the *Republic,* where the original house-builder soon gives way to the lumberman, the carpenter, the blacksmith, etc. The Stranger, in implying, for example, that there is an art of striking *(plēktikē),* from which the arts of spearing and angling split off, is going against the truth of the arts and laying himself open to the charge of making phantoms of the real.

Long before, then, the Stranger sets the sophist in the class of image-making, he has been employing the art of image-making in order to establish the kinship among the various arts to which we give the same label, sophistic. The way of discovery is productive in the class of acquisition; and the Stranger in being the hunter of the hunter-sophist uses as his nets those made up by the poetic art. The Stranger, then, practices versions of the sophist's two ways, but in neither version does he duplicate exactly the sophist. For the Stranger, hunting is a way of understanding; it assumes that the beings are not out in the open, and the way to bring them out is to illuminate them in a series of images. The Stranger's art of the image seems to be eikastics, for he is not setting things out to show them as beautiful; lice-hunting, he says, serves as well as generalship for hunting (227a9–b6). But the Stranger's art of hunting does seem to be due to phantastics, for it seems to be adjusted to Theaetetus, who is to pass for manly and brave in following the track of the sophist. Eikastics, then, is to phantastics as ontology is to psychology. If philosophy in general takes after the Stranger's double way, philosophy in its ontological aspect is not guided by anything. Its images are of its own devising and not grounded in the nature of things. In its psychology, however, there is the nature of Theaetetus, which in its moderation calls on its own for its proper corrective, just as young Socrates' boldness demands domestication through the womanly art of weaving.

Between his catching Socrates and the sophist together and his isolating the sophist in the class of making, the Stranger inserts a classification of arts that puts him and Socrates together and excludes the sophist. He begins this classification with a set of verbs that belong to the actions of several arts (226b5–c9). In labeling their common action "dividing," he shows us what he himself has been doing all along, collecting and dividing; but it is typical of the *Sophist* that the diacritical function is stressed, and it is not until the *Statesman* that its syncritical counterpart is mentioned (282b7). However that may be, the Stranger applies the single name of the diacritical art to what is done in sifting flour or carding wool. No specialist art, however, practices diacritics in itself, only the Stranger does so whenever he proceeds to cut any class in two. The Stranger comes partly into the light in these first two steps. *Sunkrinein* and *diakrinein* are the first verbs that in being comprehensive refer at the same time to particular actions. The undivided species is no longer an image of the arts in its subsets but an art in its own right. The collapse of the ethnic suffix *-ikon* into the art-suffix *-ikē* is comparable, and perhaps ultimately identical, with Socrates' persistence in refusing to separate *dialegesthai* from *dialektikē*. It is therefore surprising that the Stranger can discover a version of Socratic dialectics in a genealogical descent from *diakritikē* with which it does not link up in any obvious way.

If we start at the conclusion of his dividings, the Stranger there opposes soul-cathartics to the art of admonition that fathers practice on their sons. Since, however, those who discovered soul-cathartics started from a premise that the admonitory art rejected—every kind of folly was involuntary—and the admonitory art had long been in place before the discovery of soul-cathartics, education *(paideia)* cannot be split between an artless and an artful form. If, however, soul-cathartics moves up a level and becomes identical with education, Theaetetus must be mistaken in labeling a Socratic insight an Athenian practice (229d2). Theaetetus calls education that art which gets rid of the belief on the part of one who does not know that he knows; but that *doxosophia* is the peculiar obstacle to learning belongs to soul-cathartics and has nothing but language in common with a father's rebuke to his son, "You think you're so smart." If now, however, Socrates' way takes over as the true form of education, it is not obvious that the art of instruction *(didaskalikē)* treats two different kinds of ignorance *(agnoia)*, since the premise of the psychic counterpart to gymnastics is that every soul is involuntarily ignorant of everything (228c7–9). Theaetetus's distinction between education and demiurgic instruction cannot be maintained if the basis of the latter is mathematics, for it seems to be equally at home with education in either the ordinary or Socratic sense. If, then, soul-cathartics now treats the ugliness of soul per se, it cannot be kept out of the treatment of the illness of soul, since the Stranger ascribes to the conflict of opinions in the soul a source of its illness and assigns to soul-cathartics the task of bringing to light the conflict of opinions in the soul (228b1–4, 230b5–8). Soul-cathartics, then, takes over as the entire treatment of soul, for the Stranger's divisions have been in accordance with opinion and therefore incoherent. Soul-cathartics, however, cannot be pegged at this point either, for in order to get to the soul the Stranger had to separate the soul from the body, regardless of whether the body was ensouled or not; but such a separation of the soul from the body is nothing other than the practice of dying and being dead, which is another name for philosophy.

Even if we grant the Stranger's cut between soul and body as nothing more than a "theoretical" division, he cannot go on to split the vices of soul on the basis of a split in the vices of body without granting the body, in its apartness from soul, a theoretical determination of this structure of soul. The Stranger, moreover, identifies the soul in its separation from body as thought (*dianoia,* 227c4); and thought cannot be subject to a distinction between moral and intellectual virtue, upon which the Stranger's counterparts to medicine and gymnastics depend.[3] There is the further difficulty that though the soul is supposed to have an impulse toward truth, there is no argument that the soul has either a natural strength to attain truth or the capacity to accept the steroids of art. Indeed, soul-cathartics is described wholly in terms of medicine and not as capable of instilling beauty and strength of soul. Theaetetus indeed said that it produced the most moderate of states, but according to Theaetetus moderation should be the contrary of intemperance *(akolasia)* and therefore subject to the punishing art of *Dikē* (228e1–229a7). If, then, the Stranger's separation of soul and body cannot stand as he phrased it, soul-cathartics is now threatening the division in the arts of purification, for soul-cathartics must now have a diacritical function if it is to understand soul by itself before treating it. The Stranger's first division in the diacritical art had been between an unnamed art of separating like from like and the purificatory art of separating better from worse (226d1–5). This unnamed art is nothing but the Stranger's own procedure and identical with what soul-cathartics must also practice. It thus turns out that Socrates, rather than being a subordinate of the Stranger, usurps the Stranger's role and corrects the Stranger's divisions in light of his own resolution of the contradictory opinions at the heart of the Stranger's diacritical ontology. It now turns out that the example of spoken phantoms is that division of the Stranger's where he and Socrates both are. Its plausibility to Theaetetus is a sign of its phantom character. It is Theaetetus, after all, who insists that the Stranger's fear of confusing the sophist and the philosopher be set aside and Socrates be condemned for sophistry through a semblance (231a1–5).

Perhaps the most curious consequence of the Stranger's analysis is that Socrates' way is correctly characterized but falsely categorized. The truth is hit upon in and through a false structure. This structure is the Stranger's way, which produced the philosopher in a setting that gave him the appearance of the sophist. It is, then, the Stranger's way that fully exemplifies *phantastikē.* Previously we had thought that the Stranger's way was eikastic, since the classes he had found were the products of his own image-making; but now, in involving himself in his own classification of an art—*diakritikē*—he adopts simultaneously the perspective of Theaetetus and betrays Socrates. The Stranger's *phantastikē* corresponds rather exactly to the one he ascribes to painting, for in that case the painter makes the image ugly in order for it to appear beautiful, and here Socrates appears as completely successful, with everyone angry only at themselves and tame toward everyone else (230b8–9). The Stranger's beautification of Socrates seems to be self-defeating; it does not keep Socrates from being identified as a sophist but rather convinces Theaetetus that he is a sophist. Theaetetus cannot tell apart the elusive sophist from the beautiful Socrates. The eikastics of the Stranger's first divisions are in agreement with the phantastics of his last: the Socrates who lurks in the rejected species of acquisition—he showed up finally as the money-losing chatterbox (225d7–10)—comes into the light of opinion as the same as his own apparition. As long as Socrates is hidden in the rejected species of the Stranger's way, he is safe from being misidentified; but as soon as the Stranger sets out to stalk him alone—Socrates is like the retailer who stays at home and sells what he himself contrives (224d4–e4)—he cannot show him as he really is. It is through a set of un-Socratic distinctions that Socrates becomes as pretty as a picture.

II

At the very moment that the Stranger will abandon the image of hunting—he has just established the sophist as imitator—he becomes particularly exuberant in the exploitation of the image of hunting: "It is our job from this point forward no longer to let up on the beast *(thēra),* for we have pretty nearly encompassed *(perieilēphamen)* him in a certain kind of net *(amphiblēstrikōi tini)* that is instrumental in speeches for things of this kind (235a10–b2)." It seems, then, that we are being given a spoken phantom just before the Stranger confronts the problem of image; but it cannot be overstressed that we are given it and not Theaetetus: Theaetetus plunges into a discussion of *eidōla legomena* without having any clue as to what they are. They are there in the Stranger's language, no less than they are in Theaetetus's, but they are never brought up to the level of the argument. The one exception to this blanket concealment proves that it is not an exception. The Stranger remarks that the sophist is really *(ontōs)* amazing and very difficult to be caught sight of, and Theaetetus replies, "It seems" (*eoiken,* 236d4). The Stranger pounces on this *eoiken* without ever saying that that is what makes him suspect that Theaetetus is just going along with him and does not really recognize the problem. The Stranger is saying that unless words are taken literally their use betrays a failure to understand. Are we then to understand the Stranger's "encompassed" *(perieilēphamen)* literally? If we do, the Stranger agrees with the body-people who deny that anything is which they cannot get both their hands on (*tais khersin atekhnōs petras kai drus perilambanontes,* 246a8; cf. 265a10). And when the Stranger remarks that it was truly said that the sophist-beast was complex and not, as the saying goes, to be seized with one hand, Theaetetus's reply, "Then we have to with both" (226a8), must again be literal, and their hunting down of Socrates is not just a manner of speaking but truly means his arrest and execution. It is possible, then, to read the *Sophist* as the execution in deed of Socrates' premonition, that the Stranger has come to punish him for the poorness of his speeches, and it is no less possible to read the problem of spoken phantoms as implicitly claiming a privileged position for the identity of being and body, which is preserved as a relic in any language but which is still capable of being recovered through the pruning away of all the idealistic excrescences that a language assumes over time. Socrates, therefore, would be the appropriate target since his "philosophy" stands or falls by the priority or nonpriority of soul to body.

An immediate advantage of reading the *Sophist* in this way would be the explanation it would offer for the Stranger's silence about the meaning of *eidōla legomena. Eidōla legomena* would be language itself, which would be constantly expanding away from its literal roots and adding thereby images of bodies to the language of bodies. The sophist, then, would be each and every nonmaterialist philosopher, from Parmenides to the friends of the ideas, anyone in short who claimed either that virtue was something else than ingrained habits of the body or that numbers exist. To give to the Stranger's use of hunting a significant role would be pointless: almost any speech would betray its corporeal basis. The Stranger's elaboration of image-making in the painting done by eikastics and phantastics would thus represent the real part of imitation; all the rest would be derivative from it and as such a sign of its spuriousness. Indeed, the Stranger could not get at soul-cathartics without returning to the difference between the health and beauty of the body, and he had only confused the issue by interpolating the *stasis* of the city as a way of accounting for what he meant by illness (228a4–9).

The reductionist program that this reading of the *Sophist* suggests cannot, I think, stand up to scrutiny; but it does reinforce the peculiarity of the dialogue, where the Stranger's failure to explicate the difference between eikastic and phantastic speech entices us to a reading of everything he says in light of the body. The body is the background against which we understand what he is saying. It is therefore of the highest importance that the Stranger at the end confines the sophist to being an impersonator in his body of what he seems to know. The sophist is the sophist precisely because the noncorporeal is made corporeal and passed off as noncorporeal. The sophist embodies what in its truth cannot be embodied. He is merely a higher version of vulgar or political virtue, which mistakes images of the body for traits of the soul (cf. *Republic* 518d9–e2). The Stranger, then, must ultimately give an argument for turning language upside-down, so that the nonliteral language of soul can stand independently of its literal meaning. The argument must ground the phantastics of speech in something other than the being of body. If the argument can do so, we can then say that the Stranger fails to exemplify his meaning not because it is plain in everything he says but because it is truly hidden in everything he says. The *Sophist* is a vindication of this remark in the *Statesman:* "The bodiless things, being most beautiful and greatest, are shown plainly only in speeches and in nothing else (286a5–7)."

In order to solve the specific problem—the distinction between eikastic and phantastic speech—the Stranger has recourse to well-known philosophic issues: appearance, false opinion, and nonbeing (236e1–237a1). The specific problem seems to get lost in the Stranger's review of various answers to the philosophic issues. His experience of the perplexity of being and nonbeing takes over from Theaetetus's innocence, and from his unawareness that it was his failure to detect the difference between Socrates and the sophist that confirmed the existence of *phantastikē* in speech and supplied the evidence of its power. A series of divisions in speech was made by way of images that led to the impossibility of telling apart beast from nonbeast (nonbeast covers both god and human); but their indiscernability is nothing but an exemplification of the sophist's art of *phantastikē.* The Stranger claims he knows that the being his argument detected was the philosopher, but he cannot convince Theaetetus that he is any different from the previous series of atomic species. The very parallel between painting in deed and painting in speech seems to imply that experience, which diminishes the distance the young stand from the beings, cannot be duplicated in speech. If speech could in fact overcome the distance of innocence, one could speak of speeches in deed: "the hard facts of life" would have their equivalent in speech. We know that tragedy does have this effect with regard to the passions; but we do not know whether there is a rational counterpart. If the Platonic dialogues were such a counterpart, it would be necessary that through their speeches one would experience a turnaround of their several arguments. The Platonic dialogues would be governed by a *phantastikē* by means of which we would get nearer to the beings without ever abandoning the level of speech. For the Stranger, the Parmenidean speech, and ultimately all the speeches of philosophers up to now, are *phantasmata* in speech at a distance from the beings in speech. He proposes to narrow the distance Theaetetus stands from the beings by leading him from on high to where he is, but all within the element of speech. This movement is the Stranger's version of Socrates' second sailing, which consists in the realization that the beings are plainer to us in speeches than in deeds. The autobiography of the Stranger records for being what Socrates' does for becoming or causality; but despite this difference they are the same experientially.

In order to get at the problem of nonbeing, the Stranger establishes the arithmetical character of being and any speech about being. The characteristic prefix of his argument is *pros,* "in addition." Being is countable, nonbeing is not. It turns out, however, that the arithmetical structure of *logos* forbids the use of *logos* to show the nonsense of nonbeing, since *logos* cannot treat nonbeing if it does not give nonbeing an arithmetical structure that it then shows it cannot have. The sophist, then, if he is who he is through nonbeing, is always immune from attack. Why, however, must the sophist be assumed to have recourse to nonbeing? The sophist's claim is that he has a single science of everything. Theaetetus believes that the issue is the sophist's claim to know everything (233a3–4); his denial of that claim is not backed up by any argument, but if there were an argument, it would have to take the form of a proof that the parts of knowledge of which we are aware are two or more with two or more essentially different sets of principles, and that the sophist is involved in nonbeing and image-making by his assimilation of every other part of knowledge to one part with its unique set of principles or the comprehension of all the parts of knowledge to some unknown knowledge with an unknown set of principles. The ways of assimilation and comprehension both involve image-making. Theaetetus is asked what an image is; he speaks of images in mirrors, paintings, and statues. The Stranger asks him to imagine that the sophist is blind and that he wants a characteristic of image that does not appeal to sight. Theaetetus has no trouble in satisfying the blind sophist: whatever is another such *(heteron toiouton)* likened to the true is an image (240a7–8). Theaetetus makes up a spoken phantom. His criterion for an image in sight is an image in speech. *Heteron toiouton* entails as he says a weaving together of being and nonbeing (240c1). Through this "weaving together" *(sumplokē)* he anticipates the rest of the *Sophist* and the finale of the *Statesman.* Not only does *sumplokē* itself crop up in the Stranger's two characterizations of *logos,* but the prefix *sun* is destined to take over from the Stranger's *pros. Sun* is not subject to an arithmetical account.[4]

If *heteron toiouton* is the characteristic of any eikastic speech, and Theaetetus has no trouble in supplying it, it might seem odd that the Stranger does not follow it up with a comparable demand for the characteristic of a phantastic speech. Instead, he turns to false opinion, whose characteristic, Theaetetus agrees, involves the impossible conjunction of being and nonbeing (241a3–b3). This replacement, however, of phantastic speech by false speech and opinion does not occur; rather, false opinion is nothing but phantastic speech, for false opinion is an experience of the soul that is due to an eikastic speech.[5] There are not two kinds of speech, but there is only one speech and how that one speech appears, or the experience of falsity, that seems to make for two speeches. The experience of falsity is thus to be explained by the being of nonbeing in the image. False opinion consists in the belief that the images of beings are the beings, and—this is something new—the beings are the images of nonbeings. Nonbeings are, however, images of beings. False opinion holds that the images of the images of the beings are the beings; but *phantastikē* was precisely that art that produced images of images of the beings so adjusted to the perspective of the observer that he would take them for the beings. Accordingly, the Stranger has merely enlarged the problem with which he started and not altered it. The Stranger's final division, in which he caught Socrates, was in itself an eikastic speech; it became a phantastic speech at the very moment Theaetetus believed it described the sophist. It was geared for that mistake as well as for its own dismantling, which we did by tracing back the descent of Socrates to his origin in the Stranger. His projection of himself in another (Socrates) appeared to Theaetetus as another such of the sophist; but Socrates was the same as the Stranger and not his image.

The impasse that nonbeing makes for anyone who attempts to deny that it is suggests to the Stranger that the fault lies with an understanding of being, shared by all the philosophers, which has generated a contrary to being out of a fundamental lack of clarity about itself. The Stranger gives an arithmetical character to this misunderstanding, whereby he shows that those who say being is any number, two or more, are forced to reduce their manifold to one, and Parmenides' one in turn cannot be meaningful unless there are at least two. The precise people are opposed to the comprehensives (245e6–246a2), who do not count the beings but characterize being; but the Stranger shows that they must compromise their principles in order to find room for their own understanding, and once they do compromise, either in the direction of nonbody or in the direction of soul, they must declare that being is two and fall into the trap he had already sprung for the precise people. This argument bears directly on the sophistic claim in the following way. It supplies the proof that there is not a single science of everything, for if they were, there would have to be a coherent set of principles that would determine the number of beings. If their number jumps about between one and two, there is something in being that is recalcitrant to the unity of the science of being. The simplest example, perhaps, of the impossibility to keep the count of the beings down to the number one starts with is to be found in atomism. Its principle is, To be is to be body. Body, however, does not allow for motion unless there is space. Space, in turn, is absolute nonbeing if the atomists hold to their principle. They therefore have to weaken their principle if they are to obtain any kind of structure. This difficulty is not confined to atomism. It shows up no less in the *Republic,* where the principle one man/one art cannot establish the class-structure of the city, than in Newtonian mechanics, where the first law of motion assumes inertial frames—there are bodies that are not subject to acceleration—which the principle of gravity denies.[6]

If this is the general strategy of the Stranger—to strengthen the case of the sophist by ruining the case of the philosophers—it still does not tie in directly with the doublet eikastic-phantastic speech, for the explication of which the discussion of being is presumably an indispensable digression. The Stranger says that the philosophers tell stories (242c8–243b1). A typical story combines a count of the beings with an image of becoming, in which the philosopher who tells the story is not part of the story. The Stranger does not criticize this type of philosopher for either talking in images or leaving himself out; but in the case of the comprehensives he tells the story that puts them into one story and makes their being the issue. It thus looks as if the precise ontologists are to the comprehensives as countable being is to epistemology or psychology, for the formula "to be is to be body" really means "to be is to be touchable," and "to be is to be an idea" really means "to be is to be intelligible." The philosophers, then, are presented in such a way that eikastic speech is opposed to phantastic speech, and the Stranger's presentation of phantastic speech is itself eikastic. We can then say that the diacritical ontology of the Stranger which discovered Socratic psychology reappears in the opposition between number and soul. This opposition is at first resolved through the Stranger's proposal that rest and motion both are; but he immediately concludes that this pair must and cannot be one. The Stranger ends up by counting the beings; but his counting does not take into account what he is counting. It assumes that the two are not parts, for if they were parts of one whole, they are not necessarily together what they are apart. The body-people are body-people by themselves; when the Stranger puts them into a story, they become giants, just as the friends of the ideas cease to be nameless once they too are parts of the same story: they become gods. We therefore do not know what happens to motion and rest when they are together; but we do know that the being of the nonbeing of motion must have a cause that is not the being of rest. The absence of any causality in the Stranger's juxtaposition of rest and motion tells us that the Stranger, if he is to go on, must find a way around causality. A recourse to speeches turns out to be the Socratic way out for the Stranger.

The Stranger groups all of philosophical thought under myth, either by accusing the precise people of storytelling or by telling a story himself about gods and giants. He leaves myth behind when he turns to *logos*, which is to be discussed in light of its apparently contradictory way of postulating a one as subject which the manifold of its predicates denies (251a5–6). It is not immediately obvious that the Stranger's example—man and his predicates—is significant; but we cannot but wonder whether there is not a connection between the recourse to speeches and the citation of man, especially since they appear together after his own gigantomachy. Man had first shown up in the separation the friends of the ideas had made between body as that by means of which we partake in becoming through perception, and soul as that by means of which we are in some partnership with being through calculation (248a10–13). Man had then shown up as a possible rival to god, when the Stranger elicited Theaetetus's assent to the proposition that the being which perfectly and completely is must have mind and life in soul (248e6–249b1); but he had not gone on to ask whether soul entailed body. Man, then, is at least in the background of the discussion of *logos*. The *logos* is man's *logos*. His speech is prior to the letters that make up his speech. Its consonants are not in his speech what they are in the alphabet: "body" is the consonant of the alphabet, "ensouled body" is the consonant prior to the alphabet of the friends of the ideas. The Stranger's own alphabet accordingly is very misleading if it is not accompanied by a procedure that informs us how to translate its letters into sounds—its *aphōna* into *sumphōna.* The key to this procedure is provided by the observation that only one of the letters of his alphabet is explained. Being, motion, rest, and the same are manipulated, but nothing is further revealed about them through their manipulations. Only the other emerges with a trait it did not have as an element of the alphabet. The other thus turns out to be not a letter at all but the operator designed to transform all the other letters into sounds. Nonbeing as the other makes for the possibility of *logos.*

In his autobiography in the *Phaedo,* Socrates had compared the looking at the sun during an eclipse with the looking of his predecessors at the beings directly, and the looking at the image of the eclipsed sun in water with his looking at the beings in speeches (99d5–100a3). If the Stranger, in his turn from myth to *logos,* is going over the Socratic revolution, the region he is now looking at must be the region of nonbeing, for nonbeing belongs of necessity to *logos.* Any something looks as if it is taken up into speech without alteration; *on* has a referent that seems to be outside discourse; but *mē on* has already submitted to an operation of *logos* before it enters any *logos.* When Odysseus tells Polyphemus—he of many names—that his name is *Outis,* he has prepared the way for its being understood in the Cyclops's speech—*outis me kteinei*—"No one kills me" (*Odyssey* 9.408). The syntax of *logos* strips *outis* of a referent. Speech makes the neighbors of Polyphemus as blind as Odysseus made him.[7] Negation, then, bears the mark of man's presence in discourse. The Stranger, however, extends this to all speech regardless of whether it has a negative or not. He does this by denying that any letter of his original alphabet is what it is by itself. Motion is not the same as itself on account of its own nature but on account of its participation in the same (256b1). The participation of any element in anything denies the identity of the element with whatever it partakes in; but the principle of participation or of partial sharing is the other, for nothing is other than any other on account of its own nature but on account of its partaking in the *idea* of the other (255e3–6). The other, however, or the principle of participation, makes it possible for something to be said of something, for otherwise, as the eristical say, man would be only man and good good. The other therefore deidealizes every being and makes it not just itself but puts it in relation with other things. The other is that which adds the vocalic element to the silent consonants of being. The *Sophist* began with Socrates' suggestion that god was the philosopher. The philosopher, he implied in the argument of the Stranger, was the consonantal being with its vocalic glide already attached. The true philosopher is the only being who enters speech as just what he is. He therefore cannot but not appear as he is, for he cannot avoid being taken to be like every other being, a being in itself. The philosopher thus bears an uncanny resemblance to the lover, who despite his being equally defective comes to light as perfect and complete.[8] It is not surprising, therefore, that Theaetetus ends up by saying that the sophist impersonates the wise (268c1).

It is now possible to link the other with two prior stages of the argument. One is due to Theaetetus, the other to the Stranger. The image as *heteron toiouton,* or, as Theaetetus said, the weaving together of being and nonbeing, is no longer a marginal class among the things that are; rather, the image is that class of things acknowledged by everyone—the ease with which Theaetetus discovered the proper formula testifies to it—as not being just what it is. They are the counterparts outside of speech of what "philosopher" is within speech. Within speech, the image is necessarily double—"That's so-and-so" and "That's not so-and-so." The image creates noncontradictory doubletalk. It is thus the way into the other itself. The second step on that way is the Stranger's contribution; it comes from his attempt, easier in speech than in deed, to tame the giants. "To be is to be an agent or a patient power" was not acceptable to the friends of the ideas, who tried to restrict it to becoming; but the paradox that knowing could not be either an agent or patient power was not resolved and seemed to leave the friends of the ideas without ideas, or as least without ideas that can be known (248d4–e5). It is true that the definition of being as power, once it is split between agency and patiency, suffers from the same defect as any counting of the beings; but the definition does state that being is relational, since a power cannot be an agent unless something else is a patient. The definition thus sets the stage for the final emergence of the other. The other is the logical equivalent of the dynamical pair of being. It too makes every being relational insofar as it is in speech; but it overcomes the difficulty of power by getting rid of the contrary and including within itself a two. The not big is the equal and the small, the not beautiful the ugly and the just, the not Greek barbarian and barbaric. In the last case, the other, in cutting barbarian away from barbaric, brings "Greek" over to "not Greek" and does not exempt it from savagery. The designation "stranger" likewise bears on this designation, not only because the Spartans call barbarians strangers (Herodotus 9.11.2), but because "not stranger" includes the acquaintance and the savage. The Stranger says at any rate that not to comply with the company's request appears to him *axenon* (217e6). The Stranger is not going to be a stranger while remaining the Stranger. The Stranger's double status prepares the way for what even shocks young Socrates. "To be lawless *(anomos)*" is to be outside the law and above the law. It is to be either tyrant or philosopher (*Statesman* 301b10–c4).

The Stranger distinguishes between two kinds of weaving together. One is the weaving together of species, the other of nouns and verbs (259e5–6, 262c5–7). It is on account of the first kind of weaving that we have *logos;* but it is the second kind that constitutes the structure of *logos.* The first establishes the possibility of *logos;* it allows for things to enter *logos;* but the second distinguishes between the agent and the action of a *logos.* This distinction makes us realize that the Stranger's own divisions were primarily sets of discriminations among verbs of action, and the agent, whether angler, Socrates, or sophist, was defined by a predicate or predicates to which he could be attached. The verbs were so determinative of the agents that whoever could be plausibly said to do some action was ipso facto that agent. Accordingly, Socrates took on the guise of the sophist, for there was nothing in the verb that could declare whether the agent was spurious or not. Indeed, from this perspective, the Stranger's initial assertion that he and Theaetetus had only a name in common meant that they shared an agent-noun that had to be hooked up to an action (218c1–5). The deed *(ergon)* he there spoke of was of an action *(praxis).* To move from word to deed was simply to discover the verb. In dissolving the subject into the verb, the verb was put in the third person, in whose form a he or she that suited anyone who performed the action was concealed. Whatever this action was, knowledge had nothing to do with its character. Although the split between an artless and artful form of contradiction was strictly impossible (225b12–c9), there was nothing in "to haggle" that denied it was not fully informed by art, any more than there was in its counterpart any trace of knowledge except the label. The emergence of the agent is something we are not prepared for, since if truth or falsity is now to be found in the compound of agent and action, the Stranger is admitting that Socrates and the sophist do not do different things, and no division by itself can mark off their difference. Socrates might be as much a maker as the sophist.

After his characterization of *logos* and illustration of a false speech, the Stranger quickly dispatches thought, opinion, and *phantasia* (263d6–264b8). He asserts that thought and *logos* are the same, except that thought is the *dialogos* within the soul before itself without sound. If, then, thought and speech are the same, speech is dialogue. Speech, however, had not been dialogue but what the Stranger now calls opinion, the assertion or denial of a thought. The Stranger had indeed anticipated this revision, for he had interpolated in his example of a false speech a dialogic remark, "Theaetetus," with whom I am now conversing, "flies." What he had called speech involved two agents, the first and second persons of dialogue; but if Theaetetus is being addressed by the Stranger, the *logos* is not "Theaetetus flies" but "You fly," which in Greek has the agent built into the verb, *petesai,* or if contracted, *petēi.* Once speech becomes dialogue, the minimal speech is the verb with its proper ending. If, however, the Stranger is addressing Theaetetus, he is asking a question and expects that Theaetetus will answer it. Theaetetus is called upon to decide about his own state; whether he is right or not depends on whether the Stranger speaks an image or not, for if it is an image, it is according to Socrates, an image of those whom Theodorus calls philosophers; and we would not expect that if Theatetus were one of them his answer to the question would be true (*Theaetetus* 173e5, 175e2). However this may be, speech as dialogue alters the issue of predication. "I" and "You" seem to be resistant to their elimination through verbal action, for at first glance there seems to be no verb to specify what we do in the way that "hunts" or "sifts" does, let alone an art or science that rationalizes the human; but on reflection the verb that is predicated of man as such is *dialegesthai* and its scientific form *dialektikē.*[9] The Stranger's characterization of *logos,* then, points to a structure of *logos* in which the explicit agent—his two examples are "man" and "Theaetetus"—contains another, "You" if "I" or "I" if "You." These agents are present in any dialogue regardless of whether they are part of any *logos.* They are the object of Socrates' soul-cathartics in the double form of self-knowledge.

The Stranger concludes his account with *phantasia.* It is a mixture of opinion and perception. *Phantasia,* however, if it is to stay within the dialogic structure of speech and thought, has to be understood as the formulation of an opinion in answer to a question in light of the interlocutor's perception of the questioner. Such an answer is soon to be given by Theaetetus. The Stranger will ask him whether everything is the handicraft of a god or of thoughtless nature, and Theaetetus will say: "I, perhaps on account of my age, often have opinions on both sides; now, however, in looking at you and supposing you believe things are made in conformity with a god, I too hold in this way (265d1–4)." The most revealing thing in Theaetetus's remark is the absence of the word *phainetai,* for its absence is what makes his remark the example of a *phantasma.* Before our eyes Theaetetus banishes doubt and replaces it with a conviction that he builds out of a reading of the Stranger's face. This reading is a spoken phantom.

Regardless of whether this is a correct reading of the Stranger's face, Theaetetus is now something else than a verbal action. His conclusion has no weight unless Socratic cathartics is possible and can test whether this time Theaetetus is not pregnant with a wind-egg. The soul after all is something.

We do not know whether we are to ascribe Theaetetus's apparition of divine making to the exercise by the Stranger of *phantastikē;* but we do know that Theaetetus's apparition precedes the Stranger's reattachment of eikastics and phantastics to image-making. As the Stranger sets up the distinction between divine and human making, there is no artful kind of divine image-making, for though he alludes to dreams, his examples of the god's *phantasmata* are either shadows or mirror-images (266b9–c4). There is no suggestion that they are anything but automatic consequences of the bodies the god makes directly. Indeed, the bodies the Stranger allows to be the god's work are all on or in the earth (265c1–5); there is neither heaven nor stars, let alone an ordered cosmos (cf. 233e5–234a4). There are animals and soulless things, but there is no mention of soul; neither *psuchē* nor *empsuchon* reappears once the Stranger returns to *poiētikē* (*psuchē* last at 264a9). We are left in the dark, then, whether the god practices phantastics either in deed or in speech, and if Socrates were right, that the Stranger is a god, whether Theaetetus's *phantasma* was due to the Stranger's art. If, as it seems to be, it was Theaetetus's own offspring, there would be no divine phantastics in deed; but if it was after all a product of the Stranger's skill as of a god, there would still be no divine phantastics in speech. The Stranger's impersonation of a divine craftsman would not require more than a question to come across as an answer; it would not entail an elaborate account of divine revelation, either in the form of laws or of Socrates' *daimonion.*

The function of divine making, then, is to put the stress on the body. That the body is paramount is shown by the double use of *mimētikē,* first as the comprehensive art of *eidōla,* and then as the art of using one's own body or voice to represent someone else's (265a10, 267a7). At this point the Stranger's divisions break down, for he separates impersonators into knowers and nonknowers, even though we were dealing with kinds of productive art (267b7-8). Though nothing is said explicitly to this effect, it does seem that knowledgeable impersonators are those who imitate those they know (Theaetetus, for example), and ignorant impersonators those who imitate justice and the rest of virtue. The impersonators of virtue try to make appear in themselves the opinion they and almost everyone else have about it. They embody virtue. This kind of embodiment occurred long before men became aware of the difference between opinion and knowledge (267d4–8). What the Stranger now calls *doxomimētikē* is known to its sincere practitioners as *aretē.* It is based on the belief that virtue can appear: Theaetetus represented that belief when he read the Stranger's face as betraying his conviction about divine production. Did the Stranger then look up?

It seems at first as if the Stranger's analysis of *logos* into agent and action was designed solely for finding truth or falsity in the correct or incorrect attachment of an action to a known agent; but by his restriction of imitation to impersonation the agent becomes significant in himself and independent of what he does.[10] The sophist embodies virtue as it is understood in opinion, despite his suspicion that he does not know what his *schēma* declares he knows—Gorgias exemplifies this perfectly; but what he does is to contradict and refute the opinions about virtue the interlocutor himself maintains and believes he sees represented in the sophist. The sophist impersonates the opinions he refutes. What, then, of Socrates? He is not an impersonator. Theodorus at any rate found him poker-faced and could not figure out what Socrates believed from his totally convincing presentation of a Protagorean position (*Theaetetus* 161a6). Socrates, however, is ironical. Does his claim to ignorance come across as knowledge in light of his capacity to show up the ignorance of others? More particularly, does the incoherence in opinion about a virtue, once Socrates has exposed it, induce the impression that Socrates himself has it? It would seem impossible that Socrates could display popular virtue without its inconsistencies while showing up its inconsistencies; but Socrates the logic-chopping moralist seems to be exactly that. *Logos* as dialogue thus comes to light as the problem of Socrates the agent in his action. We can say that the *Sophist* ends at that point where the problem has been uncovered, and the *Statesman* is designed to treat Socratic agency. Socrates the agent, however, cannot show up in himself; instead, he shows up in the patient, young Socrates.

Notes

1. *to tou theou* (216c4–5) is an odd expression unless Socrates implies that beings other than god belong to the same genus; Cobet's correction *tōn theōn* is certainly what one would have expected.

2. Cf. Pierre Chantraine, *La Formation des noms en grec ancien* (Paris, 1933), 385–93.

3. N.B. *ēisthēmetha* (228b4) is used of the Stranger's and Theaetetus's "knowledge" of the conflicts in moral vice and *ismen* (228c7) of their knowledge of the soul's involuntary ignorance.

4. *Prostithenai* is at 238c1 and 239b9; *suntithesthai* at 252b1, 3, 262e12, 268d3; *summeignusthai* comes in at 252b6 and occurs four more times (cf. 264b2).

5. The Stranger's phrasing of the problem of false opinion points to this: *hotan peri to phantasma auton apatan phōmen . . ., tote poteron pseudē doxazein tēn psuchēn hēmōn phēsomen* (240d1–3).

6. Cf. Derek J. Raine and Michael Heller, *The Science of Space-Time* (Tucson, 1981), 26: "The force-free motions, the existence of which is asserted by the Law of Inertia, play a fundamental role in the theory [of Newton]. It is by means of these privileged trajectories that we map out the structure of space-time. Newton certainly did not take this next step with much success. For, in constructing a space-time arena for his dynamics, he reverts to the idea of a kinematical description of inertial motions. In doing so, . . . he arrives at a space-time structure which is not strictly consistent with his Law of Inertia."

7. It is striking that the absence of a referent for *outis* makes the neighbors speak at once of Zeus, whose afflictions it is impossible to avoid (9.409).

8. This is the gist of the argument between Agathon and Socrates in the *Symposium.*

9. Perhaps it is just an accident, but the Stranger's examples of verbs that do not constitute in succession a *logos* are all in the active voice (*badizei, trechei, katheudei*), but the two that illustrate true and false speech are both in the middle (*kathētai* and *petetai*). The middle voice is strictly used for actions that occur within the sphere of the subject; cf. Pierre Chantraine, *Grammaire homērique* (Paris, 1953), vol. 2, 174–76.

10. In the summary the Stranger gives of the sophist's genealogy (268c8–d4), all but one of his lines of descent can be rephrased as a verb: the difference between divine and human imitation resists such a rephrasing.

SEVENTEEN

The Plan of Plato's *Statesman*

IT IS NOT EASY TO follow the argument of the *Statesman.* Its difficulty seems to be due to the odd lengths of its sections, which are either too short or too long for the matter discussed. The Stranger spends two pages on a theme to which Socrates devotes two books of the *Republic,* even though it is admitted that almost everything all of us do is for the sake of what is a digression in the *Statesman* (302b8-9). Weaving takes so long to recount that the Stranger feels compelled to discuss at length the issue of length, but he never gets around to justifying the lengthiness of the section on weaving. Young Socrates is rebuffed when he wishes to learn how one can tell part and kind apart; but his mistake, which induced the Stranger to distinguish part and kind, is corrected through an elaborate myth, which, the Stranger acknowledges, for all its extensive bulk, remains incomplete (277b4-7). We seem to be given lessons in the measure of the mean by being offered swatches from a bin of odd lots and sizes. Any attempt to show the inner connection and coherence of the argument of the *Statesman* must also try to account for the appearance it has of being the Platonic dialogue with the least pleasing proportions. If a perfect writing is to resemble a living being, a committee must have put together whatever animal the *Statesman* is.

The *Statesman* begins in error. Not only does Socrates take Theodorus to task for saying that Socrates' gratitude will be triple once Theaetetus and the Stranger produce for him the statesman and the philosopher, but the Stranger denies that the order in which the statesman and the philosopher are to be discussed is, as Theodorus assumed, a matter of indifference; and Socrates and the Stranger between them arrange for Theaetetus to be set aside for the next two discussions. Theodorus's first mistake is due, according to Socrates, to an extension of his mathematical knowledge beyond its competence; and this hubris, which Socrates says is an unavoidable concomitant of any partial knowledge (*Apology of Socrates* 22c9–e5), seems to infect the starting point of the divisions of statesmanship. Arithmetic exemplifies *gnōstikē* because it is stripped of actions; and then the Stranger tries to force *politikē* into the same class, as if he wanted to vindicate Theodorus over against Socrates and show that the statesman at least is really on the same level as the mathematician. What might seem to be the pushiness of politics, as if it wanted to give itself the airs of a theoretical science, is really the Stranger's indulgence of Theodorus's desire to punish Socrates for putting him down, and which it is easy enough to imagine young Socrates as a budding mathematician shares. The Stranger himself, however, cannot be unaware that the forcing is coming from the side of mathematics, for if *politikē* were of the same theoretical order as mathematics, he could not have proposed the task he and young Socrates are undertaking to be the isolation of politics and the unification of all other sciences into one other class (258c4–8). Young Socrates' refusal to join him in this discovery forces the Stranger to win young Socrates over by letting abstraction play the role of theory. A mathematician is lured into *politikē* through a semblance of mathematical reasoning.

The Stranger's way of dividing *epistēmē* into *gnōstikē* and *praktikē* offers another possible division of each. He assigns to *gnōstikē* two characteristics; it is stripped of actions and supplies only knowledge *(gnōnai)*; and he says of *praktikē* that its knowledge inheres in its actions and brings into being previously nonexisting bodies. There could, then, be a knowledge that was *not* stripped of actions and yet supplied only knowledge, as well as a knowledge that *was* engaged in actions and yet did not handle the coming into being of bodies. A theoretical practice on souls is not an entirely inaccurate label for either Socrates' own *maieutikē* or the Stranger's version of it, the cathartics of soul (*Sophist* 230a5–e4). Indeed, it seems pretty well to fit *politikē* once the Stranger lets it drift out of *gnōstikē* and become a *praxis* (284c2). If mathematics itself, moreover, is involved in a kind of practice, too, whenever it sets for itself a construction (*Republic* 527a6–b1), *gnōstikē* could prove to be a class to which no known human science belongs.

Four different arguments establish that *politikē* belongs to *gnōstikē*. They are neither consistent with each other nor adequate for assimilating politics to arithmetic. The class of gnostics is first set up in one way, and then, when it has been reshaped to accommodate politics, it is relabeled as *kritikē* and emerges as what it was before without any connection with the gnostics that politics has now usurped for itself. No sooner does the Stranger ask whether statesman, king, master, and household manager are all one than he makes a detour into another issue, whether anyone competent to advise a public physician must be addressed with the same name as the one he advises, but the Stranger does not explain what connects the detour with the original question. The public physician does not differ from either one in private practice or one who has retired from practice and serves as a consultant in difficult cases. The political is edged out of consideration through the label "public," which no more affects the physician's knowledge than the first element in *dēmiourgos* signifies anything but the social function of the craftsman. Carpentry does not become theoretical if it is exercised in an advisory capacity. In reducing the public to the private, the Stranger can surreptitiously appeal to the fact that every adult is an *oikonomos* while he argues that knowledge is the sole title to rule. His detour thus pulls two ways at once. The Stranger strips *politikē* of practice and thereby makes it theoretical; and he puts it within the grasp of almost everyone through the indispensable practice of "economy." The Stranger leaves it at the equivalence of the *schēma* of a large household and the *onkos* of a small city, but nothing he says checks the reduction of the kingdom to the size of an individual's domain even if he rules only over himself. If, however, political knowledge includes self-rule, it cannot be unexercised; and if it does not, no proof is offered that the land *(chōra)* a king rules is the same as a *polis* or an *oikos.* The structural implications in the words *polis* and *oikos* are not evident in the featureless *chōra,* which in this respect looks much more like the self of the individual.

Once one realizes that the unemployed king could be the wise man in charge of himself, it is possible to reinterpret the Stranger's fourth piece of evidence that politics is a gnostic science. He says that the king's hands and body contribute little to the maintenance of his rule in comparison with his strength of soul and intelligence. On the surface, the Stranger is simply contradicting himself, for the knowledgeable king, who can but does not have to advise the actual king, has no rule to maintain. The inclusion of self-rule, however, within the dimensions of rule is bought at a price, for neither strength of soul nor intelligence, for all their noncorporeal character, is the same as an art or science; and if a psychic strength is needed in the science of self-rule, there must be something in such a science that has a power to corrupt whoever wields it. The *politikos* can be trivially theoretical if "theoretical" only means that he can wait in the wings without losing his knowledge; but if his knowledge extends to himself, he can no longer be theoretical without ceasing to have self-knowledge. The status of self-knowledge itself is lurking in the Stranger's depoliticization of *politikē.*

The Stranger does not want *politikē* to straddle two kinds of knowledge, so that there is "political theory," on the one hand, which speaks of various social structures, house, city, and kingdom, without ever claiming that they are ruled by the same art (let alone that they differ only in size), and, on the other, there is political flair, which shows itself in the particular judgments a sensible ruler makes in the face of unprecedented circumstances. He does not want gnostic political science to be contaminated with a kind of practical knowledge; and he tries to conceal the contamination his own account has introduced by claiming to split *gnōstikē* into *kritikē and epitaktikē.* No argument, however, is given that *epitaktikē* is a part of *gnōstikē* and not of *praktikē,* for if *epitaktikē* is modeled on the job of the *architektōn,* it has nothing to do with either *kritikē* or *gnōstikē.*[1] The master builder does not stick around after the building goes up to contemplate it, and he certainly does not rule workmen when he is out of work. Even the one trait he might share with the king—he too does not maintain his rule by brute force—separates the king from *gnōstikē* and reassigns him more plausibly to *praktikē.* The Stranger pretends, however, that the master builder, in supplying knowledge *(parechomenos gnōsin),* is doing what the mathematical sciences do, for they too supply knowledge *(to gnōnai pareschonto);* but whereas the arithmetician has the knowledge arithmetic supplies him in just the way any art is instructive, the masterbuilder can keep his knowledge to himself and still give instructions to his crew without explaining anything to them. *Gnōstikē* now seems to designate any art in which one does not work with one's hands. It has ceased to be positively determined and become merely what *praktikē* is not.

What *praktikē* itself is, or more precisely how far it extends and intrudes into *gnōstikē* becomes problematic at this point. Young Socrates agrees with the Stranger's division of *gnōstikē* into *kritikē* and *epitaktikē* with these words: *kata ge tēn emēn doxan* (280b6); and the Stranger, before he recommends the dismissal of the opinions of all others as long as they are partners *(koinōnōmen),* remarks: *alla mēn tois ge koinēi ti prattousin agapēton homonoein.* Young Socrates and the Stranger are engaged in a common action. This action has as its aim the supplying of knowledge; and since it proceeds by way of shared opinion, to the exclusion of other competing opinions, it cannot be said to be a knowledge-informed action. In its hit-and-miss way of proceeding, with all its false starts and stops, their action lies outside scientific *praktikē,* while they themselves seem to be as exclusively concerned with knowledge as any number-theoretician. The *Statesman* seems to be haunted by the ghost of its own argument. These ghosts are perhaps inevitable by-products of any argument: in the *Sophist* the Stranger drew on the image of the hunter-sophist to characterize the catching of the sophist (225e5, 226a6–8, 235b8–c6). In the *Statesman,* however, this doubling of the argument in the action of the dialogue seems to be pervasive and all the more important to understand, since when it has now emerged statesmanship is being assigned to one set of divisions and the Stranger and young Socrates find themselves imitating all that statesmanship is not. They are to observe *(theateon)* the possible split in *epitaktikē* since the statesman does not belong in *kritikē* as if he were some other observer (*theatēs,* 260c2, 6).

The next distinction the Stranger makes within *epitaktikē* is not well grounded. It cuts *epitaktikē* in itself, but not insofar as *epitaktikē* is a part of *gnōstikē,* for not only do the herald and cox use their bodies, but if they are to be understood as exercising *gnōstikē, gnōstikē* must once more alter its meaning and be equivalent to the knowledge of how to transmit knowledge; and if they are to be understood as exercising *epitaktikē, epitaktikē* must mean the art of transmitting orders and not, as we were led to believe, the knowledge of what orders are to be given. The Stranger's divisions can be saved if the herald's art is the comprehensive characteristic of *epitaktikē* and *autepitaktikē* is its precise sense. The apparent cut of a single class into two is in fact the articulation of a subset within a larger class. This too is a *diairesis. Autepitaktikē* and *epitaktikē* are not related like this—

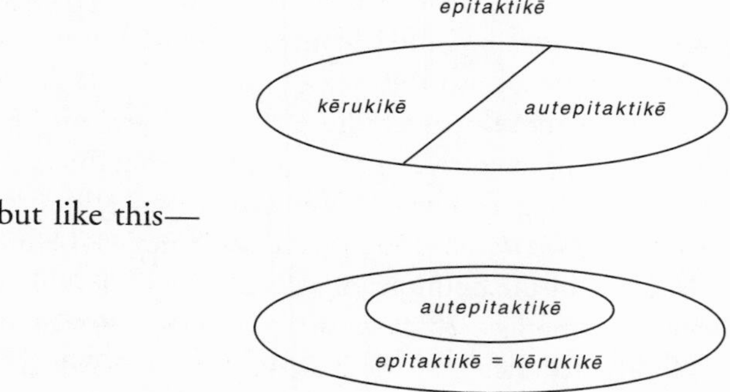

but like this—

The Stranger is peeling away outer coverings of the pith *politikē;* he is not, as he keeps on insisting he is, *mesotomei.*[2]

The soothsayer, moreover, whom the Stranger assigns to *kērukikē* and hence denies is a possible rival to the statesman, turns out to be historically the first claimant along with the priest to kingship after the god has abandoned the world (290c3-e8). In order to set aside soothsayers and priests, the Stranger takes advantage of the vestigial traces of the priest-king in Athens and elsewhere, but he does not justify his dismissal of them before the bar of reason. A theoretical *diairesis* rests on the mysterious withdrawal over time of the sacred from political life. The withdrawal, however, is not complete. Socrates just met yesterday with the *basileus archōn* to face Meletus's indictment (*Theaetetus* 210d1-4).

The Stranger appeals to the *Sophist* for his distinction between *autepitaktikē* and *kērukikē* (260c7-d6); but he does not get it quite right. *Autopōlikē* initially designated the *autourgoi* in the class of *agorastikē;* and of those who exchange the goods of others, *kapēloi* and *emporoi* were distinguished (*Sophist* 223c12-d10); and later it was admitted that it makes no difference whether one partly bought and partly made the goods one sold retail in the city (224d4-e2); but in neither case can *kapēloi* be separated from *autopōlai* unless one adds that both sell goods in their own city. The stranger had there precluded the possibility of *emporoi* with their own wares; but here, since nothing can restrict the statesman's art as an art to his own city, *autepitaktikē* should match up not with *autopōlikē* but with the missing **autemporikē.* It is the rivals to the royal art, the priests and soothsayers, who will have to claim that they are speaking in the name of the gods of their city, whereas the true statesman can very well be a stranger (cf. 295e8). It is hard not to think of the Stranger as the foreigner with the true political art, just as Socrates lurked in the notion of the stay-at-home sophist who retailed his own goods.

Prior to the removal of *kērukikē* from consideration, the *architektōn* had been said to enjoin on his workmen *to prosphoron* until they produce *(apergasōntai) to prostachthen* (260a6–7); but after *autepitaktikē* has been isolated, rulers are said to enjoin *geneseōs tinos heneka* (261b1). *Apergasōntai* was the very word and form Theodorus had used to describe the production of the statesman and the philosopher he expected Theaetetus and the Stranger to accomplish (257a4-5). Socrates as the ultimate user, with the Stranger as *architektōn* in direct charge of the workman young Socrates, is a pleasant conceit; but under no circumstances could their *apergasia* or *genesis* be understood as either *apsuchon* or *empsuchon,* into which the Stranger now asserts is the easy way to part all becoming. As soon as the Stranger makes a cut that does not allow for his own joint action with young Socrates to be thought of as running parallel with it, he makes a mistake. The expression *epi tais tōn apsuchōn genesesin* (261b12) does not have any clear sense if *empsuchōn* replaces *apsuchōn.* Neither the herdsman nor the statesman gives orders for the generation of ensouled beings. Even if the statesman arranges for the proper marriages between *andreioi* and *sōphrones* families (310e5-311a2), his arrangement cannot match the supervision a master builder exercises in the erection of a house or temple. The king has a knowledge assigned him that possesses its power *en tois zōiois kai peri auta tauta* (261d1); but this vague phrasing does not fit what presumably established half of the class of *autepitaktikē* in the first place. Indeed, the *tais* at 261c1 *(to d' epi tais tōn empsuchōn)* is an addition of the *recentiores* and missing in B and T. *To d' epi tōn empsuchōn* is translatable, "the part which is over (in charge of) the ensouled beings"; but the very suitability of the phrase deprives the part of being a section of *autepitaktikē* as designed solely *geneseōs tinos heneka.* We are given the choice of either subscribing to the Stranger's analysis despite its absurdity or of making him more sensible and obscuring or rather destroying the deduction of the *diairesis.* The Stranger, in any case, makes the choice for us, since at the very moment he denies that *basilikē epistēmē* handles lifeless things, he etymologizes *epistēmē* into *epistatein* (261c9), so that we can easily infer that it *epistatei tōn empsuchōn.* The king simply protects the herd in his care and rules it regardless of whether he orders anything to come into being or not.

In order to cut the epitactic part of *gnōstikē*—*epitaktikon* has now taken over the meaning of *autepitaktikon*—the Stranger says he will make the cut *to men epi tais tōn apsuchōn genesesin autou tattontes, to d' epi [tais] tōn empsukhōn* (261b13–c1). The Stranger decompounds *epitattein* as a way of describing his distribution of the parts of *epitaktikē.*[3] He thus calls attention to the ordering involved in the giving of orders. *Epitaktikē* is as much the science of ordering as it is the science of ordaining. *Autepitaktikē* could then be an essential part of *gnōstikē*—the distribution, on one's own, of things into their proper class. The Stranger, one might believe, is not very good at such ordering; but there is order and order, and we might not yet be in a position to judge which is which. The double sense of *epitattein,* which embraces both *politikē* and the Stranger's discovery of *politikē,* seems at any rate to be connected with the issue of the apparent defectiveness in the proportions of the *Statesman* and to hint at the lie in whose perspective its proportions might turn out right. If in just the way in which *epitaktikē* has a double sense, everything the statesman knows and practices is the same and not the same as everything the Stranger knows and practices in determining what the statesman knows and practices, the *Statesman,* it seems, must be out of joint, and the ugly the necessary by-product of the superimposition of order on order.

The Stranger's way of splitting the animal part of epitactics is inadequate. He opposes the grooming of individuals to the feeding of herds; but such an opposition lets slip out of sight the science of mating, though his own scheme requires him to make it central (v. 261d3). This is the beginning of the errors the Stranger acknowledges and goes to such lengths to correct; whether he succeeds or the project was flawed from the start cannot yet be known; but it is remarkable that at the point at which the royal art is assigned to the collective exclusively, the Stranger lets young Socrates make a division on his own only to have to exercise something like the art of statesmanship in humbling young Socrates and humiliating man in order to restore his authority over the divisions. The Stranger seems to unleash young Socrates for the sake of reining him in all the tighter. Behind the cut between herd and individual was the assumption that all herds were tame and domesticated (264a1–3); and the Stranger arranges for Socrates to see it by the confinement of humans and pig in the same class and by knocking the manly pride out of young Socrates. The actual tempering of young Socrates is imaged in the argument's discovery that man in the herd is either a two-footed pig or a plucked chicken. The barnyard section of the *Statesman* is a parody of the kind of mythology the Stranger says the statesman needs to support his rule (304c10–d2). Its pseudo-rationality, which makes it hover between the strict distinction between part and kind and the opinions the many would need to be persuaded of, illustrates how irrelevant the supposed distinctiveness of human reason is to the question of rule.[4]

Young Socrates' error does not consist in promoting man at the expense of the other animals but in believing that a division among the kinds of herd animals was the next step. The Stranger's introduction of *empsucha* misled young Socrates. This implied, he thought, that *politikē* itself had already been fully determined, and that all that remained was to designate man as the animal it rules. Young Socrates believed that there was nothing special about the science involved in *epitaktikē.* His failure to see any need to account for the manner of political reason led him to pick out reason *(phronēsis)* as the characteristic of the king's subjects. They are as rational as he and this distinguishes them from all other animals. There turns out to be something to his rash association of the ruled with the ruler (cf. 274c1–4); but there is a disproportion between the manner in which he arrives at man and the trait he ascribes tacitly to men. The manliness *(andreia)* of young Socrates is hardly the same as prudence; so that which makes him anticipate the goal of their inquiry, and which etymologically belongs to only half the human race, does not show up in his selection of human beings. His nature as a man *(anēr)* stands apart from the nature of man *(anthrōpos).* If he had attended to his own nature in his answer, he would have said *andres* (cf. *Charmides* 160d8–e5). *Andres* would have been a not-uninteresting answer, for it would have corresponded to the common notion that the city is of men, and women and children belong to a subpolitical level of the city.

Young Socrates could hardly know that the Stranger is going to propose the interweaving of manly with moderate natures. Such an interweaving seems to go some way toward settling the issue of part and kind. It suggests that male and female, which the Stranger will say would be a more "eidetic" division among animals (262e5), have their excellence in *andreia* and *sōphrosunē* respectively, and that at least politically these virtues are the highest the political herd can go in approaching the reason of the *politikos.* If we attend to the Stranger's implicit criticism of young Socrates, which entails the rule that no *diaeresis* is to be made that does not fully incorporate in the *diaeresis* that which initiated and led to the *diaeresis,* then the argument of the *Statesman* can be stated as follows: The difference between what the Stranger does and what the statesman can do defines entirely the art of statesmanship (cf. 311c5). It would necessarily follow from this rule that that difference can only be disclosed by a constant attempt on the Stranger's part to eliminate the difference. Failure and error belong of necessity to the way of the discovery of *politikē* if failure and error are not to be the statesman's lot. The first sign of the difference is the Stranger's admission that *meros* in its nonidentity with *eidos* characterizes every known political community, and a city of men, with no exclusive designation for themselves, so that no one is a stranger to them, is impossible (262e6–263a1). However *axenos* the Stranger may be, he is still a stranger in Athens (*Sophist* 217e6–7).

The Stranger's objection to the separation of men from beasts, as if this could not be done by them in speech before *politikē* had done it in deed, seems to have less to do with the definition of *politikē* than with the two lessons he can deliver to young Socrates. One lesson is a sobering *(sōphronismos)* of young Socrates toward his own pretensions in particular and those of men in general; the other lesson is an incomplete instruction in the necessity for a kind of sobriety in dialectics. For the second time we are faced with a pun that repeats on a deeper level the double sense of *epitattein. Sōphrosunē* is being displayed in its moral and intellectual senses simultaneously. It is much easier to see the simultaneity of its two senses than to discern the necessity for it. Is *mesotomein* the dialectical version of a chastened heart? To be tame and domesticated might well be the necessary condition for philosophy; but such a connection hardly warrants the collapse they have undergone in this passage, especially since the Stranger's cuts through the middle get to man in an arbitrary manner. He himself admits that whether they take the longer or shorter route is a matter of indifference (265a1–6). If, however, we consider that the Stranger is not objecting to young Socrates' isolation of man but to the concealed negation in *thēria,* which means no more than "not men," then the Stranger is demanding a unification of all nonhuman animals in positive terms. His own determination of man, once there is a shorter or longer way, is almost entirely negative: man on the longer way is *akerōs (kolobos), amigēs,* and finally alogos, since he is the square of the irrational root of two, and on the shorter way he is *psilos.* The domestication of man is achieved by turning the tables on young Socrates' negative determination of beasts. Man is "not beast." He is the other. The incorporation of *thateron* into the very constitution of man sobers man and makes him recognize the other as the other of the other (*Sophist* 255d6–7). Man thus becomes civilized and transcends the enmity of "us" against "them," which for the Athenians and others takes the form of "Greeks" and "barbarians." The evenhandedness of *thateron,* we now see, was also absent in the Stranger's very first *diaeresis. Arithmētikē* was *psilē tōn praxeōn* (258d5); it was feeding off the very *praktikē* the Stranger was desperately trying to keep *politikē* away from. The Stranger himself had started out on the wrong foot. Young Socrates' error was a consequence of following his lead. The Stranger failed to get their soul to understand all the sciences as being of two *eidē* (258c7).

The Stranger began the barnyard section with a reminder of the proverbial warning—the faster the slower *(speudē bradeōs)*—which young Socrates had just failed to heed. A theoretical procedure is put in real time and measured against the shorter time it would have taken had young Socrates given the right answer. It is not clear what the right answer should have been; it is not clear whether there was a right answer, or at least an answer that would have appreciably shortened the time. Young Socrates seems to be grateful for the delay (*kai kalōs ge, ō xene, pepoiēke,* 264b5); and he later asks for both the longer and shorter ways of division despite the time that they add (265a7–8). We are no doubt being prepared for the discussion of the measure of the mean; but in the present context the issue of length assumes a more concrete sense. As soon as land animals are separated off from birds and fishes, the Stranger says he notices two roads stretched out toward the goal their *logos* has set out for *(hōrmēken);* and he says it is possible to travel *(poreuthēnai)* on either one they wish

(265a1–6). Young Socrates' choice of both ways will cause them no trouble, the Stranger says, for they are neither at the beginning nor at the middle of their journey *(kat' archas kai mesousin [hēmin] tēs poreias),* where it would have been difficult to comply with his request. The Stranger then proposes that they go *(iōmen)* on the longer road first, since "we shall travel more easily on it while we are fresher (265b5–6)." Suddenly, the fork in the road is real, and they are obliged, once they are in real time, to calculate their strength in corporeal terms. The Stranger is intent on galvanizing back into life the original meaning of *methodos,* partly no doubt to blur the difference between the long time it took to domesticate humans and his own deliberate slowing down of young Socrates' pace; but it is also due in part to the need to arrange for his pun, as if the slowness of the pig explained why the pig *(hus)* came last *(hustata)* in the divisions (266c8). The Stranger, moreover, in mapping his *methodos* onto the *peza* he is classifying, is able to enlist young Socrates and appeal to his geometrical knowledge for the last cut (266a6–b9). Once they have isolated the hornless and nonmixing herd-animal class and set aside dogs as not worth counting, the Stranger proposes to cut the class by the diameter and the diameter of the diameter. "The nature *(phusis),*" he says, "which the race of us human beings possesses, is naturally geared to walking *(poreia)* in no other way than as the diameter two foot in power is *(hē diametros hē dunamei dipous).*" We are to imagine, it seems, our two legs as the sides of an equilateral right triangle—

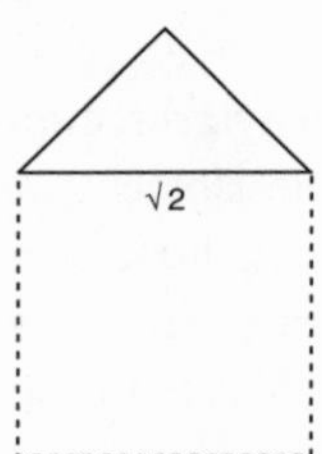

and the square on the hypotenuse makes us two feet in power. The action involved in the mathematicians' squaring *(tetragōnizein)* has restored the original meanings to their other borrowings *(dunamis* and *dipous),* so that man now moves on two feet because mathematics has recovered human rationality in a construction.[5] Metaphorical extensions of language are reliteralized in order to put man in his place and civilize him in a wholly rational manner. Man is humiliated and rationalized simultaneously. The shadowing of *politikē* in the Stranger's way of discovering *politikē* has led to a coincidence between them that could only be justified if there were literally a reversal of time, and *dipous* and *dunamis* had at the start exclusively mathematical meanings and their apparently original meanings were a derivative phenomenon. Indeed, the Stranger's first set of divisions is corrected through a myth whose most original feature is the periodic reversal of time. The myth the Stranger tells supports in retrospect what he has just done. The universe, he will say, goes on the smallest foot (270a8). This foot is the imaginary axis around which the universe revolves. If the figurative could be reliteralized, then, the Stranger implies, mathematical physics would be possible. His own contribution to that end is now before us. Whether we laugh or not depends on whether we look to its misuse of reason or its rational beating of man.

The Stranger's dishonoring of man through the indifference of his way to questions of honor has disparaged the king as well, who finds himself running alongside his herd and keeping pace with the swineherd, "the best exercised in leading the easy life" (266d1–2). We seem to be asked to put together two passages in the *Odyssey,* one in which Circe transforms half of Odysseus's men into swine, "but their mind was intact as before" (10.240);[6] and the other in which Eumaeus the swineherd forms an alliance with Odysseus against the suitors and receives in recompense his freedom, a wife, a house next to Odysseus's: he will be the comrade and brother of Telemachus (21.213–16). The radical democratization of Ithaca, Eumaeus's new status implies, has its dark side: Eumaeus chops up his enemy, the goatherd Melantheus, and feeds him to the household dogs (22.474–477). Man stripped of his pride takes a terrible vengeance. Dogs, which in the *Republic* were the models for the guardians—they were to be educated to control their canine savagery—have been canceled in the Stranger's divisions as not to be counted among herd animals. The elimination of any intermediate class between the ruler and the ruled seems to force the ruler to become one with the ruled. Differences have succumbed to the indifference of the Stranger's method. Its ruthlessness has made man either too easygoing or too ruthless. *Hus,* the Greek word for "pig," designates indifferently the shaggy wild boar and the smooth-skinned tame.

The shorter alternative to man as a twofooted pig seems to anticipate the myth, which says that in the age of Kronos men could converse with every species and learn what they severally could contribute to understanding (272b8–c4). Man could then first pair himself with each animal in turn and at the end part from all of them in order to determine both the variety of his distinctions and the manifold of his common traits. This anticipation, however, explains neither why the Stranger complies with young Socrates' request for both ways nor why the shorter way contributes to our understanding. The class of terrestrial herd animals is to be distinguished between bipeds and quadrupeds; bipeds are to be cut by the differentiae of feathered and featherless; and then, the Stranger says, one must bring the *politikos* and *basilikos* as if he were a charioteer and set him in the art of human herding *(anthrōponomikē)*, and hand the reins of the city over to him as if they were his own *(oikeia)* and this science were his (266e4–11).[7] We are asked to picture the statesman as the guide of the fallen soul, which, according to Socrates' myth in the *Phaedrus,* loses its wings and assumes a body after it has seen the hyperuranian beings. Political man, the Stranger implies, is unerotic man, for eros is the only human experience that mimics the ascent of soul. Whereas man cannot regret his not being as "rational" as the fourfooted pig, he is filled with longing for the wings of his congeners.

The Stranger had allowed there to be a double differentia of the hornless herd, either of which would distinguish man, *schiston* or *amiges (ameikton),* "with split foot" or "incapable of mating with another kind" (265d9–e9).The horse and the ass were thus separated from man. Man's exclusiveness was originally not sexual; it referred to the Greek mistake of lumping together immiscible *(ameikta)* tribes under the rubric "barbarian" (262d4).[8] One wonders whether there is a connection between the natural inability of man to mix with another kind and the political impossibility that *meros* and *eidos* could ever coincide. Whatever is man's own by nature is never man's own by law. The politically relevant "one's own" always stands between them. Socrates had beautifully expressed this first of political facts by denying in a myth that the goddess of the hearth Hestia had ever seen the hyperuranian beings (*Phaedrus* 247a1–2). For the Stranger, however, Hestia is the only god. His myth denies that Zeus and the Olympian gods are anything more than names for the absence of the gods. "Zeus" is a concealed negative; it means "not god." Heroes are not allowed in the Stranger's classification, for there is no eros (*Cratylus* 398c6–e3; cf. *Apology of Socrates* 27d4–e3).

In the course of the Stranger's discussion, two considerations become more and more prominent: the king as shepherd *(poimēn)* and his rule as a form of grazing *(nemein).* In the case of *nemein,* another deep pun is involved, for the rejection in the first part of the dialogue of the shepherd as a paradigm for the statesman is matched in the second part by the rejection of law *(nomos).* The link between herding and law is made at 295e6 *[hoposai (agelai) kata polin en hekastais nomeuontai kata tous tōn grapsontōun nomous)],* but there is throughout the dialogue a hidden reflection on the historical changes in political life that could possibly lie behind the common root of "law" and "herding" and the almost complete dissolution of their connection in contemporary linguistic experience. This historical dimension in the *Statesman's* argument is also present in the discussion of the king as shepherd. Although "flock" *(poimnē)* occurs before the myth (268b5), "shepherd" *(poimēn)* is only after it (275a1, b5), when the Stranger criticizes himself on its basis for speaking of the shepherd of the human herd at the time of the contrary revolution though he had been asked for the king and statesman of the present revolution and *genesis.* The notion of the king as shepherd of his people *(poimena laōn)* is almost confined to the Homeric epics; indeed, in the *Odyssey,* it is applied to the last representatives of the former generation (Agamemnon, Menelaus, Nestor, and even Aegisthus); Mentor, when he is Athena in disguise, gets the epithet (24.456); likewise Odysseus and Laertes when Athena has enhanced them (18.70, 24.368); and Homer speaks thus of Odysseus after Zeus has just thundered in response to his prayers and a loyal servant echoes his wish (20.106). The shepherd-king is not common in tragedy (v. Euripides *Supplices* 191); while in Plato, Socrates likens the guardians to shepherds and the auxiliaries to dogs (*Republic* 440d5–6), and in the *Minos* he again links law and shepherd and cites the Homeric phrase *poimena laōn* (321c2; cf. Aristotle *Nicomachean Ethics* 1161a10–15). Everyone is more or less aware, then, of the antiquity of the notion and the archaic or even primitive condition it represents. Its slow emergence from behind the apparently neutral designation of man as a herd animal concealed for a while that at least from the time of the introduction of the herd the paradigm of the shepherd was silently determining the understanding of statesmanship.

The Stranger's myth is primarily designed to expose the reality presupposed in his theoretical enterprise. The elimination of the difference between household and city, which looked like a case of scientific abstraction in order to be as general as possible, proves to have held in fact when there was rule without either family or regime (271e8–272a1). In a time antedating the so-called age of Zeus, a god was a shepherd of men, and his rule was indistinguishable from the divine pasturing of other kinds of flocks. The Homeric metaphor *poimena laōn* was once literally true (cf. *Republic* 382c10–d3). Then man was only a herd animal, and the absence of sexual generation did not allow mating by twos to be an awkwardness for the Stranger's divisions. That *schiston* was an alternative to *amiges* in cutting the hornless class is no longer without meaning: *amiges* holds now and *schiston* held then under the sway of divine providence. All animals were then tame, and the Stranger had made no mistake in assuming that they were (263e6–264a3, 271e1). The myth vindicates young Socrates as well, for though it seems that *thērion* was then inapplicable to any animal, still, if his real mistake was to disregard the manner of rule, it now turns out that once the rulers are gods nothing more really does need to be said. Given the self-evident superiority of the gods, perfect order follows at once without their giving any orders (cf. 301d8–e4).

The Stranger's myth accomplishes several things at once. Prospectively, it follows up his negative determination of man in the *diaeresis* with a negative determination of the *politikos* himself: the god who exemplifies the ruler as shepherd is everything the statesman is not. Retrospectively, the myth describes the conditions that must obtain if the Stranger is to justify the divisions he has already made: the soothsayers and the priests, whom the *diaeresis* of *epitaktikē* "rationally" disposed of, really cease to be troublesome through the myth's declaration that they are always impostors. Even the distinction between *gnōstikē* and *praktikē,* which seemed as if it could not be maintained for either mathematics or the Stranger's own theoretical *praxis,* is grounded in the two phases of divine activity. God either contemplates or rules; he never mixes those two activities, for when he lets go of the world, he retires to a lookout *(periōpē),* and when he is in charge, he must have his hands constantly on the controls just as he did when he made the world in the first place. It is, then, the strictness with which the myth keeps to the either/or character of the divisions that distinguishes the myth from the dialogue it rectifies. Myth as myth does not allow for the intrusion of dialogic action to contaminate the clarity of the argument of a dialogue. Myth transforms dialogue into treatise, for its narrative form lets it have only a single voice.[9] This simplicity of myth would help to explain why the Stranger cannot figure out whether men of the golden age philosophized—whether, that is, in conversing with themselves and other animals, they reflected on how their own doing was bound up with the gathering of intelligence from others. The form of the myth, then, endorses the split between *gnōstikē* and *praktikē* that the god enacts. The unphilosophic god necessarily appears in a story in which philosophy cannot be detected. He presides over a world where eros, which in the ordinary sense has vanished, is not clearly present in its true sense.

The Stranger extracts two lessons out of the myth. They had aimed too high and too low. The statesman they were after could neither emulate the god who truly is a shepherd nor compete with the various artisans who severally supply by art all that once came spontaneously for men. The Stranger does not explain why the organization of the true city, as Socrates calls it (*Republic* 372e6), could not be the unattainable ideal of the statesman. The true city had no ruler, but seems obviously enough in need of one, and the statesman should be perfect for the job. After all, the paradigm of weaving seems to be the translation inside the city of the shepherd who wanders outside. By keeping to the same animal presented under two different aspects, the Stranger lets us see that the paradigm-shift he is proposing reflects a historical shift from the apolitical pastoral life to the city of specialization. The myth had been given in order to show what would have to hold in order for the metaphor of shepherd to be true; and the Stranger had shown that its truth is embodied in myth and cannot be a guide to the age of Zeus. The Stranger has not explained in general why the poetry lingers after the reality is gone, and in particular why he has made young Socrates experience a hopeless nostalgia. The Stranger never repudiates fully the first set of divisions; he says that it served to separate the statesman from his congeners, or more exactly his fellow pasturers *(sunnomoi)*, before he was to be separated from his coefficients, the causes and co-causes of his rule (287b4–8). Just as the weaver emerges from an elaborate dichotomy, so the statesman needed the first argument and myth to stand clear of everyone else who is connected with knowledge and rule.

But this will not do. The human shepherd fulfills a variety of tasks for his flock without any competition from rival claimants precisely because he has no specialized knowledge of midwifery, medicine, or music (268a5–b6). The comprehensiveness of the shepherd's control stands over against the ever-diminishing range of each art as it becomes more refined, which needs accordingly to be set within the city in order for exchange to occur and its contribution be put together with those of others. Despite, however, the inappropriateness of the shepherd *(nomeus)* as the paradigmatic ruler, the Stranger suggests that he survives within the city in the form of law *(nomos)*. Law is the trace of the unscientific and prepolitical past with which the city of arts can never dispense. Even the young Socrates, who as a mathematician believes that life without the arts is not worth living (299c5–9), draws the line at ruling without laws (283e6–7). "Lawless" *(anomos)* does not look like "beast" and "barbarian" with their concealed negatives, but it too fails to distinguish between the arbitrariness of lawless rule and unlawful prudence. The city puts together two immiscible kinds in the label "lawless." It is as unavoidable for the city to be blind to that immiscibility as it is good for the city to be so. The failure of the

Stranger's first paradigm to reveal the true statesman is the failure of the city to accept him.[10] If the first paradigm lingers on in the later argument, it is due to the lesson it teaches about the difference between the Stranger's way and the way of the city.

The need for a new paradigm for the statesman's art is realized along with a general discussion of the nature of paradigms. As young Socrates is about to enter the city of knowledges, he is made aware of how knowledge is acquired. The Stranger has him now revert to childhood, not to recall the myths he was told, but to reflect on the letters he was taught (268e4–6, 277e3). Young Socrates is to recapitulate in remembering his own past what happened in general when men abandoned the pastoral life for cities. This recapitulation lets us see that the Stranger's remark—"Each of us probably, in knowing everything as in a dream, is once more ignorant of everything as in reality" (277d2–4)[11]—applies to the difference between their following unconsciously the paradigm of the shepherd and the Stranger's proposal to articulate a paradigm first and then match it up with the art of statesmanship. They had in fact just done the reverse. *Politikē* had been discovered first and then the myth had presented the paradigm upon which it had been based. This sequence forced the statesman to be exactly the same as the divine shepherd if he were to be a ruler at all. There were no functional analogies between shepherd and statesman. "Shepherd," one could say, was a metaphor that could not be transformed into a simile. "Weaver" is a simile that resists transformation into metaphor. Weaver and statesman link up together through the intermediaries *diakritikē* and *sunkritikē,* which cover both all of *praktikē* and *gnōstikē* without any confusion between them. "Shepherd," on the other hand, overwhelms the statesman: and nothing of a higher generality than either, in joining them, keeps them apart.

The most remarkable consequence of the paradigm-shift from the prepolitical shepherd to the urbanized weaver is that wool manufacture in general and weaving in particular illustrate in the ways in which they handle thread and cloth the very operations of dialectics itself. Philosophy in its peculiarly Socratic sense comes to light in the lengthy analysis of weaving. That analysis is in three phases: 1) the congeners of weaving; 2) its causes and co-causes; 3) the diacritical and syncritical processes in wool-working. Although the third phase belongs to the second, no attempt is made to assign *diakritikē* and *sunkritikē* to causality. *Diakritikē* and *sunkritikē* show up in the actions of carder, spinner, and weaver, but they are different from the classification of coefficients into causes and co-causes. The lengthy account of weaving discloses the *tropos* of weaving, and *tropos* becomes the common link between weaving and ruling, on the one hand,

and ruling and philosophy, on the other. The first account of *politikē* lacked an account of its *tropos,* and it seemed that no division could possibly supply what was missing. Young Socrates' mistake of dividing men from beasts looked like a mistake that belonged to *diairesis* as such, regardless of whether men and beasts were to be distinguished. *Diairesis* appeared to be capable only of distinctions among things;[12] it could not incorporate its own way into the discussion except in the highly artificial manner of the Stranger's diameter and diameter of the diameter. Unless such an incorporation could occur, the manner of *politikē* would never emerge, and the Stranger would ultimately have to resort to a description and abandon *diaeresis* as a procedure for isolating the statesman. Weaving, however, rescues the way of diairesis while it illustrates the way of *politikē.* Weaving is doubly paradigmatic; it exemplifies at once *politikē* and *dialektikē.* The length of its account therefore is both too long and too short. It is too long if it were designed only to clarify *politikē,* and it is too short in its inability to display all of *dialektikē.* Any double paradigm must have the same disproportions as weaving does. The principle of the more and less that it illustrates cannot be eliminated without its ceasing to be paradigmatic. Since the Stranger also suggests that *politikē* is paradigmatic (285d4–6), the length of the *Statesman* cannot be the right length unless it is the wrong length, for whatever of it should be expanded would risk either being a speech about *politikē* exclusively, with no paradigmatic power for *dialektikē,* or obscuring *politikē* altogether in a vain attempt to extract all of *dialektikē* out of *politikē.*

The Stranger's reflection on his own procedure emerges immediately after he has discerned in weaving the most general ways of proceeding, *diakritikē* and *sunkritikē,* or eidetic analysis. His reflection leads to a new division of sciences into that of the arithmetic measure and that of the measure of the mean. Since the sciences of relative measure are precisely the same as those in the class of *gnōstikē,* the science of the measure of the mean is the new definition of *praktikē.* Two arts are defined without either of them being negatively determined by the other. *Politikē* is now the leading candidate for being the architectonic science of the measure of the mean; but since the science of the measure of the mean regulates all paradigmatic reasoning as well, the *praxis* it determines encompasses both *politikē* and the discovery of *politikē.* The prudence of the statesman, which is displayed in the particulars of political action, is paradigmatic for the action of the Stranger. The action of the Stranger, however, is gnostic insofar as it is theoretical. It therefore redeems *gnōstikē* as the class of *politikē* while it reassigns *politikē* to the science of *praxis.* The gradual slide of *politikē* from *gnōstikē* to *praktikē* restores *politikē* to *gnōstikē* through the redetermination of *gnōstikē* and *praktikē* as the twofold science of measure. *Politikē,* then, exhibits what can only be called the indeterminate dyad of eidetic analysis.[13] It assumed this structure through its deidealization: only a god could be alternately either nothing but *gnōstikos* or nothing but *praktikos.* Man had to settle for a mixed *praxis.* This *praxis* was grounded in *sunkritikē* and *diakritikē,* which was in turn nothing but the dialogic action of *epitattein* that diverged in the original divisions of *gnōstikē* from the *autepitaktikē* of the divine shepherd. Man is *dunamei dipous:* only potentially rational.

The Stranger brings together the use of *diakrisis* and *sunkrisis* with the discovery of the two sciences of measure in the following manner: His criticism of the Pythagoreans for their failure to make the proper divisions in *metrētikē* launches him into a general proposal of how eidetic analysis is to be carried out. "Whenever one first is aware of the community of the many, one should not stand back until one sees all the differences in it that are situated in kinds *(eidē):* and, in turn, in the presence of the omnifarious dissimilarities, whenever they are seen in multitudes, one must not be able to be abashed *(dusōpoumenon)* before them and stop until one confines all the kindred within a single similarity and comprehends it with the being of a certain genus" (285a7–b6). Eidetic analysis has to persist in dividing against the appearance of unity and not be ashamed in the presence of a manifold of unlikenesses to seek the underlying unity. The first instance of a deceptive unity is presented by the law, which necessarily must homogenize the manifold of different human natures and actions (294a10–c9). To smash the law is to uncover a sea of dissimilarities, which in turn the dialectician must try to unify. Apparently, the unity must elude him; the best he can do is to discover the two kinds into which the manifold is divisible. These two kinds, which proverbially for us are represented by "He who hesitates is lost" and "Look before you leap," and in Greek are compressed into one—*speude bradeōs*—are reflected in the disjunction within another apparent unity, virtue. Virtue divides into courage and moderation, which have their natural base in the opposition, within the arithmetic measure, of relative motion, time, and power; but at the same time those virtues manifest the measure of the mean. The unity of moral virtue, which dissolves into a pair of contraries, recombines into one as the *phronēsis* of the measure of the mean that fully acknowledges the infinite diversity the law denies.

Socrates had set the problem the Stranger was to solve. His own suggestion was that the sophist and the statesman were each a *phantasma* of the true philosopher. The Stranger seemed to disagree, at least at the start, with this suggestion; in saying that the sophist and the statesman were three, he implied that they were all equally real, could be understood apart from one another (cf. *Sophist* 253c6–9), and the philosopher was certainly not the reality of which the other two were the images. In the course of the *Sophist,* however, the Stranger was forced to face the problem of image, and he discovered he did not know to which of the two arts that handled images sophistry belonged. He called one art *eikastikē,* the other *phantastikē. Eikastikē* was an art designed to give back in an image the same proportions as the original had, and *phantastikē* made an image in the proportions it would need if it were to be seen as beautiful from a certain perspective. This distinction had to be applied to the *Sophist* and every other Platonic dialogue. Were they *eikones* or *phantasmata*? If they were *phantasmata,* what were their several *eikones,* and what proportion did they have? According to the *Phaedrus,* the *eikōn* behind every dialogue was the black horse of Socrates, and the *phantasma* was the white horse, of which Phaedrus was one. The white horse was the truth of the Olympian gods. In the *Statesman,* whose action is identical with its argument, there is no white horse. The Stranger discovers to his surprise that the greatest sophists of the sophists are the spurious rivals of the statesman (303b8–c5). This discovery could not have been a surprise if the *Sophist* had already discovered this. Young Socrates' reply seems to suggest that the Stranger's discovery requires a complete turnabout of the *Sophist* if the politicians are really the sophists: *kinduneuei touto eis tous politikous legomenous periestraphthai to rhēma orthotata.* If, then, the *Statesman,* in defining the statesman, defines the sophist as well, the *Sophist* must be the *phantasma* of the *eikōn* the *Statesman* is. The disproportions of the *Statesman* are thus due to its being the only Platonic dialogue in which we are led into the workshop where dialogues are constructed. We see a dialogue put together without seeing the dialogue after it has been put in its proper place for viewing. What, then, is its proper place where the *eikōn* it is will become a *phantasma*? The Stranger solved the problem of the sophist by getting Theaetetus to agree that the god made everything. The Stranger discovers the statesman once he leaves as a myth the demiurgic god and assumes there is no Zeus. In the political sense, the *Statesman* is the only atheistic dialogue. It is not beautiful.

Notes

1. That *kritikē* is the same as *gnōstikē* is shown by the Stranger's later referring to *politikē* as *kritikē* even though it should be that part of *gnōstikē politikē* is not (292b9–10).

2. The Stranger may be hinting at this alternative when he allows someone else to assign the proper name to everything that is not *autepitaktikon: to kērukikon phulon* may not be adequate (260d7, e6–8).

3. The pun seems to explain why the Stranger uses *epitaktikē* rather than any derivative from *prostattein.* There are seventeen instances of *epitattein* and cognates before the myth and only five afterward; but there are four instances of *prostattein* before the myth but fifteen afterward.

4. Many of the distinctions of the barnyard section are said to be obvious to everyone (264e1, 3, 9; cf. 265 d3–5, e9); and its initial cuts depend in part on hearsay and trust (264b11, c5, 7–8).

5. In the *Theaetetus,* Theaetetus told Socrates how he and young Socrates had classified the roots of numbers (147d3–148b2). Their procedure involved the use of figures as images so that the square roots of 4, 9, 16, etc. were represented as the sides of squares, and 2, 3, 5, etc. were represented as rectangles and their square roots as the sides of squares whose areas were equal to those of the rectangles. Without being fully aware of it, they had managed to unify two different sciences, arithmetic and geometry, through using one as the image of the other. Their starting point had been Theodorus's proofs about the irrationality of the roots of certain magnitudes, which Theodorus had expressed in feet. In turning to numbers, they had dropped magnitudes and their measure in feet only to return to magnitudes as the images of numbers. The Stranger has now made young Socrates go one step further back than Theodorus's starting point.

6. When the Stranger summarizes the divisions after the myth, he reduces the five original differentiae to four (276a3–7), and since *pezon* here corresponds to *xērobatikon* and *aptēn* to *pezon,* he must have dropped *dipoun;* and inasmuch as he goes over again the replacement of *trophē* by *epimeleia* before he makes the cut between divine and human rule, he seems to imply that prior to that cut the division into two and four feet is irrelevant; divine rule of man corresponds exactly to Circe's rule of Odysseus's men. Circe had also tamed wolves and lions (*Odyssey* 10.212). Glaucon's rebellion against the city of pigs in the name of human pride (*Republic* 372d4–5) corresponds in the *Statesman* to the humiliation of man in light of the god. Young Socrates' pride, however, is tied directly to human reason, which in turn is also connected with Glaucon's pride but very indirectly; the length of the *Republic* is a sign of how indirect that connection is.

7. That *oikeias* is a genitive singular and agrees with *tēs poleōs* cannot be ruled out, for it would conform with the implication that the *basilikos* is the real king regardless of whether he rules or not.

8. A story in Herodotus connects these two senses of *ameikton.* The philhellenic Amasis, who usurped the throne of Egypt and to whom the Stranger possibly alludes as one who has to be enrolled in the priestly class before he could be regarded as a legitimate king (290e9–e3; cf. Herodotus 2.172.2–5), married a girl

from Cyrene, with whom, however, he could not have intercourse before she had prayed to Aphrodite (2.181.2–4).

9. In the *Critias,* Critias breaks off his narrative at the very moment he is going to quote Zeus. From this point of view, Critias conforms and Timaeus fails to conform with Socrates' requirements for poetry in the *Republic.*

10. There are two curious allusions to the present in the Stranger's revision of the final account. He speaks of those who are now statesmen (*tous enthade nun politikous,* 275c1–2), and of his comprehending by means of the same differentiae *tēn agelaiokomikēn tēn te nun kai tēn epi Kronou basileian* (276a6–7). We cannot help but think of Socrates, who like the god is not now ruling but is capable of rule. Socrates' *ta hautou prattein* is the present counterpart to the withdrawn providence of the god.

11. Whereas *hoion onar* can be paralleled in Plato (*Sophist* 266c9, *Parmenides* 164d2, *Symposium* 175e3, *Meno* 85c9), there is no other example where *hupar* is qualified with *hōsper* or the like. If we take the qualification strictly, it is not the case that we are ignorant of everything *hupar,* only in a sense are we so ignorant: the Stranger perhaps refers to the knowledge of ignorance.

12. A sign of this is the mysterious *hekousion* at 276e11 applied to *politikē* as opposed to the tyrant. The tyrant rules over *hoi biaioi* as the statesman over *hoi hekousioi,* but the voluntary nature of his art cannot be in opposition to the reluctance of the tyrant. The distinction, of course, between voluntary and forced is later admitted to be inapplicable to scientific rule (296c8–d5).

13. The Stranger begins with characterizing two different measures; after an allusion to the digression on nonbeing in the *Sophist,* the two measures are presented as two different sciences (284b7–e10). The science of nonbeing is the science of the other; the science of the other seems to be what the double character of *politikē* best illustrates.

EIGHTEEN

On the *Timaeus*

THIRTY YEARS AGO, WHEN I submitted a paper to Leo Strauss on Timaeus's science fiction, he wrote back to say that Plato's *Timaeus* for him had always been sealed with 7^7 seals, but he thought he saw two things clearly: Timaeus's account of the human soul is in agreement with Socrates' imprecise and political understanding of the soul in the *Republic*, and Timaeus's denial of *erōs* to the original constitution of man is a necessary consequence of that agreement. He might have added as well that the abstraction from the body, which he discerned to be the necessary trace of nonbeing in Socrates' anatomy of political idealism, has its counterpart in Timaeus's own procedure, whereby he begins, mistakenly as he says, with visible and tangible body, only to end up, after he has put soul first, with the five Platonic solids, which are neither visible nor tangible, in order to account for the physics of change. In what follows, I wish to look at the connections between the *Timaeus* and the *Republic* insofar as Strauss's interpretation of the *Republic* gives one a way, not to pry open the *Timaeus*, but to decipher some of its seals and read them as questions.

Strauss observed that the link between the *Timaeus* and the *Republic* seems to involve the following proportion: As Socrates presents the best city in speech, and Timaeus the best cosmos in speech, so Critias has to set Socrates' city in motion, giving it a place and a time, and Hermocrates was to set Timaeus's cosmos in motion and thereby replace Timaeus's likely story with the true cosmology. That Hermocrates has a task assigned to him, but no inkling is given of what it is, suggests that Plato thought there could not be a complete cosmology, and unlike the missing *Philoso-*

pher, which fails to complete the series *Theaetetus, Sophist, Statesman,* but which one can still figure out from the proper union of the *Sophist* and the *Statesman,* the *Hermocrates* cannot be imagined from the two and a half pieces Plato has left us. A sign of cosmology's impossibility is this: although Plato has hundreds of words with the suffix *-ikos,* which in the neuter plural can designate a field of inquiry and in the feminine singular an art or science, neither *ta phusika* nor *phusikē* appears in Plato. Aristotle is the first to coin these words, for he believes the principles of bodies in motion can be separated, at least in part, from the principles of intelligible beings. Plato's caution seems to be based on the puzzle mathematical physics has at its core. Aristotle consistently does not let mathematics have a sovereign place in his physics, and Timaeus expresses the puzzle in the phrase, "reason's persuasion of necessity." This puzzle becomes most conspicuous in elementary thermodynamics, in which the noncausal account of mathematical statistics agrees perfectly with the causally bound motions of gas molecules. Plato's own way of expressing this is to have Socrates urge mathematical education as the unique way of ascent from the Cave, only to show that all of mathematics can be done comfortably in the Cave without even a glimpse of the sun, let alone of the idea of the good. The divided line is a spurious bridge between the image of the sun and the image of the Cave.

The series *Republic, Timaeus, Critias* seems to be not only incomplete but spurious. Socrates narrates the *Republic* or *Politeia* to some unknown auditors the day after it occurred; the *Timaeus* happens one day after Socrates has feasted four men (Timaeus, Critias, Hermocrates, and an anonymous fourth) on an account of *politeia* and its best form. His summary seems to match Books 2–5 of the *Republic,* up to the point where Socrates introduced the philosopher-king; but the time of the *Timaeus* is at the Panathenaia and that of the *Republic* at the Bendideia, and these two festivals are eleven months apart. This temporal disparity appears to have a symbolic significance.[1] Whereas the revolutionary teaching of the *Republic* finds as its proper occasion a novel celebration of a goddess who was the only foreign deity Athens ever accepted into its sacred calendar, the city Socrates merely imagined turns out to be, according to Critias, the city of Athens long ago as Athena first founded it. Socrates' city, whose pattern was laid up in heaven, was once realized by a goddess whose chief characteristics were a love of war and a love of wisdom. She combines in herself what distinguishes Sparta from Athens, and these two cities signify in turn what Socrates' city in speech would have to unite. According to the principles of rationalization of myth that Critias lays down, Athena is nothing other than Socrates' philosopher-king, and who in being female but asexual comes closest to embodying the human being whom the gods according to Timaeus made first. Athena's makeup, however, in agreeing with the thrust of Socrates' argument, reveals the spuriousness of Socrates' psychology, which requires that the guardians be as savage as dogs are to strangers and as philosophic as dogs are to friends. In solving, then, symbolically the relation between the divergent settings of the *Republic* and the *Timaeus,* we come across a deeper difficulty. What did Socrates intend by proposing a city in motion that by his own argument could not possibly come to be? The complete exposure and utter explosion of political idealism, which stamps Strauss's interpretation of the *Republic* with its hallmark, seems to make the task of Socrates' hosts in the *Timaeus* futile if not impossible. It is not that the impossible cannot be the premise of an action, as Strauss showed in his interpretation of Aristophanes, but that after the *Republic* the showing of its impossibility in deed is superfluous. It thus seems that the temporal obstacle to linking the *Republic* and the *Timaeus* does have after all a symbolic meaning. It tells us that they cannot be linked because the city in speech cannot be put in place and in time. For its realization, that city requires not the cosmos we are acquainted with but a completely different one, in which Socrates could have educated the human beings Timaeus makes up and then passed them on to be enrolled in Athens by Critias. The consistency of the *Republic* and the *Timaeus* on this central point dispenses with the need for the *Timaeus.* The barbarian country Socrates thought could have contained his city merely seems to be his hometown. It is really at home in an alien cosmos.

Socrates' summary in the *Timaeus* of the best city merely seems, once again, to stop short of the philosopher-king. In concluding that marriages will be secretly arranged in order to couple the best men and women, he admits that on occasion at least golden parents will produce brazen children, and iron parents a golden child at least as often. He thus admits that his city cannot maintain order and motion perfectly, and accordingly that the rulers must be able to discern natures across classlines and correct the faults in the structure for the sake of justice. These rulers must be the philosophers, who, as Strauss showed, were indispensable to the city even prior to the introduction of the principles of equality and communism. Socrates implies in any case that order and motion are potentially inconsistent, and if there is to be a cosmology, an argument has to be given to show that either on a cosmic scale this difficulty does not arise, or, just as in the case of the city, order and motion must diverge. Timaeus begins as if he thought that constant corrections of this divergence were unnecessary—an implication that lies just behind the myth of the *Statesman*—but only because he began with body; as soon as he introduces soul, he grants a disorder in the cosmos that cannot be contained, as in Aristotle it is, within the sublunar sphere, but extends throughout the cosmos and spells of necessity the eventual disappearance of the cosmos.

Timaeus separates his account of time from his account of space. They differ from each other as much as arithmetic differs from geometry, or the discrete from the continuous. Timaeus borrows this distinction in a sense from Socrates' summary of the best city. Socrates' summary is in nine parts. The first four concern the division of natures, arts, and classes; the last four concern communism and generation. The central one describes the communized life of virtue the guardians lead. The word typical of the first part is "to speak" *(legein),* that of the second part "to remember" *(memnēsthai).* The second part deals with the transmission in time of the ordered structure of the city. We call for short the first part of the summary an eidetic analysis, the second a genetic analysis. Despite the need for Timaeus's cosmology to show the consistency of the eidetic analysis with the genetic, it does not. His demiurge starts out as both maker and father, but Timaeus is forced to admit their incoherence, which ultimately rests on his failure to solve the problem of time. A dispute going back to antiquity, which ranged Aristotle and Plutarch over against most of the neo-Platonists, turned on whether Timaeus merely for the sake of instruction put the cosmos in time or intended for it to have both a beginning and, were it not for the demiurge, a natural end. His confession that he put body before soul, even though the demiurge did not, indicates that one cannot subtract time from his account. If the order of his presentation were not that of time, Timaeus could have argued that just as the parts of a machine can be made in any order prior to its assembly, so the parts of the cosmos have only an eidetic relation to one another, and the genetic does not affect it.

If we turn from Socrates' summary to the *Republic* itself, we notice that the *Republic* too has an eidetic and genetic strain in it. Socrates proposes that they see the city coming into being and that they make the city in speech. The city they make is the best city in speech; the city they see becoming is the city to which they belong dialogically. I call it the dialogic city. The dialogic city is the only possible realization of the best city in speech. It is the city in which it is possible to ascend from the Cave, and thus realize simultaneously the eidetic and genetic analyses: the speaking that belongs to the eidetic and the transmission that belongs to the genetic are nothing other than the duality of speech itself as discrimination and communication, or dialectics. Communism is merely the defective institutionalization of dialectics. The *Republic* therefore has within itself the fulfillment of the project Socrates assigned to his guests of the day before and his hosts of today. He has given them both a city as lifeless as a painting and a city as alive as a city can be when a philosopher is in charge and his fellow citizens are the combative Thrasymachus, the manly and erotic Glaucon, and the peaceable Adimantus. Socrates and Thrasymachus are now friends. From this point of view, Socrates stops where he does in his summary because the rest is misunderstanding, and the mistake of Glaucon and Adimantus requires Socrates to enchant them with the possibility of a knowledge as impossible as the best city itself, for they do not understand that if there is an education *in* philosophy beyond their own education *to* philosophy, it consists in the understanding of their own education. No one can do that for them. It is not, then, the Athens of a remote past in which the best city in speech is in motion, but the city within the city of contemporary Athens that lasted for a day. The ephemeral of speech in action is the image of the eternal of thought.

If the best city has already been realized in motion, what exactly does Socrates expect of Timaeus and Critias? Critias, after all, does not render what Socrates said he himself was not competent to do, the city at war, for he gives the conditions for the conflict between Athens and Atlantis, but the deeds and speeches of either city are missing. Socrates likens his own incompetence to that of poets, who are best at representing whatever their own upbringing was. Poets are rooted in the morality of their own time and place. Socrates implies that he wants *per impossible* a poet born and bred in the best city to be its celebrant. He wants the Homer he censored in the second and third books of the *Republic* to sing once again of war, but he has to be "retrofited" into the mold of Socrates' imaginary city. Would this new Homer be one of those who lived his life in the Cave, or would he have ascended and understood the lesson of the tenth book, that, as Strauss said, the poets whom Socrates criticizes there are the poets he required for his own theology without justice and his own mythology without heroes? Socrates, then, seems to put to his hosts a riddle: How are they or anyone else to supply this Homer? Critias's solution is ingenious: a descendant of old Athens, who retained features of Athena's foundlings, had some poetical ability, much political experience, and wandered as far as a sophist,[2] will come as close as possible to Socrates' request. There is a sign that Critias intends to have Solon's story conform with Socrates' criteria for poetry in the *Republic:* Solon's account is solely in narrative, and at the very point Zeus would have spoken directly, the

Critias stops. Nonimitative poetry, however, cannot duplicate what Socrates did in the *Republic* or Homer in the *Iliad:* to be all the voices and keep his own. Critias's solution, then, is a nonstarter. He does not come to grips with Socrates' riddle. Socrates abstained from politics. He showed his justice by minding his own business. His incompetence therefore to describe his city at war is and is not parallel to the incompetence he ascribes to the poets: they cannot slough off their breeding, he cannot give up philosophy. Political philosophy is not to be understood as the same as the equal participation in politics and philosophy that Socrates ascribes to Timaeus, Critias, and Hermocrates. Political philosophy is the philosopher's ascent from, not his descent into, the Cave. The philosopher always looks back, he never turns back, to the Cave.

Socrates contrasts the poets with the sophists. The poets stay put, the sophists wander. The sophists are experienced in many beautiful speeches but miss the mark when it comes to the speeches and deeds of philosophers and politicians in wartime. The shape of Socrates' sentence makes it clear that speeches are not to be assigned to philosophers and deeds to politicians.[3] Socrates asks whether rest and motion can be combined. He comes forward here as Plato's spokesman. The question he poses is this. Thucydides managed to narrate the speeches and deeds of the Peloponnesian War—the greatest motion—without once mentioning Socrates, and Plato managed to represent the speeches and deeds of Socrates—a Socrates always young and beautiful—without narrating the wartime setting of most of Socrates' philosophic life. Thucydides and Plato split between them a single time-frame, so that the reader of one could discern from a unique series of events what holds forever as long as human nature remains the same, and the reader of the other could generalize about the necessary nature of philosophy from the most idiosyncratic of men, and they did so without either of them writing up the monster a political-philosophic history would be. Socrates asks, then, whether Plato was right to give the true but secret history of Athens apart from its public history, and Thucydides in turn was right to ignore its private history, in which Socrates was hidden among the silent women of Athens. The rebarbarization of Greece and the defeat of Athens were the conditions for the flight of Minerva's owl. If this is a necessity, what is its ground? Socrates' best city required, as Strauss showed, that the needs of the soul be grafted perfectly onto the needs of the body, and Thucydides and Plato, in splitting their tasks, agreed that this condition cannot be met. Timaeus silently accepts their agreement. In putting together body and soul in his cosmology, he comes up with a cosmos in which he satisfies the conditions for Socrates' best city but eliminates at the same time the possibility of Socrates being in it. Timaeus, however, does not put body and soul together smoothly. The inconsistencies of his account, which go back to his failure to put time and space together coherently, raise the question whether behind the so-called anthropic principle of contemporary cosmology there is the Socratic principle: what kind of cosmos must there be for Socrates to come to be? Can a cosmology be devised in which Socrates is a possibility but not a necessity? Socrates would be a necessity if and only if his best city in speech were possible, but its impossibility seems to entail that only the random of a certain kind could produce Socrates. It is a randomness that no one could either contrive or hope for. It is the random in the form of the teleology of evil.

Socrates' best city needed for its realization the complete triumph of art: humans would have to be made from scratch if the city were to satisfy its eidetic structure.[4] The genetic would then go by the board. Socrates' digression into philosophy in Books 5–7 testifies to his doubt whether man's elimination of man could ultimately be halted. The city of arts necessarily ends up with an artfully devised simulacrum of the human, while the sacred, which in his account only occurs in its nonutilitarian form when the city has completely degenerated into tyranny, seems ultimately too weak to put a check on the other root of the city. Nothing stands in the way of Atlantis, certainly not Athens. If philosophy were in charge of the city, this nightmare would be averted; but if this cannot be, nothing but accidents could do the work of reason. Critias's story makes out that nonperiodic cataclysms always come to the rescue of man. Timaeus's cosmos offers no such hope. It offers no such hope because Timaeus starts out with a split between being and the demiurge, or between the beautiful and the good, that must, in denying to the cosmos the necessary accident of Socrates, take away from it as well the cleansing effects of natural disasters. It is too well ordered to be good, for Timaeus professes not to know that "best men . . . for the most, become much more better for being a little bad."[5] Timaeus's overall scheme warrants this profession of ignorance, but there grows up within it another argument that can be compared to the dialogic city in its relation to the best city in speech. This alternate cosmos is far richer in sports than the official one; it has many congeners and none of them exhaust all possibilities or put man in the dilemma Timaeus's cosmos does. His cosmos is tragic for man. It can only be complete if man is unjust, and man is fated to be unjust. Man cannot say yes to Timaeus's cosmos but must wish that either it or he never come to be. Man begins to degenerate and the cosmos to be complete when some of the original men prove to be cowards and unjust. Confronted with this fate, we can surmise, men commit suicide and become women.

Timaeus begins with a prelude that contains within it all the perplexities that permeate his extended development of it. He begins with a question that he immediately answers. The question involves a division. It was already asked in antiquity what it was that he divided. It turns out that he divided the soul that the demiurge made first out of ingredients that were originally apart. Once these ingredients were in soul, they became cognitive principles; and hence Timaeus's answer to his first question is in terms of knowledge, either whatever is comprehended by intellection with logos or whatever is opined by opinion with irrational perception. In his prelude, then, Timaeus does begin in a sense with soul; but the consequence is that his original question, What is what is always? is not answered, for Timaeus never states what these eternal beings are. Indeed, in posing the question, he puts it in a nominal sentence, viz., *ti to on aei;* or "what the being always?" which implies that before answering the question what these eternal beings are, let alone how they are known, he would have to say whether they are at all.

Timaeus makes no existential statement before he asserts that the cosmos is visible and tangible, and this is his first mistake. Timaeus is well aware of the difficulties he has caused himself. At the very start he declares that he must make a division according to his opinion. He admits that he separates being from becoming by opinion and not by knowledge, for by his own division it would be impossible for mind to know of becoming. He complicates his account further by assigning to becoming the same eternity as he does to being, but again he does not ask whether what always becomes is. Instead, after answering his double-barreled question epistemically, he assigns becoming and perishing to the realm of opinion. He thus implies that within eternal becoming there is coming to be and passing away, or that, as he later puts it, space is coeval with being and not the effect of any cause. He then asserts that whatever comes to be becomes by a cause; but this can apply only to whatever perishes and not to whatever always becomes. He compounds our perplexity by declaring that if any demiurge looks at that which is always and reproduces its structure and power, the result is beautiful; but if he looks away toward becoming, the result is not beautiful. It seems very arbitrary to declare that a painting of a beautiful human being if beautifully done is not beautiful, and that if a craftsman keeps his eye on the eternal he cannot fail to produce something beautiful. Is Socrates' picture of the soul in the

Phaedrus not monstrous? After all, one of the horses of the winged chariot is as ugly as Socrates. But we do not have to go outside the *Timaeus* to know that the demiurge did not always look at being. He turned away from it and looked to himself when he decided to give the cosmos mind and was forced to give it soul. The demiurge may very well be eternal, but he cannot be what is comprehended solely by mind with logos, for the beings are not the causes of becoming without him.[6] When Timaeus gives up for a time the demiurge, he postpones any account of the causality of being.

Now as soon as Timaeus asserts that whatever becomes must have a cause, it must be as intelligible as its cause, and if the beings are its causes, it ceases to be determined solely by whatever falls under irrational perception. Timaeus asks whether the cosmos or *ouranos* came to be or not. He concludes that it came to be because it is perceptible; but the cosmos is not perceptible but the intelligible order of all becoming, and only if *kosmos,* in being the same as *ouranos,* meant the visible sky, could Timaeus draw his conclusion. Timaeus, however, cannot mean by *ouranos* "the sky," for if he did the demiurge would once more have looked away from the beings in making everything that was not sky. Cosmos is the togetherness of heaven and earth; it is not the same as heaven and earth. Timaeus later concedes as much when he replaces his false beginning with the true beginning and has the soul be the invisible envelope of the cosmos. Timaeus thus lays down three principles before he starts off on the wrong foot: being and becoming are distinct; everything that becomes has a cause; and nothing becomes beautiful if the demiurge does not look to being. These three principles do not suffice for establishing the origin of the cosmos in time, but the expression he uses for the cosmos—*tode to pan*—shows that he has jammed together a deictic pronoun that belongs to perception with a whole that does not. This unwarranted jamming haunts Timaeus throughout while it points to the ontological problem as he sees it and is the burden of his entire logos. But as it is, he has now assumed what he has to prove, that heaven and earth do form a cosmos, and he never does get around to proving it. Indeed, he later has to divorce heaven from earth in order to get the cosmos to be a one through time, but it is then no longer a whole. The sphere images the comprehensiveness of noetic animal but at the price of homogeneity: it has no proper parts.

Once Timaeus has appealed to the superlative beauty of the cosmos and the excellence of its demiurge, he says that it must be the image of some paradigm. This does not follow, for a maker could well look to the structure of something without imitating any part of that something.[7]

The sophist can display the same characteristics as the angler without bearing any resemblance to the hunter. That they share a manner of proceeding, tools for proceeding, and a subject they single out and make their exclusive concern does not establish a likeness between the hiddenness of the quarry of the angler and the secrecy of the sophist, between fishing pole and speeches, bait and talk of virtue, or between fish and rich young men. The sun is an image of the good for the sake of understanding, it is not the imagistic product of the good. If it were, Socrates would have supplied the cosmology that he confessed he could not before he embarked on his second sailing. The cosmos, then, could be a whole because there is a cosmos of the beings, and it could be good because the cosmos of the beings is a whole through the idea of the good. Timaeus, on the other hand, has the demiurge assume that the soul, in being somehow all things, is unqualifiedly the whole. In order, then, for the whole of being to be the good or the idea of the good, it would be necessary, as Strauss observed, for the cause of the being of the beings and the cause of the knowability of the beings to be one and the same. The good is the bond for the necessary distance between the beings and knowledge of them. Socrates had suggested this on the basis of the difference and sameness of the sun as the double source of heat and of light. Timaeus, however, never speaks of the sun as the cause of becoming, only as the marker of time, and he cannot unite its two roles because the demiurge is the sole cause of good, to which being contributes nothing.[8] In order, then, for Timaeus to assign a cosmos to heaven and earth, he would have had to start from the good in its relation to being and not, as he does, from the good in its relation to becoming. The cosmos as a living and thinking being takes up the slack in Timaeus's defective ontology. It replaces the idea of the good, it does not make up for it.

Timaeus says that the speeches that explicate either paradigm or image must be of the same order as either of them is. He concludes accordingly that the speeches of the likeness can be no more than a likely story, or as becoming is to being, so trust *(pistis)* is to truth. If one thinks of the divided line, where trust is between *eikasia* (likeness-making) and *dianoia* (hypothetically deductive reason), and, by the ratios Socrates sets up, *dianoia* is equal in length to *pistis,* what Timaeus sets out to do is replicate trust simultaneously on the levels of *dianoia* and *eikasia.* He gets rid of trust, or the confidence we have in the "that" of things, by linking the nonbeings of *eikasia* with the nonbeings of *dianoia,* or geometry. His argument pushes the being of becoming into the realm of nonbeing and thus confirms what he first put as a question. *Eikasia,* however, is not of the same extent as *dianoia,* and consequently the cosmos as image does not coincide with the cosmos of mathematical construction. The difficulty can be put as follows: The expression *hoi eikotes logoi* has a double sense. By itself it would mean "plausible speeches," speeches arrived at by way of conjecture, but in the context it must also mean "imagistic speeches," or, as the Eleatic Stranger calls them, "spoken phantoms" *(eidōla legomena).*[9] Timaeus uses "likely speech" and "likely myth"indifferently and never lets on except once that he has introduced this ambiguity; but if one allows it, then an imagistic speech would be a speech that expressed the logos of that of which the image was an image. "This is a picture of our dog Buckwheat." "This is our dog Buckwheat." The first speech acknowledges that one is looking at an image, the second identifies that of which it is an image, and does not in itself deny that one is looking at an image. Both are true speeches; they are not plausible speeches. If, then, the likely speech of the cosmos took after either model, the likely story of Timaeus would be true, and not, as he says, no less likely than any other. The likely speech would be about being and not about becoming. It would be likely because being and not becoming was by conjecture. The likely story, however, would be a spoken phantom if the speeches one made about it were not of the beings that they resembled but of other beings that only seemed to be the same as the others.

When the demiurge constructs the world-soul, he forces together the same and the other and mixes them with being and becoming. The nature of the soul itself entails that the other will be mistaken for the same and the same for the other. Of these two mistakes, the more fundamental is that the same is the other: the evening star and the morning star are two before they are known to be one. The world-soul consists of two circles, each of which is exactly the same as the other. When the demiurge tilts one at an angle to the other, he calls it the circle of the other, and the other the circle of the same. Despite their merely nominal difference, the demiurge assigns one to intellection and the other to perception. We are destined to take, Timaeus implies, the world of sense for the world of mind and still believe they are not the same. We are destined to do what Glaucon did, when he first shaped the perfectly just man into an artifact whose shadow he cast on the wall of the Cave and then asked Socrates to prove that he was truly happy. The first to introduce the word *eidos* into the *Republic* was Glaucon.

Both Socrates and Timaeus are violators of their own teaching. Socrates pretends that the ascent from the Cave consists in the recovery of the third dimension, but otherwise there is a one-to-one correspondence between the shadows on the wall of the Cave and the bodies of becoming, and the artifacts the puppeteers are carrying do not distort the beings in any way. Socrates pretends that law and convention do not stand in the way of the discovery of nature, or that the Cave is not, as Strauss showed, the city. Timaeus borrows this assumption for the first part of his account. The animals we see are exactly the animals that constitute the parts of noetic animal, and that the four elements we see are one through transformation, while their noetic counterparts form a whole without ever changing, does not affect the matchup between being and becoming. Timaeus, however, is even more radical than Socrates in going against his own principles. He declares that there is only one cosmos even though the notion of paradigm and image implies that images as such belong to a manifold, and the number of reproductions possible betrays their dependence on the one original. Timaeus indeed argues that noetically there can only be one being, and the demiurge made the cosmos one in order to represent symbolically the necessary oneness of its paradigm; but he soon declares that the demiurge uses up all the corporeal elements for the making of a single cosmos in order to ensure that no external forces could ever destroy it. Timaeus thus has the demiurge rid the cosmos of decay, despite the fact that becoming and corruption are an indissoluble pair within eternal becoming, and he wipes out any trace in the cosmos that it is an image.

The meaning behind Timaeus's false start emerges clearly when he says he made a mistake in starting with the transformation of the four elements rather than with the making of soul. His mistake was due, he says, to the human participation in the random, but on the face of it his excuse is absurd, for he could have as easily corrected it before he erred as correct it afterward. Timaeus begins by asking his auditors to forgive him for any inconsistencies, but they should expect from him an account inferior to no one's. He admits that there are possibly other equally plausible accounts; indeed, he himself gives two. The account that starts with corporeal becoming is his plausible alternative to that which starts with the making of soul,[10] and the account that begins with space and not with paradigm and image by themselves is his alternative to his starting with the making of soul. The inconsistencies among the three accounts is his version within plausible speech of the manifold of images that belongs to the nature of paradigm and image that he seemed at first to deny. There is no reason to believe, then, that his third correction should be his last, and any plausible account not subject to infinite revisions. Just as the making of soul does not correct entirely his starting with body, so the account of space does not correct entirely his second beginning. Two parts of the world-soul are the divisible same and the divisible other of body; but if soul is prior to body, and space prior to soul, the divisible same and other must have been incorporated into soul from space. Soul is one-third space; it is one-third irrational, or, rather, since space is formless, it is some necessarily indeterminate constituent of soul. Timaeus, however, never makes this correction in world-soul. The farthest he goes in the first part is to imply that the circle of the other in its six divisions designates the arbitrary inside the seemingly rational. Six is a number that, as the physicists say, has been fed in by hand. In the second part, Timaeus grants that there may be more than one cosmos and consequently that all of them perish. Yet these dilutions of first principles never come to grips with the true problem: whether the disorderly is as much at a discount for soul as it is for body.

The making of world-soul culminates in the establishment of time. Time is the way in which the cosmos becomes one and as close as possible to the whole that is its paradigm.[11] The oneness time imparts is in the counting of time. The intervals of time can always be brought together into one, whether it be the one of day and night, the days of one month, the months of one year, or the coincidence of all the instruments of time in one great year.[12] The one of time belongs, Timaeus says, to the parts of time. They are at odds with the species of time, for there are only two species of time, past and future, and the present between is a false insertion by men, for "is" in precise speech belongs to that which is always. The insertion of "is" between "was" and "will be" exemplifies perfectly our necessary mistaking of the other for the same. The one of time counts the past and the future. They count what is no longer and what is not yet. Time is the ultimate expression of the nonbeing of becoming. It is the truth of the myth that Kronos castrated Ouranos. Becoming only is if one speaks imprecisely. Becoming only is if the images of being can hold onto the being of space, and the being of space can be spoken of only imprecisely, by way of images, and can only be grasped by a bastard kind of reasoning.[13] All the becomings in space are bastards; their father cannot recognize them as his. The demiurge as the maker of time splits apart from the demiurge as the father of becoming, for everything that becomes is at the expense of its recognizability.

The difference between the two designations of the demiurge is the cosmological equivalent to Thrasymachus's distinction between precise and imprecise speech, which Strauss showed to be one of the fundamental keys for the understanding of the *Republic.* Thrasymachus had wanted to maintain that a ruler who made a mistake was strictly speaking no longer a ruler, any more than a doctor who erred was a doctor. Thrasymachus could not reconcile his vaunted political realism with this distinction; but Socrates was able to show that justice necessarily consisted in the dyad of imprecise and precise speech, or in the difference and sameness of justice as minding one's own business and minding one's own business well. They showed up together in the principle of the best city and its structure, for its structure was a necessary dilution of its principle. Timaeus's cosmology is likewise concerned with how cosmic principles and cosmic structures do and not fit together. Their failure to fit perfectly together shows up in the difference between time and space.

Timaeus's original distinction between being and becoming means that becoming hides its causes. It is concealed because it is manifest. The disappearance of being is the condition for the appearance of becoming. The cosmos is first a sphere because the demiurge put the visible elements into such a shape, then because the rotation of the ecliptic produces an invisible sphere, and finally because the cosmos is in fact a dodecahedron that in rotation appears spherical. As soon as Timaeus acknowledges the existence of perspective, eikastic speeches disappear as a possibility and in principle must be replaced throughout by the speeches of *phantastikē*.[14] His discussion of time first indicates what would have to be done were such a replacement possible. After asserting that no form of expression in which being and becoming are coupled—not even when that which is not is said to be what is not—is compatible with precise speech, he says that perhaps *(tach' an)* it would not be an appropriate time *(kairos prepōn)* at the present *(en tōi paronti)* to speak precisely about them. To be present *(pareinai)* is to be *(einai)* here and now. The present of discourse is the nonmeasurable interval between the two species of time. The present can be of any duration—this evening, today, this week, this year, this century, this era—but it cannot be collapsed into the nows of time. The nows of time are points that can never be set down precisely, and the swiftness of the soon *(tacha)* is always too late. All the imprecise expressions of time cast doubt on the intelligibility of *tode to pan,* the existence of which Timaeus set out to explain. The application of mind to becoming puts time in place and banishes the timely.[15]

In the *Sophist* the Eleatic Stranger distinguishes between the eikastic and the phantastic arts of painting and sculpture. The eikastic art reproduces the proportions and colors of the paradigm on any scale. It believes it is nowhere or anywhere when it makes its copies. The phantastic art realizes that if one makes a figure of colossal size, though the upper parts could be in the image in a correct proportion to the lower, the upper body would appear, from our perspective on the ground, smaller than the lower. The phantastic art thus makes an image that is not an eikastic but a phantastic image of the original, so that the appearance of the phantastic would appear eikastically beautiful. Since the cosmos is of such an immense size, one would like to know whether the demiurge practiced eikastics or phantastics. If his art were eikastical, the cosmos would appear falsely beautiful, and one could infer, if it were ever discovered to be an eikastic image, that the demiurge looked to becoming and not being. If, on the other hand, his art were phantastical, the image that copied the paradigm was disproportionate, and it would require much ingenuity to figure out how to recover the original. This difficulty is the background problem in Timaeus's discussion of space. It is not, however, the most important of the problems. As an application of a Zenonian paradox, the problem begins easily enough. If, Timaeus says, each of the four elements changes into the others through one, two, or three steps, what at any given time is the fire we see? It cannot be fire, for in respect to its future it must already be on the way to another element, and in respect to its past it must have been partly what it now appears to have ceased to be. At any moment in the cycle of transformations, each element comprises what it was and what it will be as well as what it appears to be but is not. Every element is a phantom image of itself, but it appears as what it is. What it is, is some regular solid, but at no time is it what it is. The elements are as apparitionally distinct as they are dianoetically, but they never are entirely either one.[16]

Timaeus's first solution in light of the hypothesis of change is to say that *to toiouton* (is) each element, that which is like what it is (is) what it is like. Timaeus expresses this in a nominal sentence; in asserting an identity between likeness and being, we give up being.[17] We are then asked to withdraw the deictic pronouns *tode* and *touto* from any of these *toiauta* and apply them to something else. That something else is *chōra,* or "space." Socrates was the first to use the word; he spoke of the need for offspring, who do not conform to the higher class in which they are born, to change their place with those who are coming up from below (19a5). *Chōra* can mean "country" as opposed to "town," or the "territory" of a tribe or city. It is primarily the local. Its denominative is *chōrein,* which can mean either "to leave a place and make room for something," or "to contain and have room for something." Its adverbial congener is *chōris,* "separately" or "apart"; it is constantly used in Plato for dialectical discriminations. Timaeus's first formulation of space implies that *tode to pan* or *hode ho kosmos* cannot be expressions of precise speech, for the cosmos is a collection of *toiauta* insofar as it is visible, and the cosmos, insofar as it is intelligible, does not admit the deictic pronoun. *Hode ho kosmos* and *tode to pan* look away from the beings and toward speech.[18] They are the emblematic expressions of Socrates' second sailing, which he likened to our looking at the eclipse of the sun's reflection in water.

Timaeus's second formulation for the sake of greater clarity goes like this. "Were someone," he says, "to fashion all shapes out of gold without ever stopping in refashioning each into all, and were someone or other to point to one of them and ask what in the world it is *(ti pot' esti),* far the safest thing to say is, 'Gold,' but the triangles and all the other shapes that were coming to be in it, never to speak of these as being, inasmuch as they are altering while one is positing them, but if, after all, the questioner is willing to accept securely *to toiouton,* 'the such,' one should be content" (50a5–b5). The original answer has been demoted to second place and the best answer is gold, or, in the interpretation of the image, space. The example no longer depends on the truth of the hypothesized physics of change; indeed, Timaeus will deny that the four elements do change into one another, and in place of what he calls an incorrect phantom appearance, he will take earth out of the cycle and give a stability to things in the midst of change. Earth is the physicist's substitute for the truth of *chōra.* Timaeus's example transforms the original problem of eikastics into phantastics. Space is now dialogic space. *Tode* and *touto* now have their true significance; *tode* is everything in the sphere of the speaker, *touto* everything in the sphere of the one addressed. *Tode* and *touto* are expressions of "I" and "You," respectively. "I" is not a pronoun but, as Emile Benveniste says, "*I* can be defined only in terms of 'elocution,' not in terms of objects, as is the case with a nominal sign. *I* signifies 'the person who enunciates the present instance of discourse containing *I.*' "[19] Timaeus uses "I" only once: "I the speaker" (*ho legōn egō,* 29c8). The expression occurs nowhere else in Plato. *Chōra,* then, which "I" establishes, is the nonuniversalizable. Its mythical name is Hestia, the only god who has never seen the hyperuranian beings. It is the expression for the apartness of parts insofar as they are not parts of a whole. *Chōra* is the part maker; it is that which breaks beings apart. It separates Greeks from barbarians and turns negation into constitution. There is no *eidos* or measure of place; it is the exact opposite of time. It expresses the local warp in space-time that vanishes at the moment "I" falls silent. It corresponds to the manifold of local horizons within which men are; it is Timaeus's version of the Cave in which the prisoners talk to one another and ask what each of the shadows is. The question Timaeus has his questioner put is *ti pot' esti?* "Once" *(pot')*, which is now with "is," is the indeterminable interval of time. It was that which could not be one of the parts of time and was squeezed out from the species of time only to reappear surreptitiously in the discourse on the timely.[20] To be present *(pareinai)* is to put together space and time in being insofar as being is apart *(chōris)*. It is a beautiful coincidence that the idiomatic translation of *ti pot' esti?* is, "What in the world is it?"

The truth about space was stated, according to Timaeus, when he said that it was to be a receptacle, like a nurse, of all becoming (49a5–6). The truth juxtaposes a metaphor with a simile. It juxtaposes a phantastic with an eikastic phrase. A metaphor identifies two things; it takes the other for the same. A simile acknowledges a difference in the sameness it has seen. The truth about the likely story Timaeus tells is that as metaphor it is likely *(eikōs)*, and as simile it is a phantom image. In the literal sense of metaphor, the images of being were transferred onto being and read off as if they were of that of which they were not—the ideality of the nominal sentence, *to toiouton pur*, represents this; but once in principle a simile is acknowledged to be what it is, one cannot tell how to subtract the difference the simile has from that to which it is like. If one could, there would be no need of similes.[21] Contrary, then, to one's first impression, the phantastics of the second part of the *Timaeus* is eikastical, and the eikastics of the first part phantastical.[22] This turnaround is, as Strauss illustrated, the essential trait of any Platonic argument. If it does not occur, we are still stuck in the Cave and have not yet begun to make an ascent.[23]

Notes

1. For the symbolic significance of an impossible time-frame, one might compare that of the *Gorgias*, whose setting, from the death of Pericles to the trial of the generals of Arginousae, covers almost the entire period of the Peloponnesian War: rhetoricians are inexperienced in the deeds they presume to control. The first word of the *Gorgias* is "war."

2. Herodotus 1.29.1.

3. The placement of *hama* (19e5), so that it looks as if it is in hyperbaton, with the implication that philosophers and statesmen are combined in the same persons, indicates that the actions and speeches of each are also to be taken distributively.

4. The first and last word of making in the *Timaeus* is *paidopoiïa* (18c6, 91c2);

it is the ordinary word for sexual generation, but, as Agathon indicates, it already points to Socrates' solution (*Symposium* 196e2–197a3).

5. Shakespeare, *Measure for Measure,* act 5, sc. 1, lines 441–42.

6. Atticus already asked whether the demiurge belonged to noetic animal or not. If he does, he is incomplete, since he is only a part; if he does not, there is a noetic animal that comprehends both him and the noetic animal he looked at.

7. This error has its counterpart in Timaeus's account of mathematical construction. He asserts that there must be a third element if two other elements are to be brought together beautifully (31b8–c1), but the self-binding of warp and woof in weaving shows that this does not hold in all cases. A false representation of numbers raised to the third power as equivalent to three dimensions follows on this error.

8. Timaeus can account for the difference between light and heat only by ascribing it to two different species of fire (58c5–d2); he therefore cannot account for our awareness of distance, for sight occurs when the fire within fuses with the fire outside into a single homogeneous body (45c2–d3). There is thus no "out-thereness." This mechanical explanation precedes the teleology of sight (47a1–b2), and it could not have been reversed without an admission that the making of man is not his generation. Timaeus is caught between asserting that any account of becoming is just play and for the sake of relaxation from the serious business of understanding being (59c5–d2), and conceding that there can be no understanding of the divine if one does not start from the necessary (68e1–69a5).

9. Nestor introduces the same ambiguity when he hears Telemachus (*Odyssey* 3.124–25). Telemachus's speech is as sensible as his father's, but it is still just a likeness. At *Republic* 414c8–10 there is the same juxtaposition of these two senses.

10. The account of corporeal becoming is a deduction from noetic animal and involves geometric proportions only; the account of soul evolves into an account of the solar system that involves nongeometric proportions as well: there is a surd *(leimma)* in the sectioning of soul. Since Timaeus never gives any sizes, dimensional numbers, or the constants of nature, must be inexplicable and due to *chōra.*

11. The other two cosmic unities are the unity of corporeal structure under transformation (Timaeus later abandons this) and of animal under metempsychosis. Every animal can be labeled "human" and is accordingly a *toiouton;* it is left obscure whether it can equally be called "divine." The beasts, in any case, are us: the other is the same. On the eikastic level, a recurrent "such" may be "dog," on the phantastic, "dog" is "human"; but in our failure to acknowledge this, the human being is "a son of a bitch." Accordingly, the asexual men who prove to be cowardly become women, i.e., the indignation at their cowardice relabels them. *To thumoeides,* which makes "I" possible, is the ground for all phantastic speech. Timaeus's cosmos accommodates it.

12. Insofar as time makes for the unity of the cosmos, Timaeus can speak of the time before there was time; there was then strictly relativistic time, when no interval measured for one series of events could be set in any ordered relation with any other series. This local character of time corresponds to the ineradicable localness of space and space-time.

13. Despite the number of images Timaeus applies to space, he never likens it to a mirror, for it is the ground of all orientation and consequently stands in the way of any isomorphism between being and image: the image *(eikōn),* since that for which it has come into being does not belong to itself, is a constantly moving phantom *(phantasma)* of some other *(heteron ti)* (52c2–3). We attach a condition to anything we believe to be: to be something is to be something somewhere. This somewhere *(pou)* is our acknowledgment that every something depends on something other than itself in order to be.

14. Of the forty-four instances of the root *phain-, phan-,* there are only six before the demiurge stops making the cosmos; and of these six, two belong to the prelude (28c2, 29b6), three are about the planets, and one about terrors and signs (40c9). The last occurrence of this root is at 80c8, shortly before Timaeus begins his account of disease and the degeneration of the cosmos.

15. When Solon was in Egypt, he tried to set the oldest Greek stories into measurable time (22b2–3), but he found out that though they are of the past one cannot put them on a consistent time-line. This absence of a chronology makes the Greeks, according to the Egyptians, always children: their youthful souls hold on to the truth of the never-quite-vanishing present.

16. Water is H_2O, but we always see it in some state, and as a formula it is never any of its states. In the case of smell, Timaeus does admit that we perceive nonregular solids (66d1–4). We then come closest to perceiving the truth of all change.

17. It is a nominal sentence because fire itself is a *toiouton,* for the three elements are merely rearrangements of the same triangles that constitute them; and the triangles themselves, in turn, are *toioutoi* of triangle itself, for all of the corporeal triangles are imperfect (73b5–8), and triangle itself, even if it is not just hypothetical (48c2–4), is not the same as the paradigmatic triangle selected for the construction of the elements.

18. The absence of the expressions *touto to pan* or *houtos ho kosmos* in the *Timaeus* points to the difficulty that even if there are many *kosmoi,* in accordance with the relation of paradigm and image, there is no access to them, and hence there is a fateful individuality to "this whole" that denies its intelligibility. If there were intrusions into this cosmos of others in local pockets of space-time, as the image of the *plokanon* suggests that there are, then the essential heterogeneity of the cosmos would ground the necessity for Timaeus's story to be inconsistent. It would follow that *tode to pan* is not and cannot be in the strict sense a *kosmos.*

19. Emile Benveniste, *Problèmes de linguistique générale* (Paris 1966), 252.

20. The zero of the now in the species of time seems to have its counterpart in the rapidity with which the figures in the gold change; but Timaeus implies that change is never instantaneous but always takes time, regardless of whether one can keep up with it or not.

21. Timaeus seems to imply that any mathematical model of bodies in motion will introduce a simile or a set of similes that will not admit of correction, or, as one now says, of renormalization.

22. Timaeus shows how misleading the notion of plausible speeches is as soon as he gives an account of the compounds of the four elements: his account is now fully testable, and if "water" cannot be made into gold, it is false. That he denies that his theory of colors can be tested indicates his awareness of this (68b5–8; d2–7). That "recipes" can duplicate nature does not entail that one has a true account; they could well be phantastic and not eikastic speeches.

23. Timaeus goes to great lengths to explain the experience of taking the right for the left and vice-versa (43e4–44a7; 46a2–c6). This is the experience of the baby, for whom there is no other; and it occurs later whenever one faces oneself in a mirror. The world, he implies, is not a mirror of ourselves; it is not the case that for us there is nothing out there that is not oneself looking back at oneself; but the Cave is the place where there is nothing that is not human. Our experience of weight is perhaps the most important of human disorientations. We call "down" what resists our effort to displace it more than what we call "up" does (62c3–63e8). We give an absolute designation to what solely depends on our interference with things. The third directions, front and back, have to do with time: what is *prosthen hēmōn* (before us) is the past, what is *opisthen hēmōn* (behind us) is the future. We face the past in going forward into the future. This is the species of the present.

NINETEEN

On Wisdom and Philosophy: The First Two Chapters of Aristotle's *Metaphysics A*

EACH OF ARISTOTLE'S THREE MOST theoretical writings begins with a critique of his predecessors; but whereas the second books of his *Physics* and *On Soul* present his own definitions of nature and soul respectively, the second book of the *Metaphysics* seems to be nothing but a series of questions. Nature and soul are there regardless of what anyone might say about them (cf. *Physics* 193a3); but without perplexity there is nothing to metaphysics. Metaphysics seems to be the only science that in asking questions discovers all of its own field, and so, in completing philosophy, somehow returns philosophy to its origin in wonder. Perhaps, then, being is not just in speech a question *(ti esti);* and that which was sought long ago, is sought now, and forever will be sought is precisely what being is.

I

Aristotle begins not with the question of being but with its correlative, the question of knowledge and wisdom. This question is the substitute for the lack of anything self-evidently prior to that which metaphysics itself establishes. The theme of the first chapter is delight and admiration—the delight we ourselves take in any effortless acquisition of knowledge, and the admiration we grant to anyone who is manifestly superior to ourselves in knowledge. That which unites that kind of delight with this kind of admiration is the absence in both of calculation. Without

NINETEEN

On Wisdom and Philosophy: The First Two Chapters of Aristotle's *Metaphysics A*

EACH OF ARISTOTLE'S THREE MOST theoretical writings begins with a critique of his predecessors; but whereas the second books of his *Physics* and *On Soul* present his own definitions of nature and soul respectively, the second book of the *Metaphysics* seems to be nothing but a series of questions. Nature and soul are there regardless of what anyone might say about them (cf. *Physics* 193a3); but without perplexity there is nothing to metaphysics. Metaphysics seems to be the only science that in asking questions discovers all of its own field, and so, in completing philosophy, somehow returns philosophy to its origin in wonder. Perhaps, then, being is not just in speech a question *(ti esti);* and that which was sought long ago, is sought now, and forever will be sought is precisely what being is.

I

Aristotle begins not with the question of being but with its correlative, the question of knowledge and wisdom. This question is the substitute for the lack of anything self-evidently prior to that which metaphysics itself establishes. The theme of the first chapter is delight and admiration—the delight we ourselves take in any effortless acquisition of knowledge, and the admiration we grant to anyone who is manifestly superior to ourselves in knowledge. That which unites that kind of delight with this kind of admiration is the absence in both of calculation. Without to know. If, however, speech as the species-bond for man is not just accidentally the way in which knowledge is expressed, then perhaps knowledge as that which alone is truly sharable is the ultimate ground for human society. The city as an association of free men could thus be a divination of the freedom that belongs preeminently to the highest kind of wisdom. Plato's cave is at one end open to the light.

The desire to know is not wholly a desire for power. Aristotle's evidence for this is the delight in the senses. The senses disclose to us more than we need to know, and we are attracted to their superfluous disclosures. Sight more than any other sense has this charm, even though sight is likewise the sense most indispensable for action. That one and the same sense should be most needful and most delightful perhaps reflects the fact that form *(eidos)* too is a cause. What we most need in order to act presents at the same time what is needed for most things to be and to be known. Sight shows us wholes; and those wholes are either what we most want or what we know best: "love" *(eran)* was thought to be derived from "see" *(horan)*. "See" is the only special verb of perception that has been extended to signify "know" and "understand." Latin *sapio* (taste, savor) does not argue against this privilege of sight, for to connect its extension *(sapientia)* with its root was never more than a pun; whereas the proverb "Seeing is believing" suggests that the double meanings of "see" almost always work together. To hear and not understand is no paradox, to see and not understand is.

We choose sight over almost anything else even when we do not intend to act. By nature we desire to know; but sight is by choice. The sense that in itself most delights us is the sense that most makes us know. Our choice is the perfection of natural desire. We pick the sense that has the greatest power to pick out differences. Visual differences rarely coincide as such with the range of visual pleasures and pains. "Shrill" and "jangle" belong to hearing, as "bitter" does to taste, but there seem to be no words of pleasure or pain that apply primarily to sights. Sight is pure. Oedipus's self-blinding terrifies us. How could the most innocent of the senses—we say, "I'm only looking"—ever be thought to be a source of guilt and shame? The one sense that we can turn on or off at will is the sense that puts the greatest distance between ourselves and whatever it displays. Oedipus's self-blinding, then, might signify the impossibility of cognitive distance, and while seeming to be freely chosen acknowledge instead his lack of will. There would therefore never be a time when we were not intending to act. To dream *(horan)* too is to see. Right from the start, it seems, Aristotle's *Metaphysics* calls into question tragic wisdom.

"Philosophy," at any rate, first occurs here along with the denial that wisdom is a poetic art.

"Now *(men oun)* by nature animals come into being with sensual awareness." Aristotle shifts abruptly from the nature of man to the nature of animals. The species in its highest aspiration precedes the genus in its generation. What is given by nature is both complete and incomplete. Some animals can live solely by perception; others need memory and instruction; but man seems to be more incomplete than any other animal, for even when he has supplemented the given with experience, he perfects it with the arts, whose ostensible satisfaction of his needs conceals their significance as witnesses to his desire to know. Experience and art occur together in the expert; but Aristotle exaggerates their separability in order to bring out the luxury of the knowledge in the arts. Plato speaks of the beautiful as one of the consequences of technical specialization (*Republic* 370c3). Despite the fact that textbook knowledge will not usually suffice to cure Socrates, we still believe that such knowledge is higher than experience. If we are to believe the movies, the college-educated cop is as much envied as resented. The native speaker is not a linguist, and his ability goes unnoticed. The gardener with a green thumb is not an agronomist, let alone a botanist; but the unteachability of his knowledge puts him behind the others in our esteem. Our esteem for wisdom is not strictly in proportion to its possible usefulness for us. We admire inventors more than their inventions. We are not necessarily grateful to Prometheus. The drift of Aristotle's argument forces him to be silent here about that meaning of wisdom—prudence—which predominates in most modern languages; and even when Aristotle does introduce it as the sixth characteristic of wisdom, its difference from the others stands out more plainly than its ultimate unifiability with them. Prudence, according to Aristotle, is not an art.

For the most part, experience is as far as a man can advance in knowledge by himself. Experience is deaf and dumb; it neither takes from nor shares with others. Although experience is not the same as its origin in a manifold of memories—it is an insight *(ennoēma)*—it always remains attached to a particularity of that manifold; but art is indifferent to its origin in a manifold of experiences. Art is impersonal. Its universalization of experience through the discovery of cause demotes every experience, regardless of whether it confirms the art or is in fact the source of the art. In its own eyes, art has no "history." Art is not just the last in the series of perception, imagination, memory, and experience; it is the form of the series whose matter they become. Art reverses the relation that experience sets up between "man" and "Socrates." For experience, "Socrates" is accidentally a man; for art, "man" is accidentally Socrates. Art restores to the universals of speech their primacy. In the *Republic,* the paradoxical identification of justice with an art proves to be a better basis for Socrates' inquiry into justice than his starting point in Cephalus's experience, from whom he learns that "character" is decisive for happiness or misery. Because experience is nothing but a rule of thumb, it dismisses exceptions: Cephalus does not take seriously Socrates' counter-example of the madman. Experience is the cognitive counterpart to moral virtue; but it is through art that Socrates brings Glaucon and Adimantus to philosophy.

The first chapter of Aristotle's *Metaphysics* consists of three arguments. The first argues that we naturally desire to know; the second that the degree to which rationality is present in an art matches the degree to which wisdom is credited to it; and the third that the more an art was divorced from need the wiser its practitioners were thought to be. The first and second of these arguments are linked together through the notion of nature; the second and third through the notion of development (from perception to art in the first, from the arts of necessity to the arts of leisure in the third); and the first and third are no less closely linked through the notion of the useless ("theater" and "theorem" both come from a word for "sight"); but the second argument, for all that Aristotle discerns in the arts an element of uselessness, still stands on a different level from the others. Wisdom is commonly understood in two ways. It implies, on the one hand, a knowledge of cause, and, on the other, an impractical pursuit; and whether the latter is poetry or mathematics, neither is self-evidently a knowledge of cause. Plato represents this by having the mathematician Theaetetus identify knowledge with perception right after he has failed to notice that his self-confessed ignorance of the cause of his perplexity is the answer to his perplexity (*Theaetetus* 148e8). Mathematics, it is true, is eminently teachable (its students need no experience), and it shares this trait with the arts; but poetry is held to be unteachable and impossible without inspiration, and the kind of wisdom the poet does have seems to be prudence, and prudence is just what Aristotle's argument has so far precluded. Poetry and mathematics, moreover, appear to be themselves so contrary to one another as kinds of knowledge that their common impracticality, which gets them both called wisdom, only goes to show that wisdom merely designates in their case the accident of their genesis. "Wisdom" now comprises the arts, poetry, and mathematics only because the different times at which each arose concealed the cognitive emptiness of its successive extensions. Even if poetry were irrelevant for wisdom, a wisdom that just combined the theoretical character of mathematics with the knowledge of cause the arts contain seems to be something of an oxymoron. Aristotle himself, at any rate, denies the possibility of a mathematical physics.

The arts and sciences that developed, once man had spare time, refined and articulated in a political setting men's natural curiosity. Just as man the theoretician is the perfection of man the spectator, so leisure is the political equivalent to the free play of the senses. The productive arts do not fit obviously into this schema, however indispensable they are for making leisure possible; and yet it is from then that what knowledge is came to be understood. The nature of the knower and the nature of knowledge seem to be not quite aligned with one another. A sign of their misalignment is that Egyptian priests were, according to Aristotle, among the first mathematicians, but what they knew as priests would not pass for genuine knowledge. Mathematics is a liberal science, but it is not liberating. If, moreover, the productive arts were to be considered knowledge only to the extent that they employ measure and number (cf. Plato *Philebus* 55d5–56c7), their subordination to mathematics would simultaneously deprive them of significance as representatives of causal knowledge. In Aristotle's insistence on this aspect of the arts, there seems to lurk the peculiarly modern view that we know only what we make. Aristotle therefore separates the insight, to which the arts give access, of what knowledge is from the way in which the arts apparently make over the natural to serve human needs. His distinction between art and experience, with its paradoxical suggestion that the productive arts are not primarily directed to production, is the first step in making this separation. It has to be completed with an argument that shows art to be not the conquest of nature but either its imitation or completion (cf. *Physics* 199a15–17).

II

The second chapter begins with a repetition of a difficulty in the first. Aristotle suggests that a rehearsal of our opinions about the wise man will clarify the question of which causes and principles the science that is wisdom deals with. The way to the characterization of knowledge lies through that of the knower. In the absence of any understanding in opinion of metaphysics, opinion has fragmented the unity of the wise man into six apparently independent characteristics. Aristotle implies that this incoherence, or at best this lack of mutual implication among the characteristics, preserves the truth: no known science can satisfy all that opinion demands of wisdom. Aristotle, however, does make an advance on opinion; he replaces the comparatives in his account of our opinions with superlatives in the inferences he draws from them. Our opinions express our experiences; Aristotle is about to transform them into knowledge of knowledge.

The wise man is thought (1) to know everything in its generality and (2) to have the capacity to know difficult things, or whatever is not easy for a human being to know. Furthermore, whoever has more precise knowledge (3), and whoever is more capable of teaching the causes (4) is thought to be wiser. And just as the science which is for its own sake and for the sake of knowing is thought to be wisdom to a greater degree than any science sought for the sake of its consequences (5), so the more architectonic science is thought to be wisdom rather than any science that serves it (6). The first pair of these characteristics implies that wisdom cannot be any kind of perception; the second pair that experience cannot be wisdom; and the last that wisdom is not a productive art. Aristotle, however, has paired these characteristics not only because as pairs they determine wisdom negatively but because within each pair a tension obtains between its members. The generality of wisdom is at odds with its difficulty, for the more abstracted from experience a science is the easier it seems to be to learn it. The precision of wisdom is at odds with its capacity to teach the causes of things, for mathematics exemplifies the former and seems to have no capacity for the latter. And a wisdom wholly sought for its own sake is at odds with an architectonic science of the good, for it seems that, on the one hand, whatever is sought for its own sake does not have to be good for anything, and, on the other, a good that is good for nothing is not good. If this threefold tension is to be resolved, a distinction has to be made between the universality of abstraction and the comprehensiveness of wisdom; mathematics has to be denied its exclusive claim to precision; and finally what is the good for man must be shown to be compatible with good in itself. That metaphysics is the only nonabstract science, that knowledge of the soul admits of the greatest precision (cf. *De anima* 402a1–4), and that happiness is knowledge formulate Aristotle's own resolution of this threefold tension.

Universality, difficulty, and precision seem to point to mathematics as wisdom; and, if one disregards causality, teachability and inner attractiveness do so no less. That the beautiful, however, which mathematics discovers makes it the architectonic science would not follow without a proof that the beautiful is the good; and Aristotle's argument for their coincidence for intellection presupposes their divergence everywhere else (cf. 1072a26–7). It seems, then, safer to put the fourth and sixth of wisdom's characteristics under the rubric of knowledge of cause, and assign only the first three and the fifth to mathematics. Aristotle has so far put the greater emphasis on the fifth characteristic and been wholly silent about the third, despite the fact that together they are most plainly true of mathematics. Mathematics has served as a sign of the naturalness of the desire for theoretical knowledge rather than as any indication of the content of wisdom. Its development in Egypt, prior to philosophy, is itself such a sign. Mathematics was not cultivated at first in light of any general reflection on the nature of the whole. One can even surmise that it began as a game: Palamedes was thought to have discovered numbers as well as several games at Troy. This original playfulness of mathematics—and child prodigies show that that is never lost—heightens the tension between the fifth and sixth characteristics of wisdom; but at the same time it recalls the Platonic view that wisdom is the proper union of the playful and the serious; and that union is perhaps the same as maintaining the difference and the sameness of the beautiful and the good.

On the basis of Aristotle's arguments that ethics does not admit of precision—"moral certainty" is its highest standard—wisdom is precise because (1) opinion has no part in it, and therefore it presents no conflict within itself between nature and convention, (2) it is not involved with the circumstantial, where the good, for example, can prove to be harmful, (3) its only use is for truth ("for all practical purposes" is abhorrent to it), and (4) the difference between what something is and that it is does not pertain to its subject matter (cf. *Nichomachean Ethics* 1094b14–19, 1098a26–b2, 1104a1–10). It is, however, less clear, as Aristotle states it, how wisdom is more like arithmetic than geometry, since the former is a more precise knowledge than the latter; but a non-Aristotelian example might explicate his meaning. Any desired digit in π's decimal expansion is knowable, but unless there is an actual infinite, its entire expansion must elude us. Whatever the reason for this imprecision—the not wholly geometrical principles of geometry would seem to be Aristotle's explanation—wisdom cannot contain any potentially knowable elements; all its knowledge must be present to it as a whole. The completeness of wisdom entails its rejection of every possible alternative; and this knowledge of rejected possibilities must conclude with a proof of their exhaustion. That Aristotle, however, must go through the views of his predecessors, in order to discover whether he has overlooked a fifth cause, is tantamount to an admission that he cannot prove that there are only four causes. Indeed, the problematic coherence of the four causes is the form in which Aristotle later states the problematic unity of knowledge (996a18–20). The strictest precision, moreover, is perhaps not only unattainable in itself; it seems also to be incompatible with the first characteristic of wisdom, for it is only in a sense *(pōs)* that comprehensive knowledge knows all its subordinates. A comprehensive definition of being cannot apparently be combined with a precise account of the number and kinds of being. This difficulty impinges in turn on another to which most of the perplexities of Book 2 are reducible: the principles of knowledge cannot but must be the same as the principles of being. Aristotle's use of *ousia* for both "beingness" and a being places this perplexity in being itself.

Aristotle argues that the several perfections of the opined characteristics of wisdom converge on one and the same knowledge. If, for example, wisdom is chosen for its own sake, the ultimate choice must be of the eminently knowable, for otherwise there would be a further condition attached to the reason for the choice; and a wisdom, on the other hand, which knows the good sought in any action or knowledge, would necessarily know why wisdom for its own sake is the good simply, for otherwise that wisdom is for its own sake would still be nothing but an opinion. Self-knowledge, then, completes wisdom. It gives the reason for the natural desire to know and, in establishing the good to be a knowable cause, unites the contemplative and the ratiocinative. Their union, however, occurs even before it becomes the self-knowledge of wisdom; its prior occurrence is in wonder, "on account of which men both now and at first began to philosophize." Wonder is a certain kind of conscious neediness *(aporia)*; it thus looks like the neediness that the productive arts satisfy; but unlike that neediness it is wholly selfless and thus looks like the natural desire to know. The desire to know, however, is an indiscriminate greediness to transform the opaque into the plain (information); but wonder is the recognition of the opaque in the plain. The wonderful is that which shows the hiddenness of the unhidden. It is every "that" which seems to be in itself a "why?" when seeing is not believing, and the given is a question. The wonderful is a beautiful perplexity.

If wonder is all by itself a sign that wisdom is a theoretical knowledge of causes, it seems strange that Aristotle introduces it only after he has indicated how the six characteristics of wisdom fit together in the same way. An account of what wisdom is thought to be seems to be more telling than an account of that condition without which it could never be sought. The admiration *(thaumazein)* for wisdom precedes in speech and in deed the origin of philosophy in wonder *(thaumazein)*, despite the fact that such admiration appears to be nothing but reflected wonder—the recognition that another has seen and solved a perplexity. One might argue that wonder as a certain kind of ignorance should follow even the opinions about complete knowledge; but Aristotle, I think, wanted rather to separate the essentially true opinions about wisdom from a prevalent but false one. He needs wonder now in order to confront philosophy with its chief competitor, poetry. The poets, who call themselves wise, make marvels, which are called myths. Far from such wisdom, then, putting an end to wonder, it issues in wonder. If "the lover of myth too is in a sense a lover of wisdom," and hence "myth" stands in for "wisdom," myth must be the enigmatic solution to the enigmatic: the riddle of Oedipus is bound up with oracles. The double enigmas of poetry are made by poetry; they are not found. Why men must toil and die is a biblical question that arises from its biblical answer. As a productive art, poetry is grounded in need; and the need is political (cf. 1074b3–5). It thus comes about that poetry exhibits the freedom of wisdom—poets do not toil—while it serves the city as a community of the arts of necessity (cf. Plato *Critias* 110a3–c2). Poetry, therefore, is less revealing than the other arts of what knowledge is, even though it ostensibly poses more philosophic questions than they do. If Aristotle was correct in denying production for use to the art of the productive arts, poetry only seems to be what the other arts are not while being in fact what the other arts only seem to be. That poetry has usurped the name for all of making seems to be no accident (cf. Plato *Symposium* 205b8–c9).

Aristotle cites two pieces of evidence for the view that wisdom is for its own sake. The first is essential, the second "historical," or as he says, accidental. Wonder is no less necessary now than it was at the beginning for the initiation of philosophy; but it is an accident that philosophy began once the necessities of life and the means for forgetting them (like poetry) were satisfied. He thereby implies that wonder is neither painful nor pleasant. It neither compels nor entices. There is nothing in it to be feared from which one runs away or which roots one to the spot (like awe), nor does it have the natural attractiveness of seeing. Wonder makes for self-forgetfulness. The strangeness of the strange estranges. A Greek word for the strange is the "placeless" *(atopon).* Odysseus the wandering stranger is the wonderer. He once called himself No-one (*outis*) and punned on the homonymy of "wisdom" *(mētis)* and another form of "no one" *(mētis).* Philosophic wonder induces homelessness without nostalgia (cf. Plato *Symposium* 203d11). Perhaps therefore it is too self-forgetting. Aristotle, at any rate, no sooner concludes that wisdom alone is free than he says,

"So its acquisition would justly be thought to be not human, for the nature of men is in many ways enslaved." He confirms this with a quotation from a poet: "God alone would have this honor."Whereas both poet and philosopher agree on the unlikelihood of attaining wisdom, divine jealousy is the poets', natural enslavement is the philosopher's explanation. For the poets, its appellation "not human" carries with it a prohibition and implies the criminality of its attempted acquisition; but Aristotle regards it merely as a correct designation of its excellence. The context in which Aristotle seemingly refutes the poets by a proverb, "Singers tell many lies," suggests that the lie he has in mind is the poets' identification—in honor of themselves—of the highest cause with an efficient cause, so that to seek knowledge of it looks like prying into a trade secret. The biblical story of man's fall, insofar as it points to the loss of sexual innocence, locates idolatry at the beginning: men too can make beings. The impossibility of divine jealousy thus depends on whether the highest beings are only causes as final cause, and their causality is compatible with their being for their own sake. It is, in any case, the separation between the being of the highest beings and their being as cause that lets Aristotle affirm that the origin of philosophy is essentially wonder and accidentally at a certain stage of "history." The cause of philosophy is the effect of the good.

T W E N T Y

Strauss on Plato

WHAT PHILOSOPHY IS SEEMS TO BE inseparable from the question of how to read Plato. Now almost no philosopher after Plato wrote at length about philosophy, and from antiquity at least there are few notices that inform us about the principles of Platonic writing. Three, however, stand out; the first two, in Plutarch and Cicero, respectively, point directly to the issue of esotericism; the third, in Aelian, to the very nature of philosophy. Plutarch implies that by the subordination of natural necessities to more divine principles Plato made philosophy safe for the city (*Nicias* 23.5); and in the *Tusculan Disputations* (5.4.11), Cicero remarks that he followed the way of Socrates, as it was made known by Plato, in his own dialogues, in concealing his own opinions, relieving others of error, and seeking in every dispute what is most like to the truth. Aelian tells the story of the painter Pauson who was hired to paint a racehorse rolling in dust and instead painted it running, and when his patron objected Pauson told him to turn it upside down, and Aelian says that there was much talk to the effect that this resembled the speeches of Socrates (*Varia Historia* 14.15). It was the extraordinary merit of Leo Strauss to experience the import of these three remarks (among others) and render them to the life in his own writings on Plato and elsewhere. This achievement amounts to, in my opinion, as great a recovery as that of al-Farabi, who rediscovered philosophy in the tenth century. The common thread in their recovery was no doubt their common understanding of revelation as *the* alternative to philosophy; but since after paganism the three revealed religions were already infected by philosophy to various degrees, they had to recover revelation in its true form at the same time as they recovered its opposite. For both purposes, Plato's *Laws* was their guide. As a recovery, theirs might seem of less significance than the original discovery; but as both al-Farabi and Strauss knew, the original discovery was itself not at the beginning of philosophy. Philosophy had to be rediscovered by Socrates long after there had been philosophy. Plato has Socrates call his rediscovery a second sailing. The second sailing is philosophy, and it is never first. The false start of philosophy can alone jumpstart philosophy.

The caution and the daring that characterized all of Leo Strauss's works are conspicuous in his interpretations of Plato. One could say that for Strauss the caution came from his beloved Xenophon and the daring from the divine Plato, but it would be more precise to say that Strauss always refused to separate Xenophon and Plato and in this showed especially his difference from the interpretation of Plato that had come to prevail since the time of Schleiermacher. Strauss's caution appears most obviously in the extreme reticence he maintained when it came to the so-called Platonic Forms; but his daring is thereby all the more striking when one realizes that his thought was always fixed on the beings, whether god, man, or beast, and the whole. Strauss was the master of the connection between the small and the large, or of the ways in which the one participates in and hence fails to be identical with the other. Strauss's mastery was such that its inherent difficulty does not strike home until one tries it oneself and comes up with quite arbitrary links that do not in fact encompass all of the particulars and hence fall short of the truly general. There was at least one contemporary of Strauss who had an equally uncanny eye for the unnoticed but significant detail—what he noticed was surprisingly different from what Strauss did—but his ability to work up from it to the beginning and down from the beginning to the detail was no match for Strauss's. Strauss came to almost everything experientially; he shunned "theories"; it was what he had found out for himself that he most relied on. His reading of Plato was not different from his own thinking, not in the sense that his opinions were Plato's or Plato's his, but in the element of Platonic dialectic Strauss saw and practiced his own way.

One has to turn to Xenophon in order to understand the double sense contained within Platonic dialectic (*Memorabilia* 4.5.12). Xenophon says that to converse *(dialegesthai)* meant for Socrates the coming together of men for the purpose of deliberation by dividing *(dialegein)* the things *(ta pragmata)* by kinds *(genē)*. The middle voice *dialegesthai* contains within it the active, *dialegein.* The communication among men involves the articulation of things. This Heraclitean insight into the double nature of logos was the basis for Strauss's reading of Plato. He put this double nature into the title of one of his last books, *The Argument and the Action of Plato's Laws.* The "and" in the title is misleading; it does not mean that some sort of action is represented while the argument is being developed; it means that the action has an argument, and that that argument is the true argument of the *Laws.* That Strauss did not call his book, *The Argument in the Action . . .* underlines the initial separateness of argument and action in a Platonic dialogue and the latent community between them.[1]

Strauss was not the first to notice the dramatic setting of a Platonic dialogue; he was not even the first to suggest that the drama altered the apparent meaning of the argument; but what is peculiarly his discovery was that once argument and action are properly put together an entirely new argument emerges that could never have been expected from the argument on the written page. Something happens in a Platonic dialogue that in its revolutionary unexpectedness is the equivalent to the *periagōgē,* as Socrates calls it, of philosophy itself. This turnaround has a peculiar structure. It has to be experienced and can never be formulated in such a way as to allow one anything more than anticipation of an equivalent turnaround in another dialogue. There cannot be a method *(methodos)* of thought in the thoughtful going after *(metienai)* of thought. The complete rationality of the ineffable seems to be around the bend and open to the charge of mysticism and obscurantism; but Strauss saw that such a consequence of Platonic dialectic was nothing other than the sobriety of the highest kind of madness, which is philosophy, that Socrates celebrates in the *Phaedrus.*

There are two kinds of esotericism, ancient and modern. Swift represented one by the bee, which out of the sweet produces the sweet, and the other by the spider, which out of the foulest things produces the most beautiful web. The first kind is metaphysical esotericism, the second political. The first kind necessarily includes the second, the second necessarily denies the first. The first says that it is in the nature of things that things are hidden; the second says that it is in the nature of the city as now constituted that this is so. The second proposes enlightenment, the lighting up of things until nothing and no one are in the dark; the first sets out to disclose things in their hiddenness and show the reality of what appears. Strauss put this as follows: "The problem inherent in the surface of things and only in the surface of things is the heart of things." This sentence is merely a rendering of what al-Farabi says is the way to interpret Plato.

The first thing Strauss was always doing in his study of Plato was to be a beginner. He knew how to start again, not as if he were starting for the first time, but really starting for the first time. It is what Strauss must have had in mind when he wrote to Gadamer that he could not recognize in Gadamer's "theory of hermeneutic experience," which as such is a universal theory, his own experience as an interpreter, which made him feel "the irretrievably 'occasional' character of every worthwhile interpretation."[2] This experience calls for a practice of being without habits; Socrates called it "the practice of dying and being dead" and identified it with philosophy. This experience would be impossible were there not a hiddenness to things that metaphysical esotericism recognizes and reproduces through trapdoors in arguments. Socrates' account of the structure of the soul in the *Republic* is one such example. Only if one follows patiently Socrates' argument about desire can one see it turn upside down and discover that it is the presentation of desire by the thumoeidetic that has put on the mask of reason. It is then but a small step to apply this *periagōgē* to the Thrasymachus of the first book and realize that in the soul structure of Book 4 there culminates one part of the Thrasymachean principle of the *Republic,* and such a culmination prepares the way for its elimination and the emergence of philosophy. All of this was known to al-Farabi, who remarked that Plato combined the way of Socrates with the way of Thrasymachus; but it was Strauss who gave the full argument and indicated how one has to proceed beyond what al-Farabi had written.

What is most remarkable in the history of philosophy is the simultaneous dominance and absence of Plato. It is as impossible to conceive of Aristotle without Plato as to recall Plato while reading Aristotle. The Platonic Forms show up in the manifold of treatises Aristotle wrote, and Plato disappears from the apparent separateness of those treatises, only to show up once more in the incoherence of the principles that do not allow Aristotle's treatises on the soul, on nature, and on being to be put together, even though they severally demand to be put together. It is this kind of separation and combination that we are left to acomplish on our own when we come to Aristotle and that Plato's Socrates practices continuously. Strauss realized that this is what it meant for Socrates to replace efficient, material, and final causation with his hypothesis of "ideas," which Aristotle pretends to be a fourth modality of causation that can readily be added to the other three rather than an abandonment of causality as it was known before Socrates. This second sailing of the ideas was inseparable from the promotion by Socrates of the soul as a nonderivative principle. Ontology, epistemology, and psychology were thereby joined and hence transformed, and it was one of Strauss's most beautiful discoveries to put together logos, being, and soul.

Strauss wrote up his interpretations of Plato's *Euthyphro, Apology of Socrates, Crito, Euthydemus, Republic, Statesman, Minos,* and *Laws.* It is not unreasonable to ask whether analyses so heavily weighted in favor of the political can do justice to Plato and do not distort Plato as much as the contemporary tilt in favor of the *Phaedo, Theaetetus, Sophist, Parmenides,* and *Timaeus.* It turns out, however, that what seems to be the unavoidable bias of the professional put Strauss in a unique position to return to Plato in his entire range through political philosophy. The subtitle of Strauss's course on Plato's political philosophy was "Its Metaphysical Foundations." In his time, political philosophy had decayed so completely as to cease to be a part of philosophy. It had decayed so completely because philosophy itself had decayed so completely. The connection between political philosophy and ontology was not obvious, and the reason was the vanishing of the primary phenomena of the Cave and their replacement by what Strauss called "the Cave beneath the Cave." Strauss had to recover the Cave in all its shadowiness before he could show the way out of the Cave. This entailed the establishment of the fundamental character of the political in its double aspect: the nature of political things and the best form of the city. This double aspect can be said to show the simultaneous empiricism and idealism of Plato. Machiavelli understood the idealism by itself and accordingly failed to understand either its political ground or its philosophic purpose. The starting point for Strauss was simply the two questions Glaucon posed at the beginning of the second book of the *Republic;* but this starting point does not hold just for political philosophy but for philosophy as such: the nature of the beings, on the one hand, and, on the other, the nature of the good. Forms of these two questions inform all of Plato's writings, and all of human life. Of the two questions the good is always first for us. We are willy-nilly oriented by the good. Philosophy after Plato had tended to forget this, partly because Plato had been so persuasive about the human good, and partly because the separation of philosophical disciplines could not keep the good as an essential part of each of them. The dialectical success of Plato in the articulation of things could not preserve the comprehensive reflection of Plato which alone had made his success possible. The tradition of philosophy thus became unphilosophic, and philosophy could not be restored unless one could go back to Plato, where the part that is being and the whole that is the good are constantly shown in their mutual interference. Strauss therefore was always turning away from Plato to return to Plato and turning back to Plato after the obstacles to such a return had been faced. In the history of scholarship, it is not easy to find anyone with as wide a range and depth of understanding throughout that range as Strauss; and such a successful union of disparate features speaks in a peculiar way for the soundness of his view that political philosophy is the eccentric core of philosophy.

Strauss often spoke of his subjective certainty. What he meant was the experimental nature of his way of interpretation. Once he could hypothesize about the drift of an entire dialogue or a sufficiently complex argument, he would deduce from it the consequences that should hold in the text if the hypothesis were sound. The consequences could range from a word to an entire argument that should be present or absent from the dialogue. Strauss was thus able to deduce that "soul" does not appear in the *Euthyphro.* What made this deduction subjective was not its willfulness but that it could never carry the same conviction to anyone else who had not proceeded in the same way as Strauss had done. Indeed, some of these deductions would appear in print as spurious, as if what Strauss had really done was merely to construct a hypothesis to fit his observation. This appearance of specious serendipity is a necessity.

Once, when Strauss was discussing the *Republic,* he listed seven examples that Socrates had given in the course of an argument, and remarked that from his experience he had learned that the center in an odd number of items turned out to be the most important, either in the immediate sequel or in the larger scheme of things. We were bemused and impressed when in this particular case the argument unfolded in the way Strauss had anticipated. A friend of mine, who was more skeptical than the rest of us, went home and took down from the shelf Montaigne's *Essays,* counted their number, and looked up the central one. It was entitled *On Vain Subtleties,* and its theme was the importance of being in the middle.

Perhaps the principle Strauss invoked most consistently in his interpretation of Plato was that of "abstraction." On the basis of his long experience with the dialogues, he thought that the key to each was something absent from the dialogue, which was necessary for understanding the issue at hand. This principle is the hermeneutic equivalent to the difference between a being as a part of the whole and a being apart from its being a part of the whole. Aristotle, for example, discusses being in the *Metaphysics* in such a way that it would make no difference whether there was only one being in the universe; but he pays heavily for this assumption, since he must end up with only one kind of being which strictly is and from which the universe necessarily falls away. In Plato, however, the abstraction from something essential to the issue turns out to be the revelation of the issue, and its apparent absence a sign of the failure on our part to effect the turnaround of the argument. The most obvious question to raise about Strauss's principle is this: what is the principle that governs what Plato chooses to omit? After all, it would seem that any essential omission guarantees that nothing will be understood. There must be, then, reasonable grounds for the omission, and these grounds must lie in the nature of the thing as it initially comes to light. The abstraction must be grounded in an abstraction by opinion, which has failed to take something decisive into account. Plato's procedure is based on the idealism of opinion, or the vulgar Platonism of opinion, which is checked in turn by the Platonic doctrine of participation. It thus turns out that abstraction in Platonic dialogues brings together two principles: nothing can be understood if everything must be understood, and nothing can be properly understood if one does not take one's bearings by the necessarily improper starting point of understanding.

Strauss's most startling illustration of his principle is in his discussion of the *Republic.* What the *Republic* abstracts from, he says, is the body, the most obvious sign of which is that the city, which is formed to supply bodily needs and does so perfectly, has a class-structure based on the soul by itself, and this despite the fact that Socrates introduced the city as the analogue of the individual and not his body or soul. The city, then, is the locus of idealism. It is shot through and necessarily shot through with self-misunderstanding. It is geared for the body and lays claim to the soul. In its usurpation, the city is essentially the locus of alienation. It follows therefore that the city cannot make for happiness, and only if justice is radically reinterpreted as philosophy is Thrasymachus refuted on this issue.

This last allusion to justice as philosophy, which occurs quite late in the *Republic,* calls attention to the most obvious character of Platonic arguments. They keep on moving and changing in the course of a single dialogue, so that one can legitimately ask whether it is ever possible to single out anything as conclusive, or whether we must simply go with the flow and not bother to pull together beginning, middle, and end. Does a dialogue make a whole, or is it rather an ever-moving series of insights and arguments that are not meant to come to an end? Or what exactly is gained in understanding a Platonic dialogue if the temporal flux of argument is integrated into the parts of a single whole? What Strauss came to see was that only if one were able to link up the temporal order with the part-whole order would the true argument ever emerge. The dissonance of pattern and sequence is of a different order than their coincidence. It was through the transformation that a temporal segment underwent when it became part of the whole that Plato imitated the relation that always obtains between a part apart from the whole and a part as part of the whole. This imitation, which never ceases to amaze, made it possible for Plato to preserve the Socrates who in never writing represents the truth that philosophy alone has no tradition within the perpetuation of philosophy in its necessary decline. Strauss's deconstruction of philosophy is thus not Heidegger's, who hurried past Plato to Parmenides and Heraclitus, bypassing Socrates.

Strauss's second most important principle for the interpretation of Plato was the more obvious one. The dialogues were imitations because nothing in them was left to chance, but everything was in order even though the circumstances of reason should not, it seems, partake of the same order as reason itself. The elevation of the circumstantial into the inevitable pointed in two ways: First, it reflected the fact that for us the starting point is always our interest; and this good, however conceived, is the engine of all serious discourse. What is true for life is as true for philosophy, which alone among the scientific disciplines has no principles from which to start except from life itself. To begin to philosophize, then, is to encounter a question that has been incorrectly formulated. The question reflects the true question, but it is not the true question. A Socratic discussion always moves toward a disclosure of the true question and its answer that determines at the same time the degree of displacement that was in the original question, and without which one could never have started. Plato's imitation of the relation between the beings and the good as it first comes to light confronts us with certain difficulties: Once we have come to know the character of the perspectival, are we allowed to discard it and come face-to-face with the beings in themselves? Strauss's short answer is, Only if the soul can be discounted at the same time and shown to be a derivative phenomenon. Granted that the occasion Plato fixed upon does not and cannot stand in for all other possible occasions in which an issue arises comparable to the one he chose, it still must be the case that the occasion for all its apparent particularity is susceptible to thematization, i.e., to a structural extension that is as general as any argument. This is where an interpreter can most easily go astray and where Strauss was most surefooted. His reflection on the setting of the *Laws,* in which the Athenian Stranger is and is not Socrates, leads him to show the structural resemblance between wine-drinking and a discussion of wine-drinking, on the one hand, and, on the other, the descent of the Stranger and the ascent of Megillus the Spartan and Clinias the Cretan. Such a reflection led him in turn to the *Phaedrus,* through which Strauss could understand why Cicero began his *Laws* with borrowings in equal measure from Plato's *Phaedrus* and Plato's *Laws.*

Strauss's way of interpreting Plato, so that he became the model of all genuine philosophy, raises the question of poetry and its ancient quarrel with philosophy. Just as it is easy to recognize the difference between post-Platonic and pre-Platonic philosophy, despite the poorness of our sources for both, so it is no less facile to distinguish between poetry and philosophy, as long as one does not look to Plato and wonder whether he is a hybrid who, in putting paid to the issue of poetry for all subsequent philosophy until Nietzsche and Heidegger, did not resolve the tension between the poet and the philosopher in himself. Strauss was alone, I suspect, in showing the spuriousness of this apparently self-evident divide in Plato. One way of stating the issue is to raise the question of translation, for if one renders Plato idiomatically, so that one conveys what one believes is the sense and not the words, one has already decided that the poet Plato, who is a legitimate subject of this kind of rendering, is irreconcilable with the philosopher, whose arguments, everyone would agree, should be presented as exactly as possible. In a recent translation of the *Symposium,* the translator puts into a heroic couplet two lines of epic verse that Agathon made up in honor of Eros. Eros "brings," Agathon says,

> "Sweet peace to men, and calm o'er all the deep,
> Rest to the winds, to those who sorrow, sleep."

The translation seems flawless until one notices that "rest" is not the same as *koitē,* which means either "sleep" or "bedtime." "The sleep of the winds" points directly to Agathon's argument, that Eros is the god of poetic production, by whose agency the metaphorical becomes literal. It seems therefore almost inevitable that that translator introduces the couplet with the words "[Eros] brings," and not with "[Eros] makes." Perhaps one could come to understand Agathon even through a nonliteral translation; but Strauss alone, as far as I know, did understand him because he followed the argument down to and from the details.

Perhaps the most puzzling as well as the most unexpected aspect in Strauss's recovery of Plato and philosophy concerns the status of the Greek poets before Plato. Even if Plato does not open up the only way to them, it is certainly the most accessible. Without Plato, the tragedies of Sophocles, to say nothing of Aristophanes, are almost lost to us. Their understanding of the city, particularly of its subpolitical foundations, and of the law, particularly the sacred law, would remain in darkness were it not for the light Plato brings to them. The logos of Plato unveils the muthos of poetry for the logos that it is. Once, however, this is acknowledged, the Socratic revolution in philosophy seems to be coeval with Greek poetry, which had realized from the start, with its principle of telling lies like the truth, the relation of argument and action. Homer and Hesiod, then, would have to be recognized as already within the orbit of philosophy. It is a remarkable fact, whose significance Strauss was the first or the last to see, that the only mention of "nature" in Homer has this meaning in Plato but not the philosophers who preceded him. Strauss's recovery of Plato opened up the possibility of gathering into the fold of philosophy more than philosophy had ever dreamed of.

I cannot end this discussion of Strauss on Plato without quoting Strauss's account of Plato's understanding of the philosopher, for it applies no less to Strauss in himself than to Strauss in his understanding of Plato:

> To articulate the problem of cosmology means to answer the question of what philosophy is or what a philosopher is. Plato refrained from entrusting the thematic discussion of this question to Socrates. He entrusted it to a stranger from Elea. But even that stranger did not discuss explicitly what a philosopher is. He discussed explicitly two kinds of men which are easily mistaken for the philosopher, the sophist and the statesman: by understanding both sophistry (in its highest as well as its lowest meaning) and statesmanship, one will understand what philosophy is. Philosophy strives for knowledge of the whole. The whole is the totality of the parts. The whole eludes us but we know parts: we possess partial knowledge of parts. The knowledge which we possess is characterized by a fundamental dualism which has never been overcome. At one pole we find knowledge of homogeneity: above all in arithmetic, but also in the other branches of mathematics, and derivatively in all productive arts or crafts. At the opposite pole we find knowledge of heterogeneity, and in particular of heterogeneous ends; the highest form of this kind of knowledge is the art of the statesman and of the educator. The latter kind of knowledge is superior to the former for this reason. As knowledge of the ends of human life, it is knowledge of what makes human life complete or whole; it is therefore knowledge of a whole. Knowledge of the ends of man implies knowledge of the human soul; and the human soul is the only part of the whole which is open to the whole and therefore more akin to the whole than anything else is. But this knowledge—the political art in the highest sense—is not knowledge of *the* whole. It seems that knowledge of the whole would have to combine somehow political knowledge in the highest sense with knowledge of homogeneity. And this combination is not at our disposal. Men are therefore constantly tempted to force the issue by imposing unity on the phenomena by absolutizing either knowledge of homogeneity or knowledge of ends. Men are constantly attracted and deluded by two opposite charms: the charm of competence which is engendered by mathematics and everything akin to mathematics, and the charm of humble awe, which is engendered by meditation on the human soul and its experiences. Philosophy is characterized by the gentle, if firm, refusal to

succumb to either charm. It is the highest form of the mating of courage and moderation. In spite of its highness or nobility, it could appear as Sisyphean or ugly, when one contrasts its achievement with its goal. Yet it is necessarily accompanied, sustained and elevated by *eros.* It is graced by nature's grace.[3]

Notes

1. For the expression "the deeds in the speeches," see *Euthyphro* 11c3.

2. "Correspondence Concerning *Wahrheit und Methode,*" *The Independent Journal of Philosophy* 2 (1978): 5–6.

3. *What Is Political Philosophy?* (Glencoe, IL, 1959), 39–40.

SELECTED WORKS BY SETH BENARDETE

Entries marked by an asterisk (*) are reprinted in the present volume.

"The Daimonion of Socrates: A Study of Plato's *Theages*." Master's thesis. University of Chicago, 1953.

"Achilles and Hector: The Homeric Hero." Ph.D. dissertation. University of Chicago, 1955. Reprinted in *St. John's Review* in two parts: Spring 1985: 31–58, Summer 1985: 85–114.

Aeschylus, *Suppliant Maidens* and *Persians*. Translation, Chicago: The University of Chicago Press, 1957.

"Plato *Sophist* 231b1–7." *Phronesis* 5, no. 2 (1960):129–39.

"Vat. Gr. 2181: An Unknown Aristophanes MS." *Harvard Studies in Classical Philology* (1962): 241–48.

*"Achilles and the *Iliad*." *Hermes* 91, no. 1 (1963): 1–16.

"The Right, the True, and the Beautiful." *Glotta* 41, nos. 1–2 (1963): 54–62.

"*Eidos* and *Diaeresis* in Plato's *Statesman*." *Philologus* 107, nos. 3–4 (1963): 193–226.

"The Crimes and Arts of Prometheus." *Rheinisches Museum für Philologie* 107, no. 2 (1964): 126–39.

*"Sophocles' *Oedipus Tyrannus*." In *Ancients and Moderns*, 1–15. New York: Basic Books, 1964. Reprinted in *Sophocles: Twentieth Century Views*, ed. Thomas Woodard. Englewood Cliffs, NJ: Prentice Hall, 1966.

"Some Misquotations of Homer in Plato." *Phronesis* 8, no. 2 (1963): 173–78.

"XRH and ΔEI in Plato and Others." *Glotta* 43, nos. 3–4 (1965): 285–98.

"Two Passages in Aeschylus' *Septem*." In two parts: *Wiener Studien* NF 1 (1967): 22–30, NF 2 (1968): 5–17.

"Hesiod's *Works and Days*: A First Reading." *Agon* 1 (1967): 150–74.

*"The *Aristeia* of Diomedes and the Plot of the *Iliad*." *Agon* 2 (1968): 10–38.

Herodotean Inquiries. The Hague: Martinus Nijhoff, 1969. New edition with "Second Thoughts." South Bend: St. Augustine's Press, 1999.

"On Plato's *Timaeus* and Timaeus' Science Fiction." *Interpretation* 2, no. 1 (Summer 1971): 21–63.

Review of H. Lloyd-Jones's translation of Aeschylus' *Oresteia*. *American Journal of Philology* 93, no. 4 (1972): 633–35.

"Aristotle *de anima* III.3–5." *Review of Metaphysics* 28, no. 4 (June 1975): 611–22.

"A Reading of Sophocles' *Antigone*." In three parts: *Interpretation* 4, no. 3 (Spring 1975): 148–196; 5, no. 1 (Summer 1975): 1–55; 5, no. 2 (Winter 1975): 148–84. Reprinted as *Sacred Transgressions: A Reading of Sophocles' Antigone*. South Bend: St. Augustine's Press, 1999.

*"Euripides' *Hippolytus*." In *Essays in Honor of Jacob Klein*, 21–27. Annapolis: St. John's College Press, 1976.

"The Grammar of Being." *Review of Metaphysics* 30, no. 3 (1977): 486–96.

*"On Wisdom and Philosophy: The First Two Chapters of Aristotle's *Metaphysics* A." *Review of Metaphysics* 32, no. 2 (December 1978): 205–15.

"Leo Strauss's *The City and Man.*" *Political Science Reviewer* 8 (1978): 1–20.

*"On Greek Tragedy." In *The Great Ideas Today,* 102–43. Chicago: Encyclopaedia Britannica, Inc., 1980.

*"Plato's *Phaedo.*" Manuscript. 1980.

*"Physics and Tragedy: On Plato's *Cratylus.*" *Ancient Philosophy* 1, no. 2 (1981): 127–40.

*"The Furies of Aeschylus." Manuscript. 1982.

The Being of the Beautiful: Plato's "Theaetetus," "Sophist," and "Statesman." Translation and commentary. Chicago: University of Chicago Press, 1984. Paperback in 3 volumes with a new introduction, 1986.

*"On Interpreting Plato's *Charmides.*" *New School Graduate Faculty Philosophy Journal* 11 (1986): 9–36.

Symposium. Translation. In *The Dialogues of Plato,* 231–86. New York: Bantam Books, 1986.

Review of M. Giraudeau, *Les notions juridiques et sociales chez Herodote. Gnomon* 58, no. 5 (1986): 546–47.

"Cicero's *de legibus* I: Its Plan and Intention." *American Journal of Philology* 108, no. 2 (1987): 295–309.

*"Protagoras' Myth and Logos." Manuscript. 1988.

Socrates' Second Sailing: On Plato's Republic. Chicago: University of Chicago Press, 1989. Paperback 1992.

The Rhetoric of Morality and Philosophy: Plato's "Gorgias" and "Phaedrus." Chicago: University of Chicago Press, 1991.

*"The Plan of Plato's *Statesman.*" *Metis: Revue d'anthropologie du monde grec ancien,* 7, nos. 1–2 (1992): 25–47.

*"Plato's *Laches:* A Question of Definition." Manuscript. 1992.

The Tragedy and Comedy of Life: Plato's "Philebus." Translation and commentary. Chicago: University of Chicago Press, 1993.

*"On Plato's *Sophist.*" *Review of Metaphysics* 46, no. 4 (June 1993): 747–80.

"The Poet-Merchant and the Stranger from the Sea." *The Greeks and the Sea,* 59–65. New York: Caratzas, 1993.

*"Strauss on Plato." A lecture in the series, "The Legacy of Leo Strauss," University of Chicago, 1993.

*"On Plato's *Symposium.*" Munich: Carl Friedrich von Siemens Stiftung, 1994.

*"On Plato's *Lysis.*" Manuscript. 1994.

*"The First Crisis in First Philosophy." *Graduate Faculty Philosophy Journal* 18, no. 1 (1995): 237–48.

The Bow and the Lyre: A Platonic Reading of the "Odyssey." Lanham, MD: Rowman and Littlefield, 1997.

*"Plato's *Theaetetus:* On the Way of the Logos." *Review of Metaphysics* 51, no. 1 (September 1997): 25–53.

"Plato, True and False." *The New Criterion,* February 1998, 70–74.

*"On the *Timaeus.*" Lecture at The Hannah Arendt/Reiner Schürmann Memorial Symposium in Political Philosophy: "The Philosophy of Leo Strauss," New School for Social Research, 1999.

"Metamorphosis and Conversion: Apuleius's *Metamorphoses*." In *Literary Imagination, Ancient and Modern: Essays in Honor of David Grene,* ed. Todd Breyfogle, 155–76. Chicago: University of Chicago Press, 1999.

"Socrates and Plato: The Dialectics of *Erōs*." German translation in *Über die Liebe,* ed. Heinrich Meier and Gerhardt Neumann. Munich: Pieper Verlag, 2000.

INDEX